The Practice of
Collaborative
Counseling &
Psychotherapy

The Practice of
Collaborative Counseling &
Psychotherapy

Developing Skills in
Culturally Mindful Helping

David A. Paré

University of Ottawa

Los Angeles | London | New Delhi
Singapore | Washington DC

Los Angeles | London | New Delhi
Singapore | Washington DC

FOR INFORMATION:

SAGE Publications, Inc.
2455 Teller Road
Thousand Oaks, California 91320
E-mail: order@sagepub.com

SAGE Publications Ltd.
1 Oliver's Yard
55 City Road
London EC1Y 1SP
United Kingdom

SAGE Publications India Pvt. Ltd.
B 1/I 1 Mohan Cooperative Industrial Area
Mathura Road, New Delhi 110 044
India

SAGE Publications Asia-Pacific Pte. Ltd.
3 Church Street
#10-04 Samsung Hub
Singapore 049483

Acquisitions Editor: Kassie Graves
Editorial Assistant: Elizabeth Luizzi
Production Editor: Laura Barrett
Copy Editor: Barbara Corrigan
Typesetter: C&M Digitals (P) Ltd.
Proofreader: Theresa Kay
Indexer: Michael Ferreira
Cover Designer: Anupama Krishnan
Marketing Manager: Lisa Sheldon Brown
Permissions Editor: Adele Hutchinson

Copyright © 2013 by SAGE Publications, Inc.

Library of Congress Cataloging-in-Publication Data

Pare, David.

The practice of collaborative counseling and psychotherapy: developing skills in culturally mindful helping / David Pare.

p. cm.

Includes bibliographical references and index.

ISBN 978-1-4129-9509-2 (pbk.)

1. Psychotherapy—Cross-cultural studies. 2. Counseling psychology. 3. Ethnopsychology. 4. Counseling psychologist and client. 5. Psychotherapist and patient. I. Title.

RC455.4.E8P37 2013

616.89′1408—dc23   2012037012

Photo Credits: 44: (clockwise from left) Thinkstock/Photos.com, Thinkstock/altrendo images, Istockphoto/RichVintage, Istockphoto/StanleyPhotography, Istockphoto/RapidEye, Istockphoto/macniak; 220: Istockphoto/Nikada (left), Istockphoto/FreeSoulProduction (right)

All *Student Voices* boxes are reproduced with consent from anonymous students.

12 13 14 15 16 10 9 8 7 6 5 4 3 2 1

BRIEF CONTENTS

CONTENTS

FOREWORD

At last! The textbook I have been waiting for!

It's hard these days to write a counseling textbook that is fresh and doesn›t read like a rehash of existing texts. David Paré has done it.

Many textbooks teach the practice of counseling to new learners by relying on basic ideas generated before the 1970s and graft more recent developments onto this foundation as optional modalities. David Paré avoids this shortcoming. He has written a text that incorporates some of the best of contemporary practices while avoiding the arbitrary cobbling together of unrelated ideas that can result in a sort of eclectic counseling stir-fry. The problem with doing this is that practices that are incompatible often get stirred in and the overall taste is spoiled.

There are also those who advocate dropping a range of practices into a 'toolkit' and pulling out the ones that seem most appropriate for the occasion. The problem with such an approach is that it does not represent a unified perspective which gives practitioners the opportunity to improvise in accordance with a coherent set of values. In fact practices are always linked to philosophical frameworks and these are rooted in perspectives on living that, in order to be useful, have to be espoused with some depth. Without careful learning of the framework as well as the immediate tool, practitioners can actually do damage. It is as hard to be completely eclectic in this sense as it is to be Christian, Muslim, Buddhist and Jewish at the same time. David Paré does not ask students to attempt the impossible.

David Paré does not try to be all things to all people. Instead, he draws carefully from theoretical frameworks that hang together coherently. He explains his own preferences along the way and students are therefore able to critically engage with the material as they formulate their own forms of practice. This transparency is a refreshing alternative to implausible "neutrality" that wears a mask of purported objectivity while secretly turned in one theoretical direction.

Much of the professional and academic energy in the counseling professions has been dedicated in recent years to strengthening the structure of the profession through establishing licensing standards, credentialling processes, codes of ethics or laws, and extending the reach of professional bodies. There has also been a concerted effort to attend to long overdue issues of diversity and social justice. As a result, concerns about the basic foundations of practice have often remained neglected. By default, counselor education has fallen back on teaching practices established long ago. It often appears to be assumed that you can just paint a coat of diversity on top of the usual basic practices and add on a few 'evidence-based' tools from the toolkit and all will be okay.

The problem is that the world has changed. People's lives are different from when Freud wrote and also from when Carl Rogers constructed his 'core conditions' for the counseling relationship. Problems people experience are constructed differently and philosophical developments have taken place that move us inot new territories of meaning and practice. Cultural forces have shifted the ground on which learning counseling has to take place.

What I like most about this book is that it recognizes these shifts. David Paré does not assume that the world has not changed in recent decades. He draws on a wide range of innovative ideas and practices well suited to addressing the challenges people face in the contemporary world, weaving them into a potent foundational mix for practice. The approach taught here actually has much to offer the cause of social justice through doing counseling itself with more understanding of the effects of power, rather than seeing social justice as mainly relevant to what counselors do outside the counseling room.

Neither does David Paré dismiss the foundations of counseling laid a generation or two ago as irrelevant. Instead he connects them judiciously with new emphases drawn from the most creative practices of recent decades and makes them relevant to students learning counseling. His effort can be summarized by saying that ideas drawn from the turn to meaning are placed alongside many well-established traditions of counselling which are reworked and retained in new formats.

Remarkably, David Paré both draws from sophisticated philosophical thought but avoids heady jargon. He speaks to the reader in a very direct, practical, and accessible way. This book guides students through the complex process of learning to be a counselor without hurrying understanding along or glossing over knotty issues. There is plenty of invitation to reflect, to loiter with a poignant metaphor, to discuss subtle nuances, and to incorporate both accumulated wisdom and vigorous new ideas into creative practice.

There are also many useful suggestions for practice exercises to use in class and invitations to discussions worth having. This book will help enthusiastic and caring practitioners become skilled, intentional and up-to-date in their practice. I am very grateful for the work that this book does, and I can't wait to share it with classes.

John Winsladee
Professor and Associate Dean, College of Education,
California State University, San Bernardino
September 2012

PREFACE

It would be difficult to marshal the staying power to complete a text like this one without the conviction that one had something new to say. This book has been a long time coming—many years in gestation and a few in the birthing phase, too. It's precisely because I believed I had something urgently worth sharing that I was able to keep at the project despite many other duties, obligations, and distractions. But I'd like to be clear that I don't see this book as a compilation of my ideas; the something new that I have taken great pleasure in articulating derives from the work of countless theorists and practitioners I have had the privilege of encountering over the past two decades.

I won't fill this early preview of what lies ahead with a detailed account of what those novel ideas and practices are—there is plenty of space ahead for that—but let me provide you with a brief glimpse. The idea for the book sprung from my noticing that none of the counseling skills textbooks I was acquainted with through my role as a counselor educator paid sufficient tribute to the dazzling array of innovative approaches to counseling and therapy I was familiar with through my role as a counseling practitioner keeping up with contemporary work in the field. I noticed the textbooks were still informed by a highly individualistic view of people, whereas so many forward-looking practitioners had moved well beyond that perspective.

As you will see in the pages ahead, that single shift to a view of person-in-context sets off a domino effect of other important shifts that distinguish this book in may ways from traditional counseling texts. For starters, counseling is unveiled as a cultural practice, and clients are seen as cultural beings. That move away from individualism precipitates a lessening of the focus on individual pathology because it opens up a view of people's taking on the diverse contextual challenges of their lives in a variety of resourceful ways. Counseling comes to be seen less as an exercise in correcting dysfunction or promoting personal growth and more as a cross-cultural collaboration capitalizing on people's unique knowledges and competencies.

The book is divided into sections that roughly parallel phases of the work, with the first section devoted to preparation for practice. Chapter 1 provides a tour of some of the key new ideas I referred to above; it may be worth returning to from time to time as the issues highlighted there become foregrounded through the practices outlined in later chapters. This first chapter introduces one of two counselors, Maria, whose therapeutic conversations will be featured in transcript form throughout the text. Maria is represented in each of the ongoing scenarios—as both a counselor to Jorge and a client of Daniel. She is included in both roles as a reminder that like clients, counselors face ongoing challenges themselves that hover in the background of the work they do.

The second section of the book is devoted to constructing a foundation of collaboration. Chapter 3, on receiving and listening, emphasizes the critical importance of skills that are less overt but fundamental to creating a safe and receptive context for sharing. The fourth chapter examines the role of the therapeutic relationship, which has been repeatedly shown to play a crucial role in effective helping.

Section 3 of the book takes on the task of mapping the client's experience, reminding readers to be mindful of cultural diversity and to approach each new client with an attitude of open-minded curiosity. Achieving shared understanding is a subtle art that includes both receptive and expressive skills. The section is divided by these, starting with skills for reading experience, followed by skills for conveying that reading back to clients to coordinate meaning making.

The fourth section of the book focuses on assessment. This is where some of the more striking divergences from some other texts appear. Whereas assessment typically emphasizes a scoping out of personal deficit, these chapters provide ideas for separating persons from the challenges they face, a practice that diminishes the focus on pathology and opens space for more optimistic and productive conversations. Chapter 7, about defining problems and preferences, reminds readers that assessment should never lose sight of what people are striving for because clients' hopes and aspirations are the compass for the work. The following two chapters expand on assessment practices that situate challenges in context and keep a view of client competencies alongside an account of what is troubling them.

The book's final section, about promoting change, moves into the more proactive task of joining persons in making shifts in the ways they act, think, feel, and make meaning of their lives. The section begins with the topic of collaborative influence, an orientation to practice that facilitates change while keeping the client at the center of the process. The chapters to follow in this section offer a diverse range of practices for joining clients in making changes in particular areas. The chapters portray possibilities for creatively linking practices associated with dominant contemporary models of counseling and psychotherapy. Chapter 14, "Working With Stories," is particularly integrative because it demonstrates opportunities for bringing together gains made in the various domains of living, making meaning of changes, and reflecting on what they say about clients' values, skills, and identity. The book's final chapter, "Endings and Beginnings," emphasizes that the termination of work with a counselor is the beginning of a new era of living for clients—cause for both thoughtful reflection as well as acknowledgment and celebration.

As the book unfolds, you will notice some other features worthy of mention. The chapters include boxes designated as "Student Voices"—passages written by graduate students in the thick of their counselor training. These will give readers cause for reflection as they witness accounts of counselors' experience both resonant with, and different from, their own. The chapters are also interspersed with further opportunities for contemplation: watch for the gray boxes that invite reflection on personal experiences tied to the material at hand. The text is also broken up at times with boxes focusing in on particular elements and presented in the form of vignettes, in-depth explanations of key concepts, tables and charts, and so on. Each chapter closes with a pair of other features: sets of questions for discussion, and activities for bringing an experiential element to the learning.

Writing this book has been a rewarding experience for me, consolidating my respect for the infinite diversity and resourcefulness of the people I encounter as a practitioner. I hope it serves to invigorate your own practice.

ACKNOWLEDGMENTS

The chapters to come reflect my journey as a student, therapist, counselor educator, researcher and supervisor. The ideas and practices that fill these pages derive from the many sources cited throughout the text, of course, but also from countless interactions with colleagues who have stoked my curiosity and inspired me to further exploration and learning.

I'd like to pay a particular tribute to the late Michael White. His work courageously challenges the taken for granted and has been profoundly inspiring to me and thousands of others. Thanks as well to his colleague David Epston, whose unwavering energy and optimism have given birth to so many joyful practices and who generously provided feedback to earlier drafts of this book. Michael White and David Epston belong among the pantheon of seminal contributors to counseling and psychotherapy. I would also like to acknowledge the clear-eyed and steady vision of Cheryl White, David Denborough, Jill Freedman, Gene Combs, Harlene Anderson, Ken Gergen, and Mary Gergen, prime movers behind international communities of theorists and practitioners devoted to countering oppressive practices and celebrating the knowledges of diverse peoples.

I'd like to mention fellow teachers and writers who have served as mentors, intellectual role models, and conversational partners over the years. Thank you to Don Sawatzky, my original mentor who set me on my path, and to Stephen Madigan, whose riveting Vancouver conferences provided so much early learning. I'm grateful to the Waikato community, which inspired me at the time the idea for this book was hatched: Kathie Crockett, Wendy Drury, Wally McKenzie, Gerald Monk, and John Winslade. Mishka Lysack welcomed me into his Ottawa community and joined me in growing that community over the years. Glen Larner teamed up with me at a great distance on an edited volume. Tom Strong did the same and continues to be a continual source of inspiration through his prolific writings. André Gregoire provided thoughtful commentary on earlier drafts and has nourished me over the years through our ever-animated bilingual discussions. Jim Duvall, Texan "Jimbob" to my "Slim," has shown me how therapist training and guitar picking can go hand in hand. And Vikki Reynolds continues to energize me with her moral courage and passionate solidarity.

An Ottawa-and-area community of practitioners has been a constant source of inspiration and support. May it continue! My deep gratitude goes out to Aimee Anderson, Don Baker, Lynn Bloom, Bonney Elliott, Karen Hill, Margaret Kelly, Rena Lafleur, Alice Layiki-Dehne, Marc Leger, Heidi Mack, Karen McRae, Mego Nerses, Christine Novy, Maureen Parker, Linda Smith, Noah Spector, Pamela Story-Baker, and Francine Titley.

Thanks to those who contributed feedback and reflections for the text and help with the accompanying videos, including Mohamoud Adam, Emely Alcina, Mary Alexandrou, Cristelle Audet, Magda Baczkowska, Janet Balfour, Patricia Bernier, Shaofan Bu, Kevin Chaves, Katie Crosby, Jessica Diener, Christy Etienne, Tara Findlay, Maria Franchina, James Galipeau, Cheryl Gaumont, Frances Hancock, Victoria Homan, Samantha Johnson, Lauren Joly, Genevieve Killulark, Peter Kiriakopolis, Tracie Lee, Nicole Lewis, Tapio Malinen, Gaya Mallya, Talia Nadler, Julia Paré, Jill Peckham, Jessica Poloz, Chelsea Purcell, Peggy Sax, Melanie Stubbing, Jacqui Synard, and Tina Wilston.

I'd like to tip my hat to my good humored and ever supportive colleagues at the University of Ottawa: Cristelle Audet, Nick Gazzola, Diana Koszycki, André Samson, David Smith, Anne Thériault, and Tracy Vaillancourt. I had special hands-on help pulling the manuscript together from Sheena Sumarah and Jessica Chew Leung, assistants who patiently juggled multiple inquiries and diligently dug up obscure sources. Thanks to the SAGE team including Lisa Brown, Barbara Corrigan, Lauren Habib, Elizabeth Luizzi, Laura Barrett, Adele Hutchinson, Anupama Krishan, and in particular, Kassie Graves. Kassie, you were always available for consultation and reassurance while gently steering the process forward; it's been a real pleasure working with you.

My final words of acknowledgment go to my children Casey and Liam and my wife Susan Peet, who have spent recent years witnessing my preoccupation— sometimes to the point of distraction—with what turned out to be a formidable project. Susan, I'm not quite sure how I would have pulled this off without you. I am forever grateful.

Section One

Preparing for Practice

Chapter 1

CULTURE, COUNSELING, AND CARE

INTRODUCTION: COUNSELING AS A CULTURAL PRACTICE

As the elevator door closes, Maria takes a deep breath and tries to shed some of the day's hectic energy. This next hour is supposed to be for her. She turns her attention inward for a moment and notices she's feeling some complicated emotions on the verge of her first therapy session ever. For the past 2 years she has been training as a counselor and has come to appreciate the complexity and sensitivity of the craft. But today she will sit in the other chair. Maria is immediately aware of a sense of vulnerability: As much as she looks forward to the chance to talk about the various challenges she's dealing with in her life, she's also aware she'll be opening up to someone she's never met. She pulls the slip of paper out of her pocket and glances at it one last time: Daniel Brooks, Suite 345.

In the waiting area, Maria's phone rings as she sits down. Her husband Azim wants her to pick up some milk on the way home. He's talkative on the other end of the line, and Maria feels she's attracting unwanted attention.

"Okay, honey, gotta run. I'll see you at dinner. Make sure to change Kyla."

Maria turns the ringer off and puts her phone away as a tall African American man steps into the waiting area.

"Maria?" he says, scanning the faces around the room.

"That would be me," says Maria, standing and extending her hand.

"Good to meet you; I'm Daniel Brooks. My office is just down this way."

Maria follows Daniel down the hall, marvelling at what feels like a curious mixture of excitement and dread as she prepares to put words to the various stressors that led her to this moment.

And thus begins a conversation with a purpose. In the exchange about to unfold, Maria as the client[1] will seek help with challenges she faces, and Daniel as the counselor will attempt to support Maria in diminishing her distress. This book is devoted to a detailed examination of the multiplicity of skills that Daniel and other counselors employ in this critical work.

As we shall see, rigorous and specialized as many of the skills are, they also have a familiarity about them because they are centered on a practice widely employed by the general public, namely, talk. This makes them less mysterious than, say, the skills required to isolate a gene from a strand of chromosomes or to etch microscopic circuits onto carbon wafers. Counseling and psychotherapy[2] are highly refined disciplines, yet conversation more generally is a practice engaged in by virtually all human beings. In addition to that, many stereotypical depictions of counseling and psychotherapy have seeped into popular culture, making the practices that much more familiar, although tailored for popular consumption. And finally, most readers of this text will have had some previous academic exposure to counseling theories and practice. This all adds up to a lot of assumptions about a topic that deserves a more open-minded inquiry in preparation for practice.

And so as tempting as it is to plunge immediately into exploring the diversity of counseling skills, I invite you to pause for a moment to reflect on what sets therapeutic conversation apart from ordinary talk. Just what is it that practitioners are attempting to accomplish, and what are key issues and ideas that demand our attention before we proceed? To rush forward without asking these key questions is to treat therapeutic conversation like a recipe-driven, formulaic, linear task—a gravely simplistic view of the practice. Instead, this book begins with reflections designed to prepare the way for developing skills that are used thoughtfully, with an eye to the big picture. This involves looking at counseling with fresh eyes, holding on for a little longer to the desire to refine the skills of the craft. Have no fear, we will soon get to those skills—the book is devoted to them. But for now let's just behold the practice called counseling, in both its beautiful simplicity and its intriguing complexity.

Remembering that counseling and psychotherapy are cultural practices is a useful way to examine them with a discerning eye. Imagine for a moment that we venture forth as anthropologists encountering an unfamiliar social ritual for the first time. As mentioned, this is not easy: The media are awash with portrayals of counseling and therapy, and your own education to this point has added further impressions. It's difficult to bring a genuine curiosity to a cultural activity not entirely new to us. But shed your knowledge and assumptions for a moment, and you will see a cultural ritual increasingly prevalent among industrialized nations and less so in the developing world. The ritual has many variations, but all are born of a desire to offer support and comfort to those who are experiencing some form of distress. Broadly speaking, the practice is a response to human suffering (Gehart & Paré, 2008).

Look more closely and you will notice that although there are many approaches to counseling and therapy—hundreds of them by some counts (Duncan & Miller, 2000)—they all feature an encounter between people relying on language as a central tool of the craft. Things quickly become more complex on closer inspection because unlike numbers, language isn't stable and universal. Words express lived experience, yet their meanings curiously vary from person to person, capturing the nuance of unique cultural contexts. What we notice is that counseling inevitably involves speakers and listeners with distinct backgrounds—it's a social practice that involves the coming together of cultures or, as Courtland Lee and colleagues (2009) point out, "all counseling interactions are cross-cultural" (p. xix).

The implication of this, of course, is that multicultural counseling is not a subdiscipline of counseling in general. Culture is not a variable or factor but the space in which counseling conversations—all conversations for that matter—happen. A saying that helps to capture this idea is, "We are the fish; culture is the water." Culture is all around us, influencing how we think, feel, and act—the backdrop to, or context for, each of our conversations.

The view of counseling as cross-cultural conversation gives rise to a number of important themes that will be threaded throughout the chapters of this book. Like the construct of culture, the themes are not isolated issues to consider or specialized practices to apply in narrowly defined situations: They suffuse the work and are always at play. These themes will not be referred to constantly throughout this text but will be the backdrop to the many counseling exchanges depicted throughout the book.

In the rest of this chapter, I'll say a few words about these themes as a way to prepare the ground for your encounters with them later. You may find that some speak to you immediately, whereas others require further reflection. My intention in providing capsule descriptions of these themes up front is to orient you to ideas that will be revisited and developed more fully as the chapters unfold. So I encourage you to let the themes wash over you, knowing you can flip back to this introduction at any time as you progress through the book.

CONVERSATION

Talk as Intervention

Curious as it may seem, the emphasis on counseling as conversation is so far virtually absent within the field. More often, counseling conversations are depicted as vehicles for delivering some form of helpful intervention distinct from the conversation itself. But counseling differs from other helping professions in that the conversation *is* the intervention. As Friedman (1993) says, "therapy is a conversation in which dialogue between therapist and client leads to the generation of new meanings, understandings, and options for action" (p. 273). Counselors talk with clients, and the talk *itself* is what is helpful.

If this seems confusing, a sideways glance at other professions helps. In many helping professions, the intervention or treatment is not primarily about speech: Consider the wielding of a scalpel or the scribbling of a prescription. In other cases, the intervention is delivered through words (as an exercise plan or dietary regime, for example), but it's the plan or regime and not the words used to convey it that are seen as the intervention. With counseling, it is the words themselves, and of course the nonverbals, that are also a key element of conversation, that are central to the professional practice. We might not blink if someone were to say, "She's an excellent doctor, but a lousy talker and listener." Make the same comment about a counselor, and it begs the question of on what possible grounds they're being evaluated. Counselors talk and listen, and these exchanges are the cornerstone of their professional skill.

Honing Familiar Skills to a New Level

Counseling conversations share many features with other forms of conversation. And so students new to the profession arrive with a lifetime of experience. In some ways, refining one's counseling practice is more about further mastering a long-developed skill than taking on some arcane practice foreign to the uninitiated. Nevertheless, just because we've always conversed doesn't mean that there isn't a great deal to learn and refine. There's a story about Margaret Atwood, the acclaimed Canadian novelist, being told by a neurosurgeon at a cocktail party of his plans to write novels upon retiring. Atwood paused to sip from her drink before responding, "Yes, and I think I'll take up neurosurgery."

We assume neurosurgery requires knowledge and skills that take years to acquire, yet most of us already know how to write. If you've tried writing a novel, you probably know it takes far more than the ability to string words together. So too for conversation. We may be reasonably adept at participating in conversations—after all, it's a familiar practice we've engaged in since the age of about 2. But are these conversations helpful to others? Learning to have helpful conversations with clients facing diverse mental, emotional, relational, physical, and spiritual challenges is a lifetime's project. Counseling is founded on a great many skills used in daily life but involves using the familiar tool of language for some highly particular purposes. And as much as those purposes may vary, they always happen in the context of culture.

CULTURE

Recognizing the Role of Culture

Counseling and psychotherapy have developed amid a long Western tradition of individualism that places primary emphasis on people as distinct and self-contained entities. This is changing as rapid globalization puts us face to face with the cultural imbeddedness of our experience and the critical importance of intercultural relationships. There's been a striking growth in the attention paid to culture as it relates to counseling in recent years (cf. Arthur & Collins, 2010; Baruth & Manning, 2007; Ivey, Ivey, & Zalaquett, 2009; Lee et al., 2009; Lee & Ramsey, 2006; McAuliffe, 2007; Monk, Winslade, & Sinclair, 2008; Pedersen, Draguns, Lonner, & Trimble, 2008; Ponterotto, Casas, Suzuki, & Alexander, 2010; Sue, Ivey, & Pedersen, 2009). Yet the field struggles to incorporate culture into the center of the practice: to understand culture not as an add-on to attend to when doing a specialized form of counseling designated as multicultural but rather as the substance of the practice itself. Culture permeates counseling in countless ways:

1. Counseling is a practice with cultural origins that is understood and performed differently (if at all) in different geographic locations and at different historical moments.

2. Counseling theories are discourses developed in the context of various cultural institutions such as psychology, psychiatry, and education, reflecting the values and beliefs associated with those points of origin.

3. When counselor and client(s) meet, they always bring their diverse cultural understandings and meanings to the conversation.

4. Counseling is practiced in language, a cultural creation itself that is the primary vehicle for the expression of and construction of meaning.

Culture in Pluralistic Terms

No doubt the previous list can be extended in various ways. On close inspection, it seems culture permeates not just counseling but all human affairs. But what exactly am I referring to in referencing *culture*? The word has a long history and a surprisingly diverse array of meanings attached to it (cf. Monk et al., 2008). Historically, culture has most often been tied to the notion of ethnicity or race but in a manner that fails to capture the complexity of our diverse social locations (Arthur & Collins, 2010; Lee et al., 2009; Monk et al., 2008; Paré, 1996, 2008). A more useful way forward is to understand culture in pluralistic terms. In other words, we all inhabit many cultural subgroups, and our participation in these groups shifts over time and across contexts.

Student Voices

Talia: Changing Identities

I was recently told by a new friend that I was the first Jewish person they had ever met, but that I did not "look or act the part." Being someone who is opened minded and accepting, I responded by asking, "What were you expecting Jews to be like?" She told me she thought all Jews had dark hair, big noses and are rich—all stereotypical characteristics I had heard linked to Jewish people in the past. My friend's response struck me for a number of reasons. First of all, I was surprised that at 24-year, having lived her whole life in big cities, I was the first Jew she had ever met. This situation made me want to introduce my friend to a variety of Jewish people to show her that we are just like everyone else: We come in all colors, shapes and sizes. Within the counselling profession, we need to be mindful of our own stereotypes and make sure that we remain curious, and remember that just like us, our clients have multiple stories.

Some sources (cf. MacCluskie, 2010; Miraglia, Law, & Collins, 2006) refer to culture as the rituals and traditions, beliefs, behaviors, lifestyles, and so on in which various groups of clients engage. This is one familiar way to talk of culture; this book uses another familiar connotation of the word. It refers to the groups themselves: the people who share and engage in the various traditions. Lee's (2006) definition fits with this view: "Culture can be broadly defined as any group of clients who identify or associate with one another on the basis of some common purpose, need or similarity of background" (p. 179).

Looked at this way, we can see that all of us simultaneously inhabit a multiplicity of subcultures—or as Pedersen (1991) puts it, "each of us belongs to many different cultures at different times, in different environments and in different roles" (p. 4). Box 1.1 shows what this looks like graphically. It may be easier to picture when attached to an example, however. Box 1.2 depicts Maria, whom we met at the opening of the chapter and whom we will follow throughout this book. Her brief vignette is intended to demonstrate the many subgroups of society she inhabits: the multiplicity of her cultural locations.

BOX 1.1

Multiple Cultural Locations

This is a graphic depiction of the multiplicity of identity. Each of the elongated ovals depicts some group to which this person belongs. The number of groups is arbitrary, and belonging to some groups may come and go. The person is represented at the center, where all groups overlap, because they simultaneously inhabit each of these.

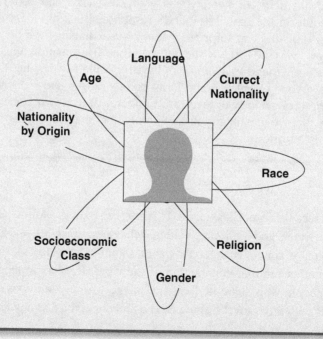

BOX 1.2

Wearing Many Hats: Maria's Multiple Cultural Locations

Like all of us, Maria occupies multiple cultural locations. As a mother, wife, employee, daughter, counselor, colleague, and so on, she wears many hats, and her relationships with others can be understood in terms of those hats. They influence how she makes sense of things and how she reads others' meanings. In each encounter, her cultural location also has implications for power relations—placing her sometimes in a position of power and at other times in a position of subordination. As she goes through her day, all of this shifts in relation to those around her—cultural location is a fluid and ever-changing thing.

At 6:00 a.m. her alarm goes off, and Maria rises groggily. She's still nursing her infant girl, Kyla, and her nights tend to be interrupted. Her partner Azim does what he can, but as a man he can't be with their daughter in some ways. Maria and Azim share domestic duties and have what some might call an "equal relationship." But their gender differences nevertheless can't be erased: There are biological and social distinctions between the two cultural sub-groups they inhabit that both add interest and present challenges to their relationship.

She leans down to kiss Kyla before heading out the door. The bond between her and her daughter is the most intense relationship in her life; at times she feels as though they are one. Yet as a 28-year-old woman, Maria is a long way from infanthood. It takes care and attention to anticipate her baby's experience of the world. There are dramatic asymmetries to their relationship as well: In many ways, the baby's survival depends on her mother, whereas Kyla can't offer any deliberate support or protection to her mother in return.

As she steps into the foyer of the apartment building Maria greets Juanita, who is vacuuming the carpet. Juanita also has a young child. As young mothers, Maria and Juanita have an easy point of connection. Maria speaks English whereas Juanita shares her experience in her second language. Maria has to work hard to imagine the threat of one's life unraveling over citizenship and immigration issues. She and Juanita laugh about Maria's counseling studies—to Juanita, sitting and talking to clients sounds like an easy way to earn grocery money.

As she unlocks her office door, Maria is greeted by Myriam, the director of the counseling center where Maria is doing her practicum placement. As women, mothers, and counselors, they have a lot in common and have found many points of connection. But at the same time there's no escaping their differences. Myriam's children are almost Maria's age, and she and Maria have occasionally found themselves in awkward conversational moments, stumbling on some very different ideas about parenting. Because Myriam is

(Continued)

(Continued)

her supervisor's boss, Maria is aware she sometimes frets about how she's presenting to Myriam, who might one day write a letter of reference or even be a prospective employer.

Inside the office, Maria removes her coat as the phone rings. It's Maria's mother, who's been having some medical problems lately. She's calling to tell Maria about some recent tests she's had. For most of her life, Maria's mother loomed as an imposing figure in her life, a strong woman who ran a tight ship at home. A few months ago, Maria's father died, and Maria is aware of a change in their relationship. Her mother turns to her more now for support and guidance as she copes with health concerns and fears about her own mortality.

At 10 o'clock her first client, Niall, arrives. Niall comes from a very wealthy family. His parents donated a large sum of money to the university, some of which helped to pay for the construction of the counseling center. He's never had to worry about money, unlike Maria, who has lost sleep over mounting student loans. Lately Niall's become concerned he may be developing a drug habit. He's confused about many choices he's been making, and he looks to Maria for guidance, seeing her counselor status as evidence of a psychological expertise and emotional stability he feels he's lacking.

One way to make sense of Maria's experience is to understand her as a member of many cultural subgroups, with the significance of some of those groups coming to the foreground in various encounters she has. Throughout her day, different aspects of her cultural location are highlighted, positioning her differently in relation to others in her life. What goes on between Maria and others, including her clients, is much easier to understand when we take their cultural locations into account.

Maria is a woman; she is Caucasian, middle class, English speaking, able bodied, and heterosexual; she is a mother, daughter, wife, friend, employee, supervisee, and counselor—she stands in many places relative to those around her. Which of her cultural locations is most relevant at any time depends on the immediate context in which she finds herself. In some contexts she is at an advantage and derives power from her cultural location. In other contexts, her cultural location puts her in a one-down position. When Maria engages in a counseling session, both she and her client bring these and many more cultural locations to the conversation. This is critical because—just as in any other conversation—counselors need to think about cultural location in deciding what to say and how to say it (Robinson-Wood, 2009). Culture-blind counseling conversations are likely to be unhelpful at best and harmful at worst.

Counseling and Colonization

Without considering culture, it is easy to inadvertently underestimate or over-look the knowledge of the clients who consult counselors. This is what the colonial powers did in relation to the cultural groups they colonized. Through their training, counselors are introduced to vast vocabularies and conceptual frameworks in some ways analogous to the "advanced" learnings that Europeans brought overseas. These professional knowledges are always available to coun-selors although often unfamiliar to the clients with whom they work. They can be useful to clients, but they can also obscure the rich specificity of clients' experience, just as the ways of colonizing powers have typically supplanted local knowledges and tradition.

And so counselors can't escape a challenge faced by any colonial culture as its citizens step ashore on some foreign land: How does one contribute helpfully to a client's quality of life without "colonizing" them with ideas and practices that obscure or eradicate their local knowledge? Western colonizers generally had a dismal record on this count; the challenge endures in the multicontextual practice of counseling.

Context as Cultural Location

Among many reasons it is so important to consider culture is its role in deter-mining the meaning of words spoken by clients. Word meanings can differ dramatically depending on where the speaker or listener is coming from—their cultural location. Although cultural location is not literally a geographic place, geography is a helpful frame for understanding the notion of cultural location. Consider the experience of a Bronx cab driver accustomed to weaving the can-yon streets of Manhattan; compare his experience to that of a bewildered Japanese farmer riding a flatbed truck into the neon of Tokyo for the first time. The word *city* has a very different meaning for each of these two people. The world looks like a very different place depending on where you are rooted.

Of course cultural diversity goes beyond urban versus rural. From the moment an infant is dressed in pink or baby blue, two more distinct territories are staked out—these having to do with cultural location within gender rather than geogra-phy. So it's not necessary to travel any distance to encounter cultures whose rituals and traditions, styles of speech, and modes of dress vary. Just ask a young boy on his way home from his first ballet class or a woman after her first day on the job as a diesel mechanic.

Clients are cultural beings. The things they think and feel, say and do, can't be dissected from the contexts in which they live their lives. It's impossible to make sense of exchanges in counseling conversations without keeping this in mind. This idea will become clearer as we follow the examples of clients throughout the book.

competent @ work
insecure @ school

Reflection 1.1

When you reflect on your own identity—your sense of who you are—which variations do you notice over time and across locations? For instance, are there contexts in which you feel more or less confident, more or less vital, more or less funny, more or less attractive, and so on? Which sorts of contextual factors do you see contributing to the variations?

CARE

Care as a Guiding Compass

Each of the hundreds of various approaches to counseling puts its emphasis in a somewhat different place. The practices vary widely, if not wildly. Some pay limited attention to the content of what clients say while honing in on feelings, whereas others key into cognitive patterns and downplay emotional expression. Some focus almost exclusively on behavior and devote virtually no attention to accompanying thoughts and feelings. As varied as these disparate models are, they share a common purpose. They're intended to be helpful to clients, to relieve them, at least in part, of their suffering. Each of these approaches is ultimately founded on an ethic of care.

The notion of care has been dissected minutely in countless thoughtful ways (cf. Dalmiya, 2002; Hoagland, 1991; Noddings, 2002; Sevenhuijsen, 1998; Tronto, 1993) that bring nuances to the concept that I won't attempt to duplicate here. But I would like to say a little more about *care* as it's used here because like all words, it resonates in many ways depending on the contexts in which it finds itself.

In simple terms, care is about attempting to be helpful to another in the other's terms. In counseling, that *other* is the client, and the reference to the other's terms is a reminder of the importance of keeping the client's purposes and intentions at the center of counseling conversations. It is also a reminder that the client inhabits a distinct cultural location. Although this may seem evident, it is not uncommon for counseling conversations to undergo a sort of slippage so the interaction is centered elsewhere—on strictly following a model, staying true to a theory, adhering to an ideology, complying with the demands of an insurance company, impressing a supervisor, satisfying a manager. This is what happens, for example, when a counselor attempts to "convert" a gay client to heterosexuality because of the counselor's religious beliefs or when a counselor subjects a client to a vivid reliving of some past trauma when the client has clearly indicated he or she prefers a future focus to the work. Centering the client in the process is critical, and less straightforward than it sounds, especially given the complexities of culture described earlier. An ethic of care involves more than simply the aspiration to be helpful or an empathic disposition; it requires ongoing reflection on practice that takes into account both the client's and the counselor's contexts, plus a whole lot more.

Over the decades, the counseling profession has introduced many theories and practices, models and protocols, taxonomies and instruments. Many students of counseling are both seduced and overwhelmed by the choices available to them for engaging with clients. In the earnestness to put these frameworks into practice, it's easy to forget they are tools forged for responding to and collaborating with clients of diverse backgrounds—not for erasing their diversity through the blind application of protocols. When seeking guidance as to a way forward, the first place to look is the client across from you because an ethic of care involves keeping the client's unique purposes and interests at the center of the work. Care for the unique other is counseling's guiding compass.

Centering clients' concerns is not about abandoning theories or models but about adapting them to the context at hand. A practice is effective if it is useful to this unique client, at this specific time, in this particular context. As the early American psychologist William James (1890/1981) said, truth is the compliment we pay to an idea that earns its keep. And so I encourage you to hold on lightly to all that you find between these covers. Try out the ideas and practices, and join with your clients in evaluating their helpfulness in the conversations where these words will have their true test.

MEANING AND STORY

Reality Through a Human Lens

Counseling conversations always unfold in the context of the very real challenges of living. Fact is, life brings us up against violence, illness, conflict, injustice, loss. But unlike many professions that seek an objective account of these, counseling is more concerned with the subjective way that clients make sense of the realities they inhabit. This starts with deriving a description of what people experience and continues into an exploration of the meaning they make of it.

Meaning is the spin people put on their experience. It isn't *reality* in the scientist's sense of the word, but it constitutes their *lived reality*. In this respect, meaning is reality through a human lens. And the primary vehicle for conveying that reality always has been stories. As we listen to peoples' stories, we discover how they make meaning and are invited into the territory of interpretations, values, aspirations, and memories, making it both endlessly fascinating and complex.

Meanings behave quite differently than objects; they're fluid and changeable. To put it differently, we are all "multi-storied" (White, 2007; Winslade & Williams, 2012). A person's subjective experience is never static, and a client's meaning for an event or circumstance may change year by year, week by week, even minute by minute. Today Zack sees his layoff from his job as an act of racism; a few weeks ago, he looked at it as the fallout of a recession. Last year when the incident happened, he viewed it as evidence of his own incompetence. The reality is that Zack was laid off, but to get at his lived reality, we have to understand the meaning he makes of it. And there are always many meanings available to him—many stories to tell—which is key to what makes counseling and psychotherapy helpful.

Reflection 1.2

Can you think of some significant event in your life about which you have made meaning differently at different times? Which sorts of emotions and thoughts were tied to the different readings of the event? Which reading do you prefer? Which reading seems to give you more energy and hopefulness? What, if anything, makes it a challenge to keep your preferred reading to the forefront?

divorce =
failure
— or —
success

Meaning and Culture

We don't make meaning out of thin air. Instead, we draw from the interpretations and stories available to us. These are typically constrained by the cultural locations that provide vantage points for the events of our lives. That's why the upper-middle-class son of a professor has little trouble making sense of his A+ grade in physics as evidence he'll teach at Harvard some day. The same conclusion seems like naïve grandiosity to an inner-city kid whose grades are just as high but whose horizons are more limited.

This doesn't mean those horizons can't be expanded; indeed that's one of the beautiful accomplishments of helpful counseling conversations. The point is that apparently identical circumstances can give rise to multiple meanings—lived realities are fluid and amenable to change in a way that physical matter is not. For Nora, a cancer diagnosis is seen as a betrayal by God, whereas for Heidi it's the beginning of a spiritual opening, a door to reconnection. Brian understands the end of a marriage as evidence of failure, whereas Gareth sees it as an opportunity for a new beginning. Discrete events may provide the raw material for meaning making, but it's the way we weave these together and make sense of them—the stories we tell and the stories we live—that determines our lived realities.

Student Voices

Rahima: The Meaning of *Weekend*

Last Friday, my colleagues and I were chatting before the end of a very long day. In this conversation, I wished one of my colleagues a relaxing weekend at home. She replied by saying that she rarely, if ever, has the opportunity to relax on the weekend since she has two sons. This exchange illustrates that our cultural locations—myself, as a single individual, and she, as a mother of two boys—influenced the different meanings we associate with "the weekend." For me, the weekend is a time to relax, and for her, the weekend is the time when she fulfills the majority of her responsibilities as a mother, which does not, as a rule, facilitate a great deal of relaxation. The multitude of cultural locations we inhabit—such as gender, socio-economic status, relational identities, et cetera—can impact the meanings exchanged and created within a conversation.

Counseling and Psychotherapy as World Making

Counselors trade in those lived realities, supporting others in narrating their lives according to their values and preferences, stepping into the stories that speak to the longings of their hearts. Those stories are filled with thoughts and feelings, actions and relationships; they constitute a client's world. That world changes as meanings shift throughout (and between) conversations. And so a view of a counseling conversation as "information exchange" fails to capture the richness of a practice more akin to world making (Goodman, 1978; Paré, 2001). Counseling sessions are fertile gardens, places where new worlds of meaning emerge from the soil of therapeutic conversation.

Centering Client Meanings

The point of reminding ourselves as counselors of the importance of attending to a client's meanings is directly tied to the subject of care. When we gauge the effectiveness of our actions primarily by the logical clarity of a favored theory or the purportedly objective evidence of a tested model, we neglect the subjective experience of the unique client before us. A care-filled practice keeps the client's preferred stories at the center of the activity. At the end of the day, it's the movement in the client's lived reality and not our technical virtuosity that determines whether the process is helpful.

POWER

A Process Both Generative and Oppressive

The topic of power is not often discussed in the professional counseling literature. I don't know if this is related to Law and Madigan's (1994) observation that "the idea that power doesn't exist tends to be quite popular among middle-class white persons. However, it seems not so popular an idea among the poor, the oppressed and the marginalised" (p. 3). In any case, this omission is difficult to understand because without careful consideration of issues of power, therapy can easily devolve into an imposition of professional expertise, the muting of a client's voice by a therapist's voice. Of course this wouldn't be the deliberate aim of a competent practitioner, but it's impossible to hold clients' purposes and intentions at the center of counseling conversations without considering the way power works to foreground certain versions of reality and marginalize others. The consideration of power is a natural outgrowth of discussions about culture, care, and meaning making. It's also central to an understanding of ethical practice.

Power as a construct is often oversimplified to the point of the recommendation that counselors give it up so that clients can take it on. *Empowerment* is a useful shorthand, but power is not a commodity that can be handed to others. Power is tied to context and relationship, as we saw earlier in the example of Maria (see Box 1.2). It's less like a thing and more like a process that can be both generative and oppressive: the leverage to make things happen, to uphold certain views, to influence others. In counseling conversations, it's important to pay attention to both how power plays out in interactions with clients and how power relations operate in their lives.

Not All Stories Are Created Equally

The complexities of power relations will unfold through the accounts of counseling practice in these pages, so I won't attempt to elaborate in full here. However, a key concern that will frequently surface is the legitimacy granted to certain meanings (and the corresponding delegitimizing of others).

We live in a world characterized by multiple meanings, an ever-fluctuating diversity of perspectives and representations available to us. We draw on these to make sense of our lives. Some are helpful and hope sustaining; others lead to discouragement and despair. It would be nice to think these meanings are equally accessible. However, certain views are relegated to back alleys and underground hideaways, pushed to the margins, whereas others are trumpeted from the towers of mass media. There are many versions of reality available to us, but the marketplace of meaning is not a democratic forum, and some versions tend to dominate. The topic of power invites curiosity about whose versions of reality are upheld as real and legitimate.

Claire stands in front of a mirror. Is she beautiful? The answer to this question is certainly not a fact. Claire's height and weight, the color of her hair, and the shape of her nose might all be measured and documented, but it's her subjective evaluation of all of these, rather than an objective accounting of the facts, that will constitute her experience and answer her question. And she's free to evaluate her looks any way she chooses. Or is she? As she glances at her reflection, Claire considers her appearance relative to images bombarding her from billboards, in supermarket checkout lines, on the Internet, and on film and television screens. These particular versions of what constitutes beauty are omnipresent and skillfully executed. To the degree that Claire doesn't match these specifications, she deviates from a widely circulated norm, a version of reality backed by profoundly influential social forces. She's tried reciting the mantra "I am beautiful" repeatedly, but the words stick in her throat, and she remains unconvinced.

This is about power, the way certain versions of reality gain credibility and influence through their association with potent social forces. These versions exert normative pressure on all of us: They influence the way we construct our very identities. Not all stories are created and distributed equally. Some are like pop songs that rule the airwaves, infiltrating our consciousness so that no other melodies come to our lips when we're moved to hum a tune. For example, it is difficult to consider accounts of morality or the afterlife beyond versions disseminated for centuries by world religions. That's because these particular stories are burned into cultural consciousness. Similarly, it's hard to think about and talk about intelligence in a way that's different from how the topic has been characterized by psychology. It's a challenge to make meaning in an original way, outside the influence of dominant stories—like imagining a new color.

Power also plays out in the relationship between counselors and clients. Disciplines like psychology and psychiatry have contributed to making certain constructs so prevalent they're regarded by many as universal realities: distorted cognitions, personal growth, superego, and so on. These stories about people and how they operate are upheld by academic tomes and organizations. The stories that clients share will contain strands of these but will also contain unique perspectives that are not legitimized in the same way by professional institutions. Making room for these is part of what is involved in negotiating power relations in counseling and psychotherapy.

The Role of Power in Ethics

There are key implications here for ethical therapeutic conversations. To practice ethically involves more than adherence to a disciplinary code of conduct or guideline. It involves vigilance about the impact of our words and actions on those who consult us, the influence we impart—whether intended or not. As counselors and therapists, we meet our clients backed by academic disciplines, regulatory bodies, and professional affiliations. Much as we may embrace diversity and encourage creative lifestyle choices, we speak from an institutional location. We inhabit a professional culture branded as credible and competent by the titles and degrees conferred on practitioners. This relates to power because that credibility is a capacity to influence the lived realities of others—a very potent capacity indeed. When we forget this, we underestimate our own potential dominance in a therapeutic conversation.

That real possibility of hijacking our clients' attempts to express their experience is there simply by virtue of the role we play. Wally McKenzie (Hancock & Epston, 2010) points to how this is also a dilemma for physicians, who may inadvertently intimidate patients due to their expert knowledges. He recounts how he carries a list of questions in his back pocket before visiting the doctor because he loses a sense of his own authority once he sits down in the consulting room.

This is not to say clients are clay in the hands of counselors, but to point to the influence that comes from being branded a professional helper. Few clients who engage in counseling by choice will dismiss the credibility of the profession—otherwise, why would they come? This is not all bad news: Our credibility increases our chances of being helpful. But it can also contribute to a sort of professional complacency. When we take the pronouncements of the discipline to be given truths, we pitch these at clients and stop inviting them to evaluate their own positions on topics critical to their dignity and emotional well-being.

This would be less of a concern if we could be assured disciplinary truths always offer ready relief for human suffering. But a review of the field's history suggests otherwise. We might easily forget, to choose one example, that homosexuality was officially designated a mental disorder until 1973 (cf. Spitzer, 1981). It's interesting to consider which currently dominant disciplinary ideas about health, functionality, normal development, and so on are more a reflection of social, political, or institutional agendas rather than expressions of care for the clients who seek services. In this respect, considerations of power are ever present in counseling, and counseling work begins to look inseparable from the domain of social justice.

Reflection 1.3

Can you think of relationships in which you feel you are in a one-down position by virtue, for example, of the other person's authority, education, age, gender, and so forth? How about ones wherein you are in the one-up position? To make things more complicated—appropriate to the complex topic of power—if you revisit these examples, can you identity how the power relations shift depending on the context in which you and the other person meet?

(handwritten margin notes)
One down:
boss
professor
parent

One up
boss
professor
parent

Shift
mom ♦ parent
♦ grandparent
to her g. kids

SOCIAL JUSTICE

Making Meaning, Doing Justice

The World Health Organization (n.d.) takes the position that "a *lack of access* to basic mental health care and treatment" (p. 1) is a basic violation of human rights. Access to services is part of the picture, but a social justice orientation to counseling takes it a step further. It leads us to the social inequities in clients' lives that give rise to the distress that brings them to counselors. When we move away from an individualistic view of clients, and understand personal experience as always strongly influenced by cultural context, we bump into the relationship between mental health and social justice.

By now it should be clear that the marketplace of meaning we call the wider culture doesn't operate by fully democratic means. Meanings are not granted equal say and are not distributed evenly through society. Dominant representations of cultural subgroups are often not generated by the groups themselves but by mass media driven by agendas that often have little to do with those groups' interests. As we've seen, representations—pictures and language, interpretations, views, stories, and so on—are the tools of meaning making. They constitute clients' lived realities. This is the stuff of counseling conversations, which inescapably happen in the context of issues of fairness, equity, and hence social justice (Zalaquett, Fuerth, Stein, Ivey, & Ivey, 2008).

The way clients make sense of who they are—views that can be painful indeed when things are not going well—is related to the distinctions available to them.

These include familiar binaries such as healthy/unhealthy, normal/abnormal, and functional/dysfunctional. It's easy to take these distinctions for granted; after all, they're enshrined in traditions inherited from prestigious disciplines such as medicine and psychology. But the criteria for what constitutes the second half of each of these binaries have typically been defined by those who purport to represent the first half. This leads one to wonder about who gets to characterize whom when it comes to what we call mental health.

This is a social justice issue because it relates to the politics of meaning. The various definitions of clients that circulate in society and are available for use by counselors and clients serve a variety of interests and purposes, not all of them guided by an ethic of care. For this reason, supporting clients in making meaning and taking action is an expression of solidarity (Reynolds, 2010), a facet of what therapist and activist Vikki Reynolds (2009) calls "doing justice" (p. 5).

Individualism and a Deficit Focus

During many decades, the helping professions have developed monumental systems for assessing deficit. Their many contributions include detailed protocols for distinguishing disorders and describing pathology. In some instances, these distinctions can be helpful revelations to clients struggling to make sense of a painful experience they can't seem to change. When Shania discovers that erratic mood shifts from manic highs to despairing lows have been given a name, she experiences relief from the sense that she's a failure for not getting her emotional life in order. On top of that, her diagnosis points to medications that can help to moderate painful mood swings. This is helpful; what is not helpful is our professional and cultural preoccupation with holding people up against countless norms, which feeds self-critique and feelings of inadequacy. Helping clients to critically evaluate normative judgments is an aspect of social justice work.

The prevalent focus on dysfunction and deficit is just one variety of world making, one way to make meaning of clients' lives, and it can be traced to long-standing traditions of individualism in psychology (Gergen, 2006; Iversen, Gergen, & Fairbanks, 2005; Rose, 1990, 1998). When we overlook culture, we have nowhere to turn to explain people's difficulties but the people themselves. What gets rendered invisible are the countless contextual factors that contribute to struggle and distress. These include violence on the streets of a poorly funded housing project, expectations of regimented behavior in overcrowded classrooms, media presentations equating thinness with beauty, homophobic messages from public figures, and so on. Understanding the problems clients face as evidence of their shortcomings is one way to join the conversation, but it fails to acknowledge the very real challenges that litter the road of life.

Responding to Injustice

The movement from an individualist view to one of clients as cultural beings leads to a significant shift in the focus of counseling interventions. This includes joining clients in critically evaluating the various accounts available in the wider culture for making sense of their lives and identities. It also includes understanding their actions as more than mere expressions of their "natures," seeing them instead as responses to circumstances, including violence and other forms of injustice (Todd & Wade, 2004; Wade, 1997, 2007; Yuen, 2007, 2009). Erving Goffman (1961) noticed these responses in his study of what were once called "insane asylums"—he spoke of the "small acts of living" that residents engaged in as expressions of human dignity. Attending to these as expressions of personal agency (Davies, 1991) and choice helps to counteract the debilitating inertia of victimhood.

An orientation to social justice plays out in the kinds of conversations counselors have with clients, but it goes beyond that too: Sometimes talk just isn't enough. Given the very real social barriers to mental health and emotional well-being, it's worth speculating about whether counseling work is complete if it stops at the office door. An emerging view is that a commitment to clients implies a willingness to use the leverage afforded counseling professionals to challenge injustices and to seek basic rights denied to clients.

COLLABORATIVE DIALOGUE

Tapping Insider Knowledge

A lot of the discussion about meaning and power relations to this point is cautionary in tone, pointing to processes compromising, rather than supporting, helpful counseling conversations. But this is certainly not the whole story. The power to construct meaning is held by not just cultural institutions and mass media; everyone has the capacity, and one of the great privileges of counseling is the opportunity to join with clients in reclaiming the richness of their lives. *Collaboration* and *dialogue* are two more terms that describe how that unfolds.

Collaboration is a prominent word in the contemporary professional vocabulary, and for good reasons. Vast resources are squandered when we fail to work together. This could be across geographical settings or professional disciplines. At the global level, collaboration includes respectful dialogue across national boundaries; locally, it might involve coordinating activities within an agency or teaming up with a colleague in the next office. Collaboration makes a wider selection of options available. It also provides useful safeguards because more pairs of eyes are likely to spot potential hazards otherwise overlooked.

In counseling, *collaboration* is an apt word to describe a way of working that pools the rich contributions clients and counselors bring to the conversation. Collaboration is a way of going forward that stays true to the themes explored to this point. It involves orienting to competence, tapping into skills and resources that may not always be particularly visible to clients in the midst of their struggles. In a sense, then, collaboration is an expression of cultural respect, a way of working *with* rather than working *on* the clients who consult us.

Dialogue is a key feature of collaborative practice. The word reminds us that two or more voices are present and that the process is about mutual exchange. Terms such as *counsel, treat,* and *intervene* fall short of capturing a collaborative spirit; they convey images of one-way transmission—the dispensing, the applying, the doing of something by one person to another. To be helpful, counseling needs to be more than that, a *doing with*. This is what Freeman and Lobovits (1993) mean in calling the work a "co-creative" process (p. 219). When we fail to consult our clients on their preferred directions and on the outcomes of our work with them, we relegate their points of view to the margins, duplicating a dilemma they experience elsewhere in their lives. You can probably see how this relates to an ethic of care.

Resistance as a Lapse in Collaboration

There are also pragmatic reasons for ensuring counseling conversations are dialogic. Think about times someone has pressed their ideas on you with no curiosity about your own point of view. We are naturally more open to listening when we feel listened to ourselves. On the other hand, we more often push back when someone foists their views on us. In the professional vocabulary this pushing back is sometimes characterized as resistance, as an indication of a client's intransigence. I prefer to see it as a lapse in collaboration. And it can be a useful moment in the longer term, as well, because it helps the counselor develop a better sense of the client's point of view.

Collaborative dialogue doesn't compel us to abandon theories or models or preferred frames for making sense of the complex work of counseling. The word *dialogue* suggests two or more voices are present, the counselor's among them. A simplistic view of counseling as being solely about inviting forward the client's voice fails to acknowledge this. But when it's collaborative, dialogue does involve being open to being surprised. It calls on counselors to be ready to shift gears: to be responsive, utterance by utterance, to clients. There's an improvisatory aspect to this that renders each conversation as unique as the clients participating. Responsive, collaborative practice unfolds differently than manualized treatment, which is informed primarily by statistical outcome measures rather than the unique person in the chair opposite the counselor.

From Discovery to Creation

There is another dimension to collaboration worth mentioning—its additive quality. Building on the metaphor of counseling as world making, a counseling dialogue involves two or more people constructing meaning sentence by sentence, glance by glance, heartbeat by heartbeat. This is different than other familiar views of therapeutic conversations as a process of peeling an onion, digging to a core, uncovering a nugget obscured by distracting surface features. The distinction is far from trivial: It shifts the task from one of discovery to one of creation. This shift links back to the more promising dimension of power mentioned earlier. It reminds us that more than merely coming to terms with who they *are,* clients can strive to become who they *wish to be.* Counseling becomes a constructive and forward-looking enterprise.

RELATIONSHIP

Natural Science Versus Cultural Exchange

The counseling and psychotherapy field has a long and still thriving tradition of searching for the "curative factors" (cf. Bachar, 1998; Kessler, 1994; Wilkins, 2000) that render therapeutic conversations effective. But whereas a very extensive body of research has clearly shown counseling and therapy work—they make a helpful difference in the lives of clients—the quest for curative factors continues to be mired in ambiguity (Wampold, 2000, 2001, 2010). I think this is because of a tendency to treat counseling like a natural science rather than to understand it in cultural terms. The quest for an active ingredient makes a good deal of sense in metallurgy or pharmaceuticals, where one element may be key to a chemical reaction, one molecule critical to targeting a specific organ or bodily process. However, the notion of isolating the key factor that works across contexts ignores the infinite cultural variability of counseling conversations and their dialogic character as well.

In the natural world, compounds are stable: Sodium and chloride make salt anywhere on Earth. But as we shall explore in more detail in Chapter 2, words and gestures have multiple meanings; the cultural world of lived realities is ever changing. Just what is going on when you combine a counselor, intervention, and client is different every time. A second problem with viewing counseling as akin to, say, administering a pill is that it construes the process as a one-way transaction, something we do *to* rather than do *with* others. Missing is the collaborative, responsive aspect of the craft that gives rise to the construction of unique and unanticipated ways forward that are often completely specific to one time, one place, one set of circumstances.

This is not to suggest counseling and therapy are mystical arts or that there are no useful guides to competent practice. What is helpful? is one of the most important questions counselors should ask. However, in addition to gaining some useful perspectives from statisticians, we can speak directly to the clients who seek our services. This is a form of evidence not founded on studies that amalgamate findings from dozens, hundreds, or even thousands of separate cases, which smooth flat cultural variability.

Practice-Based Evidence

To seek "evidence" of the helpfulness of our work by consulting clients is to acknowledge their "author-ity" (Crocket, 1999, 2004), to count on their judgment in discerning what is useful to them. Jim Duvall (2010) captures this in suggesting clients are our best supervisors: Their input is the best gauge of the effectiveness of our practice. The centering of client voices in evaluating therapy outcomes is a form of "practice-based evidence" (Fox, 2003). It is also a powerful relationship practice, and despite the enduring frustration of quests for the active ingredient that makes therapy work, a substantial body of accumulated research shows the relationship between counselors and clients is critical to helpful outcomes (Hubble, Duncan, & Miller, 1999; Wampold, 2001, 2010).

Think about conversations that have made a difference in your life. More likely than not, these have been with people you've trusted, people you respect and who respect you in turn. It's a risky venture to share one's experience of struggle and suffering; respect helps to create the safety to do that because it conveys the belief that a person is far more than the problems they face. Counselors who see themselves as "practitioners of respect" (Hancock & Epston, 2010) create a fertile territory for productive problem solving and the healing of sorrows.

Relationship as Process

Traditions of breaking the relationship down into component parts run the risk of turning it into a static variable, a magic bullet, an active ingredient. More useful, I think, is to remember that relationship is about an ethical interpersonal process because how counselors relate always has the potential to be helpful or hurtful for the people who consult them. Rather than attempt to tease out the components of a thing called a relationship, we focus on relational practices and the effects of our actions as counselors on the people who consult us.

It's common to speak of the importance of building rapport as a precursor to more productive counseling work. It might be helpful to add the phrase *and maintaining;* it is not as though, rapport having been built, we then get around to doing the work. Just as talk is the intervention rather than its delivery mechanism, doing relationship is the practice rather than an ingredient of counseling. And it's a doing that is never done; relationship is an ongoing, mutual process negotiated sentence by sentence in therapeutic conversations.

MINDFULNESS

High-Stakes Conversations

It's been mentioned a few times by now that despite distinctions that mark it as a specialized activity, counseling is fundamentally conversation—a familiar process to all of us. But in the conversations we partake in most days of our lives, we don't typically focus our attention carefully and deliberately. We talk to pass the time, to entertain ourselves or express affection, to convey or receive information.

This changes when we have more at stake in the conversation. We heighten our attention when the outcome of the conversation depends on it. When trying to persuade a reluctant friend to join us on a trip, we watch their reactions carefully to help us guide the pace of our unfolding pitch. Sitting in a job interview, we're vigilant about self-defeating thoughts that might erode our confidence and sabotage our presentation. These are examples of attending to the information available—in the first case external and in the second case internal—to inform us in going forward as effectively as possible. When the stakes are high, we draw on all the resources available to us in the moment.

In counseling conversations, the stakes are *always* high—at least to the degree that the outcome of the conversation has very real effects in the life of an individual reporting some form of distress. For that reason, it's important that counselors work at being as mindful as they can of all of the information coming to them through their senses. This may start with visual cues, such as a slump in a client's posture, and it may also include noticing the feel of a handshake or the tone of a voice. The field of awareness extends beyond raw sensory data as well and includes an internal realm of thoughts, ideas, and feelings that also has the potential to influence the direction of the unfolding conversation.

Mindfulness is sometimes described as a state of awareness and at other times as a discipline or practice. Later in the book we'll look at these descriptions in more detail. I include mindfulness as a theme here because I don't believe it can be separated from the ethic of care. To effectively care for another, we need to make deliberate and informed choices, and this is very difficult to do when we aren't paying attention.

Attending Inwardly and Outwardly

"Know thyself" is a sensible recommendation for helpers, and mindfulness is a useful tool for doing that. It's remarkable how the world can be born anew in the eyes of someone who cultivates careful attention. If you direct your awareness to what is going on inside your body in the midst of a difficult conversation, you will be sure to discover places of tightness that speak to you in ways that words do not. Attend to your feelings, and you may come upon anger, frustration, or sadness you hadn't previously noticed. Listen to the internal voices that feed you hypotheses and commentary, and you may become aware of promising options and unhelpful judgments, all of which can inform you as the conversation unfolds.

There is also a wealth of useful information available to us as we fine-tune the attention we direct outward. Various studies have shown that nonverbal cues contribute more than words themselves to the meaning that speakers convey (Bavelas, Coates, & Johnson, 2000). But of course, to be effective in conveying meaning, these cues—the flush of the cheek, an acceleration in speech—have to be picked up by the conversational partner. This is another place where a discipline of mindful attention supports practice.

Reflection 1.4

Take a moment to pause in your reading. Allow yourself to go quiet momentarily, and turn your attention to your sense of hearing. Close your eyes if it helps to focus. What do you hear? Can you separate out more than one sound? What are the qualities of these sounds? How many of these sounds were you consciously aware of before being invited to attend in this way? What other information might be available to you if you were to enlarge your awareness?

*[handwritten margin note: copier * voices ac]*

Mindfulness and Ethical Caring

Mindful attention is a critical tool at the service of responsible and ethical caring. Although we can never guarantee the impact of our part in a therapeutic conversation, we can reduce the chances of being neglectful or harmful by attending to the range of information available to us. So too for the development of our skills as counselors: The more we can notice, the more we can adjust our responses in accord with our intentions. In this sense, "attention supports intention" (Paré, Richardson, & Tarragona, 2009).

CHAPTER ONE RECAP

If you're feeling somewhat overwhelmed at this point, it isn't surprising. We've covered a very large territory. As I mentioned in the beginning, this chapter was designed as a preview of themes that will appear and reappear throughout the text. Some of the material may already be familiar to you, although it's likely some poses questions not raised in your training to this point. It would be nice if reflecting on ideas that challenge common assumptions did not bring on a certain temporary unbalancing. But I'm not sure it can be helped. It may reassure you to know that these themes will appear and reappear throughout the text, so if you're struggling to comprehend some of the material, you'll have many further chances.

Before moving to a look at the craft underlying counseling practice—conversation—I'd like to connect the themes introduced in this chapter to the writing and reading of this book as well. In sharing these words, I draw on my cumulative experience, all of it resonant of places I have journeyed, clients I have met, books I have read. It's also impossible to step outside of human society in writing a book, so this text comes from a perspective that reflects my various cultural locations. I have worked hard to present a balanced perspective of the practice of counseling here, but I make no claims to objectivity. Objectivity suggests the absence of cultural influences; but it isn't possible to stand nowhere. We are all multicultured (N. Spector, personal communication, October 23, 2009).

And so the words I've chosen to include within these covers reflect my training as a counseling psychologist and family therapist. They're the product of countless interactions I've had as a counseling practitioner and as a university-based counselor educator. They can't be separated from my identity as a white, middle-class, heterosexual man in North American society. Each of those aspects of my cultural location, and many more, help to account for the details I've chosen to bring forward.

The words I have chosen also reflect my values and commitments. I don't believe a stance of neutrality helps to move our profession forward. I resonate with Salaman, Grevelius, and Andersson (1993), who argue that "neutrality objectifies the persons we are trying to help, reducing them to objects for strategic manipulation rather than partners in a mutual undertaking" (p. 335). How can we be helpful to the people who seek out our services without being passionately committed to honoring them in their exquisite uniqueness?

This textbook is therefore the product of a commitment to a multiplicity of ideas and practices circulating our professional community and beyond. I've chosen not to brand these because I think this would not do service to their diversity. But the sources of these ideas are readily available to you, if you're curious, by exploring the literature I cite as you come upon passages that fascinate or infuriate you. There you'll find further accounts of practices and ideas—more eloquent and detailed than I'm able to include in this book. These all speak to the various locations from which I write.

The writer Salman Rushdie (1983) has said that every story is a form of censorship, meaning that in telling one account, we exclude endless possible others. So too for this book. I encourage you to retain a constructively critical viewpoint that allows you to evaluate the usefulness of all you encounter here and to consider what else might be useful to the practice of counseling and psychotherapy.

NOTES

1. Because it foregrounds the commercial aspect of the relationship, the word *client* does a poor job of characterizing clients who consult counselors. However, it does provide a shorthand and is a word in wide circulation. For that reason, it will be used throughout the text despite its deficiencies.

2. The terms *counseling* and *therapy* are used interchangeably in the literature. More often than not, *counseling* will appear here. When *therapy* is used in its place, it will be for no reason other than to match the content of a quote or to provide variety.

CHAPTER ONE DISCUSSION QUESTIONS

1. **Counseling as conversation.** What does it mean to say talk is the intervention? What shifts (if anything) in your view of counseling to see it as fundamentally a conversational practice? What are some preexisting skills most counselors can count on having? Which skills may be most in need of honing due to the specialized nature of counseling?

2. **Maria's multiple cultural locations.** Review Maria's story in Box 1.2. Can you identify shifts in power relations between Maria and others? Describe how those power relations might conceivably shift, even within a single relationship. Explain in which contexts they might reverse themselves. Which are some of the cultural subgroups Maria shares with others that seem to promote understanding and connection? Which are some of the cultural subgroupings that distinguish her from others? Can you identify how these differing cultural locations might pose power asymmetries or challenges to mutual understanding?

3. **Exploring your cultural identity.** Make a list of the main cultural subgroups you occupy. Some, such as gender or age, may be relatively easy. Others may be more subtle—think about the groups of which you are a member that contribute the most to the meaning of your life, that constitute significant communities for you. Pair up with a partner and discuss the process of making the list. Compare your cultural locations, noticing overlaps and differences.

4. **Care.** The word *care* is often used in the phrase *take care of.* Can you identify how the connotation of this phrase differs from the way the word is used in this chapter?

5. **Meaning.** How would you characterize the difference between the term *reality* and the term *lived reality* used in this chapter?

   temp

   felt hot/cool

6. **Power.** The word *power* rarely comes up in counseling textbooks. What are the consequences of not thinking about and attending to power differentials both in clients' lives and in the relationship between counselor and client?

7. **Exploiting personal knowledges.** Form pairs. Name a particular gift, skill, knowledge, or resource of your own that helps/has helped you to deal with some challenge in your life. What was the situation, and how do/did you exploit this resource?

   time mgmt

8. **Collaborative dialogue.** In collaborative dialogue, the knowledge and resources of both counselor and client are exploited in therapeutic conversations. What are conceivable examples of client resources/knowledges? What might be examples of counselor resources/knowledges?

9. **Mindfulness.** Which activities do you engage in with a heightened mindfulness and attention? Which do you take on in a distracted or absentminded manner?

Chapter 2

THERAPEUTIC CONVERSATION

INTRODUCTION

"Come on in," says Daniel, hovering at his office door as Maria enters and stops to scan the room. It's not a large space, but there's lots of light from the window and a handful of comfortable-looking chairs from which to choose. Maria spots one with an invitingly round contour and heads for it, aware again of the fatigue that seems to have taken her over lately.

"Aha! The gray chair," says Daniel, smiling as he sits.

"It's a popular one, and some people say it bothers their backs after a while. I promise I won't tag you with being indecisive if you decide to switch seats at any time."

Developing competence in counseling and psychotherapy involves refining new skills, but it also calls for becoming conscious of existing skills and using them with purpose. In the example above, it's arguable the session is yet to begin, yet Daniel is already skillfully employing talk to get something done. Look closely and you will see he helps Maria relax into the space by leaving it to her to decide where to settle in. At the same time, he supports her in making an informed choice about her options while also ensuring she won't have to worry about changing her mind later. These are conversational skills employed for creating comfort. Daniel does this intentionally, at the service of an ethic of care. But he is not executing a technique introduced in his training. Counselors employ a wide variety of conversational skills, some highly specialized and others, like these, honed over years of using talk to get something done.

Reflection 2.1

What are some contexts in which you help to create comfort with others? Which skills do you use? What sorts of things do you say, and how do you say them, to create a noncompetitive atmosphere of safety and trust?

Counseling and psychotherapy are sometimes portrayed as highly specialized ways of relating, informed by theories and laden with techniques. Not surprisingly, this view dramatically deflates the confidence of many counselors in training. It also fails to account for various research that has indicated novice counselors can be more effective than highly trained professionals (Bickman, 1999; Luborsky et al., 1980; Stein & Lambert, 1984). How can this be? As useful as theory and technique can be, they do not constitute the full repertoire of an effective practitioner, employing conversational skills developed over the course of a lifetime. All of us—trained as counselors or not—use talk skillfully in a wide variety of ways to get things done. This does not mean, however, that we are always aware of the skills we are employing: Conversation is something we take for granted, and it takes concentrated attention to begin to notice and refine the skills we often use automatically to get things done.

And so counseling and therapy share much with regular talk, but of course they also differ in some key ways from most other conversations we have in our daily lives. Counseling is a professional activity, with one person designated to be helped by another, most often for a fee. It involves intimate sharing between a client and a counselor without family, friendship, or collegial bonds. And there is often more at stake than the circumstances surrounding most verbal exchanges we have in the course of a day. Examining what sets counseling apart is just as important as noticing what it shares with nonprofessional, daily discourse. That's where this chapter starts, followed by an examination of the way talk, including therapeutic talk, operates to construct meaning and shape experience.

THERAPEUTIC CONVERSATION AS A SPECIALIZED FORM OF TALK

Many of the skills introduced throughout this book are widely employed by non-counselors. The difference here is that counseling calls for a purposefulness that only occasionally characterizes ordinary talk. It is therapeutic conversation:

dialogical exchange engaged in with the purpose of being helpful to someone reporting distress or facing some challenge. When I ask students to reflect on what distinguishes therapeutic conversation as a form of talk, they quickly generate a list that includes the items listed in Box 2.1.

BOX 2.1

The Distinct Features of Therapeutic Conversation

Features that distinguish therapeutic conversation as a form of talk include the following:

1. It takes place at regularly scheduled times and places.

2. It is between people who typically have no relationship links beyond the conversations.

3. It is for a specific purpose:
   a. includes a helper designated to assist a client struggling or suffering in some way and
   b. involves some description of goals, objectives, preferred states of being, and so forth.

4. It is a professional activity:
   a. usually involves a monetary transaction;
   b. is subject to ethics codes, legislation, and so forth;
   c. is bound by confidentiality; and
   d. gains legitimacy from the profession and academy.

5. It is informed by theories.

I haven't attempted to be comprehensive here; no doubt you can generate more items to add to the list. But these items highlight a few of the distinctive features that characterize counseling conversations. Item 1 in Box 2.1, for instance, reminds us that counseling is less off the cuff than some conversations, yet scheduled conversations nevertheless occur in other areas of our lives. It's not unusual for busy colleagues to pull out their Day-Timers or handheld devices in arranging a time to talk. Sunday dinners with family are another venue for prescheduled conversation. Item 2 captures a characteristic of therapeutic conversations not typical of much of our talk; on the other hand, we all occasionally have conversations with people we don't otherwise know. Many commercial transactions involve talking with people we have not previously met. As for Item 3, the notion of having a specific purpose, this should be a characteristic of all counseling exchanges, although less so for ordinary talk. Yet even a seemingly idle chat over coffee with a friend may be at the service of catching up and maintaining a connection. When pressed, we can usually identify some purpose to our use of talk, including seeking and conveying information, offering encouragement, planning future activities, and so on.

In the case of counseling, the purpose of the conversation is explicitly tied up with being helpful (see Item 3a in Box 2.1). This, too, is something we do in a variety of ways outside of professional activity, but just how being helpful works is something we'll examine in great detail because the habits we fall back on for being helpful in other contexts are not always effective in counseling conversations. I think it's fair to say that we also devote less attention to establishing objectives (see Item 3b) in many of our day-to-day helping conversations. So at this point in the list, we're beginning to see some features that more starkly distinguish therapeutic conversation from ordinary talk.

The differences become more pronounced by Item 4 in Box 2.1, although less so for readers already attached to various disciplines. Engineers, child care workers, lawyers, nurses, social workers, doctors, accountants, and many others experience talking and listening within a professional context, surrounded by considerations (codes, rules, guidelines, etc.) not present in casual daily conversations. Interestingly, many of these focus more on the kinds of talk they forbid than on those they encourage. We will look at these because they relate, for instance, to professional ethics and occasional dilemmas associated with adhering to codes while doing what seems best for the clients with whom we work.

Professional Activity, Shared Expertise

Item 4 in Box 2.1 deserves some careful attention because it speaks of a pronounced difference in the cultural locations of counselors and clients, regardless of overlapping locations (ethnicity, age, gender, etc.) they may share. Consider the issue of legitimacy (see Item 4d). The culture of counseling is one legitimated by professional credentials and academic degrees. These add a certain kind of weight that, if not attended to carefully, can unbalance conversations intended to be collaborative.

This unbalancing can happen outside of a professional domain as well, of course: You may have had the experience in a conversation with someone relatively new to a topic about which you're particularly knowledgeable. It can be difficult for the novices to acknowledge their existing knowledge as they're busy being impressed with—maybe even discouraged by—your knowledge. With professionals, the deference to expert knowledge can play out more starkly, points out Wally McKenzie:

> When I go to the doctor, I usually write the three things I want to talk to him about on a piece of paper and put it in my back pocket. Otherwise, I will forget. My ability to be assertive and thoughtful seems to disappear when I enter the doctor's office. (Hancock & Epston, 2010, p. 10)

Our broader culture has well-entrenched traditions of deferring to experts, relying on them to make sense of events we might otherwise have much to say about ourselves. The authority attached to professional expertise may look like a prize won by diligent study and practice, but in many ways it can act as an impediment to collaborative work with clients.

Invisible Hierarchies

The term *invisible hierarchies* relates to the topic of power, of course—a professional can't make invisible hierarchies disappear simply by adopting an inviting or jovial air.

As an African American, Daniel is accustomed to situations in which he's in a one-down position due to his skin color. But here in his office, other aspects of Daniel's identity come to the foreground in his conversations with Maria. He makes an effort to level the counselor-client hierarchy by urging Maria to let him know when she feels her main concerns are not being addressed. But Daniel has a PhD and has been practicing for many years the profession in which Maria is currently training. He drives an SUV, whereas Maria and her husband Azim are scraping by on student loans. To the extent Maria downplays her point of view in favor of Daniel's—assuming he knows what's best for her—she will be adhering to a long-standing cultural tradition of deferring to professional knowledge. Daniel will need to keep this invisible hierarchy in mind throughout his work with Maria if he wants to support her in actively evaluating her situation in her terms, rather than merely capitulating to what she sees as his expertise.

When professional knowledge remains at the center of therapeutic exchanges, the conversation is decidedly unbalanced. Harlene Anderson (2007) says therapeutic competence involves countering this drift away from client knowledges, "fostering an environment and conditions that naturally invite collaborative relationships and generative conversational processes" (p. 47). Put this way, a central facet of the counselor's skill is the invoking of the client's expertise.

Reflection 2.2

Have you ever had the experience of feeling your point of view was muted in a one-on-one or group conversation even though no one literally discouraged you from speaking? If you try to make sense of this situation in terms of a power differential, can you identify any invisible hierarchies that were at play?

LANGUAGE GAMES: WORKING WITH THEORY

Moving to Item 5 in Box 2.1, we come across a consideration (theory) that typically looms large for students as they prepare to hone their counseling skills. After all, what distinguishes counseling conversations more than their reliance on knowledge enshrined in the 400 or so theories and models (Karasu, 1986) developed in the past hundred years? As much as counseling shares many features with other forms of talk, the proliferation of theories about why people act, what makes them change, and so on offers up a vast range of ideas and practices to incorporate in conversations with clients. Good news, perhaps, but theory can both be helpful and disabling, depending on how it's treated.

One useful way to think about theory comes from the philosopher Ludwig Wittgenstein's (1953) notion of "language games." Wittgenstein paid careful attention to how language works and noticed that we use talk for different purposes, each of which are bound by unspoken guidelines, as it were, much like the rules of a game. When we're debating, we listen to detect holes in arguments, and we exploit the rhetorical power of words and nonverbal expression to make points. When we use language for consoling, of course, none of these rules apply, and the purpose of our words and gestures is different altogether because the game is different.

Counseling theories invite us to enact conversation with clients according to a strikingly varied array of rules. Some theories call for listening to interpret and speaking to explain. Others prescribe the use of language for releasing strong emotion. Still others make the central task the disputing of certain ideas deemed irrational, to be replaced with more functional thoughts, and so on. Each theory introduces a language game that ascribes rules for what speakers and listeners can say and do as well as what is to count as detail worthy of attention. The theory therefore strongly influences what we pay attention to, what we notice, and what we ignore.

Theories can bring great richness to therapeutic conversations, but when they are taken on with uncritical fervor, they also present challenges. For one, the elevated prestige they're granted through association with psychological traditions can lead us to neglect many other forms of knowing at our disposal. These could include knowledge from spiritual traditions, literature, popular culture, family traditions, and so on. They could include bodily knowing less associated with theoretical ideas than with a felt sense of things grounded in our biological natures. These are additional resources available to counselors beyond the theories they turn to to help organize their practices.

A second challenge associated with theories is that they can lead counselors to orient to books on a shelf rather than the clients in front of them. Like any source of knowledge, it's more helpful to use theories with clients rather than on them, to treat theories as what Sheila McNamee (2004) calls conversational "resources for action," where the action is "*joint* [italics added] action" (Shotter, 1993) in which clients are full participants.

This is about drawing on theory in the context of an ethic of care. There is no one-to-one correspondence between theories and lived experience, but theories add useful grist for the mill of critical reflection (Fook & Gardner, 2007)—a reflection best undertaken alongside clients. Later we'll look in more detail at how counselors can collaborate with clients by inviting them to evaluate the applicability of theory to their own unique circumstances.

COUNSELING AND PSYCHOTHERAPY AS VENUES FOR WORLD MAKING

> *As Maria exits the building, she is engulfed by the blare of traffic horns amid the brisk movement of people and vehicles around her. It's too early for her to say what exactly she takes away from this first counseling session, but she feels wide open and overwhelmed by the energy on the street. She and Daniel covered a lot of ground. They held her life to the light and examined it from several angles— some familiar and some novel. Just a conversation, she thinks, but she can't help noticing that something feels different as she heads home.*

More than any other activity, the complex use of language distinguishes humans from other living beings. Within weeks of coming into the world, we begin to reproduce the sounds made by those around us, associating them with things both tangible and intangible. We learn to use symbols as stand-ins for things themselves. As Berger and Luckmann (1967) put it, "language marks the co-ordinates of my life in society and fills that life with meaningful objects" (p. 22). Sharing this system of symbols, Daniel and Maria were able to visit the past, present, and future—both remembered and imagined—without leaving their chairs.

Language makes this exploration possible and constrains it at the same time. Language constrains us in that we are a little like what Wittgenstein (1953) described as flies in a bottle: we can't get out of the enclosure language creates. John Shotter (1993) used a different metaphor to capture this, likening language to a prosthetic tool we use to touch the world, much as a blind person feels the ground through the tip of a cane. This is useful because it helps to distinguish counseling and psychotherapy from the natural sciences. That ground, the material world beyond the tip of the cane, beyond language, is the one in which most physicists, chemists, and biologists will tell you they're interested. This is sometimes called the objective reality and is not the primary focus of counseling conversations, which are centered on clients' subjective experience. For counselors and therapists, the primary site of activity is a world mediated by language, a lived reality. This is something different indeed, a dynamic and shape-shifting world that takes new form even in the uttering of a word.

This all says something about the profound role conversation plays in contributing to human experience. When we talk with each other—face to face or through print, broadcast, or digital media—we don't merely refer to things; we shape our experience of them, sentence by sentence. Geologists can speak and write about iron for centuries, and the iron molecule will still be composed of 26 atoms. But a charismatic public speaker may refashion social attitudes, literally moving a nation to action, with carefully chosen words.

This constructive power of talk is equally evident in private, one-on-one conversation—counseling or otherwise. When Maria divulges her anxiety about her abilities as a novice counselor to an empathetic and curious Daniel, her practicum transforms from an object of fear to an intriguing challenge. The facts of the situation remain the same, but her experience of the situation has shifted. We construct and reconstruct our lived realities through talking and listening. Thinking about language this way, counseling is a world-making activity.

Reflection 2.3

Think about a momentous conversation you had at some time in your life—one that sticks out in your memory because of its impact on you. What shifted for you in that exchange of words? If conversation has the ability to move us to a new place, how would you describe what was different about where you ended up as a result of that exchange?

THERAPEUTIC CONVERSATION AND CULTURE

As useful a tool as language is, it also poses significant challenges when it comes to understanding someone else's experience. Words mean different things to people depending on their cultural location as described in Chapter 1. That location includes ethnic cultures, of course, which develop specialized vocabularies to suit local circumstances. Witness the wide variety of forms of English spoken by diverse groups throughout the world.

Words aren't mapped, one on one, onto the world. When Maria and Juanita, who works on the night cleaning staff in Maria's building, utter the same syllable—*job*—the word reverberates in very different ways for each of them. For Maria, it has echoes of *career, profession,* and *self-expression.* For Juanita, the word's overtones are closer to *green card, paycheck,* and *rent.*

The influence of cultural location on meaning goes beyond ethnicity or nationality, however. Cultural location comes in many forms. Consider our location in time, in a particular era. A century ago, *gay* described an upbeat disposition; now it's more likely to refer to sexual orientation. Age is another location that affects the meaning of language: no matter how I may try, I can't seem to make the word *sick* work to describe a piece of music I like, whereas the word flows effortlessly off the tongue of my 21-year-old son. Or perhaps the cultural location in question is distinguished by gender: Associations with words like *love* and *sex* are often quite different for men and women, something screenwriters exploit to amusing effect in romantic comedies.

Given that conversation always has a cross-cultural element, it calls for complex skills in discerning a speaker's intended meanings. To simply assume that another's words mean to them precisely what they mean to us is clearly not enough. In the chapters to come, we'll look at the skills involved in coming to shared understandings between speakers and listeners.

TALK AS POETRY

"So, how was it?" asks Azim, cradling Kyla in one arm and clutching a bottle in the other. Maria kicks off her shoes and reaches for her daughter.

"Well, interesting. . . ."

"Interesting as in good and helpful or interesting as in a weird waste of time?" asks Azim as he heats up the bottle.

"Interesting as in that new soup we had the other night. I talked a lot, and the pot got fuller and fuller. He threw in a few seasonings I'm not familiar with, and I stirred. Smelled interesting but it's a little early to say what we're making."

Counseling is a field rife with intriguing paradoxes, and they come up often in any discussion about language. I've been describing challenges associated with language due to its imprecision—meanings depend on where the speaker is coming from. But there is a built-in ambiguity to language that also gives it much of its richness and supports the expression of lived realities in ways dry facts or numbers never could. If words meant just one thing, and one thing only, they would be more precise and yet curiously handicapped in evoking lived reality. In this sense, we rely on the poetic quality of language to capture the complexity and subtlety of our experience. Does it fully succeed? When it comes close, we are struck with the resonance of an account, but as Spence (1982) says, "language is both too rich and too poor to represent experience adequately" (p. 49).

Maria's afternoon conversation with Daniel was an experience not quite like any she's had before. Not only that—because it was Maria's experience and no one else's, it was not precisely like what anyone else has ever had either. Short of inventing words to capture this exquisitely unique moment (something poets are apt to do) Maria chooses a word used by others—*interesting*. She settles on language that suffices, that's good enough, knowing she can't quite express the uniqueness of the moment.

Despite its shape-shifting qualities, language is our best tool for getting to know each other, making and maintaining connections. We'll look at this in more detail in coming chapters; for here, it's worth mentioning that although we all use language in different ways, it's language that builds bridges between us. Words are entry points into one another's experience, portals into each other's cultures. They are also remarkably helpful for constructing doorways to new territories of living.

MEANING: BEYOND INFORMATION TRANSMISSION

In her afternoon session, Maria shared various details of her life, but her conversation with Daniel was about far more than the transmission of information, which is a thin way to describe what happens when we talk to each other (Bavelas, 2012; Bavelas, McGee, Phillips, & Routledge, 2000). Mind you, it's a view with a long track record: As Lock and Strong (2010) point out, the "prevailing western view sees minds as information processors and communications as involving transmissions and receptions of information" (p. 155). But the notion of information transmission falls short of describing what Maria did in sharing or in capturing what counselors and clients do each time they talk. When someone tells me they've been hurt, they've transmitted a sound, but I'll usually need to hear more before I'm satisfied I understand what is meant. Assaulted? Disappointed? Abandoned?

Dismissed? To unpack the meaning of words conveyed through sound, we associate them with more words, often conveying some of these back to the speaker. In doing so, we give the speaker an idea of how we are receiving their account while also providing the speaker with an extended vocabulary for describing what he or she just shared. This is what brings us closer into each other's lived experience. For this reason, it's more useful to think of conversation, including therapeutic conversation, in terms of construction of meaning rather than transmission of information.

The notion of construction adds an important element not captured by transmission. For one thing, speaking not only conveys experience but can give birth to it. You've probably noticed that you sometimes formulate what you think by saying it (or writing it). This is the generative aspect of language. We shape experience in the speaking of it. This process gets heightened even further when we talk together. In conversation, we convey and generate experience, and we also shape each other's experience in the process. When a child reports she's scraped her knee, we might say, "You poor thing!" or perhaps we respond with, "Aren't you brave!" By the time our response leaves our lips, the child's lived reality has shifted in some way as a consequence of our contribution. Imagine telling a friend about an achievement of yours: Depending on the friend's response, you may experience a swell of pride in your accomplishment or perhaps a wave of shame for your self-indulgence. There is a lot more than information transmission going on here.

Co-construction of Meaning

Thinking about the way two people affect each other's experience as they talk together, it makes sense to go even further and describe therapeutic conversation as the co-construction of meaning through dialogue (Gergen, 2009; McNamee & Gergen, 1992). de Jong, Bavelas, and Korman (2012) described co-construction this way: "The speaker and listener produce the information together, continuously coordinating and collaborating to shape a mutually agreed-upon version to which both contribute" (p. 6). Another way to say this is that not one speaker or the other, but the conversation they create, is the author of whatever emerges out of a productive exchange (Hoffman, 1993; Walter & Peller, 2000). Smith (1991) captures this in poetic terms:

> The truth that is realized in the conversation is never the possession of any one of the speakers or camps, but rather is something that all concerned realize they share in together. This is a point well stated by Thomas Merton: "If I give you my truth but do not receive your truth in return, then there can be no truth between us." (p. 196)

This is about dialogue, about the whole being more than the sum of the parts. To accomplish this dialogue, therapeutic conversations need to be two-way exchanges. One of the two most common challenges I witness among novice counselors is the tendency to fall back on blunt advice giving, reducing therapeutic conversation to one-way information transmission when it could involve the rich co-construction of meaning. This is not synonymous with abandoning one's purpose—the second major challenge I frequently witness among counselors in training. The choice to engage in two-way exchanges calls for the same degree of intentionality as unilateral advice giving. Without intentionality, counseling conversations are at risk of aimless meandering, squandering the opportunity for productive dialogue.

INTENTIONALITY: DOING THINGS WITH WORDS

In his book *How to Do Things With Words* (1965), John Austin reminded us that we use talk purposively all day long, that words are prime tools for accomplishing things. This includes making up (and breaking up), rejecting offers, killing time, offering consolation, building relationships, and so on. The list is endless; we are always using language for various purposes. Ludwig Wittgenstein, who liked to use as few words as possible when contributing his momentous insights, put it this way: "Words are deeds" (cited in Lock & Strong, 2010, p. 157). Talking is in a very palpable sense *doing*, not merely the outward expression of some inner state.

To do things effectively with words calls for intention on the part of the speaker. Chapter 1 introduced the notion that our attention goes up when the stakes are high in a conversation; the same can be said of our intention. Whereas we are content to let many daily conversations take their own course, we become more intentional when we are clearly trying to accomplish something through talk. Consider persuasion: You likely know the experience of mentally rehearsing a conversation you hope will go your way. You ponder the appropriate setting, reflect on the most fortuitous way to start, prepare to adopt the proper tone of voice. This intentionality continues once the conversation begins: You listen for changes in the other's inflection, keep stock of their points in preparation for presenting your counterpoints, inject humor to reduce the tension.

As noted in Chapter 1, the stakes are always high in therapeutic conversation, and one of the great challenges in developing one's practice is to not lose sight of one's purpose, interacting with intentionality even as the conversation takes you to unexpected places.

As you engage in practice as part of the training that accompanies this text, you will be called on to employ all sorts of skills with intentionality. Several of these have been part of your repertoire for many years, although you may never have examined them. Becoming conscious of them and attaching names to them may initially be disorienting, as it was for Kira (see Student Voices), who expected counseling to be a practice largely unfamiliar to her, a process characterized by specialized techniques not used in everyday talk.

Student Voices

Kira: Putting Hands in the Dough

The idea that she already had all sorts of skills coming into her first counseling skills course took Kira by surprise. *I guess it was more an expectation of getting the theorists' techniques rather than really examining my own.* She says she expected a kind of recipe—a list of tried and true techniques—and was taken off guard when the class was asked to *put our hands in the dough and feel around and see what do you feel? What's in there? To try to distinguish the ingredients on their own.*

The conversations we have in our daily lives may be our richest source of learning, sites for many skills involved in being helpful to others. Naming, and reclaiming, these is just as useful as learning new practices in developing counseling skills.

CHAPTER TWO RECAP

In this chapter, we exoticized conversation in the sense of taking pause to examine it as an anthropologist might study an unfamiliar, and hence exotic, culture. In doing so, a number of features of conversation not often talked about became visible. We looked at how language is used to make meaning and how meaning is the foundation for experience, our lived realities. Our experience is inescapably cultural because the very language we use as a tool with which to reach out and touch the world is a communal creation; words have ancient histories that disappear into the undocumented past.

Because of the diverse cultural contexts in which language is employed, grasping another's meaning is always an approximate task. Yet the ambiguity of language also lends it richness: Words themselves reverberate with multiple meanings—a feature that grants great poetic power to language and helps us in evoking descriptions of our infinitely varied experience.

We don't just pitch information at each other when we talk; we do things, and we do them together because conversation is a back-and-forth process that generates meanings and perspectives frequently unanticipated at the outset. Counseling is a particular cultural variety of conversation and shares more with ordinary talk than differs from it. So students come to counseling with a wide range of useful skills they may not be accustomed to noticing or naming. The process of doing that can be both intriguing and disconcerting.

Counseling conversations also differ in many ways from other forms of talk. They are oriented to being helpful to another client, and they unfold in the context of an implicit hierarchy that can't be erased, although its potentially negative repercussions can be minimized with care-filled practice. Rather than wishing away the contextual factors that distinguish counseling conversations from other daily encounters, a practice of care involves attending mindfully to what sets counseling apart. There is no single formula for this because it involves a knowing-in-action, a responsiveness to the particularities of the moment. A good starting point is to create an inviting and safe space for clients to share their deepest concerns and longings: to receive them with openness, to listen and attend generously. We'll begin to look at these practices in the next chapter.

CHAPTER TWO DISCUSSION QUESTIONS

1. **Purposeful conversation.** Pay attention to the conversations you have during the day. How often do you have an explicit or implicit purpose? Is anything accomplished through the conversations? What effect do the conversations have on your relationship with the others? In which ways do views of the conversation topics change in the course of the exchanges?

2. **Conversational skills.** Listen to or watch an interview on the radio, on TV, or via the Internet. Which cues tell what the intention of the interviewer is? Which conversational skills can you name? What do they accomplish that tells you they were successful? What do you notice in the interviewee's responses that indicates whether the interviewer is effective?

3. **Language and culture.** What are examples of words that have highly specific meanings within particular cultural contexts and very different meanings outside of those contexts? Examples of cultural contexts include youth culture, legal culture, psychotherapy culture, (your) family culture.

4. **Language as poetry.** Pay attention to the way words are employed in conversations you participate in and witness, whether via media or live. Which ones capture a unique sense of what is being described? Which jump out at you because they are used in novel or creative ways? How do these words contribute to the expression of meaning?

5. **Transmission and co-construction.** Identify venues in which the transmission of information is the central purpose of talk versus situations wherein the co-construction of meaning is higher on the agenda.

6. **Popularized theoretical ideas.** What are examples of widely circulated and influential psychological ideas and constructs that have become part of popular culture, of folk wisdom? From which theory traditions do they come?

BOX 2.2

Topics for Practice Conversations

- My experience of the change of seasons in this city
- What is most stressful about pursuing studies right now
- The way music affects me—which responses it evokes in me
- My thoughts about the trend toward sensitivity to cultural diversity
- My concerns about the state of the environment
- How September 11 affected me
- What is valuable to me about family
- What I like/don't like about traveling
- How it feels to know somebody who has a serious disease or ailment
- My thoughts about the architecture and layout of this educational institution
- My experience of my counselor training to this point
- What I appreciate/don't appreciate about living in this country
- A rich description of a kind of mood I don't like that I fall into from time to time
- A rich description of a kind of mood I do like that I fall into from time to time

---

CHAPTER TWO ACTIVITIES

1. Pair up with a partner. Jointly choose one of the following words: *Christmas, home, peace, success,* or *beauty.* Each partner writes the chosen word, followed by the five first words that come to mind in association with that word. Share lists. Discuss the differences and similarities between the five associated words. How do they contribute to an understanding of each partner's experiences around the thing referred to by the original word?

2. Pair up with a partner. Jointly choose 1 of the following words: *Christmas, home, peace, success,* or *beauty.* Write the word and take turns adding associated words that come to mind, one a time, until there are 10 words. Debrief: How did each partner's

associations influence the direction of the other partner's words? Which of the other's associations unexpectedly enriched your own experience of a word?

3. Group of three, with one observer and two conversational partners. In three consecutive 3-minute segments, Partner 1 will do things with words: (a) make a case for the excellence of their favorite band or singer, (b) seek sympathy for their heavy workload, and (c) evoke enthusiasm about the change of seasons. Partner 2 mostly listens, responding only when Partner 1 is clearly faltering, while loosely keeping time. The observer watches mindfully, taking notes to jog the memory. Three-way debrief, guided by the following question: What were the most striking differences in skills used by Partner 1 to accomplish these three tasks? (Break these down by verbals and nonverbals, and be as specific as possible.)

4. Groups of four, with two observers and two conversational partners. Partners discuss one of the topics in Box 2.2 of this chapter (Topics for Practice Conversations), making an effort both to express their experience and to learn about the others'. Observer 1 attends mindfully. Debrief, starting with Observer 1: (a) Which key words struck you as either suggesting a shared meaning between the partners or pointing to differences? (b) Which words or phrases, if any, suggested a cross-fertilization or co-construction of meaning as one partner took up aspects of the other's account? and (c) Which words or phrases, if any, demonstrated a reshaping in the moment of the experience of the topic as a result of the dialogue?

SECTION TWO

CONSTRUCTING A FOUNDATION FOR COLLABORATION

In this section we move on from an overview designed to orient you to issues and themes associated with counseling and plunge into the practice itself. From this point forward, samples of counseling scenarios and conversations will provide concrete illustrations to support the discussion. Before continuing, though, I'd like to share with you a dilemma associated with writing a book like this to give you an inside view of how the sections were organized.

Counseling is a complex craft that requires quite specialized skills. However, whereas certain other fields are renowned for the specialization needed to pursue them ("You don't have to be a rocket scientist to know . . . "), they're technical crafts and of a very different character than counseling. They're organized around factual information, featuring procedures that can generally be mapped on flow charts designating clear decision points along the way. Steps follow each other relatively sequentially, and usually one backtracks only because things are going wrong—to start over or undo what's been done.

Counseling is fundamentally different for all sorts of reasons. First, it deals with perspectives and interpretation, which makes the subject at hand shape shifting in a way that facts are not. Second, it's not a linear, sequential procedure. Although it can be broken down roughly into phases (which I have done by inserting sections into the book and sequencing the chapters), one step may accomplish the ends of many steps all at the same time. When I ask Perry how he managed to keep his fear of flying at bay, I'm simultaneously (a) acknowledging his success, (b) gathering information, (c) consolidating a positive development, and (d) helping him prepare for a possible relapse of the fears, among other things. And in counseling there's often cause for not keeping steps in sequence, for the reason that may distinguish counseling most markedly from technical crafts—because counseling involves a dialogic interplay, a conversational dance with another person. This brings me back to the dilemmas I encountered in organizing the book. If I were to lay things out in a sequence of distinct linear steps, I would grossly misrepresent the craft and perpetuate a myth that I see many counselors fretting over—critiquing themselves for not proceeding in the tidy linear fashion demonstrated in workshops and outlined in textbooks. On the other hand, if I were to ignore order and sequence, and merely demonstrate examples of counselors' improvising in the moment to whatever comes up, I would fail to capture the structures and sequences that lurk in the background and inform practice.

To deal with these dilemmas, I've chosen a middle path. The sections of the book point to phases of the work, and I hope these will help organize your thinking and practice in useful ways. At the same time, it has taken some strenuous, disciplined labor to tease apart practices into distinct phases because we're typically accomplishing several things simultaneously at any moment in a counseling conversation. Nonetheless, it's possible to point to certain sequences in counseling work, as it is in day-to-day conversations. For instance, we don't attempt to explore solutions to problems with friends before we get a description of what's troubling them. So the sections point to rough phases of work with clients during a number of sessions. At the same time, they also mirror to some extent the movement that happens within sessions because single conversations also often have discernible patterns that to some extent mimic the movement that occurs across sessions.

Still on the topic of the book's construction, I'd like to add a note here about the vignettes about Daniel and Maria and, in this chapter, Maria and her client Jorge. To preserve a sequence throughout the book from the start of therapeutic work to its conclusion, the vignettes at this early point in the book represent exchanges early in the collaboration between counselor and client. Therapeutic work has an overall arc, as explained above, and I have tried to capture that arc in the samples of practice. Could some of these exchanges have occurred in another phase of the work between counselor and client? To use a phrase that is a useful qualifier for discussing a practice as context dependent as therapeutic conversation, *it all depends*.

The two chapters in this second section are about building the trust and rapport that make helpful collaborations possible. You'll notice that this includes projecting both compassion and curiosity so that clients can sense the counselor's concern and interest. It also involves conveying respect and a profound faith in clients' preexisting knowledges, skills, and abilities because these will play a key role in making change possible.

Some of the counseling examples interspersed throughout the text from now on are scenarios from my practice and the practice of colleagues; others were created to illustrate the topics at hand. All names are pseudonyms, and all transcripts have been modified to preserve anonymity. It's important to emphasize the transcripts are not presented as formulae to adhere to or as templates to duplicate. As tempting as it is to view counseling as a practice guided by strict protocols, its complexity calls for thoughtful adaptation to each unique situation, accommodating the multicultured identities of counselor and client and other circumstances background to the conversation. The transcripts provide concrete illustrations of ideas addressed more abstractly in the text. They are examples of certain ways forward among many others and are not intended as so-called best practice. So I encourage you to view the transcripts critically and to consider what *other* practices might be effective and appropriate to the circumstance at hand. There are always various ways forward, many roads to Rome.

Chapter 3

RECEIVING AND LISTENING

INTRODUCTION

> *Jorge sits in the waiting area, a* Sports Illustrated *magazine on his lap. He's flipping pages, but the words and pictures aren't registering; Jorge has never sat down with a counselor, and he's feeling distracted and uncomfortable. His older sister Catalina told him it's just like talking to a friend, but Jorge hasn't even met the counselor he arranged to see through a phone conversation. It seems like a strange idea to have a friend you've never met.*

Counseling conversations may be among the most intimate talks anyone has in their lives, but this shouldn't obscure the fact that they're more often than not between people who've never met and whose connection initially rests on a professional arrangement. Receiving, listening to, and attending to clients are critical first steps in counseling—critical because they lay the foundation for the unfolding relationship and prepare the ground for the coordination of meaning that is the intricate dance step of therapeutic conversation.

In this chapter, we look at the beginning of a therapeutic relationship. But the skills we'll explore here are not reserved for first sessions, and there are no hard lines between the topic of listening and other important topics to come, including making meaning, assessing, establishing preferences and setting goals, and influencing. Listening alone may seem less active than some forms of intervention, but that doesn't mean it's an inconsequential aspect of the counseling craft, a holding pattern between bursts of activity. Listening is an intentional activity in itself, and the way we receive, listen, and attend—our very presence to the other's experience—has significant repercussions for clients.

RECEIVING: CREATING A HOSPITABLE SPACE FOR SHARING

> *Maria checks her online calendar to confirm she has a 3 o'clock appointment. Although she's been at this practicum placement for a couple of months, she notices her mouth is dry as she makes her way to the waiting area to meet her new client, Jorge. She stops at the water fountain where a young man is taking a drink. Is this Jorge? Maybe. But there are others sitting nearby. Maria watches him return to his seat and takes a drink herself before stepping forward. "Jorge?" she asks, scanning the faces around the room. As she suspected, the young man from the fountain nods nervously. Maria smiles and extends her hand. "Hello, I'm Maria Gazzola; good to meet you."*

The notion of hospitality, usually reserved for clients visiting our homes, is a useful metaphor for describing a manner of receiving clients that embraces their uniqueness and reassures them of their welcome (Paré & Larner, 2004). Anderson (2007) uses a host/guest metaphor and suggests it's helpful to think of counselors as hosts to clients and simultaneously guests in their lives. Before the first session starts—sometimes before meeting, if there's been a phone exchange prior to the first session—the collaborative partnership with clients commences.

As Maria and Jorge walk the few steps to Maria's office, that partnership begins to form. Maria is aware it will happen in the context of an asymmetry built into the relationship. After all, Jorge is a customer seeking help even though he doesn't pay fees directly for the service because Maria works in a university setting. Maria is a professional agreeing to provide help. This is the backdrop to the conversations they will have, a hierarchy that will endure even though they may discover they share various cultural locations as they get to know each other, an asymmetry that can't be erased despite any amount of rapport they develop in their work together.

They do share one obvious overlapping territory—the university setting—and Maria chooses to key in on that as a way to help Jorge feel at ease. She remarks on impending exams as they approach her office, and Jorge is reminded that although she is a stranger, Maria is already somewhat familiar with the world he inhabits. This reduces the strangeness of the situation for him, letting him drop his guard ever so slightly.

The shared setting of the university aside, there are many noteworthy differences between Jorge and Maria that are background to this encounter. Maria is female; Jorge is male. Near the end of her program, Maria has a number of years of university education behind her, whereas Jorge is a freshman in his first year of an engineering degree. Maria is 28 years old, married, and has one child, whereas

Jorge is 22 years old and single. She was born and grew up in North America, with parents of European descent. Jorge was born in Mexico. His mother is of indigenous Mayan descent, and his father is a third-generation Mexican, first-generation American, whose family roots are in Spain.

Here at the counseling center, Jorge is among unfamiliar clients, hallways, and rooms, whereas Maria is surrounded by colleagues in an environment she was invited to decorate when she started at the beginning of the term. This is Maria's territory, her professional home, and Jorge is her guest.

> *"Here's my room," says Maria, stepping sideways as Jorge enters. In a quick glance around he notices walls covered with posters and hangings, a bookshelf and desk, and three chairs. "Make yourself comfortable, wherever you like," says Maria, gesturing to the chairs. She waits for him to choose, then rolls a second chair a few feet away and sits, turning to face him.*

The opening moments of a first counseling session are usually a very vulnerable time for clients who've chosen (or in some cases have been mandated) to share their struggles with a stranger. Of course no two clients are alike, but it's probably fair to say most want first of all to feel welcomed, to not be pressured to perform, to know the time is theirs to use in a manner that fits their needs and temperament. Providing that reassurance is all about receiving a client with hospitality and a beginning step by the counselor in an evolving relationship.

USING TRANSPARENCY TO CREATE TRUST AND ENABLE INFORMED CONSENT

Jorge isn't quite sure how this session will unfold, but he is not without expectations. As much as any of the conversations we have may venture off in countless directions, they're also bound in some ways by cultural rules that, although unnamed, are implicit in the words spoken. This is true of informal talk: In a conversation devoted to making up, for instance, we break the rules when we veer into trading insults. It's also true of professional exchanges such as counseling. This is Wittgenstein's (1953) notion of "language games" mentioned in the second chapter in reference to theories. We enter conversations—even varieties of conversations we've never had—with some expectations, and perhaps some uncertainties, about the unspoken rules of the game.

Jorge's expectations are the product of his witnessing therapy sessions on TV and in film, reading the Client Bill of Rights on the wall of the waiting room, and being coached by his sister Catalina who was a client of the center 2 years earlier. As he sits down with Maria, he commences a cultural ritual widely (if not well) represented in the popular media and framed by a number of legal and ethical considerations. He is likely to have many ideas about what should happen next, and he is just as likely to be uncertain about how to proceed.

For Maria, the situation is less novel. Although she is relatively new to counseling, this is what she does for several hours, 2 days a week. She can stay silent and leave Jorge to wallow in his doubt and discomfort, or she can render some of the implicit rules visible—put some cards on the table, as it were—in a gesture of transparency (see Box 3.1). By doing the latter, she helps to redress an imbalance between herself and Jorge around their unequal familiarity with the process as well as ensure he enters into their work together with some understanding of what it entails. In reminding Jorge about what stands behind the process they're about to undertake, Maria conveys a spirit of openness, and perhaps more important, she increases the opportunity for Jorge to make an informed choice about what he will share as they continue to talk.

BOX 3.1

Transparency

You've likely had the experience from time to time of talking with someone who's holding onto some information, concealing some knowledge, keeping their cards close to the chest. The experience can be uncomfortable, leaving you with a sense of being at a disadvantage. In counseling conversations, this feeling of being left in the dark can understandably lead to clients' putting a lot of energy into wondering what their counselor is thinking—about them, about the challenges they're facing, about their prospects.

Freeman and Lobovits (1993) describe transparency as a hallmark of "co-creative" counseling practice, "a methodological guideline that allows for the therapeutic process to be shared between therapists and clients" (p. 219). Transparency involves making the covert overt—sharing thought processes and information so clients draw from a shared well of knowledge to inform them as the conversation unfolds. This might involve the counselor's sharing the thinking behind a question or explaining a theoretical idea that sheds light on the conversation at hand.

In a care-filled practice, transparency is employed judiciously, at the service of the client, and is not the mechanical sharing of everything that comes to mind. You might prefer your client's previous haircut, or you may disagree with their taste in music, but in most cases, sharing these thoughts is not likely to be helpful. There is no formula for transparency; it is always tailored to the

(Continued)

(Continued)

situation at hand, informed by an ethic of care. W. H. O'Hanlon (1993) likens it to a "sculpture board with pins through it: if you put your hand on the back side of it, the pins take on the shape of your hand on the front" (p. 83). For counselors, the choice of which pins to foreground is based on consideration of the impact on clients.

Parallel with the transparency of therapeutic practice, you'll notice places throughout this book where I share some of my thoughts about the writing of the book so readers have a look at how the structure emerged. The impulse behind this is the same: to ensure that you know what's going on behind the scenes to maximize the chances of your exercising your critical judgment about what you read.

Reflection 3.1

Have you ever been in a conversation with someone and felt there was some hidden agenda, some ideas or facts not spoken but influencing what was being said? What was this like for you? How did it affect your sense of trust in the person and your willingness to share your experience?

"Welcome, Jorge!" says Maria, "I'm glad we were finally able to catch up—we both seem to have crazy busy schedules!" She notices that Jorge exhales a breath as he sits back in his seat. Maria continues, "I'm sure you have lots to share, and I want to be sure we make the space for it. But I'd like to run through a few important reflections on this process we're about to embark on before I hand it over to you. That way I won't need to interrupt our talk later. How's that sound?"

For some clients, it's a relief to have the counselor doing the talking at the outset, whereas others prepped to unload their worries and concerns may feel temporarily hijacked. Either way, Maria routinely opens her sessions this way; she wants to ensure Jorge has a full opportunity to proceed in an informed way. She's deliberate in choosing this opening moment to speak to Jorge about the limits to confidentiality so he's aware at the outset of the circumstances in which she may have reason to disclose details of their conversation with others.

The information she'll share here is also included on a sheet of paper the receptionist handed to Jorge in the waiting area. But Maria can't be sure he's read or understood the material, and regardless, he hasn't had an opportunity to pose questions for clarification. She reviews this material up front because it may be difficult to bring up the topic later in the hour if Jorge plunges into an emotional account of his story. By then he may have disclosed something he might otherwise have chosen to reserve. Maria is interested in maximizing Jorge's chances of participating with informed consent. Her transparency is intended to get her relationship with Jorge off to a good start, and it is also in accordance with professional codes of ethics and the law.

Legislation varies from context to context, so the transcript, below, of Maria's sharing of limits to confidentiality may not adhere precisely to all jurisdictions. But this transcript covers the main items of concern. It's important that clients understand the limits to confidentiality up front so that they engage in the process knowingly—this is what's meant by *informed consent.*

> Maria: Jorge, as you know, counseling conversations are confidential, and that's what's special about them. What you share with me stays with me. At the same time, there are certain limits to confidentiality that are set down by legislation and by professional guidelines, and it's important I let you know about these now, before we continue. For starters, I'm required by law to let Child Protective Services know when I have information that a child is being abused or is at risk of abuse. So if I learn of a situation like that, I'll make sure to report it to ensure the safety of that child. Do you have any questions about that?

> Jorge: Not really. Makes sense.

> Maria: Okay. I may also let someone know if I learn you're at risk of doing serious harm to, or killing, yourself or someone else.

> Jorge: Who would you tell?

> Maria: It depends on the situation. I might turn to a family member, or a friend, or the police, whatever it takes to ensure your safety or the safety of the person in question.

It's not uncommon for counselors on practicum training—sometimes on the direction of the sites where they're working—to gloss over details about their training and supervision on the assumption clients may form the impression they aren't getting full service. The decision about whether to mention supervision may happen in isolation from clients, but it affects them directly. They can't be fully informed about what they are committing to if they are unaware of the supervision arrangement. In addition, concealing this arrangement could have dire repercussions for the therapeutic relationship. Counselors need to weigh the consequences of being forthright about their status as practitioners-in-training against the consequences for a client in learning this secondhand.

> *"There's one more thing I'd like to mention,"* says Maria after sharing the limits to confidentiality and checking to see if Jorge has any questions. *"I'm working here at the center 2 days a week as part of my counselor training."* She names the program and explains it involves a couple of supervision contexts. *"I sit down once a week with my supervisor here, Dr. Sheila Granden, to catch her up on my work and to brainstorm possibilities."*
>
> *"And Dr. Granden?"* asks Jorge. *"What does she do with the information?"*
>
> *"It stays with her. She's ultimately responsible for the work I do here, so she has access to my files, which are stored in the main office in a locked filing cabinet. In some rare instances I might be subpoenaed by the courts to release those files, which would be another instance when the confidentiality of our conversations would be broken."*
>
> *"Hmm. I don't think the law is after me,"* says Jorge dryly.
>
> Maria smiles. *"Well, that's a good thing. One final thing: I'm also fortunate enough to have access to additional input from colleagues and a professor in the program at a weekly seminar, where I sometimes get a chance to share my work. There's a chance some of what we talk about might come up in those contexts, and I wanted to reassure you those conversations are bound by the same confidentiality as this one. So . . . many heads are better than one! We've got lots of help we can rely on when we're feeling stuck. Do you have questions about any of what I've told you here?"*

The sharing of the limits to confidentiality is a good example of intentional practice in that a lot hinges on every word spoken. Despite repeated reminders that counseling is an improvisational craft, this is one piece that is best rehearsed both to reduce the stress on the novice counselor and to ensure the message is clear and the tone appropriate. By now Maria has settled into a standard script that she can recite effortlessly, but she has given some careful thought to its contents. She introduces the elements with few wasted words and provides Jorge a chance to seek clarification. You may also notice that rather than apologizing for being a student under supervision—which would only detract from Jorge's confidence in the process—she sells the supervision as added value while being clear about its implications.

With these words behind them, the deck is cleared for an exploration of Jorge's concerns. The sharing of limits to confidentiality and the description of supervision arrangements takes about 5 minutes of the first session. In one's earnestness to get on with it, these may seem like precious minutes that might have been spent on Jorge's story. But they're an investment in the relationship and help to build a solid foundation for the work to follow.

Student Voices

Margaret: First-Session Nerves

My first session with my client left me with a whirlwind of emotions. At first, I was so nervous that I stumbled with my limits to confidentiality and I was feeling so anxious that even going through something so rehearsed and calculated was hard and challenging. I composed myself and apologized for being nervous and gave myself a little pep-talk and reminded myself that although these sessions are new to me, they are for my skill development and being nervous is quite normal. Therefore, I started over and this time around felt much better. I went through the limits to confidentiality smoothly and from there started gathering information about my client. Strangely enough, I found the "getting to know" part of the session much easier on my nerves. My nerves had slowly disappeared and I found myself intrigued by my client and wanted to know more about her.

Reflection 3.2

By now you may have had a chance to take on the role of counselor in a role-play if not a genuine session. What was it like to enter a conversation with a deliberate purpose? To what extent were you able to tap your natural conversational skills? To what extent were these hampered by your preoccupation with getting something specific done? What did you take away from the experience?

BEING PRESENT WITH COMPASSION AND EMPATHY

"So I wonder if you can tell me why you came in today, Jorge." Maria notices an indistinct flicker of emotion pass across Jorge's eyes. He shifts in his chair, a strained look on his face. She sits in stillness. A moment passes. Suddenly and unexpectedly, Jorge lets out a plaintive sound from deep in his abdomen, a sob. Maria releases a breath, leans forward in her chair, and waits for more.

Compassion as Shared Humanity

Identifying a shared interest or hobby with someone we haven't previously met helps to lift the initial feeling of strangeness. Talking about shared common experiences such as the weather or traffic jams also helps to stake out a shared territory.

But a deeper sense of trust and connection comes from a more fundamental openness to the other's shared humanity. This is what compassion is about. The Dalai Lama, who travels the world in seemingly perennial joviality, speaks of how he feels instant connection with others—old friend and complete stranger alike. For him, the connection stems from a fundamental recognition, cultivated by much deep reflection, that all humans walk together on a path that includes the vitality of youth as well as the deterioration of the body and of death. Compassion involves recognizing and accepting this in ourselves and others.

BOX 3.2

Suffering and Connection

A fundamental conclusion that arises in both Eastern and Western thought is that suffering is an inescapable aspect of human experience. Janet Surrey (2005) recaps an ancient tale that captures the ubiquity of suffering. Gotami's beloved son died as a child while playing. Grief stricken, she carried his dead body from person to person in search of a cure, even though he was clearly dead. She was sent to the Buddha. He proposed that in exchange for medicine, she first bring him a mustard seed from a household that had never experienced death. (Mustard seeds were very common in India.) Gotami went from household to household telling her story, and hearing others' stories of death. Eventually she went back to the Buddha, not one mustard seed in hand, and told him she understood.

A counseling student, Mohamoud, captured the relationship between suffering and connection in his account of coming home from work after a hectic day. With much still undone after dinner, he disconnected from his family, burying his face in his laptop to catch up on unprocessed e-mail. At one point his wife caught his attention, telling him his infant daughter was still being bothered by a mosquito bite from earlier in the day. Mohamoud recounted how in that very instance, his feeling of disconnection evaporated as he turned his attention to his daughter. He said the disconnection never returned that evening, which was devoted to compassionate concern for a child he loved.

Compassion is awareness of and feeling for the suffering of others (Germer, Siegel, & Fulton, 2005). Steven Levine (1987), who spent many years working in palliative care, writes eloquently about the role of compassion in being present to another's pain. Compassion is quite unlike pity. Levine says we express pity when we meet pain with fear and that it "makes one want to change the givens of the moment: 'I want you out of your pain because I want me out of my pain'" (Levine, 1987, p. 10). Levine recaps how patients will lucidly distinguish between visitors who seem to take their energy away (through pity) versus others who seem to lend them their life force through a compassionate presence. He describes pity as promoting a sort of contraction of the heart, whereas compassion is an opening that leads to something more like a loving connectedness.

The open and loving disposition Levine (1987) describes is closely related to what Carl Rogers (1957/1992) has called unconditional positive regard—a posture of profound acceptance and nonjudgment. Levine describes it as the "opposite of judgment . . . a kindness of the mind that mirrors the spaciousness of the heart . . . the quality of non-injury, of kindness" (p. 15). Compassion is a vehicle for connection because it eases arbitrary distinctions between us and them, reminding us that "no one is exempt from suffering and that everyone wishes to be safe from it" (Germer et al., 2005, p. 63).

Jack Kornfield (2000) tells the story of an elderly man walking a beach strewn with dying starfish after a spring storm. He tosses one at a time into the water. When asked by a visitor what he's doing, he answers, "I'm trying to help these starfish." The visitor challenges him: "There are tens of thousands of them washed up; throwing a handful back doesn't matter." The old man reaches down for another starfish. "Matters to this one," he says as he tosses it into the surf.

> *"Take your time," says Maria gently, while Jorge regroups. "Sometimes we just need a chance to release some pent-up emotion. You and I can take as long as we need to sort it out."*
>
> *Maria takes a breath to settle herself. She is struck by how Jorge's response has evoked deep feelings in her. She's been struggling on a number of fronts lately, and she almost envies the way that Jorge has found a way to express his own struggle. But just what is that struggle, and how similar is it to her own? In time, she and Jorge will make meaning of the feeling he is sharing. For now, she is content to be with him and to honor his struggle.*

Although we can learn various communication skills and develop the ability to adapt to various clients, compassion is not a technique to refine or a stance to adapt to suit the purposes at hand. It's more like the expression of a way of being cultivated through "the practice of opening to our own suffering" (Fulton, 2005, p. 63).

To meet clients where they are, we need to be present not only to possibility but to pain. And that involves engaging with the breadth of our own experience of suffering, not always an easy companion. If we have difficulty sitting with ourselves, we will have difficulty sitting with others. To be compassionately present to another's experience—their joy and hope but also their suffering—we have to be compassionately present to our own.

Empathy: Walking in Another's Shoes

Although compassion is a global disposition that builds a bridge between human hearts, empathy is more particular in its focus and relates specifically to the person across from you. Empathy, described so richly by Carl Rogers (1957/1992), is the ability to resonate with the other's experience, to imagine walking in their shoes. Rogers depicted empathy as "entering the private perceptual world of the other . . . being sensitive, moment by moment, to the changing felt meanings which flow in this other client" (quoted in Gazzola & Stalikas, 2003, p. 250). Mearns (1997) describes empathy as "the ability to understand how the other person feels in his or her world" (p. 112). He makes the point that this is not the same as imagining how we or others would feel in the same situation. To do this involves appreciating that as much as another person shares their humanity with us, they also experience their lives in unique ways that may be unfamiliar to us. This calls on us to let go of our ethnocentricity—the tendency to see the world only from the perspective of one's own cultural standpoint. This is an important point: As much as empathy helps us to identify with another, it opens us to what might be different and unique in their experience, making it possible to revel in the infinite cultural diversity of the world.

Later chapters present examples of practices associated with expressing compassion and empathy, but I'd like to emphasize here that these are not techniques—they are orientations to others. You may benefit from practice examples of these, but I also encourage you to tap into these dispositions in yourself and to convey them, relying on modes of expression you have developed during decades of relating to others.

Student Voices

Inez: Being a Client for the First Time

At first, the idea that the entire hour was "all about me" was difficult and uncomfortable for me to accept. I felt guilty that my counselor had to listen to me talk on and on about myself the whole time. However, these initial feelings about being the client took an interesting shift when I started being a counselor to my own client. After our sessions I would reflect on how I felt towards my client while in the counselor's seat: my unconditional positive regard, and my genuine interest and curiosity surrounding their experiences. I realized we have chosen this profession because we care about others, and hope to be able to be helpful to them. I now realize that my counselor probably feels the same way about me as I feel about my client. Since then, I decided to get everything from my counseling sessions that I can. . . . As the semester's progressed, I've been able to appreciate the benefit of simply having someone with no biases to talk to, giving me the space to discuss various concerns, and allowing me the opportunity to gain insight.

Reflection 3.3

By now you've likely had the chance to be the client in a role-play, or perhaps you have occupied the client's chair in a genuine counseling relationship. Do you remember those first moments when you began to share details of your personal life? What was that like for you? Was there anything the counselor did that helped you to feel comfortable? Was there anything they did that made you uneasy? What learning for your role as counselor did you take away from the experience?

DOCUMENTING CLIENTS' LIVES: NOTES AND RECORDS

In the wake of an outburst he hadn't anticipated, Jorge looks apologetic, perhaps embarrassed. Maria is in no hurry. "Seems like a lot going on. We've got lots of time. Do you want to say more about what that was about for you . . . or maybe get to it later?" Jorge smiles sheepishly and asks for a glass of water. He says he wasn't expecting to get emotional and that maybe it'll all make more sense if he tells Maria more about why he's there.

"Do you mind if I jot a few notes, Jorge?" Jorge waves his consent and Maria reaches for a pad. "I do this to jog my memory. Highlights . . . anything that might seem helpful. It's especially useful when I'm first getting to know someone because it helps me track details of who's in your family and so on. Before a session I like to review the notes from our last conversation as a reminder of where we left off. There's nothing secret about the notes—if you'd like to see them or have a copy of them just ask me at any time. I keep them here in a locked filing cabinet, and they're bound by the same confidentiality I told you about earlier. Sound all right?"

Jorge nods, now looking more relaxed.

"So I wonder where is a good place to start," says Maria.

As a society, we've developed long-standing traditions of documenting details about clients' lives—confidential dossiers stored in cabinets, often for the eyes of professionals and never seen by the subjects themselves. Michel Foucault (1965, 1979, 1980) wrote widely about the way these practices reinforce normative judgment—that is, arbitrary standards of what is normal and what is abnormal. The official quality of documentation adds further credibility to accounts of identities that often feature deficit, misdemeanor, and pathology. Think about the ominous ring associated with the statement from a school principal, police officer, or psychiatrist that "we've got a file an inch thick on you."

White and Epston (1990) seized on this tradition to instigate a range of alternate uses for the written word (some of which we'll explore later) and to invite critical reflection on the role of documentation in counseling and therapy. They remind us that Hare-Mustin's (1994) "mirrored room" where counseling conversations occur reflects dominant ideas about clients as disordered and dysfunctional and counselors as expert and healthy. In this setting, the site of a professional's scribbling into a pad is almost certain to suggest the creation of a new file focused on what is not working in a client's life. When the contents are withheld from the client, the process further heightens a hierarchical gap and reinforces an image of the client as the object of normative scrutiny.

Yet counselors are typically required by workplaces and regulatory bodies to keep detailed records of their work, and it can be difficult to remember details from sessions without jotting periodically during conversations. Maria deals with this by being transparent about the process and soliciting Jorge's permission as well as letting him know he can look at what she's writing any time he is curious. In my own experience, it is extremely rare either for a client to deny permission for note taking or for a client to ask to see what is written. But the acts of asking and offering speak volumes and help to address many of the dilemmas associated with notes mentioned above.

A variety of approaches to note taking are written about in the counseling literature (cf. Baird, 2005; Crocket, 2010). It is best to adapt the practice to your own processing style and workplace requirements while ensuring thorough documentation of what transpires from session to session. Decisions about note taking should be made with considerations of care in the foreground: record-keeping practices have an immediate impact on clients and—as much as the words spoken—are relational acts.

LISTENING: ATTENDING TO THE MOMENT

Jorge looks as though he's working on an answer for Maria, but he doesn't speak. Her question lingers in the air and seems to gain gravity with each tick of the clock. He looks at Maria, and the clear delineation of roles that accompanied the almost businesslike exchange about confidentiality of moments ago is now gone. Jorge becomes aware for the first time of the length of her brunette hair, just as Maria notices Jorge's slender hands and the portfolio case leaning against his chair. Maria smiles gently as Jorge gives himself permission to speak.

More than any other, the 21st century is an era of divided attention. New media have vastly multiplied the places available to direct our attention, fragmenting it in the process. Where the invention of the printing press multiplied our choices for distraction, print media are now joined by film, TV, and radio (both now available on hundreds of digitized channels); e-mail, text messaging, blogs, social networking sites, cell phones, MP3 players, handheld devices, and car DVDs; not to mention the new communication gadgets that will have taken the market by storm in the time it's taken to write, edit, and publish this book.

It's been estimated that more than 90% of North American adults have cell phones, that we now have access to more than a trillion webpages and 200 million blogs, and that we're bombarded by about 100,000 words a day, or 2.3 every second. And these information sources have generally become louder, faster, and busier for fear of losing viewers/listeners increasingly accustomed to high stimulation. Compare contemporary children's programming or television news to earlier versions and you'll notice shorter items and quicker edits. Contemporary media also increase the speed of our conversations. The posting of a letter used to be followed by a few days' wait for a reply; now we receive mail moments after it is sent, with the expectation we'll respond again without delay. These multiple information sources stimulate the mind and in many instances build community across vast distances. They also give us little opportunity to remain fully present to any one source for more than a passing moment. We live in an era that discourages close and careful listening.

Listening attentively is an act of focused concentration. It's a training of the spotlight, a reining in of the restless impulse to crowd the incoming channels. The brain can process about 500 words a minute, and clients typically speak at a rate of about a quarter as many (Shaffir, 2000). While we sit listening, there's lots of space left to anticipate our next meal, fret about our bills, soar off into the theoretical heavens, and plan our next response. To listen attentively is to exercise a skill no less demanding than playing chess, driving in a snowstorm, or writing an exam. Shaffir (2000) notes that the Chinese pictogram for "listening attentively" includes what at first appears like an odd assembly of characters including images for (a) the ear, (b) standing still, (c) 10, and (d) heart and mind. Zen master Dae Gak explains this means "when in stillness, one listens with the heart. The ear is worth 10 eyes" (Shaffir, 2000, p. 42).

If you think back on conversations that have touched you in meaningful ways, that have been useful in dealing with troubling matters of the heart, my guess is most didn't happen on the fly, at high volume, in a brief spurt. Helpful conversations typically share little with the brisk, busy, and fragmented media phenomena I described above. To notice and articulate embodied experience usually involves slowing down, giving each word and silent pause its due. Counseling at its most effective can be a very patient endeavor, quiet and slow. These are not words that come up much in reference to recent trends in communication. To listen fully and patiently with an open heart is a rare and generous gift.

Student Voices

Margaret: Handing Over the Spotlight

My roommate was eager to talk about her new love interest, a guy she'd recently met on campus. The conversation started off with her sharing her many doubts about her new relationship. She looked at me and asked "Does he really like me?" Already in a committed relationship, I wanted to jump in and share my thoughts and stories with her, but made a conscious point of handing the spotlight over to her and becoming the active listener. Was that ever challenging! It is hard for me to do this because I feel I can empathize more with the person I'm conversing with if I share my feelings too. However, something quite remarkable happened during our conversation. At many times, I wanted to say "Me too, I felt the exact same way when Brian and I started dating," but I refrained. As much as I thought keeping out of the spotlight would hinder our conversation and limit it, it did not. My roommate kept the conversation alive by talking about this new boyfriend, her concerns and excitement. I kept my stories to myself and gave my roommate a chance to explore her own feelings and her own concerns in a detailed and passionate way. It made me realize a conversation can still be very engaging when one person becomes the active listener while the other speaks. When one truly listens, it is more than just listening—we put our own needs aside to help that other person. This does not go unnoticed. My roommate thanked me for my time and for being "a great ear."

Reflection 3.4

Think back to a conversation in which you felt the other person truly put their needs aside to attend to yours, when you felt truly listened to. What was this like for you? Was there any impact from the other's mute attention and caring alone? How would you describe the benefit to you of listening? What do you take away for your own counseling practice?

HEARING OURSELVES

Daniel steps into his supervisor's office after a particularly difficult session. His client, a middle-aged man mandated for counseling after he was charged with assault, had once again focused on how he was provoked by his wife's "passive aggressive behavior." As he sits down to debrief on his work, Daniel's first inclination is to vent steam by putting down his client.

"How was the session?" asks his supervisor, who is aware of the challenge Daniel is up against.

"Frustrating, as usual," says Daniel. He's about to make the case that the man clearly doesn't want to change, that he has no empathy and is only out for himself. In the short term, Daniel realizes this version of events will assuage his doubts about his ability by branding this an impossible case. Instead, he puts his need for affirmation aside and reflects on what his client is up against.

"This guy's spent his lifetime being told he's right and everyone else is wrong—especially women, whose point of view he automatically assumes holds less weight. I think I've got him twisted in a knot, inviting him to consider his part in things. Besides, I could see how difficult it was for him when I asked him about his wife's broken arm. It must take a whole lot of courage to face up to the shame attached to that."

"Doesn't sound like a whole lot of fun."

"Nope. Tough stuff. Sometimes I just want to give him a shake. It's exhausting."

Amid all the emphasis on listening throughout much of this chapter, it's worth remembering that counselors are speakers, too, and along with listening to clients, it's important that we *listen to ourselves*. In addition to conversing with individuals, couples, and families behind the closed doors of consulting rooms, counselors speak to colleagues in supervision and case conferences, to fellow professionals in consultations and information sharing, to parents of younger clients, and to fellow practitioners or members of the public in educational talks and workshops. In each of these situations, paying attention to the impact of our contributions is helpful. As we saw in Chapter 1, attention supports intention—the intention to interact mindfully in accord with an ethic of care.

In the example above, Daniel catches himself on the verge of pitching one particular version of his client's identity. As we've seen elsewhere, this is one take among many, and it reinforces a picture of his client as intractable, immune to reflection, doomed to a lifetime of abusive behavior. This is a view that saps Daniel of energy and promotes a self-defeating pessimism, all of which detracts from the work he's attempting to accomplish. This kind of talk is not unusual among practitioners frustrated by challenging clients, and it becomes a vehicle for venting frustration. But it paints a narrow view of events and is ultimately dishonoring of clients. In choosing his words, Daniel does not whitewash the situation or repress his feelings, but he finds a way to speak of events that leaves the possibility of progress open while respecting his client's humanity.

Imagine a world in which all speakers paused momentarily prior to each utterance to reflect on their intentions and to anticipate the effects of their speaking. No doubt this world would be filled with more words of compassion and empathy—caring and constructive talk that adds possibilities rather than taking them away. To listen to ourselves is to adopt a reflexive position (Béres, 2009), to hold a mirror up (metaphorically speaking) as we interact in our work (see Chapter 10 for more on reflexivity). This is what Donald Schön (1983) has called "reflection-in-action" and is about paying attention, bringing consciousness to the task at hand. It's what mindful practice is all about.

USING SILENCE

> Jorge puts down his glass and looks toward Maria's feet. "I can't sleep," he says, glancing at Maria momentarily as though to confirm this is an appropriate opening for a client of counseling.
>
> "You're experiencing insomnia?" asks Maria. Jorge nods. "How much sleep are you getting?"
>
> The conversation unfolds. Maria learns that Jorge has been fretting about school for the entire semester, that he is plagued with doubts about whether engineering is the right field, and that he's fearful of his parents' reaction if he were to quit or change programs.
>
> "They don't understand me," says Jorge, diverting his eyes back to the floor. "They have no idea who I am."
>
> "What don't they know about you, Jorge?" asks Maria.
>
> The question seems to blanket Jorge in an analgesic mist. He stops fidgeting and sits immobile, looking at Maria and then away. She notices he seems to be working at a response, chooses not to rush him. The clock on Maria's shelf becomes louder as a stillness settles over the room.

The opportunities to experience silence seem to grow fewer year by year. Our populations are increasingly urbanized, and our cities are increasingly plugged in. For many clients accustomed to filling the air with talk or music, sheer silence can be an unnerving thing. Yet there are some striking qualities to silence, a fact that virtually all of the spiritual traditions worldwide have been onto for millennia. Being still and silent affords the opportunity to settle and to regroup. It provides a break between what has been and what is yet to come. It turns off the background noise, clearing space for reflection. And it creates space for meaning to be born and shared. As the medieval poet Rumi (2005) said, "There is a way between voice and presence where information flows. In disciplined silence it opens" (p. 32).

Jack Goldstein (2002) captures the way silence "speaks" in recapping an exchange between Mother Teresa and an interviewer who was interested in what she says to God when she prays. "I don't say anything," she replied. "I just listen." So the interviewer asked what God says to her. "He doesn't say anything," said Mother Teresa. "He just listens" (p. 51).

Musicians famously claim that it's the silence between the notes that adds the nuance to their playing, and it's interesting what you notice when you pay attention to those similar gaps in spoken conversation. Silence punctuates and adds pacing to what might otherwise be a relentless tumbling forth of words. If you listen to accomplished orators like Barack Obama, you will notice this punctuation at work. In slowing things down, silence adds gravity to what is said. It gives pause for reflection and invites a lingering that can give birth to unanticipated thoughts, feelings, sensations, and images. Longer silences do more than this, too. An extended silence signals a stopping place. When the back and forth of words ceases, we are left in the here and now—at this time, in this place, in this body. That presence can be a useful moment in a counseling conversation.

Student Voices

Talia and Margaret: Growing Accustomed to Silence

Talia: The thought of using silence during a session with a client who may not be familiar with the benefits of silence brings back memories of an unhelpful counseling experience I had recently. The sessions I had with my counselor were filled with many silences that felt awkward on my end. Perhaps the timing was wrong, or maybe I would have benefited from more active questioning, or maybe it would have helped if my counselor explained the purpose of silence. As a result of this experience, when I noticed a silent moment with my own client, I found myself rushing to ask my client a question rather than taking the time to think and reflect on what was just said. This is something I've become aware of, and I'm now working on becoming more comfortable with moments of silence.

(Continued)

(Continued)

Margaret: Silence frightens me in day-to-day conversations. I've been told that whenever I'm around there is never a moment of silence because I always keep the conversation going. In counseling I'm sometimes uncomfortable with silence, too. Whenever I am the client and I feel there is a long pause, I sometimes conclude (wrongly) that my counselor thinks my problems or emotions may be a little too much to cope with. I do think silence is useful in counseling, but to a limit. On the one hand, it's necessary to give your client moments of self-reflection. But if you give someone too much time, they start over-analyzing the silence and fear something isn't right.

Despite these observations, my client reported in our first session debriefing that I had given her many good moments of silence. My great learning about this is not rely on your own judgment about how much silence should be being used in counseling. Instead, check in with your client every now and then to ensure that you are giving them enough silence, because in the end, the silence won't benefit you, it will benefit them.

Reflection 3.5

What's your own experience of silence? When you encounter it in day-to-day conversations, do you rush to fill it, or are you comfortable with spaces between speaking turns? What are the traditions around silence in your family, in your cultural subgroups? How have you dealt with silence as a counselor? What's it been like to encounter it in session as a client?

Many counselors new to the craft experience discomfort around silence in their sessions. They speak of how it feels as though the conversation's ground to a halt and describe searching their minds for something new to say or ask. This no doubt has something to do with the expectation that therapeutic change is more about *doing* than *being*. It probably also relates to intimacy. To sit in silence with a client is an intimate thing. There's a sense of the roles dissolving, of immediate contact between fellow humans who know both joy and hardship.

It's one thing for lovers, or parents and their children, to sit together in stillness, punctuating the silence with intermittent remarks, but another thing for two people without a shared social history to do this. If we gazed mutely across the counter at a pharmacist, we'd typically provoke curiosity, discomfort, possibly even alarm. Like language, the absence of language—stillness, silence—means something.

When silence appears in an unexpected context, the meaning is murky, the message confusing or unsettling.

Silence, like words, has multiple meanings, reflecting the cultural traditions of which it is an expression. For this reason, it's best not to assume in any conversation that a silence for one means the same as it does for the other. Not all cultures are as talk oriented as Europeans, both at home and in the many countries Europeans have colonized around the world. In many indigenous cultures, silence is a more familiar punctuation. Extended pauses are seen not as pregnant but as merely part of the rhythm of daily speech.

Even within the culture of counseling, silence speaks differently from counselor to counselor. A novice counselor's inadvertent silence may mean something like, "I'm brain-dead and can't think of anything useful to say. Help me out!" A more experienced practitioner who's become accustomed to silence may use it deliberately to convey, "This seems important and deserves a pause." In either of these cases, an extended silence—unusual in most mundane conversational exchanges—runs the risk of putting pressure on the client to deliver, as if to say, "The ball is now in your court, and I await your insightful response."

When entered into with an ethic of care, silence is something done with clients and not to them. The choice to suspend speech shouldn't be based on an abstract theory or manualized instruction but should arise in response to the particularities of the moment. Curiously, this suspension of active work is sometimes the most productive thing counselors can do, making space for what Anderson and Goolishian (1988) call "the unsaid"—the hope never uttered, the word never spoken, the feeling never named. A moment of stillness prepares both speaker and listener to experience something lurking between the lines of dialogue.

CHAPTER THREE RECAP

The starting point of therapeutic conversations is the gathering of the client's lived experience. We can't go there (a preferred future) until we are here (the present, as it's currently experienced). Care-filled listening is key to creating an inviting space for clients to enter. In truly listening, we suspend our own needs on behalf of the other, initiating a journey of mutual discovery. Listening poorly mires the process by prompting false starts founded on misunderstandings, or worse, it erodes the sense of trust needed to venture forward on roads rarely traveled.

Although the importance of listening attentively never goes away, it may be most critical at the onset of the relationship. The feeling of being heard by their counselors is frequently cited by clients as key to relationships that work. There is a certain healing that comes with the mere sharing of suffering (Pennebaker, 1997). A counselor who does nothing but devote time to sitting in stillness and opening to the heartfelt expression of another's experience provides a precious gift. In fact, this compassionate presence is a good place to return to when conversations become tangled in confusion or seem to be drifting into unhelpful territory. To know that one other person is witness to and identifies with one's struggles can be an antidote to isolation and a powerful comfort in itself (Myerhoff, 1979, 1986).

A thin description of listening portrays it as a passive act, to be contrasted with the active process of responding. But as we'll see throughout this book, there is no place to be with clients devoid of impact on their experience of themselves and of their challenges. Listening is more than a preparation for being helpful—it's a complex and compassionate task central to the therapeutic process.

Listening alone is itself influential, although less actively so than the combination of listening and responding, which we will explore in future chapters. I'm often astounded (occasionally amused, sometimes alarmed) when I check in with clients who consult me about what's been useful in our work together and they say it was when I "told" them they should do X, Y, or Z. Given that I work hard at not telling clients what they should do, this is a reminder of the influential quality of less directive participation—including posing tentative ideas, asking questions, or even attending in thoughtful silence.

CHAPTER THREE DISCUSSION QUESTIONS

1. **Hospitality.** What are some of the things a good host says and does that help to promote comfort among visitors and allow them to relax into the space? Which of these are transferable to therapeutic practice? Which don't fit?

2. **Compassion.** Think of a time when you have found yourself open to experiencing the suffering of others . . . whether an individual, a community, or even a nation of people. Perhaps in some instances you experienced this as personal guilt or as pity whereas in others it was more an opening of your heart to a human condition that you yourself share. Provide examples and reflect on possible differences between these experiences.

3. **Limits to confidentiality.** In the case of Jorge and Maria, Jorge is not given a chance to open up immediately with his concerns. Instead Maria launches into her description of the limits of confidentiality. What are the pros and cons of routinely starting each first session with sharing the limits of confidentiality?

4. **Transparency.** Transparency sometimes involves an element of self-disclosure. What are some useful guidelines for deciding whether an act of transparency is helpful? Give an example of a personal sharing that might be helpful and one that seems ill advised.

5. **Silence.** Prior to the discussion period, clear the time to spend an hour in deliberate silence in a context wherein you would normally be engaged in conversation or would fill the air with music, entertainment, or information. Pay attention to what you experience. What do you notice in your thoughts, your feelings, your body? Discuss the experience with a partner.

6. **Stillness.** Where do you find stillness? Think of time (of day, of year, of life, etc.) and of place (in house, in city, in nature, etc.). Are there ways you can evoke that sense of stillness? How can you bring it to your listening practice?

CHAPTER THREE ACTIVITIES

1. **Listening with compassion.** In pairs, take turns listening to your partner as they tell you about something they've struggled with in the past, something that caused your partner suffering that is not currently a significant problem for them. Listener, open your heart to your partner's account of their suffering. Ask questions as necessary to help your partner describe their struggle in rich detail. Allow yourself to identify the links between your partner's suffering and your own to experience your shared humanity. What was it like to listen in this manner? Were you able to experience a kinship based on your shared suffering? How did this focus affect the quality of your listening? Speaker, what did you notice about the quality of the listening? Did you feel that the listener identified with your suffering? Can you identify what the listener did that made a helpful difference for you?

2. **Noticing and suspending judgment.** Watch or listen to a radio or television personality, a professor, anyone who is "talking at you" for an extended period. Pay attention to judgments that may arise. These might be about the speaker's appearance or style of speech; they might relate to your evaluation of their intelligence or acuity. If you discern judgments, take note of them and let them go, returning your full attention to the speaker. Which sorts of judgments come up? How did the judgments affect the quality of your listening? What is it like for you to let go of the judgments, and how does that affect how you hear the speaker?

3. **Listening in silence.** Pair up. Take turns being listener and speaker. The listener's job is to be fully present to the speaker while remaining virtually silent. The speaker may draw from suggested topics listed in Box 2.2 at the end of Chapter 2 or may choose any other topic of meaning to them. The listener primarily remains silent, although occasional questions to clarify a point or support the speaker in saying more may help to diminish potentially awkward silences. The listener's task is to center the speaker's experience, to relinquish the desire to comment, provide comfort, debate, and so forth, instead merely providing a quietly empathic ear. Listener,

what was it like staying silent? If you were tempted to speak more than you did, which sorts of things did you feel tempted to say? What impact on your listening did the silence have? Were there details, either verbal or nonverbal, that you noticed that you might not have otherwise? If so, describe them in detail. Speaker, what was it like for you to have a virtually silent listener—what impact on your experience of being listened to? Were there moments of discomfort when it felt awkward that the listener did not respond? Would you say the listener's silence contributed to or detracted from your exploring your own experience? Listener and speaker, among the unwritten rules of ordinary conversation, both speakers are usually expected to contribute to a certain degree. Were there moments when it felt you were violating this rule, and if so, did this detract from the quality of the exchange or support it?

4. **Generous listening.** At a party or some social gathering, or over coffee or drinks with a friend or colleague, make a point of centering the other's experience as fully as you can. Suspend the temptation to shift to your concerns, your agenda, and provide the speaker with all the space they need to describe their experience. Pay attention to what this is like for you as a listener. Are you tempted to blurt out your own experience? Do you feel the urge to take the spotlight away from the other? What's it like for you to remain mute with regard to your own experience? What impact on the speaker does your posture of generous listening seem to have?

5. **The quality of being heard.** Identify a time when you've felt profoundly listened to. This may have been one instance or perhaps many conversations with a particular person. Describe the experience. What did the listener do that led you to feel heard? Which adjectives might you use to describe the quality of the person's listening? What was it like for you to feel you were being so carefully listened to? What impact did this have on your experience of the conversation(s)?

6. **The quality of not being heard.** In pairs, discuss the same questions as in Activity 5, but focus on an instance of feeling *not* heard.

7. **The context of being heard.** Following on the previous two activities, which contextual conditions supported or interfered with the listening? Which conditions in general support good listening? Which conditions are barriers?

Chapter 4

BUILDING THE RELATIONSHIP

INTRODUCTION

A striking finding of meta-analyses of counseling and psychotherapy studies is that the therapeutic relationship contributes far more substantially to outcomes than do theories or models. Considering the attention devoted to theories, and the competition among proponents of the many models of practice circulating the professional community, this may come as a surprise. On the other hand, when you consider the practice of counseling in the terms laid out here, understanding it as the collaborative co-construction of meaning through dialogue, the finding that the relationship is central is less surprising. As noted elsewhere, therapeutic conversations are akin to relational dances. Adroit practitioners need to respond to their clients throughout their work together, adjusting their course in accord with shifts in nonverbals, altering the focus in the wake of new information revealed, and so on. This is relationship in action.

Relationship is not a thing; it is a practice. It is ultimately not who we are but how we are that defines the relationships we enact with clients. In later chapters we will explore practices associated with a number of prevalent theories and models in wide circulation today because these help to bring form and substance to therapeutic conversations. But at the heart of counseling and psychotherapy is that relational dance, and it is ultimately a responsive, care-filled give and take that should characterize therapeutic practice, including practice strongly informed by theory. This chapter is devoted to exploring relationship because of its preeminent importance to practice and because it begins with the first contact between counselor and client and continues to the final parting.

RESEARCH ON THERAPEUTIC OUTCOMES

In recent years, there's been an accumulating body of research linking the counseling relationship and favorable therapeutic outcomes (Duncan, Miller, & Sparks, 2004; Lambert, 2004; Wampold, 2001). With hundreds of therapeutic models in use, and sprawling variation in client populations and contexts, these various studies of research studies—or meta-analyses—have had little success in isolating specific interventions that make the difference (in the way that medical and pharmaceutical studies sometimes do). Instead, this research repeatedly demonstrates there is no significant variation in the effectiveness of the interventions themselves (Lambert & Bergin, 1994; Wampold, 2010). Variations in theories don't make a substantial difference. The dominant treatment approaches produce approximately equal benefits, both in reference to particular client complaints and generally (Duncan et al., 2004; Wampold, 2010; Wampold et al., 1997). In other words, although the models may contribute to the overall efficacy of therapy, they aren't significantly differentiated one from another.

Encouragingly, what the meta-analyses do demonstrate is that counseling and therapy are consistently helpful (Duncan et al., 2004; Lambert, 2004; Wampold, 2001, 2010). They also produce some other interesting findings. When the data are analyzed to tease out elements correlated with favorable outcomes, certain important factors emerge. The most significant factor is clients themselves. Variability in their situations, their support networks, their ways of being, and so on have a key impact on how therapeutic practice works out (Bohart & Tallman, 1999; Prochaska, Norcross, & DiClemente, 1994; Wampold, 2010).

For those inclined to inflate the importance of therapist knowledge, the finding that it's clients who make the biggest difference might be regarded as a humbling discovery. On the other hand, if you consider that all approaches to counseling and therapy arguably strive to support the autonomy and self-sufficiency of clients, this is welcome news indeed. It suggests the most useful place to look for resources, insights, and solutions may be within the repertoires of the clients who consult us.

This does not mean the counselor's task becomes less complex or challenging, but it suggests we should spend less time scouring our own personal experiences and accumulated book knowledge for answers to client dilemmas and turn our attention to uncovering what is useful in the lives of our clients instead. This source of knowledge is gaining growing attention with the proliferation of traditions of positive psychology (Biswas-Diener, 2010; Peterson, 2006; Snyder & Lopez, 2009; Snyder, Lopez, & Pedrotti, 2010) and a variety of counseling and psychotherapy approaches oriented more toward psychological and social resources than deficits (cf. Anderson & Gehart, 2007; de Jong & Berg, 2007; Madsen, 2007; Saleebey,

2008; Ungar, 2005; 2006; White, 2007). But these increasingly widespread practices and the aforementioned research findings are not particularly well represented in popular depictions of therapy, and many people do not come to counselors with the expectation that they hold the biggest key to resolving their distress. To effectively tap into client knowledge therefore requires significant relational skill and is itself a significant relational act because it signals to clients that their knowledges, skills, and abilities are valued and respected.

THE IMPORTANCE OF THE THERAPEUTIC RELATIONSHIP

A second significant factor uncovered by research into counseling outcomes is the therapeutic relationship (Cochran & Cochran, 2006; Horvath & Greenberg, 1994; Horvath & Symonds, 1991; Martin, Garske, & Davis, 2000; Norcross, 2001; Wampold, 2001, 2010). This may come as less of a surprise considering that counseling is fundamentally a relational process and given the emphasis throughout these pages on the practical importance of collaboration and the co-construction of meaning.

There are many ways to unpack the workings of the therapeutic relationship, reflecting the variety of theoretical traditions within which that analysis occurs. These perspectives range from the notion that the relationship is a critical replaying of other significant relationships in the client's life (Wiener & Rosen, 2009) to the more pragmatic notion that counselor and client are trying to accomplish a practical task and depend on a "working alliance" (Horvath & Greenberg, 1994) to get it done.

My preferred emphasis in this book is on the counselor's contribution to the relationship as the outward expression of an ethic of care. This is in contrast to the notion of practitioners' using the relationship as a strategic tool to effect change—a description that overlooks the counselor's emotional participation and the vulnerability associated with opening to another's experience. It is not possible to do relationship while hiding behind a professional fortification. To be engaged in a relationship, we need to step forward and stand in relation to the other. Counseling is not an objective practice.

Maria is aware that although she and Jorge have been talking for only half an hour, they've covered a lot of ground. Jorge's disclosure that he's been wrestling with whether to come out to his parents was followed by his account of various run-ins with homophobia. For years he endured bullying in grade school, and for a long time his harshest critic was himself as he struggled to reconcile his feelings with the conservative religious tenets he was brought up on and his father's macho attitudes.

As she listens, Maria is struck by the way society at large has let Jorge down since he was a vulnerable child first discovering what made him different and unique. She notices a rising anger in herself as Jorge recaps stories of exclusion and rejection. Jorge's account casts her own challenges in new light: As difficult as it's been raising a young child and negotiating her busy schedule with her husband, all of this has unfolded in a heterosexual nuclear family that is sanctioned, even celebrated, by the wider culture.

The Myth of Neutrality

It's not uncommon to read about the importance of maintaining objectivity as we listen to clients, about why it's critical that we adopt a neutral stance as they share their stories. Descriptions like these are intended as reminders that it is not helpful to be judgmental or to impose values on clients—both important reminders. But at the same time, they convey a confusing message about a practice devoted to the relief of human distress. Nobel Peace Prize winner Elie Wiesel described therapy as a "moral quest" (Wylie, 1994, p. 10) because it involves "actively taking sides on behalf of those who suffer" (p. 10). Counseling would not be seen as worth the bother if it weren't for our very subjective experience of being human. And how would it be experienced by a client if we were to be steadfastly neutral in relation to their hardship and pain?

Far from objectivity and neutrality, counseling calls for a passionate commitment to others. And this commitment is not a theoretical idea. No theory will unfailingly illuminate the passage through the intricate maze of relationship; no model will guarantee sure navigation through the sometimes murky waters of therapeutic conversations. The compass of the work is ultimately not theory but care. This calls for a clear expression of subjectivity.

A care-filled orientation to the other is not the payment for an endearing personality or an offer of consolation for a tragic circumstance. It's not dependent on how clients present or what they're facing. Instead, it comes from a commitment that precedes getting to know any particular client. This may seem confusing, given that some clients may be hostile to counselors and, worse, might inflict harm on others. To actively participate in the therapeutic process, counselors must be willing to stand beside their clients and against violence and abuse in all their forms. Notions of neutrality fail to capture this spirit.

One-Way and Two-Way Accounts of Therapy

Michael White (1997) describes most familiar accounts of therapy as "one way" in that they depict a professional with expert knowledges administering a series of interventions to a client. There is rarely a mention of what clients contribute to the lives of therapists or descriptions of how therapists learn, grow, and develop alongside clients when they take the risk of engaging in therapeutic relationships. And it is a risk. As Bill Madsen (2007) points out,

> there is a certain amount of vulnerability when we step out from behind our professional roles. We run the risk of not knowing ahead of time how to respond to clients, of feeling on the spot, and of having to acknowledge our own uncertainties. We also run the risk of more deeply connecting to clients' painful experiences as well as to our own feelings that get triggered in the process. (p. 38)

Counseling conversations are inherently cross-cultural encounters (Howard, 1991; Lee et al., 2009; Paré, 1996; Pedersen, 1991; Speight, Myers, Cox, & Highlen, 1991), and like any meeting of cultures they're mutually influencing events (Harkaway & Madsen, 1989) with learnings on both sides. To acknowledge this does not mean to suggest the aim of counseling is to be helpful to counselors. But it's a reminder of the richness clients bring to the lives of the professionals they consult and the rare privilege it is to be intimately present to their lives.

In my own therapeutic work using a reflecting team format (which involves the active participation of a number of counselors who reflect aloud on a live session), I've frequently heard clients declare the most useful moment was when one of the counselors was visibly moved and shared their own experience in relation to the client's story. This is an example of compassionate connection, and it also goes against the grain of a variety of well-entrenched ideas about the risks of self-disclosure, blurred boundaries, therapist overinvolvement, and so on. These issues deserve further attention, and I would like to tease out some distinctions about them due to their importance and because the issue of self-disclosure is sometimes presented with a highly cautionary tone that is incompatible with the kind of openness and presence described above.

Reflection 4.1

Have you ever lent your help to someone struggling with a significant challenge, perhaps over a prolonged period of time? In addition to identifying what you were able to contribute to this person's life, can you identify what you got back from this relationship? Is there anything you learned, anything you took away from the experience?

Self-Disclosure and the Therapeutic Relationship

Much has been written on the topic of therapist self-disclosure, which occurs when the counselor divulges details of their personal life and experience with clients (Audet & Everall, 2010; Knight, 2012; Ofer, Williams, Lehavot, & Knapp, 2009). A counselor's indiscriminate and repeated sharing of their personal experiences, emotions, and so on is clearly unhelpful—if for no other reason than that the conversation should center on the client.

Making deliberate choices about self-disclosure can be very challenging for novice counselors. After all, in daily conversation, we often indiscriminately share our personal experience, as in, "I know what you mean. The same thing happened to me," and so on. The account from Estrella in the Student Voices box below shows the effort it took for her to deliberately refrain from recapping her personal experience of chronic illness. By keeping this out of the conversation, she ensured her own considerable challenges did not have the effect of minimizing her client's concerns or upstaging her client as the primary focus of attention. She also avoided inciting an undue sense of responsibility in the client to take care of the counselor.

Estrella's choice made sense with this client and at this stage of their work together but does not speak to some universal axiom regarding self-disclosure. Here, as in relation to many decisions of this sort, the "it depends" rule comes into play: It depends on the context. With another client, or at another moment, sharing her experience of illness might contribute to the therapeutic relationship and be useful to the moment at hand. Indeed, at other times in her work, Estrella does disclose her own chronic illness while assuring clients she has reliable and competent support. This sharing sometimes leads to a palpable shift in relationship and a strengthening of the collaboration with clients. Talia's reflections in the second Student Voices box below demonstrate a shift from indiscriminate to intentional personal sharing. When it is at the service of the client and the relationship, self-disclosure has a useful role in therapeutic work.

Student Voices

Estrella: Withholding Her Illness Story

I recently met with a young woman who I will be working with on a project for youth with chronic illness. Before our meeting, I decided I would work on my counselling skills by withholding my opinions and personal experiences. Our meeting started off well as I asked her to tell me about herself, how she spends her time, and what motivated her to get involved with this project. When I asked about her motivation, she said she wanted to get involved in working with youth because she too suffered from a chronic illness as a child and wanted to get involved in this project as a way of making some sense out of her own experience. It took everything in my power to not share my similar experiences with chronic illness right away. Instead, I asked her to explain what she meant by making sense of her own experience. It suddenly became apparent to me how engaged she was in this conversation. It took her a second to answer my question and it seemed to me nobody had asked her to explain herself in this way before. When she did answer, I paid attention to her body language. She sat a little straighter and smiled as she talked. She seemed to have pride in her answer and seemed grateful for the opportunity to express herself.

Student Voices

Talia: From Indiscriminate to Intentional Sharing

When we were discussing self-disclosure during class, I assumed it would be difficult to withhold my own personal experiences when conversing with others because it was something I frequently did. But over the past few weeks, my perception of sharing experiences has shifted. I used to find that sharing was a way of connecting, building rapport, and that it was necessary to do in order to make the other feel that I am actively listening and interested. However, I have realised that self-disclosing personal information is not always necessary. I am still practicing strategically using self-disclosure and have noticed that with time, it gets easier and feels more natural. I find I am more conscious and aware of whom I select to share personal information with. For example, I have gotten in the habit of asking myself, "Why am I feeling the urge to reveal this information about myself?", "How may this impact the conversation?", etc. I now disclose only if I have a valid reason.

The issue of therapeutic boundaries (Daly & Mallinckrodt, 2009; Gabbard & Crisp-Han, 2010; Yonan, Bardick, & Willment, 2011) is related to self-disclosure and also touches on the topic of the therapeutic relationship. Counseling is a professional activity, and a professional relationship differs in some key ways from other relationships in our lives. When the center of therapeutic conversations drifts from the client's presenting concerns, it can detract from the helpfulness of the work. But this does not suggest a chain-link fence between counselor and client. An overly rigid conception of a boundary can lead to the adoption of a sort of fortified position that discourages counselors from sharing their humanity with the people who consult them. Here again, the key consideration is the impact of our sharing on clients: What kinds of sharing help to promote connection while keeping the client centered and not placing responsibility on the client to take care of the caregiver?

Last on the topic of self-disclosure and the relationship is the caution of therapist overinvolvement. To the extent the phrase reminds us of the dangers of burnout and the importance of counselor self-care, it is useful. But like the notion of boundaries, the term *overinvolvement* is at risk of painting the picture of neutral practitioners' reserving narrow slivers of themselves for their work while expecting the clients who consult them to wear their hearts on their sleeves and bare their darkest secrets.

These are highly complex issues, and the intention here is not to unpack them in detail but to make the point that it takes the involvement of two or more to have a relationship. Given the central importance of the therapeutic relationship, it is not reasonable to strive for a sort of clinical detachment. A committed counselor is in it for the pain and sadness along with the joy and inspiration, or what John Kabat-Zinn (1990), borrowing from the film character Zorba the Greek, likes to call "the full catastrophe."

AUTHENTICITY AND GENUINENESS REVISITED

The discussion about therapeutic relationship and self-disclosure is a stark illustration of the intentionality associated with therapeutic work. The sorts of deliberate decisions about what, when, and how much to share only rarely come up in our day-to-day encounters. As you can see, care-filled practice demands a large degree of reflexive self-awareness. It calls on us to ask what face we want to present to clients, which version of ourselves we want to be present in the consulting room. A familiar response to this question that you may have encountered in prior training is that the counselor should present their *authentic* and *genuine* self. These terms capture the spirit of acting naturally—of not hiding one's personality behind a professional veneer—and are of some use for that. But the terms derive from individualistic traditions that are limited in their scope for describing the cultural dimension of counseling and psychotherapy and the relational responsiveness of practice. They also posit a sort of fixed, essential self that prompts practitioners to preoccupy themselves about *who they are* when attention should more appropriately be directed to *what they do*. As mentioned earlier, relationship is a practice, not a thing.

> *Daniel tends to lapse into playful jive talk with his young nephews, of whom he is very fond. With his clients, he comes across as thoughtful and measured, weighing his words and listening more than he speaks. Maria, herself prone to expressive outbursts, notices what she would call a certain reserve in Daniel. She also notices a shift in his demeanor as their conversations continue, and she sees more glimpses of Daniel's wry sense of humor. In conversations with his supervisor, Daniel reports feeling impatient with Maria's partner Azim based on Maria's accounts of their home life: "I think he needs to step up to the plate more." With Maria, Daniel adopts a more patiently curious stance, asking questions to help Maria reflect on the events she recaps.*

The monolithic notion of an authentic, genuine self fails to capture the complex diversity of identities—the ways in which we are multicultured, reflecting different facets at different times, in different contexts and relationships. In the example above, Daniel adjust how he relates and what he says according to each context in which he finds himself. To view one of these various versions of himself as the true Daniel would be to cast doubt on the veracity or substance of the self he presents in the alternate contexts. When we think of relationship as something Daniel does, we see him making adjustments, context by context, reflecting the pluralism of the many cultural locations he inhabits. For Daniel, the more pertinent question is not, *Am I being authentic?* but rather, *What impact is my way of relating having on the other person in the relationship?* This latter question is congruent with an ethic of care and is consistent with the view of relationship as multicultured.

A second reason an appeal to authenticity or genuineness is limited for monitoring therapeutic relationships is that it inadvertently encourages a sort of either/or regime, vigilant for contradictions that are arguably typical of lived experience. If a counselor is *either* authentic or inauthentic, how might it be possible, for instance, to project one sentiment ("It's good to see the changes you're making") while withholding another ("I preferred your former haircut")? And how could one account for experience that contains contradictory elements, such as when Daniel, his stomach growling as lunch approaches, feels *both* empathetic concern and impatience while Maria recaps a rambling story of her failed shopping trip?

Later in this chapter we'll explore the distinction between either/or and both/and in more detail; for now you might want to look at the following Student Voices box, Bella. The issue here is that the notion of an authentic and true self doesn't sit well with the familiar experience that sometimes our thoughts or feelings don't add up. The emphasis on being who we are overshadows more important questions about the impact on the other person of our participation in a relationship.

Relationship is the word we use for the sum of our mutual interactions; in this sense a relationship is about actions, about how we relate to each other. Building and nurturing a therapeutic relationship involves an ongoing mindfulness about how our verbal and nonverbal actions are playing out for our clients. To do this doesn't imply abandoning our unique personal styles or withholding our playfulness or sense of humor. But it does suggest making deliberate choices about how we will speak and act. This entails shifting attention from a preoccupation with being our true selves to asking how the client is being affected by any particular version of self that we bring forward.

Student Voices

Bella: Shifting Relationships, Shifting Identities

I often have conversations with friends about the different identities, or aspects of our identities, that come to the forefront depending on the situation we find ourselves in. I often joke that I have my "teacher face," and my otherwise "responsible face," which is not to be confused with my "friends and family face," and of course, the ever important "in-law face!"

I feel that identity changes depending on how professional and responsible we need to be in a situation. It all just depends on the image we wish to portray to our social audience. I don't think any of these identities are unauthentic, just that real elements of an entire person come out at different times and in different situations and environments. I know that during the time I lived in Ireland, my main and almost only identity became "I am Canadian," and I did not want anyone to mistake that. By contrast, when my dad made a speech at my wedding this past summer, he referred to me as a jazz dancer (not a particularly good one, mind you), an artist, a public speaker, an author, a scholar, a volunteer, an athlete, a world traveler, a sister, and a daughter. I feel that in many ways my own identity is determined by the life role I'm presently engaged in, and by the perceptions of the people around me while I'm engaged in that particular role. When asked to define who I am, I am not sure where I would start. I don't think my first response would be to declare I am a soccer player, and yet on Monday nights in the summer time, that is exactly who I am, and I would imagine that is how my teammates would identify me, since that is the social context in which we know each other.

Reflection 4.2

Think about the contradictions that exist in your relationship with some key person in your life. Can you identify ways in which you hold a variety of apparently incompatible feelings about that person? Can you identify choices you make about which feelings you share, and when, in consideration of preserving and nurturing the relationship?

THERAPEUTIC STANCE: RELATING AS AN ALLY

Setting aside the quest for defining an essential, individualistic, therapist self makes room for attending to the self in relationship. This fits the topic at hand, which is relationship building. Working on the relationship is about doing rather than being. We build relationship moment by moment in our interactions. But there's an enormous amount going on at any moment in a conversation, and it can be challenging to consciously attend, moment by moment, to the impact of this on clients. So it can be helpful to reflect on the stance you'd like to occupy in relation to clients because a clarity about that preferred position can point the way forward in moments when you might otherwise be overwhelmed by the possibilities for responding.

There are many metaphors available to capture the stances counselors might occupy in relation to their clients, including teacher, mentor, guide, advisor, facilitator, and healer. If you spend some time reflecting on which sorts of relationship configurations they suggest—such as Maria's various relationships in Box 1.2 in Chapter 1—you'll notice the terms say something about the roles of each partner and of the distribution of power between partners as well.

Choosing how to relate to clients has significant repercussions for how they experience themselves because of the relational quality of self. Think about your experience of yourself through the eyes of someone who admires you and believes in your best intentions, and compare that with your identity in the presence of someone who doubts your capability or intent. Madsen (2007) says, "Our most important clinical quality is the attitude, stance, or emotional posture we take in relation to clients. That stance is the foundation for all our subsequent clinical work" (p. 19). How we relate is key.

Relating or orienting to clients with a focus on deficit or pathology invites deficits or pathologies forward. Milton Erickson used to say, "If the only tool you have is a hammer, then all your clients will look like nails" (Walter & Peller, 2000, p. 43). Orienting toward what is not working will turn up innumerable instances of problems and confirm to clients that they indeed need help. Relating as an ally involves standing beside clients, seeing them as active agents of their lives, and attempting to enact choices that fit with their values and intentions in the face of challenges.

Note this is not quite the same as focusing on strengths—an orientation that can inadvertently downplay the severity of the difficulties with which clients may be dealing. It's probably closer to say it's relating in a way that helps clients to connect with their strengths because it involves standing at their sides as they engage with the struggles and joys of living.

BOX 4.1

An Appreciative Ally

William Madsen (2007) uses the term "appreciative ally" in his description of a therapeutic stance. He refers to it as a "stance in which we position ourselves in alliance with clients and in which clients experience us as 'in their corner' or 'on their side'" (p. 22). This approach necessitates a continual search for elements of competence, connection, vision, and hope. Madsen regularly interviews clients in the quest to understand their experience of service providers so he can adjust his own orientation in ways that are helpful. This account from his client Karen helps to capture the importance of the counselor's stance:

When you're sitting in a therapist's office and the therapist is sitting across from you in his or her professional attire and you're the client with the problems and you're feeling very ashamed about yourself in the first place, there's a definite hierarchy. It feels like this person sitting across from you has his or her life all together and I'm a mess even though rationally we know that's not true. But that's what it feels like, and to have somebody be able to meet you on an equal footing and connect as a human being, well it just changes everything. . . . It decreases the feelings of shame and helplessness. To me, it gets rid of the feeling of I'll never be able to live up to where this person is or I'll never be able to get it together. (p. 37)

To relate as an ally doesn't mean to ignore or underestimate difficulties or to pretend that everything is okay. Instead, it's a holding of faith—a belief in the good intentions of clients and in their abilities to surmount challenges. This is easier to do when we hold a little lighter to our accumulated professional knowledges and make more space for being curious about what clients themselves bring to the challenges at hand.

BRINGING FORWARD LOCAL KNOWLEDGE

One consequence of the prolonged studies preceding counselor preparation is the accumulation of a huge body of psychological information that can lead to an understanding of people as particular *types*. Thinking this way, a counselor engages with clients as though in reference to mental file cards, experiencing them as "categories" (Anderson, 2009) rather than unique individuals. This way of relating detracts from being curious about how people make meaning in distinct ways and about what informs their particular understandings because it relies on abstracted academic and professional knowledge.

The metaphor of colonization serves as a reminder of the consequences of relying on generalized psychological knowledge at the expense of being curious about client knowledges. If you think of counselors as the emissaries of an imperial power and clients as the inhabitants of an island not previously visited by the colonizers, it creates a picture of what can happen when one set of cultural meanings overlooks another. There is a coherence to the beliefs and practices of the island dwellers' lives. Their symbols, stories, rituals, and ceremonies have long traditions and infuse their lives with meaning and richness. Their ways of life work. The colonizers arrive, brandishing their own foundational religious and scientific texts, and build churches and schools as vehicles for replacing indigenous ways with the colonizers' ways. This is a scenario that's been replayed countless times across the globe. The negative repercussions for the colonized are well known.

It's worth reflecting on how a version of this scenario can be replayed in counseling practice when encounters between practitioners and clients are dominated by professional meanings—when client experience is categorized, analyzed, understood, and explained in specialized professional terms and concepts foreign to the clients themselves.

Clients show up for counseling with knowledge accumulated over a lifetime. A 40-year-old has lived 350,400 hours, whereas a counselor meeting with a client for 1 hour once a week for 1 year would spend an accumulated 52 hours with that same client. This is not to suggest that clients aren't seeking outside input—otherwise why would they consult counselors?—or that counselors don't have something to offer. However, it's worth remembering that the view from the inside and the view from the outside are not the same thing. As Duvall and Béres (2011) put it, "totalizing, global categories invite therapists to relate to abstract concepts rather than relating to the specific people seeking assistance" (p. 48).

There is a wealth of what anthropologist Clifford Geertz (1983) called "local knowledge" available to clients. How does Maggie manage to feed four kids on her marginal income and keep them healthy? What does Pepe know about geriatrics that enables him to successfully share a tiny apartment with his 92-year-old mother? Which subtle signs that an anxiety attack is coming on does Daphne read that help her to take countermeasures?

The honoring of local knowledge is in contrast to the tradition of what Todd and Wade (1994) have called "psycholonization" and what Madsen (2007) refers to as "therapeucentrism" (p. 27). These authors' plays on words are attempts to capture the habit of conferring truth status to institutional concepts, constructs, procedures, and so forth and in the process overlooking the unique knowledges of individuals.

If these cautionary words seem to dismiss the knowledges that counselors accumulate during years of study and practice, that's not the point. However, counseling skill transcends book knowledge; it's relational expertise and calls on the ability to join with clients in evaluating the multiple knowledges available to therapeutic conversations. A distinction about forms of knowing might help to clarify this point: the contrast between *knowing that* and *knowing with*. *Knowing that* is knowledge one brings to a conversation, whereas *knowing with* is an expertise shared between counselor and client and makes room for both what counselors bring and also the accumulated wisdom clients have at their disposal.

Revisiting the island culture metaphor for a moment presents a picture of visitors from a foreign land arriving to offer support to local inhabitants. In doing so, they share understandings developed elsewhere. They also draw on the freshness of their perspectives as recent arrivals to help the island dwellers capitalize on indigenous, local knowledges they may have come to overlook or to dismiss. Notice it sometimes takes an outsider to remind an insider of what they already know. Facilitating the resurrection of local knowledges is the satisfying and fruitful outgrowth of relating as an ally.

Clearly, there are many metaphorical ways to talk about and write about orientating as an ally. Ultimately, however, assuming the stance of ally is a relational posture realized in the doing; if you're having difficulty picturing what it looks like, the following sections may help you to see how it plays out from the very beginning of contact with clients.

BOTH/AND: LISTENING FOR POSSIBILITIES AND PREFERENCES

In our daily conversations, it's not unusual to sit on something someone tells us, waiting for an opportune time to bring it up. That time could be moments later or days later. When a child is crying over a knee scrape after her first successful bike ride ever, we first commiserate and apply a bandage. Later, we joyfully congratulate her on her momentous accomplishment. This same filing away of something we've heard so that we might respond later is probably even more common in counseling conversations because they're invariably intentional and purposeful. Listening in the absence of responding is never a passive task, and even in silence there's a lot going on.

Chapter 3 limited itself to reflections and practice on the craft of listening, saving an exploration of the many options for responding to later chapters. Similarly, this chapter has been focused on the therapeutic relationship, without yet moving forward into an examination of the active skills of responding to clients. The intention of this sequencing is to focus on the skills that counselors primarily employ from the outset—skills they of course continue to employ throughout their work.

As a starting point, we bear compassionate witness to clients as they begin to tell their stories, acknowledging their experience in some cases for the first time. This can be powerfully therapeutic. But to acknowledge suffering is not to resign oneself (or another) to it, and this is what distinguishes a relationship founded on being an ally. Even in the moment of compassionate presence to what *is*, we are also witness to what *can be*.

As we listen to expressions of what has been lost, we also hear echoes of what is yearned for and cherished. Descriptions of purported failures are also accounts of actions that thumb their noses at arbitrary social markers of success. Stories of hardship include instances of courage and persistence in the face of daunting challenges. Confessions of moral lapses are simultaneously expressions of commitment to change. When we orient as allies, we hear client stories from a both/and perspective that you will see repeatedly throughout this book (see Box 4.2).

BOX 4.2

Both/And (And, And . . .)

Human knowledge made some dramatic leaps starting in the 18th century. Scientific methods began to produce dramatic results, ushering in an era of unprecedented technological innovation that continues to this day. The practical success of this particular way of engaging with the world elevated reason and rationality as keys to a universe of possibility. Although these habits of thought and practice have contributed to progress in many key areas, it's arguable the

(Continued)

(Continued)

focus on classification and measurement has had the unfortunate effect of crowding out other highly useful modes of engaging with the world.

Science earns tremendous mileage from distinguishing one thing from another, developing detailed descriptions of what makes them different, and affixing labels to each so they are forever distinct. Classifying things this way is known as Cartesian dualism, after the French philosopher René Descartes who famously divided mind from body—a division not common until that time and one still not made in many cultures around the world. Classifying things as distinct from one another, as mutually exclusive, relies on treating them as binary opposites (Fook & Gardner, 2007): as *either* X *or* Y. Enduring binary opposites relevant to counseling include illness versus health, thoughts versus feelings, nature versus nurture. This dualistic worldview has become dominant throughout societies striving to progress by tapping the momentum of the technology tsunami.

It's arguable that with the success of science and technology, we have come to turn to dualistic thinking for solutions to all that ails us, regardless of whether the issue at hand involves mechanics, emotions, relationships, or imagination. For instance, in identifying medical pathology, it's helpful to know a tumor is *either* malignant *or* benign. But this either/or perspective can also lead us to view clients as either ill or well, either angry or sad, either capable or incapable. Dualism is comforting in its simplicity, but it blinds us to the multiple possibilities always present alongside the challenges, difficulties, and problems clients face. What dualism gains in achieving order and control, it loses through its inability to capture the fluidity and diversity of lived human experience. An either/or perspective constrains the generation of new perspectives. Think about acquaintances you may have pegged with certain qualities: He's a bully. She's a worrier. The labels instantly reduce the scope of behaviors you anticipate and induce a blindness to actions that stand outside of them.

When we adopt a both/and perspective with clients, we don't rush to define, to achieve closure. Instead we remain open to the unexpected, to new options for going forward not immediately evident. This is an orientation that celebrates multiplicity, one ill suited to technology yet remarkably practical in the realm of human relations.

The phrase *both/and* reminds us of the possibility of two apparently contradictory elements being simultaneously present, but it isn't intended to draw the line at two. Letting go of the constraints of an either/or perspective opens space for multiple options. There is always another view, another description, another possibility. In this sense, it's not so much *both/and* as *both and, and, and.* . . .

Reflection 4.3

Do you ever peg yourself narrowly in terms of your own weaknesses, foibles, deficits, and so on? What happens when you open up your view of yourself, adopting a both/and perspective? What else do you see when you consider that you are X, and Y, and Z, and so forth? Is it challenging to hold this view of contrasting and multiple dimensions of yourself? What is the effect of entertaining this expanded perspective of your identity?

A both/and view of clients recognizes that pain can exist alongside pleasure, and sadness alongside joy. It allows us to listen with two ears, as it were—first to the distress that difficulties bring to clients' lives, and second to the hopes and purposes, skills and abilities, clients bring to these difficulties. Without this second ear, we hear only stories of passive victimization.

DOUBLE LISTENING: LISTENING AS AN ALLY

White (Carey, Walther, & Russell, 2009; White, 2000, 2003) used the term "double listening" to describe the practice of staying open to the hopeful possibilities always on the other side of struggle. This is relating in a manner that prepares the ground for constructive collaboration; later we'll explore the many directions it can lead. To stay true to the sequencing of sections that organize this book, I will save the discussion about active responding and concentrate for the remainder of this chapter exclusively on listening as an ally.

Even in silence we actively gather much that will later prove useful. But this doesn't just happen. The choice of what in particular to listen for is a deliberate act and happens in the context of traditions that place more focus on deficits than on possibilities. Kenneth Gergen (1994) uses the term "progressive infirmity" for a widespread social trend that owes much to psychiatry and psychology, continuing to define and measure purported mental disorders. Especially when done under the influence of dichotomous thinking (*either* A *or* B), this perspective leads to clients' capacities and resources being minimized, if not rendered fully invisible. This outcome may well be inadvertent, but the dominant emphasis on deficit leads to the downplaying of capacity.

The practice of making sense of certain forms of human experience in terms of psychopathology arose in the 20th century and is foreign to virtually all indigenous cultural traditions around the world. It has proven useful for many clients dealing with serious disturbances—for instance, in helping identify medications that can diminish problematic symptoms. An unfortunate outgrowth of these developments, however, is that they have fueled the almost exponential growth of newly designated mental disorders[1] with no corresponding collective enterprise dedicated to classifying the endless skills and qualities that people draw on in the face of what Shakespeare called the "slings and arrows of outrageous fortune" (*Hamlet*, 3.1.66). A consequence of this trend in the therapeutic domain is a thinning of our view of clients: Rather than seeing them as acting from intention in the face of contextual challenges (Bruner, 1990), we characterize them primarily as passive victims of circumstance.

The choice of therapeutic stance is not about what is really *true* about a client; it is a decision about how and what to orient to for ethical and pragmatic reasons. Double listening is a practice associated with a stance of appreciative ally, opening up an alternate view of the people who consult counselors:

1. kindred human beings who share with us and, like us, experience distress and suffering;

2. agents of their actions, exercising purposes and intentions in the face of life challenges;

3. actors in the context of cultural influences, material constraints, and power relations;

4. experts in their own lives;

5. people making meaning of their experience according to values; and

6. people possessing skills and abilities not always immediately evident in the midst of struggles.

These aren't factual claims. Like a diagnostic label, each is closer to what Madsen (1999) calls "a story we tell to organize our understanding" (p. 44). Their intent is to support an ethical stance vis-à-vis clients that influences what we see, hear, and feel as we sit with the clients who consult us. They orient us to possibilities, offering a rich palate of colors even as discouragement and dichotomous thinking urge clients to see their circumstances in black and white. Early in our work we gather accounts of these possibilities; in time we join with clients in painting new futures.

In the beginning, we listen—to the client and to ourselves. Fully present to the moment, we orient to all that we see and hear, witnessing expressions of distress as well as openings to new territories of living. There are many ways of creatively exploring these openings, and we will look at many of them later in the book. But even before that active responding happens, we prepare ourselves for constructive collaboration through the practice of double listening.

In the remainder of this chapter, you're invited to engage in double listening in relation to the story of Maria (whom you have met as both a client and a counselor) and her client Jorge. You may want to review what happened in the first exchanges between Maria and Jorge: You'll find them throughout Chapter 3. After reviewing the following additional vignette, read the sections that follow it, engaging with the questions at the end of each section.

> *Jorge says getting to the gym regularly helps with the insomnia, when he can pull together the discipline to do it. But he still can't escape what he describes as the "dread" that comes over him in the middle of the night and lingers throughout the day. He says that it scatters his attention and that he's having trouble getting anything done.*
>
> *"This is what I've been wasting my time with," says Jorge, unzipping a worn and overstuffed backpack at the foot of his chair. Maria had commented on the backpack earlier when he mentioned his full work plate but hadn't expected him to spill its contents on the floor between them. She looks down at a striking collection of cityscapes in charcoal and ink. Several of the pieces feature a tall young man set against the city's historical quarter.*
>
> *"Jorge! They're beautiful. Are these yours?"*
>
> *"Keeps me away from my studying! I'm a procrastinator," says Jorge, rolling his eyes. "This is why I'm going to flunk out of engineering. It might be forgivable if I were any good."*
>
> *Jorge says he drew a lot when he was younger but gave it up for a time, and recently reclaimed his passion for visual expression. A few months earlier, he was sitting in a café popular among gay men. He noticed Richard, the man depicted in Jorge's drawing, doodling in a notepad. They struck up a friendship and later started a relationship. Since then Jorge's been dabbling with ink, charcoal, and more recently watercolor. He grimaces ironically as he adds that taking up another medium gives him one more option for avoiding "real work."*
>
> *As it turns out, Richard's doodling was mostly to pass the time while waiting for his coffee, and he has little to say about Jorge's sketches. But Jorge recently joined a drawing club through a friend studying fine arts.*

RELATING TO VALUES

Values are the blood of stories, says screenwriter Robert McKee (1997), who's spent his lifetime studying how screenplays are constructed. Writers do a poor job bringing stories to life when they fail to give us a sense of what matters to the characters they create. Directors are famous for berating wooden actors with the question, "What's your motivation?!" Clients—and lives—appear two-dimensional until we get a sense of the purposes that drive action.

When clients share their stories, they provide a glimpse of the elaborate network of values that inform and give life to their thoughts, feelings, and actions. But they don't necessarily display these on a silver platter, any more than a film's protagonist (those in cheesy films excepted) might explicitly proclaim, "I stand for justice, freedom, and moral redemption."

Read the previous vignettes again, placing yourself in Maria's position. As you listen, ask yourself, What does Jorge want? Which expressions of value, hope, purpose, and desire can you discern amid his mostly defeatist account of his circumstances? After you've done this, revisit the vignettes one more time after reading the questions below to see if any new material comes to light.

What might Jorge's revealing his art to a stranger say about his interest in sharing it?

What might his belittling of his technique say about a desire to refine his craft?

What might the presence of Richard in several drawings say about his care for his partner?

How might Jorge's experimenting with solutions to insomnia speak of the importance to him of health?

What might Jorge's joining an art club signify in terms of an interest in connection with others?

Reflection 4.4

We are not always inclined to identify the values we are enacting as we engage in our own lives. However, momentary reflection can bring these to the foreground. Consider some challenge you are currently facing or have recently faced in your life—some issue that has called on you to exert considerable effort, perhaps in the face of adverse physical circumstances or uncomfortable emotional ones. Your actions have been on behalf of something that presumably matters enough to you that you would endure these. How would you name the values by which you have been standing? What has been important to you that has kept you engaged?

RELATING TO SKILLS AND ABILITIES

People have all kinds of skills and abilities available to bring to bear on challenges, many of which don't even appear on the radar screen because of their (and sometimes our) preoccupation with what isn't working. And then there are the skills and abilities that seem to contribute to problems that, with creativity and vision, can be useful for distancing from problems. Consider the example of Ramos: He relied on his stunningly gregarious nature to raise money in support of a volunteering trip overseas. He thus ended a lot of trouble associated with his drug-dealing habit that owed its success to his . . . yup, his stunningly gregarious nature.

David Epston likes to have playful conversations with young clients about how they're "weirdly abled" (Freeman, Epston, & Lobovits, 1997), another way to exploit qualities that may be overlooked or even maligned. Consider Zack, who displays the spectacular ability to send 31 text messages during one class while listening to an MP3 player, playing an app, and jotting the occasional note. How these abilities might be harnessed is an intriguing question, but just the noticing of them prepares fertile ground for further exploration—something difficult to do when we're mostly preoccupied with, for example, deficits in attention or defiant behavior.

As you revisit Jorge and Maria once more, look for skills and abilities of Jorge's that might be harnessed. One of these is quite explicit—his artistic ability. How, in the longer term, might he put this ability to use in helpful ways? Others are to be found between the lines, to be mined with careful attention. What other abilities do you notice, remembering there are many skills of living that we're unaccustomed to noticing and naming? Once again, after you've done this on your own, read the question prompts below, and go back to the vignettes one more time to see what else might come to light.

> Which abilities do you notice in Jorge when you think of various initiatives he's taken such as meeting strangers, tapping organizational resources, maintaining relationships, as performing tasks requiring particular interpersonal skills?
>
> What becomes visible if you think of his efforts to deal with sleep disturbances as empirical research projects of sorts?
>
> Which particular qualities are needed to stick to dietary regimes, sit in silence daily, or lace on runners when the weather's grim or the bones are weary?
>
> Which role do you imagine art could play in addressing insomnia or building relationship bridges with parents?

RELATING TO AGENCY

When things are going poorly in our lives, it's easy to feel things are happening to us with no sense of our agency, our own volitional action in the face of the challenges bearing down on us. This pervasive sense of victimization is not uncommon among clients, because they meet with counselors when they are up against it. At the time they choose to consult therapists they are frequently caught up in what White and Epston (1990) call "problem-saturated" accounts of their experience—stories that highlight their victimhood and all that is not working in their lives.

But there are always other views available to a compassionate witness willing to hold open other possibilities—because regardless of the hardships and calamities befalling clients, they do continue to make active choices in the face of them. We cannot escape our own agency, as elusive as it may seem. In fact, times when things are particularly difficult for clients (when they may be most likely to feel they're victims of circumstance) are also times when they arguably exhibit more striking exertions of will. Getting out of bed to face a day of relentless physical pain or crippling fears is akin to an act of heroism. When clients appear on our doorsteps, they have enacted a series of actions in the face of various constraints to avail themselves of support and assistance. This is agency.

Allan Wade (1997) has explored these ideas richly, drawing on Erving Goffman's (1961) phrase "small acts of living" to depict the acts of agency in which clients engage regardless of the obstacles they face. He takes a broader cultural view to remind us that wherever there is oppression in the world—European Jewish enclaves under Nazism, the black majority under South African apartheid—there is resistance. When the oppressive forces are large, the power imbalances severe, that resistance is understandably difficult to discern—*underground,* to use a familiar wartime term. Identifying those acts that defy victimization is what relating to agency is all about.

This time as you review the vignettes of Jorge and Maria, orient yourself to the expressions of agency in Jorge's account of his experience. Listen for actions he's taken that can be understood as instances of personal agency in the face of challenges. It may also help to consider the scope of the challenges themselves, to reflect on how they might discourage action, because this may help to highlight Jorge's efforts in the face of them. As before, after you've done this on your own, review the question prompts below. They'll orient you to other possibilities when you return to the vignettes one last time.

Which steps does one have to take to meet with a counselor for the first time ever? See if you can anticipate a series of actions this would involve by breaking things down into steps.

Here and in the questions to follow, always think of not only the actions taken but the forces (ideas, feelings, relationships, etc.) that might constrain the actions and make them more difficult to achieve. For instance, which social forces constrain the open expression of homosexuality, and what does it take to come out?

Which actions are involved in resurrecting a drawing and painting hobby?

What do you have to do to connect with a like-minded community?

What does it take to meet and connect with a stranger and to develop this acquaintance into an intimate relationship?

Relationships are about relating—they are constructed in a series of actions and are not mere by-products of the compatibility between two people. When clients share their stories, we have innumerable options for how to relate, choices about the sort of relationship we want to foster. The way we position ourselves vis-à-vis the other is written across our faces; it resonates in our tone of voice and of course is apparent in how we actively respond by adding our words to theirs. This chapter began to talk about this with the reminder that how we orient influences what we see and hear and what clients see and hear in our eyes and our voice. The discussion of responding, the active dimension of relating, will be taken up in more detail starting in Chapter 6.

CHAPTER FOUR RECAP

It may not come as a surprise that meta-analyses of counseling outcome studies repeatedly show the relationship with clients is critical to helpful counseling outcomes. After all, the craft of counseling is inherently a relational profession. Counselors prepare for years, acquiring an assortment of useful knowledge in the process, but they don't get a chance to hone the relational craft until they engage in the actual practice of therapeutic conversation with clients.

It requires considerable skill to bring those knowledges to therapeutic conversations without erasing the wide range of other knowledges of potential use to the situation at hand. Drawing on a cultural metaphor, this points to the local, indigenous knowledges easily overlooked by colonial visitors entranced by their own advanced technologies. When we relate to clients as allies, we're poised to discern the threads of local understandings and corresponding activity that might offer alternatives to the dominant accounts of their experience. Ironically, clients will often overlook these local knowledges, caught up in problem-saturated accounts of their experience.

Relating as an ally involves listening in a very particular way. Rather than listening to categorize—to determine if clients are either X or Y—it's an orientation to multiplicity, always open to noticing and contemplating an additional possibility that might prove useful to the conversation at hand.

Relating as an ally is more than a passive, receptive act. Although it creates space for the expression of what is, it also begins the movement toward what can be. In sitting in compassionate presence with clients, we commit to witnessing their distress and suffering. However, in being an ally, we commit to joining them on a journey to a preferred place resonant with their hopes, intentions, and values. So in addition to holding (and voicing when and if appropriate) the question, How does it hurt? we also hold another key curiosity: What do you want? In the coming chapters we'll look at ways of responding to clients that point the way to preferred futures. The process starts with discerning a client's intended meaning, the focus of Chapter 5.

NOTE

1. The first *Diagnostic and Statistical Manual of Mental Disorders* (American Psychiatric Association, 1952) was published in 1952. It was 130 pages long and listed 106 disorders. Since that time, several committees have been busy developing descriptions of new disorders, with each subsequent edition of the *Diagnostic and Statistical Manual* containing further entries. The latest version (American Psychiatric Association, 2000), a revision of the 1994 version, lists more than 300 mental disorders in 993 pages.

CHAPTER FOUR DISCUSSION QUESTIONS

1. **Nonneutrality and professionalism.** Is it possible to be professional without being neutral? Which expressions of subjectivity or bias might be professional? Which expressions of these might be unprofessional? How could self-disclosure play a useful role in responsible practice, and how might self-disclosure be counterproductive?

2. **Two-way experience of therapy.** It's common to speak of what clients gain from therapeutic services. What might counselors gain? What difference does it make to the way we look at the role of clients in therapy when we entertain their contribution to therapists' lives?

3. **Authenticity and genuineness.** Which aspects of these terms are useful in considering how to relate to clients? In which ways are the terms limiting in providing guides for practice?

4. **Multiplicity of identity.** Identify ways that your own identity shifts depending on (a) the social context in which you are situated, (b) the time period in your life that you are considering, and (c) the physical context in which you are located.

5. **The complex self.** What is to be gained through the reminder that selves are complex and varied? Which advantages does this view present in relation to counselors? Which advantages does it present in relation to clients?

6. **Metaphors for the counselor's positioning.** Consider the following list of metaphors—teacher, mentor, guide, advisor, facilitator, healer, ally—and describe (a) what distinguishes the roles of counselor and client and (b) what the metaphors connote about power relations between counselor and client. For example, whose ideas are given higher status, and who has more say in the shaping of the relationship, the direction conversations take, and so on?

7. **Your experience through the eyes of an ally.** Identify some challenge you have struggled with or are struggling with. Think of the efforts you have made or are making in the face of difficulties. Look at these efforts through the eyes of someone who you know admires you and stands beside you. What impact does this have on your experience of your experience? Look at these same efforts through the eyes of someone who you feel may doubt you or is not in touch with your intentions, purposes, and values. How do you experience yourself in this instance? What is different about the two views in terms of your energy for engaging with your challenges and moving forward in life? Discuss the impact of these two views on your sense of yourself.

8. **Relating as an ally.** Discuss the list of assumptions about clients in the section titled Therapeutic Stance: Relating as an Ally. Which resonate most strongly for you? Which common views of clients (for better or worse) do these assumptions exclude? Are there items you would remove from the list or items you would add? What does it mean to say, These are not factual claims?

9. **Psycholonization.** Consider some of the most dominant constructs emerging from roughly a century's worth of psychology. In which ways do these constructs distract from the local knowledges that clients might bring to their situations?

10. **Knowing *that* and knowing *with*.** Describe what a therapeutic conversation would look like if it mostly featured *knowing that* and was centered on counselor knowledge. Contrast this with a description of a conversation featuring *knowing with*, which features the intermingling of counselor and client knowledges.

11. **Both/And.** Identify some apparent contradictions of your own identity. Consider, for example, a particular attribute, and ask yourself if in some ways you also experience the opposite of this attribute in certain contexts.

12. **Orienting as constructing.** Discuss the ways that we invite forward particular attributes in people by the way we orient to them. Give examples from your own life. In which ways does our orienting contribute to the construction of identities?

CHAPTER FOUR ACTIVITIES

1. **One-way and two-way accounts of therapy.** In pairs, speakers share their experience of overcoming a challenge in their life. Listener, help the speaker recount their stories. Afterward, the listener debriefs on what they took away from listening to the speaker.

2. **Relating to values.** In pairs, take turns sharing with each other. You may want to use a topic listed in Box 2.2 at the end of Chapter 2. Listener, listen for what is important to the speaker as they share with you. Ask yourself, What is it they want? What is it they value? What is it they cherish or yearn for that is between the lines of the account? In the debrief that follows, the listener shares their impressions, and the speaker comments on them.

3. **Relating to skills of living.** Even when clients are struggling, we can understand them as relying on various skills of living to cope with challenging circumstances. In pairs, take turns describing some difficulties you faced in the past. The speaker should not conclude with a happy ending by providing an account of how they solved or dealt with the challenges; the task here is for the listener to discern various skills of living that the speaker may have brought to bear on the challenges even in the midst of the struggle. Listener, ask questions as necessary to help the speaker evoke a rich account. In the debrief, the listener may share some ideas about skills of living they identified. The speaker may comment on these.

4. **Relating to agency.** In pairs, take turns describing some difficulties you faced in the past. This may be a situation wherein you primarily felt a victim of circumstances. Listener, ask questions as necessary to help the speaker identity the actions they took in response to the challenges faced. In the debrief, the listener and speaker compare notes on expressions of agency in the midst of challenging circumstances.

SECTION THREE

MAPPING CLIENTS' EXPERIENCE

Y ou may remember that at the start of the previous section, "Constructing a Foundation for Collaboration," I wrote about the pedagogical challenge of breaking down the craft of counseling into separate elements without straying too far from what actually happens in practice. We bump into this challenge again in the relationship between the two chapters of this section about mapping clients' experience because the skills introduced are not necessarily sharply differentiated in practice. Nevertheless, as stated elsewhere, the chapters adhere to a general arc of practice. Chapter 5 covers two primary tasks: (a) We ask about the other's experience, and (b) we do an initial interpretation of the meaning of what they share. Chapter 6 is devoted to a third task: (c) We respond, offering back our take on what we have heard and inviting the client to correct it.

The first of this section's two chapters is therefore devoted to the skills involved in coaxing an account of a client's experience, as well as the receptive skills of reading that experience, an internal process of discernment that happens as we listen and attend, even prior to responding. This is followed in Chapter 6 with a look at what happens once the counselor enters the conversation to negotiate understanding. Things quickly get more complex here due to the ambiguity of both nonverbals and spoken language; in effect, the counselor's voice is added to the client's, and the process of co-construction of meaning is well under way.

The skills in these two chapters are foundational to developing a picture of clients' experience and beginning the process of working more actively on the issues brought to the conversation. They are particularly central at the outset of the work, when a key task is to get a reading of where clients currently "are at." The skills continue to be the backbone of helping conversations because constructive collaboration is impossible without some degree of shared understanding but are joined later by other skills, including those devoted to promoting movement or change.

Maps help us to develop a picture of a territory, so they serve as a useful metaphor for the skills to be explored in this section of the book. The division into distinct chapters is to help you engage with the skills sequentially, to build gradually toward greater complexity. I'll say again, however, that any compartmentalization of counseling skills is always somewhat artificial because responsive dialogue is always improvisational. We can rarely count on things to unfold in tidy sequences.

So although Chapter 5 looks at the receptive aspect of mapping experience, there's no expectation that in a typical counseling exchange, the counselor would merely invoke input without responding as well for any extended period. As we'll see throughout Chapter 5, we can get only so far in receptively understanding without also responding to clarify distinctions, coax out details, inquire as to the meaning of certain words and phrases, and so on—all skills to be explored in more detail in Chapter 6.

You'll notice that these two chapters are devoted to developing an understanding of clients' experience in general, even prior to working at developing a detailed account of the concerns or issues they may have brought to counseling. That more specific focus on what is often called client problems will be taken up in Section 4, en route to an exploration in Section 5 of the skills used to help clients move in their preferred directions.

Chapter 5

RECEIVING AND READING MEANING

INTRODUCTION

So far we've explored the role of compassionate and mindful listening in creating a space for helpful conversations. We've also looked at the central importance of relationship, which more than any other identifiable aspect of practice has been linked to favorable outcomes. The chapter about relationship emphasized the importance of the counselor's attitudinal stance, with the reminder that as counselors we actively contribute to clients' experience of themselves when we interact with them. This is not always foregrounded in the psychological literature, which frequently refers to "individual experience" and can inadvertently suggest an image of each of us experiencing the world in totally distinct ways, isolated from each other, sealed away in our own private bathyspheres (Hoffman, 2002).

In fact our mere presence to another in any social interaction, including a counseling conversation, has an impact in itself. In this sense, we never fully encounter another's individual, raw experience because we contribute in some measure to that experience, moment by moment. Nevertheless, clients do arrive with their own personal histories, and the ways they express their experience both verbally and nonverbally are unique to them. And so this chapter deliberately lingers on the practices of seeking to understand prior to actively responding to clients. This includes the receptive skills involved in reading the client's account and questioning skills for encouraging sharing and seeking clarification.

In exploring the territory of clients' experience, we begin with the task of discerning meaning, based on a careful consideration of three key elements: (a) the words clients use to convey their experience, (b) their nonverbal expression, and (c) the wider context in which they are speaking.

VERBAL EXPRESSION

A key opening task in counseling is achieving an understanding of the client's account as a precursor to collaborating to address their concerns. A substantial amount of that account is conveyed through words. Given the ambiguity of language and the inevitable cultural differences between counselor and client, this process deserves patient attention.

Cultural Curiosity

Getting There From Here

Maria suddenly yawns heavily and rubs her eyes, interrupting what until then has been a brisk speaking pace.

"Tired on top of these other things?" asks Daniel.

"I don't know. Fed up. Baffled. Messed up. Crazy. Take your pick."

Daniel smiles and waits for more, not certain what would be the most helpful addition at this point. Maria heaves a resigned sigh and shrugs her shoulders.

"So, where were we?" she asks, preparing to resume.

A sensible question to ask when setting out to get to some destination is, Where am I starting from? Establishing how to get somewhere involves knowing where the start point is. So too for counseling conversations, whose purpose is ultimately to be of some help to a client, to effect some change or movement from here to there.

What the *there* is and what shape that movement will take is not clear at the outset: It might involve significant action, like choosing a career path or getting a divorce. Or maybe it's movement of a less visible variety: a shift in attitude, the gaining of a new understanding. Whichever form the movement takes, the starting point is the client's current experience because this constitutes their reality, their point of departure.

Developing Understanding Over Time

Language is the prime tool clients use to share their experience. As we've seen, it's a flawed tool, although those flaws curiously account for its ability to express a poetic richness and complexity no mathematical system or logistical model could ever match. The difficulty, you'll remember, is that there is no one-to-one correspondence between words and things. When clients share detailed descriptions of their experience, we're filled with thoughts and feelings, images and sensations, but we can't be sure how closely our reading fits theirs. Although we may know the definitions of the words clients use, it's another matter to know what the words mean for them (Gadamer, 1988).

It takes time to develop understanding. A fundamental challenge of counseling is to contain the impulse to rush to get there—an impulse that is particularly strong when we feel we identify with the client. This most often happens when we share a variety of cultural locations with someone, which leads us to conclude we know where they're coming from.

Assuming Cultural Differences

This assumption that we've *got it* happens less often when we encounter someone whose cultural location is clearly very different from our own—an indigenous tribal client in native headdress from a recently "discovered" island performing a ritual in an unfamiliar language, for example. We fully expect not to understand many of this person's meanings. We are prepared to go slowly, to learn about their world, to set aside our understandings to make room for theirs. This is much less the case in the company of others who appear to share our cultural locations—for instance, a neighbor who dresses similarly, speaks the same language, votes for the same political party, and drives the same model car. Here we are less primed for an anthropological adventure. But there are always cultural divides. Even with those closest to us, the task of deciphering the other's meaning is a challenge that never truly ends, as you may agree if you reflect on misunderstandings you've had with partners, family members, or friends.

In Daniel and Maria's case, a lot of evocative words have already been spilled, and their possible meanings are many. "Fed up" may be a precursor to quitting practicum or merely the expression of a passing irritation. "Baffled" might mean thoroughly perplexed or mildly bemused. "Messed up" could denote emotional unraveling or having a bad day. And "crazy" is a widely circulated word with a broad range of possible meanings, some of them associated with mental health and others having to do with whimsy, eccentricity, spontaneity, and so on. Daniel is familiar with the words and uses them himself, but not in precisely the same way.

Language as a Secondhand Tool

Language is our key resource for conveying meaning. However, it's only half ours, said Mikhail Bakhtin (1986), reminding us no single speaker has a monopoly on its use. Words are our tools, but they don't come sparkling new out of plastic shrink-wrap, to be put to the test for the first time. Instead, they come "second-hand," as it were (A. Gregoire, personal communication, June 4, 2011).

They've been used in a variety of ways for a very long time, and they'll continue to be used in ways both familiar and idiosyncratic. For someone on the listening end, it's usually possible to notice both an identification with how someone uses a word and a sense of how the other's use differs from our own. The craft of counseling would be a lot easier, although perhaps less interesting, if words simply corresponded, one on one, to objects in the world the way a label such as "2-inch brass, Phillips head, size 12 screw" denotes a particular piece of hardware. Language is nested within the multiple and diverse cultural contexts from which it emerges. When the context is not immediately familiar to us, our grasp of the meaning is also more tentative.

When we first meet someone, we're less sure about what the person means by the words they use. For this reason, early in getting to know someone, we're less inclined to jump to conclusions about their intentions. Think about ironic remarks made by strangers: When we don't have a sense of where they're coming from we're less likely to laugh (genuinely, that is) along with them. When a new client says, "Tony hurt me," we can't know if this is about physical assault or an overlooked birthday. Even once we learn more context, it's another matter to gauge the nuance of a word like *hurt,* which is rife with meaning. Between speaker and listener there are inevitable gaps in the sense of the language used to convey and construct experience.

Adopting a posture of cultural curiosity (Madsen, 2007) narrows that gap when it's turned into the practice of patient inquiry about another's experience, much like an anthropologist's investigations of cultural meanings and traditions. Cultural curiosity is not about professional humility: It's a deliberate posture intended to evoke rich accounts of clients' experience.

Reflection 5.1

Have you ever had the experience of an aha moment when you suddenly discovered your take on someone's opinion or experience was inaccurate? Perhaps this was when someone did something out of sync with your expectations, raising a flag and inviting you to reexamine your assumptions about them. Or maybe it was something someone said that seemed to contradict everything they had previously said—or at least everything you *thought* they'd said until you adjusted your reading. Junctures like these can make for momentous shifts in understanding, the way plot twists in movies get the audience members reevaluating the assumptions that have carried their reading of the plot to that point.

Avoiding the Rush to Understanding

It's an interesting thing: At the moment we decide we understand, we cease our inquiry into the client's experience. It's like taking a snapshot, freezing the image. Life is a very complicated business, and so is the work of counseling. As Rønnestad and Skovholt (2003) put it, "an attitude of respect for the complexity of counseling/ therapy work lies at the base of ethical practice and also for a constructive professional developmental process" (p. 38). Describing counselors' process broadly, Rønnestad and Skovholt speak of "premature closure" to capture the notion of hastily settling on a particular reading of things to cope with the anxiety that arises in the face of complexity. In counseling conversations, this can convert into a rush to understanding. We prematurely assume we've arrived at a shared territory, foreclosing on capturing the richness of the other's experience by attaching a significance to their words that fits for us although it may not have been intended.

> *"The way I'm living is wrong," says Jorge, more forcefully than Maria expects.*
>
> *In this university setting, Maria has often worked with young clients struggling to consolidate their identities in the face of pressure to conform to cultural expectations. Sometimes she watches as they reclaim values they rejected for many of their adolescent years. More often, she sees clients deny deeper longings or dispositions in an effort to placate their parents, with the effect of dishonoring themselves. It seems to Maria that Jorge is doing this, but she needs to hear more and chooses not to assume she understands.*
>
> *"Can you tell me more about 'wrong,' Jorge?"*
>
> *Jorge goes on to explain he's been hiding from his parents for too long, that he knows his gay sexuality reflects a way of being and not some passing fad, that he wants to embrace his sexual orientation and share the news joyously with his parents.*

Striving, Not Arriving

Because a sense of connection often emerges from a place of common ground, it can be tempting to assume we've reached that place. A shared understanding, we think, will no doubt prepare the way for fruitful conversation. But "understanding too quickly runs the risk of blocking the development of new meaning," write Anderson and Goolishian (1988, p. 382). It also hampers the expression of a current meaning still forming for the client and not yet fully articulated.

Zali Gurevitch (1989) deals with the challenge of prematurely foreclosing on meaning by proposing a sort of paradox. He advocates a posture of what he calls "not understanding" because this helps to ensure the speaker (client in our case) is "liberated from the image that one has projected onto [their] experience from the center of one's self" (p. 163). Expanding on this idea, he says, "The power to not understand is based on the essential morality of dialogue and human relations, which is the obligation to recognize the other as an other. This is the foundation of honor and respect" (p. 166).

Gurevitch's quest is to avoid what has been called the "linguistic violence" (Strong & Zeman, 2005, p. 247) of denying difference and otherness (cf. Derrida, 1976; Larner, 1996; Levinas, 1985). All of the authors cited are acutely attuned to an ethic of care, depicting an almost reverential quality to dialogue that acknowledges each client's uniqueness. The practice supporting this is a persistent curiosity that brings forth the richness of the other's experience—a striving to understand without the expectation of ever fully arriving.

Beginner's Mind

Early in their training, I often witness counselors illuminated by a spark of recognition in something their clients say. In their excitement at this moment of identification and their earnestness to bridge the gap between themselves and their clients, they sometimes respond, "I've experienced that too" or "I know exactly what you mean." This is not *always* an unhelpful moment, but the rest of the conversation is most often hijacked in this rush to connection. From that point forward, the counselor has difficulty absorbing aspects of the client's experience that are different from their own, and the client struggles to articulate what makes their own experience exclusive to themselves. When we greet client experiences as familiar, it sometimes has the effect of turning what for the client is a unique experience into a more commonplace thing known to many.

Eastern traditions have a term, *beginner's mind,* for referring to a childlike state of awareness in which our preunderstandings are suspended and our hearts, minds, and senses are open to being surprised (Epston, 1993; Goodman, 2005). Entering counseling conversations with beginner's mind is like walking through the woods, the senses finely tuned to nature's stunning biodiversity. Cultures and clients are also infinitely diverse, and no client's story is quite the same as any ever told before.

And What Else? Refraining From Concluding

When a client conveys the counselor is on the right track, a connection is made, and a space closes between them. Among other things, it's a mutual territory of language, a shared vocabulary. This could be the "dread" that a client named Anita talks about as a feeling in the pit of her stomach before exams or the "old runaround" Jackson refers to in descriptions of his increasingly frustrating exchanges with his boss. Achieving some degree of understanding is a crucial task and one that continues indefinitely. For the counselor, getting it should not be reason to suspend curiosity, to seize the quest for further understanding. When we do that, we fix the other—like substituting a freeze-frame for a flowing video. We run the risk of experiencing them as an instance of a category (Anderson, 2009) that our diligent inquiry has uncovered rather than a unique, ever-changing, and never fully knowable person. We come to a conclusion, and the curious thing about conclusions is they conclude. They bring to an end a fruitful mutual inquiry into further possibilities. There is always more to understand; we can always wonder, And what else? There is no contradiction between curiosity and connection. Curiosity conveys a desire to acquaint oneself more fully with another in their glorious uniqueness.

Student Voices

Lydia: The Impact of Curiosity

A favorable moment as a client occurred in my second session with my counsellor. My struggles of attending university are centred on homesickness and the feeling of not being where I belong. I unexpectedly became emotional while telling my story, then I quickly became embarrassed. My counsellor appeared comfortable and calm while I was going through these unexpected emotions. My counsellor was with me with every step and allowed me to talk through my emotionality and embarrassment without rushing in to try to fix me, nor did she give me any suggestions how to get through this. She was just there with me, as an ally, allowing me to speak about my thoughts and feelings while reflecting her understanding of my experiences. The way she composed herself gave me comfort to just keep on talking.

After this emotional rush was over, my counsellor asked me what exactly I missed about home. This conveyed she was genuinely interested in hearing my story. She asked about every new person I brought up and what role they played in my life. This curiosity about my experiences left me feeling heard. Because "home" plays such a big part in my life, it left me feeling empowered. Through my counsellor's curiosity, empathy, and responsiveness during this one session, I left feeling emotionally lighter and hopeful that future sessions would be beneficial.

Minimizing Misreadings

As crucial as it is to strive for mutual understanding, getting it wrong is not necessarily a problem as long as counselors build in the opportunity for clients to set them straight. Discovering and owning up to an error can strengthen the sense of trust in the relationship. But it's also worth remembering that counselors and clients speak from different cultural locations by virtue of their roles, although they walk the path together. Correcting a professional viewed as steeped in knowledge about human nature and knowing more about us than we know about ourselves—common cultural assumptions reinforced by popular media—is easier said than done. As often as not, the client may assume the counselor is onto something by virtue of their expert knowledge. When the counselor's misreading is not corrected, the conversation may be temporarily derailed—an unfortunate waste of time—or worse, it might plunge down innumerable blind alleys as the client forfeits their understandings and the counselor's meanings are centered. So it is important that counselors convey their readings in a manner that invites correction.

Conveying Tentativeness to Invite the Client's Corrections

The question is, What does it take to ensure this happens? At a time when Jorge is struggling and confused, he may uncritically buy a pronouncement by Maria of her current reading of his experience, such as "You clearly seem to be judging your sexuality." In his respect for Maria's professional authority, Jorge might begin to wonder whether there are in fact feelings he hasn't come to terms with yet—unresolved moral issues stemming from his Catholic upbringing. This would be counterproductive, eroding Jorge's confidence in the values he is professing—the product of many years of soul-searching and reflection. The exchange would be unhelpful at a time when Jorge is preparing to celebrate his identity by coming out to his parents.

The alternative is for Maria to offer her readings in a tentative manner. If she were to say, "Jorge, I'm wondering if you're saying you feel a gay lifestyle's wrong?" this would leave far more space for Jorge to say something like "I don't! That's my point! I'm proud of who I am, and I want my parents to be proud of me too." Exchanges like this help to align meanings. Chapter 6 will explore this critical issue in more detail.

Reflection 5.2

Think back to some conversation you've had with someone in authority. Perhaps this was someone who held a certain power over you associated with their position, or maybe you assigned this person authority based on your respect for their knowledge or experience. Can you picture what happens in a conversation like this when the other person projects an image of you that does not fit with your view of yourself? How easy is it to speak up and correct them? To what extent does this person's authority lead you to doubt your own point of view, perhaps discarding it in favor of the other's interpretation?

NONVERBAL EXPRESSION

To this point in the chapter, the focus has been on verbal expression—the use of words—to express experience and the challenges associated with reading spoken language. But we speak with more than words. Nonverbal expression is a key component of any message conveyed. It is just as important to attend to nonverbals in the effort to approximate understanding. And it is equally challenging because nonverbals are also subject to cultural variation and thus open to multiple interpretations.

Reading Nonverbals

Conveying Meaning Without Words

Broadly speaking, language constitutes more than just words. All cultures develop elaborate systems of nonverbal cues—including facial expressions, voice tones, and body language—to convey meaning. We both read and employ all of these aspects of language in conversation.

The verbal content of messages typically gets the most explicit attention. When someone asks what someone said, the expected response is to repeat the sequence of words that were spoken as well as we can remember. Verbal content alone sometimes suffices to discern a message's meaning. For example, when a friend misses a public address announcement, it's enough to repeat, "The train for Toronto leaves at 3:17 p.m. from Track Number 5." We leave out "spoken in a flat, yet authoritative, professional tone." A recapping of just the words often does it, especially when the message's intent is to convey information.

But language often is used for much more than simply conveying information, and in those cases, the verbal content may not be enough to convey meaning. This is certainly true for most counseling conversations. If a colleague were to ask, "What did Maria say to her counselor Daniel?" the answer, "She said she's crazy," would get their attention but hardly suffice to capture Maria's meaning. More often we need to attend to nonverbals and to consider the context in which words are spoken to discern their meaning. This section addresses the issue of nonverbals; considerations of context will be taken up in the section to follow.

The Ambiguity of Nonverbals

The nonverbals we use to express meaning are outgrowths of particular cultural traditions, as natural as they may feel. Consider Daniel and Maria. He's African American and male, and she is Caucasian, of Italian descent, and female. These make for some differences, but both are middle class, university educated—even to the point of a shared profession. Daniel automatically assumes he and Maria have some degree of shared nonverbal communication repertoire when it comes to conveying meaning. He asks if she has to go back to work today, and she shakes her head sideways. Daniel takes that as a "no" although he realizes from his travels in India that in some cultures the same gesture has the opposite meaning. Things are less straightforward, though, when questions seek more than facts or information. When it comes to the meanings Maria attaches to her experience, Daniel is less quick to assume understanding. Like words, nonverbal language is multilayered and laden with ambiguity.

> *"I always figured I was born to be a counselor because I love listening to other peoples' stories. I guess it never occurred to me that there'd be sad stories, confusing stories, and desperate stories, and I wouldn't necessarily have any answers!"*
>
> *Maria pauses and shakes her head. "Maria, what were you thinking?!" She throws her head back and laughs with gusto, then reaches over and blows her nose into a tissue.*

Daniel relies on various sources of knowledge as he tries to understand what's going on for Maria. Her words alone seem to suggest discouragement, perhaps disillusionment, maybe even embitterment about her career choice. Yet she laughs heartily—a form of expression not normally expected when things are going badly. And then her laughter appears to turn to tears. Clearly there is more inquiry ahead of Daniel to coordinate his talk with Maria. He'll need to respond, to join with her in evoking a rich description of her experience. In the next chapter we'll look at responsive skills—the more active dimension of making meaning—in detail, but for now I'd like to continue with the exploration of the challenges associated with reading meaning. In addition to the vagaries of words themselves, nonverbal expression clearly plays a key role in contributing to the meaning expressed.

Student Voices

Inez: Attending to Nonverbals

I took some time to consciously focus on how I interact with others both at work (as a customer service representative and fitness instructor at a gym) and with my family. I noticed I try to acquire and maintain eye contact, and I also nod a lot. Over the years, both peers and acquaintances have mentioned how expressive I am through my words and gestures. I think that by consistently seeking eye contact and nodding, I'm trying to validate the other person and develop a connection with them. Two examples include discussing a customer's weight loss goals at work, and listening to my mother tell me how her authority was being undermined by one of her employees. In both scenarios, I found myself concerned about making the other person feel I was not judging them. I wanted them to know that their worries and stresses were normal.

At first I didn't consider my conversational "habits" to be "skills" in any way, however upon some thoughtful reflection, I am beginning to feel nonverbal conversational behaviour will benefit me in building a helpful environment for my clients.

Cultural Variations in Nonverbals

The Global Diversity of Nonverbals

It's often said that nonverbals contribute more to the meanings we convey than the words themselves (Bavelas, McGee, Phillips, & Routledge, 2000). A fellow driver who extends his middle finger after you cut him off doesn't have to use words to say something to you. Lovers who embrace after a long absence don't need to exchange words to convey their joy in being reunited. Tones of voice and inflections, physical gestures and expressions speak fluently.

Although their meanings are not laid out systematically in dictionaries the way words are, nonverbal cues constitute languages of themselves. Just as we often converse without consciously choosing our words, we most often use these languages without deliberately adopting a tone of voice, facial expression, and so on. But we can't escape the use of nonverbals or the meanings they connote. For instance, a flat tone of voice—in dominant Western culture at any rate—is usually taken as an expression of fatigue or depression.

We're accustomed to think of verbal languages' developing historically around the globe as local, culturally distinct codes for conveying experience. However, we're less likely to think about nonverbals that way. It's understandable: Many nonverbal gestures certainly come close to being universal. I recently watched a soccer match between teams with very international rosters; every time the referee made a penalty call, the players on the offending team all threw their hands up in the air in a (seemingly universal) gesture of exasperated protest. When traveling in countries where we don't speak the local language, we often rely on nonverbals to help us through. And it would be an anthropological rarity to find a culture where the mouth with upturned corners that we call a smile is used primarily to convey grief and loss or where a clenched fist signifies tenderness.

But as much as it's possible to identify a variety of near-universal nonverbal expressions, it's not difficult to point to exceptions either. Nonverbals also exhibit massive cultural variation. Certainly smiles around the world convey different meanings, many of them unrelated to mirth or happiness. What constitutes lively and friendly discussion in Mediterranean and Middle Eastern contexts may look more like hostile conflict to a northern European or North American. Silence in the presence of another is an expression of comfort and intimacy in many aboriginal cultures, whereas in more verbally inclined contexts, it speaks of shyness or even grief. Implicit codes of appropriateness of physical proximity between speakers differ the world over. Standing close in some contexts conveys respect and connection; in others, it's an indication of insensitivity—even aggression.

Sometimes a Furrowed Brow Is Just . . .

Besides variations associated with more clearly delineated cultural groups, there are other reasons for variations in the meaning of gestures and other nonverbals. Clients' personal styles of expression are varied. The crossing of the arms may signify someone's reluctance to open up, or it may just be a comfortable position for the limbs. Or perhaps it says something about a chilly room temperature. As Freud is said (apparently inaccurately) to have mused in exasperation with people's reading Freudian symbolism into every possible dream image, "Sometimes a cigar is just a cigar." As crucial as is the role played by nonverbals in conveying meaning, there is no code to break the endless variation of nonverbal expressions. Thinking about cultural context helps, but at the same time, one can't reliably assume any particular nonverbal is the expression of a cultural tradition. This brings the discussion back to a familiar place: The achievement of mutual understanding emerges out of dialogue, and when you aren't sure, you should ask. Chapter 6 will explore the role of responding to clients to confirm readings; the intention here is to remind readers of the importance of attending to nonverbals in the quest for understanding.

Because of the variation in cultural and individual expression, this book offers no categories of the meaning of particular nonverbals exhibited by clients, just as Chapter 6 includes no recommendations for the use of set nonverbals in response to clients. This isn't to say nonverbals don't deserve much attention though: You may be surprised by what you learn about how nonverbals are used to communicate meaning if you engage in the exercises related to nonverbals at the end of this chapter or those included in Chapter 2. Cultivating mindfulness in regard to nonverbal communication will expand your awareness of the nonverbals you and others employ in conveying meaning.

CONTEXT AND MEANING

To this point we've looked at how both verbal and nonverbal content constitute culturally imbedded languages, with both the richness and the ambiguity of meaning associated with cultural diversity. Attending and listening on these two channels, as it were, are central tasks in discerning the meaning of the messages conveyed to us. But in addition to verbals and nonverbals, there is one more significant dimension of the reading of meaning to contemplate—the consideration of the circumstances surrounding the message, the context.

Words Among Words

Jacques Derrida (cf. 1976) wrote extensively about the topic of meaning, and two of his ideas will help here to illustrate the part context contributes to understanding an utterance. For one, Derrida reminds us of an idea mentioned earlier—that to understand what a word means, we refer to other words. We look in a dictionary, which provides a series of related words, and if we want a richer sense of the meaning of the original word, we look up some of these related words, and so on, potentially ad infinitum. The meaning of one word rests on the meaning of others. Hold that thought.

The second observation is related to the first and shows how we determine the meaning of a word by looking at words around it. This happens all the time when we read, although we don't consciously think about it. We discern the meaning of a word lodged in a sentence partly by reference to the words around it. If this seems implausible, consider what helps you determine the meaning of the word *right* in the following sentences:

As a taxpayer, I have a **right** to speak!

Don't forget to turn **right** at the intersection.

He insisted he was **right,** although his argument made no sense.

To make a decision like that he couldn't have been in his **right** mind.

The **right** time to retire is when you still have your health.

Without the words around them, the five letters that make up the word *right* aren't enough for us to know which of the word's many possible meanings are intended. That's why we ask someone to give us the word in a sentence before we offer a definition. Voice recognition software borrows from this principal: When the user dictates into a microphone, the software waits until it hears other words before it "decides" which word was intended, at which time it displays the word on the computer screen.

Considering context is always part of reading meaning. The same goes for discerning meaning at a broader level, as when Daniel tries to discern what's going on for his client Maria. Besides attending to any particular utterance, such as her statement, "Maria, what were you thinking?!" Daniel absorbs all she's said leading up to this. This is the third time they've spoken, after all, which provides lots of additional context for Maria's verbal and nonverbal expressions.

> *Daniel knows Maria quit a secure job to return to graduate school and study counseling. With a partner not finished with his own studies and a baby to feed and care for, Maria's apparent disillusionment could speak of a challenge of crisis proportions. Yet despite these contextual details, this conclusion seems implausible to Daniel. That's because he has additional context through witnessing Maria in action and has come to see how she quickly "puts it all out there" when she steps into his room, often in theatrical fashion. She tends to describe things in dire terms initially, seemingly as a warm-up to engaging with them more thoughtfully later in the conversation. Later, she presents the contours as less jagged, the options less limited, the situation less grave. Daniel is also aware of Maria's Italian heritage and considers the possibility that the dramatic flare with which she expresses herself may be characteristic of that particular cultural subgroup. Or not—time and further conversation will tell. All of this figures in Daniel's reading of Maria's meanings. And it is all subject to revision as she continues to speak—even before he responds more actively to clarify her meanings.*

The Hermeneutic Circle

The term "hermeneutic circle" (Kvale, 1983) refers to this search for understanding as it was employed to interpret ancient religious texts. Separate parts of the text are understood in reference to the whole text. This is what Maria relied on when Jorge shared the fruits of his creativity with her—one part of his overall account of his life. On their own, the drawings certainly looked competent to Maria, but they took on an extraordinary quality in the context of his broader situation, which featured insomnia, gnawing self-doubts, anxiety, and so on.

The *circle* in *hermeneutic circle* refers to the cycling between the part and the whole and vice versa. Just as the broader context can affect how we understand one piece, so can a reading of one part influence the understanding of the whole. This also happened when Jorge clarified for Maria that it wasn't his gay lifestyle he felt was wrong but his hiding it from his parents. In one utterance, Maria's overall reading of his experience (that he was experiencing self-judgment about his sexual orientation) changed. Walsh (2008) describes how the hermeneutic circle leads to greater understanding, but by a spiraling loop that passes through a lot of uncertainty along the way:

> With each attempt at empathy, listeners are (or should be) made aware of how little they do in fact understand. As a result, each pass through the circle leads to greater uncertainty about the other along with increased sensitivity to the biases that are projected. This in turn leads to further scrutiny of those presup-positions, an increasingly complex picture of the other, and subsequent attempts to further project understanding. (p. 77)

On first reading this may sound like a discouraging account of an attempt to understand, but the increased complexity that Walsh (2008) speaks of is therapeu-tic gold. People are complex, and our pictures of them should be as well. Having a sense of a person's uniqueness makes it possible to join them in taking steps well matched to their distinct experience—as opposed to issuing formulaic, off-the-shelf prescriptions. Attaining that complexity comes with "reflection, skepticism, and humility" (Walsh, 2008, p. 77), attention that alternates between the specific instance and the general context. We see that in the following exchange between Maria and her client Jorge as he fills in the background to his family relationships.

Maria listens as Jorge describes the ups and downs of his relationship with his parents. He tells Maria that his father works for an appliance repair shop and that he used to bring Jorge to the shop on Saturday mornings, hoping his son would take an interest and pick up the trade. For years, the family story was that one day Jorge and his father would own their own shop together. But Jorge was never interested in things mechanical, and as that became apparent to his father in Jorge's early teens, Jorge felt distance opening up between them.

They began to argue over things. Jorge couldn't always explain what the argument was about—he was just aware of a tension that never seemed to dissipate and sometimes culminated in an outburst of rage from his father. Eventually the argu-ments stopped—not because they worked things out but because they avoided each other, both sensing, says Jorge, that their differences might lead to a violent confrontation.

Jorge's mother most often went silent when things heated up. When Jorge spent most of one winter sleeping on the couch at his friend's house, she would often make tortillas for him on schooldays when her husband was out, but she never begged him to move back home.

When he was 18, Jorge's paternal grandfather died and left a modest inheritance for each of his five grandchildren. Jorge describes seeing his father tearful for the

> *first time ever when he announced this gift to Jorge and his sister Catalina. It was a rare family dinner after Jorge had moved back home, where he spent most of his time in his room on his computer when he wasn't working at a part-time job at a nearby supermarket. His father pulled out a letter and read it aloud, his voice trembling throughout, eventually sliding it across the table to his children when he was unable to finish.*

As Jorge recaps his experience to Maria, he shares details of a series of events in an effort to explain his distress. At this point Maria and Jorge haven't come to any mutual understanding about what his main concerns are, on what they are working on together, on what the problem is that brings him in. And Jorge himself may not be certain either. Neither of them can be sure if the events he's recapping will be central to their unfolding conversation. But he's engaged in retelling these events—they clearly seem important to him—and at this point Maria is mostly relying on receptive skills to discern the meaning of these events for him.

Some of this happens in Maria's reading of his nonverbals. Watching Jorge's face and the clenching and unclenching of his hands, Maria doesn't need Jorge to clarify that "it hurts." In a sense he's commented on his experience through nonverbal language. Connecting with her own experience of connection and disconnection with loved ones help Maria to empathize with his plight as well, to imagine what these events may mean to him.

The nonverbals alone aren't enough, however, and in this particular anecdote Jorge hasn't provided much in the way of verbal commentary on his subjective experience of these events. So Maria turns to context. In attempting to make sense of this anecdote but also his experience generally, Maria considers cultural differences between Jorge and herself. Gender is one cultural location that provides some insight. Reflecting on her past experiences and her counseling practicum work to date, Maria has found males are often, though not always, less emotionally expressive than females. This is not surprising, considering the messages they receive from an early age that crying is for sissies. It's important not to expect to find generalized characteristics for all members of any cultural subgroup, though, and Jorge's case is an example. Earlier, he was quite emotionally expressive with her, so she thinks it's unlikely that his lack of commentary is the playing out of a sort of male stoicism. She decides not to interrupt just yet; perhaps he'll tell her more about what this has all been like for him in a moment.

Maria considers other contextual factors, thinking about Jorge's ethnic cultural location, his Mexican heritage, which differs from her own. She wonders about patterns of relationships between Mexican men and their sons, whether this alienation that Jorge describes is more common in his ethnic and linguistic cultural subgroup. The answer to this would not finally confirm anything but would add more texture, provide more context to his story as she works at understanding. As she ponders these various contextual considerations, Maria's breadth of understanding increases, but at no point does she assume she's got it; understanding is an ongoing process and not a point of arrival.

Of course this fine-grained analysis is only an attempt to approximate the way, as counselors, both Daniel and Maria consider context in reading their clients' expressions. It only half captures the way we rely on various "ways of knowing" (Smith, 2004) in counseling conversations. Not all of this knowing unfolds within our field of awareness: It would certainly take up a lot of mental hard drive if it did. In addition to the deliberate weighing of multiple possibilities, we're also processing at various levels in the background throughout our conversational exchanges. Because this processing is more difficult to describe and account for, it's a form of knowing sometimes referred to as intuition.

Intuition and Accountability

Accountability as the Ability to Account

It's not uncommon to hear a counselor describe how they responded to a client in a particular way based on intuition—that they listened *with their gut*. This is a way of ascribing the basis for an intervention to a mysterious process that almost by definition cannot be explained. The difficulty with this sort of explanation is that it virtually rules out the possibility of being accountable—of offering an account of our actions to the clients who consult us or to anyone else. The invoking of intuition as the foundation for therapeutic interactions also fails to provide a rationale for ethical decisions—another form of accountability inseparable from professional practice.

This is not to suggest that counselors can be expected at all times to provide detailed explanations of every minute factor guiding their decisions. But I do suggest that this form of accountability is at least an aspirational goal, one that becomes increasingly achievable with practice and experience. In instances in which one's first instinct is to attribute a question or comment to intuition, it's useful to deliberately extend the inquiry—to ask further what informs the intuition. In a profession wherein our actions have very clear stakes for the clients who consult us, to do otherwise is to neglect our ethical responsibility.

A second reflection on intuition pertains to the distinction mentioned previously between *knowing that* and *knowing with.* Like any knowledge we rely on to inform our work, we may choose between hoarding a private hypothesis about a client and inviting the client to evaluate it with us. In the latter case, intuitions, like other sources of knowledge, can be brought to the dialogue and weighed for their usefulness in collaboration with clients.

ENCOURAGING SHARING

To this point in the chapter, we've been mostly reviewing the issues associated with reading meaning and the receptive skills used to make it happen. But what happens when a client is struggling to share their story with a counselor who sits in stony silence? Even prior to actively responding to confirm meaning (a topic saved for Chapter 6), there are times when a client needs encouragement and affirmation. Sometimes the counselor's nonverbals suffice; at other times statements and questions help evoke accounts of clients' concerns.

Conveying Attention and Concern Nonverbally

Jorge's earlier reticence seems to have evaporated. Perhaps he's experiencing the relief of getting his story out; he speaks rapidly now, describing the chasm that he says opened up between him and his father over the years. Maria listens intently as he speaks about his painful relationship, reading Jorge's nonverbal and verbal cues and considering the context of his words.

By attending to, listening to, and reflecting on what she hears, Maria is beginning to develop a picture of what's going on for Jorge. But she also realizes listening without responding both nonverbally and verbally won't be enough. As vital as it is that she attends with care, it's just as important that Jorge senses this. Her face conveys compassion as she leans in to hear his story, and at times a wordless sound of concern and caring passes her lips. Rothman and Nowicki (2004) found that nonverbals are probably more reliable for conveying the emotional state of a speaker than the words the speaker actually says. This probably comes as no surprise; we all know the experience of being confused or uneasy when someone's spoken message doesn't seem to fit with facial expression, voice tone, or other body language. Vulnerable sharing by clients calls for a tender reception by counselors, and nonverbal expression plays a key role in making this happen.

In the domain of nonverbals, facial expressions, voice tone, and body posture all contribute significantly to the expression of empathy and concern (Hofstede, 2001). These encourage others to share, as do wordless murmurs of acknowledgment (*mhmm, unhhuh, ahh,* etc.) sometimes called "minimal encouragers" (Young, 2009, p. 38).

The question of how deliberate to get about the expression of nonverbals is an interesting one. As noted earlier, nonverbals are a language in themselves, and no two people express themselves in identical fashion (Hofstede, 2001); as a result, we cannot reliably assume that the intent of our expression matches the client's reading of it. We can't refrain from nonverbals, either: Every presentation, either animated or passive, is open to interpretation by others. On the basis of these reflections, it makes sense to exercise care in nonverbal expression.

At the same time, an excessive preoccupation with nonverbals can severely constrain spontaneity. Generally speaking, if counselors are reflexive—that is, if they regularly monitor their practices to ensure their intentions and actions are aligned—they can usually be assured that their nonverbals are congruent with what they hope to project to clients. But how will the client read what is projected? It can be useful to review practice tapes and to make adjustments if you feel you are not conveying the emotion you intend through your nonverbals. Even then, keeping in mind inevitable cultural and individual variations in nonverbal expression (Hofstede, 2001), it's a good idea never to assume that what is sent is what is received.

Reflection 5.3

Think about a time—perhaps a situation that comes up repeatedly—when you were attempting to share something important to you and indications were the other person was paying little attention. What does the other's apparent inattention convey about their respect for and interest in you? How does the person's behavior affect your willingness to be vulnerable and open in your sharing? What emotions do you feel now as you think back to this experience?

Using Language to Solicit the Client's Account

As a tool, language is far more versatile than nonverbals, and words present endless options for responding to clients. This part of the chapter is limited to the use of words to support clients in getting their stories out. As mentioned elsewhere, we'll take up the task of confirming the meaning of that story in the next chapter.

Statements Versus Questions

Loosely speaking, verbal contributions can be divided into statements and questions. Both forms of verbals have their purposes. Statements convey information; they tell someone something.

The office is open only on Tuesdays and Thursdays.

I have never heard of that and will have to look it up.

I think you've handled this very well and predict it will work out tomorrow.

Statements don't necessarily solicit an answer, unless the telling is in the form of, "I'd like you to X, Y, and Z." They may or may not evoke a response, but they don't demand one. They also have more of a closed quality than questions because they are more like the issuing of a conclusion than the posing of a wondering. Related to this, statements generally tend to center the counselor's knowledge because that is what they convey. Questions are less centered in that they direct more of the attention toward the client's knowledge, point of view, experience, and so on.

Open Versus Closed Questions

It's interesting what you notice when you take a close look at questions, as I have in training counselors for many years. It's common to categorize questions as *either* open or closed, but a more accurate depiction is to place them along a spectrum, from fairly open to very closed. No question is completely open because just in posing it, we ask someone to restrict their response to some territory. "What would you like to talk about?" leaves a client with a wide range of possibilities but rules out sitting in silence, leaving the room, singing an operatic aria, and so on. "How are you feeling?" is arguably less open because the boundaries of possible responses narrow further—this is not an invitation to talk about abstract ideas or to speculate about the future, for instance. It is open in that many possible responses would not evoke arched eyebrows, but many more have been ruled out. Questions toward the open end of the spectrum lead to more uncertain outcomes because they are less determining of the direction of the talk.

Continuing along the spectrum in the other direction, questions denoted as closed give very little leeway for responses. Examples include questions such as "How old are you?" or "Would you like to book another session?" Questions that are more closed often demand yes/no or single-word answers. They significantly control the range of talk and get things done. For this reason they're more useful for efficient information gathering.

Whether they tend toward the open or the closed end of the spectrum, questions promote the involvement of clients—they call on clients to think, feel, and reflect. When used excessively, this can feel like interrogation; but the skillful use of questions is central to effective practice because it both conveys a spirit of curiosity and actively engages clients in processing their experience.

The distinction between statements and questions and between varieties of questions is of more than academic fascination because a counselor's choice of verbals inevitably has a very real impact on clients. Attempts to assist a self-professed unfocused client to make concrete plans will not be very helpful if they rest on mostly wide-open questions. On the other hand, the intention to empower a client by soliciting their input into the direction of a therapeutic conversation can be thwarted by an excessive use of statements or closed questions that constrain the range of possible responses.

Verbal Expressions of Attention, Concern, and Affirmation

You may have had the experience of a partner or friend asking you, perhaps in a slightly petulant tone, "Are you listening?" Questions like this usually follow long stretches of silence on your part, and they happen more often over the phone, when the listener can't share visual nonverbals indicating engagement. But even in face-to-face conversations, body language and facial expressions combined with nonverbal voice tones have their limitations when it comes to communicating engagement. Think about a listener who employs stylized grunts and glazed nods of acknowledgment but who's mostly busy playing with their handheld device: These responses may not be convincing, and they certainly don't convey understanding or compassion.

Of course counselors are (one hopes) more engaged and thus convey more without speaking, but nonverbals communicate a general response and can't differentiate the finer points of a client's account. Responding verbally takes acknowledgment a step further because it's specific to what a client is saying. As Jorge recaps his experiences with his father, he's aware his counselor Maria is attending because of her verbal expression of attention, concern, and affirmation. Likewise, Maria as client feels encouraged in sharing details of her busy life—juggling internship and parenting and a young marriage—because of Daniel's occasional interjections, which are not aimed at interpretation or influence but merely support her in sharing. What follows are a number of examples of the ways verbals can be used to encourage clients to share their accounts.

Clarifying

Is your father still working at the same shop?
To whom did you say you've come out so far?
How many credits does that leave you before you get your degree?

Expressing Concern

That must have been very hard for you.
I'm sorry to hear that.
Wow, that's a lot to take on.

It can be a momentous task to sit and divulge one's story to a stranger, especially when that story is "problem saturated" (White & Epston, 1990), as is often the case for clients of counseling. Well before teaming up with clients to effect changes, counselors can make the task of sharing less daunting by the interjection of a few words of affirmation.

Affirmation

> *You've managed remarkably well considering the circumstances.*
> *Good for you; that's quite an accomplishment.*

Reflection 5.4

Have you ever been plagued by doubt about something—perhaps an action you took in full earnestness about which you later felt uncertain? In sharing that doubt with someone, can you remember the feeling of vulnerability that accompanied the sharing? (Will I be judged? Will they discover who I really am?) How was your sharing met? If in silence, did it leave you guessing? What was it like to be unsure about the other's reaction? If it was met with affirmation, what was it like being acknowledged for your thoughtfulness or reassured that your wonderings made sense?

The sense that's one's experience is far from the norm, which in literal terms makes it abnormal, is not unusual when things aren't going well. Understandably, this discourages personal sharing. A normalizing response can counteract this, as seen in Daniel's response to Maria, below, which invites her to continue. Rushing to normalize all expressions of unease or discomfort is not a good idea for a couple of reasons, however. For one, it can be experienced by clients as minimizing because it might seem to convey the thought, *What's your problem? You're just like everyone else.* And rushing to normalize any expression of discomfort or concern can also jeopardize the opportunity for a client to reflect on their experience or sit with and familiarize themselves with an emotion. In the example below, though, Maria does indeed find herself faced with a range of challenges, and Daniel's affirmation of this encourages further exploration.

Normalizing

> *I can imagine what that must be like. Internships are usually pretty stressful times. Throw in a young daughter, and you've got a lot on your plate.*

Sometimes just encouraging or asking a client to say more is effective in soliciting more of their experience. Later chapters will introduce a range of these sorts of questions with highly particular ends in mind; the examples of probing statements and questions below are more general and designed to expand on client accounts.

Probing

Tell me more about that.
What was that like? Could you give me a picture of that experience?
It would help me to hear more about that.

Of course there are always many more possible statements and questions available for encouraging sharing by clients; perhaps you can list some yourself on reflection and study of your own work. That multiplicity of options is one of the pleasures of a creative and improvisational craft like counseling. In the chapters to come, the intent of counselor contributions becomes more narrowly focused on highly specific agendas, starting with the crucial task of coordinating understanding with clients by confirming readings of what they have shared.

CHAPTER FIVE RECAP

If counseling involves accompanying clients as fellow travelers (Weingarten, 1998) on the way to preferred destinations, the place to start is here in the moment. Determining what that *here* is involves gathering up and striving to understand clients' accounts of their experience, reading the meanings of the words they share.

This is a deliberate task, requiring patience and the willingness to "loiter" (M. White, speaking at an intensive training titled "Mapping Narrative Conversations," April 2005) as meanings congeal. It is fortunate that curiosity about clients and their stories draws many counselors to the profession because curiosity is a key attribute in the quest for understanding. When we don't assume we understand another's experience, we "dignify" (Epston & Marsten, in press) the other—we convey respect for the uniqueness of their experience. This willingness to be surprised is an antidote to a classificatory mindset that views clients as instances of a category. It keeps us open to endless unanticipated possibilities lurking beyond the next utterance.

It helps to keep the anthropological metaphor in mind. The effort to discern another's meaning is very much like the anthropologist's task: attempting to get inside the experience of a cultural group that shares a common humanity but has its distinct traditions of making meaning. These traditions are evident in the use of language, and they also show in bodily expression, the way nonverbals are used to convey experience.

Another important practice in discerning meaning is the cycling between any particular utterance of the client's and the larger context of the conversation. Isolated words, statements, and nonverbals can take on startling new meaning when they're considered in the wider context of what is going on more broadly in the client's life and which events are precursors to the current moment.

After reviewing the three key facets of discerning meaning (nonverbals, verbals, and context), the chapter introduced some practices for supporting clients in sharing their accounts. Some of these practices are themselves nonverbal, whereas others rely on statements and questions from the counselor. The chapter reflected on the distinction between statements and questions before making the point that conventional dichotomies of open versus closed questions overlook that questions are never fully open and that all questions lie on a spectrum from more open to more closed. Choosing between statements and questions and between more open and more closed questions is key because these various verbal tools operate differently and are useful for distinct purposes.

To this point in the book we've looked at therapeutic conversation primarily in terms of client as speaker and counselor as listener. But of course dialogue, by definition, involves a two-way exchange. With that exchange, meanings transform, which is one of the marvelous features of therapeutic conversation. As the counselor inquires further—to express concern, to share thoughts, to avoid misreadings, to seek expanded descriptions—counselor and client collaborate in shaping what comes out of the dialogue.

The next chapter moves further into that collaborative territory. From receiving and reading meaning, the focus turns to responding to confirm that reading. This more active engagement by the counselor instantly adds complexity to the therapeutic exchange. In a sense, the task moves from reading to writing, or perhaps more accurately to coauthoring—a collaboration of counselor and client.

CHAPTER FIVE DISCUSSION QUESTIONS

1. **Being understood.** When you don't feel understood in a conversation, how does it influence your receptivity to the other person? How open are you to considering alternative views and possibilities? What happens to your engagement in a conversation when you don't feel understood?

2. **Not understanding.** In a craft so reliant on understanding clients to be helpful to them, what could possibly be the usefulness of Gurevitch's (1989) posture of "not understanding"? What does he see as the benefits (for clients) of this position?

3. **Linguistic violence.** What does it mean to engage in "linguistic violence" as described by Derrida (1976), Levinas (1985), and Larner (1996), among others? What are examples of this?

4. **Nonverbals.** Make a list of all the nonverbal cues you can think of that contribute to meaning. Include both auditory and visual cues. Compare lists.

5. **Cultural variations in nonverbals.** Using the same list of cues, discuss which ones are particularly prone to cultural variation. What are some stereotypical characterizations of the nonverbals (auditory and visual) of particular cultural groups?

6. **Clashes in nonverbal style.** Give examples from your own experience of conversing with others with different nonverbal styles that may have promoted discomfort in you or led you to struggle either in conveying your meaning or in discerning the others' meanings.

7. **Noticing nonverbals.** Watch a movie, TV show, or newscast, and pay primary attention to the nonverbals conveyed by speakers. Which nonverbals do you notice, and what impact do they have on the meanings conveyed? What difference does paying attention to these have on how you receive the message?

8. **Using nonverbals.** Pay attention to your own use of nonverbals. What are some of the primary auditory and visual cues you rely on? How do the nonverbal aspects of your conversational style vary from context to context?

9. **Cultural variation in nonverbals.** Tell a story of a time you've had difficulty understanding someone due to different nonverbal styles. See if you can relate the differences between you and the other person to different cultural locations—this could be ethnicity or nationality, but it might also include, for instance, gender, socioeconomic class, or sexual orientation. Discuss.

10. **Context and meaning.** Choose a commonly used word with multiple connotations, and see how many sentences you can generate that each demonstrates a distinct meaning of the word. Make up a simple statement, and make a list of different contexts that would give the statement a very different meaning or implication. Compare what you have with others and discuss.

11. **Intuition.** Identify a process or practice for which you feel you have an "intuitive" knack. See if you can identify information and forms of knowing you may be drawing on that you don't normally identify that might be contributing to your abilities in this area. Discuss.

CHAPTER FIVE ACTIVITIES

1. **Cultural curiosity.** Pair up with a partner, and take turns sharing about one of the topics listed in Box 2.2 at the end of Chapter 2. Treat the speaker as someone from an exotic culture whose ways of life, although apparently similar, differ in substantial ways. Avoid the tendency to conclude that you've got it, and instead continually ask yourself, *What else don't I know about what makes this person's experience different?*

Debrief with your partner. Listener, what was it like refraining from concluding you understood? What additional things did you learn when you refrained? Speaker, what was it like having someone so persistently curious about your experience? What impact did this have on your experience of your experience?

2. **The multiple meanings of words.** In triads, pick a word that seems rich with meaning—a word that comes up often in the culture and is used in a variety of ways. Generate five sentences, using the word differently each time, bringing out different shades of meaning. Compare your sentences with others.

3. **Nonverbal expression and meaning.** In groups of four, generate a statement and deliver it in a variety of ways, playing with tone of voice, inflection, pace, and volume of speech. Reflect on the different apparent meanings of the words spoken, depending on the nonverbals. Speculate on the various contexts in which the various versions would be spoken.

4. **Inventing a cultural nonverbal.** In groups of four, team up with one partner and together decide on some nonverbal traditions for your own miniculture that are different in some distinct ways from dominant nonverbals you're used to. This could include tone of voice, body language, facial expressions, gestures, and so on. Once you've established these, one team takes a turn interviewing the other team about an agreed-on topic (see Box 2.2 in Chapter 2 if you need ideas). The interviewee minicultures adhere to their agreed-on nonverbals; the interviewing teams save their invented nonverbals for when they're being interviewed. Try to play it straight although it's bound to be funny. After a few minutes, stop and debrief. Speakers, what was it like to change the default setting on some established nonverbals? Interviewers, what was it like to try to make sense of the others' experience given their unusual nonverbals?

5. **Words in context.** Form pairs or triads. In this exercise, you'll be free-associating— listing five words that come up in response to one word provided to you. The catch is you will do this three times. Each time the same word provided will be nested in a different context. The word is *diet*. First, free-associate five words in response to the word *diet* in the context of Beverly Hills, California. Jot these down. Second, free-associate five words in response to the word *diet* in the context of rural Somalia. Third, do the same for the word *diet* in the context of an orbiting space station. Compare your lists with your partners'.

6. **Referring to context to read meaning.** Form pairs. Identify an issue or story about which you'd like to speak. Before sharing it with your partner, come up with a statement that speaks to your experience of the issue/story. This might include a value you hold, a feeling associated with it, a thought or opinion you have about it, and so forth. Tell the interviewer just the general topic of the issue/story, and then give them this

single statement first. Interviewer, write down the statement, attending to how you currently read the meaning of this statement, taking notes if it helps. Then interview the speaker about the issue/story for a few minutes, taking notes if it helps. Debrief. Interviewer, how did your understanding of the original statement change as you gathered more context? Can you name specific contextual ingredients (other factual information, nonverbals, and so on) that contributed to your new understanding of the meaning of the speaker's original statement?

7. **Responding/not responding to expressions of meaning.** Form groups of four. Work in pairs. In each pair, students take turns being the speaker—telling the other a story about something important to them. In the first round, the listener does not respond verbally at all. Switch partners. Speaker, tell roughly the same story to your new partner. In this case, the listener responds, asking questions to clarify and expand descriptions but not centering their own experience in the conversation. Debrief. Speaker, what was different about your experience of the events in the story depending on whether or not your listener was responding? All, how does responding expand the story? In what ways may it add meaning not originally visible or intended?

8. **Encouraging sharing.** In pairs, pick a topic to discuss from the list in Chapter 2, Box 2.2. Take turns being the speaker and listener. Listener, actively encourage sharing using some of the skills for doing that listed in this chapter. Debrief. Listener, what were the challenges associated with doing this? Which encouragers seemed to be helpful? Speaker, what did you notice about the efforts to encourage your sharing, and what effect did they have?

Chapter 6

RESPONDING TO AND CONFIRMING MEANING

INTRODUCTION

Chapter 5 looked at the receptive dimension of therapeutic conversation, focusing on how counselors read meaning into the text of a client's sharing. The chapter also concluded with some practices for encouraging that sharing. This chapter introduces ways of responding that go further—practices for engaging in a back and forth with clients to consolidate mutual understanding. When counselors respond to confirm their reading of the client's experience, there is a switch from (primarily) monologue on the part of the client to dialogue between counselor and client, a movement from one voice to two.

On first meeting a client, or early in a repeat conversation with a client, it's usually appropriate to do more listening than speaking, reading meaning and encouraging sharing as described in Chapter 5. However, as mentioned in the introduction to this section, counseling is never neatly compartmentalized or sequenced, and the skills introduced in this chapter are typically mixed in with those explored in the previous one. The skills in Chapters 5 and 6 are separated from each other here to tease out what makes them different: Responding to confirm meanings (featured in this chapter) begins to complicate the process, and that's why it's treated separately here from the covert, receptive practice of discerning meaning introduced in the previous chapter.

Reflection 6.1

Have you ever had a conversation in which you felt vulnerable and exposed as you shared something close to your heart and yet were not sure if the listener was understanding what you were trying to convey? What told you they weren't understanding? What in the listener's nonverbals stood out? What did they say, or not say, that suggested they were not getting it? What impact did this have on you? Did it encourage or discourage sharing, for instance? How did it affect your sense of safety to disclose, your willingness to take risks?

No conversation is likely to be productive if one of the speakers feels misunderstood. When someone you are talking to fails to "get" you, you experience a growing sense of futility—especially when they don't appear to be making the effort. As you see or hear evidence the other is missing your meaning, you may also become protective of your experience, shielding yourself from the possibility of being misrepresented even further. You become less interested if not downright wary of what the other has to say, and the foundation for constructive collaboration crumbles. This all hinges on whether you perceive that the other is understanding you, so for that reason, a skillful reading of meaning is helpful only if the counselor lets the client know what that reading is.

The term *active listening* is often used to describe the skills explored in the coming pages. The phrase half works. The word *active* helps to characterize how responding to confirm meaning goes beyond merely signaling that one is attending or conveying empathy. However, *listening* falls short of capturing the scope of these practices. In responding verbally to a client, beyond encouraging them to go on, the counselor adds their words to the client's. As a result, the meanings forged in the dialogue emerge from two speakers, two voices, two sets of language. This is despite the fact that in these early moments, the counselor's energy is often exclusively on helping the client to describe what is going on for them.

This blending of voices is what characterizes constructive dialogue and is central to what makes counseling useful. But taking a more active part increases not only opportunities to be helpful but prospects for harm. That's because the addition of the counselor's voice raises issues associated with power differentials and colonization discussed earlier. This relates to the inescapable asymmetry of therapeutic conversations. The counselor participates in the conversation as a professional helper, and the client as a help seeker. Because of this asymmetry, the language and images the counselor generates for what the client is experiencing may come to dominate—not necessarily because they resonate strongly with the client but because of the authority granted the counselor due to their perceived expert status. And so the act of responding to the client calls for a mindful accountability on the part of the counselor—keeping the client's purposes and intentions at the center of the conversation, proceeding with an ethic of care.

"A gay guy I went to high school with, he went through something like this," says Jorge. "He changed his name and pretty well erased his family from his life. Hasn't seen them in years. Sometimes I think he's onto something."

Maria feels a certain alarm at Jorge's words. She has an impulse to comment on the value of family ties. But if Jorge is going to embrace family he needs to do it on his terms, and besides, Maria is aware she still has only a thin idea of where Jorge's at around this distressing rift.

"I'm wondering if sometimes it seems that it would be easier to cut off altogether," she offers.

"Crosses my mind."

"I imagine you must feel caught between the urge to escape the hurt and your love for your family."

"Yeah, I often imagine what it would be like to just disappear on them. But then what would that solve?" Jorge pauses and lets out an ironic laugh. "Besides, I'd miss my mom's green tomato salsa!"

THE RELATIONAL DANCE OF DIALOGUE

Because they both involve responding to and coordinating with another, dialogue and dance have a lot in common. They demand relational skills. Moving from monologue to dialogue is like the difference between executing dance steps in front of a mirror and trying them out with a partner. This chapter introduces a number of steps—that is, specific conversational practices—and I would like to comment on that now because in my experience, it's not uncommon at this point in their learning for counselors to become preoccupied with technique. Staying with the dance metaphor, they begin to worry about forgetting footwork sequences and not executing the moves correctly. This can have a crippling effect on practice. An undue focus on techniques can distract counselors from the relational dimension of counseling and may help to explain why in some studies on counseling outcomes, practitioners with less formal training in "advanced techniques" proved to be more helpful than their highly trained colleagues (Strupp & Hadley, 1979).

Counseling conversations are like a dance of sorts, but it's helpful to remember the task at hand is not the display of individual virtuosity. It doesn't matter how flashy a counselor's routine is if she doesn't coordinate with her partner. In a dialogic dance, the important moves are not precisely executed solo techniques but relational practices. These include conveying empathy, compassion, respect, and curiosity; attending to and listening for meaning; responding in a way that helps the other to speak their truths in an atmosphere of safety; and many more relational practices we've looked at so far and will explore in later chapters.

A preoccupation with therapy as technique can distract practitioners from the task of coordinating with their partners. My recommendation is that you study and practice the skills with diligence, doing your best to integrate them into your conversational repertoire, but do not forget that counseling is more of a relational practice than a set of techniques. If your intention is to attend with care to the relationship, the two of you not only will survive but will have some moments of grace and beauty on the dance floor.

Reflection 6.2

Have you ever interacted with a professional—nurse, doctor, lawyer, psychologist, accountant, professor, and so forth—who seemed to know their stuff but who was ultimately not helpful to you? What do you notice when you try to make sense of this? For instance, what convinced you of this person's knowledge or expertise? And why was this not enough? What did they do, or not do, that left you feeling ultimately dissatisfied with the services?

Response-Ability and Improvisation

I'd like to say more here about relationally responsive practice because of an apparent contradiction between (a) using particular skills with specific names and (b) being responsive to the client and the particularities of the moment. The first point seems to suggest sticking to the script, whereas the second seems to imply going with the flow. To understand how these are not incompatible, another metaphor—this one of musical improvisation in jazz—might help.

The interplay between the counselor and client is not formless; if it were, there might not be much of a role for a book like this. Counseling and psychotherapy contain phases, various types of questions, interventions, and so on—just as jazz music is built around keys, chord progressions, and rhythms that can be charted for the players to follow. But jazz improvisers aren't wholly bound by these structures: They listen to and respond to each other, not knowing precisely which notes they'll play until they're in the thick of a musical exchange. That is what the art of jazz improvisation is all about: working with predetermined and coherent structures while bending these to spontaneous musical purposes along with other musicians sharing the creative process. So too, skillful counselors improvise in response to what arises in the conversation, exchange by exchange, despite having a range of honed practices from which to draw. This is about response-ability, the readiness and ability to respond.

VERIFYING CLIENTS' INTENDED MESSAGES

In striving to coordinate meaning making, the task will quickly go awry if clients and counselors are missing each other. Earlier, we looked at where the conversation might have veered if Maria had misread Jorge's statement that the way he was living was wrong. Counselors need to let their clients know what they're picking up so clients can recalibrate, as it were, by offering corrections. Without this, it is difficult to know if the message received is the one the client intended to convey: Each new utterance from the client can lead a counselor further and further down a side alley of misunderstanding, and depending on the degree to which the client defers to the counselor, it could drag the client down there too. So Maria periodically responds to Jorge—not to influence deliberately his telling but to confirm that her current readings reasonably match his intended meanings.

The remainder of this chapter introduces specific skills for responding to clients to convey and confirm understanding in the sense of checking to ensure the counselor's reading of the client's account fits for the client. The last two, recapping and summarizing, also involve summing up a chunk of a therapeutic conversation or an entire session. These are the key skills that will be explored in detail:

1. **Restating**—using the client's specific words and phrases (this is a surprisingly powerful way to acknowledge the other's experience);

2. **Paraphrasing**—altering the client's wording while trying to stay as close as possible to the perceived meaning;

3. **Confirming understandings**—explicitly or implicitly inviting the client to correct the counselor's reading of what the client intends to convey;

4. **Recapping**—periodically taking stock of the unfolding conversation, providing a summary of the most recent portion of the exchange; and

5. **Summarizing**—providing an account of an entire conversation by way of achieving closure or introducing a subsequent conversation.

Restating

Giving Back the Client's Words

To ensure she's following Jorge's concerns, Maria gives him back his words from time to time. In hearing these repeated, Jorge is able to know which aspects of his message she's keying in on, what she hears as important in what he has to share. In sharing her current understanding of Jorge's experience, Maria chooses to stay close to his language, using his very words at times, and doing her best nonverbally to convey the gravity Jorge attaches to his account of his relationship with his parents.

> *Maria feels she's generally following the facts of Jorge's story, and she feels she has a reasonable read on his experience based on his rich retelling. But she's also aware of diverse possible shades of meaning and decides it would be helpful to share some of her reading with Jorge in case her understanding is beginning to diverge from Jorge's intentions.*
>
> *"Jorge, can I ask you to pause for a moment; I just want to make sure I'm understanding what you're saying," says Maria. Caught up in the telling, Jorge hasn't offered many openings. Maria's question breaks his flow, but her expression of wanting to get it right tempers the sense of being interrupted because it tells him she's listening attentively and with interest.*
>
> *Jorge nods and sits back. Maria glances at a few key words she jotted as she listened to Jorge, sprinkling them into her statement.*
>
> *"You were saying the 'tension eased' between you and your dad but not because you were getting along better, more a case of 'staying out of each other's way.' And that your mom 'stuck by you,' mostly in the way of what you called 'quiet support.' How am I doing?"*

You may have had the experience of hearing your own words reflected back at you—perhaps at a meeting where your comments were acknowledged prior to a speaker's taking the discussion one step further. Something more than mere repetition happens in these cases; it's as though you are being paid tribute, an acknowledgment that gives your words substance and significance.

Reflection 6.3

Have you ever thought your voice was lost in a discussion or your experience was being overlooked only to hear some of your words repeated verbatim by someone you thought had not truly been attending? What was this like? How did it alter your impression of the degree to which you previously had been listened to? What did it tell you about the level of the other's attention? How did it influence your willingness to share more of your experience?

The Multiple Skills in Restating

Restating seems simple but takes a good deal of skill: skill in listening, skill in discerning, skill in remembering, and skill in selecting language from the client's account. Because restating doesn't involve repeating all that someone has said, the counselor selects the words that seem to speak most resonantly of the client's experience, of what the client most wants to convey. This selection is about more than mere efficiency: It identifies the substance of the client's account. To be absurd for a moment, consider the ineffectiveness of the following restating:

> Client: *I'm filled with anguish each time I enter that building. I can feel my raw nerve endings as I stoop to get a drink of water to try and calm myself.*
>
> Counselor: *So, if I've got it right, you stop for a drink of water every time you show up for work.*

As ambiguous as language can be, certain words and phrases speak more powerfully of someone's experience. The counselor in this case restated a few words that were spoken but missed the significant ones. Restating is discriminatory. There are always many aspects of a client's experience one could possibly key in on; the selection of words for restating involves resonance with what the client is going through. When we listen with compassion, we identify our shared human experience. With empathy, we can imagine, approximately, what it would be like to be the client and experience what they are going through. Compassion and empathy support the practice of restating because they are necessary for picking up what matters most to the client.

The following examples demonstrate the difference between restating that appears to miss vital aspects of the client's experience and restating that appears to nail it. I say "appears" because ultimately it is the client who will judge the degree of resonance in the counselor's restating.

> Client: *Sure, he seems nice enough, bought me the tickets, tells me I'm special. But it wouldn't be the first time some guy sweet-talked me before dumping me. Why should I trust him? Why should I trust me for that matter? I've got a history of picking losers. It can't last.*

Restatement Number 1

> Counselor: *He bought you tickets and sweet-talked you, and others guys have done that before too. But you think he may turn out to be a loser.*

Restatement Number 2

> Counselor: *You have doubts it'll last. He seems nice, based on what he's saying and doing, but you're not sure you can trust your own judgment after a history of hooking up with guys you later decide are losers.*

As you can see, restating involves far more than selecting and repeating a few words and phrases; it calls for discernment of the client's central message. In the first example, the restating fails to capture the client's lack of faith in her judgment based on past experience. The second example hones in on this idea and makes it more central.

A dilemma in laying out specific examples like these is that it may inadvertently suggest there is *either* a right way or a wrong way to respond to clients, which is not the case: There are always many options. It may also leave the impression that the counselor needs to be a cognitive virtuoso, memorizing words and phrases, reordering them, and repeating them in neat packages that perfectly capture the client's intentions. Remember that these examples involve analyzing what was said *after* it was said: Conversation analysis always reveals complexities—even the analysis of casual exchanges.

This relates to the point about the distinction between being technique focused and being relationship focused. If you are working hard to understand and to convey your understanding, the skills of restating and most other skills introduced throughout this book will already be somewhat evident in your speech. Breaking them down and naming them, however, increases the chances that you can be more intentional in implementing them in future conversations.

Why Restating Is Useful

Here are a few reasons restating is useful to the client:

1. *It lets the client know what the counselor considers important.* The counselor's inclusion of some words/details and exclusion of others gives the client a picture of what the counselor considers central to the story.

2. *It provides the opportunity for the client to say more about elements neglected or underemphasized by the counselor.* If a restating is devoid of a detail—factual, emotional, or otherwise—the client feels is important, the client can adjust their account to emphasize the neglected material. This is good news because it means that thin restating may still serve some purpose, provided the client feels empowered to expand further.

3. *It encourages the client in the telling.* The client feels acknowledged because the restating lets them know the counselor is attending and listening carefully. This will make it easier to share more freely.

4. *It deepens a sense of trust in the relationship.* In selecting the client's very words, the counselor makes the effort not to interpret the story but just to capture it. This reassures the client that the counselor's intention is to understand the unique experience rather than to prescribe one-size-fits-all solutions.

Limitations of Restating

Hearing our own words come back to us in the voice of another is a reassurance that we've been listened to attentively by someone seeking to understand our experience. This is what restating accomplishes, but it can still beg the question of what exactly the other person understood. Going back to the earlier exchange between Jorge and Maria, you'll remember he said, "The way I'm living is wrong." If Maria had only restated here, she might have said something like, "Jorge, it sounds like you feel the 'way you're living is wrong.'" But this might have falsely conveyed to Jorge that he and Maria were on the same page. As became clear as that conversation unfolded, her initial take on what he meant by "wrong" was off target. Because words have multiple meanings, they may mean one thing to the speaker and one thing quite different to the listener. In those cases, restating may not be sufficient to ensure the listener understands what the speaker intends.

Another reason restating *alone* is not enough for coordinating meaning is that it can be done in a mechanical way. This can lead the client to wonder if the counselor is merely feeding words and phrases back without attempting to understand them. You may know the experience yourself of a partner or friend repeating your own phrases to you to assure you they're paying attention. Sometimes the result is that the person convinces you they're not attending, because a computer could do the job just as well. This mechanical repetition is sometimes known as "parroting", for obvious reasons.

As seen above, restating has many useful purposes, but it also has limitations that can be addressed by the closely related practice of paraphrasing. When paraphrasing, a listener demonstrates they're doing something parrots *can't* do: processing what is heard and reformulating it in different words that express similar meanings. This is helpful in coordinating understanding. It's also more prone to a different sort of risk than restating because paraphrases stray from the original words, increasing the chance of misrepresenting the speaker's intentions. If we had complete reassurance that clients would correct all misrepresentations, this might not be a concern, but as we've seen this is never a sure thing.

Paraphrasing

Using Alternate Language to Convey the Client's Experience

When paraphrasing, the counselor offers *different* words back to the client as a way of conveying the counselor's reading of what the client is saying. The client can then evaluate whether the counselor's words resonate with the client's intended meanings. This is easier to appreciate with an example:

> *Jorge:*   *I feel sick when I think of how my mother is suffering through all of this.*
>
> *Maria:*   *Wow, it sounds tough, Jorge. It drives you almost to the point of nausea.*
>
> *Jorge:*   *No, not nauseous sick. It's just so worrisome. I feel bad that she has to deal with all this on her own. It kind of gnaws at me.*

In this example, Maria's paraphrase misses the mark. Sick with nausea and sick with worry are different senses of *sick*. Maria offers her version, and Jorge quickly sees she's not quite understanding how he's feeling. This would not have occurred if she had responded by saying the following:

> *Maria:*   *Wow, it sounds tough, Jorge. You feel sick when you think of how your mother is suffering through all of this.*

This literal restatement might lead Jorge to assume Maria has got it because he hears his precise words coming back at him. On the other hand, hearing Maria's paraphrased version of his remark gives him the opportunity to correct her. Maria seizes on this and offers an alternate paraphrase:

> *Maria:*   *Oh, okay. Is it more like sick with worry, then? You're concerned she keeps it out of view and bottled inside. Is that about right?*
>
> *Jorge:*   *Yeah, bottled up describes it. She's got no one to share things with. My mom has high blood pressure, and it's not good holding onto things like that.*

Because paraphrasing deviates from the exact wording that the client shares, there is a higher risk that the counselor's meaning will not match the client's intentions than there is with restating. As mentioned in Chapter 5, a misreading by the counselor can nevertheless serve the relationship and move the conversation toward mutual understanding if the client is explicitly or implicitly invited to let the counselor know they've got it wrong. In the example above, the invitation is explicit because Maria invites Jorge to confirm her understanding is accurate by asking him if he is sick with worry. I will say more about this practice of confirming understandings in the next section because it plays a key role in minimizing the chances of misreadings.

Reflection 6.4

If you reflect on the words you use in your various conversations with people throughout the day, no doubt you can identify times when you rely on the tool of paraphrasing. In which sorts of exchanges does this happen? What would prompt you to paraphrase the words of the person you are talking to? What does paraphrasing achieve in those situations?

Paraphrasing is a conversational skill used widely by counselors and noncounselors alike when the task at hand is to ensure a close reading of another's experience. Because it involves the counselor's introducing additional words to the description of what's going on for the client, it also multiplies the linguistic tools available for both client and counselor to talk about the topic at hand. In cases wherein the client is struggling to find words to depict their experience, the additional language supplied by a counselor's paraphrase can add useful new vocabulary to the ongoing conversation. Below are examples of paraphrases that seem to miss a key dimension of the client's shared experience on the left, alongside some that come closer to the mark on the right.

| *Client:* | *I've been worried sick about that exam for weeks.* |

Paraphrase Number 1	Paraphrase Number 2
Counselor: You're not so sure you'll ace that test.	Counselor: Knowing that test is coming up, you're fretting about it all the time.

| *Client:* | *Have you ever heard such BS? What right do they have to stop us from protesting?* |

Paraphrase Number 1	Paraphrase Number 2
Counselor: It irritates you the way the police hover around.	Counselor: Sounds like you're pretty angry about the way they're being heavy-handed; they're denying you your fundamental rights.

Generating Experience-Near Description

Paraphrasing involves more than drily relating the facts as you hear them. People consult counselors because, as therapist Stephen Gilligan likes to say, they're "up to something big." The stories they relate and the concerns they share mean a great deal to them. This investment in their lives is best conveyed back to them in what anthropologist Geertz (1976) called "experience-near," contrasting it with "experience-distant" description (p. 223).

Experience-near description contains language that captures persons' purposes and intentions, values, and feelings (Epston, 2008; Paré, 2002). If not containing some of their own words, it contains words they can relate to that capture the tone and color of what they are trying to convey. To get a handle on what that looks like, consider the opposite: jargon-laden psychological reports about the intimate details of clients' or patients' experience that are impenetrable to the people about whom they are written. Or consider the two examples below, one clearly absurd:

> Client: *I haven't been able to concentrate since the accident. I keep revisiting it and worry about getting on with my life.*

Experience-Distant	Experience-Near
Counselor: You are clearly exhibiting the sequalae of trauma with symptomatology reminiscent of, but not strictly congruent with, posttraumatic stress disorder.	Counselor: Sounds like the images and memories of that frightening scene are staying with you, and it gets you wondering if you won't be able to move forward from it.

Experience-near description evokes an aha from a person, the sense that someone finally heard them. That's why restating is one reliable practice—because the language came from the client in the first place. But paraphrasing adds rich texture to this task with the expressive use of language that evokes the client's experience.

Generating experience-near language is easy enough when clients hit the nail on the head and name their feelings and commitments outright. Other times, these are between the lines. Skillful paraphrasing involves identifying subtle expressions of emotion and value and bringing them into the room, even when clients have not named them explicitly. In doing this, it's critical not to get ahead of clients in the sense of speculating about what's going on for them, only very loosely based on what they have actually conveyed. That's because unless they correct your paraphrase, you may continue to assume your description covers it—an assumption that could blind you to aspects of their experience not captured by your words. The second version of paraphrases below are more experience-near.

> Client: *Angie and I haven't talked in years, since we had that big falling out. I just hope that by the end of the visit some of that is water under the bridge.*

Paraphrase Number 1	Paraphrase Number 2
Counselor: You haven't spoken to her since the fight. You'd prefer it if you didn't argue when you meet her again.	Counselor: You're braced for some awkwardness when you get together. And I guess you're hoping the visit will help to resolve the bad feelings.

> Client: *I spent 2 years training and a whole pile of hard-earned cash getting ready for the climb. Now the expedition's been canceled on a very flimsy premise if you ask me. Kind of leaves me in a funny place.*

Paraphrase Number 1	Paraphrase Number 2
Counselor: For a long time your life revolved around getting ready for the expedition. Now that it's not going ahead, there's no need to be training any more.	Counselor: Wow. Your whole life's been built around that expedition—you've put out tons of effort and lots of money too. I imagine you're very upset with the way things were handled.

The addition of new language through paraphrasing requires skills not demanded of restating. Although both practices call for empathic understanding—the ability to identify what is of most consequence for the client—paraphrasing involves creative word use. Different kinds of language use can be helpful in this regard. A counselor who has the ability to organize a disjointed account and present it in clear, distilled language can offer a client a way out of a confusing maze of jumbled thoughts, images, and feelings. And a counselor with a poetic gift can add new resonance to the description of events, possibly helping clients identify experience long unexamined due to a lack of language to describe it. Either way, paraphrasing extends the vocabulary shared by both speakers for talking about, thinking about, and feeling the issues at hand.

My House, Your House, Our House

Tom Strong (2001) has written about how this collaborative interplay of language happens, using the metaphor of a shared house constructed by two speakers. Clients and counselors inhabit separate houses as it were in that they come to the conversation with two distinct sets of experience leading up to the moment they meet. Strong refers to these as "My House" and "Your House." This is similar to the notion of the distinct cultural locations of counselor and client, as discussed earlier. In the course of their conversations, they have shared experiences, exchanging words and phrases, borrowing language from each other, and coordinating ways of speaking about things. This becomes "Our House," a mutual construction. As Lock and Strong (2010) put it, "we do more than merely receive experience via our sense organs; we participate in its creation" (p. 195).

Student Voices

Rachelle: Clarity Through Dialogue

The first thing that struck me as the client is the fact that just having the opportunity to discuss certain issues can bring a great deal of clarity. For example, during the beginning sessions I was discussing how it stresses me out when my house is not clean and tidy. During this discussion it came to me that the untidy house stresses me out because if my house is untidy, it is usually because I have many other stressors on my plate that I need to attend to first (i.e., school, kids, sick husband, deadlines at work, and other sick family members). As a result the house gets tended to last. The messy house is a visual depiction of the chaos in my life, and it is not the mess that is stressing me out, it is what the mess means: I have too much on my plate. This realization has made me stress less about the mess, instead realizing that maybe I have a lot on my plate at the moment and when I can, I will get to the mess of the house.

My realization has led me to see how important it is for the counsellor to listen and stay curious. I used to believe that the counsellor should always be attempting to initiate change in the client. However, after experiencing the role of client, I see that having my counsellor compassionately listen enabled me to make some great progress without her direct intervention.

This cocreation of a shared expression happens all the time when friends develop a mutual shtick for talking about something—some word or phrase richly laden with mutual meaning that may be opaque to an outsider. To a small degree this happened when Jorge and Maria arrived at the notion of his mother's bottled-up stress. The word *bottled* came from Maria, who described Jorge's mother's experience as "bottled inside." Jorge picked up on it and turned it into "bottled up." The phrase *bottled up* was mutually constructed and became part of Our House, their shared vocabulary. We'll look at how this happens in various ways throughout the book because it's a central feature of what happens in any conversation, therapeutic or otherwise.

Why Paraphrasing Is Useful

Paraphrasing is critical to negotiating shared understanding with the client, an essential tool of collaborative meaning making. Among other things, paraphrasing accomplishes the following:

1. *It indicates the counselor is listening.* Because paraphrasing involves generating new language, it cannot be done as mechanically as is possible with restating (e.g., parroting). It therefore demonstrates the counselor's engagement.

2. *It paints a picture for the client of what the counselor is understanding.* Because the counselor uses their own words to capture the client's meanings, the client gets to see how the counselor is making sense of what he or she is hearing. In this way it gives the client a fuller picture of the counselor's reading than restating does.

3. *It multiplies the vocabulary for speaking about the client's experience.* Paraphrasing involves bringing additional words to the task of depicting what's going on for the client. These words become part of Our House, a shared vocabulary.

Limitations of Paraphrasing

One potential downside of paraphrasing, when used too liberally, is that it may crowd out the opportunity to coax richer descriptions from clients. It is a useful moment when the counselor generates a word that the client indicates fits, but at the same time it raises the question of which word the *client* might have used if given sufficient time and space. Paraphrasing should be used primarily to coordinate understanding and evoke rich description about what people have shared, not to get ahead of them, generating description based on hypotheses of what they might be experiencing. This is a topic to be explored in greater detail in the next chapter.

The limitations of paraphrasing as a practice for coordinating meaning making are different from those of restating. Whereas restating raises the possibility the client will hear the counselor as merely repeating their words without being genuinely engaged as an empathic listener, paraphrasing presents a different challenge. As mentioned, it poses a greater risk of misrepresenting a client's experience.

True, this can be averted, and misreading can actually lead to increased mutual understanding when clients let their counselor know they are getting it wrong and the counselor makes adjustments accordingly. This is likely to happen between friends or in exchanges that are relatively symmetrical vis-à-vis power differentials. However, in therapeutic conversations, clients will often neglect to point out misreadings due to discomfort challenging the professional helpers. Alternately, at a time in their lives when they are struggling and unsure of themselves, clients may defer to therapists' versions of events even when they differ from descriptions the clients themselves have offered. To counteract this dilemma, it's important to complement restating, and even more so paraphrasing, with the practice of confirming understanding.

Confirming the Counselor's Understanding

You may have noticed that in examples in this chapter, when Maria presented Jorge with her version of things, she tagged on phrases such as *How am I doing?* and *Is that about right?* In each case, Maria is giving Jorge a chance to let her know if she is missing the mark, explicitly inviting him to confirm her understanding of events. This is to avoid the trap of assuming she is on track, only to dig a deeper and deeper hole of misunderstanding as the conversation proceeds.

Confirming one's understandings involves more than striving to understand. What distinguishes this skill is that it involves intermittently offering up those understandings so their accuracy can be verified (Mearns, 1997).

BOX 6.1

Confirming the Counselor's Understanding in Three Steps

1. Listen empathetically to formulate a reading of what the client is experiencing, based on what the client has said.

2. Hand a version of that reading to the client by restating or paraphrasing.

3. Explicitly or implicitly check the reading's accuracy by inviting the client to make adjustments to the picture presented.

By virtue of her association with a profession, her higher education, and her role of helper to her clients, if Maria doesn't signal to Jorge that her restatings are subject to his correction, they may come across as pronouncements instead, effectively terminating the back-and-forth exchange involved in coordinating meanings. I don't believe this point is emphasized sufficiently in the counseling literature, with the result that reflecting skills are sometimes portrayed as *telling* the client what they are thinking and feeling rather than *checking in with them* about the counselor's reading.

Explicit and Implicit Checks

The two phrases *How am I doing?* and *Is that about right?* are explicit invitations to Jorge, and for that reason they minimize the chances he will let a misreading slide. But if counselors explicitly checked in with clients after each of their utterances, the exchange would get boring or annoying very quickly—and probably unhelpful too. If you pay careful attention to the way you conduct yourself in conversations in which you're working hard to ensure you aren't missing the point, you will notice there are other, more subtle ways to invite the other to correct you.

As we saw in the previous chapter, meaning is a function of verbals, nonverbals, and context. So there are various ways counselors can communicate their readings of meaning to check for the fit between their versions and clients' versions. Some of these are implicit and do not involve posing a specific question (e.g., How am I doing?), as Maria does.

Tone of voice varies the meaning of utterances in a dramatic way. The exact same words can come across as definitive declarations that leave room for no challenges or lightly held ideas offered up for correction or modification. The identical phrase can be read as a closed statement or a question depending on tone. Because of this, it's possible to nonverbally invite the client's correction by raising one's voice to form a question or adjusting one's tone to indicate uncertainty or curiosity. It is difficult to demonstrate this in print and best to try it to experience the distinction.

Student Voices

Talia: When Counselors Don't Confirm Their Understandings

I know my counsellor had my best interests in mind in our first two sessions; however he tended to make sweeping generalizations based on some of the information and stories I shared with him. In so doing, he also did not invite me to offer alternate explanations in case his interpretation did not match my intended message. Being in the client's chair in these moments, I did not feel comfortable correcting him because I was worried this would insult him. I was experiencing what a client/counsellor hierarchical relation or power imbalance might at times feel like, where the client defers to the counsellor as the expert. As a result, I now consciously try not to make sweeping generalizations about my client during my sessions. Instead, I summarise different parts of our conversation and invite my client to let me know whether or not I am capturing what she is trying to convey, and give her the space to clarify if necessary.

I'm happy to say that in more recent sessions, my counsellor has invited me to clarify whether his interpretations are in line with my experiences, and I have been comfortable providing him with feedback.

Reflection 6.5

The easiest way to identify how to turn what looks like a statement into an invitation for correction is to try it. Take the statement, *You're feeling better this week*. Without altering the wording, deliver it three ways: (a) as a definitive statement, with no invitation for correction or challenge; (b) as a question, clearly inviting a response; and (c) in a wondering tone, indicating you are uncertain rather than sure you understand.

What do you notice? Do the three sentences sound different? How do you think they would be received differently by a client?

Other Strategies for Confirming Understandings

Two other strategies for confirming one's current reading of another's experience that we use all the time in regular conversation as well as counseling are (a) reading nonverbals and (b) considering context. The reading of client nonverbals, although it offers less reliable input, is a way to preclude the need to constantly confirm your understanding. When Jorge's face lights up with recognition, Maria is less inclined to check if she got it right because his expression in effect tells her this already. Because nonverbal cues such as facial expressions are ambiguous, however, overrelying on them for confirming understanding is ill advised, especially as this approach doesn't explicitly offer invitations to clients to correct counselor meanings.

Another strategy to confirm one's emerging reading of the other's experience is to consider context. This is precisely what the hermeneutic circle mentioned in Chapter 5 refers to. Returning to Maria and Jorge, Maria has a steadily accumulating body of information about Jorge—what he is concerned about, what he is hoping for, and so on. At times, this contextual knowledge is enough for her to gauge the significance of events for Jorge without having to ask him. For instance, if he tells her his father sent him a warm birthday card, Maria can assume this is momentous without needing to confirm that hunch. This doesn't mean she won't explore the development with Jorge, though, because it is rich with possibility. And it also doesn't mean she cannot remain open to revising her understanding of the meaning of the event to Jorge.

Reflecting on Intentions to Guide Practice

Restating, paraphrasing, and confirming understandings are more than the mechanical repetition of key words and phrases to clients. They're nuanced language practices used to coordinate meanings in conversational exchanges. Breaking things down systematically as I've done here distinguishes the various practices involved but may also give the impression they are conversational skills you haven't used previously, which is certainly not the case. If you're having difficulty isolating the various practices involved in confirming understanding, try focusing your attention on your *relational stance* instead. Listen with the intention of understanding the client in the client's terms. To your possible surprise, you may find yourself performing the very practices above without having to think of them. Like all the conversational practices explored in this book, confirming understanding unfolds from an ethic of care because it seeks to ensure we don't supplant clients' meanings with our own.

Why Confirming the Counselor's Understanding Is Useful

Responding by restating and paraphrasing, and then confirming one's understanding, accomplishes more than merely helping the client to articulate experience; it also contributes to a migration of that experience through the fertile process of therapeutic exchange. We never simply find out what a client is experiencing; we always actively contribute to that experience. That's why it's so important to be mindful of where we direct our attention and how we respond. You can see this in action by revisiting Maria and Jorge's exchange earlier in this chapter. Jorge starts by saying he was "sick" because of the "suffering" his mother was doing. After Maria's misstep, Jorge clarifies that for him this means *worry,* an expanded description of the original word, *sick.* The migration of meaning begins. He adds that her suffering is something his mother has to contend with all on her own. The depiction of his mother's situation is evolving, and so is Jorge's experience as he adds another new phrase, saying "it kind of gnaws at me." This is where Maria introduces the phrase "bottled inside" to depict Jorge's mother's stress, and he modifies it slightly to say it is "bottled up." Together, Maria and Jorge are developing a shared vocabulary that will continue to evolve as their conversation unfolds. As the description evolves, so does their experience of the subject at hand.

If Maria had sat in empathetic silence, would Jorge have arrived at this expanded description of his mood and his mother's situation? It's not likely. Dialogue promotes movement in meaning, whereas monologue is more vulnerable to staying in a stuck place. Meaning is more like a verb than a noun. It's always moving and evolving as the conversation unfolds, and the counselor is always actively affecting the direction of that migration.

Confirming one's understanding after restating and paraphrasing serves another important purpose: They're accountability practices. They let the client know how their story is being taken up by the counselor—something not possible if the counselor doesn't actively respond. Certainly at times an appropriate response to a client's sharing may be to listen in empathetic silence. In these cases the counselor's nonverbals indicate, if somewhat vaguely, how they are receiving the client's account. But silent witnessing alone is insufficient for coordinating meanings, as you may have discovered if you've ever had a silent reception to something you've shared with passion or commitment. Silence alone can sometimes be discomforting, provoking a sense of being ignored or judged.

Restating and paraphrasing avoid this dilemma by making it possible for the counselor to be accountable to the client through intermittent offerings of the counselor's readings of the client's experience. Both practices feature transparency, as described in Chapter 3, providing glimpses of the counselor's internal process. Harlene Anderson (1997) calls this "going public" because it offers a public account of how the counselor is making sense of the client's story.

Confirming understanding achieves the following:

1. *It helps to confirm the counselor's reading is close to the client's intention.* It therefore supports coordinated meaning making.

2. *It conveys a tentativeness versus a certainty.* This encourages the client to critically evaluate the accuracy of a restatement or paraphrase and gives them greater permission to correct.

3. *It is an important element of restating and paraphrasing as well as other counselor interactions (as we shall see).* It addresses power related imbalances in the degree of authority granted counselor versus client utterances.

4. *It can be done explicitly as well as implicitly.* It's possible to convey questions through nonverbals and to read responses conveyed in nonverbals. Considering the broader context, including past client utterances, can also inform counselors of how necessary it is to confirm their understandings. Explicit verbal checking in with the client is the best safeguard against misreadings, however.

SUMMING UP

Recapping

Tracking the Journey

We've been looking at how clients' accounts of their lives and identities have a fluid quality to them, at how clients' stories evolve and transform as they engage in dialogue with counselors. Because of this changeable flow of meaning, a lot of movement can happen in a short period of time. It's useful to track this journey with clients as a way to coordinate the unfolding exchange. This is done by reviewing some of the conversation intermittently—the practice of recapping.

Reflection 6.6

Have you ever had a conversation with friends that took you to unexpected places? Reflect on one of these talks. Can you picture how this happens—how one topic transforms into another, perhaps prompted by a wry remark that sets the talk off in a new but related direction? Working backward from what may have been an insightful, humorous, or simply unexpected comment, can you remember where you started in the first place? This is about the movement of meaning. In therapeutic conversations this process is invaluable because it provides what White (2007) calls "transport" from unhelpful to helpful thoughts, feelings, and understandings.

Pausing to Take Stock

Recapping involves summarizing a recent stretch of conversation. It always involves a combination of restating and paraphrasing, but whereas those two practices happen in response to brief exchanges—often single client utterances—recapping covers a longer stretch of the conversation.

> After an intense outpouring of words during which Daniel sat in attentive silence, Maria pauses and takes a deep breath.
>
> "Lots going on today," says Daniel. "It sounds as though you've been unexpectedly plagued with doubts about your career choice lately." In the rhythm of the exchange, Daniel now has the floor. He glances at his notes as he recaps Maria's recent sharing, and she sits back, taking in his words.
>
> "It seems you're experiencing doubts on various fronts—feeling you're not able to devote as much attention to clients and tasks that are important to you. You described saying good-bye to your daughter Kyla this week and how you felt going to your practicum was like 'abandoning her to indulge yourself.' You described how your preoccupation with your work at the counseling center has you feeling 'guilty' about your role as a mother. You've also been talking about how your studies feel like a wedge between you and your partner Azim. And with all of this going on for you, you've been finding it hard to concentrate in your sessions, which isn't the attention you want to devote to your clients and has got you wondering about your suitability for counseling in the first place. Am I catching the highlights?"

Recapping serves a variety of purposes:

1. *It provides a window to confirm understanding after a client's monologue.* After a stretch where there are few opportunities to restate or paraphrase, recapping offers up the counselor's understanding of what they've just heard.

2. *It offers a moment's respite from the generation of new meaning.* It can be difficult to process what is being said and felt if a conversation lurches forward headlong without moments of pause and reflection. Recaps provide these.

3. *It slows the conversation down.* In taking the floor momentarily while recapping, the counselor has the opportunity to moderate the pace of exchanges that feel unhelpfully hurried.

4. *It gives counselor and client a pause to consider where to go next.* For the counselor, this is useful in moments when they draw a blank and are uncertain how to proceed. The regrouping that happens as the counselor recaps constructs a base camp for further joint meaning-making expeditions.

5. *It provides the opportunity to highlight the client's agency.* In recapping, the counselor can foreground the client's expressions of value and intention, which are always present but not always explicit.

Recapping is a selective process, just as restating and paraphrasing are. It involves judgment on the counselor's part to decide which aspects of the exchange to review. In the example above, Daniel combines restating—deliberately using Maria's exact words (e.g., "guilty," "abandoning her to indulge yourself")—and paraphrasing, wherein he uses his own language to capture what he feels he's hearing (e.g., "plagued with doubts"). Because he is recapping more than five continuous minutes of virtual monologue from Maria, there's lots of selection at work. He closes by explicitly confirming his understanding with Maria: "Am I catching the highlights?"

This recapping gives Maria and Daniel a breather, but it accomplishes much more than that. On a day when her experience is a jumble of thoughts and feelings, it reflects a coherence Maria is having difficulty discerning. But which coherence, which version of the past few minutes, does Daniel choose to bring forward? The counselor's role inevitably involves judgment and intentionality. Daniel is deliberate about staying close to Maria's account, but he's also deliberate about placing Maria's concerns in context and foregrounding the values she's attempting to uphold in her life. Her judgment of her role as a parent and partner is in the context of a demanding practicum and speaks to her desire to be present for her loved ones. Her concern about her difficulties concentrating with clients reflects her desire to practice professionally. Daniel's recap has a thematic unity that honors Maria in her attempts to uphold her values. His account escapes the notion that Maria's struggles are all about what's wrong with her, an unhelpful conclusion likely to promote discouragement and hopelessness.

It's important to remember there are always many ways to hear a story and many ways to respond to it. When counselors are oriented as allies, their responses are always in relation to clients' expressed concerns and aspirations. Efforts to be helpful hinge on a clear mutual understanding of, for shorthand's sake, clients' problems and preferences. This point will be taken up in much greater detail in subsequent chapters.

The Natural and Not-So-Natural Flow of Conversation

In the preceding vignette, you may have noticed a reference to the rhythm of the exchange between Daniel and Maria. I was tempted to call it the "natural rhythm," but if we mystify conversation as happening according to some purported natural flow, decisions about when to intervene might be made on the basis of what is gauged to be natural rather than what is helpful.

In some counseling conversations, the back and forth feels effortless and somehow balanced, but this isn't always the case. Sometimes a client may be inclined to speak for an hour straight if not interrupted. A very common shortcoming I have witnessed in the work of novice counselors is the tendency to let this happen by not intervening to restate, paraphrase, and recap. One downside of this is that an extended client monologue often further consolidates a problem-saturated or otherwise unhelpful view. A second concern is that if the counselor does not confirm their understanding periodically, the counselor will never know which aspects of the story they got and which ones they misread. Having the ear of a compassionate witness is often comfort in itself, but in this case, the counselor should make occasional opportunities to restate, paraphrase, and recap—even at the risk of feeling they are interrupting the flow.

Of course, not all counseling exchanges are at risk of devolving into uninterrupted monologues; in some cases, the challenge may be virtually the opposite. When a client is very short on words, the counselor isn't presented with much to restate, paraphrase, or recap! These instances call for the sort of encouragers introduced in Chapter 5. The task here is to draw forth richer accounts from the client. The next chapter reviews a number of practices that facilitate this.

Summarizing

Summarizing is (literally) an extension of the former practices: a summing up from the counselor, more often at the end but sometimes at the beginning of a session. At the beginning of a conversation, summarizing (perhaps while scanning process notes) can provide a way for both counselor and client to catch up on where they were last time they talked. This can be useful when there's been a big gap between sessions. Even then, it will depend on a number of things: A client who comes poised and ready to talk may prefer to share new developments now preoccupying them. In this case, an opening summary might be counterproductive. At other times, however, the distractions of a hectic week may have erased details of a useful exchange in the previous session. Here, a summary provides a useful linkage.

Toward the end of a session, summarizing is helpful for giving counselor and client a moment to reflect on where the conversation has taken them and perhaps to speculate about future possible directions. In this respect it operates similarly to recapping but on a larger scale because it reviews the entire conversation and looks ahead at the next meeting.

> Maria: Jorge, I see we're almost out of time, and I thought it might be useful to spend a moment looking back on what we've been talking about. How's that sound?

Jorge: Sure. I'm feeling kind of talked out anyway.

Maria: You started out by speaking about the trouble you've been having sleeping, and your doubts about the program you're in. You used the word "dread" to describe a feeling that comes over you sometimes and makes it hard to concentrate. That led us to your parents, who you said have always expected you to do engineering. You talked about your dad in particular—how for a long time he assumed you'd join him in starting up an appliance repair shop, how you've had your tensions for a long time.

But I guess we probably spent most of our time today on the dilemma you described of being in the closet around your mom and dad. You said—let me look at my notes here—you said, "the way I'm living is wrong." For a moment I wondered if you were judging your sexual orientation, but you explained that it doesn't feel right to hide such an important aspect of who you are from your own parents.

Jorge: What kind of a relationship are we supposed to have with me carrying a secret like that?

Maria: Mmhmm. You described that image of the "glass wall" between you and talked about all the stress of not being out with them.

Jorge: But my father would friggin' freak out.

Maria: Yeah, sounds like you're in a real dilemma: Hiding isn't working but the prospect of coming out seems momentous. My impression is this is all having some pretty serious consequences on your health.

Jorge: It is.

Maria: Anything else I missed?

Jorge: Nothing comes to mind right now.

Maria (pausing to give Jorge time to reflect): Any thoughts on next steps?

Jorge: I'd like to talk again if that's possible.

Maria: Sure, we can set up an appointment for next week. It would be useful for me to hear more about your relationship with your parents, especially your dad.

Jorge: We could do that.

Maria: Anything in the meantime?

Jorge: I think I'm going to get back to the gym, like I said. I'll get Richard to nag me; that always helps. And I guess I'll study for that midterm if I can't find anything better to do!

Maria: Workouts and readings—sounds like a plan.

Maria's summary distills the conversation, which ranged over a lot of territory but clustered around the theme of Jorge's alienation from his parents. She selects some of Jorge's exact words, consulting her notes at times. She also confirms her understanding in inviting him to add anything she may have missed. The summary provides a platform for pondering where to go from here. Maria doesn't rush Jorge by speculating about coming out to his parents; she prefers to *lead from behind* (Cantwell & Holmes, 1994), letting Jorge set the pace rather than pressing him toward an encounter that today at least seems like more than he can handle. The summary concludes with speculation about the focus of the next conversation and a look ahead at Jorge's week.

HOW ARE WE DOING? CONSULTING CLIENTS ON THE JOINT PROCESS

One of the biggest burdens counselors often take on is the belief that the outcome of counseling sessions depends solely on them. If you reflect on this, you may agree this minimizes the clients' contributions, not to mention that it overlooks the two-way aspect of conversations. Counseling is a dialogic process, and all partners in the dialogue contribute to its outcome. For this reason, it's helpful to check in with clients toward the end of sessions to consult with them on the process so that adjustments can be made. Barry Duncan and Scott Miller (Duncan, Miller, & Sparks, 2004; Duncan, Miller, Wampold, & Hubble, 2010) have written extensively about the usefulness of doing this every session with the use of a very simple Likert-type scale (cf. Campbell & Hemsley, 2009; Tilsen & Nylund, 2008). Consulting clients on the work you're doing with them is an example of what I referred to earlier as "practice-based evidence"—it gives voice to clients' experiences and honors clients' points of view. In the example below, Daniel does this with Maria informally, moments before the session wraps up.

> *Daniel: Maria, before you go, I wanted to check in with you briefly about our work together. As you know, there are lots of ways counseling conversations can unfold. We did it our way today, and I'm wondering about your thoughts on the process. Anything you'd like more of or less of?*

There's more going on in Daniel's question than immediately meets the eye. First, he acknowledges there's a wide variety of styles and schools of therapy in circulation. This gives Maria a chance to contemplate her own expectations. Clients always have some expectations, however vague, of what counseling will be like; these are fed by media representations, anecdotal reports, and of course in Maria's case, her own training in the area. Second, Daniel depicts what they have done as "our work" rather than suggesting that all that transpired in the hour was a function of unilateral decisions on his part. This affirms Maria's active role in the process. Third, Daniel gives Maria a chance to comment on what she'd like more of or less of. By starting with "more of," he makes it clear this is not only about inviting negative critique but also about the chance to take note of what's been particularly helpful. And by offering Maria the more/less distinction, Daniel gives her room to come up with constructive input without reducing it to a simplistic and unspecific dichotomy of good versus bad. In this case, Daniel's carefully worded question draws a blank from Maria, but his invitation alone conveys the importance of his input and also prepares Maria to reflect on their process. Perhaps next time she'll have more to say.

CHAPTER SIX RECAP

In this chapter, we've examined in detail what happens once counselors start responding actively to coordinate understanding. More so than listening mostly silently, responding nonverbally while offering occasional encouragers, this more active verbal responding complicates the process in dramatic and fascinating ways. It initiates a dialogic dance, a two-way co-construction of meaning. Power relations are typically at risk of tipping the balance toward counselor meanings, so along with responding, counselors need to attend to the potential mismatch between their intentions and the effects of their contributions. So the chapter reviews an assortment of skills for coordinating meaning making along with accountability practices to ensure clients have input into the overall process.

For many counselors, the introduction to a wide range of skills at this point in their training prompts a feeling of technique overload. Which technique should I use? How can I possibly attend with care and empathy while also trying to ensure I execute with precision? To address these concerns, the chapter introduced a distinction between focusing on relational practices and focusing on techniques. Attending to relationship, to the way we orient to clients, can take care of much of the small stuff. It's remarkable what scintillating "techniques" counselors come up with when they adopt a disposition of respect, hopefulness, and curiosity! Of course this is not to say skill development isn't critical; rather it is a reminder that an ethic of care *gives rise* to particular skills. It's therefore as useful working on your attitude toward clients as it is tinkering with your nonverbals or word sequences.

The chapter covered what is sometimes called active listening, with the reminder that as counselors check in with clients to minimize misreadings, the conversation moves to places that the word *listening* doesn't capture. Both the client's experience and our own evolve continuously as the conversation unfolds.

You may notice there has been less space devoted to nonverbals here than in some similar texts. This is not to downplay their significance; rather, I don't believe a specific focus on our nonverbals is usually necessary so long as we are mindful of our preferred orientation to clients. If we're deliberate in being attentive and empathetic, we will typically present as attentive and empathetic. Early in my own training I agonized briefly about whether my trunk was sufficiently "square" to the client until I realized that a "square trunk" is just one of many subtle nonverbal cues clients read to determine how someone is attending to them. That said, if you see yourself on video and it appears your nonverbals are not expressing the attitude you intend, you can choose to break some habit and alter an aspect of your nonverbal expression. I have worked with many practitioners who reported how conversations deepened when they slowed down their speech. I've heard counselors describe how they noticed a shift in their feeling of presence to their clients when they put aside their notepads or leaned forward in their chairs. So adjusting a nonverbal may bring you closer in line with your intentions. In other cases, it may end up being more useful to commit to the intention itself more fully, and the nonverbals may fall into line. Some counselors describe how, as they let go of their compulsion to share their own experiences, they notice a shift in the way they speak and listen, right down to the inflections in their voices and their postures in their chairs.

Another reason this chapter put more emphasis on verbals than nonverbals is because words lead us into potentially tangled forests of meaning. As with nonverbals, intentions and attitudes go a long way, but so do fundamental practices such as confirming one's understanding because an outlet for the client's point of view is built right into them. This is another topic not always stressed in the counseling literature. My own emphasis on it is prompted by witnessing many examples of practice by "master counselors" who essentially told their clients what they were thinking and feeling.

The distinctions between the related practices of restating and paraphrasing lead into some fine-grained territory, and I hope you will develop a taste for splitting hairs over certain choices of words and phrases because they make a world of difference in counseling conversations. The skills involved in recapping and summarizing have a lot in common with storytelling, which in some ways is what counseling is all about. When meanings are woven together by clients and counselors, they constitute narratives with particular coherence: Much more of this is to come in the pages ahead.

The chapter ended with the practice of consulting clients about the counseling process. In some ways, this simple act embodies the intended spirit of this book. To orient to another as an expert in their own life, fully expecting that person to hold many useful knowledges to draw on, is to join with them in stepping into an empowered version of their identity. Bill Madsen (2007) refers to this when he speaks of moving "from technique to attitude." Curiously, this does not diminish a focus on the development of skills, but it does call for skills not usually associated with the word *technique*. In the next chapter, we'll examine the skills involved in helping clients to name their concerns and in the process to begin speaking about their hopes and values.

CHAPTER SIX DISCUSSION QUESTIONS

1. **Listening for the skills in practice.** Watch or listen to an interviewer (skilled or unskilled—both are productive!) on the radio, TV, or the web. How do they bring/fail to bring the experience of the interviewee to the forefront? See if you can identify the effective/ineffective use of skills introduced in this chapter. Take note of specific examples, both effective and ineffective, and discuss.

2. **Power relations and voice.** In some conversations we feel our voice is being given particular credence; at other times we may feel the opposite, and our point of view seems minimized or overlooked. Identify and describe richly an example of each from your own life. What insight does this give you into the client's experience?

3. **From technique to relationship practice.** Reflect on a person in your life for whom you have a great deal of compassion and admiration. How do your feelings affect the way you listen to this person, your curiosity about and your confidence in their point of view? How do you imagine your attitudinal stance affects this person's sense of themselves and their knowledges?

4. **Dancing missteps and relational repair.** Discuss how a misstep in the form of a botched intervention may provide the opportunity to strengthen a working relationship and build a sense of trust. Provide examples. In what ways can this understanding reduce the pressure on the counselor to always have the facts and get it right?

5. **Co-constructing meaning.** The term *active listening* has been around for a very long time. Discuss the reasons for introducing the additional term *co-constructing meaning*. Which aspects of the conversational process does the term capture that are overlooked by *active listening*? What are the downsides of the term *co-constructing meaning*?

6. **Coordinating meaning.** What does it mean to coordinate meaning in a conversation with a client?

7. **The importance of responding.** Chapter 5 had a lot to say about how we read a client's experience by receptive skills of discernment. Why is this insufficient for coordinating meaning and approaching mutual understanding? Why does this question employ the word *approaching* rather than *achieving* in terms of mutual understanding?

8. **Hearing your own words.** Describe an instance when someone repeated your very own words to capture your point of view or to express their own. What was that like for you?

9. **Acknowledgment versus interpretation.** In which ways does the precise use of someone's language—restating—convey acknowledgment rather than the effort to interpret another's experience?

10. **Confirming the counselor's understanding.** In which ways could restating without confirming your understanding attach importance to details that are not aligned with the client's experiences and priorities?

11. **My House, Your House, Our House.** Read over Activities 1 and 2 in Chapter 2. How do these relate to what happens between Jorge and Maria in the examples of paraphrasing in this chapter?

12. **Paraphrasing and poetry.** How does paraphrasing capitalize on the poetic aspect of language discussed in Chapter 2?

13. **Capturing a picture of the counselor's reading.** Why does paraphrasing capture a picture of the counselor's reading more thoroughly than restating?

14. **Accountability to clients.** Discuss what it means to characterize both restating and paraphrasing as accountability practices. What role does transparency play in this?

15. **Consulting clients.** Think back to an instance when you were collaborating with someone—perhaps you were making or writing something together or engaged in a joint project. Can you remember being consulted about how the process was going and what you might like to do differently? If so, what was that like? How did it affect your sense of your own point of view, your comfort in the working relationship? If not, what difference might that have made in these respects?

CHAPTER SIX ACTIVITIES

1. **Restating.** Pair up. Speaker, describe your experience of something meaningful to you. Listener, periodically restate some of what you hear, using some of what you take to be the most significant language shared by the speaker. You may be restating the speaker's ideas and thoughts, expressions of feeling, statements of value, bodily sensations, and so forth. Do this for about 5 minutes prior to debriefing, and then later switch roles. Listeners and speakers, debrief on the impact of this restating. Listeners, was it hard to track key words and phrases? What was it like using these rather than your own paraphrases? How did you decide which words and phrases to restate? Did you notice any patterns as to which elements were restated and which excluded? Speakers, what was it like hearing your precise words come back to you? Did they affect your sense of whether you were being listened to? Did they feel like the highlights of your experience, or were there key elements that seemed missing?

2. **Confirming your understanding explicitly.** Pair up. This is an extension of the former exercise. Listener, ensure that you not only restate but explicitly check to see if your restating matches the speaker's intentions. Do this for about 5 minutes prior to debriefing, and then later switch roles. Debrief. Listeners, what was it like asking if your restating fit? Was it awkward, comfortable? Did asking take the pressure off to make sure you had it right the first time? Which phrases did you use to confirm your understanding? Speakers, what was it like to be asked explicitly if a restating fit? Did it affect in any way your sense of having a voice in the exchange?

3. **Confirming understanding implicitly.** Pair up. This is another extension of the previous exercises. This time the listener will restate but will not *explicitly* check for understanding. Instead, checking with the speaker will be *implicit* in the tone of voice offered for the restating. Do this for about 5 minutes prior to debriefing, and then later switch roles. Listeners, what was it like conveying permission to be corrected nonverbally rather than explicitly? How did you do it? Speakers, what conveyed that you were being given permission to correct the restating? What was it like to hear the tentative quality of the restating—did it affect your willingness to comment or correct?

4. **Restating: The role of voice tone.** Pair up. This is again an extension of the preceding exercises. This is about noticing the different impacts of restatings made as definitive statements versus those done with a tentative tone that invites correction. Speaker, describe your experience of something meaningful to you. Listener, periodically restate some of what you hear. For the first half, restate in the form of authoritarian pronouncements as to the speaker's intended meaning. In the second half, restate in a tentative tone. Do this prior to debriefing for about 5 minutes, and then later switch roles. Listeners, what did you notice about how it felt to restate authoritatively versus tentatively? Did one come easier? Speakers, what was different for you in the two forms of restating?

5. **Paraphrasing.** Pair up. This is similar to the above exercises, but the listener will paraphrase rather than restating from time to time, substituting their own words for the speaker's, attempting to capture the speaker's experience. Do this for about 5 minutes prior to debriefing, and then later switch roles. Listeners, was it challenging or did it feel natural to find alternate ways to describe what the speaker was experiencing? How did you decide which words and phrases to paraphrase? Did you notice any patterns as to which elements were paraphrased and which excluded? Speakers, what was it like hearing your experience come back to you in different words? Did it affect your sense of whether you were being listened to? Did you feel the listener captured the highlights of your experience, or were there key elements that seemed missing?

6. **Achieving conversational practices through collaborative intention.** In groups of four, take turns in the roles of (a) speaker, (b) listener, and (c) observer. Speakers, share something of importance to you. Listeners, focus exclusively on understanding and conveying the speakers' experiences in the speakers' terms *without deliberately focusing on technique.* Observers, split roles: One watches for examples of restating and/or paraphrasing, and the other looks for and records examples of explicit and implicit checking for fit. Debrief. Observers, report in concrete and literal terms what you witnessed. Listeners, were you aware of using these practices? Speakers, what contributed to and what detracted from feeling understood?

7. **Recapping.** Pair up. Take turns expressing your experience of some topic of concern to you or telling a story about something meaningful that happened to you. Listeners, periodically recap what you've been hearing as the stories are extended, and check for fit. Listeners and speakers, debrief. Listeners, what were the challenges associated with recapping? Speakers, did the recapping seem accurate? What difference did it make to your experience of the conversation?

8. **Summarizing.** Pair up. Take turns expressing your experience of some topic of concern to you or telling a story about something meaningful that happened to you. Listeners, toward the end of the speakers' turns, summarize what the two of you have been talking about, and check for fit. Listeners and speakers, debrief. Listeners, what were the challenges associated with summarizing? Speakers, did the summarizing seem accurate? What difference did it make to your experience of the conversation?

SECTION FOUR

ASSESSING CHALLENGES, PREFERENCES, AND OPPORTUNITIES

The previous section, "Mapping Clients' Experience," introduced a range of skills useful for coming to an understanding of a client's experience and conveying that understanding as part of the fundamental process of coordinating counseling conversations. If you've been reading the text and trying out some of the activities to this point, you have likely already discovered that you already employ these practices in your day-to-day conversations. We are always coordinating talk, so most of the skills examined here are used by all of us, to some extent, in conversations both professional and personal.

This section of the book moves deeper into territory that we all venture into from time to time in our daily lives but that is the stock and trade of counseling and psychotherapy: talking to people about some concern they are hoping to remedy. That concern might be an open-ended interest in self-exploration, but much more frequently it's the expression of some challenge or issue—often referred to, for shorthand's sake, as *the problem*.

In the previous chapter we talked about experience-near description that captures someone's purposes and intentions, feelings and values. These are not always evident in dry accounts of facts, but they quickly become starker once clients report on the problems that have brought them to counseling. In declaring that there are aspects of their experience that are difficult, painful, and/or aversive in some way, they are stating their position in relation to what's going on in their lives. And at the same time, they are explicitly or implicitly reporting on how they would like things to be—their *preferred experience*. This information is critical to the counselor interested in relating according to an ethic of care because, in effect, it erects signposts indicating which avenues are likely to be helpful and which hurtful to the client. The client's articulation of problems and preferences therefore provides the counselor with a foundation for collaborative practice.

The chapters in this section are devoted to practices for developing detailed and concrete pictures of client concerns. As described in the "Mapping Clients' Experience" section, getting this picture—and getting it (sufficiently) right—both reassures clients that they are being heard and prepares the ground for coordinating the talk to follow. Descriptions of problems and preferences do more than that too—they establish a direction for the conversation. And when assessment is thorough and ongoing, it contributes a lot of useful additional information. It points to resources and opportunities that can be brought to bear on the situation, and it flags the possibility of harm to the client or others, making it possible to anticipate and respond to risk factors preventively.

Chapter 7

DEFINING AND DESCRIBING PROBLEMS AND PREFERENCES

INTRODUCTION

Chapters 5 and 6 demonstrated how receiving and reading meanings and relaying them back to the client accomplish a number of important things:

1. signal the counselor is attending and listening;

2. acknowledge the client's experience;

3. encourage the client to share their stories;

4. create opportunities for reflecting on a client's experience by putting it out there where it can be observed;

5. promote a sense of unburdening as the client gives voice to previously unspoken experience;

6. sum up, identifying thematic threads and foregrounding agency;

7. provide the client the opportunity to correct counselor misreadings; and

8. help to coordinate the ongoing conversation by promoting mutual understanding.

So far, the sorts of responses introduced have mostly involved statements offered back to clients by way of verifying our take on their meanings, with the occasional question or encourager used to stimulate further sharing. Practices such as restating, paraphrasing, recapping, and summarizing accomplish this by offering either key words and phrases already used by clients or contributing paraphrased words and phrases with shades of meaning closely related to those presented by clients. The practice of confirming understanding, which is tagged onto the tail end of any of these former four, is a way of ensuring we and our clients are on similar tracks.

These are skills you have used extensively since long before your counselor training, although perhaps you've never attached any terminology to them— they're foundational to any conversation intent on sensitivity and understanding. By naming the skills precisely and differentiating them from each other, Chapters 5 and 6 encouraged a refinement of the practices and made it more possible for you to use them intentionally and purposively.

The skills introduced in the past two chapters are critical to meeting clients where they are—crucial to ensuring they feel heard and understood as they relate their experiences. In the rush to make things happen, counselors often skim over the practices involved in creating a foundation for useful change to occur. This is something like rushing to scramble up a rock face without establishing a firm footing. Climbers make sure they've got a reliable grip on each foothold before reaching for the next one. When counselors convey experience-near understanding, they provide the foothold that supports clients in undertaking the ascent to higher ground. It calls on a counselor's patience and generosity to suspend the desire for outcomes, to pause in the present moment, to pay witness to the other's experience. This brings counselors and clients to a safe plateau, a place of departure for further forays. This is a helpful start, but it is far from the end of the expedition.

In this chapter, the focus of the collaborative work that lies ahead begins to emerge through naming the client's specific concern(s) and starting to paint a picture of how they would prefer things to be. Ensuring that our understanding fits the client's to coordinate meaning making is foundational to this, but the skills here go beyond those covered in Chapters 5 and 6. The talk now becomes more explicitly outcome focused, where *outcome* can have a range of meanings depending on the person at hand.

Earlier, introducing an ethic of care, I challenged notions of objectivity and neutrality, suggesting instead that a counselor needs to take a position—to relate to the client as an ally. To do this requires having the client's inside view of the events they recount. When Resha says the evening didn't go at all the way she'd anticipated, I don't know whether an offer of comfort or a celebration is more in order. Fewer people showed than she expected; was that to her liking? The conversation went in unexpected directions; was that a favorable development? Without an inside view of the significance of these events for her, I am at a loss as to where to stand. This chapter demonstrates how important it is for the counselor to have a sense of the client's subjective experience of events to position themselves in relation to the unfolding story.

In some cases, people will explicitly name the temperature (e.g., positive, neutral, negative) of events they recount. This happens when a client not only recounts events but also provides an insider's view of their experience of these events, in effect saying, "This has been happening, I don't like it, and I'd like that instead." Problems and preferences are all there. When this happens, the practices introduced in the previous chapter will generally suffice in laying the ground for working actively with the client to effect some sort of change. However, when this insider view is absent or vague, the counselor needs to take a more active role. The term *problem definition* is often used to depict this skill and serves as a useful shorthand. But it tells only half the story because every expression of distress or suffering also indicates the desire for something different, some preferred state of affairs. Ultimately the preferences will become a central focus of the work, the beacon that calls the conversation forward. So this chapter includes a look at both the skills involved in developing a clear problem definition and, equally, a statement of client preferences.

PROBLEM DEFINITION AS A STARTING POINT FOR CONSTRUCTIVE COLLABORATION

Conversation With a Purpose

One thing that can be reliably assumed about counseling conversations—less so for many other conversations we have during the day—is that they're intended to accomplish something, to be helpful. Clients generally show up because they're seeking support in dealing with challenges in their lives. Regardless of what brings clients for counseling, it's critical to elicit their expression of what they would like different in their lives to begin the process of being helpful to them.

The term *problem definition* is shorthand for denoting how counselor and client come to an agreement about the purpose of their conversations. In some cases, this may begin moments into a session; but in other situations, it may take time to distill a description of the client's primary concern or concerns. In joining with clients in the process of problem definition, the counselor's role goes beyond the coordination of understanding featured in the previous two chapters. Reading and confirming meaning empathically is almost invariably comforting and supportive in itself and is certainly foundational to all counseling practice, but determining clients' specific concerns makes it possible to be more proactively helpful. Problem definition leads counselors and clients into more task-oriented territory and forms the basis for constructive collaboration.

Suppose a stranger approaches you for help. She says, "It's been a lovely afternoon watching my children playing in the park on this gorgeous summer day." Drawing on skills introduced in the previous chapter, you might be able to convey a certain amount of understanding by restating ("You've found it lovely to witness your children's happiness as you've enjoyed this gorgeous afternoon") or paraphrasing ("It sounds like you've treasured watching your children enjoying themselves"). But because you so far haven't heard the woman's description of a concern or problem, you would be at a loss for ideas about how to *help*. You would need to ask for more, to initiate the process of problem definition.

The counselor's role is to be helpful, to provide a service; for counselor and client to evaluate the usefulness of their exchange, there needs to be some sense of what they are trying to *accomplish* together. As we shall see, this purpose can take many forms, but it is the shared understanding of a purpose that makes helpful collaboration possible, and the purpose relates to what the client is finding problematic, what they would like changed. Returning to the woman in the park, suppose she then elaborates: She needs to breast-feed her infant immediately so is unable to gather up the other two children and their things in time to board the last bus of the day that will get them home. In providing a picture of the problem (she's unable to round up the kids in time), she conveys what you need to begin collaborating with her. Karl Tomm (1987b) said, "To not take a position is to take the position of not taking one, that is, to be noncommittal" (p. 4). The intent to be helpful implies adopting a position in relation to the experiences being described, and that's where problem definition comes in.

TAKING A TEMPERATURE READING

You've probably heard or watched exchanges in which an interviewer is drawing out an interviewee's account of surviving some natural disaster. Sometimes the interviewee relates the facts of the event without locating themselves in the account. This makes for a bland exchange when it could be an exciting and fascinating story. Here, a competent interviewer typically comes to the rescue with questions such as, *What was going through your mind at that moment?* or *How did you feel when that happened?* These questions help get inside the event by presenting the events from the interviewee's perspective. The story springs to life because it is no longer a dry enumeration of facts but an account of someone's subjective experience. Until the client provides a temperature reading of events—are they good, bad, indifferent?—there is not yet a definition of problems and preferences, and it is therefore difficult to team up with the client to effect change.

Without a sense of a client's subjective experience, a counselor sometimes decides for themselves, making an educated guess based on personal and professional experience. Shirley, who drops in from time to time to an inner-city detoxification center, announces, "My boyfriend moved out on the weekend." A counselor's quick reading of the temperature of this event for Shirley, based on a previous breakup of their own, might be that this was a sad event. But for Shirley, whose bruised arms are testament to ongoing violent conflict, this is an announcement of liberation from an abusive relationship. When a counselor defines problems unilaterally, it sets the counselor and their clients on potentially divergent train tracks, neglecting the relationship and failing to capitalize on the client's expertise in relation to their own life (Duncan, Miller, & Sparks, 2004; Duncan, Miller, Wampold, & Hubble, 2010). Making guesses based on one's own experience to determine what is problematic for the client is never sufficient; the client needs to have a central role in problem definition.

Sometimes clients convey problems and preferences through a flicker of strain in the eyes, a playful lilt in the voice, an angry tone of voice, a relaxed posture, and so on. Nonverbals are useful cues. But as we've seen, they alone are open to misinterpretation, so it's important to actively solicit the client's subjective experience—taking a temperature reading, as it were, of events as they are recounted. To echo the tale about bears and porridge, are things too hot, too cold, or just about right? There are infinite ways to find out; Box 7.1 gives a sample of a few.

BOX 7.1

Getting at Clients' Subjectivity
How does that make you feel?

When clients report on events and experiences without conveying their sense of where they stand in relation to them, it's difficult for counselors to know how to position themselves to be helpful. Questions help to determine where the client's at and provide a basis for collaboration.

What do you think about that as you describe it to me now?

If those tears could talk, what would they say about this?

I notice you laugh when you describe the e-mail she sent. What's that say about how you feel about it?

What's it like for you dealing with the challenges you've been describing?

(Continued)

(Continued)

So where does that leave you now?

How did you sit with the news?

How was that for you when she left?

If there were one point you'd want me to get from that story, what would you say it was?

What do you think is the key message in your description of that incident?

Would you say this event drew you together or pushed you apart?

How did that affect you?

The quest to help a client convey their subjective experience lies behind what is arguably the most stereotypical counseling question of all time: *How does that make you feel?* As you can see in Box 7.1, there are many ways to elicit the temperature of a client's experience, and the language of feelings is only one of the ways in. Nevertheless, emotion is a powerful barometer of a person's experience, so watching for nonverbal expressions of feeling and inquiring about emotional experience are two very useful ways to join a client in defining problems.

Student Voices

Inez: Slowing Down to Watch the Picture Develop

In the first session or two with my client I was struggling with which aspects of her story I should ask for elaboration on, and which I should not. I always felt I was missing something important, or was not focusing on what she wanted to focus on. But in reflection, I realize I'm rushing the process. I am too caught up on trying to find "positives" for my client, instead of taking the time to truly grasp what she is saying. I now think by slowing down and seeking out deeper descriptions from my clients, we will naturally begin to paint a picture of the things they favour, and the aspects to their stories that resonate most for them. By noticing which questions evoke a strong verbal or nonverbal responses I will begin to determine what my clients' preferences are.

INCLUDING THE CLIENT'S VOICE IN PROBLEM DEFINITION

Whose Problem Is It Anyway?

I often hear counselors in training disputing what is really going on in a session, which leads to some simple but important questions, some of which are outlined in Box 7.2. Leaning toward airtight, one-sided conclusions about clients instead of joining clients where they're at runs the risk of opening schisms in the working relationship.

BOX 7.2

What's Really Going on Here?

Counselors are trained in scientific traditions that adopt rigorous methods to seek answers to fundamental questions about human behavior. A potential downside of this accumulated body of knowledge about psychological content is that it sometimes gets precedence over the process of collaborative conversation and meaning making. Instead of asking, *What is my client's experience?* counselors ask, *What's really going on here?* This preoccupation with what is true can jeopardize the therapeutic relationship and hamper the possibility of collaboration. Here are some useful questions to ponder in response to the question of what is "really going on" for any client:

Real according to whom?

Should we assume anyone sufficiently clearheaded and knowledgeable would come to the same conclusion about the situation at hand? If so, how are we to make sense of things when our clients don't see the situation the way we do?

In these instances, should we conclude that one of us is right and one of us is wrong? What sorts of conversations ensue when this assumption is the basis?

How might one determine in any final way what is actually going on for a client?

What impact does it have on attempts to coordinate collaborative conversation when counselors assume the role of arbiters of what is real/unreal, true/false?

Naming Rights

Throughout this text you will continue to find reminders about privileging (seeing as credible, devoting primary attention to) clients' accounts of what is problematic for them and what they would like to experience instead. In effect, this implies giving clients the naming rights to their experiences. This differs from a familiar assumption you may have encountered in your studies: that clients' judgment is questionable, as evidenced by the fact they have come for counseling—that the reason "clients get into trouble in the first place is that they make poor decisions" (Egan, 1995, cited in Strong, 2000, p. 147).

Collaborative problem definition goes beyond merely assuming that clients are always right; it depends on careful attention to clients' characterizations of problems and preferences. This means not getting ahead of clients in understanding the issues at hand. Otherwise counselors sometimes charge headlong down a path, filled with the satisfaction that liberation from the problem is at hand, only to turn around and find their clients are nowhere to be seen. Lipchik (1994) says one of the "greatest pitfalls" for therapists is

> subtly or unwittingly imposing their own goals on their clients. This can happen early in therapy or later because the therapist does not hear, or does not want to hear the client's own changing and evolving understanding of what he or she wants and needs. (p. 38)

To ensure counselor and client are walking together involves a persistent curiosity to learn more about what the client takes to be problematic. Mind you, this is rarely a static process, as we shall see shortly. With the unfolding dialogue, problem definitions typically evolve as the client comes to a deeper and broader understanding of their experience, partly under the influence of the counselor's outside perspective.

Reflection 7.1

Have you ever turned to a friend or family member for help with some challenge, only to find that their take on what constituted the problem differed from yours, despite your attempts to articulate your point of view? If so, what was this like for you? Did you hang in or back out of the conversation? If you hung in, do you remember if the person engaged you in dialogue about their alternate perspective, or pushed it on you without inviting your input? How did you respond to the other's defining of your experience?

WHAT'S UP? ASKING ABOUT CLIENTS' CONCERNS

Clients come for counseling for a wide range of reasons (see Box 7.3). Finding out what they want to accomplish is an early task because as we saw earlier, it helps counselors to position themselves for constructive collaboration. Once the patter of getting-acquainted talk is over and the counselor has shared the limits to confidentiality and any other up-front business needing attention, it's time to hear from the client.

BOX 7.3

Problem Definition and Diversity

The reasons clients come for counseling are as diverse as the clients themselves. Some are very goal oriented with concrete objectives, and others are heavily process oriented, with objectives more difficult to summarize in a brief phrase.

- Ali wants to develop more disciplined study habits.
- Sarah is hoping to get over a breakup with her boyfriend.
- Justin is feeling directionless and wants to find some focus in his life.
- Marla's husband is abusing drugs and alcohol and has been threatening her in front of their two children.
- Selma is angry and confused following an abortion she didn't want to have.
- Rafael is tired of the endless self-critique he subjects himself to and is hoping to improve his relationship with himself.
- Wei wants to make sense of her recent troubles concentrating at work.
- Yolande says she's determined to give up drinking but feels she needs support and guidance.
- Frank came because it's a condition of the courts: He's been violent with his partner, and counseling is a requirement if he wants to have access to his two daughters.
- Margarita says she can't name one issue in particular but wants to use the conversations as a vehicle for getting to know herself better.

Opening the Conversation

There are many ways of opening a counseling conversation, some of which zero in on problem definition immediately and some of which leave the agenda up for grabs. *How would you like to start?* is open ended and allows for the possibility the client will save the naming of an issue for later. In that case, the client might opt to hear more about the counselor first *(Could you tell me more about how you work?)* or to provide more general background about themselves *(I'm a mother of two teenagers, married to John for 23 years. I work as an accountant at a local biotech firm).*

Questions as simple as, *What brings you in?* or *How can I be of help?* steer the exchange more to a presenting concern but don't require a description of a problem *(I'm depressed)* and could be as easily answered with an expression of a preference *(I'd like to feel better about myself).*

Some questions are more deliberate in helping clients to connect with their intentions in seeking counseling, such as, *What are you hoping to accomplish by meeting with me? How would you like to use this meeting?* or *What would you like to work on today?* Alternately, the counselor can be deliberate in avoiding a focus on problems by eliciting a description of a preferred destination: *How will we know when we no longer need to keep meeting?* Speaking of problems is one way to identify what the client would like to change, but for some clients the language of problems does not resonate with their purposes in consulting a counselor.

BOX 7.4

Language Diversity to Match Client Diversity

The word *problem* is most typically used in the counseling literature to denote the concern a client brings forward, and it is employed here for shorthand sake. It does come with baggage, however. As Bakhtin (1981) said, "each word tastes of the contexts in which it has lived its socially charged life" (p. 293). *Problem* leans toward what is *not* working, failing to highlight the active, purposeful dimension of experience. Some clients come to counseling because they want to achieve something or work something out—not because they view themselves as having problems. So you may have noticed the text includes a variety of words to depict what brings people to counseling. Throughout this book, the word *problem* will continue to play a central role, but it will occasionally alternate with other words such as *concern, difficulty,* and *challenge.* Although there is nothing exhaustive about this alternative list, it promotes a diversity to match the various ways clients prefer to speak of what they are up against. It also serves as a reminder that each word conjures up other words and of the central role of language in making meaning.

Student Voices

Handing Over the Spotlight

It takes discipline and purpose to keep the spotlight on the other person throughout a conversation. That's what the following counselors in training discovered. Rasni tried this out in a talk with a friend, while Serena made this a central objective of her first session.

Rasni: As my friend started to talk I focused on offering non-verbal supportive gestures and paraphrasing questions to encourage her. After speaking for a few minutes, my friend asked me "Why are you so quiet?" and seemed puzzled at my lack of "opinion." I said I wanted to be there for her and really understand and hear what she had to say. My friend seemed really happy that my focus was on her. I found that by handing over the spotlight my friend said she felt more heard and supported than in the past. This surprised me in some ways as I previously thought that offering my experiences showed her my understanding, but I've become more aware of what simply letting a person just talk can accomplish. I now find that I try to focus on offering my listening skills, rather than my dialogue in conversation, but I find it hard not to revert back to old patterns, especially with close friends.

Serena: After the first session with my client I walked away with a realization of the urge to self disclose when I am told about circumstances that I feel I relate to. Although I "held back the reins" in not disclosing, I felt that I had to consciously put effort into making sure I kept my comments to myself. When I left the session I felt that much of my energy was focused on this aspect when it should have been 100% focused on listening attentively to my client. I would advise myself in the future to approach all clients, those culturally similar to myself and those not, with the same degree of curiosity. There will always be a different twist to everybody's story no matter if the client and counsellor share for example, the same race, socio-economic status, or educational background. In looking back on the video of our first session it was very evident that my client's feelings towards her similar experience were quite different from my own. In the future, I will work on entering my sessions with open, fresh eyes so that I can fully empathize with how my clients experience their stories.

THE SHIFTING DEFINITION OF PROBLEMS

For simplicity's sake, the implication so far has been that clients and counselors determine what the problem is and then get on with the work of addressing it. In practice, counseling is usually more complex. Clients rarely present with a single solitary problem they are intent on addressing. Even a complaint as apparently straightforward as nail biting can quickly expand to a discussion of anxiety, relational conflict, lifestyle choices, and so on. The same sort of range of related concerns is evident in the opening conversations between Daniel as counselor to Maria. Maria has expressed guilt about her role as mother while she is preoccupied with the demands of graduate school, conflict with her partner Azim, and difficulties concentrating with clients. Jorge, too, in his sessions with his counselor Maria, has named a range of concerns, including insomnia, doubts about his career trajectory, and the dilemma that he has not come out to his parents. In time it is conceivable that each of these various concerns will be addressed in their sessions, although not simultaneously because each concern, although related, has its distinct features. And no doubt, new concerns and topics worthy of exploration will arise. Helpful counseling conversations are never static: They're more like rivers than lakes, flowing from moment to moment, week to week, month to month. As important as it is to agree on some sense of direction near the outset, it's also important to be prepared to move with that changeable flow.

> *In her first session, Karyn looked haggard, and her speech was labored after she dropped heavily into the chair. She said she was there to deal with her chronic insomnia, launching into a detailed description of sleepless nights. But before the hour was up, the conversation turned to the worry and anxiety she said follows her throughout her days. The following week, an exploration of Karyn's distress led to her sharing that she'd been sexually assaulted a few months earlier. Discussion of this brought her and her counselor a week later to recent conflict with her boyfriend about their sexual relationship.*

Because counseling involves a process of ongoing meaning construction through dialogue between counselors and client, the definition of problems morphs as therapeutic conversations unfold. Client and counselors come to see particular concerns in a new light as they actively explore them. It is not unusual to discuss roughly the same concern over many conversations—challenges with mood, relationship difficulties, destructive habits, and so on—and to simultaneously reinvent ways of speaking and thinking about the concern from session to session.

Like assessment in general, problem definition is an important part of the work early in the process, but it is also an ongoing activity necessary for coordinating a series of conversations. The experience counselors sometimes report of feeling lost in the middle of an exchange with a client is often the result of losing sight of a mutual purpose. It would probably be easier if clients always came for counseling because they had a set of bangs they wanted shortened or a nagging cough they wanted soothed. But counseling is more complex than hairdressing—and yes, medicine too—due to the infinite variation and changeability of human experience. This may explain why counselors never seem to lose their thirst for professional development. It may also explain the deep resonance that many counselors describe having with their work (Rønnestad & Orlinsky, 2005).

Reflection 7.2

Think back to a problem you previously dealt with that you no longer describe as a problem. Which word or phrase would you use for it? Was it related to or did it emerge from some previous problem? Did it disappear overnight? Did it transform over time into a different problem or challenge or do you now use a different word for it than you previously did?

CO-CONSTRUCTING LANGUAGE FOR PROBLEMS

When we remember that the concept of a presenting problem is itself an idea embedded in the culture of counseling and therapy, it comes as less of a surprise that some clients are not prepared to distill their distress into a few words. Sometimes the counselor needs to take more of an active role in focusing the collaboration to come. When this is done skillfully, the client stays at the center but may draw on the counselor's support in focusing their concerns.

Maria (counselor):	*Sounds like the silence between you and your parents is weighing heavily on you, Jorge.*
Jorge (client):	*Yeah, it hangs in the air between us. It seems it's there no matter what we're talking about; it hovers there and makes it impossible to just chill and have fun together.*
Maria:	*I'm wondering if that's something you'd like to deal with. I don't know if it would be about breaking the silence or just accepting it.*
Jorge (shaking his head):	*I've tried the acceptance route. Doesn't work. No, the silence has got to come to an end. Just not so sure when, or where, or how.*

Here, Maria invites to the foreground the issue of Jorge's nondisclosure to his parents, although he's also spoken of other concerns such as insomnia and a lack of motivation for his studies. In raising this as a potential candidate for further discussion, she does not convey the notion that nondisclosure is *the* problem, his one and only concern. Nor does she assume what the most appropriate way forward would be, leaving open whether he'd like to deal with it or accept it—two distinct avenues. For his part, Jorge picks up on the silence as an issue worthy of attention and further clarifies that accepting it has not been helpful. Together, they begin to consolidate a direction for their work.

Loaning Descriptive Support to Clients

Sometimes it is difficult for a client to find a word or phrase for a concern, and again, the counselor can help in this respect. For instance, in her role as client, Maria is struggling to pinpoint what is distressing her. She has provided Daniel a picture of being simultaneously torn between being a mother and a counselor in training, with 2 days a week devoted to seeing clients at the university counseling center. She's referred to tensions with her partner, Azim, who is under similar stress as a lawyer in training. She's spoken of difficulties concentrating with her clients and of creeping doubts about her suitability to the profession altogether.

But for various reasons, clients may not always generate vivid language to capture their primary preoccupations, and in some cases, the most resonant words or phrases for their concerns may emerge from the back-and-forth dialogue with the counselor. Is it a problem if the client didn't initially generate a word or phrase that ultimately gets used repeatedly to talk about the client's concern? The more important question may be whether the word resonates for the client and speaks to their concerns.

Maria: *It's that nagging feeling that I'm violating the rules when I go into work.*

Daniel: *The rules?*

Maria: *The rules for motherhood—you know, mothers are supposed to be all-nurturing, selfless providers, all that stuff. [laughs] Those are the rules, aren't they?*

Daniel: *Sounds like mother guilt to me.*

Maria: *Mother guilt?*

Daniel: *I talk to lots of mothers caught up in the idea that any "good" mother wouldn't venture out of the home, that any step to expand their identities beyond providing directly for their kids is just plain selfish. Big-time guilt. Does that fit for you?*

Maria: *Mother guilt. Ha! Yeah, by the barrelful, I'd say.*

ESCAPING PROBLEM IDENTITIES:
SEPARATING PERSON AND PROBLEM

White and Epston (1990) describe how many clients arrive for counseling with a "problem saturated story" ready at hand. A central feature of this story is that it characterizes the client themself as the problem: *I'm codependent, I'm the product of a dysfunctional family, I'm a failure, I'm a bad parent*, and so on. In medical contexts, this collapsing of problem and person is sometimes expressed in the language used to describe patients: *Mr. Spinelli is a diabetic. Ms. McGrath is a schizophrenic.* These descriptions are totalizing in the sense that they exclude other aspects of persons' identities beyond the problems they face. Problem-saturated accounts present a challenging start to a counseling collaboration because they carry an implicit assumption that the task at hand is nothing short of personality reconstruction. In these cases, it can be useful to join the client in finding language that separates them from the problem. This practice of "externalizing" the problem (Freedman & Combs, 1996; White, 2007; White & Epston, 1990) opens a metaphorical space between person and problem, creating room for new choices. When clients experience themselves as being in relation to problems rather than the problems themselves, novel avenues for action present themselves.

As we shall see here (and expand on in future chapters), externalizing can be turned into a conversational practice, but it is more than a mere technique. The separation of people and problems is not just a way of speaking; it's also a way to conceptualize the challenges clients present. In effect, it embodies a stance taken by the counselor—a stance of refusing to see problems as expressions of fundamental deficiencies of character but seeing them instead as difficulties clients are encountering for which exceptions can invariably be identified. Note that externalizing is incompatible with an individualistic view: It characterizes people in context and in relation to their surroundings.

To hold a view of people as separate from the problems they are dealing with is not a neutral stance: It means orienting as an ally, holding the torch for possibilities in the face of discouragement and distress. That separation helps clients move from a world of problems to "a world of experience, a world of flux. In this world, persons find new possibilities for affirmative action, new opportunities to act flexibly" (White & Epston, 1990, p. 42).

Michael White (1984) spontaneously introduced the practice of externalizing in a conversation with a family whose members had become convinced there was something deeply wrong with them because one of the children was having trouble controlling his bowel movements. The boy was excreting in his pants and on occasion had even smeared the feces on the walls of his room. The family's account of itself was profoundly problem saturated; White was aware of how this distressing situation was causing the family members to lose sight of their own resources and the various options for responding to them. He made a deliberate choice to orient to his clients as an ally and introduced a playful twist to the conversation, becoming curious about the effects of "Sneaky Poo" on their lives. From here the conversation evolved from an account of their various trials to a description of how the family had had some measure of success in not letting Sneaky Poo lead them to lose touch with their caring for each other. Before long, the family developed strategies for "tricking" Sneaky Poo, and the problematic behavior ended. White's separation of the family from the problem through the practice of externalizing helped each member to extend on their successes rather than getting bogged down in endless soul-searching about what was wrong about them that would give rise to this serious "condition."

BOX 7.5

Externalizing: Separating People and Problems

When faced with big challenges, clients sometimes make themselves out to be the problem. This is a painful and discouraging place to be and a difficult starting point for constructive collaboration. In these situations, it can be helpful to think about and talk about challenges in a way that separates them from people. This practice of externalizing makes room for helpful conversations about what people *have* done, *are* doing, or *will* do in the face of challenges. It can be a helpful conceptual and verbal tool when defining problems with clients. To experience the effect of externalizing, choose a challenge you face, and reflect on it, guided by the following two sets of questions. What is different about your experience of yourself depending on the questions guiding you?

A. **Problem X as identity** (e.g., worrier, problem drinker, nail biter, person with an anger control problem).

   1. How did you become an X?

   2. What kinds of things happen that particularly prove you are an X?

   3. What is it about your own genetics, neurology, biochemistry, and so forth that makes you an X?

   4. What effect has being an X had in general in your life and relationships?

   5. Are there times when being an X is less of an issue for you? What is going
      on then?

B. **Problem Y as separate from identity** (e.g., worry, drinking [or
alcohol], nail biting, anger).

   1. When did Y enter your life?

   2. In what contexts is Y most likely to take over?

   3. Can you identify ways in which cultural beliefs or other dominant ideas,
      images, and stories stoke the Y as it were when it's operating in your life?

   4. What effect does Y have on your life and relationships?

   5. Are there times when you manage not to let Y discourage you or hold
      you back? How do you manage to do that?

Source: Adapted from Freedman and Combs (1996).

Reflection 7.3

Think about a problem that a friend or family member has—perhaps even a
problem you see as a deep expression of this person's fundamental being.
Think about words for externalizing this problem so that you can separate your
friend or family member from it and see them as facing it as a challenge in their
life. Consider the ways the (externalized) problem affects the person and
detracts from their quality of life. Think about how they sometimes cope with
it, stand up to it, or successfully rise above it, if only momentarily. What shifts
in your view of that friend or family member? What is different about your
sense of hopefulness and possibility on their behalf?

Any persistent curiosity on the part of the counselor about clients' abilities or
successes in the face of problems has an externalizing quality because it involves
seeing clients as separate from the challenges confronting them. In cases in which
clients seem to make sense of their problems as evidence of what's wrong with
them, it can be useful to make the separation of person from problem more
explicit by the linguistic practice of externalizing. In effect, Daniel and Maria did
that when they settled on the term *mother guilt* as a way to describe one of the

challenges Maria is facing. In the excerpt below, Daniel is persistent in separating Maria from the problem at hand by periodically reintroducing the term *mother guilt* into the conversation.

> Maria: There I go again: It's all about me, me, me.
>
> Daniel: I may have missed something: I didn't catch how worrying about whether you're being helpful to your clients is all about you.
>
> Maria: I should be thinking about my daughter Kyla, poor kid, not obsessing about my practicum.
>
> Daniel: I wonder if you're speculating about quitting the program.
>
> Maria: No! I want this; I definitely want this. I'm not saying that. It's just that I feel so guilty when I find myself focusing on the client work. Some mom.
>
> Daniel: Sounds like doing grad school is bringing up a lot of self-doubts about your role as a parent. Do I hear the voice of mother guilt whispering in your ear?
>
> Maria: Shouting is more like it! Yeah, the mother guilt thing again for sure. It has a way of hounding me, all right.

As Maria and Daniel talk about Maria's situation, there's a shift in the definition of the problem. It begins as something like "Maria is a bad mother"; when Daniel introduces language to separate Maria from the problem, it becomes something closer to "mother guilt is impairing Maria in her roles as counselor, partner, and mother." This separation of Maria from the problem comes from externalizing mother guilt. It does not preclude the possibility of her carefully examining her values around parenting and graduate work—externalizing is about understanding clients as being in relation to problems, not about pretending problems don't exist. The shift that externalizing achieves here allows Maria to step back from her situation and make active choices in line with her values rather than wallowing in unhelpful self-critique.

BOX 7.6

Internalized and Externalized Problem Descriptions

Externalizing involves thinking about and in some cases speaking about problems as separate from people. When using language in deliberately externalizing ways, it's best to collaboratively decide on appropriate language to ensure the language fits for clients. Below, the left column captures snatches of clients' descriptions of their concerns. The right column presents words and phrases that might be used to separate the problem from the client. It's important to note these are not diagnoses but merely ways of thinking and talking about problems that put some space between them and the people experiencing them.

It's hard to say it, but the fact is I'm a failure. My two marriages failed, and now I've been laid off. I can't seem to get anything right. Everywhere I turn I find myself bumping up against the same thing.	self-doubt, the critical voice, the failure story
It's this heavy sensation in my chest and the feeling of being slowed down, like my feet are in mud. Nothing seems interesting. I feel flat and can't find any energy for life.	depression, the blues, the heaviness
I can't seem to put it all out of my head. I wake up thinking about it; I dwell on it all day; I go to bed with it on my mind. It makes me so tense, I can't sleep. I worry about my health.	fretting, anxiety, worry, racing thoughts

As mentioned, externalizing is the expression of both a stance and an accompanying linguistic practice. The stance alone supports counselors in staying alert to clients' successful expressions of value and intention in relation to challenges in their lives. When the stance is combined with explicit use of externalizing (Brown & Augusta-Scott, 2007; Duvall & Béres, 2011; Freedman & Combs, 1996; Freeman, Epston, & Lobovits, 1997; White, 2007; Winslade & Williams, 2012), the separation of persona and problem is more pervasive and visible to clients:

When did the preoccupation first become evident to you?

Are there times when your temper acts like a wedge between you and your partner?

How have you managed not to let the fear take over?

If worry had a voice, what would it be telling you?

Would you be interested in cohabitating with the sadness, or is it more like wanting to kick it out of the house altogether?

As you can see, explicitly externalizing language introduces a twist on our usual way of making sense of problems. Once clients get past the unfamiliarity of these creative ways of speaking, they often discover the separation of person and problem opens gaps they overlooked when caught up in understanding problems as expressions of who they are. We'll revisit externalizing in later chapters because it is a useful practice in both assessment and active intervention.

PROBLEMS AND PREFERENCES: TWO SIDES OF A COIN

So far, this chapter has been devoted to the skills involved in defining problems collaboratively with clients. Achieving a picture of what is problematic helps clarify what the client would like less of in their life. But helpful change is not merely the extinction of unwanted experience: It involves replacing problems with something different, something more in line with client preferences. As Salaman, Grevelius, and Andersson (1993) put it, "a problem is a person's wish for a change that he or she does not know how to achieve" (p. 334).

> ### Student Voices
> ### Nadia: Problems and Preferences, Flip Sides of the Coin
>
> When working with my client, I found throughout our sessions we were continuously "flipping" between the problem and her preferences. As we worked through expanding the description of what has been problematic for my client, I couldn't help but notice she was also expressing what she wanted more of and less of in her life. For example, when my client expressed her concern of not feeling balanced in her multiple responsibilities, I could tell just from this that she would prefer a more balanced lifestyle. As we continued to explore this concern, my client shared that she was not feeling fully present in class, which was thereby affecting her schooling. She elaborated on the notion of being fully present, stating that lately she's been distracted during class and has not been able to participate as much. From sharing this concern, I truly got a better sense of how my client would like things to be. I could tell that my client wished to be more engaged during class as a way to get the most out of her schooling. Thus, the more my client talked about her concerns, the more I got a better sense of how she would like things to be. I truly do believe that the two go hand-in-hand. You cannot develop a rich description of the problem without uncovering a picture of what the client would like his/her life to be like.

Pointing in a Direction: Client Preferences as a Compass for the Journey

Drawing on the familiar metaphor of counseling as a journey, an account of problems indicates where clients don't want to travel, whereas an account of preferences points to where they do want to venture. So it's just as important to determine preferences as it is to name problems. Client preferences act as a sort of compass for the journey in the sense that they indicate which direction counselor and client will be going. Anderson (1997) characterizes this mutual journey as "shared intentionality."

The issue of client naming rights arises in relation to preferences just as it does with problem definition. If counselors are intent only on collaborating with clients in defining problems, but not on soliciting descriptions of preferences, they may rely on their own ideas about what clients need—ideas that may be out of step with clients' points of view. Or seeking guidance on the topic, counselors might turn instead to generic sources of information that, although potentially useful, are decontextualized and as yet untailored to the specifics of the situations at hand.

Consider how this would play out in Maria's counseling work with Jorge. Early in their first conversation, Maria and Jorge developed a description of the distress Jorge feels in his relationship with his parents—not a thorough problem definition, but a start. At this point, Maria might turn to her own experience and conclude the most helpful way forward would be for Jorge to do what she herself had done a few years earlier: move to a city across the country as a show of autonomy. Or she might consult the literature on gay and lesbian issues and propose a highly specific plan for Jorge to come out to his parents, based on a documented case study. In each instance, however, Maria would be excluding Jorge's voice and abandoning the collaborative process of establishing preferences. This would greatly diminish the odds of arriving at a helpful way forward that is closely tailored to Jorge's unique experience.

To plunge into offering solutions without soliciting a clear account of client preferences is like flipping to the troubleshooting section of a manual without turning to the consultant most intimately familiar with the situation: the client. When Duncan and Miller (2000) speak of attending to the client's theory of change, they mean counselors should primarily rely on the person before them not only for clarification of what is problematic but also for accounts of where the client would like to go and thoughts about how they might get there.

In Maria and Jorge's case, some persistently curious work by Maria led to further problem definition—the silence between Jorge and his parents. Even here, Maria does not assume what Jorge's preference would be, so she pitches a couple of options: breaking the silence or accepting it. At this point, Jorge makes it clear that acceptance is not an option, pointing the compass needle in a clear direction. Although there will no doubt be many twists and turns in the road ahead, counselor and client are walking side by side.

Invoking Preferences Through Questions

In some cases, a client may state outright a preferred destination—skipping a description of the problem altogether—such as Abdul, who says, "I want to be more playful and relaxed with my little daughter." But more often, clients speak of what is troubling them rather than paint a picture of a preferred state of affairs. As we've seen, client preferences often begin to come into focus as concerns and challenges are described because preferences are the flipside of the coin. But although a description of a problem may hint at a preferred state of affairs, it does not necessarily name it explicitly. Consider Daniel and his client Maria. They come to the conclusion that mother guilt is problematic for Maria; this suggests Maria would prefer a life free of guilt or at least less troubled by chronic self-critique. Precisely what this looks like—which actions, thoughts, feelings, relationships, and so on she would be experiencing instead—is as yet unclear because more energy has gone into identifying the problem. It will be important to keep Maria's preferences in the foreground as the conversation evolves because there is no formula for a model of motherhood unfettered by relentless guilt. The following questions all provide possibilities for enhancing this side of Maria's account. Notice the first and last use explicitly externalizing language.

> *How would you like to treat yourself instead in those moments when the guilt drops by for a visit?*
>
> *What do you prefer to believe about the dual role of mother and student?*
>
> *What sorts of ideas about motherhood make more sense to you?*
>
> *What would you like to feel instead when caught between your child and your work?*
>
> *Do you have any images of where you'd like to be when this issue is behind you?*
>
> *Can you think of any role models—working mothers—you'd like to emulate?*
>
> *You mentioned that tension that comes over you. How would you like to feel in your body instead?*
>
> *Can you paint a picture of an exchange with Azim without mother guilt in the room?*

Although each of these questions is different, they share some common features. Each attempts to draw forth from Maria some alternative to the problem experience she is reporting. And none of them assumes what that might look like; instead, they are open-ended explorations along a variety of lines, including inquiries into possible preferred actions, beliefs, thoughts, feelings, images, body sensations, and relationship practices. When clients respond readily to these sorts of questions, the way is cleared quickly for moving forward. However, in the midst of the distress and confusion that accompany problems, it is often difficult to pinpoint preferences. In these cases, stylized questions can be useful to stimulate clients' imaginations and descriptions of a preferred state of affairs.

Reflection 7.4

Think of some challenge or problem with which you are dealing. Once you have a sense of it, allow yourself to let go of it, and imagine a time in the future when that concern is no longer an issue for you. Perhaps it is absent, or perhaps it just isn't a problem any more. Without trying to think through how you got there, allow yourself to bask in the satisfaction of being free of the problem's negative influence. What does it feel like in your body? What is different about your attitude, your mental habits, your emotional temperament? Linger in this space for a moment before stepping back and asking yourself what effect, if any, this leap of imagination had on your experience of the concern at hand.

Describing a Preferred Outcome

The slip of paper in a fortune cookie reads, "The first step to better times is to imagine them" (Friedman, 1993). The imagination is a potent resource for generating images of other times—different, more favorable situations beyond the here and now (cf. Hall, Hall, Stradling, & Young, 2006; Yapko, 2003). When clients struggle to name what a preferred state of affairs might look like, questions tapping into their imaginations can help them.

de Shazer (1985, 1988, 1991) introduced a number of ingenious questions for accomplishing this. He prepared clients for his "crystal ball question" by introducing the notion that unaccountably, they uncover a real working crystal ball that can provide them with a picture of the future. The question to follow adds just enough of an imaginative twist to help some clients invoke a picture when otherwise their efforts to name preferences might draw a blank:

Imagine you look into the crystal ball and mysteriously an image materializes of you at a time in the future, a time when the problem is absent or perhaps still there in some form but somehow less of a problem for you. Describe to me what's going on for you—what you're doing, thinking, feeling, and so on—in that future moment.

Pichot and Dolan (2003) use a variation of this in which the crystal ball is replaced by a magic wand. Here they seek the description of just one change and use it as a starting point for developing a broader picture of a preferred outcome.

If you could wave a magic wand and change just one thing about yourself/your situation, what would it be?

Pichot and Dolan (2003) recount the example of receiving the answer, "I would be taller," which created an opening where none existed, but clearly one with limitations. They followed up with, "What difference would it make if you were taller?" With the response, "People would respect me more," they were on their way to articulating what in effect constitutes the flip side of a problem. But what, in real terms, would that increased respect look like in this man's day-to-day life? To answer this, they continued their inquiry by using the "Miracle Question" developed by colleagues Berg and de Shazer (cf. Berg, 1994; de Shazer, 1985) to help their client develop a detailed description of what a day would look like if he were respected more. The miracle question is not about solving problems miraculously, but it playfully draws on the notion of a miracle to conjure up imaginative exploration (see Box 7.7).

BOX 7.7

The Miracle Question

Suppose someone asked you to respond—quickly and off the cuff—with a clear and precise account of what the better person you've professed you want to be would actually do on a daily basis. Chances are you'd struggle to fill in the detail. The miracle question (de Shazer, 1985) was conceived by a team of counselors interested in helping clients to develop rich accounts of preferred outcomes. In effect, it involves "therapists and clients address[ing] the question, 'How do we know when to stop meeting like this?'" (de Shazer, 1991, 112). The miracle question skips over abstract talk by evoking a blow-by-blow account of a day on which the problem is absent or at least not the problem it has been. It is really the framework for a very detailed conversation, and it starts with some variation on the following.

Suppose you were to go to sleep tonight, and in the middle of the night, a kind of miracle were to happen so that even though your overall situation wouldn't change radically, the problem no longer would be in your life or at least wouldn't be a problem any more. There's a catch though: You don't know this has happened. What do you notice in the morning that begins to tell you this miracle has happened?

There are various ways to phrase this question; there are two noteworthy features of this version. First, to avoid answers like, "I'd be a successful and attractive movie star," it's emphasized that the client's overall life situation is not necessarily radically changed. The second point is related to the first: Certain problems (physical disabilities, loss of a loved one, etc.) can't realistically be expected to go away, but conceivably they could be less of a problem than they currently are.

Using the miracle question effectively involves breaking things down into small steps, paradoxically slowing down to speed up by evoking details that might otherwise be hard to access. Chapter 10 begins with the summary of Jorge's response to a miracle question posed by Maria.

Student Voices

Serena: Vivid Imagery Through the Miracle Question

In my work with my counselor we've focused on what I see as my over-analysing the relationship with my boyfriend. A moment that really resonated with me was when my counsellor asked me a Miracle Question. It was centered on me waking up and having a feeling that my analyzing mind, and the feelings and thoughts surrounding it, were at bay. My counselor helped to facilitate a vivid imagining of how that day would play out. I felt her curiosity surrounding the details of the day made the experience very real and tangible in my mind. I was able to physically feel what it would be like to carry out my day with a sense of security and calmness. Furthermore, her curiosity played a large part in my discovery that my boyfriend and I care so much about each other.

Letter From the Future

For some practitioners, the notion of a miracle runs the risk of suggesting an unrealistic quick fix to clients who may be reluctant for some reason to take concrete steps. An alternative means of evoking a description of preferences is to invite them to view the changes they will make from the other side—that is, to look back on them after the steps have been taken:

> *Suppose it's 5 years from now, and you've made a number of changes in your life so that [the problem] is gone or at least it's no longer a problem in your life. Things are going well for you; you're feeling good about yourself, your situation, and your relationships, and you sit down one sunny day to compose a letter to [a family member or close friend identified by the client or perhaps the client themselves]. The catch is that you're writing the letter* then *but it's to be read* now—*you're sending the letter back in time to describe your life in rich detail. How do you start?*

There are various ways to work with this: The client could take the time to compose the letter on the spot, the client could do this between sessions, or the counselor could walk the client through a verbal description of what the letter would contain by providing prompts:

> *Are you working? Retired?*
>
> *Where are you living? What country, area, city, neighborhood?*
>
> *What does your street, your home, the room you're sitting in look like?*
>
> *Do you live alone or with somebody?*
>
> *Who are your friends?*
>
> *What is different about your relationship with [the problem] at this time in the future? Is it out of your life altogether or present in a different way?*
>
> *What habits and practices do you have to cultivate good physical and mental health?*
>
> *What can you tell [your friend, your family member, yourself] about how you managed to deal with the problems/challenges you faced in the past?*
>
> *And so forth.*

Like the miracle question, this letter from the future relies on gathering plenty of concrete description, and it's the counselor's job to coach the client to attend to the detail. Many creative variations of these questions are possible; what they share is a playfulness that may uncover helpful concrete description harder to access through abstract questioning.

CHAPTER SEVEN RECAP

It's conceivable that an empathic presence suffices to reduce or eliminate some clients' concerns and helps them on the path to new horizons. But peoples' lives and the challenges they face are typically complex, and more often counselors need to rely on a broad range of skills to be helpful. Clients are usually hoping for some form of change to occur, and to help make that happen, counselors need to support clients in articulating both what is distressing them and what in particular they would like to be different.

This chapter introduced skills for supporting clients in defining problems and preferences. When clients name these explicitly without deliberate prompting, the foundational skills for reading and coordinating meaning introduced in Chapters 5 and 6 may suffice to establish a clear direction for the work. More often, though, it takes some active work by the counselor to conjointly define challenges and identify preferences. This happens early in the work and continues throughout because the landscape changes as counselor and client collaborate over time.

Problems and preferences are imbedded in clients' accounts, which typically speak to what they want less of and what they want more of. But the naming of problems and preferences is not always explicit, and it's sometimes necessary to get inside client stories, to draw forth their subjective experience by asking questions that place them squarely in the middle of the events they're describing.

When a client construes themselves as fundamentally the problem, both client and counselor can be pulled into an unproductive, problem-saturated view. Thinking about the person as separate from the problem(s) helps the counselor notice expressions of value and intention in the face of challenges rather than slide into a self-fulfilling, pathology-focused perspective. This possibility-oriented stance can be taken further with the linguistic practice of externalizing, involving the counselor's deliberate introduction of language that separates client and problem(s). Externalizing is particularly helpful in situations in which problems are pervasive in a client's consciousness, making it difficult for the client to notice experiences and events that stand outside of their difficulties.

Every expression of what is problematic is also the expression of a preference, though not always named explicitly, because it's more typical for clients to name problems than preferences. So the counselor often plays a key role in facilitating this by engaging the client's imagination and coaxing forth a detailed and concrete image of a preferred future. There are a number of playful, stylized options for doing this, including the crystal ball question, the magic wand question, the miracle question, and the letter from the future.

Once counselor and client have some starting definitions of problems and preferences, they're in a position to venture forward together, gauging the scope of both challenges and opportunities as they collaborate on achieving helpful change. The next two chapters introduce the skills involved in conducting this broader assessment. It's a process that typically reaps a bounty of unforeseen possibilities.

CHAPTER SEVEN DISCUSSION QUESTIONS

1. **Inside view.** Some books provide an outside-in view of the subject matter, never venturing into the subjectivity of the people featured. Others provide an inside view of the experience of the subjects, describing their experience and including their voices. Which sorts of books adopt each of these approaches? What characterizes each?

2. **Taking a position 1.** What does Karl Tomm (1987b) mean when he says, "To not take a position is to take the position of not taking one, that is, to be noncommittal" (p. 4)? What might be an example of a counselor's adopting a noncommittal position in relation to a client's reporting they had been sexually assaulted, for example? What might the counselor say or do (or not say and not do)?

3. **Taking a position 2.** What would be different about taking a position in relation to a client's account if (a) you did not know what within that account concerned the client versus (b) you did know what concerned the client? Provide an example.

4. **Collaboration and the client's subjective experience.** Why is it necessary to be aware of a client's subjective experience on an ongoing basis to collaborate with them? If not "collaboration," how would you describe the process if you were attempting to be helpful to the client without having a reading of the temperature of their experience? Provide an example.

5. **Foregrounding the client's voice.** What are the potential downsides of defining problems without adequately consulting the client? How about doing the same thing in relation to making conclusions about preferences?

6. **Problems and preferences.** Select one problem, concern, or challenge you face in your life. What is the flip side of the coin? When you consider your dissatisfaction with the problem, what does it say about what you want different, what you would prefer?

7. **Invoking imagination.** The examples of practices for envisioning preferences in this chapter feature stylized questions that set up a particular imaginative frame. Why do you think it helps to use this form of structured question?

CHAPTER SEVEN ACTIVITIES

1. **Withholding the temperature of a story.** In pairs, one person tells a brief story about some event that affected them significantly. The speaker does not reveal what the event was like for them: The speaker excludes any reference to what they were feeling, thinking, sensing, and so on, merely recapping "what happened." The listener does not intervene but takes note of (a) impressions of how the speaker experienced the event (positively, negatively, neutrally, etc.) and (b) what the listener sees and hears from the speaker that leads the listener to these conclusions. Debrief. Speaker, talk about what it was like to withhold your subjective experience. Were there ways you inadvertently shared your subjectivity, and if so, what was it you said or did? Listener, reflect on what it was like to not be told explicitly what the speaker's position was on events and on what basis you came to any conclusions about the speaker's subjective experience of the events.

2. **Getting inside the story.** Form pairs. Similar to the previous activity, the speaker tells the story of some significant event they experienced, attempting to exclude the subjective experience of the event. The listener asks questions to *actively elicit an inside view* of the events—that is, to get an account of what the experience was like for the speaker. Debrief. Speaker, comment on your experience of the listener's questions. How did the questions affect your connection to the story you were telling? Were there certain questions that were particularly helpful in locating you inside your own story? Listener, what was it like trying to come up with questions? Which aspects of the speaker's experience did you most often hone in on (e.g., feelings, thoughts, beliefs, images, sensations). What shifted for you as you gained more of an inside view of the speaker's experience?

3. **Externalizing 1: Restating.** In pairs, the speaker recaps some difficulty they have experienced or are experiencing without deliberately naming any problem in particular. Listener, pay attention to words or phrases used by the speaker (restating) that may be candidates for naming as externalized problems. Debrief after a few minutes. Listener, share the words and phrases that struck you. Speaker and listener, discuss which words or phrases might be useful in naming a problem or problems that are separate from the speaker.

4. **Externalizing 2: Paraphrasing.** Form pairs. This is the same as the previous activity, but this time the listener attends to and considers words or phrases *not* used by the speaker that might be useful in naming a problem or problems the speaker is dealing with (paraphrasing). Debrief after a few minutes. Listener, share the words or phrases that came to mind. Speaker, comment on the resonance and potential utility of these terms.

5. **Magic wand.** Form pairs. The speaker identifies some area they are struggling with somewhat that is suitable for sharing in this activity and responds to the question, If a wave of a magic wand could change just one thing for the better in your life, what would it be? The listener inquires about what difference that would make in the speaker's life, drawing on variations of the questions in the *Invoking Preferences Through Questions* section of this chapter as a way of expanding the speaker's account. Debrief. In which ways does the magic wand question lead to an expansion of preferences versus problems? What was challenging about sustaining this exploration, and what would have enhanced it further?

6. **Miracle question.** In pairs, the speaker identifies some area they are struggling with somewhat that is suitable for sharing in this activity. The listener poses the miracle question (see Box 7.7) and leads the speaker through a methodical description of their day in the wake of this unanticipated change. (For ideas about breaking down the day, see the account of Maria and Jorge's miracle question exchange at the beginning of Chapter 10.) Debrief. Speaker, what difference did it make to slowly and methodically outline a day on which the problem is absent or less problematic? Listener, what were the challenges associated with this practice? What seemed helpful and what tripped you up?

7. **Letter from the future.** Form pairs. The speaker identifies some area they are struggling with somewhat that is suitable for sharing in this activity. The listener presents the notion of composing a letter from the future, guided by the description in the Letter From the Future section of this chapter. The speaker writes the letter or is coached through what it would contain by the listener. Debrief. Speaker, what difference did it make to describe your new life situation by recounting it from the future? Listener, what was it like engaging in this practice? What seemed helpful and what challenged you?

Chapter 8

ASSESSMENT I

EVALUATING CHALLENGES AND COMPETENCIES

INTRODUCTION

Chapter 7 introduced skills for joining clients in identifying problems and preferences, a practice that accomplishes a number of important things:

1. clarifies what clients want more of/less of, thereby defining a direction for the work;

2. constructs a foundation for collaboration;

3. provides a temperature reading of events as they are recounted;

4. helps counselors position themselves relative to clients' accounts; and

5. captures clients' positions in relation to events they recount.

This chapter and the one after it are devoted to expanding those descriptions, rendering them in full color. The word *assessment* is a staple of the counseling literature, and so it is used here to describe the skills involved in expanding clients' accounts of their experiences. Typically, the word refers to gathering up a detailed picture of the client's overall situation, with a particular emphasis on problems and challenges. A broader view of the term adopted here reaches for a balance between (a) problems and challenges and (b) possibilities and opportunities. The difficulties people contend with are only one aspect of their diverse experiences. There is the very real danger of amplifying these through conversations that characterize clients' lives as problem saturated or their identities as damaged in some way (Frank, 1995, 2004; Lindemann-Nelson, 2001).

The term *assessment* is sometimes taken to mean a process primarily at the front end of a linear sequence of steps in engaging with clients, as in (a) assess and (b) treat. Although it is important to do a substantial amount of assessment up front for reasons we will explore, it is also important to *continue* assessing: People are moving pictures. Box 8.1 advocates for a broad approach to assessment that counterbalances the up-front documentation of problems with the ongoing generation of possibilities.

BOX 8.1

Narrow and Broad Versions of Assessment

The traditional view of assessment—whether it is formal, up front, and document-based or informal, ongoing, and verbal—tends to place the vast majority of focus on what is *not* working. A broader approach counterbalances this description of difficulties with an inventory of resources and opportunities and is more deliberate about capturing these in clients' language.

Narrow

- Focused on pathology, deficits, dysfunction

- Assigns problem-focused, codified labels

- Mostly up-front practice associated with client intake
- Precedes intervention
- Prime emphasis on formal protocols, questionnaires, forms, and so forth
- One-way information gathering

Broad

- Focused on challenges as well as exceptions, competencies, values, responses, preferences
- Solicits clients' experience of labels as well as self-descriptions in clients' language
- Ongoing practice never completed
- Is a form of intervention
- Balances formal and informal

- Two-way generation of rich description

As we shall see, assessment serves the important role of keeping an eye out for problems—both current concerns and potential problems that might exacerbate the client's situation. But assessment as it is presented in this chapter is far more than the identification of what is wrong. It pays just as much attention to what is right. And because genuine curiosity about what is right is itself influential and sets thoughts, feelings, and actions in motion, assessment is more than merely taking stock. It is also active intervention that begins the process of moving clients to preferred territory.

In many counseling contexts, assessment is associated with client intake. Often, before clients meet the counselors they will be working with, they are asked to complete a form by an intake worker, who may also solicit a verbal description of the presenting concerns. Alternately, counselors themselves may be expected to ask for this information. Depending on the requirements of the workplace and the regulatory context, practitioners may also be required to supply a diagnosis for clients, referencing the *Diagnostic and Statistical Manual of Mental Disorders* (text revision) (American Psychiatric Association, 2000). See Box 9.7 in Chapter 9 for more on working with the *Diagnostic and Statistical Manual of Mental Disorders.* Diagnoses are typically imbedded in formal assessment protocols. Appendix 1 provides one example of an assessment format that touches on the main areas of inquiry typically included in a formal protocol. Appendix 1 outlines potential areas of inquiry but does not provide a picture of the conversational processes involved in conducting that assessment; this chapter and the next take up that task.

A Moving Target

Whether assessment is done in a highly structured, formal manner or is a practice blended into a conversational exchange, the job of assessment is never completed; assessment is an ongoing practice. We don't blink when we notice this morning's prediction for the weekend weather is different than yesterday's—we expect the forecasts to evolve continuously because weather patterns are complex and in constant flux. *Complex* and *in constant flux* are good descriptors for peoples' lives as well. To count on an initial assessment to provide a workable snapshot that will serve the duration of a counseling collaboration is like expecting the long-range weather forecast for a special event 1 month away to hold consistent up to the day itself.

That flow of client experience outside of the counseling relationship also happens within it. So the picture of the client's experience shifts as client and counselor are transformed through their working relationship (Thomas, 2007). Over time, the task or tasks at hand may shift as the alleviation of one concern makes room for another. In addition to that, therapeutic conversations often uncover unanticipated concerns and yearnings worthy of expanded description. Safety and trust play roles in this: Imagine a complete stranger asking you to open up to them on your personal experience of shame, regret, loss, and so on. Not likely—we generally parse out such intimate sharing only after gauging the safety of the context, and this usually takes time. For all of these reasons, it's important that counselors continue to gauge the scope of their clients' experience throughout their work together, on the expectation that the picture will continue to change.

Identifying Problems and Challenges Early in the Process

As Box 8.1 indicates, both narrow and broad understandings of assessment feature the identification of problems. It is important for the following reasons to identify problems early in the process:

1. **To convey a concern for client welfare.** Inquiring about problems and challenges early is akin to asking, Where does it hurt?—it gives people a sense that "their experience is known" (Madigan, 2011, p. 87).

2. **To solicit clients' theories of change.** Finding out about past counseling experiences prepares counselors to adapt to clients' preferred ways of working and provides insight into their views about what makes a difference.

3. **To identify risk to others.** Counselors may be called on to protect the public, for instance, in cases wherein clients express violent intentions or make choices that could endanger others.

4. **To identify risk to clients.** Clients may be at risk of harm from others or to themselves. This includes potential physical or sexual abuse by adults on children, as well as suicidal ideation, substance abuse, or unprotected sex, among other reasons. Identifying these early may prevent a mishap or a tragedy.

5. **To uncover obstacles to therapeutic change.** Undetected, challenges such as health concerns, substance dependence, and so on can hamper forward movement.

You will notice that Box 8.1 also points to the formal assignment of a diagnostic label. Although this may be a requirement of counselors in some jurisdictions, in many others, counselors are not authorized to conduct formal diagnosis. In these latter cases, it's usually helpful to develop terminology with clients to designate problems or concerns for the reasons cited above. Although it's important to identify challenges likely to impair forward movement, it's also important to remember that a persistent focus on problems may affirm the problem-saturated accounts frequently brought to the counselor's door. Client experience is not merely *discovered* in counseling but *constructed* as well through interactions with the counselor. Everything the counselor says and does has an impact on the client's experience, and ongoing assessment that is all about problems constructs a bleak picture not likely to incite much positive energy for change.

Discussion of assessment in this and the next chapter is centered on what goes on face-to-face between therapist and client, most often after a formal, structured intake assessment done by a different practitioner. The information garnered in that prior assessment adds useful context to the conversations to follow and may provide a starting point for a face-to-face meeting. The sections that follow feature ideas and practices for engaging with clients directly around key questions worthy of assessment, regardless of what has previously been garnered through formal protocols.

PREVIOUS COUNSELING AND THE CLIENT'S THEORY OF CHANGE

Even before talk of problems or concerns begins, assessment is under way. Asking the client, "Did you have any problems finding your way here?" begins to provide a picture of the client's lifestyle (e.g., did the client walk, bike, take a bus, or drive? Did they skip out from work or secure a babysitter for young children? etc.). Inquiring about whether the client has consulted a counselor previously provides more useful information. When the client has, it makes sense to follow up with questions about whether they found the process helpful. If the process was helpful, what exactly made the difference? The answer to this is of course a gold mine to a counselor hoping to facilitate a productive collaboration. If the process wasn't helpful, what did they find unhelpful? This may be equally helpful in suggesting practices to avoid. In the excerpt from their first session, below, Daniel mines the exchange with Maria about her previous counseling experience, collecting a lot of useful information that will inform his work with her.

Daniel: *Have you ever been to a counselor before, Maria?*

Maria: *Yeah, that's part of the reason I got interested in becoming a counselor myself. Whoops [laughs and then grows serious]. I was 17 and very mixed up after breaking up with a boyfriend.*

Daniel: *How was that experience for you?*

Maria: *Good. Definitely helped me get through a rough patch.*

Daniel: *What was helpful?*

Maria: *The counselor was a good listener. She made a lot of space for me to process things. She didn't judge me.*

Daniel: *So you felt heard. [Maria nods.] And understood? [She nods again.] If you could point to one thing that seemed particularly helpful, what would it be?*

Maria: *She helped me see that a lot of my emotions made sense. That was a relief.*

Daniel: *Sounds like you'd been carrying around a lot of self-judgment.*

Maria: *A backpack full.*

Daniel: *And your counselor helped you revise your relationship with yourself.*

Mara: *That's a good way to put it.*

Daniel: *Anything that didn't work for you? I'd like to avoid more of the same!*

Maria: *She could get a little preachy at times. Not a huge problem. I just tuned out when she did.*

Daniel: *If you could replay that counseling experience, what would you do differently? What would your counselor do differently?*

Maria: *Not too much. I think I'd be quicker to name what was bothering me most. Not sure what she would do differently, other than fewer speeches about what it's like to be an adolescent.*

Daniel: *So you've been a client, and now you're studying counseling. I don't know if you have any ideas about how the process works. What do you see your role as, and how do you see my role?*

Maria: *I think my job is to do most of the talking, to let you know what's on my mind and, with your help, to work it through.*

Daniel: *Work it through?*

Maria: *Sort it out, I guess. I can get overwhelmed and have trouble seeing things from a distance.*

Daniel: *So I can help you do that? What would that take?*

Maria: *Mostly asking questions to help me make connections between things.*

Daniel: *Okay. We could give that a shot. I'm assuming you have some degree of hopefulness in coming here today. Could you tell me more about that hope?*

Maria: *I just think the process works—though I've been having doubts at my practicum lately! I don't think there's anything seriously wrong with me. But I do think I need some support sorting out my thoughts and feelings.*

In inquiring about a client's previous experience with counseling, the counselor is also beginning to develop a picture of what Duncan and Miller (2000) call the "client's theory of change." This uncovers the client's ideas about what makes counseling helpful and indicates what they expect from the counseling process. All of this is useful to the counselor, who can make adjustments to how they proceed as a result.

It would be unreasonable to expect counselors to be chameleonlike, radically modifying their practices to match each new client. But even though counselors develop their own styles—influenced by personal histories, dispositions, values, role models and mentors, philosophical perspectives, theoretical influences, and so on—there is always room for adjusting practice in accordance with the unique expectations and learning styles of clients. If a client reports they "learned to talk myself down" last time, it may be helpful this time to explore the internalized messages or self-talk currently hampering them, with an eye to generating alternatives. If the client says, "I just needed a place to vent and to shed all those pent-up tears," the counselor might prepare to make plenty of space for expressing emotion.

Reflection 8.1

If you have been or currently are a client of therapy yourself, reflect on what seems to make a difference for you in working on challenges in your life. Is it important for you to lay things out logically and organize your thinking? Or perhaps you find it most useful to have a venue to vent strong emotion. Maybe it's having an empathetic listener who helps you to regroup and move forward. If you haven't consulted a therapist before, reflect on what processes you rely on to get you through your biggest stresses and challenges. For instance, do you "talk to yourself," or is it more important to discuss things with others? Are you more inclined to seek solutions, or do you prefer to let things go on the assumption that "this too shall pass"? Your reflections on all of these questions constitute your theory of change.

EVALUATING RISK OF HARM

The previous chapter explored the importance of problem definition for preparing to work constructively with clients. The evaluation of risk is another important reason for developing a picture of what is problematic early in the process. Counselors have an ethical obligation to protect against harm—both harm perpetrated on members of the public and harm against clients themselves. As indicated above, there is far more to assessment than measuring problems, but the importance of evaluating risk should not be underestimated. In some cases, this evaluation may begin with formal assessments that precede the first sessions with clients, but in these cases it's still important that counselors clarify and expand on indications of risk that might be contained in intake summaries.

Harm to Others

The possibility of violence and abuse against others is an obvious risk. In cases in which clients report challenges with temper or anger or speak of relational conflicts, it's a good idea to gather an expanded description of these. Here are some questions that may be useful in doing that:

> *Could you paint a picture of what you do when, as you said, your "temper gets the better of you"?*
>
> *What would I see if I were watching you at a time when the anger was at its greatest?*
>
> *You mentioned Irene has expressed concern about those mood swings you talked about. What would she say are the most serious effects of these on her?*
>
> *Which kinds of things have you done under the influence of that anger that you regret the most?*
>
> *Do you worry that the temper could get out of hand? If so, what picture do you have of what might happen?*
>
> *You talked of saying hurtful things to the kids. Could you give me examples?*
>
> *You said the rage sometimes expresses itself in abusive language. How about action? Have you ever hit or assaulted anyone during these rages?*
>
> *Would you say any of this happens within earshot of the children?*
>
> *You talked of "nonstop partying." Where are the children when this is going on?*
>
> *How do you manage to provide for the kids when you're using?*
>
> *When you say that sometimes "you really want to hurt her," what's your image of what that would look like?*
>
> *You mentioned a [weapon]. Do you have access to one?*

Notice that in the examples above, the questions are often linked to specific things clients have already said (i.e., preceded by paraphrasing and restating), so they are less likely to be experienced as intrusions into their private lives. Because of shame and concerns about judgment, it can be very difficult to speak about violence and abuse; it takes sensitivity and skill on the part of counselors to ensure these topics are not glossed over and simultaneously avoid a tone of interrogation that runs the risk of shutting down that conversation. To engage clients in evaluating their potentially hurtful actions, it helps to simultaneously investigate "signs of safety" (Turnell & Edwards, 1999;

Turnell & Hogg, 2007)—the steps they are already taking to reduce the risk of harm to loved ones.

> *Where did you get the idea about taking a "time-out"? What difference has it made?*
>
> *How have you been able to remember the time-outs even when the anger grabs hold of you?*
>
> *What difference has it made in the tension between you to create space, those holidays from the relationship you were talking about?*
>
> *If you decided you needed to leave, whom would you call, and where would you go?*

The risk of physical abuse is always an important concern. With children, counselors have additional responsibilities to ensure the children are protected against emotional abuse, which includes the witnessing of violence and verbal attacks, and neglect, which is the failure to provide the necessary care.

The risk of sexual abuse is another area of concern that can be particularly difficult to talk about because this form of abuse most often occurs in private and is shrouded in secrecy. An in-depth exploration of that topic is beyond the scope of this text; however, many resources are available (cf. Calder, 2008; Smith, 1995). As with any form of harm, it is useful to catch up on current circumstances if a client reports a past history of difficulty in relation to abuse.

Besides the usual conceptions of violence and abuse, there are other ways in which one's actions can be harmful to others. One example that's become far more prevalent in the wake of AIDS is engaging in unprotected sex. This is clearly harmful behavior, particularly in a case wherein a client has tested positive for HIV or has been diagnosed with AIDS and especially if partners are not notified. Gathering relevant details in this instance provides the opportunity to educate the client about risks they may or may not have anticipated.

Harm to the Client

Alongside the possibility that clients may be deliberately or inadvertently posing a risk to others, they may themselves currently be the targets of violence or abuse or at risk of harm. For the reasons cited above, clients will not always be forthcoming about this. Significant power differentials may be at play in their situation, and thus a disclosure would escalate the harm. This is particularly the case with younger clients, for whom a range of indicators may signal abuse and are worthy of further exploration. Some of these are detailed in Appendix 2. Because of the risk of escalation in harm, it isn't enough to press for further details without being prepared to address client safety. In many cases, it will be important to collaborate with clients in developing "safety plans" (Niolan et al., 2009) to ensure they have options to fall back on to remove themselves from dangerous situations. With younger clients, counselors are required to contact the appropriate authorities to secure help when abuse is happening or at risk of occurring.

Self-Harm

It's also possible that clients are at risk of inflicting serious harm on themselves. Depending on the policies of particular workplaces, counselors may be required to check for suicidality in initial meetings with clients if this was not addressed in previous intake assessments. In other situations, detailed assessment for this form of risk is initiated when clients indicate serious depression, sadness, loss, discouragement, self-critique, and so on.

It is very common for counselors in training to feel the burden of concern associated with the possibility of working with suicidal clients. Being prepared for this eventuality through prior reading and training helps to diminish this worry. There are many useful written resources available on this topic (cf. Newman, 2004; Sommers-Flanagan & Sommers-Flanagan, 1995), and many communities have organizations devoted to ongoing training for responding to suicidality. The most important resource—and one that greatly relieves an undue sense of individual responsibility—is consultation: As with other challenging therapeutic situations, practitioners should remember that they can and should always consult colleagues and supervisors in gauging a helpful response to a suicidal client. Appendix 3 provides an outline of some key steps in the assessment of suicidality.

KEEPING DIVERSITY VISIBLE THROUGH A STANCE OF CURIOSITY

The practice of assessment can restrict or expand our view of clients, depending on the assumptions guiding the process. Following on the assumption that people are representative of relatively clearly defined, universal "types" (cf. Donnellan & Robins, 2010; Thomson, 1998), assessment becomes focused on ascertaining which type sits across from you. Such an approach is efficiently streamlined but dishonors cultural diversity—not just at the level of race or ethnicity but extending to each individual client (Arthur & Collins, 2010; Lee et al., 2009; Monk, Winslade, & Sinclair, 2008; Pope-Davis & Coleman, 2001; Robinson, 2005; Robinson-Wood, 2009).

Although there is usefulness in identifying similarities in problems faced by diverse clients, the expectation that any particular client fits the category in mind tends to dull the senses as far as attending to what makes this particular client different. Rosenhan (1973) and colleagues dramatically illustrated this phenomenon in a landmark study with confederate psychiatric patients. These pseudo-patients exhibited no symptoms of mental illness but gained admission to several psychiatric institutions after (falsely) claiming they were hearing voices. After being admitted, the research participants responded honestly to psychiatric staff member questions, reporting no further problems, and made no efforts to portray themselves as people dealing with mental illness. Afterward, staff reports of these pseudo-patients described them as exhibiting the features of serious psychopathology. This was a case of what is known as confirmatory bias: Research participants were assumed to inhabit the category of the mentally ill, and psychiatric staff members interpreted what they saw as evidence of that illness, thereby confirming their assumptions.

There is always a risk of looking past clients, caught in the headlights of some category; we all do this on a daily basis with friends and family when we assume we have heard enough to "get it" and we stop listening. This is where the quality of beginner's mind and the practice of not understanding—both introduced in Chapter 5—are particularly useful. So is the fundamental stance of curiosity—a suspension of assumptions that uncovers the unexpected. To look beyond neat categories is to defy a steadily growing expectation of insurance companies, managed care organizations, and so on to provide a tidy snapshot of people and their situations. As such, it is an ethical stance vis-à-vis clients because assessment is far more than the mere gathering of information—it is inescapably active intervention with real repercussions for the lives of the people assessed.

ASSESSMENT AS INTERVENTION: SELECTIVE CURIOSITY

There is no more useful tool of assessment then curiosity itself. You may know someone—or perhaps you're such a person yourself—with an abiding interest in people that expresses itself through ongoing questions about career, hobbies, families, personal histories, and so on. Questions like these expand the picture of peoples' lives, providing useful information to anyone intending to be helpful. Later in this chapter you'll be introduced to frameworks for guiding those questions.

Curiosity—but not an indiscriminate curiosity—is an indispensable attribute for the thorough practice of assessment. Assessment is more than mere information gathering; it's more accurately intervention in itself (Madsen, 2007) because all of our interactions with clients influence how they experience themselves and the issues that confront them. Curiosity can be experienced as discouraging or empowering, depending on its focus. As a result, assessment needs to be conducted with the same ethic of care that informs any other aspect of practice.

Reflection 8.2

Think about some problem or challenge you have faced or are currently facing. Be highly deliberate in your curiosity about your engagement with this challenge, asking yourself only the following questions:

Despite any discouragement and setbacks, which important personal values did I/do I attempt to uphold and realize in my engagement with this challenge?

What difference does it make to you—to your energy, your hopefulness, your morale, and so forth—when your curiosity is focused on this question? How does it lead you to feel about yourself and about your prospects for dealing with further challenges in the future?

BOX 8.2

Who's in the Mirror? Generating Experience Through Assessment

Madsen (2007) reminds us that "the questions we ask in assessment not only collect information but also generate experience" (p. 45). When counselors characterize clients based on assessments, they shape the way they think about their clients and influence their colleagues' views of the clients. Perhaps most important, they also influence clients' views of themselves. As Adrienne Rich put it, when someone in authority such as a teacher or a counselor "describes the world and you're not in it, there is a moment of psychic disequilibrium, as if you looked into a mirror and saw nothing" (cited in Bruner, 1990, p. 32). Here are some questions for ensuring this does not happen:

- What are the effects of our characterizations of clients on our view of them?
- How are their perspectives and language built into our characterizations?
- What are the effects of our characterizations on our clients' views of themselves?
- How do our characterizations affect our relationships with our clients?
- How do our characterizations lead our colleagues to think about our clients?
- Which sorts of conversations do our characterizations encourage with and about our clients?
- Do our characterizations invite connection, respectful curiosity, openness, and hope?
- Do our characterizations encourage the enactment of our preferred relational stance with clients?

Source: Adapted and expanded from Madsen (2007).

As seen in Chapter 2, John Austin (1965) provided some intriguing reminders about the way our utterances are actions themselves. They do things; they set off chains of events; they have very real implications in the world. This is more obvious perhaps when a judge announces a verdict or an influential investment tycoon makes a pronouncement about the prognosis of the stock markets. But it also happens when we distill clients' lives when sharing in case conferences or assign labels to meet institutional requirements. Many people who consult counselors are experiencing discouragement in their lives, bumping up against what they take to be evidence that they are not capable, not worthy. Do our assessments confirm those sentiments or provide hopeful alternatives by highlighting not just challenges but also possibilities? Assessment involves selective curiosity because, like all therapeutic interactions, its purpose is not merely to gather information but to be helpful to the person before us.

ASSESSING COMPETENCE

Madsen (2007) laments the lost opportunities associated with the practice of assessment, saying, "The most frequent misuse of assessments is when they become a list of all the things that are wrong with clients" (p. 72). Berg (1994) provides an example of this sort of assessment, frequently confronted in frontline practice:

> You will often see a detailed account of what a poor childhood a client had: how she was abused, grew up in a foster home, has no contact with her mother, and was "hooked up" with shady characters who used her. This assessment may go on to describe how she had four children by different men, and how she neglects and abuses her children now. (p. 17)

The single-minded focus on deficit in Berg's (1994) example is unfortunately not unusual. As Madsen (2007) has said,

> ironically, the field of mental health has been much better at emphasizing illness than health. We have many more tools for discovering how things went wrong with clients than for developing develop steps to help them do better in their lives. (p. 72)

Madsen (2007) offers a clear-headed critique of tendencies to "pathologize" clients—indeed, not just clients but *ourselves* and *each other* in a society that Gergen (1994) says has been overrun with "progressive infirmity"—the tendency to proliferate more and more categories for naming our deficits and deficiencies. Counselors can offer an antidote to these trends through assessment practices designed to take stock of all that will be useful to clients as they strive to move forward in life.

When you consider that clients consult counselors when faced with challenges in their lives, it makes sense to conclude they must already be drawing on some competencies by virtue of their coping sufficiently to arrange and show up for an appointment. Which qualities did it take to make the call despite a pervasive sense of discouragement? Which skills did they call on to locate help in the midst of chaotic circumstances? The answers to these and other questions oriented to what clients bring to challenging situations are equally part of *assessment*, in a broad sense of the word.

The assessment of competence requires being on the lookout for examples of client skills, knowledges, qualities, resources, and so on that may not be named explicitly but lurk between the lines. Box 8.3 provides an example of a client's story, with a challenge to readers to uncover competencies not named explicitly. After all, clients don't normally tell counselors outright about the skills and knowledges they bring to bear on the situation at hand.

BOX 8.3

Resha's Story: Competence Amid Challenges

Resha arrives late for her session, out of breath and clearly distraught. She says she's been sleeping badly, worried about her children, ages 2, 4, and 7. Resha's estranged husband has been telephoning her at all hours to unleash angry tirades and has dropped by unexpectedly more than once, threatening physical violence in front of their children. Resha says these incidents haven't escalated because she's refrained from responding to his taunts, but she's aware the children are "not themselves," so she decided she needed to seek help.

The receptionist at the counseling service seemed to struggle with Resha's Arabic accent and originally suggested she contact a local agency offering services to immigrants. Resha persisted, asking to speak to an intake worker. She told the intake worker there is a long waiting list at the other agency and said she'd been told she falls within the counseling agency's catchment area for services. This morning, Resha arranged for her sister to walk the eldest child to school and dropped the other two at the home of a friend for whom she often offers child care. She says after a sleepless night it was difficult holding it together when her 7-year-old asked why his "daddy was mad," but she told him, "Daddy is having a hard time," before giving him a hug as he walked out the door. At her friend's house, Resha borrowed enough money for return bus fare, offering the reassurance that she would pay her back Tuesday, when she'll earn 3 hours' wages for cleaning a neighbor's apartment. As she relates this last detail, Resha laughs as she tells her counselor her family will be "going on a diet" until next Tuesday.

At first glance, Resha's account is the story of a marginalized woman struggling with difficult life circumstances—certainly a plausible description, but one that does not encompass the possibilities also imbedded in her story. Look more closely, and you'll discover the following competencies, among others:

- bilingualism;
- the ability to placate an aggressive or violent person in order to deescalate the situation;
- the capacity to discern her children's emotional/psychological states and to make decisions accordingly on their behalf;
- the use of language to soften an abrasive situation for her children without misrepresenting the seriousness of the situation;
- the capacity to offer physical comfort to her child;
- the personal insight to identify her need for help;
- the knowledge of appropriate services offered in her area along with the awareness of her right to services at the agency she contacted;
- persistence and persuasiveness in the face of attempts to direct her elsewhere;
- the maintenance of reciprocal, supportive family and community relationships;
- the ability to secure part-time work for wages; and
- a sense of humor.

We are more inclined to take notice of competencies such as the ability to operate heavy equipment, fly a light airplane, or cook French cuisine than to identify the pervasive "skills of living" (White, 2007) that people draw on regularly for their day-to-day survival. Discerning these latter competencies is a key aspect of assessment, broadly defined, and inevitably becomes easier with practice. Later chapters will introduce skills for capitalizing on competencies in a variety of ways.

Maria (counselor):	*Jorge, I understand that one of the dilemmas you're facing now is the question of how and when to come out to your parents—your dad in particular.*
Jorge:	*Yup. "How and when," but not if.*
Maria:	*No, you've made that clear: You said something has to change here, and accepting the situation is not going to do it. How did you come to that conclusion?*
Jorge:	*It's time.*
Maria:	*It's time?*

Jorge:	*I just know it's the right thing and the right time.*
Maria:	*What tells you that?*
Jorge:	*It's a sense I have. I know I can trust it.*
Maria:	*Can you tell me more about that sense? What kind of a sense is it?*
Jorge:	*It's a feeling I get; I don't know how to describe it—just a feeling. Like a certainty. It tells me the decision's made, no need for more turning it over and over in my mind.*
Maria:	*Wow, sounds like a useful thing. And it's something you can trust?*
Jorge:	*I have so far. Hasn't steered me wrong.*
Maria:	*It just comes out of the blue?*
Jorge:	*No, nothing like that. I have to work on an issue myself before it comes.*
Maria:	*Work on it?*
Jorge:	*Mull it over, look at it from different angles, talk to a friend. That gives the feeling a chance to come up.*
Maria:	*You've got to do your homework. What would you call that feeling?*
Jorge:	*I don't know. It's the sense of being sure about something. Sureness maybe. Is that a word?*
Maria:	*Hmmm. Sureness. It is now! How would it be if we keep on the lookout for the sureness as we work together? Sounds like a useful resource.*
Jorge:	*Sounds good to me.*

An interesting thing happens when we begin to pay attention to competencies, and not just problems, when engaged in assessment. We start to notice insights people have, decisions they arrive at, steps they take. We begin to see them as agents of their lives rather than embattled victims of challenging circumstances. This change in perspective uncovers critical detail often left out of conventional assessment: peoples' responses to the challenges they face. A general orientation to competence is more likely to uncover these, but more helpful still is a repertoire of questions deliberately aimed at inviting forward accounts of peoples' active agency. To understand how this line of inquiry works, it will be useful to look at the distinction between (a) questions focused on effects and (b) response-based questions.

Reflection 8.3

Think about some significant challenge you have confronted in your own life—something that you may not have defeated or entirely vanquished from your life but that you survived, learned from, overcame in the sense that it is not currently the issue it once was. Allow yourself to limit your curiosity to just one thread:

Which abilities or competencies did you draw on to cope with this challenge?

You may find yourself being able to itemize things you did, said, or felt that helped; see if you can take it a step further and give a name to the skill that you identify, even if you have to make up a term. Once you have done this, ask yourself,

What difference does it make to isolate and name a life skill that you brought to bear? Is this a revelation to you or the affirmation of something you already knew?

EFFECTS AND RESPONSES: FOREGROUNDING ACTION

Effects Questions

There are various reasons for asking about the effects of distressing events in a person's life when engaged in assessment. A client describes an incident, and we become curious about its impact on them. We ask, "How did you feel about that? What was that like for you?" Questions that solicit the effects of events on a person's life have a role in therapeutic conversations for the following reasons, among others:

1. They confirm whether an incident was favorable or not, providing the temperature reading referred to in Chapter 7.

2. They communicate empathic acknowledgment of the client's distress, providing a venue for the client to share their concerns in safety and to a compassionate audience.

3. Learning about the impacts of events contributes to a broader understanding of the dimensions of the client's experience, which is important for the ongoing coordination of meaning between counselor and client.

All of this is useful; however, a single-minded focus on effects can inadvertently position the client as a passive recipient of hardship, thereby obscuring their actions—their responses to these events. Note how this operates in the effects-focused questions below:

What idea did that put into your head?

How is your appetite since she died?

What was the fallout of that incident?

What became of your enthusiasm as a result of that failure?

How's your confidence in the wake of being rejected?

Look closely and you'll see the wording of the above questions paints a picture of the client as the passive recipient of repercussions emanating from a precipitating event. The very simple graphic in Box 8.4 captures this. Without saying so explicitly, the questions imply a causal connection between the event and some effect, portraying the client as docile or submissive, someone who had something happen to them. However, as Foucault (1980, cited in Carey, Walther, & Russell, 2009) compellingly demonstrated, "people are never just passive receivers of what life throws at them, there is always some point of resistance" (p. 322). Questions that solely focus on effects overlook this active quality of a person's experience. As a result, they may inadvertently confirm passivity—a familiar sense for a person struggling with challenges—through the absence of attention to the client's responses to the trials facing them.

BOX 8.4

Effects-Focused Questioning

CLIENT ← EVENT

Questions that are preoccupied with what events did to clients help to convey concern and provide part of the picture necessary for a thorough assessment of a person's situation. However, excessive reliance on effects-focused questioning may inadvertently construe people as passive, making the effects out to be inevitable because they are causally determined. An unintended consequence of this form of questioning is that it may reinforce a sense of passive victimization at a time when people are struggling with life events.

Allan Wade (Todd & Wade, 2004; Wade, 1997, 2007) provides rich possibilities for addressing this dilemma. His work is inspired by, among other sources, James Scott's (cf. 1990, 2009) observation that wherever there is oppression, there is resistance. To put this differently, when things happen to people, they respond. Inquiring about responses is a powerful way to highlight and build on action that makes a difference.

Response-Based Questioning

Wade and his colleagues (Coates, 1997; Coates, Bavelas, & Gibson, 1994; Coates & Wade, 2007; Todd & Wade, 2004) have conducted extensive research on the language used by judicial systems in the wake of violent events, noting that accounts of victims' active responses in the face of these are conspicuously absent. Yet they point out that "resistance to violence is ubiquitous" (cf. Campbell, Rose, Kub, & Nedd, 1998; Epston, 1989; Epston, Maisel, & Borden, 2004; Goffman, 1961; Lempert, 1996; White, 2007).

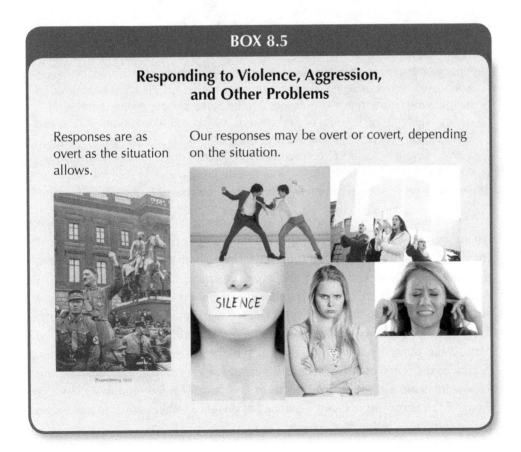

BOX 8.5

Responding to Violence, Aggression, and Other Problems

Responses are as overt as the situation allows.

Our responses may be overt or covert, depending on the situation.

SILENCE

Look carefully and you will find that when people are transgressed against—whether it is whole societies oppressed by occupying military forces (Churchill, 1993; Scott, 1990) or individuals battered by violent partners (Campbell et al., 1998; Lempert, 1996)—they don't merely take it but exhibit resistance in proportion to the danger at hand. In other words, people respond but will usually take steps to ensure their responses don't further jeopardize their safety. So not all responses are equally overt, but they are substantial nevertheless. These observations suggest that an overemphasis on effects can blind counselors and clients to clients' active responses to events.

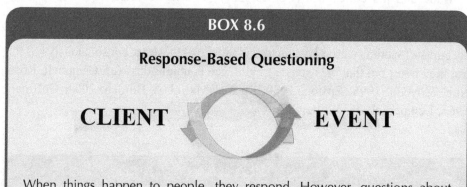

BOX 8.6

Response-Based Questioning

CLIENT   **EVENT**

When things happen to people, they respond. However, questions about these responses are often left out of standard assessment practices, which have a tendency to focus solely on the effects of events on clients. Determining people's responses to events provides a fuller picture of the events themselves. It may highlight the severity of the situation by foregrounding efforts taken to resist violence or overcome obstacles. The addition of curiosity about clients' active responses to life circumstances foregrounds their agency and avoids corroborating accounts of passive victimization.

This change of focus is illustrated by the graphic in Box 8.6, which does not ignore the impact of events on people but moves the primary emphasis to the client's response to the event. It is through attention to both dimensions of the description that the fullest account of the event emerges. Consider that the client's description of the severity of the impact of an event ("I was completely terrified," "It left me feeling worthless," "I felt beaten down," etc.) illuminates what might fairly be called the heroic (Duncan & Miller, 2000) quality of any response on their part. At the same time, a rich account of the client's response helps to fill out a picture of the scope of what the client is up against ("I stayed very quiet because I knew he could kill me," "I would sit in my yard for a few minutes a day even though I felt terror just opening the door," "I bought an alarm clock to make sure I got myself out of bed in the morning," etc.).

Reflection 8.4

Think of a time when someone transgressed against you. This need not be an instance of violence or abuse; if it is, consider first whether you feel it would be safe and potentially helpful to reflect on it privately and briefly here as you pause from your reading. Choose an incident about which a thin account might easily depict you as the passive recipient of the transgression. Ask yourself the following questions:

What was it about the circumstances that may have made it difficult or inappropriate to respond in a particularly overt manner?

What did you do (or not do) that reflected your unwillingness to participate in the transgression as a willing recipient?

What might you have felt, thought, or done that showed you were not colluding with the transgression but rather protesting or resisting it in some way—whether obvious or subtle?

What impact did these reflections have for you? Were you able to identify your responses to the transgression? Did they confirm something you already knew or help you tap into understandings previously unavailable to you?

One reason clients' responses are typically overlooked in assessment is the preoccupation with pathology mentioned earlier—a focus on dysfunction purportedly caused by trauma and other precipitating circumstances. A second reason is the subtlety of many responses. As Nora's story in Box 8.7 illustrates, transgressions of all sorts occur in situations in which there is a significant power differential between perpetrator and perpetrated, and in these circumstances, it makes sense that responses are subtle, if not downright covert.

BOX 8.7

Nora's Story: From Effects to Responses

Allan Wade (speaking at a seminar titled "Witnessing Victims' Resistance to Violence and Oppression," October 2010) has countless anecdotes illustrating the common tendency to see people's behavior, thoughts, and emotions as effects of trauma or other negative events. At the same time, these stories highlight the possibility of making sense of things in a different and more helpful way. The story of Nora exemplifies a response-based account of her experience.

(Continued)

(Continued)

Nora is a middle-aged Native elder, a respected educational administrator, who shared with Wade that throughout her life she had been "unable" to cry, including in circumstances wherein expressions of loss or grief seemed the appropriate response. As Nora expanded her account of her experience, Wade learned that she had been a student in a residential school characterized by a culture of strict discipline and corporal punishment. This was a topic Nora had chosen never to speak about in public settings.

One way of making sense of Nora's failure to cry might have been to see it as a deficit in affect caused by early childhood trauma. With persistent curiosity about Nora's responses to the transgressions against her, Wade invited forward a very different story. Nora recalled an incident in which she and her classmates stole a few apples from a neighbor's tree overlooking the school grounds. When they were caught, they were called before the nun in charge of meting out discipline—more accurately, physical assault—to the schoolchildren. They stood in a line, awaiting their punishment, which was typically to be strapped until their hands bled onto the floor. One by one, the children whispered supportive directives to each other down the line until they reached Nora's ears: "Don't cry."

It is not hard to see the children's behavior in this situation as active resistance in the face of violence perpetrated against them. Like much resistance, it was improvised in the moment with no guarantee that the response would lessen the harm perpetrated (in this case, there was a high risk of further harm as a consequence). It was an expression of dignity: Nora's comment on the children's withholding of their tears was, "We would never give them that."

This childhood account also makes it possible to understand Nora's current actions as a continuation of that resistance—in other words, to understand her withholding of her tears as a response to, rather than the effect of, events in her life. Is this the "true" interpretation of her experience? Perhaps that's the wrong question, and it would make more sense to wonder whether this equally plausible account is useful in the circumstances. Wade recaps how, in the wake of his conversations with Nora, she took up the invitation for the first time to speak in public about her experience of residential schooling. When Wade phoned her later for a recap, she said it didn't go quite as expected. She cried repeatedly during the presentation.

In deriving a full picture of what is going on in the life of a person, it is useful to consider various "biopsychosocial factors" (Rosen & Callaly, 2005) operating in their lives. However, this curiosity is counterproductive when limited to measuring, categorizing, quantifying, and naming only the *effects* of these. Too often assessment highlights events that happen to people, making childhood events out to be causal determinants of adult "disorders" (cf. Spitzer, 1981), at the expense of attending to the active steps people take to overcome the many obstacles in their path.

This is about personal agency as an alternative to passive victimhood. If there is any often-repeated cliché about counseling, it is the counselor's mantra, "I can't do it for you; it's up to you to change." In other words, counselors can provide all kinds of facilitative support, but it's clients who ultimately need to act in some way if they wish things to be different. In fact, of the many ways to describe counseling, one version is to depict it as a practice focused on supporting people in reconnecting with their personal agency. Counseling conversations dominated by language that characterizes clients as passive recipients of effects do not call forth agency and are less likely to promote change.

This is not to suggest counselors should interrupt clients who seem to want to speak about what they take to be the consequences of events in their lives. But it does mean listening with a second ear, what White (2007) calls "double listening," holding onto a curiosity about clients' personal agency—their active assertions of will—which may well have become invisible to them in the midst of difficulties. Box 8.8 shows how this curiosity can be turned into questions. You'll notice these questions often get at similar topics as do effects-focused questions, but they and also convey the expectation that what people do, say, think, and feel is not merely an outcome of an event but the expression of purpose and intention.

BOX 8.8

Foregrounding Responses

The gentle but persistent foregrounding of client agency is the expression of an ethic of care, a counselor's refusal to give up on a person who may be on the verge of giving up on themselves. There are always many ways to pose questions. Although the pairs of questions below touch on similar topics, you'll notice the response-based ones hone in on the client's personal agency. They are not neutral. They reflect an ongoing challenge to the view of the client as a passive victim of difficult circumstances.

The questions here are meant to give a taste of what changes when the counselor orients toward client agency, not to provide a formula. The skillful use of questions in general requires a careful responsivity to the client and lots of practice.

(Continued)

(Continued)

Effects-Focused Questions	*Response-Based Questions*
How did that affect you?	What did you do next?
What caused you to shut down emotionally?	How did you manage to withhold your emotions from him in the moment?
What did that get you thinking?	What sense did you make of that?
Why did you quit?	How did you know the time wasn't right for you to go on?
What was it like to be rendered helpless like that?	How do you think keeping quiet and still saved you from further harm?

Finding a balance between effects-focused questions and response-based questions is one of various challenges associated with generating a rich and useful picture of the client's situation. So the next chapter will revisit the topic, providing further ideas and practices associated with assessment.

CHAPTER EIGHT RECAP

Like many familiar counseling terms, the word *assessment* comes with some strong associations. In this case, the association is to pathology and dysfunction, so in this chapter I have worked hard to portray a wider approach to assessment—to demonstrate that it is not just about finding out what is going wrong but also thickening accounts of what is going right. Assessment is sometimes characterized as information gathering that precedes intervention; this chapter presents the alternate view that it is intervention. And it is never over: The practice of assessment is a multidimensional process that infuses all counseling conversations, offering the opportunity to affirm and amplify possibilities in addition to providing space for the client to speak about how they are struggling.

Assessment offers the possibility to celebrate the human capacity for growth and generativity (cf. Lopez, 2008; Snyder, Lopez, & Pedrotti, 2010; Southwick, Litz, Charney, & Friedman, 2012). This does not occur simply by adopting an optimistic demeanor, however; it involves an ongoing curiosity and well-crafted questions that elicit accounts of people as agents of their lives. This means inquiring not only about the effects of problems but also about clients' active responses to difficulties (Todd & Wade, 2004; Wade, 2007).

Another key point visited within this chapter is the reminder that assessment is not simply an up-front activity but rather an ongoing practice that happens session to session and even utterance to utterance. It's the practice of joining with clients in evaluating where things are at (this month, this week, this moment) and doing it in a way that points to where clients want to go.

This first of two chapters devoted to assessment has emphasized the possibilities inherent in an expanded view of assessment that incorporates an exploration of competence and agency. The next chapter continues the exploration of assessment, introducing skills for developing rich, multifaceted views of client experience.

CHAPTER EIGHT DISCUSSION QUESTIONS

1. **Uncovering problems.** Why is it important to identify the scope of problems early in conversations with clients? Provide examples of the repercussions of not doing this.

2. **Client theory of change.** What does this phrase point to? As a prospective client yourself, how would you characterize your own theory of change?

3. **Assessing risk.** Assessment has many facets, one of which is about minimizing potential harm. In this role, counselors are accountable not only to their clients but to the general public. Discuss.

4. **Assessment as intervention.** Why is it unfeasible to assess clients *prior* to intervening? What is the meaning of the phrase *assessment is intervention*?

5. **Doing things with words.** Austin (1965) writes of how speech is itself action that not only conveys impressions but sets off a series of events. Drawing from your own experience, provide an example of a label assigned to a child or adult, and describe some key events that unfolded in the wake of this practice.

6. **Labels: pros and cons.** Discuss the advantages and disadvantages of diagnostic labeling. In what ways might a diagnosis empower a person or open up possibilities? In what ways might it discourage a person or delimit their possibilities?

7. **Alternate labels.** Think of someone you know who has some formal label attached to them—perhaps a label around which the person organizes their identity. Reflect on the skills and qualities they bring to bear in dealing with challenges, and concoct alternate competence-oriented labels for the person.

8. **Confirmatory bias.** To what does this term refer? Describe an instance in your own life in which you have confirmed expectations about someone (whether favorable or unfavorable) by looking for evidence in support of your view and ignoring evidence to the contrary.

9. **From effects to responses.** Discuss the story of Nora in Box 8.7. What sense do you imagine she was making of her failure to cry when she came to see Allan Wade? Which prevalent ideas—both professional and popular—might have been influencing her self-judgment? What do you think may have shifted in her view of herself as a result of her response-based conversations with Wade?

CHAPTER EIGHT ACTIVITIES

1. **Theory of change.** Form pairs. Speaker, relate your theory of change based on your experience as a client or your experience having had someone be helpful to you through conversation. Listener, use the skills introduced in the previous chapters to develop a rich account with the speaker. Elicit a description of the previous helpful conversations and the specific aspects that proved helpful. Debrief. Once both partners have shared, compare notes about similarities and differences between the experiences.

2. **Noticing competence.** Form pairs. Speaker, recount the story of dealing with a significant life challenge. Listener, support the speaker in telling the story. Pay attention to (taking notes if necessary) the skills, qualities, resources, and so forth required by the speaker to cope with or overcome the challenge. Debrief. Listener, list the skills and so forth you witnessed, explaining how you identified these by drawing on specific material from the original story. Speaker, what was it like to have these skills and so forth recounted to you?

3. **Foregrounding competence.** This is the same as the previous activity, except the listener plays a more *active role* inquiring about skills, abilities, values, resources, and so forth that were actively employed by the speaker. Debrief. Speaker, what was it like to have the listener actively draw out your competencies? Listener, how did this orientation to ability and so forth affect your view of the speaker and shape the conversation?

4. **Response-based inquiry.** Form pairs. Speaker, share the description of a challenging event you experienced. If this was somewhat traumatic, please exercise judgment about disclosing in this context. Listener, inquire about the event, centering questions on the speaker's responses. Debrief. Listener, which challenges were associated with focusing on responses, and which responses did you identify? Speaker, what was the impact of having your responses foregrounded? What was it like to have less attention given to effects?

5. **Responses versus effects.** Form threesomes. As above, the speaker recaps a challenging event. Listener 1 asks about the event, focusing on the *effect* on the speaker of various incidents and interactions, while Listener 2 observes, taking note silently of the speaker's *responses* to the event. Listener 2, then takes over (while Listener 1 observes), drawing draws out an account of the speaker's responses. Debrief. Speaker, what was different about your experience of the two modes of inquiry? Listener 1, what was it like to focus exclusively on effects? What was it like to later witness the uncovering of responses? Listener 2, what was it like attending for responses in the original recounting that was focused on effects?

Chapter 9

ASSESSMENT II

ATTENDING TO THE WIDER CONTEXT

INTRODUCTION

Chapter 8 introduced an expansion of conventional views of assessment that makes lots of space for learning about client competences along with difficulties. This expanded approach to assessment is deliberately nonneutral—it takes a position *alongside* people versus the challenges they face, foregrounding skills and abilities often overlooked in the focus on deficit, holding to a view of people as agents in their own lives rather than passive victims of circumstances. Among its various features and purposes as described so far, assessment

1. sheds light on barriers and obstacles hampering change;

2. identifies areas of potential harm to clients or others;

3. uncovers resources, including client values, abilities, and key relationships;

4. provides a venue for clients' airing of effects, or repercussions, of events; and

5. renders visible clients' agency by highlighting active responses to circumstances.

This chapter introduces further skills associated with assessment. Here, the lens is widened, and its power is turned up as it were: Counselor and client team up to generate a view that encompasses the broader context and also has three-dimensionality.

The breadth of description referred to here pertains to context. Under the influence of individualistic Western traditions, conventional assessment sometimes halts its inquiry at the boundary of the skin, overlooking the contextual details that illuminate our understanding of why people act the way they do. When people's actions are seen in context, behaviors that at first appeared mystifying or even bizarre suddenly make sense.

The depth or three-dimensionality of description relates to the richness of accounts evoked in assessment. Evoking textured descriptions takes active work on the counselor's part: inviting an exploration of ideas and beliefs accompanying actions, inquiring about emotion associated with particular thoughts, and so on. Scanning the surrounding environment adds scope, but so does multilayered inquiry that portrays experience in the complexity worthy of a well-crafted novel.

This chapter adds a couple of other key considerations to the topic of assessment. The first relates to culture. It's important to remember that when we evaluate how someone is doing, we do this against some reference point. In a profession with well-established traditions of categorizing health and illness, practitioners are always at risk of gauging clients' experience against some normative yardstick. To counteract this, counselors must pay attention to the biases they hold while actively seeking to understand clients' cultural assumptions—assumptions that may not reflect socially dominant ideas and traditions and that in some cases may bump them up against local laws or expectations.

The chapter also touches briefly on the issue of trauma as it relates to assessment. Given that assessment is inescapably an intervention in itself, it's critical to avoid reperpetrating trauma through insensitive probing into painful memories.

CONSIDERING CONTEXT

The man stands in the pitch dark for most of his waking hours, tossing a button from one hand to the other. Most times, he fails. It falls to the floor, bouncing erratically, spinning off to some obscure corner before coming to rest. Each time, the man crouches on his hands and knees, feeling the cement floor with his fingers, seeking out the plastic disc. Reclaiming the button, he stands again and resumes the ritual, which he will repeat over and over again until exhaustion delivers sleep.

Sensible Accounts of Client Action

The above description, devoid of contextual detail, renders a man's actions utterly senseless—even bizarre. To gain insight into people's experience, we need to gain a picture of what phenomenologists call the "lifeworlds" they inhabit, to consider their thoughts, feelings, and actions in the context in which they occur. In sharing this example, A. Wade, speaking at an October 2010 seminar titled "Witnessing Victims' Resistance to Violence and Oppression," went on to reveal this is a factual account of a political prisoner's desperate effort to retain his sanity during a prolonged solitary confinement—an objective he achieved through unfathomable persistence and determination.

Stripped of their context, the man's actions may lead us to conclude he suffers from mental illness. Situated in the environment where they took place, the same actions lead us to diametrically opposed conclusions. As we learn more, the man's behavior becomes sensible—even heroic in proportions. There is an important lesson here for the practice of assessment. Research indicates that as many as 80% of people diagnosed with mental illness may have experienced major trauma in their lives (A. Wade, speaking at a seminar titled "Witnessing Victims' Resistance to Violence and Oppression," October 2010). As Victoria White (2001) points out, "the woman who was a victim of domestic violence may exhibit muscle tension, irritability, and sleep disturbance and would meet the criteria for generalized anxiety disorder" (p. 205). Gathering an enlarged picture of the context shifts our view of her. Understanding the context of people's experience allows us to see their actions as meaningful responses to circumstances, suggesting different avenues for going forward.

Reflection 9.1

Think of your initial encounter or encounters with someone you now know reasonably well and with whom you even may be quite close. Reflect on the things the person said and did when you first met them that were difficult for you to get a read on because you did not have much context for their life: You didn't have a sense of the family they came from, the person's living arrangements, their personal history, and so on. Do you remember any conclusions you came to at that time that no longer fit for you? What difference has it made to your view of the person to know more about the context of their life?

Countering Traditions of Individualism

The eminent anthropologist Clifford Geertz once said, "There is no such thing as human nature independent of culture" (cited in Bruner, 1990, p. 12). Nevertheless, popular representations would have us think otherwise. We are surrounded by individualistic portrayals of people, personified repeatedly by Hollywood as the rugged, gun-wielding hero who takes on the enemy single-handedly. Listen carefully to movie trailer voice-overs, and you may notice how often they open with variations on "One man. . . ." From the dusty, pistol-packing cowboy to the suave, tuxedoed secret agent, the lone character (usually male) relying on no one but himself is an enduring story motif.

The discipline of psychology, which plays a key role in influencing how counselors think and how they listen, mirrors this tradition in a variety of ways (Gergen, 1985, 1994, 2001). Psychology is more inclined to make sense of people's actions as expressions of their personalities than to understand them as responses to the wider ecology (Wade, 1997; A. Wade, speaking at a seminar titled "Witnessing Victims' Resistance to Violence and Oppression," October 2010). In this tradition, clients are frequently referred to as "individuals" and traits or types are often categorized and measured (cf. Matthews, Deary, & Whiteman, 2009; Mroczek & Little, 2006; Sloan, 2009; Thomson, 1998) at the expense of attending to the client in context (Brown & Augusta-Scott, 2007; Hoffman, 2002; Monk, Winslade, & Sinclair, 2008). This is not to suggest the focus on the individual is somehow wrong but just that it obscures some very useful elements of the wider picture.

Living things are relational beings. Consider, for example, the irregular pattern of rings in a tree's core: In addition to providing a window into the tree's makeup, the pattern provides a history of the tree's relationship with and responses within its ecological setting. One ring speaks of the fire that scorched the forest, and another is a reminder of the drought that killed off the less hardy trees. We are able to make sense of how the tree has developed when we gain a picture of the context of its growth. To merely acknowledge a client's expression of their experience without joining them in contextualizing it is to overlook critical information that makes the story sensible.

BOX 9.1

The Relational Self: Context and Assessment

first year growth

scar from forest fire

dry season

rainy season

People are relational beings. To gain a rich picture of the self, it's important to look beyond individuals to observe them, as we do other living things, in the ecologies they inhabit.

When Maria reports she has been late for work a few times, Daniel restates and paraphrases her expressions of concern. He does not stop there, however. He also becomes curious about the context of these events, helping Maria to make sense of her actions.

> Daniel: *So what's going on?*
>
> Maria: *I guess I'm not the 9 to 5 type.*
>
> Daniel: *Can you paint a picture for me of one of those mornings when you show up late?*
>
> Maria: *Well, they start with Kyla wailing away while I'm trying to dress. She's colicky, you know.*

Notice that Maria's initial response is to account for her actions as the expression of a personality type, with no reference to context. It's not inconceivable that a later conversation might lead to Maria's concluding a 9 to 5 schedule doesn't suit her. But to assume this is all about personality without exploring the context would be to arrive at what Geertz (1983) would call "thin description" (more on this shortly) because it excludes the surrounding circumstances that make sense of Maria's actions. So Daniel persists, soliciting more detail. Together, Daniel and Maria make a connection between being late and having a distressed baby. Now we see Maria making an active response in line with what is important to her rather than merely manifesting some hardwired disposition. Although this does not solve the problem, it sheds new light on the situation. In addition to opening up new options (e.g., Maria's partner Azim might stay home until the babysitter arrives), this expanded view is a helpful alternative to the notion that Maria is fundamentally not cut out for a 9 to 5 job.

Cultural Constraints and Supports

A thorough assessment attends to both the client and the client's wider context. Within that context, there are always challenges to contend with—external factors such as poverty, relational conflict, and racism. Madsen (2007) refers to these as "cultural constraints." This is to avoid casting any as the *cause* of a client's current experience—a perspective that makes an open and shut case for staying stuck in an unhappy place. Thinking of challenges as constraints rather than causes is a heuristic, or conceptual frame, that helps to keep alive a curiosity about people's agency.

In the previous chapter we saw how assessment can include an inventory of personal competencies; in a similar vein, a scan of the broader context can include vigilance for opportunities to be exploited in the broader context—what Madsen (2007) calls "cultural supports." Box 9.2 expands on constraints and supports in Resha's broader context, building on the scenario introduced in Box 8.3 in Chapter 8.

BOX 9.2

Resha's Constraints and Supports

Cultural Constraints

- Poverty
- Violence
- Sexism
- Domestic responsibilities
- Tight labor market

Cultural Supports

- Sister and extended family
- Loving children
- Neighborhood friends
- General and Arabic community services

There is a place for attending to and noting both cultural constraints and cultural supports in clients' wider contexts. Identifying the constraints helps to paint a picture of what people are up against and diminishes the chances of writing off their struggles as the consequence of poor motivation, weak character, or other personal deficits. At the same time, it can be invaluable to note cultural supports that surround a client, providing solidarity and backup when the going is tough.

THE ECOLOGY OF EXPERIENCE: SCOPING THE IMMEDIATE AND WIDER TERRAINS

Once you make the shift to thinking of a person as a relational being, a variety of territories come into view. We all inhabit multiple contexts. Assessment that ignores these in a single-minded focus on the individual neglects to note important constraints and also many helpful possibilities. Bronfenbrenner (1977, 1979) uses what he calls a socioecological model as a way of organizing the view of a person nested amid multiple contexts. Box 9.3 renders a simplified view of this. The concentric circles depict the contexts people inhabit, the details of which have much to offer by way of thickening the view of a client's experience.

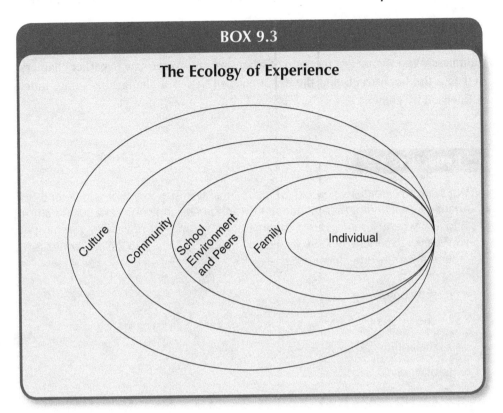

BOX 9.3

The Ecology of Experience

Culture

Community

School Environment and Peers

Family

Individual

Bronfenbrenner (1977, 1979) reminds us that what happens in one context has a ripple effect in other contexts, and the influence is reciprocal. When a young client reports a serious loss in the family, we grow curious about how this plays out at home, among peers, and at school. On the other hand, the description of a factory shutdown—an event happening in the wider context—will often manifest in the client's smaller circle. Assessment that attends to the full ecology of experience calls for a curiosity about how events and developments in one context manifest in another.

Multiple Contexts, Multiple Selves

One reason it's important to inquire about experience across multiple contexts is that it provides a fuller picture of a client's experience. If *self* refers to the totality of a person's being, *identity* is probably a more useful word to capture the variations of self that clients actually experience across contexts and over time. Many people have the experience of feeling a change come over them—almost at the cellular level—as they cross the threshold of their childhood homes when visiting their parents as adults. One person's sense of confidence in their career path goes up in smoke; another's edgy restlessness gets replaced by a soothing calmness. Who we are is a function of where we are: As we saw in earlier chapters, self is a fluid construct, and the experience of self is a changeable thing, much influenced by context.

Reflection 9.2

What are two contexts you occasionally inhabit in which you feel differently about yourself and/or present differently to those around you? On a scale from 1 to 10, where 1 represents a minimal amount and 10 represents the most you've ever experienced, how would you compare yourself in the two contexts around the following characteristics?

1. self-confidence

2. energy level

3. sociability

4. playfulness

5. anxiety

Do these two sets of ratings apply equally well to your experience of yourself and *others'* experience of you in these contexts? Is there one version of yourself you prefer? What constrains your expression of the qualities you prefer in the one context? What supports the expression of those preferred qualities in the other context?

This points to another important reason to engage in an ecological inquiry into a person's experience as part of the practice of assessment. For some clients, this will mean generating questions to extend the inquiry outward into additional contexts they inhabit: to get a sense of what a client's mood is like at school or work, for instance, after hearing about long lethargic hours in front of the TV. For others, an expanded ecological view might mean inquiring about what goes on closer to home: asking a client dealing with workplace stress about interactions with a partner and children, for example. Box 9.4 provides examples of questions that can be used to bridge the various contexts of a client's life to develop a rounded view of their experience.

BOX 9.4

Generating Questions Across Contexts

People don't always cover the broader ecological landscape of their lives when talking about the challenges they face. Part of the skill of assessment is to pose questions that help to draw out a wider view, based on curiosity about how particular experiences play out in other contexts of clients' lives.

Would you say that moodiness shows up at work as well?

What would I see if I watched you with your friends?

How does this play out in the classroom?

It sounds like things are pretty turbulent at work. Does that turbulence come home with you?

Does that pattern look the same with your friends as it does with your siblings?

How would you describe the version of you that people see in the workplace?

Seems like the neighborhood's going through a lot of changes. Are there ways that's reflected in your home life?

Painting Pictures: In Praise of Specificity

As we saw in Chapter 2, despite the thousands of words available for describing experience, spoken language is generally ambiguous and often vague. If all counselors did were to help clients articulate their experience in more precise terms, they would be providing a considerable service. Whole universes of possibilities open up in the process of refining descriptions and identifying optimal words to capture clients' subjectivity.

Clients often describe what's going on in their lives in broad terms, and it takes alertness on the part of the counselor to notice the fuzzy edges and press for further detail. Consider each trio of statements below.

1. My partner and I are not getting along.

2. My wife and I shout at each other virtually every night.

3. My marriage is in trouble. When I come home from work, I'm grumpy and not very talkative. She tries to engage me and gets upset when I open the newspaper. Once she raises her voice, I get defensive, and it turns into a shouting match, ending with both of us withdrawing to separate rooms.

1. I'm depressed.

2. Lately my mood has been kind of flat, and I've lost interest in people and activities.

3. For almost a year now I've been struggling big time. There's just no joy in anything; I feel like I'm going through the motions. I've got no appetite to speak of—I eat because I'm supposed to. I've lost touch with most of my friends. Most nights I just come home and sit in front of reruns. Sometimes I wonder if I really want this to go on; I've been thinking about stockpiling a bunch of pills.

Each consecutive description, above, becomes more specific, offering the counselor more with which to work. If you take another look at Box 9.4, you will get ideas for how you could extend the inquiry further still, getting a sense of what is going on for these clients across multiple contexts. However, inquiring across multiple contexts alone will not ensure the descriptions are concrete, so it can be useful to deliberately invite clients to paint a picture of what you would be seeing as an observer:

> *If I were a fly on the wall while this was happening, what would I witness?*
>
> *Suppose a documentary crew were following you all day and a producer were reviewing the footage at night. The problem is the audio isn't working. What would the producer actually see at the end of the day that would give them insight into your experience?*
>
> *What would _____ tell me about what they see when they're with you and this is going on?*

Scaling questions (Berg & de Shazer, 1993; de Shazer, 1994) are another useful way to support someone in moving from vague to specific accounts. By placing a number on one's experience, one gains a reference point against which to gauge past, present, and future developments. Box 9.5 provides some ideas about using scaling questions to evoke concrete descriptions.

BOX 9.5

Scaling Experience to Evoke Concrete Description

Not all clients are likely to produce rich, multilayered accounts of their experience. It's not uncommon to hear vague accounts that provide little for counselor and client to work with: "Things are going a little better." "I'm feeling off this week." "We're not getting along." Inviting a client to put a number to some aspect of their experience is a way to create a sort of benchmark—a reference point against which developments can be gauged. The key skill in asking scaling questions is to ensure the client understands what the bottom and the top of the scale represent. Without this, the client (and you) won't appreciate the significance of any particular number. Notice how the various questions here offer up ideas for assessing both problems and positive developments.

> *On a scale from 1 to 10, where 1 is the worst* [the problem] *has ever been for you and 10 is the best, how would you rate* [the problem] *this week?*
>
> *How does that compare to where it was last week/month/year?*
>
> [If the number is lower] *Could you say more about what's gotten worse for you? Have there been any developments that might help us understand this better?*
>
> [If the number is higher] *How did you get from there to here? What did you do that made the difference? What skills did that take on your part? How does that leave you feeling?*

Scaling questions have a number of useful applications, and they will be revisited in later chapters.

Using Genograms to Locate Experience in Social Contexts

Another useful tool for locating a client's experience in the broader context is the genogram. Genograms are widely used in family therapy for developing a pictorial representation of the people in a client's life—a sort of relationship map (Papadopolous, Bor, & Stanion, 1997a, 1997b). They are equally useful in individual counseling, however, because social relations (including relations with absent or deceased family members, friends, colleagues, and acquaintances) contribute significantly to a person's experience.

There are many ways to adapt genograms (cf. Duba, Graham, Britzman, & Minatrea, 2009; Frame, 2000; Hardy & Laszloffy, 1995; Kuehl, 1995; Thomas, 1998) to suit the purpose at hand. At their most basic, genograms are useful for jogging a counselor's memory *(What's the name of the sister-in-law? When did the parents divorce?)* when a client reintroduces characters or situations not spoken about in recent exchanges. They can also be used as a key reference point when jotting notes to develop a complex picture of the client situated within a matrix of social relations. This makes it possible to explore the relational aspect of experience, joining the client in evaluating the influence of their family of origin, for instance, on their current thoughts, feelings, and actions. Box 9.6 provides a rudimentary view of a genogram.

BOX 9.6

Mapping Social Relations With a Genogram

If for nothing else, genograms are very useful for tracking multiple relationships in blended families, which are common to a high percentage of clients. The simple genogram below situates the client, Sara, among family members. It indicates genders; ages; dates of deaths, marriages, and divorces; natural and step-siblings, parents, and step-parents.

THE SINGH FAMILY (genogram demo)

b. 1900 d. 1984

Jane McNally — 84

John Singh — 78

Janis Jones — 37   m. 2010

Tim Singh — 46   m. 1992 s. 2000 d.2008

Sara Harding — 42   m. 2008

Stephen Butters — 39

James Singh — 18

Sara Singh — 16

Janice Butters — 3

Jane Butters — 1

Legend:

	18	Male, age 18
	(X in oval)	Female, died at 84
	m. 1992	Married, year
	s. 2000	Separated, year.
	d. 2008	Divorced, year.

(double circle) Female, 16 focus of clinical attention
/ Separated couple
// Divorced couple
(dashed loop) Surrounds people in the current household

THIN AND THICK DESCRIPTION

The various proactive practices for gathering a picture of a person's situation are offered here because there is no reason to expect the client will necessarily provide a comprehensive description of their experience without some effort on the counselor's part. For starters, some people are more verbal or extroverted than others. If counseling is happening in a second language, that's a further barrier to expression. And as mentioned earlier, when challenges are significant, a person's account of their experience may be contained to what is not working, saturated with descriptions of problems and self-critique.

A central task of assessment is to join clients in developing what the anthropologist Clifford Geertz (1983) described as "thick description" of their lives. Geertz contrasted this with thin description, which is what we produce when attempting to describe other cultures but failing to get inside of the events we witness, failing to at least try to see them and experience them as the locals do. He critiqued what he saw as anthropology's tendency to depict less industrialized cultures as operating from a sort of naïve irrationality—portrayals that offered up descriptions rife with detail (the color of the costume, the sequence of the ritual, etc.) but lacking the insider's perspective and thus failing to capture the significance of the actions.

M. White (2004b, 2004c) applies these ideas to counseling, saying thin descriptions of clients' lives omit accounts of their purposes and intentions. Thin description is what we get when we maintain a professional distance, tallying behaviors rather than coming to see them as meaningful actions—performed by personal agents, by actors—in their local settings. Labels—diagnostic or otherwise—are occasionally useful shorthand but on their own offer thin description. They don't provide an inside view of what's important to people, of the intentions behind their actions, as in the conclusion that Mary does so much for Maurice because she is codependent or that Sherman distrusts his physician because he has a borderline personality. These accounts close down inquiry in the manner of a statement such as "Harry smokes because he's a smoker." In the quest to understand people's lived realities and to support them in more fully reflecting on them as well, labels may provide the beginning of the journey. But explorations that end there affix a brand from the outside, overlooking the uniqueness of the person before us. One useful practice that moves from thin to thick description is to engage clients around their experience of the labels assigned to them.

Engaging Clients in Critical Reflection on Diagnostic Labels

One reason labels are commonly used in any field is that they provide shorthand descriptions. Consider what it would be like to have to describe in detail each physical challenge faced by members of a large group pushing for policy to ensure equal access: Instead, we say "people with disabilities" are advocating for their rights. But the very thing that makes labels occasionally useful is also a serious limitation because it fails to highlight what makes people different and unique—such as a person with a visual impairment versus someone with a brain injury. Taken further, it becomes clear that there are many varieties of visual impairments, just as the consequences of brain injury vary widely. Each time, the summarizing label achieves an efficiency at the expense of erasing individuality.

Another dilemma associated with the shorthand that labels of all sorts supply is that they have the air of officialdom about them—especially when they're assigned by professionals. This can lead clients to treat them as monolithic and beyond critique, evaluation, or even reflection. Although the criteria for being included in certain medical categories (cancer, diabetes, and so on) are far more concrete and measurable than most psychological categories, clients may not make these distinctions and may understand the labels assigned to them as somehow capturing the *essence* of who they are. When this happens, they are operating on thin description.

BOX 9.7

Therapeutic Conversation and the *Diagnostic and Statistical Manual of Mental Disorders* (DSM)

The *Diagnostic and Statistical Manual of Mental Disorders* (text revision) (American Psychiatric Association, 2000) has become an increasingly influential document in relation to the practice of counseling and psychotherapy in North America and around the world (Watters, 2010). This development has widespread implications for a range of stakeholders associated with therapeutic practice. For those holding the purse strings, the document offers leverage for "rationing of therapy" (Strong, n.d., p. 7) by drawing hard-edged lines between well and ill. For pharmaceutical companies, the proliferation of diagnoses is a windfall because the medicalization of problems legitimizes pharmaceutical solutions. For some practitioners, diagnosis decreases the discomforts of ambiguity and complexity by distilling people's lives to leaner accounts built around psychopathology. For others, the *DSM* is an intrusion into therapist-client dialogue, a protocol they accommodate for bureaucratic purposes but subvert at the level of practice (Strong, n.d.).

These observations reflect the diversity of opinion about the *DSM* among various stakeholders; ultimately, however, an ethic of care calls for consideration of the impact of the *DSM* in the lives of clients, and it is probably fair to say that impact is mixed. For some clients, a diagnosis may provide access to mental health or accommodation services not otherwise available. For others, it may represent respite by giving names to ongoing, vexing concerns, perhaps relieving them of a crippling sense of self-blame in the process. At the same time, diagnosis alone offers thin description of people's lives, overlooking both people's diversity and their resourcefulness by assigning them to reductionist categories highlighting deficit. Given this potentially unhelpful feature of the *DSM,* it requires therapeutic skill to speak about and around diagnostic labeling.

It goes without saying that practitioners mandated to diagnose clients need to be thoroughly trained in the practice, one hopes in a manner that never loses sight of the fact that the *DSM* represents one of many ways of talking/ thinking about people. As seen earlier, to equate the *DSM* with (apparently) similar taxonomies in the physical sciences is to overlook the way that categories of mental illness are arrived at through a consultative process not infrequently questioned by insiders (cf. Caplan, 1996; Frances, 2012; Spitzer, 1981) and observers (cf. Greenberg, 2010; Horowitz & Wakefield, 2012) alike.

Part of the skill of working with diagnoses is in explaining to clients what they represent, clarifying that statements such as "You have cancer" and "You have depression" are of a different order of meaning. Another skill involves anticipating how diagnoses, once issued, have a tendency to influence both the outer and the inner dialogue of therapeutic conversation. In the overt outer realm, they risk curtailing generative, possibility-oriented talk, reducing the therapeutic focus to coping with purported inevitabilities. Formal diagnoses also influence what goes on in the covert inner dialogic realm (Strong, n.d.). Clients may hear praise as therapists' attempts to perk them up despite their purported dysfunctions rather than genuine witnessing of their life-affirming accomplishments. Under the sway of deficit-focused discourses, therapists may lose sight of clients' agency, hearing what might otherwise be understood as active responses to life challenges as symptomatic expressions of illness. As Strong (n.d.) says, "It is one thing to welcome clients' concerns, but another to actively join in co-authoring problem-saturated and deficit-enabled storylines that clients may take with them beyond therapy" (p. 8). With these various provisos in mind, Box 9.8 suggests some carefully crafted questions for inviting clients inside conversations from which they are too often excluded so they can reflect on their positions in relation to the labels assigned to them.

Explaining how psychological categories are arrived at and defined—on the basis of observed clusters of behaviors, thoughts, and feelings—helps clients to appreciate how the categories generally differ from medical disease designations. This supports them in engaging in critical reflection—where *critical* does not necessarily imply criticism but thoughtful analysis that maximizes their opportunity to make informed choices (Fook & Gardner, 2007). For clients who take diagnostic labels as given truth, understanding that the labels are invented, not discovered (Parker, 1999; Parker, Georgaca, Harper, McLaughlin, & Stowell-Smith, 1996), enables them to step back and identity their experience of the diagnostic process as well as generate their own language to describe themselves. This addition of clients' voices contributes to the movement from thin to thick description. Box 9.8 provides some ideas about how to engage clients in thick description when they arrive with ready-made accounts of who they are in the form of labels assigned by professionals, colleagues, family, or friends.

BOX 9.8

Generating Thick Description in Relation to Diagnostic Labels

A person who might otherwise have a lot to say about what makes them different from others may sometimes lose sight of their own uniqueness once a diagnostic label is affixed by a professional seen to be an expert in psychological categorization. Inviting clients to reflect on labels is an antidote to a hardening of the categories and enriches the assessment process. It involves a movement from thin to thick description because it centers clients' voices in their self-accounts.

When did this diagnosis first enter your life? How did you respond at the time? What are your thoughts and feelings about it now?

What impact has the label had on you and the people around you?

How well does the diagnosis fit your own experience of your challenges?

Which aspects of the diagnosis seem closest to your experience, and which ones furthest from your experience?

What's your own definition of [the disorder], and how is it similar and different from what you're being told about it?

If you were diagnosing yourself in your own language, which words might you use to describe the challenge you've been telling me about?

What do you see as some of the advantages and disadvantages of having this label assigned?

Which special skills and abilities that have proven useful to you in dealing with your challenges are overlooked by the diagnosis?

Are there new options for you emerging from having this diagnosis?

Reflection 9.3

Reflect on a label assigned to you. This may be a label associated with mental functioning, such as learning disabled or ADHD, or a medical label, such as diabetic or anemic. If you can't come up with any of these, consider other sorts of labels such as family labels (the trouble maker, the peacemaker) or labels assigned by friends or social acquaintances (the big guy, the bully, etc.). Take a moment to review the questions in Box 9.8, substituting the label in question for the word *diagnosis* in the questions. What difference does it make to engage critically with the label rather than to take it as the way things are?

Dignifying Clients: Thick Description and Insider Knowledge

Thick description provides something closer to the insider's view—a view we arrive at only with patient and persistent exploration of a client's experience (D. Epston, speaking at a training intensive titled "Insider Knowledges," May 2009). Think of some cultural or religious ritual you once encountered as unfamiliar (maybe even bizarre) that you have since come to know and perhaps participate in. This is the movement from a thin to a thick view. To join a client in rendering a thick description of their life means dropping the urge for final conclusions that, after all, conclude inquiry. Instead, it involves persisting in the quest to understand what for the client makes their actions, thoughts, and feelings meaningful. Assessment that strives for thick description is less concerned with categorization and more focused on eliciting insider knowledge, according to Epston. As A. Wade (speaking at a seminar titled "Witnessing Victims' Resistance to Violence and Oppression," October 2010) said, it honors the dignity of persons, something too often overlooked by systems preoccupied with efficiencies and classification.

CAPTURING THREE-DIMENSIONALITY THROUGH LAYERED DESCRIPTION

A familiar reaction from a director exasperated by the thin portrayal of a part is to shout at the actor, "What does this character *want?*" An actor who engages in a series of interactions without giving us a glimpse of how they are invested comes across as two-dimensional—not real somehow. These kinds of portrayals are common in action movies, which depend on plot momentum and special effects rather than character to engage audiences. This may work for Hollywood, but it's not helpful when trying to gain a complex picture of what is going on for a client. Assessment is about developing three-dimensional descriptions of character, and practitioners have more to learn from novelists than action-adventure screenwriters.

If you think about an impactful novel you've read, you're likely to notice the characters stand out from the page because the writer not only captured what they *did* but provided many more layers in their descriptions. We understand what it feels like to be lost in a jungle, what thoughts and ideas preoccupy the politician plotting a campaign bid, how the relationship between lovers contributes to the argument, what the sensation of being pinned in a collapsed building is like. Invoking these additional dimensions gives clients the opportunity to reflect widely and deeply on their experiences, adding texture and substance to their accounts. Box 9.9 includes a list (inevitably partial) of some of these potential layers, along with questions for evoking them.

BOX 9.9

Multilayered Descriptions in Assessment

Developing a rich account of a client's experience through assessment is similar to painting an evocative picture of a character in a coauthored novel. Rich and evocative writing is multilayered, not just capturing what characters *do* but combining this with accounts of many other dimensions of their experience.

| Feelings | Hopes | Memories | | Beliefs | Sensations | Morals |
| Thoughts | Values | Relationships | Images | Dreams | | Philosophies |

Multilayered assessment involves the use of questions to expand on accounts and invite forward dimensions not always explicitly named by the client. When a client reports on any of the dimensions above, there are openings to get a broader and deeper picture by asking follow-up questions such as those listed below.

Feelings—How did you feel after doing that?

Thoughts—What were you thinking about when you made that decision?

Hopes—Sounds like you're hoping for something different. Could you describe what that is?

Values—What do you think that says about what's important to you?

Memories—What sorts of memories come to mind as you describe it?

Relationships—What does that say about your marriage at this point in your life?

Beliefs—My sense is there's conviction hovering behind that gesture. What belief is that?

Images—Does any image come to mind that would help give me a sense of what it was like?

Sensations—How does that show up in your body? Is there a place where that fear lives?

Dreams—Where do you see all this going? Do you have a picture of where you'd like to end up?

Morals—My impression is this is about doing what's right. Could you tell me more about that?

Philosophies—Sounds like you've done some deep thinking about that. Is this something about your ideas about how to be in the world?

In the excerpt from Maria and Jorge's second session, below, Maria helps Jorge to expand the description of his experience by evoking layers in the manner of the questions in Box 9.9 and by inquiring about his experience across multiple contexts, as demonstrated in Box 9.4. When counselor and client act like coauthors of a rich and complex novel, they produce descriptions that begin to do justice to the complexity of lived experience.

Maria (counselor):	*You mentioned that feeling of dread, Jorge, and said it comes up most often when you anticipate visits home. Are there any thoughts that go along with it?*
Jorge:	*What do you mean?*
Maria:	*Anything you find yourself telling yourself before those weekend visits?*
Jorge:	*That my father will criticize something I say or do as soon as I walk in the door.*
Maria:	*That you'll be under attack the moment you step into the house.*
Jorge:	*Exactly. Crazy idea.*
Maria:	*Why crazy?*

Jorge:	*It's not like that. My mom and dad are always happy to see me. They worry about me being away at college.*
Maria:	*So the thoughts about getting criticized aren't realistic, but they happen anyway? What effect do they have on you?*
Jorge:	*I get anxious. Screws up my Fridays.*
Maria:	*Tell me about "anxious."*
Jorge:	*Like, nervous. Preoccupied. I can't concentrate.*
Maria:	*What would I see if I saw you being anxious?*
Jorge:	*I'm restless. I don't sit still. I start something then drop it and start something else.*
Maria:	*And is it the anxious Jorge that your parents see when you show up?*
Jorge:	*Not so much. I think I pull it together. I mask it. I present like everything's fine. I don't know if they see the anxiety.*
Maria:	*Everything's fine. And when you present that, is that what you're feeling inside?*
Jorge:	*Nada! No, "fine" doesn't do it. I'm not sure how to describe it. Maybe a bit like being numb. Playing a role but holding a lot back.*
Maria:	*How would you describe the difference between that version of Jorge and the Jorge who sits in a café with Richard?*

Maria invokes multiple dimensions of Jorge's account. At various key junctures, she

1. asks if there are any thoughts that go along with the feeling of dread,
2. unpacks the meaning of the word *crazy,*
3. inquires about the effects on Jorge of the idea that he'll be under attack,
4. unpacks the word *anxious,*
5. evokes a description of what being anxious looks like,
6. solicits a perception of Jorge from his parents' point of view,
7. inquires about what's going on inside for Jorge when this unfolds, and
8. invites a comparison of two versions of Jorge in two distinct contexts.

CULTURAL CONSIDERATIONS IN ASSESSMENT

Normal According to Whom?

As discussed elsewhere, it's impossible to stand nowhere when engaged in therapeutic conversation, so the practice of assessment inescapably happens within a cultural context. In North America and western Europe, when we hear that a family of children is fed the same meatless, starchy dish every day, we are inclined to wonder about the parent's capacity for caregiving. In sub-Saharan Africa, where dietary choices are minimal, however, we might not blink in response to the same account. When the context shifts, the meaning shifts. The sense we make of client accounts is always a function of cultural context, and it's important to keep culture in mind when engaging in assessment.

This includes attending to which assumptions of our own lurk in the background as we listen to people tell the stories of their lives. Which accounts do we embrace and view as positive developments? Which raise concerns? And how do these responses reflect cultural assumptions—deeply ingrained beliefs about, for instance, healthy emotions, normal development, appropriate relationships, competent parenting, and so on? Cultural assumptions vary the world over—across geographic locations and within them as well. For instance, in Western societies a dominant perspective puts high value on autonomy and individuality, but a substantial segment of the population takes an alternate view—indeed for many, these qualities may be seen as barriers to growth and actualization (Sue & Sue, 2003).

It's easy to forget that what we take to be normal and abnormal are reflections of understandings that are widely circulated but by no means universal. This pertains to values, of course, but also to the categories that we call "mental illness" under the influence of Western traditions of categorization. Box 9.10 outlines a small sampling of the countless syndromes specific to particular areas in the world. The names and descriptions have an exotic ring to ears accustomed to Western medical terminology, but to local inhabitants, these conditions may be as real as depression and schizophrenia.

BOX 9.10

Culture-Specific Syndromes

Condition	Location	Description
Amok or meta elap	Malaysia	An episode characterized by a period of brooding (usually instigated by actions interpreted as insult or betrayal) followed by a violent outburst
Irarata	Meru tribe of Northern Tanzania	Severe reactionary depression, usually affecting menopausal women who have lost a spouse; often results in death from loss of appetite and thus loss of body weight

(Continued)

Condition	Location	Description
Taijin kyofusho	Japan	A syndrome of intense fear that one's body, body parts, or bodily functions are displeasing, embarrassing, or offensive to other people
Zar	North Africa and Middle East	Spirit possession—the person often acts totally unlike himself or herself, with symptoms including laughing, shouting, hitting the head against a wall, singing, or weeping

Source: Adapted from Hamid (2000).

The culture-specific terms and descriptions listed in Box 9.10 are not likely to come up often while counseling in Western contexts but are a reminder that there are many ways to speak about and conceptualize the subject of people's distress, and these are expressions of local traditions. When counselors assess the scope of client challenges, they always do so under the influence of dominant cultural understandings. For clients who did not grow up in the context in which the counseling is taking place, these understandings and the language that goes with them may seem as exotic or unfamiliar as the terms above are to many readers.

Reflection 9.4

Think about a time you visited or lived in a place that you consider most culturally different from where you currently live. If you have not traveled widely, this could be a rural location if you live in a city now or an urban setting if you live in the countryside, and so on.

What leads you to choose this place as most culturally different? If you were to nail down what constitutes the differences from what you are accustomed to in the way people act, think, feel, and so on, which stories or examples could you come up with? Did you ever have the experience of coming to realize that some way of acting (talking, feeling, etc.) in that culturally different setting was considered normal locally, even though it seemed strange or exotic to you? What implications does this have for how one goes about ascertaining normality—to which yardsticks do we turn?

Client Acculturation and Assessment

Most of all, this discussion about the cultural variability of meaning making is a reminder of the importance of mining local knowledge—turning to clients themselves to determine what is in fact problematic in their lives. In an increasingly diverse society, those local knowledges may sometimes reflect understandings not widely circulated, depending on the degree to which clients are acculturated to the dominant culture (Chun, Organista, & Marin, 2003; Kosutic & McDowell, 2008; Lonner, Dinnel, Forgays, & Hayes, 1999). If we merely hold client accounts against a dominant cultural yardstick, we may render clients' actions senseless. Behaviors, thoughts, and emotions that may appear bewildering to the counselor will often make eminent sense in light of the cultural assumptions underlying them. But curiosity and openness to cultural variation does not suggest dismissing dominant cultural norms when engaged in assessment, because regardless of their origins, clients are bound to some degree to local norms as a consequence of their relocations.

Consider Hamid, who erupts into intense shouting matches with his 17-year-old daughter Afifah and who locked her in her room when she insisted she was going on a date with a boy from her school. In addition to asking the kinds of questions outlined throughout this chapter to develop a multidimensional picture of Hamid's experience, it would be important to understand how his behavior fits with norms in the country in which he grew up. It would also help to get a sense of his appreciation of differences between his culture of origin and the cultural context he now inhabits. Countries, states, and provinces all have legal sanctions designed to prevent certain behaviors in their own jurisdictions. These reflect dominant local norms. Although these norms may sometimes appear to betray an intolerance for cultural variation, they are nevertheless the law, and violating them can have significant repercussions for people. In a situation such as Hamid's, questions like the ones below not only clarify what his understandings are but also help him to reflect on his actions in light of values and laws in his current location.

> *Hamid, where did you learn your ideas about parenting your children? Who were your role models? What were their ideas?*
>
> *What is it about your way of parenting Afifah that is similar to/different from the way your friends and neighbors parented in* [country of origin]?
>
> *What have you noticed about the ideas here about parenting? What differences do you notice? What do you see as similar?*
>
> *Are you familiar with the laws in* [current location] *about the protection of children? Are they similar to/different from the laws in* [country of origin]?

When migrating from one location to another, it's necessary—for one's own well-being and thriving—to become familiar with local cultural understandings. In some cases, clients may be blind to the ways their culture-bound assumptions or practices are potentially problematic in their new context. Culturally conscious assessment therefore has more than one facet: It hones in on local knowledge to understand clients' experience in their own terms and also keeps in mind dominant cultural expectations (including laws) that might be problematic for clients who may not notice the discrepancies. Attending to cultural context is therefore always critical; in the case of assessment it can be particularly important when the difficulties clients face are directly related to straddling differing sets of cultural norms.

CONSIDERATIONS IN ASSESSING TRAUMA

Among the many remarkable features of conversation is the way it can capture distant events and bring them into the room. Reminiscing with friends about old times, the past becomes the present. Our heads are flooded with thoughts and images, our hearts refilled with dimly remembered emotion. When the moment being recalled is intense, we may even experience the bodily sensations—racing pulse, tightness in the temples, sweaty palms—that accompanied the original event. In conversations with clients, counselors are always revisiting events and bringing them into the room. And because those conversations are sometimes focused on traumatic events that clients are currently facing or have experienced in the past, there is always the risk of re-creating the trauma by not exercising sufficient care in asking about and speaking about it.

If you pay attention to day-to-day conversations about traumatic events—someone's car accident or someone's miscarriage, for instance—you will notice this care in action: It's reflected in tone, pace, and body language but also in the sorts of questions that are asked—the gentle probing to confirm the speaker's willingness to go on. In daily conversation, we don't typically assume a person wants to revisit a trauma, and we take our cues from them as to how much they'd like to share. In counseling conversations, there is the risk of neglecting this care, based on the unquestioned assumption that clients consult counselors primed to talk about difficult things, whether trauma or milder concerns. But consent to counseling is not a commitment to plunge headlong into painful and frightening territory. Care-filled assessment keeps the client's welfare at the center and proceeds at a pace that avoids duplicating the trauma that often brings the client to counseling in the first place.

One important consideration, then, is what the client wants to share and at what pace. In some cases, the client may have been asked outright on a printed intake assessment form whether they have experienced violence, sexual abuse, or other trauma. Although gathering this information may serve institutional demands for efficiency, it's an example of the abrupt directness around tender subjects that is more often avoided in day-to-day encounters. For a client who has experienced a crossing of boundaries and a sense of powerlessness in relation to a personal transgression, this sort of documentation is often experienced as intrusive and might naturally encourage the client to be on their guard from the outset in a therapeutic relationship. Nevertheless, if organizational protocols are such that this information is solicited up front, the counselor need not take the client's written responses as an indication of what they wish to talk about and in which order. Better to turn to the client and take a cue from them as to how to proceed:

> *I have a copy of the intake form you filled out, but I haven't had a chance to check with you about what you'd like to work on. How'd you like to use our time together?*

A client who comes for counseling around career indecision will not normally be counting on exploring a childhood sexual assault, for instance. Knowing that the assault occurred provides the counselor with some context that may or may not become relevant, depending on how the conversations unfold. When, at the outset, the counselor assumes connections between certain life events (noted on intake forms) and current distress, they are getting ahead of the client—centering their private assumptions when it would be more helpful to facilitate the client's exploration of their own experience.

A second key consideration around assessment of trauma relates to the building of secure base camps, as it were, for forays into sensitive territory. Joining with the client in cataloguing that which is working in their life can be a useful precursor to examining difficult topics. For instance, a client struggling with a significant loss may be feeling a loneliness that leads them to lose sight of valuable and enduring relationships. To immediately join the client in painting a picture of their loss might deepen the feeling of isolation. This can be counterbalanced by an inquiry into the client's existing social network—their "club of life" (Duvall & Béres, 2011; M. White, 2007)—providing a comforting reminder that they are not alone in the world. This is not about avoiding painful experience but instead building a foundation for processing loss without being engulfed by it.

> *Who is there for you when you're struggling? Who is supporting you through this?*

> *Could you tell me about who are the important people in your life?*

> *Who have you been able to talk to about this?*
>
> *What are the relationships that sustain you most in your life?*

A third important consideration in relation to assessing trauma is the way that actual events are talked about. If you have ever been subjected to violence or other trauma, you likely know the experience of feeling helpless or overpowered. Talking about trauma in a way that situates clients as passive victims can inadvertently consolidate a story of victimization. One way of addressing this dilemma is to not talk about the traumatic event(s) explicitly at all. It is not necessary to gather minute detail about past events to develop a thorough picture of where a client is now in their life. This way of going forward might involve referring to trauma abstractly or simply speaking about how things are now:

> *How have you been coping since it happened?*
>
> *What would you say are some of the lingering effects of the incident?*
>
> *On a scale of 1 to 10, where 1 is when you have been struggling most in your life and 10 is when you have been doing your best, where would you put yourself now? Where would you put yourself at the time the incident happened?*

In other cases, you and your client may find reason to develop a more detailed account of what happened. As mentioned in Chapter 8, this is when the distinction between a language of effects and a language of responses can be helpful (Wade, 1997, 2007). A client may want to seize the opportunity of having an empathic listener to report on effects or may feel this is expected of them as part of the cultural ritual of therapy. Checking on where the client stands in relation to this helps support them in making informed choices:

> *I'm wondering if you feel it would be useful to you to revisit some of what happened. Or perhaps you're more interested in exploring where you're at now and looking forward to where you want to go.*

When revisiting the details of traumatic events, asking the client about how they responded positions the client as the agent rather than the victim and greatly diminishes the chances that the process of gathering details will exacerbate the trauma. Unfortunately, this practice is not widespread, with the result that people frequently describe being subjected to interrogations following violent incidents that only make a bad situation worse (A. Wade, speaking at a seminar titled "Witnessing Victims' Resistance to Violence and Oppression," October 2010).

CHAPTER NINE RECAP

This concludes two full chapters on assessment skills. Readers chafing at the bit for intervention skills may be wondering when their opportunity comes to deliberately facilitate change in their clients' lives. I hope by now it will be clear that this happens from the first moment of contact—that all interactions are interventions and that counselors and clients are potentially working on change from the moment they meet. These two chapters have been filled with skills devoted to effecting change while simultaneously painting a picture of current circumstances.

The discussion about assessment blossomed from one chapter into two through the addition of dimensions left out of more narrow accounts. Conventional readings of assessment sometimes characterize objective counselors as honing in exclusively on problems, gathering lists of symptoms, and affixing off-the-shelf categories to these clusters. In some cases, these practices can be useful: for instance, in identifying medications that may help to moderate particular forms of distress and in providing persons with frameworks for making sense of a bewildering array of experience that leaves them feeling isolated and misunderstood. However, there is clearly a lot more that assessment can achieve, and much of Chapters 8 and 9 introduced skills for capitalizing on the possibilities inherent in rendering client experience eminently sensible by considering it in context and regarding actions as expressions of personal agency rather than seeing them as the effects of external or internal causes.

Nevertheless, assessment's primary motive is not to influence but to scope out the territory—even if the mode of scoping itself can be change inducing. In the next section, we turn to practices more explicitly associated with intervention and promoting change. The chapters in the section have been organized to isolate skills associated with intervening in relation to actions, thoughts, emotions, and story, roughly paralleling four dominant strands of theory informing a large body of counseling practice. But first, Chapter 10 takes a look at what is arguably the most fundamental task of counseling itself, the practice of influencing. The chapter will emphasize counseling's central purpose of supporting clients in moving to a preferred territory of experience. Doing this involves "leading from behind" (Cantwell & Holmes, 1994; de Jong & Berg, 2007)—a subtle skill that is central to collaborative counseling.

CHAPTER NINE DISCUSSION QUESTIONS

1. **Western individualism.** What are some major symbols, traditions, and/or stories associated with individualist values in Western societies? What alternative symbols, traditions, and/or stories are more evident in non-Western cultures?

2. **Rendering actions sensible.** How is it that a person's actions may seem to make little or no sense when they are evaluated in isolation from the context in which they occur? What difference does it make to widen the view to include contextual detail related to the actions? Can you provide examples?

3. **Multiple selves.** Describe the shifts in your identity that have occurred across time periods in your life or that occur from context to context in the present time. Which aspects of yourself are brought to the foreground, and which recede in these varying contexts?

4. **Thin versus thick description.** Pick some flamboyant cultural ritual and discuss what it would look like to someone from a foreign culture completely unfamiliar with local beliefs, customs, symbols, traditions, and so forth. What is missing in the outsider's view? What effect does the person's being on the outside have on their characterization of the people involved in the ritual? How does this relate to the difference between thin and thick descriptions of clients' experiences?

5. **Assessment and culture.** Why is attention to cultural assumptions (the counselor's and the client's) so important in assessment? Give examples of what can go wrong when (a) a counselor fails to identify their own cultural assumptions in assessing a client's situation and (b) a counselor fails to explore assumptions from a client's culture of origin in assessing the client's situation.

6. **Trauma and assessment.** Describe an experience you have had of someone's pressing you to speak about an unpleasant experience either (a) before you were ready or (b) in more detail than you were willing to share. What was this like for you? What effect did it have on your openness to share and receive comfort from that person? What does it mean to say that a counseling conversation could inadvertently reperpetrate trauma?

CHAPTER NINE ACTIVITIES

1. **Sensible accounts.** Form pairs. Speaker, provide a description of an unusual (apparently senseless) action, thought, feeling, and so forth that you have experienced at some point, restricting your description to just the action, thought, or feeling and excluding all contextual detail. Listener, first take note of how you receive this decontextualized story, and then help the speaker to fill in the contextual details surrounding the event. Debrief. Both speaker and listener, what shifts in the view of the action, thought, or feeling as context is added?

2. **The ecology of experience.** Form pairs. The speaker briefly describes a challenge occurring in some single context of their life. The listener poses questions to extend

the description to other domains, developing a view of both what happened and the speaker themselves in various contexts. Speaker, what was the impact of having the exploration widened to various contexts of experience? Listener, what were the challenges associated with widening the exploration?

3. **Constraints and supports.** Form pairs. The speaker shares about some challenge in their life. Together, the speaker and listener explore the various obstacles or constraints that accompany this challenge, making sure to construe these as separate from the speaker's identity. The speaker and listener also reflect on the various supports that surround the speaker in their life. Debrief. Speaker, what difference did it make to separate constraints and supports? Listener, what challenges were associated with making these distinctions?

4. **Scaling questions.** Form pairs. Speaker, briefly describe some negative incident in your life and your response to it. Listener, introduce a scaling question by first establishing what 1 and 10 on the scale represent and then inviting the speaker to identify which number they would assign to the experience at the time of the event. You can expand this activity by further inquiry; for example, if the speaker is at a higher number now, what have they done to make this difference? If the speaker is at a lower number, what circumstances are contributing to this? Debrief. Speaker, in what ways was it helpful to have a number on which to hang your experience? Listener, what were the challenges associated with introducing and working with a scaling question?

5. **Working with genograms.** Form pairs. Speaker, describe your extended family configuration to the listener. Listener, draw a rudimentary diagram as you listen, asking questions to clarify details to be inserted into the emerging genogram. Debrief. Speaker, what was it like to see your family map? Listener, what were the challenges associated with doing this?

6. **Multilayered descriptions.** Form pairs. The speaker describes a challenge occurring in some context of their life. The listener asks questions to evoke additional dimensions of the speaker's experience, guided by Box 9.9 regarding multilayered descriptions. Speaker, how did you experience your challenge differently when describing it across various dimensions? Listener, what challenges were associated with evoking various dimensions of the speaker's experience?

7. **Cultural considerations in assessment.** Form pairs. Speaker, describe some ritual particular to your cultural subgroup, broadly speaking. This could be an ethnic or linguistic subgroup, for example, but it could also be the subgroup of your family of origin or a particular set of friends. Describe the ritual or tradition without elaborating

on the beliefs, values, or history behind it. Listener, take note of how you initially respond to what makes this ritual or tradition unusual or even abnormal relative to the norms you are used to. Then ask questions to draw out a rich account of the speaker's assumptions, values, and history associated with this ritual or tradition. Debrief. Speaker, what difference did it make to be asked questions that helped you to contextualize the tradition or ritual? Listener, what was your initial reaction to hearing of the tradition or ritual? What difference did it make once you drew out a description of the assumptions, values, and history associated with it?

Section Five

Promoting Change

This fifth section of the book makes more explicit the focus on what is arguably the central purpose of counseling: change. You may notice I didn't say the section *introduces* the topic, because the numerous skills already featured in the text are ultimately aimed at promoting change. That's because they're devoted to a movement away from distress or suffering, a movement that suggests some form of change in acting, thinking, feeling, and so on.

Spatial metaphors have appeared from time to time in these pages to capture that sense of movement: Weingarten's (1998) reference to clients as "fellow travelers," the idea of helping clients move forward, the notion of seeking out new territories of living. White (2007) uses the term "transport" to speak of what happens when we have experiences that seem to deposit us in a new location, a vantage point from which nothing looks quite the same. That movement underlies all counseling practices, showing up in how counselors listen to and think about clients, what they say, when they say it, how they say it, why they remain silent.

So the previous four sections of the book have also been devoted to change. But until now, that impetus toward change has been the background to practices explicitly devoted to more immediate aims: to ensure clients feel witnessed and understood, to clarify the focus of their concerns, to develop a context-rich description of their challenges, and so on. What is different about Section 5 is that from this point forward, that background agenda of therapeutic change comes to the foreground. In the remaining pages, the skills featured are more explicitly devoted to facilitating movement—the counselor is more actively influential. The chapters to come introduce skills for supporting clients in acting differently, thinking differently, feeling differently, making meaning differently.

The word *intervention* is sometimes used to describe these skills and to differentiate them from the sorts of listening, attending, and assessing skills featured to this point. This comes from what I think is an overly simple depiction of the practice of counseling: The counselor first finds out what is wrong and then intervenes to change things to make it right. It is fairer to say the intervening begins with the very first contact with clients—that one cannot interact without intervening (Tomm, 1987a, 1987b, 1988). Thus, the chapters to come differ from those that preceded them only in the kinds of interventions they feature, interventions more *explicitly* devoted to facilitating movement or change.

The section starts with an in-depth look at the issue of influencing. Whichever style counselors choose to work in, they are ineffectual unless they are influencing clients in some way. As de Shazer (1991) says, "clients are seeking practical results when they come to therapy; they are pragmatists. They are 'in pain' and they want to get rid of [the problem], plain and simple" (p. 110). An effective counselor is an influential counselor. But as Chapter 10 will demonstrate, influence comes in various forms. Collaborative influence keeps client values and aspirations at the center of the conversation.

The chapters that follow Chapter 10 focus on facilitating influence in different dimensions of clients' lives. This is where readers are likely to recognize ideas and practices associated with some of the more prevalent models of counseling and therapy circulating at this time. Chapters 11 to 13 focus on actions, thoughts, and emotions, respectively; Chapter 14 introduces skills for integrating all three of these in helping clients "story" their lives in ways more aligned with their preferences.

Chapter 10

COLLABORATIVE INFLUENCE

ACHIEVABLE GOALS TOWARD PREFERRED OUTCOMES

INTRODUCTION

The practices of problem definition and assessment generate a rich picture of the current terrain, a clear statement of where we are now. This includes an account of what clients want *less* of in their lives and what they would like *instead.* These descriptions make it possible to take a more active role in facilitating movement because with understandings well coordinated between client and counselor, the risk of imposing solutions out of step with client purposes and preferences is greatly reduced.

This does not mean the practices associated with coordinating meanings with clients now come to an end, because the terrain will always continue shifting as the conversations progress. But the careful application of the skills featured to this point solidifies a mutual understanding between counselor and client that sets the stage for the more active pursuit of change. With a reasonable account of the situation at hand, the counselor is in a position to support and encourage movement in the direction of client preferences. This is where the counselor explicitly seeks to be influential.

The first part of this chapter clarifies the meaning of *collaborative influence,* a phrase that depicts a partnership in meaning making between counselor and client (collaborative) that aims to alter some aspect of the status quo (influence) en route to a preferred outcome. Later the chapter turns to the process of identifying potential steps—achievable goals—along that aspirational pathway.

IN THE CLIENT'S FAVOR: COLLABORATIVE INFLUENCE

The word *influence,* like all words, comes with its own baggage (S. R. Strong, 1969; Sutherland & Strong, 2012; Zimmerman, 2011). In some contexts, the word evokes the image of a powerful person who is able to steer the course of events in their own favor. With the addition of the qualifier *collaborative* (T. Strong, 2000, 2002), the combined term comes closer to depicting the role of an effective counselor. Effective counseling is influential counseling (Sue & Sue, 2008), but the client's purposes and understandings are at the center of the process. Collaborative influence is about steering events in the client's favor.

This is not directiveness in the conventional sense, which is more like a counselor's nudging a client toward a prescribed destination. Instead, it's more like codirectiveness, or what John Shotter (1995) calls "shared intentionality," with client and counselor sitting side by side like copilots in a cockpit. Collaborative influence involves engaging in ongoing responsive dialogue.

It's important to note that although collaborative influence can be distinguished from conventional notions of directive practice, it does not imply that the counselor relinquishes their point of view or abstains from bringing their perspective into therapeutic conversations. Although the practice of collaborative influence keeps client preferences central—respecting, as T. Strong (2000) puts it, "their primary authorship over their lives" (p. 144)—it need not feature the client's point of view to the exclusion of the counselor's. After all, the client comes to the counselor because they wish to benefit from the input of a professional. But the counselor's input comes in a different form than the client's. It is primarily facilitative in nature, directed to helping the client martial their own knowledge and resources to realize their aspirations. This client-centered, facilitative role sets collaborative influence apart from simple advice giving. Collaborative influence finds a balance that includes both the client's voice and the counselor's point of view. Establishing that balance is one of the more challenging tasks reported by counselors in training.

Overbalanced one way, we see the exclusion of the client's voice and the unilateral imposition of counselor prescriptions disconnected from local knowledges—a version of colonization, writ small. In practice, this is the inattentive counselor who jumps to conclusions about what the client needs and pitches advice without checking to see how it fits for the client. Overbalanced the other way, the counselor's point of view is excluded, leaving the client wallowing in the very difficulties that brought them to counseling in the first place. In practice this looks like directionless conversations that recycle problem-saturated accounts without moving forward into preferred territory. This chapter introduces a range of skills for achieving the balanced facilitative task of collaborative influence.

ADVICE GIVING VERSUS FACILITATIVE QUESTIONING

Facilitation and advice giving are very different practices. Unsolicited advice giving projects the message that the recipient of the gift is somehow incompetent to address the challenge at hand on their own. As a result, it is common for people to uphold their dignity by tuning out advice or acting in a contrary manner, according to A. Wade, speaking at an October 2010 seminar titled "Witnessing Victims' Resistance to Violence and Oppression." In their study of public health nurses doing home visits, Drew and Heritage (1993) describe how, on receiving direct advice, clients acknowledged the suggestions but countered by saying they'd "tried that already." The nurses may actually have minimized the chances of potential useful practices' being adopted through their manner of suggesting them.

Reflection 10.1

Think about a time you encountered straight advice giving when you had given something a great deal of thought and were looking for someone to bounce ideas off instead. How did this leave you feeling about your own efforts toward solving the issue at hand? How would you describe your sense of the other's respect for your intelligence and insight? How receptive were you to the advice being offered?

In some cases, however, clients may explicitly ask for advice. A request like this deserves serious consideration because it is a clear expression of what someone feels they need at that moment. A simple refusal on the basis that the client knows best would be paradoxical because it would project the message that the client *doesn't* know best in thinking advice would be helpful. Nevertheless, a request for advice deserves further exploration because it provides an opportunity to support a client in examining what the request says about their current experience. The questions below give some indication of the various considerations that might accompany a direct request for advice:

What do you understand about your situation that tells you it would be useful to seek some direct professional advice?

What steps have you taken so far that led you to that conclusion?

What's been your experience in the past of professional advice?

How would you know if my advice didn't fit for you?

Would it be okay for us to explore this issue in more detail so that I feel more equipped to add my commentary?

These various possible responses share one feature: Rather than rushing to add counselor knowledge to the situation at hand, they use questions to keep the client's knowledge at the center of the conversation, a defining feature of collaborative influence. As Tomm and Lannamann (1988) put it, "the therapists' job is not to make choices for people but to help them arrive at a position from which they can make choices for themselves" (p. 41). Elsewhere, family therapist Karl Tomm is reputed to have said, "Statements set forth; questions draw forth"—a simple distinction that goes a long way to delineating what distinguishes the two forms of utterances. Freedman and Combs (1996) capture another aspect of the statement-question distinction in recapping how over the years, they came to see questions as "a way of *generating experience* rather than a way of gathering information" (p. 293). As to which experiences would be helpful to generate, it depends on the person and the context. As Anderson (1997) says, "right questions are the ones that emerge from being immersed in a client's world" (p. 148).

Posing questions does not imply censoring one's ideas or adopting a passive stance. But questions hand the work back to the client. Regardless of one's theoretical orientation, the centering of client knowledge is a fundamental attribute of therapeutic interactions intended to promote autonomy and personal agency (Paré & Lysack, 2006). The use of questions is key to this process.

BOX 10.1

The Dilemma of the Meandering Conversation

Among the various challenges that counselors in training confront, two stand out. One is the tendency to dispense advice without inviting clients to participate actively in evaluating the prescriptions. Antidotes to this practice are spoken of in many places throughout this book. The second challenge is of a very different sort and is in some ways antithetical to the excessive taking charge represented by rampant advice giving. Instead, it is the dilemma of the meandering conversation.

In everyday conversation, it is typically considered rude to interrupt someone who is on a roll—long-windedly recounting a story or otherwise monopolizing what was ostensibly intended to be a two-way exchange. For this reason, novice counselors sometimes find themselves tongue-tied when encountering a client whose speaking patterns leave virtually no entry points. The counselor sits on the edge of their chair, poised to ask a question or otherwise respond, but the opportunity rarely presents itself. The conversation—something closer to a monologue—comes to an end with the sense (on the counselor's part) that there has been a somewhat undifferentiated venting but little in the way of constructive dialogue. Of course there is no formula for determining when this is the case; for some clients, something approaching a monologue may be particularly therapeutic. It is always important to read each situation individually and to consult from time to time with clients about what is helpful to them.

When it does appear that a conversation lacks direction and that the time together could be spent more productively, one apparent remedy is to interrupt the client and get things back on some mutually agreed-on and productive track. However, this could be perceived by the client as dismissive—not a favorable outcome. The reason a counselor shies away from this option is their respect for and deference to the client, and a remedy fortunately lies there as well.

Considering that an ethic of care calls on counselors to ensure their interactions with clients are helpful, it makes sense for a practitioner to take note when they feel like a passive witness to an extended monologue that at best appears not to be advancing things and at worst may even be reinforcing a problem-saturated narrative. In other words, far from being a rude dismissal, an interruption can sometimes be at the service of the client. The challenge is to execute the interruption in such a manner that the client can experience it as a collaborative gesture. The example below provides one of many ways to respond to the dilemma of the meandering conversation.

Rejean:	*[in the midst of a long account about a mixup about misdirected mail, the purpose of which is unclear to the counselor]*
Counselor:	*Excuse me, Rejean, do you mind if I stop you there for a moment?*
Rejean:	*[looking slightly flustered, pauses and waits for more]*
Counselor:	*I'm aware we were earlier talking about what you called the "blues" and your mood swings, and I wasn't sure if this is related to that in some way that you wanted to explore.*
Rejean:	*[reflects] No, not so much; I just wanted to catch you up on things.*
Counselor:	*So you don't see this mail mixup on the weekend as shedding light on your moods, but there's something in it you thought would be useful to discuss?*

(Continued)

(Continued)

> Rejean: *I don't know. It was just on my mind.*
>
> Counselor: *It does sound frustrating. I'm wondering whether you think it would be helpful to explore that more now, or to pick up on the thread of the mood swings we've been talking about. I think I can be more helpful to you if I have a sense of what we're focusing on together.*
>
> Rejean: *Yeah; I can see your point.*
>
> Counselor: *Any idea which you'd like to work on right now?*
>
> Rejean: *I think for now I'd like to get back to the moods; the whole mail thing with the neighbor was pretty crazy, but I'm not sure I need to do anything about it right now at least.*
>
> Counselor: *Okay, and as I said I'm happy to go there as well if you feel it would be useful; just that it's helpful if we do that deliberately. How about we get back to the issue of your mood swings for now, and if I get the impression we're veering off the track I might check in again just to make sure we're on the same page?*

The counselor accomplishes a couple of key things here: In addition to clarifying what it is that Rejean wants to focus on, she solicits permission to interrupt again if she feels the conversation is veering off topic. This will make it much easier for her to speak up the next time and will diminish the chances Rejean will experience it negatively. In effect, the act of interrupting is transformed from a rude dismissal to a collaborative gesture. It is worth noting again that initiating an exchange like this is always subject to a careful reading of the context and is founded on a respectful relationship. After all, who ultimately gets to decide what is off topic and thus not useful? Ultimately, this question should be addressed by both counselor and client so they can move forward with a unified purpose.

SCAFFOLDING CLIENT LEARNING THROUGH QUESTIONS

White (2007) developed a compelling account of how questions are used in counseling conversations to expand client learnings. His account of the "scaffolding" of therapeutic conversations captures the practice of collaborative influence and deserves further exploration here. White's contribution draws on some key ideas from a seminal figure who influenced his work—the developmental psychologist Lev Vygotsky (see Box 10.2).

BOX 10.2

Scaffolding: The Heart of Outcome-Oriented Collaborative Dialogue

Psychologist Lev Vygotsky's (1986) research provided an influential alternative to what was at the time the more dominant developmental account of Jean Piaget (Piaget & Inhelder, 1962). Piaget's work focused on how new behaviors appear in a child's repertoire when the child attains a certain developmental readiness. Vygotsky acknowledged that biological readiness cannot be ignored—it sets certain limits on what can be learned. But rather than seeing new behaviors as "the unfolding of some genetic or neurological imperative" (White, 2007, p. 271), Vygotsky saw them as more often the product of learning. His observations therefore differed from the classical view that development precedes learning. Instead, he said that learning contributes to development, that children inhabit a sort of territory of possible development—he called it the *zone of proximal development*—and how much they develop depends on how much they learn.

This has some very compelling implications for counseling, as White (2007) pointed out. To appreciate the link, consider one more relevant feature of Vygotsky's work, another key distinction from the conventional Piagetian view. Vygotsky saw learning not so much as an individual achievement but instead as the product of social collaboration. When a child is engaged with colored blocks of different shapes, for instance, an adult might ask, "What makes the red ones different from the blue ones?" Questions like this contribute to the child's making a conceptual leap they would not have made at that moment on their own. White talks about this as a movement within the zone of proximal development from the "known and familiar" to "what is possible to know" (p. 271). That movement is facilitated through questions that provide a "scaffold" that supports the learning. Vygotsky's work vividly applies to skillful counseling conversations in which counselors collaborate with clients to (a) facilitate new learning, founded on (b) knowledge at hand that they are in a position to draw from, that (c) moves them toward new possibilities. In this influencing process, questions are the primary vehicle for scaffolding that movement.

all the yes!

Although focused on human development, Vygotsky's research, reconceived by White (2007), contributes useful language for making sense of what goes on in effective outcome-oriented collaborative dialogue. The vocabulary of scaffolding conversations describes a central feature of the practice. Using questions to invite consideration of what it is possible to know, counselors promote learning and forward momentum without getting in front of clients. This practice of "leading from behind" (Cantwell & Holmes, 1994; de Jong & Berg, 2007) is evident in the right-hand column below.

Advice Giving Through Direct Statements	Collaborative Influence Through Scaffolded Conversation
You should get more exercise; research shows lack of exercise is a factor in insomnia.	Are there any differences in your sleep patterns at the end of an active day?
I would tell him you're not interested in seeing him and he should stop calling.	What do you think it would take from you for him to get the message you aren't interested?
You shouldn't talk to your teen like that; it will only make him push back harder.	Would you say your son tends to get more or less cooperative when you talk to him like that?
You need to look at the bright side of things instead of always thinking the glass is half empty.	You mentioned your mood can vary depending on what you focus on. What might you focus on here that will keep you from sliding into that dark place?

[Handwritten margin note: Howard Barrows would say the client should generate the questions! Facilitator reframes as Learning Issue (scaffolding question)]

The counselor's point of view is as present in the column on the right as it is in the column on the left. In scaffolding inquiry, counselors don't relinquish their knowledge. But notice how the questions on the right offer that knowledge in such a way that clients can critically engage with it. The questions bring informed hunches to the conversation but do not assume universal truth. In this respect, they honor the client's unique perspective and keep the counselor open to alternative views. The following are some of the key benefits of scaffolded inquiry:

1. It helps to keep client meanings at the center of the conversation.

2. It capitalizes on clients' potential to think/feel/act differently by activating latent knowledge.

3. It ensures that clients, and not counselors, are doing most of the work.

4. It avoids the risk of counselors' getting ahead of clients by facilitating change in incremental steps.

CHANGE IN MANAGEABLE INCREMENTS

When a client is struggling with a dilemma, potentially useful actions, thoughts, emotional responses, and so forth may seem indistinct or out of reach to them although they are visible to the counselor. Continuing with the metaphor of scaffolding, the counselor's questions act as an infrastructure to bridge the client to those possibilities. A key aspect of this practice is the discernment of how far from the client's current experience the questions should extend. As Andersen (1987, 1995) has said, "not unusual enough" and the question is unhelpful; "too unusual" and it sets the client up for failure. Change may sometimes happen in a blinding flash, but more often it unfolds in increments, and the counselor's task is to support movement in that direction.

This will be clearer with examples. Returning for a moment to the case of an adult's supporting a young person's learning, the increments are too small with a question such as, *Where are the blocks?* It fails to prompt any new learnings because it doesn't bridge beyond the known and familiar for a child who is already engaged with the objects in front of her. An example of this in Maria's conversations with her client Jorge might be, *What are your Dad's ideas about homosexuality?* Jorge has already reflected on this deeply: In fact, his knowledge about his father's views is central to his dilemma about coming out. The question does not facilitate movement.

Alternately, a question that reaches too far will be equally unhelpful. Asking, *What's the relationship here between shape and color?* might overwhelm the child just getting a handle on the distinction between square and round. In the realm of therapy, Andersen (1995) talks about this in terms of questions that are not resonant and thus not useful because they are "too unusual." Returning to Maria and Jorge, an equivalent question might be, *What would it take to repair your relationship with your father?* The question reaches too far; if Jorge had a ready answer to this, he probably wouldn't be meeting with Maria. I often witness practitioners in training posing questions of this sort—asking clients to identify what they need to do to resolve a problem they brought to counseling. That the client has come seeking help is evidence they currently don't know or at least believe they don't know; the counselor's task is to scaffold an inquiry that will lead the client from where they are at (the known and familiar) to helpful alternatives (what it is possible to know).

A COLLABORATIVE RELATIONAL POSTURE

Toward the end of his life, Albert Einstein reflected on what led him to what were among the most consequential scientific insights uncovered by a single human being:

> I have no special talents. . . . I am only passionately curious. . . . Curiosity has its own reason for existing. . . . One cannot but be in awe when one contemplates the mysteries of eternity, of life, of the marvellous structures of reality. (Isaacson, 2007, p. 548)

Curiosity is a compelling feature of a collaborative relational posture because it refuses to fall into the complacent assumption that the client's universe has been thoroughly scoped, that all that remains is to settle for the status quo. Curiosity has a forward-looking quality to it, patient and receptive to as-yet-undiscovered possibilities, filled with anticipation of the "not yet said" (Katz & Shotter, 1996; Rober, 2002). In adopting a stance of curiosity, counselor and client become "co-researchers" (Epston, 1999, 2001, 2009; Speedy et al., 2005) joined in a mutually supportive quest for preferred futures. Counseling becomes a venue for, as George Kelly put it, "co-investigating testable hypotheses about productive ways to live" (cited in Efran, Lukens, & Lukens, 1988, p. 32).

Counselors who adopt a curious stance do not rest on professional pronouncements, devoting their energies instead to clients' learning and development. In Vygotsky's (1986) terms, this leads to self-mastery; in relation to counseling, White (2007) adopts the term *personal agency*. Both descriptions highlight a fundamental aspect of practice fueled by curiosity: It involves active facilitation by the counselor, but primary attention falls on the client's knowledge, with energy devoted to invoking rather than transmitting learning.

It is important to note once again that a collaborative posture does not exclude instances wherein counselors have specific knowledge or insight to share. What is different from an expert-oriented stance, as mentioned above, is that this material is not taken to represent given truth and is brought to the conversation for clients to engage, evaluate, and make their own. This is about learning but reflects a distinction made by Sfard (1998) between learning as acquisition and learning through participation. Collaborative practice is participatory. Box 10.3 presents a schematic that may help to shed light on a relational posture that combines collaboration and influence.

BOX 10.3

Collaborative Influence and Relational Posture

For visual learners, the figure below may help to clarify distinctions around a relational posture associated with the practice of collaborative influence and the repercussions for the counseling practitioner. The left-to-right axis represents a continuum from practice centered primarily on counselor knowledge (expert driven, directive) to practice oriented toward foregrounding client knowledge (collaborative, curious, invitational). The bottom-to-top continuum ranges from noninfluential practice (despite the counselor's efforts, not much change occurs) to influential practice (helpful change occurs). Each combination of attributes (described in each of the four quadrants) manifests as a different variety of practice with different repercussions. The lower half of the chart depicts varieties of ineffectual practice—unhelpful for client and counselor alike. The upper half discriminates two forms of influential practice. In the upper left, the therapist takes "authorship" (White, 2007) such that "the door closes on collaboration, and the therapist is set up to feel burdened and exhausted while the people who are seeking consultation feel impotent" (p. 40). In the upper right, clients "define their own position in relation to their problems" (White, 2007, p. 39), which is energizing for therapists and empowering for clients.

Influential
Counselor facilitates change

Counselor dispenses unsolicited advice and feels responsible for finding solutions	Counselor scaffolds inquiry to help client connect with their own knowledge and resources
Burdensome for counselor	**Energizing for counselor**
Counselor provides many suggestions that are not adopted	Counselor follows client without facilitating, problems continue to dominate
Dismissive of counselor	**Discouraging for counselor**

Centered
Counselor knowledge dominates

Decentered
Client knowledge is foregrounded

Noninfluential
Counselor fails to facilitate change

Source: Adapted from Michael White (see http://www.dulwichcentre.com.au/michael-white-workshop-notes.pdf).

A popular axiom associated with a collaborative practice is that the client is the expert. This speaks to the effort to privilege the client's voice but is ultimately a thin description because it renders the counselor's practice of decentered influencing invisible. It also fails to describe the back and forth between counselor and client that leads to therapeutic gain. Steve de Shazer (1993) comes closer to capturing the co-constructive work of counseling by describing it as "a mutual, cooperative, collaborative conversation between two or more experts" (p. 89).

Clients' expertise rests on their intimate knowledge of their bodies and minds, their connection to their social networks and physical contexts, their accumulated learnings from repeated encounters with the challenges they bring to counseling. Like clients', counselors' expertise derives from their own lived experience and includes their formal education and training in facilitative relational skills. However, as T. Strong (2000) points out, these skills involve "expertise about collaborative processes . . . not about win-lose negotiations or about therapists by force of enthusiasm securing the consent of their clients to adopt a particular intervention strategy" (p. 145). Lynn Hoffman (Hoffman-Hennessy & Davis, 1993) is more blunt in characterizing the nature of therapist expertise:

> I would like to see banished once and for all the idea of therapists as doctors, healers, or priests. This would not mean abandoning our hard-won skills: it would mean that instead of subjecting people to them we would explain them and teach people how to use them. (p. 372)

Inevitably, there will be times in this meeting of experts when one's understanding does not match the other's: After all, why would one expect experts to perennially agree? There are many ways to make sense of these moments, each leading to different sets of responses. A collaborative orientation suggests possibilities beyond merely labeling breaches in understanding as resistance, which construes the event exclusively in the counselor's terms and sets the stage for confrontation—another mainstay of some approaches to counselor skills training (cf. Corey, 2005; Egan, 2002; Hackney & Cormier, 2008; Young, 2009). Given that practitioners have choices about how to construct moments of impasse, it makes more sense to see them as instances when clients vividly convey where they're at, providing fertile soil for further collaboration.

RESISTANCE AND COLLABORATION

Madsen (speaking at a workshop titled "An Afternoon With Bill Madsen," April 2009) humorously recapped the example of a female client depicted as resistant who refuses to attend an assertiveness training program recommended by her counselor. What makes this ironic? The woman described above is doing a splendid job demonstrating assertiveness in the face of a power differential associated with her counselor's professional status. When we stop regarding client differences with professionals as evidence of contrariness, something quite different comes into view: We see expressions of value and personal agency.

The notion of client resistance has a long history in counseling, stretching back to Freudian ideas about patients' working overtime to avoid confronting emotional material repressed in the unconscious (Beels, 2001; Madsen, 2007). A review of the counseling literature shows that resistance is regularly measured (Mahalik, 1994), predicted (Bischoff & Tracey, 1995), and explained (Beutler, Moleiro, & Talebi, 2002).

The intent here—and throughout this text—is to do none of those things. Measuring, predicting, and explaining people's actions without engaging them actively in the process are the sorts of behaviors that promote push-back in the first place. Instead, the aim here is to propose a useful way forward when counselor and client do not see eye to eye.

The designation of a client as "resistant" grants primacy to the counselor's point of view and gives rise to talk of "strategies" (Walitzer, Dermen, & Connors, 1999) to "overcome" (Ellis, 2007) the resistance. This is a recipe for constructing a confrontational relationship. When a supervisor tells an intern, "I would call [the client] on her behavior"—as reported by a student recently—the comment conjures images of a punitive parent-child relationship. Portraying the unreceptive client as resistant is certainly one of many options for going forward, but it positions the counselor in a top-down relationship to the client and is at odds with a collaborative relational stance.

How, then, do we make sense of instances when the client refuses to accept the counselor's interpretations, when they see things differently and are unwilling to acknowledge what seems apparent? For starters, these moments stand out because they are interruptions in the back-and-forth flow of conversation. It's as though a wall goes up, and *working together* starts to feel like *pushing against*. The flow of dialogue comes to a halt. As discussed in Chapter 1, this can be understood as a lapse in collaboration—a juncture at which counselor and client temporarily lose a grip on the co-constructive process. Viewing resistance in this way trains the attention on a mutual process rather than locating it in client attributes. It provides an impetus to recover the working connection rather than do battle with resistant clients and risk further erosion of the working partnership.

> # BOX 10.4
>
> ## Encountering Resistance
>
> Steve de Shazer (1993) talks about being "resistance informed" in the sense of taking a cue from clients when they seem not to be engaging—at least not engaging in a manner expected by their counselors. Rather than seeing this as noncooperation, these instances can be understood as just the opposite: moments when clients are letting counselors know where they are. This information supports the movement toward working together collaboratively and is readily available—with the right questions.
>
> *I'm noticing you haven't followed up on talking to Chantal as we discussed last week. Can we unpack that? I'm thinking it might clarify where you're at around working things out with her.*
>
> *I'm getting a sense that I'm pushing you in a direction you don't want to go in right now. Am I off base? How are you doing with the direction we're going right now?*
>
> *So that doesn't fit for you. How about if we explore this further and get a better handle on what your take on the situation is?*
>
> *It seems that right now your first choice wouldn't be [working on X problem]. What would be the most useful way to use this conversation?*

Staying with this mode of understanding resistance, what at first glance looks like an impasse can be seen as an opportunity. When you consider how much careful attention goes into helping a client articulate their experience and identify their values, a client's failure to agree or refusal to act offers the counselor a prime opportunity to refine their understanding of where the client stands. There is little more useful to the process of change than when a client forthrightly states what is important to them, when the client shares their voice and proclaims their allegiances. This not only happens when a client says "yes" but also happens when a client says "no."

To characterize that "no" as resistance puts the counselor's point of view at the center because it highlights the way the client's experience deviates from the counselor's when it could instead accentuate what makes the client's perspective unique. To say "no" is to express one's voice. Consider the following, from sessions with Daniel in the role of counselor and Maria as client.

> *Maria says she wants to put an end to her angry outbursts with her husband Azim because she's concerned they're hurtful to him and in turn to their daughter Kyla. Recently, Maria's father, with whom Maria had a very conflictual relationship, died unexpectedly. Maria has expressed no grief in the wake of his passing. In conversations with her counselor Daniel, Maria tries to keep the focus on her interactions with her husband Azim. When exchanges with Azim go poorly, she seeks to identify alternatives. When things go well, she's interested in figuring out what enabled her to interact in a manner closer to her stated preference. For a time, Daniel repeatedly attempts to refocus their sessions on an exploration of Maria's relationship with her deceased father. In particular, he tries to help Maria get in touch with feelings of hurt and sadness so she can process unfinished business. Maria says she would prefer not to talk about her father at this time. Instead, she repeatedly tries to steer the conversation back to her interactions with her husband. In sharing his work with his supervisor, Daniel says vulnerability and loss always lie beneath anger and that Maria is resistant to exploring the real problem at hand.*

In this situation, Daniel is suffering from a dearth of curiosity, caught up in selling Maria his perspective. Rather than seeking to understand Maria's experience, he has come to a conclusion about what's really going on and is trying to effect change around an issue he has defined unilaterally. This is not to say Daniel's view is senseless, but it doesn't match what Maria currently regards as her central concern. As the work continues, Maria's view may change, as may Daniel's; for the time being the more fruitful way forward would be to explore Maria's aim to change the way she interacts with her husband Azim.

> *What makes those breaches in your communication with Azim your top priority right now?*
>
> *I've been suggesting this may be mostly about your relationship with your dad; what tells you there's something different going on?*
>
> *What comes up for you when I turn the conversation to talk of your dad?*
>
> *When you and I seem to disagree on how we interpret things, where do you turn to identify your point of view?*
>
> *Some people I meet with spend a lot of time processing the relationship with a parent in the aftermath of their parent's death. What does it say about where you're at that you're putting work on your relationship with Azim ahead of that?*

Rather than viewing Maria's position as resistant, one might understand her as standing by what is most important to her at this time, despite the counselor's attempts to recruit her into an alternate agenda. In this respect, what might otherwise be seen as a resistance can be understood not only as a lapse in collaboration but as an offering by the client that, when taken up, provides an opening for getting the working relationship back on track. Extending this idea even further, de Shazer (1993) inverts the traditional conception of resistance and suggests these are instances of "cooperation" by clients, arguing that the responsive, pragmatic counselor is "resistance informed." Certainly there are times when clients do not share their counselors' perceptions of things or exhibit reluctance to move into some territory of feeling, thinking, or acting. These present prime opportunities for recalibrating understandings.

Reflection 10.2

Think of someone whom you've been trying to persuade of something but who so far has pushed back and not shown a willingness to take on your point of view. Put aside the notion that they are being stubborn or obstinate and instead think of the person as feeding you rich information about what is important to them, what they are uncomfortable with, what they fear, and so on. Be open to learning more about the person's experience. As you do so, what if anything shifts in your quest to persuade the person of your perspective? Does it help you to let go of it, for instance, or does it perhaps give you different ideas about how to bring your thoughts forward in such a manner that the person would be more likely to hear them?

PREFERRED OUTCOME AS DESTINATION

Having engaged in a fine-grained examination of the practice of collaborative influence, we turn now to the question, *Where to?* because influence implies movement toward a destination. Section 4 of this text featured assorted practices for establishing where that *isn't* (problem definition) and where that *is* (preferences). In conjointly painting a rich picture of problems and preferences, counselor and client chart a map for their journey. It is the picture of what the client values and cherishes, hopes for and strives for—their preferred outcome—that constitutes the destination. The role of collaborative influence is to nudge the client in that direction.

Using a Miracle Question to Paint a Picture of a Preferred Outcome

To develop a picture of Jorge's preferred outcome, Maria introduced him to the miracle question (see Box 7.6 in Chapter 7). She preceded the question by conceding,

> *I have an unusual question for you, Jorge. It involves plunging into your imagination a little. I'll share the question; let me know if it sounds interesting.*

It's usually a good idea to point out when stylized practices deviate from more typical conversation—that way, clients can signal their willingness to participate and are able to engage more fully because the unusual quality of the practice has been acknowledged. Throughout the exchange, Maria invites Jorge to provide concrete descriptions in the present tense. Whereas the miracle question is more typically oriented to a description of action specifically (cf. Berg, 1994; de Shazer, 1985, 1988), Maria widens her inquiry to elicit multilayered description, drawing on the sorts of questions outlined in Box 9.9 in Chapter 9. Below is an excerpt of the exchange.

Maria:	*What's the first thing you notice when you wake up, Jorge?*
Jorge:	*I feel good.*
Maria:	*"Good," okay. Can you say more about that feeling?*
Jorge:	*I don't feel that sense of dread I'm used to at the start of the day.*
Maria:	*What's in its place?*
Jorge:	*I feel energized, well rested. I'm looking forward to my day.*
Maria:	*Where do you notice that energy in your body?*
Jorge:	*[pauses to turn his attention inward] It's a feeling of lightness. I feel lighter, looser, ready to move.*
Maria:	*Are you up earlier, later, same time?*
Jorge:	*It's maybe a little bit earlier.*
Maria:	*Is Richard with you?*
Jorge:	*No, he's at home. I get up and grab a quick shower. Then I text him. Might set up a time to meet or maybe just checking what's up.*
Maria:	*Okay. Now remember you don't know that something happened overnight. You discover what's different only as you go through your day. What do you notice next?*
Jorge:	*I'm hungry! I head for the fridge.*
Maria:	*What do you eat?*
Jorge:	*Not cold pizza. No, I have a decent breakfast. Yogurt, fruit, maybe some muesli.*
Maria:	*Do you do anything while you eat? Or just eat?*

> *Jorge:*   Just think. Eat and think.
>
> *Maria:*   Is that different?
>
> *Jorge:*   Yeah, I usually turn on the TV.
>
> *Mara:*   What's it like having the TV off?
>
> *Jorge:*   I feel less scattered, more focused.
>
> *Maria:*   What are you thinking about?

As mentioned, actions may be the backbone of the miracle question, but Maria does more than elicit a description of what Jorge does on this day following the event that happened unbeknownst to him. She expands the questioning to include, for instance, feelings, bodily sensations, thoughts, and so on. She occasionally reminds him that on this day he doesn't know the miracle occurred. And she periodically checks to confirm whether what Jorge reports is different than usual so they can compare this scenario with the problem scenario.

This sort of future-focused inquiry, whether stylized in the form of a miracle question or not, identifies the end point of a shared journey. It is the detailed description of a preferred outcome. But how does one get there? If it is a destination never before visited, it may be helpful to identify milestones to aim for along the way. That is where goals come in, and we will look at those in more detail momentarily. But it is not uncommon for clients *already* to have experienced many or all aspects of their preferred outcomes. In these cases, counselors have gold veins to tap and can exert collaborative influence by helping clients to reconnect with the knowledges, skills, abilities, and actions that got them to that preferred place previously.

EXCEPTIONS: FRAGMENTS OF PREFERRED OUTCOMES

The novelist Ursula K. le Guin (1984) tells the story of Ged, a talented sorcerer from Earthsea who is confronted by an intransigent Doorkeeper when he tries to enter the venerable House of Roke, where he once trained as young apprentice. He is told he may not pass unless he can tell the Doorkeeper his True Name. This presents a real challenge for Ged: In Earthsea, all of sorcery rests on knowing the True Names of things. Understandably, True Names are jealously protected. If Ged draws on a spell, he can be sure the Doorkeeper—himself a master sorcerer—will have a more powerful spell to counter it. If he tries a ruse, the Doorkeeper will certainly see through it. If he tries to use force, Ged can be sure the Doorkeeper will respond with greater force. Ged sits under a tree to ponder this puzzle. Several days and nights go by, and he is exhausted and despairing when, in a moment of insight, he resolves the puzzle. He stands before the Doorkeeper and utters five words: "What is your True Name?" The Doorkeeper responds, Ged repeats the words, the door swings open, and he enters. There was no conjuring to be done: All Ged needed to do was *ask*.

This story made an impression on me when I first encountered it many years ago because it's a compelling reminder that we often get busy trying to solve dilemmas when the answer is already at hand. I was thinking of counseling and therapy in particular: So many traditions seem oriented to making headway *despite* clients rather than *with* them. So much energy goes into figuring out clients at the expense of relying on their expertise on their own experience. When it comes to the topic of influence, the learning here is that one of the key influential roles counselors can play is to support clients in exploiting knowledge they already have.

Berg (1993) and many others have made a similar point with one simple phrase: "If it ain't broke, don't fix it" (p. 15). If a client already displays the ability to deal with the challenges they report, why work to replace the existing repertoire? It is not uncommon to notice gaps in the problem-saturated story (Epston, 2008) at the very moment of its telling. Shaquille, for instance, is having angry outbursts verging on violence in his marriage, but the relationship was peaceful and loving for many years. Maya reports chronic depression but also tells the story of how she recently played joyfully with her grandchildren. These exceptions deserve further inquiry.

Exceptions to the problem may have occurred in the past, or they may be occurring now, at the time the client is consulting you. Rather than working overtime to fix the situation by conjuring up ideas for what the client needs to do differently, it makes more sense to learn from the client what they have done or are doing now—at least occasionally—that keeps the problem at bay. In effect, exceptions are fragments of preferred outcomes and are as available as Ged's password.

Many widely circulated accounts of counseling practice—including the approaches you may have been exposed to so far in your training—pay what I believe is insufficient attention to exceptions as central to therapeutic change. This is because of a dominant strain of thought focused on pathology and deficit—one that borrows heavily from medical traditions that are inadequate models for the practice of counseling and therapy (Gergen, 1994). If a medical patient who has been shown to have advanced multiple sclerosis reports a day virtually devoid of symptoms, the physician may celebrate their relief but will not normally anticipate much more of this unless the root of the symptoms is eradicated. In other words, the symptomless day is seen not as evidence of change but as an aberration unlikely to persist without the elimination of the underlying disease.

In some cases, clients are dealing with mental illness, some forms of which have been shown to be linked to medical factors. But the counselor's primary task is to provide help in relation to the client's subjective experience and not to treat organic disease—the mandate of a medical practitioner. The counselor's task is to collaborate with the client to seek relief from distress and suffering. When a client reports a diminishment of the concerns that brought them to counseling, this constitutes change itself. To minimize such a development is to squander a valuable opportunity. Consider the following examples of exceptions:

> *Sandip complains he is tongue-tied with women despite his desire to have a partner and raise a family. He reports that he recently enjoyed making somewhat awkward small talk at a party with a woman and has arranged to meet her for coffee.*

> *Ursula has been losing sleep about school. She says she hasn't been able to bear down on studying and is getting poor grades, which will prevent her from enrolling in a graduate program. On the weekend, she shut off her Internet wireless, made a pot of tea, and spent 2 consecutive hours reading her textbook in preparation for an upcoming exam.*

> *Laurent was diagnosed with cancer several months ago and is undergoing treatment. So far, the tumor has not shown signs of shrinkage. Since the diagnosis, Laurent has been overwhelmed by feelings of self-pity and dark moods. This week he was reading a book about spirituality, and a passage about compassionate acceptance jumped out at him, leaving him with a momentary feeling of peacefulness.*

In each of the above examples, the client reports a development that is, in effect, a fragment of the outcome they came to counseling to achieve. In each case, the client exhibits the ability to contend successfully with the source of their distress. This does not mean the challenge has evaporated, but it certainly indicates possibilities not evident in any description of their situation limited to problem definition. To regard these developments as merely symptomatic change unrelated to root causes is to misapply a medical mode of understanding to the practice of counseling and therapy.

Perhaps this is clearest in the example of Laurent because he is both a medical patient and a counseling client. For the medical practitioner whose task is to treat his cancer, an exception of note would be a pathology report indicating the tumor has lost mass. But the problem outlined by Laurent the counseling client is not the tumor but rather his mood. And so Laurent's attitude shift is a key exception. In the counseling context, this week's development is worthy of much further exploration.

There are many ways to talk about and make sense of exceptions. Below are a few; readers may have ideas about other descriptions that might be added to the list:

1. times when problems are absent or diminished,

2. gaps in a problem-saturated story,

3. instances of clients' living aspects of previously described preferred futures,

4. moments when clients experience what is valued by them or important to them, and

5. clients' enactments of personal agency.

Sykes Wylie (1994) described inquiry into exceptions as "panning for gold." However they are characterized, exceptions present a golden opportunity for therapeutic conversations. Working with them is a key influencing task, regardless of the practitioner's preferred theoretical orientation. It is a form of influence that strikes the balance between the client's and the counselor's points of view that is a feature of collaborative influence. Inquiring into and building on exceptions are collaborative because they draw from the client's knowledge and preferences and influential because they call on the counselor to consciously seek out and maintain a persistent curiosity about developments the client may have difficulty noticing at the time of sharing. The chapters to come will feature a wide variety of practices for working with exceptions.

ESTABLISHING ACHIEVABLE GOALS

There is a growing body of compelling literature demonstrating the utility of single sessions (Bobele, Servin-Guerrero Lopez, Scamardo, & Solorzano, 2008; Harper-Jaques, McElheran, Slive, & Leahey, 2008; Slive & Bobele, 2011; Young, 2008, 2011), a distilled form of practice typically organized around highlighting and building on exceptions. In some cases, clients may need no more than to reconnect with what has worked or is currently working (to some degree) in their lives to rekindle a sense of hopefulness and forward momentum. Remember, though, that exceptions are only fragments of preferred outcomes, and for many people, the experience of those breaks from their distress are a welcome respite but do not indicate they've reached their destinations. Put differently, it's one thing to experience moments when things are working as desired and another to render counseling superfluous because one's concerns have generally receded to the background. For this reason, in addition to encouraging clients to do more of what is already working, it is often useful to join clients in identifying additional actions they can initiate so the fragments of preferred outcomes can occupy increasingly more space in their lives. Counseling goals are those concrete steps.

Student Voices

Razni: Preferences, Goals, and Preferred Outcomes

As the client in my previous counselling, I found myself going round in circles, absorbed by critical analysis and intrusive thoughts. This made it difficult to effectively and rationally look at challenges. With my current counselor, however, I feel that defining my preferences (what I would like things to be like) and setting small, incremental goals to get there has been extremely valuable to my self-development. I feel that approaching my challenges in this way has helped me to focus specifically on the main issues and also on the underlying themes, such as developing self- confidence. By having this focus I've been able to look at my problems from a more external, rational and logical position, break down my issues into separate parts and devise an organized plan (my goals) to overcome them. I have therefore been able to avoid getting emotionally overwhelmed by all my thoughts and self-criticism. . . . I feel highlighting preferences can provide the client with motivation and hope for the future and that goals can help the client to feel equipped to take the necessary steps to head towards their preferred outcome.

It's worth noting that in daily usage, the words *goal* and *outcome* are sometimes taken to be synonymous. In this book, they are not. A *preferred outcome* is the overall state of being at the conclusion of a successful therapeutic collaboration. A detailed account of a preferred outcome has the multifaceted quality of thick description, as explored in Chapter 9. A counseling *goal* is an achievable step, a milestone along the road, something a client can do to move closer to their preferred outcome. Achievability is therefore the hallmark of effective goal setting. Box 10.5 outlines some features of well-defined goals.

BOX 10.5

Well-Defined Goals

Like the practice of developing accounts of challenges and preferences, goal setting is typically a methodical process aimed at detailed, concrete descriptions. Goals are steps to a destination and should be things clients can do, not end results. Effective goals give clients concrete bases for action. When goal setting is unhelpful, it is often because the goals are vague and ill defined. The list below provides some ideas to keep in mind when defining goals with clients.

Positive Representation

The client describes what they will be doing, feeling, thinking, and so forth in explicit terms rather than in terms of the absence of a problem.

"I will phone friends more" rather than "I won't be lonely."

Process Form

Verbs are better than nouns because they describe actions, not states of being.

"I will jog every second morning" rather than "More fitness."

Here and Now

The client describes something they can start when they walk away from the conversation or even during the conversation.

"I will research universities online" rather than "I will decide where I want to go."

As Specific as Possible

Generalizations blur the picture.

"I will watch videos with my kids on weekends" versus "I will connect with my children more."

Achievable

Reaching too far backfires.

"I will take time to meditate" rather than "I will attain total peace."

Measurable Frequency

Establishing how often something will be done makes it possible to achieve a target.

"I will jog for half an hour three times a week" rather than "I will go for more runs."

Within the Client's Control

The client describes something they can do rather than something different in the world.

"I will say 'no' more often" rather than "The pace of life won't be so fast and hectic."

In the Client's Language

The goal is based on the client's, rather than the counselor's, worldview, preferences, and ways of speaking.

"I will hang out with my friends" rather than "I will break my habit of isolation."

Reflection 10.3

Perhaps you have certain preferred outcomes, but you have not yet taken the time to consider the steps that might incrementally move you in those directions. Reflect on one outcome that currently comes to mind: How vivid is your picture of that end destination? A clearer image of where you want to go will help you make your way there. What would a step in that direction look like—not a giant leap to an end place but some small gesture that would begin the movement toward that preferred outcome? What might you do, how often, at what time, and in what context? What is the impact of reflecting this way on potential goals?

BOX 10.6

To Goal or Not to Goal?

Although most counseling skills texts (this one included) feature a section on goal setting, there are differences of opinion among practitioners as to the utility of setting detailed goals near the outset of the work with a client. For instance, Walter and Peller (2000) describe the evolution of their practice away from the up-front setting of concrete goals and into something more like an ongoing, future-oriented process they call "goaling."

There are compelling views on both sides of this issue. Having goals to aim for suggests specific behaviors clients can engage in as they move toward preferred futures. Because goals are steps that clients actually take, establishing goals helps to circumvent the risk of counseling's being all talk and no action. Goals also provide a reference point for gauging how the work is progressing. For this reason most institutional settings require some form of goal setting for evaluating outcomes.

On the other hand, setting goals near the front end of a therapeutic collaboration can lock down the conversations that follow, constraining the possibility of changes in direction and new angles. If lived experience is ever-flowing, as it has been described here, then a client's experience shifts from session to session, and what was resonant or significant at one time may be less so at another. In addition, some client concerns are less about action and more about meaning (see Box 7.3): Coming to terms with a loss may not involve doing anything more than reflecting on it, talking about it, and being with it.

It probably makes sense to approach the issue of goal setting in the spirit of both/and discussed in Chapter 4. In other words, it's not necessary that one of these two perspectives prevail. The degree of goal setting and its specificity can be adjusted according to the specific situation and institutional requirements.

Maria and Jorge's Collaboration on Goal Setting

As the picture emerges of a client's preferred outcome, counselor and client can speculate about steps in that direction. When Maria and her client Jorge spent the better part of a session exploring a miracle scenario, they significantly expanded the picture of Jorge's preferred outcome. Their conversation started with a detailed account of the beginning of Jorge's day but continued to include descriptions of Jorge at school, Jorge with Richard, and Jorge with friends and even an account of a visit home to his parents. Box 10.7 contains highlights of that conversation, parts of his picture of a preferred outcome. Note that the descriptions featured are those that relate to what he has described as his central concerns: his career uncertainty, his insomnia, the relationship with his parents, and the issue of coming out to them.

BOX 10.7

Highlights of Jorge's Miracle Scenario

"I'm in a program that fits my passions and talents."

"I'm in good physical shape."

"I have a good handle on career options ahead of me."

"I don't feel I'm living two lives or that I have to hide a big part of who I am when I'm with my parents."

"My dad is aware of my sexual identity and comfortable with it. We can laugh together."

"I'm sleeping well and feel refreshed."

This exchange painted a far more vivid picture of Jorge's preferred outcome and generated lots of ideas about possible goals. Around each point, Maria and Jorge first considered whether he currently experiences or previously had experienced anything listed above. If so, which actions helped him achieve those experiences? There is a great deal of productive conversation that can accompany this sort of inquiry, and the chapters that follow will explore further possibilities related to building on exceptions: For now, the topic at hand is goal setting.

Considering past successes is an important part of setting goals because it provides a barometer of what has worked previously. In the case of sleeping, Jorge has noticed he gets a better night's sleep if he lays off caffeinated beverages. So it makes sense to build this into a plan. He also sleeps better when he gets regular exercise, and he's less prone to anxiety at those times too. All of this figured in the goals outlined in Box 10.5.

The issues of career/school and his relationship with his parents are more complex and interrelated than Jorge's sleep challenges. Jorge realizes he needs to explore his own talents and passions more, as well as get a picture of career profiles, on the road to studying/working in an area that fits him better. It's still not clear what that might be. Around career, he says he has to sort out his values from his father's, not to mention evaluate his position on the widespread cultural idea that success is equated with income. Goals around career involve further exploration that will help him move closer to his preferred outcome.

Jorge's miracle scenario depicts a quantum shift in Jorge's relationship with his father. In that scenario he's now out to his father, but he's not sure how he got there. After much discussion, Jorge concludes he doesn't feel ready to take on that one; it makes more sense to him to work on his relationship with his parents in preparation for coming out in a manner that feels comfortable.

The list of goals in Box 10.8 gives Jorge some things he can work on prior to the next session; he and Maria recognize they will likely revise the list as the picture evolves. Jorge came up with some of the ideas without prompting; in other cases, Maria made suggestions that were modified by Jorge. Some steps involve doing more of what's been helpful up to now; others involve new initiatives. The goals vary in specificity. It's not assumed these will solve Jorge's problems or launch him overnight into his preferred future, but Maria and Jorge agree they will move things in a favorable direction.

BOX 10.8

Jorge's Goals

1. Jog or go to the gym four times per week.
2. Don't drink coffee or pop after supper.
3. Cut back on takeout junk food, and cook at home more.
4. Meet with university career counselor.
5. Review university calendar to learn about programs offered, rules for switching, and so forth.
6. Have Sunday dinners with parents, and arrive early enough to talk and catch up.

Notice this list does not include "Switch university programs" or "Introduce Richard to parents." Remember, goals are steps *toward* preferred outcomes—not the outcomes themselves. A key to setting achievable goals is to reflect on which steps the client feels ready to undertake at the present time. In this case, Jorge indicated he has some information gathering and reflection to do before making any career moves. He also concluded he would prefer to spend time with his parents after a period of disconnection in preparation for sharing news that will likely be complicated for them.

It's important that Maria pay close attention to where Jorge is as she walks alongside him in this process. A different client in a situation similar to Jorge's might feel he's already expended all options and that it's time for his parents to deal with reality, regardless of the consequences. To push Jorge in this direction could have long-term repercussions on his family relationships. In collaborating on goal setting, it's important to calibrate the brainstorming in relation to each unique client. This involves helping each client to consider their experience in detail, considering the various options available, and anticipating the consequences of choices they might make. This is the practice of promoting critical reflection, another key feature of collaborative influence.

INVITATION TO CRITICAL REFLECTION

You may have had the experience at some time in your life of being overwhelmed by some situation, at a loss for words to describe your experience. You're enveloped in an amorphous mass of thought, feeling, image, and sensation, and you can't separate one from the other. Talking things through at moments like these can be very useful, and a key aspect of the counselor's influencing role is to help clients to step back (Young, 2011) from their experience—to survey it from afar, as it were, revealing its contours and bringing details into focus.

The distancing that makes room for the examination of experience is sometimes referred to as "reflexivity" (Béres, 2009). It's like the difference between being carried in a river's currents versus watching the river from the bank. In the current, one is caught in the torrent, out of control and preoccupied with staying afloat. From the bank, one surveys the passing flow but is separate from it. Reflexivity provides a useful vantage point for both clients and counselors.

BOX 10.9

Eyes Wide Open: Critical Reflection

If counseling involves influence, it also involves risk—at least the appearance of risk—because it usually feels safer to do nothing than to take a step. Despite the mantra, "Change is good," change is also threatening because it

(Continued)

(Continued)

upsets the status quo and does not come with guarantees that things will be better. For all of these reasons, it's important that counselors and clients keep their eyes on the road as they move forward, critically reflecting on the challenges and opportunities that present themselves.

To do this requires the ability to make one's experience the object of attention. In this sense, it is a lot like mindfulness (Béres, 2009; Hick, 2009), as described in earlier chapters. Imagine the counseling room has mirrored walls (Hare-Mustin, 1994), and counselor and client observe at a glance their own personal experience, their interactions, and the broader social context in which their conversations are taking place. Critical reflection involves turning your gaze to yourself and the situation at hand to not only experience it but observe your experience of it. This is about getting a distance on things, as we do on a holiday away, the experience of seeing the forest when we're lost in the trees.

For clients, critical reflection is very useful. Instead of *being* their experience, they are *in relation to* their experience, sifting through it to determine what fits and what they would like to discard. It also allows them to play out various scenarios, anticipating obstacles and negative repercussions. Inviting critical reflection is similar to what feminists called "consciousness raising" (Brown, 2006) and what the emancipatory educator Paulo Freire (1972) called "conscientization"—identifying and naming oppression as a step toward achieving freedom. Reflecting critically on options creates the opportunity to make informed choices, guided by values. This is self-determination, the sort of client autonomy that Madsen (1999) playfully suggests is a desirable aspect of a therapy founded on the "planned obsolescence" (p. 129) of the counselor. It is also agency—the antithesis of a stance of passive victimhood and a useful position from which to deal with challenges and problems.

Critical reflection is equally useful to practitioners. When we think about, write about, and talk about our practice, we hold a mirror to the ideas and beliefs deriving from professional sources, our families and personal histories, the wider culture, and so on, which influence our interactions in helpful and unhelpful directions (Duvall & Béres, 2011; Fook & Gardner, 2007). Attending to these and doing our best to track their influence helps us make deliberate choices informed by judgment, to stay truer to an ethic of care (Paré, Richardson, & Tarragona, 2009).

Epston (2008) captures the shared, reflexive quality of counseling in depicting counselors and clients as "co-researchers." When both are scanning the horizon, open to possibilities and vigilant about obstacles, they are engaged in a mutual practice of critical reflection.

Like the patient and persistent inquiry into exceptions, critical reflection is another invaluable skill that balances collaboration and influence. It supports clients in drawing on their local knowledge, but in a selective and discerning manner specific to the challenge at hand. Effective goal setting calls for critical reflection because without it, steps for the road ahead are identified without thoughtful consideration of how particular choices might play out both personally and socially. For example, Jorge's miracle scenario provided him and Maria with a lot of material for setting possible goals, but discerning what would be achievable and appropriate at this time involved reflecting critically on options. Maria helped Jorge do this through questions inviting him to turn options over in his mind's eye, the way a jeweler examines the various facets of a gem. Notice that some questions encourage him to pay careful attention to his immediate experience, and others to cast his view more widely, imagining how various scenarios might unfold and considering the ramifications of certain choices.

> *What steps would be most doable right now, Jorge?*
>
> *What's the relationship between physical fitness and a good night's sleep?*
>
> *How would it affect your budget if you started buying more fresh food?*
>
> *What's helped calm you down when the anxiety's come on in the past?*
>
> *What could you do to widen your picture of the career options out there?*
>
> *What do you notice coming up for you as you contemplate coming out to your dad?*
>
> *What do you imagine would happen if you just showed up for dinner with Richard and announced he's your partner?*
>
> *What gestures by you might begin to repair what sounds like an abrasive relationship with your dad?*
>
> *How would you know the time is ripe for coming out to your folks?*

Critical Reflection and Mindful Practice

Inviting clients to critically reflect on their experience supports the goal-setting process, but so does critical self-reflection by counselors (Duvall & Béres, 2011). That same discerning eye that Maria invites Jorge to train on his own life can be adopted by Maria as a key tool of accountable practice. Critical self-reflection allows Maria to ensure her counseling interactions are aligned with her purposes and intentions and enables her to scan the wider horizon for both opportunities and threats. This is mindful practice. It calls for an attention to experience that can be cultivated through the conscious commitment to an ethic of care and by engaging in meditation and other practices that promote self-awareness (Germer, Siegel, & Fulton, 2005; Hick, 2009). At the same time that Maria is inviting Jorge to reflect critically on his situation, she is also turning her gaze on herself:

> *Am I pushing Jorge too hard out of frustration with my own struggles lately?*
>
> *Is my knowledge about nutrition and sleep getting in the way of Jorge's discovering what works best for him?*
>
> *How is my own experience with anxiety influencing the sorts of options I'm inviting Jorge to consider?*
>
> *How am I dealing with my discomfort with silences?*
>
> *I'm currently having a sort of career crisis of my own; is that influencing me to encourage Jorge to switch programs?*
>
> *What do I feel in my gut when Jorge talks about his alienation from his father and their stark differences?*
>
> *Is my passion for social justice making me overlook how difficult it would be for Jorge to simply come out to his parents overnight?*

Reflection as Inquiry

Readers may notice that whether it takes place in the form of clients' examining their own experience or counselors' monitoring their practices, critical reflection consists of ongoing inquiry. It is not founded on closed conclusions or final answers; on the contrary, it is, as Walsh (2008) puts it,

> the ultimate impossibility of understanding that keeps the reflective process going. Hence, while therapists may gain a deeper appreciation for the complexity of their clients' experience, that appreciation should be accompanied by an equally growing sense of humility and awe in the face of that experience. (p. 78)

Inviting clients to reflect critically is a collaborative process because it centers clients' understandings, but it is also influential because it ensures clients are actively engaged in finding ways out of their distress. To do this effectively involves the skillful use of one of counseling's most versatile tools: the *question.* You may have noticed that most of the session excerpts presented throughout the book feature clients responding to counselors' questions. Questions are the core of scaffolded therapeutic conversation. As we turn to theoretically informed modes of influencing in the next four chapters, you will notice that questions continue to play a central role. Curiosity is the motor of all the approaches; it is what one is curious *about* that distinguishes the various models of practice.

THE ROLE OF THEORY IN COLLABORATIVE INFLUENCE

As discussed earlier, the term *intervention* often comes up when describing practice that explicitly and actively seeks to promote change. In the literature, intervention is often depicted as something the counselor brings to the conversation and is typically associated with theory-driven practice. What is different here is that a chapter about influencing clients is wrapping up without reference to any particular theory or model. That's because the chapter has explored the many ways of influencing movement toward change by working with what clients bring *to* the conversation—the knowledges, abilities, resources, and so on that are available but frequently overlooked by clients in the midst of challenges. Put simply, there is a lot that counselors can do to move conversations forward without relying on specific, theory-informed protocols to facilitate change.

That said, de Shazer's (1993) notion that therapy involves dialogue between *two or more* experts is useful. Not only clients bring resources to the conversation—so too do counselors. And there are certainly many resources for counselors out there; by any count more than 350 models of therapeutic practice are described in the literature (Duncan, Miller, Wampold, & Hubble, 2010). These offer potentially helpful conversational "resources for action" (McNamee, 2004) that counselors can draw on to enhance the movement toward helpful change.

Avoiding Culture-Bound Myopia

Counseling theories are typically focused on ideas (e.g., about growth and human development, personality, psychopathology) and practices for intervening in highly specific ways with clients. As helpful as these can be, there is always the risk of regarding these ideas and practices as given truth, which leads to interactions highly centered on counselor knowledge, as explored in Box 10.3 in this chapter. The downside of this has been described in various ways. Hoyt (1994) and many others have equated a strict allegiance to theory to condemning the client to a Procrustean bed. Procrustes was a mythological figure who stretched his victims or cut off their limbs to make them fit into an iron bed he had welded. The therapist Milton Erickson is said to have issued a similar warning, saying that when the only tool you have is a hammer, everything looks like a nail. Either way, the client is made to adapt to the counselor's viewpoint or to adhere to a prescribed set of actions.

There are remedies for the loss of flexibility that come from holding too tight to theory. One helpful tack to adopt is an anthropological perspective, remembering that a theory is introduced by a person of a certain race, ethnicity, age, gender, sexual orientation, and so forth inhabiting a singular geographical location at a particular time in history. In that sense, theories are culture-bound creations (Stuart, 2004). When speaking with local inhabitants of foreign countries, only naïve travelers expect to encounter ideas and practices just like those at home. Why should it be different with therapeutic conversations, given that counseling theories are generated in specific contexts that can't be expected to match the day-to-day life of all people? Pedersen (1995) takes this further in suggesting that counselors who expect their ideas to apply to clients regardless of context are acting in a racist manner, although of course this may not be deliberate: "The unintentional racist may behave in ways that are even contradictory to that person's underlying intended motives" (p. 197). The consciousness of cultural diversity can be a reminder to invite clients to participate actively and critically in evaluating the applicability of theory to their unique circumstances. The skills associated with this attitude are similar to those shared in Chapter 9, Box 9.8, for inviting clients to reflect on the impact of diagnostic labels in their lives. The introduction of theoretical ideas doesn't have to be like an announcement of how things are but can be an invitation to further dialogue:

> *You've probably heard* [ideas associated with a well-known theory]. *I wonder, how do you think they might fit in this circumstance?*
>
> *There is an interesting notion from* [a counseling theory] *that I think could be useful here. How about if I tell you more about it, and we can evaluate whether it might apply?*
>
> *You know, the research literature often points to* [some theoretical or empirically demonstrated point]. *I'm wondering if that might be a useful way to make sense of what's going on here? Any thoughts?*

These questions suggest a particular spin on the role of theory: the notion that theories can be something we *invent with* rather than *do to* clients, at least to the extent that we invite them to reflect critically on the ideas we bring forward, to adapt them and make them their own. As Bohart (2006) says, therapies and the theories that inform them "are not really treatments that operate on clients to change them but rather tools used by clients in their self-healing and problem-solving efforts. Techniques do not operate on clients so much as clients operate on techniques" (p. 223).

Bohart's (2006) conception of what he calls an "active client" fits well with the emphasis throughout these pages on practice that invokes client agency and choice. There is no need for clients to be relegated to submissive roles once theory-informed interventions are brought to the conversation. But there are many skills involved in realizing Bohart's vision. The chapters to come will introduce practices associated with a variety of widely used counseling theories, along with demonstrations of how these can be integrated into fluid, responsive, and collaborative dialogue.

CHAPTER TEN RECAP

This chapter carefully teased out a description of collaborative influence as a precursor to presenting skills for identifying steps along the path to preferred outcomes. The hallmark of collaborative influence is a relational posture that centers the client in an ongoing process of critical reflection. This facilitated reflection builds a bridge between what is already known and familiar to the client and what it is possible for them to know. Questions play a key role in the process—whether questions that draw forth preexisting knowledge and abilities or questions that invite clients to critically reflect on material the counselor brings to the conversation.

Establishing a vivid picture of a preferred state of affairs, as introduced in Chapter 9, provides a destination for the work but does not automatically reveal the steps necessary to get there. Identifying and honing those steps is the practice of establishing well-defined, achievable goals. Depending on the client and the presenting concern at hand, goal definition may be more or less pronounced. In any case, the practice of goal setting is an expectation of most counseling and psychotherapy workplaces.

Collaborative influence constitutes foundational counseling practice and does not depend on specific theoretical models to facilitate change. Instead, it relies on an attitude of hopefulness and a relational posture that invites clients to connect with their knowledges and to critically reflect on their options. It does not exclude the option of counselors' drawing on professional (e.g., theories) or individual (e.g., personal experience) knowledge but involves holding these tentatively and offering them up in a manner that gives clients the opportunity to evaluate their usefulness and applicability.

The book's having established a broad base founded on client resources, the coming chapters will present options for bringing theoretical ideas and practices to therapeutic conversations. Although no chapter is exclusively linked to any particular theory, each explores skills associated with a domain of therapeutic change predominantly featured in contemporary counseling practice: (a) action, (b) thoughts and beliefs, (c) emotion and values, and (d) story.

CHAPTER TEN DISCUSSION QUESTIONS

1. **Balancing advice and passivity.** Think about times you've sought support for a challenge you were trying to work out. Can you remember a time when someone's response was unsolicited advice giving? What was this like? Alternately, can you remember a time when your listener remained passive in a way that left you wondering what their perspective was on the issue? What was that like?

2. **Maria and Jorge's miracle question.** What difference does it make having Jorge answer in the present tense? Why does Maria intermittently remind Jorge that in this scenario, he's unaware the miracle occurred overnight? What does she gain or lose by her expanded version of the miracle question that goes beyond the more typical focus on client actions? Why does she ask about whether certain experiences are different than usual?

3. **Goals as milestones toward destinations.** What does it mean to suggest counseling goals are milestones on the way toward the multilayered description of a preferred outcome gained by a miracle question? What is the difference between a counseling goal and an outcome? Why is the description of a preferred outcome multilayered whereas the description of a goal is focused on concrete action?

4. **Goals and preferred outcomes.** The word *goal* in everyday use sometimes suggests an endpoint (i.e., "My goal is to retire at sixty."). Discuss what is different about the way the word is used here and its relationship to the term *preferred outcome*.

5. **To goal or not to goal.** Discuss the advantages and disadvantages of establishing goals early in the work with clients. What practices would make it possible to capitalize on the advantages of goal setting while sidestepping the disadvantages?

6. **Reflexivity.** Reflect on and discuss a time you managed to get a distance on an issue, how you were able to break it down into parts and to make sense of what may at first have been an undifferentiated conglomerate of thoughts and feelings. What changed for you as you were able to step back and reflect on this? What sorts of dialogue did you rely on—inner dialogue such as thinking and writing or outer dialogue such as drawing or talking? How did these processes help?

7. **Critical reflection and risk.** Given that striving for any sort of change involves some degree of risk, what role in mitigating risk does critical reflection play?

8. **Resistance and cooperation.** In which sense could what is normally called client resistance be seen as cooperation instead? What could be useful in exploring a client's reluctance to assume language or engage in actions proposed by the counselor?

9. **Learning, development, and context.** How do Vygotsky's notions of scaffolding and zone of proximal development help to explain positive correlations between (a) IQ and academic achievement and (b) socioeconomic class?

10. **Two experts.** Discuss the difference between the notion that the client is the expert and de Shazer's (1993) notion that counseling is a "conversation between two or more experts" (p. 89). How would this difference play out in counseling practice?

11. **The role of theory.** Provide an example of a client's being forced to fit a particular theory, following on the myth of Procrustes. What happens to the client's sense of agency and connection to their own knowledge when this happens? What impact might it have on the therapeutic relationship?

CHAPTER TEN ACTIVITIES

1. **Advice giving.** Form pairs. Speaker, talk about some challenge you are currently dealing with, choosing a topic appropriate to the context, or make up an issue for the purposes of this activity. Listener, attend with an ear to solving the issue on the spot, deliberately giving blunt advice as quickly as it comes to mind—even if it feels abrupt and perhaps half-baked. (Warning: This may be humorous! Try to make it somewhat believable.) Debrief. Speaker, what was it like to have advice pitched at you so quickly? How did it leave you feeling about the listener's estimation of your own judgment or the complexity of your challenge? Listener, what was it like to stifle the urge to keep listening and to plunge directly into advice giving? If it was challenging, which concerns held you back?

2. **Exceptions.** Pair up. Speaker, share the details of some challenge you face appropriate to the context at hand. Listener, join with the speaker in examining their past and recent history with this challenge, with a deliberate focus on exceptions to the problem-saturated account. Debrief. Speaker, what was it like to have exceptions noted by the listener? How did this affect your experience of the issue? Listener, which sorts of challenges were involved in keeping an ear and eye out for exceptions? How did this affect the way you experienced the speaker?

3. **Goals and preferred outcomes.** Form groups of three. From the following list, identify which items describe preferred outcomes and which represent goals. Compare your responses and debrief. How did you decide which is which?

    1. To study 1 hour per night

    2. To get along well with my roommate

3. To feel good about my body shape

4. To talk to a police officer's supervisor about racist treatment

5. To have regularly scheduled dates with my partner

6. To appreciate my family for who they are

7. To let go of my guilt about my affair

8. To be rid of my nagging anxiety

9. To talk to my roommate about how her untidiness bothers me

10. To meditate for 20 minutes a day

4. **Relating goals and preferred outcomes.** In groups of three, revisit the list of 10 goals and preferred outcomes, above. For the preferred outcomes, invent some possible goals that would move a client in that direction. For the goals, speculate about which preferred outcome might be the end point achieved by taking that step. Debrief. Compare the goals you came up with: similar and different roads to Rome. How might these reflect your own personal experience? Compare the hypothetical preferred outcomes: Did you describe these primarily in actions, feelings, thoughts, or other ways?

5. **Preferred outcomes and goals.** Form pairs. Speaker, describe your preferred outcome in relation to the challenge described in Activity 1 or 2. If it helps, have the listener help you explore this by using a miracle question or letter from the future (see Chapter 7). Listener, support the describing of the preferred outcome, and work collaboratively with the speaker to speculate about achievable steps toward the destination. Debrief. How did the description of the preferred outcome suggest possible goals? How did you determine what might be achievable?

6. **Goal setting and critical reflection.** Form pairs. Speaker, select goals that seem at first glance to be most appropriate and achievable in relation to the challenge identified in the previous activity. Listener, invite the speaker to critically reflect on the goals named by asking questions to encourage the speaker to consider obstacles, consequences, the wider context, and so on. Debrief. Speaker, how did critical reflection temper your goal setting? Listener, which sorts of questions seemed to invite critical review of possible goals?

7. **Scaffolding in daily life.** Form small groups. Scaffolding inquiry is a skill widely used in daily life, although not typically named as such. Come up with specific examples of scaffolding in the following situations: (a) adult with young child, (b) parent with young adult, (c) teacher with student, and (d) peer with peer. Generate examples of actual questions that would exemplify the practice of scaffolding.

8. **Increments of change.** Pair up. Speaker, recount your experience around some life learning—a challenge you confronted and overcame over time, learning some valuable lessons in the process. Speaker and listener, break down the learnings into those that involved smaller, incremental learnings and those that were the product of larger leaps. Develop questions that would invoke both sorts of learnings. Debrief. Both speaker and listener, which questions are more challenging to answer? In which ways do answers to questions about smaller increments of learning make it possible to answer those calling for larger leaps?

9. **Scaffolding inquiry.** Form pairs. Speaker, describe some current challenge appropriate to the context. Provide a rich description of the situation and your efforts to contend with it. Listener, pay attention to possibilities for addressing the challenge imbedded in the speaker's story (vs. ideas parachuted in by you). After supporting a rich recapping of the situation, ask questions that invite the speaker to expand on their learnings around the subject at hand. Debrief. Listener, which challenges were associated with posing questions versus offering advice? Speaker, which questions got you actively engaged in your learning? Which came across as more like veiled advice? Both speaker and listener, what is different about these two sets of questions?

10. **Theory as done *to* clients.** Pair up. Listener, privately conceive of some theory about what people need to do with their anger. Don't worry if it is plausible or not; it should suffice for this activity. Speaker, discuss something you are currently angry about or describe an unresolved incident in which your anger played a significant role. Listener, without sharing your theory with the speaker, coach them in acting, thinking, or feeling in a particular way that adheres to your theory about what people need to do to resolve anger. Debrief. Speaker, what was it like to be prescribed a particular way of dealing with your anger? What impact did it have on your working relationship with the listener? Listener, what was it like to impose your process on the speaker? What did you notice about how they took it up (or did not take it up)?

Chapter 11

WORKING WITH ACTIONS

INTRODUCTION

If readers of this text were surveyed about what has been helpful to them—outside of counseling—in dealing with various life challenges, the answers no doubt would vary widely. Some would report it was all about taking action—talking to someone, leaving a relationship, applying for a job, and so on. Others would speak about thinking about things in a new way, talking to themselves differently, challenging an entrenched belief. Some would describe making an emotional shift—getting in touch with some lingering anger, letting go of a grudge, expressing withheld affection. And finally, others would speak about coming to new understandings, formulating alternate accounts of their identities, making different meanings around key events.

There is no singular or universal path to preferred outcomes. Change happens in countless ways, reflecting the diversity of the human population. That's why it makes sense to attend carefully to clients' unique experience in the quest to determine what is helpful. At the same time, however, practitioners and theorists have for many decades developed and refined models—hundreds of them at last count—for counseling practice. Although any claims to all-inclusiveness ("It fixes all that ails you, no matter who you are") should be looked at with grave suspicion, many of these approaches offer useful resources for clients and counselors. Examining specific models in detail is beyond the scope of this text, but the vast majority of models can be grouped according to which dimensions of experience they key in on. This chapter and the three to follow it are organized around groupings widely applied in the field.

Research on Counseling Theories and Models

Various meta-analyses of the accumulated body of research into the effectiveness of counseling models have demonstrated some consistent findings. For one, they confirm that counseling itself is clearly helpful (Duncan, Miller,

Wampold, & Hubble, 2010; Lambert, 2004; Lambert & Bergin, 1994; Wampold, 2001). Despite the ongoing quest for a gold standard among "treatment options," however, the research does not indicate significant variability in the efficacy of the various models (Tilsen & Nylund, 2008). Nor does it point to a particular "active ingredient," akin to the key component of a pharmaceutical, that accounts for what makes counseling helpful (Duncan, Miller, & Sparks, 2004; Hyun-Nie & Wampold, 2001). As Wampold (2001) concludes, "decades of psychotherapy research have failed to find a scintilla of evidence that any specific ingredient is necessary for therapeutic change" (p. 204). Instead, the research indicates a variety of factors present to some degree in all approaches contributes to therapeutic change, with the therapeutic relationship and qualities specific to particular clients figuring most significantly (Duncan et al., 2010; Wampold, 2001). Theories and models come up third as having some influence on counseling outcomes.

A theory, according to the Oxford dictionary (Soanes, 2003), is "a system of ideas intended to explain something" (p. 1195). Without coherent frames or "lenses" for looking at/talking about things, we are confronted by the "buzzing confusion" that James (1890/1981) described as the infant's view of the world. In that respect, this entire book to this point is informed by theory because the text introduces innumerable ideas for making sense of the practice of counseling.

However, as discussed in the closing reflection in Chapter 10, the word *theory* sometimes applies to theoretical models that provide templates for counseling practice—complete with explanations for why people act the way they do and guidelines for interacting with clients in highly specific ways. Each of the innumerable models in circulation keys in on particular aspects of clients' experience as crucial to facilitating change; they provide ideas for engaging clients in distinct ways. Mastery of the models involves different approaches to looking, listening, and responding, depending on the change processes emphasized by the particular model. These various approaches to engaging clients represent expertise the counselor brings to the conversation, to add to clients' expertise, which is more focused on the unique particularities of their personal lives.

Chapter 10 explored the centrality of client knowledge and resources, generally speaking, in the process of collaborative influence. In the next four chapters, things get more specific: Attention turns to tapping relatively distinct aspects of client experience: (a) action, (b) thoughts and beliefs, and (c) feelings and values. I say relatively distinct aspects because lived experience is not compartmentalized and is simultaneously awash with actions, thoughts, feelings, bodily sensations, images, and so much more. The fourth chapter in this sequence (Chapter 14) introduces practices for bringing those diverse elements of experience together by helping clients identify through-lines or stories—narratives that capture the thematic unity of their varied experiences.

The breadth of experience notwithstanding, it is often helpful to keep a counseling conversation focused on one aspect of experience for a time, and this chapter and those to follow provide ideas and examples for doing that. Focusing a therapeutic conversation by keying in on particular dimensions of experience offers clients comforting coherence in the face of the chaos that sometimes accompanies distressful situations. It's also useful to practitioners, providing conceptual roadmaps to guide practice. So of the various features of human experience that models of therapeutic practice hone in on, this chapter features just one: action.

DO SOMETHING DIFFERENT: KEYING IN ON ACTION

Working with action may be the most direct way forward because ultimately, helpful change involves a client's doing something different (Nelson, 2010; O'Hanlon, 2000). An orientation to action is pragmatic, less concerned with explaining where problems come from and more concerned with encouraging steps forward toward preferred outcomes. Supporting clients in doing more of what works involves posing questions that generate and consolidate action, motivated by the belief that people are agents of their own actions—an alternative to the preoccupation with the purported causal origins of behavior.

Causality and Human Action

Causality is a staple of a scientific worldview and makes eminent sense in reference to the interaction of physical substances. When dealing with the biochemical determinants of health, for instance, it makes sense to identify causal links between symptoms and some organic dysfunction because correcting the underlying dysfunction usually makes the symptoms go away. That's why, in the pharmaceutical domain, the notion of the active ingredient mentioned in the introduction to this chapter is so important. Drugs are designed to target and eradicate or repair causes. As discussed earlier, however, an overreliance on medicine's causal way of thinking can lead to the squandering of many helpful opportunities in counseling.

We all are accustomed to thinking in causal terms. If you polled the general public with the question, What causes the problems people bring to counseling? you'd likely get responses ranging from "the early lack of bonding between mother and child, to genetic predispositions, to chemical imbalances, to the social environment, to personality disturbances" (Walter & Peller, 2000, p. 9). This sort of thinking makes for reassuring explanations, but it completely fails to account for the innumerable examples of people who triumph over adversity, leading rich and fulfilling lives despite childhood hardships and trauma, physical disabilities, or medical conditions. (Liebenberg & Ungar, 2008; Reich, Zautra, & Hall, 2010).

A second reason an action orientation is not preoccupied with causality is that there is not necessarily a tidy one-on-one relationship between a problem and its resolution (Gehart & Paré, 2008; Lipchik, 1999, 2002). Steve de Shazer (1988) vividly illustrates this with his story of a Japanese coastal village threatened with an approaching tsunami. A villager spies the oncoming wave, which is sure to decimate all the homes clustered along the steep-walled shoreline. He rushes to the hillside above the town and sets fire to the crops growing there. On seeing their livelihood going up in flames, all of the other villagers rush en masse up the hill to put out the fire. The wave hits the town, wiping out the deserted homes. All are saved.

de Shazer's (1988) point is that the action (dousing a burning crop) that achieved the preferred outcome (survival of the villagers) is not necessarily related to the problem itself (the tsunami) in any obvious or direct way. This constitutes a key idea behind approaches to counseling less concerned with determining causes and more concerned with encouraging action: supporting clients in taking steps toward preferred futures (cf. de Jong & Berg, 2007; de Shazer & Dolan, 2007; Guterman, 2006; Nelson, 2010; O'Hanlon, 2000; Walter & Peller, 2000).

Action Versus Explanation

The word *why* can be used for many purposes. White (2007) suggested the word has become devalued in therapeutic circles and puts it to fertile use with questions that invite people to name values and commitments, such as, *Why is it important for you to carry on despite the discouragement you're feeling?* Note, however, that this is a very different *why* than the version imbedded in the question, *Why do you have this problem?* which seeks an explanation of circumstances on the premise that it will furnish a solution. As the philosopher Wittgenstein said, "It's a mistake to look for an explanation when all you need is a description of how things work" (cited in Ward & Reuter, 2011, p. 78). A focus on supporting people in doing something different sidesteps the "why" associated with explanatory quests.

A much-circulated story about the famous therapist Milton Erickson helps illustrate what can come of encouraging more of what seems to make a difference without seeking an explanation for why a person is struggling in the first place. Erickson was in Milwaukee for a speaking engagement when a colleague asked if he would pay a visit to a disabled aunt who was housebound and depressed. Never one to fret about conventional protocol, Erickson was happy to take up the request and paid the woman a visit at her home. He discovered a heavily curtained Victorian mansion inhabited by a sad woman in a wheelchair. As this one-time client took Erickson on a tour of the vast dwelling, he found each room gloomier than the previous, mirroring his host's dark mood, until they arrived at a sun porch attached to the house.

In this bright space, the woman introduced Erickson to a project she'd initiated— starting African violets from cuttings. The vivid purple flowers, and his host's apparent pride in them, were in stark contrast to the general melancholy of the house. As Erickson inquired further he learned the woman was a member of a church congregation and that her weekly attendance at church was her lone regular social activity. His visit done, Erickson took his leave after conveying one simple directive. He suggested that whenever a member of the congregation got married or baptized a baby, the woman should mark the occasion by delivering an African violet from her nursery.

Two decades later, when this client died at the age of 76, the Milwaukee newspapers featured a bold headline indicating the "African Violet Queen of Milwaukee" had passed way. Erickson could rightly take credit for contributing to the fortuitous turnaround in the woman's life. He had put little energy into explaining his client's problem; instead he had encouraged her merely to take action in line with her apparent passion. Reflecting back on the case, Erickson commented, "I never did know what was wrong with that woman" (Capps, 1998, p. 60). O'Connell (1998) captures the spirit of Erickson's approach this way:

> Knowing intellectually how to solve a problem does not always motivate us to act. In fact, it can allow us to retreat into rationalizations of the status quote. Anyone who has fought against an unwanted habit, whether it be food, cigarettes, alcohol or anything else, has experienced the gulf between intellectual understanding and ability to act. (p. 70)

Reflection 11.1

Do you have your own African violet story? Think of something in your life that currently supports your image of who you are and fills your days with meaning—a hobby, relationship, project, pastime, habit, or crusade. What was the equivalent of those plant cuttings Erickson spotted that have since blossomed and multiplied? Who bore witness to your initial forays into this territory? What difference did it make to have a witness to something close to your heart?

[handwritten margin note: So, he just told her what to do...?]

O'Hanlon (2000) reflects the pragmatic spirit of future-focused, action-oriented therapies in saying, "Explanations often give us an illusion of help by enabling us to understand we have a problem but not giving us any concrete ways to actually solve it" (p. 2). Ample insight into problems doesn't necessarily make them go away. Sometimes the most useful way forward is to suspend reflection and rumination and simply do something different.

CAPITALIZING ON THE CONSTANCY OF CHANGE

The impulse to categorize and label discussed elsewhere in this text has a tendency to blind us to the changeability of things. Yet physicists increasingly describe a universe in constant motion and development, and biologists remind us of how living things constantly renew themselves by replacing the very cells of which they are made. This fundamental observation of the constancy of change has been a central facet of Eastern thought for centuries and is becoming increasingly evident in the Western literature on counseling and therapy (cf. Baer, 2003; Germer, Siegel, & Fulton, 2005; Hofmann, Sawyer, Witt, & Oh, 2010). Pay very close attention to any aspect of lived experience, and you will discover that nothing remains quite the same—change is ubiquitous.

Although elsewhere we've explored the importance of acknowledging clients' concerns and struggles, it is also helpful to maintain an ongoing expectancy of change—the belief that change is possible and, more than that, the assumption it is likely already occurring, although perhaps not noticed at this time by the client. As Hudson O'Hanlon and Weiner-Davis (1989) put it,

> as therapists we help to create a particular reality by the questions we ask and the topics we choose to focus upon, as well as those we choose to ignore. In the smorgasbord of information supplied to us by our clients, we think it is important to focus on what seems to be working, however small, to label it as worthwhile, and to work toward amplifying it. (p. 37)

The constancy of change is very real in the lives of clients, but therapeutic conversations won't turn toward change if the therapist does not anticipate change; as Weiner-Davis (1993) observes, you're not likely to hear about change unless you ask. Beyond conveying a curiosity about change, the asking itself can telegraph an expectancy: Note the difference between, for instance, *Have you noticed anything different this week?* and *What have you done differently this week?* This orientation to what is different can be a useful thread linking weekly conversations, and first sessions provide a rich opportunity to develop a shared curiosity about change with clients (de Shazer & Dolan, 2007; Guterman, 2006; Sharry, Darmody, & Madden, 2008).

Inquiring About Presession Change

When Weiner-Davis and colleagues (Weiner-Davis, de Shazer, & Gingerich, 1987) decided to conduct research into the relationship between how their clients were doing at the time they took the initiative to book a counseling appointment and how they were doing once they arrived for the first session, they made a fascinating discovery. About two thirds of the clients were doing better. It is interesting to note that in a follow-up study in which the therapist asked about this "pre-session change" while projecting an expectancy that it did not happen, about the same number of clients reported no change (O'Connell, 1998). The counselor's expectancy of change contributes to uncovering it.

Scaling questions, first visited in Chapter 9, are useful for tracking presession change because they quantify differences that can later be expanded on qualitatively through further exploration:

> Counselor: On a scale from 1 to 10, where 1 represents where you were at the day you decided to seek help and 10 represents the best you feel you've ever been doing, where would you say you're at today? Where were you when you called for the appointment?

If these questions are preceded by the miracle question or one of the related questions discussed in Chapter 7, the counselor and client already have the description of a preferred state of affairs as a point of reference. Rather than asking about the best a client has been doing, the counselor can inquire instead about that version of an ideal situation (e.g., the day after the miracle). When there has been any favorable movement, action-oriented questions seek a detailed inventory of client actions:

> What have you been doing to move from X to Y?
>
> How did you manage that?
>
> What steps did you take?
>
> If I were watching you during these developments, what would I see?

Projecting Change Into the Future

Keeping with the notion that change is constant, one can anticipate not only that change has happened since a person made the decision to consult a counselor but also that change will continue to happen in the future. Curiosity about changes leading up to now shines a light on actions the client is *currently* taking that make a positive difference, and these in turn point to future possibilities. Another way to put this is to say that the hunt for exceptions needn't only focus on the past or present: Speculating about *exceptions not yet enacted* can provide a powerful pull toward a preferred future:

> *Where do you see yourself by the end of the semester if you keep "sticking to the books," as you put it?*
>
> *If this "peacemaking" you both described keeps happening, how do you picture your relationship a year from now?*
>
> *If I checked in on you a few months from now (assuming these steps you've been taking continue) what kind of lifestyle would I see you engaged in?*
>
> *What will you have more of in your life, and what will you have less of, if you keep on this track?*

WHEN CHANGE ISN'T EVIDENT: COPING QUESTIONS

When there is evidence of forward progress, action-oriented questions place client and counselor squarely on a path to preferred outcomes. However, even when progress seems absent, there is no need to abandon a view of people as agents, even though movement is less evident. For starters, if a person reports doing the same or worse, their struggle deserves an acknowledgment—for example, through empathetic restating or paraphrasing. But surviving—no less than thriving—is a considerable feat in the face of difficult circumstances. Consider Odette, who has struggled on and off with depression for several years and whose 12-year-old son is currently dealing with a serious health issue that's keeping him home from school. She says she was at a 4 when she called for the appointment but is at a 2 since having learned her plans for an in-home caretaker have fallen through. The following questions are oriented more toward coping than progress, but they foreground the actions Odette has managed to take despite her challenges.

> *How have you managed to cope with this tough situation?*
>
> *What have you been doing to keep things from getting worse?*
>
> *What did you do to get yourself here with this going on?*
>
> *What keeps you going right now?*

Coping questions don't seek out exceptions, but they often provide a foundation for exceptions by fortifying a person's sense of their own agency. The questions above prompted Odette to identify a tenacity she had never previously named: I'm like a mother bear who swims into the rapids to retrieve her lost cub. Fortified with that image in her mind, Odette pored through her union agreement, marched into the office of her human resources manager, and emerged with a plan to take a limited paid leave to attend to her sick child.

PROMOTING INTRINSIC MOTIVATION

Alternatives to Cheerleading

Action-oriented questions help plant the realization that favorable developments happen without the counselor's intervention, so "the credit belongs solely to the client" (O'Connell, 1998, p. 44). These are moments worthy of celebration, and it can be tempting to cheerlead with comments such as "Good for you!" or "That's terrific!" Although the affirmation is certainly appropriate, there are a number of reasons there is more to be gained from refraining from simple cheerleading in these situations.

First, a favorable development is a prime opportunity for developing thick description (see Chapter 9). Simple praise is supportive, but it can *conclude* inquiry by rating an event. As an alternative, engaging with the development by asking more about it is a way to capitalize on a moment fertile with possibility and learn from its implications.

> *Interesting! Tell me more about what you did.*
>
> *This sounds like a whole new development. Can you lead me through it?*

Second, inquiring further into successful action helps the client get in touch with their own—as opposed to the counselor's—experience of positive developments. Noticing the rewards of one's actions fortifies intrinsic motivation, encouraging more of the same:

> *What was it like for you to stand on that weigh scale and see that number?*
>
> *How did you feel, seeing that surprised look in her eyes, when you simply said "no"?*
>
> *It seems you reaped a few rewards for all that effort this week. What's it like to savor that now?*

> *What difference does it make to your sense of hopefulness, having taken those steps despite the challenges?*

Cade (1997) cautions that it's "important to never be more enthusiastic about change than your clients" (cited in de Shazer & Dolan, 2007, p. 64). Centering *clients' own evaluations* sidesteps that trap. It provides incontrovertible proof of their own accomplishments, and it avoids setting clients up for a sense of failure when they fall short of counselor benchmarks.

White (1995) raises a third point with regard to the downsides of issuing simple praise for preferred developments in his consideration of the possible ill effects of cheerleading. He points out that simple compliments—although well intentioned—are nevertheless expressions of normative judgment. Elsewhere in this text we've looked at the predominance of negative judgment associated with deviations from "normal"; but as White points out, straight-up praise not accompanied by an invitation to clients to evaluate developments in their own terms is also a form of judgment, albeit of a positive variety. It positions clients as subject to their counselors' scorecards. More helpful is inquiry that implicitly celebrates some turn of events not by dishing out gold stickers but by seeking a richer account of how clients managed to achieve some steps.

I'd like to emphasize there is no suggestion here that positive developments are not cause for celebration or that the people achieving them should not be acknowledged. It is the form in which these acknowledgments happen that is at issue. Without offering their own judgment of developments, counselors can nevertheless celebrate developments by seeking fine-grained descriptions of actions taken. Without explicit praise, curiosity is its own compliment.

> *How did you manage it?*
>
> *What did it take to pull this off?*
>
> *What skills did you draw on?*
>
> *What does this say about your ability to overcome the problem?*

In a playful mood, Michael White used to mimic falling off his chair to register surprise at some step a client had taken, but he also made sure to invite the client to evaluate that step. Insoo Kim Berg's implicit compliment was more muted: She would greet new developments with a look of pleasant surprise and respond with one simple word: *wow.* Witnessing a person's actions with a sense of wonder affirms the scope of the life project they've undertaken.

Action in the Face of Adversity

Tapping into a person's motivation for change by deliberately foregrounding helpful actions is sometimes more difficult than it sounds—especially in conversations with a person beset by challenges. When difficult things happen to us, it can feel we are helpless victims of circumstances or guilty purveyors of wrongdoing. Acknowledging the discouragement and even hopelessness in a client's account is important, as we've already seen. But to leave it there can reinforce a sense of passive victimization or fuel destructive self-critique.

> Ralph has been living on the street since he started hearing voices 13 years ago. He comes in and out of an inner-city health facility where he meets with one of the counselors and a physician who has prescribed medication that he takes only intermittently. He's tried a number of substances to mute the sometimes terrifying mental activity but has largely settled on alcohol as his drug of choice. Last week Ralph met with a social worker to talk about some potential housing, but he showed up drunk and is doubtful anything will come of it. Today he's noticeably down on himself and discouraged about his prospects.

Fortunately, the magnitude of a person's efforts only grows as the challenges mount. So occasions of great adversity offer the opportunity for a shared inquiry into how someone manages to persist in the face of daunting circumstances.

Counselor:	Ralph, I can hear your frustration.
Ralph:	I don't think I came off too good.
Counselor:	You wanted to make a good impression.
Ralph:	[points to his worn clothing] Well I don't know about that!
Counselor:	That housing office is on Sparks Street. How'd you get there?
Ralph:	I got chauffeured. Courtesy of City Transit.
Counselor:	A bus! When was the last time you did that?
Ralph:	Don't ask me.
Counselor:	How'd you figure out the route?
Ralph:	They've got those maps plastered all over the place.
Counselor:	I can never make any sense of them.
Ralph:	You gotta study them. Two buses, one transfer. I got directions along the way.
Counselor:	Whoa. I guess it mattered to you to get there.

Ralph:	Yeah, I got that part right.
Counselor:	I'm thinking about how last time you were telling me you get paranoid talking to strangers. How'd you manage to overcome that?
Ralph:	No small talk. I just got the info I needed and skedaddled.
Counselor:	Ralph, I understand you figure you didn't come across the way you wanted to, but I'm kind of curious to learn more about what you did to find the place, make the appointment, get yourself back, and all of that. Is it okay if I ask you more about that?

There are many ways to make sense of these events in Ralph's life and many potential inquiries into them. The counselor could see this as a lapse on Ralph's part and gently chide him for his drinking. The effect of that exchange would likely be a deepening of Ralph's self-critique: just the sort of thing that another drink might mute. Instead, the counselor holds to a view of Ralph's making active choices, informed by values, in the face of challenges. It's a perspective that dignifies Ralph by implicitly acknowledging the obstacles he faced and the steps he took to overcome them. An exchange like this builds a foundation for further constructive dialogue with Ralph—including, for instance, conversations about what he needs to do next time to avoid sabotaging his efforts to solicit housing.

Reflection 11.2

Think about some small efforts you've been making to deal with some substantial challenge in your life, steps that may sometimes seem insignificant and perhaps even disheartening compared to the scope of the challenge. Ask yourself these questions:

Considering the magnitude of [the challenge at hand], what keeps you at it? What do your actions say about how committed you are to making changes?

Which kinds of qualities have been required to take the steps you've taken in light of the scope of what you're up against?

How have you managed to take the steps you have despite the possible temptation to give up on trying and pack it in?

What difference, if any, has it made to your experience of yourself and this challenge in your life to reflect on these questions?

When people's lives appear to be unraveling, counselors can let discouragement get the better of them and get busy telling clients what to do—so much for agency. Beyond conveying an attitude of respect, there is great pragmatic utility to the conviction that people invariably respond in the face of challenges, even in circumstances in which their choices are severely delimited.

ACTION AND THE LANGUAGE OF CHANGE

Earlier in this chapter we looked at how the application of a causal analysis to human action severely restricts the productive possibilities of therapeutic conversations. Another common perspective that borrows from the physical sciences is the notion of therapeutic conversation as an archaeological dig, the therapist's probing to uncover some subterranean truth. The metaphor reflects the aspect of discovery that comes with stumbling on new personal insights but in doing so obscures the constructive dimension—the way insights become *manifest* through the creative and collaborative use of language. There are ways to talk that reinforce the status quo and ways to talk that promote change. The expectancy of change mentioned earlier is more than an attitude that encourages an atmosphere of optimism: It is a way of directing attention through language that foregrounds possibility, constructing a highway to preferred outcomes.

Constructing What You Look For

Take a moment to cast your eyes about, on the lookout for anything blue within your field of vision, in preparation for reporting back a moment from now. Chances are you'll spot items you may not have previously noticed because the intention to find something in particular invites forward just that, makes it stand out from the background. And now it's time to report back: What did you see that was *red?* A dirty trick perhaps, but it's illustrative of an interesting observation: When our eyes and ears are trained on a problem, it seems to be everywhere and we're not likely to notice instances when the problem is absent.

The language we use to talk about the events of our lives guides our attention and shapes our experience. This is less about uncovering a hidden truth and more about drawing attention to what often lies in full view yet unnoticed. This requires measured attention. Taking note is very difficult to do at high velocity, like trying to spot wildflowers while speeding down a highway. Of the various features that effective therapeutic conversations of all theoretical persuasions share, one of them is the speed of their unfolding: They proceed at a thoughtful and attentive pace.

Slowing Down the Image

Although a well-placed question brings an exception to the foreground, carefully measured follow-ups ensure a golden opportunity is not squandered. An exchange that plunges forward too quickly overlooks the diamonds in the rough. You can't appreciate a gem at a glance; you have to cradle it in your palm, hold it to the light, admire its many facets. In Chapter 3 we looked at the utility of slowing down, becoming comfortable with silences that make room for unuttered thoughts and feelings to enter the conversation. Slowing down is useful for another reason as well: It creates space for observing experience at a level of detail that's impossible amid a fast-moving torrent of words.

In the very early days of photography, British photographer Edward Muybridge was able to determine with precision for the first time the complex movement of a horse's limbs in full gallop by setting up trip wires attached to a series of still cameras. Break things down into discrete pictures, and much is revealed. Muybridge discovered galloping horses do indeed have all four hooves off the ground at once—once the subject of much debate. When a client describes acting in ways that are in effect exceptions to the problem originally reported, there are a number of creative ways to break their actions down too:

> *Were there any steps you took to prepare for the changes you've made in the past few days?*
>
> *What were the first things you did differently?*
>
> *Who's been witness to these developments? What would they tell me about what they've seen?*
>
> *If I were a fly on the wall while this was going on, what would I have witnessed?*
>
> *Suppose a documentary film crew were following you around in the days since you made that phone call. When it comes time to review all of the recording, they discover there's no sound. What pictures would tell them that they indeed managed to document some of the changes you've been making? What would they see on the tape?*

The orientation to possibilities is not about seeking an *explanation* for things but about stepping back from experience and becoming more familiar with successful action.

In the following exchange with her counselor Daniel, Maria reviews highlights of her week. A week contains 10,080 minutes, however; deciding which ones to focus on depends on how Daniel wishes to orient to Maria's account. Notice here how Daniel foregrounds some of these moments with Maria and slows down her account to ensure he and she identify key actions by Maria that made a difference.

Maria:	*Well, no flare-ups at home this week anyway, although I'm still stressed out about that counseling practicum.*
Daniel:	*Hmm. How'd you create that pocket of calm?*
Maria:	*Huh? As in . . . ?*
Daniel:	*You've managed not to let that stress incite one of those famous arguments with Azim. Is that fair to say?*
Maria:	*Yeah, s'pose that's true.*
Daniel:	*How'd you pull that off?*
Maria:	*Not sure I've given it any thought, really.*
Daniel:	*Would you be interested in exploring it further? Sounds like a favorable turn, based on our last conversation.*
Maria:	*Yeah, I'd have to agree with that. Okay, shoot.*
Daniel:	*When would you say the flare-ups have been most common?*
Maria:	*Oh, probably me coming home from the counseling center, a little fried, hungry, and tired and having just picked up Kyla (also hungry!) from my sister's. Azim's reading the sports page, and I start banging things around while I heat up the bottle. I'm feeling hard done by—understandably in my opinion—and just waiting for him to offer to help, which I fully expect he won't do. And before you know it, we're shouting at each other.*
Daniel:	*Okay, and this week?*
Maria:	*[pausing to reflect on her week] Well, I was at the practicum Tuesday and Wednesday.*
Daniel:	*You picked up Kyla as usual?*
Maria:	*Yeah, picked her up—she had a cold this week, which made things worse. Brought her home.*
Daniel:	*Was Azim there when you got there?*
Maria:	*Yup, usual scene. He grabs the paper first thing he gets home, gives him a bit of a bridge into the evening after his day at work.*
Daniel:	*So what did you do when you stepped into the apartment?*
Maria:	*[more reflecting] Let's see. Tuesday, not much different. "Hi, Honey"— that sort of thing.*
Daniel:	*What were you feeling at that point?*

Maria: *Oh, braced for the dustup.*

Daniel: *What did you do next?*

Maria: *Oh, I held it together like a true Mother Teresa. Sat Kyla on the cushions and did the bottle as usual.*

Daniel: *So you chose to bite the bullet. What did that take?*

Maria: *I didn't want Kyla subjected to a bunch of shouting.*

Daniel: *So keeping her in mind helped. How did it play out?*

Maria: *No fireworks, but it didn't make for a very relaxed night. Although he did cook eventually.*

Daniel: *You kept things peaceful for Kyla, and for the three of you really. Progress?*

Maria: *Yeah, progress. But no marital bliss, that's for sure.*

Daniel: *Okay, step forward but not ideal. And Wednesday?*

Maria: *Wednesday I handed Kyla over to Azim, reminded him about the bottle, and took a shower.*

Daniel: *Wow, that sounds like a change.*

Maria: *Yeah, it was a little disorientating!*

Daniel: *How did you manage that with all the tension between you?*

Maria: *I just decided that's what I'd do when I was parking the car.*

Daniel: *So you made a deliberate plan beforehand to do things differently. How did you avoid falling back on old habits when you stepped into the apartment?*

Maria: *That was the harder bit! I came close to dropping my game plan when I saw his head over the top of the sports page.*

Daniel: *What did you do to hold onto it?*

Maria: *I just decided to stick to the plan, hell or high water. I was genuinely exhausted. So I told him I needed some support, even though he'd probably had a tough day himself.*

Daniel: *Something there about acknowledging to yourself that you needed a break? Did that make your voice clearer do you think?*

Maria: *Makes sense when I look at it now. At the moment it was a bit like closing my eyes and jumping.*

Daniel: *[laughs] And you hit the water, not a rock. What effect did asking him to take over have?*

> *Maria:*   He seemed okay with it. Kyla cried a little while he got the bottle thing organized, but it worked out. The world didn't come to an end. We ended up having a good evening, actually.
>
> *Daniel:*   So you did things differently Wednesday. What would you call what you did?
>
> *Maria:*   Hmmm. Sharing the load, maybe?
>
> *Daniel:*   Sharing the load. Sounds like you managed to keep that resentment at bay by inviting Azim into more of the parenting action.
>
> *Maria:*   Yeah, true, but I wish he'd step up to the plate without being invited.
>
> *Daniel:*   Would you say Wednesday made that more or less likely to happen?

In this exchange, Maria's opening comment that there were no flare-ups this week is an announcement of a noteworthy exception to a problem that's been troubling her. Daniel is immediately poised to explore what Maria did differently: Ask about action, and action will show itself. Subject to her confirmation, he portrays Maria as creating a pocket of calm. Rather than risking the events being depicted as random developments (e.g., "How did that happen?"), Daniel keeps Maria squarely in the middle as an agent of change: "What did you do?" "You chose to bite the bullet," "How did you manage that?" "You made a deliberate plan," and "What did you do to hold onto it?" He slows down the account to render visible the choices Maria made: "Was Azim there when you got there?" "What did you do when you stepped into the apartment?" "What were you feeling at that point?" and "What did you do next?" After Daniel confirms these are favorable developments by asking about their effects, Maria says it would be preferable if Azim took the initiative himself ("I wish he'd step up to the plate") rather than being asked. This is a reminder for Daniel that it is still Maria who is taking the primary responsibility for the changes in the couple's interactions. Without disagreeing with this point, he invites Maria to consider whether the steps she has taken nevertheless increase the odds of Azim's initiating change on his own.

Reflection 11.3

Think back on some success you had in recent memory—for instance, working out a difference with a partner, friend, or colleague; weathering a computer meltdown; or achieving a task new to you. Zero in on a particular event or moment rather than a series of things. Allow yourself to slow down to a snail's pace as you review what you did to achieve this:

What steps did you take to prepare?

What was the very first thing you did that set you on the right path?

If someone were videotaping this event, what would the tape show?

What were you thinking, feeling, and sensing in the midst of this event?

If someone were watching you, what would they have noticed?

Which skill did you need to apply?

What impact, if any, does this fine-grained inquiry have on your experience of yourself in the wake of this accomplishment?

It's worth noting again that this exchange, although clearly useful, does not rest on developing elaborate explanations for Maria's or Azim's behavior. Certainly various explanations come to mind, including, among others, gendered socialization patterns as they relate to parental roles. As an action-oriented person, Maria has indicated a lack of interest in seeking explanations: She wants to do something different, and Daniel scaffolds a step-by-step inquiry of her actions to help her do that.

Maria's conversations with Daniel help her to unload some frustrations, clarify her positions, and prepare for future interactions with her partner. As she herself relates, she comes close to dropping her objective in the heat of the moment, but she manages to follow through on her plan. For Maria, talking about what she will do differently is sufficient to do it on her own, and she doesn't need to rehearse. Other clients may find it difficult to follow through on intended action in the heat of the moment. In these instances, it can be useful to enact the exchange with the counselor in preparation for the actual encounter.

REHEARSAL FOR ACTION: IN-SESSION ENACTMENTS

It's not uncommon to engage in habitual patterns of interaction with an almost trancelike automaticity—complaining to a partner, showing deference to a superior, being irritated with a younger sibling, flirting with a friend's partner, and so on. These styles of relating are prompted by the context of the exchange and of course the identity of the other person: Without planning to do so, one finds oneself acting in a familiar way, as though adhering to a script.

This is not necessarily a problem. But when the interactions are out of step with one's intentions—for instance, when they are unproductive or unpleasant, hurtful to the other party or oneself there may develop the resolve to act differently. Unfortunately, this is sometimes easier said than done. Patterns of relating are often deeply ingrained and resistant to change. Added to this, certain relationships give rise to intensely emotional responses that hamper attempts to relate differently. Despite the aspiration to break the pattern, it's as though a default setting takes over in the actual moment of encounter. Sometimes talking *about* alternate actions without trying them out beforehand just does not suffice.

In situations like these, it can be helpful to engage in a sort of dry run with a counselor—a rehearsal for the real thing. There are a few things worth keeping in mind in doing this, as portrayed in the exchange between counselor Maria and her client Jorge in the excerpt below. Roughly speaking, the exchange unfolds in the following phases:

1. Determine whether it might be useful to enact the exchange on the spot by way of rehearsal.

2. Achieve some clarity about what is not working in these exchanges and how the client would prefer to relate.

3. Evoke a description of how the other party tends to respond so that the counselor knows what their role is.

4. Clarify the context of the enactment.

5. Provide the client with an out in case they find the exchange overly upsetting or otherwise unhelpful.

6. Enact the exchange, staying in role.

7. Debrief.

In the following example, Jorge has been talking about what happens when he has one-on-one conversations with his father. This is a relationship he would like to change, but he has felt helpless to do so all his life and finds that virtually all encounters leave him feeling empty or hurt.

> Jorge: So, more of the same. We'd already talked about football for 15 minutes. I know nothing about football, and I couldn't care less. But I hung in there. Then I tried to tell him about this amazing art exhibit I'd been at on the weekend, and before I know it, we're talking about oil leaks!
>
> Maria: And I guess you're saying you weren't in the mood to indulge him.
>
> Jorge: No! I'd been indulging him all afternoon, talking about carburetors and transmissions, field goals and touchdowns. I figured it was my turn. But it always turns out the same way.

Maria: And how would you describe "the same way"?

Jorge: I feel invisible. No, it's worse than that: I feel like I'm not being myself. I'm just being busy keeping him happy. Avoiding his wrath.

Maria: Hmm. His wrath. Do you think that's what you would have coming if you tried to relate differently?

Jorge: Maybe. I'm not really sure. But it doesn't feel right, and it has to change.

Maria: Would you be interested in trying out something different with me?

Jorge: Not sure what you mean.

Maria: We could rehearse an exchange here, in this room, as a way for you to try out responding to your father in a different way.

Jorge: Like, I talk to you like you're my dad?

Maria: Exactly. I'd need some coaching from you, and you'd have to adjust to the fact that my mustache isn't as full as his.

Jorge: [laughs] I'll squint.

Maria: How would you prefer to respond to your father when this sort of thing happens?

Jorge: I guess I'd like to figure out how I can keep the conversation on my agenda, at least for a little while.

Maria: Okay. We can play with it. You don't necessarily have to know up front what you would do differently. Sometimes it just happens. If not, we can always brainstorm. So, the situation is . . . ?

Jorge: Sitting on the deck, end of a weekend, on a visit home.

Maria: Okay. Can you give me more of a picture of how your father would talk to you in a situation like this?

Jorge: It's not that he isn't friendly or fun. He's just caught up in his own world and tunes out quickly when the topic doesn't interest him.

Maria: I imagine at those moments it must feel like you don't interest him. That must be difficult.

Jorge: It sucks. But I know that at some level he cares. He just doesn't know how to do it any other way.

Maria: All right, why don't we give it a shot and see how it unfolds? I find these things usually go better if we stay in role for a few minutes to capture an approximation of what actually goes on. But if for some reason something comes up for you and you'd like to ditch it, please do. We can always use that as an opportunity to debrief.

At this point, Maria and Jorge get started. Maria launches into talk about the weekend's football game. She doesn't try to imitate Mr. Gonzales's Mexican accent, but she does try to approximate his style of interacting by drawing on what she's learned from previous conversations with Jorge. Jorge joins this exchange about football, but at a pause, he introduces his preferred topic. Here, Maria wants to make sure that it is Jorge and not his father who does something different, so she responds as she believes his father would in this sort of dissatisfying exchange Jorge has told her about.

Jorge:	*Hey, I went to that new art gallery on the weekend.*
Maria as Mr. Gonzales:	*What gallery?*
Jorge:	*There's a big new art gallery downtown.*
Maria/Mr. G.:	*They charge you to get in?*
Jorge:	*Ten bucks. It was worth it. Fantastic stuff.*
Maria/Mr. G.:	*The city—always trying to soak the taxpayer.*
Jorge:	*Dad, artists should get paid for what they do, don't you think?*
Maria/Mr. G.:	*I guess so. I bring the car in for an oil change yesterday, and they tell me it's leaking.*

At this point, Jorge suddenly realizes he feels stuck. This is just the kind of exchange he's been talking about. He breaks out of role to announce this to Maria.

Maria:	*So what's going on for you right now?*
Jorge:	*I feel like I just got shut down, cut off. It's this feeling of "Whatever." I don't want to continue.*
Maria:	*But you do. This is where the conversation goes off the rails, and you feel like you're not being true to yourself?*
Jorge:	*Right. But what am I supposed to do?*
Maria:	*Do you want to tell him about the art show?*
Jorge:	*Yes and no. I don't want to fight him for center stage.*
Maria:	*Do you want to tell him that?*
Jorge:	*Tell him what?*
Maria:	*Do you want to bring it to his attention that this is happening, that this happens all the time?*

Jorge: *Okay, sure. But how?*

Maria: *I don't know. Do you want to try it out?*

Notice Maria doesn't advise Jorge about how to respond; she can't know as well as he does what would feel right and fit for his relationship with his father. They resume the enactment. When Maria as Mr. Gonzales changes topic, Jorge interrupts him to say he wants to tell him more about the art show—that they just spent 15 minutes talking football and now he'd like to tell his father about his weekend. As Mr. Gonzales, Maria's response is somewhat gruff, but she grudgingly poses a few questions as Jorge describes the show. In the debrief, Maria first checks to see whether Jorge feels her response as his father was plausible.

Jorge: *Unfortunately, yes. It would probably piss him off or at least confuse him.*

Maria: *So what was that like for you?*

Jorge: *Definitely uncomfortable. It felt like I kinda burst a bubble and we weren't about to put the bubble back together again. But what in its place?*

Maria: *Sitting in the suds. Sounds stressful. Is it worth it? Would there be anything to gain? Could it be the beginning of a shift, do you think?*

Jorge: *I can't say for sure. But I know I don't want things to go on the way they are. Maybe it would be a wake-up call for him. Maybe it would just remind us both how different we are. But at least I wouldn't be pretending that we're not! I've had it with the pretending.*

Maria: *So there's a risk here. How big a risk?*

Jorge: *It could be awkward, but it's not like it would be the end of our relationship, such as it is lately.*

In-session enactments like this one are opportunities to experiment with new actions in the safety of the therapeutic relationship. They provide a first stab at acting differently in challenging situations. They are rehearsals, but they are more than that: They often uncover unanticipated angles and in so doing provide additional insight into relationship impasses. At the same time, they have their limitations: They cannot hope to be more than rough approximations of the real-life situations they mimic. As a result, an apparently smooth and effective substitute exchange in session may play out quite differently once the client encounters the actual person with whom they are having difficulty. An alternate option for trying out new responses is for clients to try out new behaviors between sessions, in the contexts in which they live. This is one option of many between-session client tasks sometimes known as homework.

TRYING IT OUT BETWEEN SESSIONS: HOMEWORK

Considering that a 1-hour session represents 1/168 of a person's week raises the possibility of capitalizing on some of that time between meetings to sustain and perhaps build on helpful changes—that is, if the client thinks so. I've often had the experience—and frequently witnessed it among colleagues—of a client departing a session with carefully reviewed tasks for the days ahead, only to come back a week later to announce they forgot the homework completely or just couldn't seem to get around to it. Does this mean the client never intended to follow through in the first place? Perhaps, if the working relationship is such that they don't feel free to confess their disinterest in homework. More often, I think the intentions may be there, but life takes over between sessions. One of the challenges in using homework as an additional venue for a client to do some work is therefore to determine how interested the client is in between-session tasks and how feasible it is that they will be able to follow through. If the answer is "yes" on both counts, another challenge is to tailor tasks to the client's disposition and the opportunities available to them.

Homework can take an endless variety of forms (Detwiler & Whisman, 1999; Hertlein, 2002; Piercy, 2002; Sori & Hecker, 2008). Below, for instance, is a hypothetical list of tasks for Jorge that might emerge from a discussion between Maria and Jorge about things to do in the week ahead:

- Make a list of activities of mutual interest that you could engage in with your father.
- Go through your old photographs, and bring in a picture of you with your father that says something about how you'd like the relationship to be.
- Spend at least half an hour of one-on-one time with your father; don't worry about doing anything differently. Imagine you're a researcher studying the relationship, and take detailed notes afterward. We can talk these over when you come in next time.
- Draw up a list of qualities and characteristics you share with your father and a second list of those that differentiate you.
- Talk to at least one of your male friends about his relationship with his father, taking note of both the disappointments and the rewards.
- Read [a book recommended by the counselor] about fathers and sons, and we'll talk it over next time.
- Draw a picture of you and your father spending rewarding time together at some imagined time in the future. Bring it in, and you can tell me about it.
- Start a journal about the issues we've been discussing, and commit to writing in it for at least 15 minutes a day.

- Spend time with your father. When you reach one of those junctures where he switches topics midstream, point it out to him, and ask him if he's ever noticed how he does this. Pay careful attention to how the exchange unfolds so that we can debrief about it next time.

Homework, like goal setting, should happen in close collaboration with the client. This helps to avoid the client's having the experience of being in school, compelled to fulfill some task of someone else's choosing. As important as is the up-front reflection on the viability and appropriateness of homework is the attention to debriefing afterward. Like in-session enactments, between-session activities are a gold mine of information. It's useful to review homework at a slow tempo, examining what was done along with the client's experience of doing it. And in those instances wherein a client embarked the week before with a task that seemed destined to crack open the mystery of their life only to return empty-handed—having been sideswiped by life's daily demands—it's important for the counselor to let go of expectations so they can plunge into the new conversation fully present.

CHAPTER ELEVEN RECAP

Action is just one dimension of a person's repertoire that also includes thoughts, feelings, bodily sensations, and so on: The list is infinite. Lived experience does not unfold in discrete packets; nevertheless, it's sometimes useful to keep therapeutic conversations focused on one dimension of experience by drawing on practices oriented to that dimension. This chapter drew on a number of practices that are useful for amplifying actions to consolidate favorable changes.

The focus on action is a highly pragmatic orientation unconcerned with explanation and causal attribution and more interested in doing something different or—in cases wherein things have taken a favorable turn—doing more of what works. There is no expectation that helpful changes will necessarily be directly linked to the problem itself; the more important consideration is whether things have gotten better. Speaking of expectations, this orientation to action features an abiding assumption that change is inevitable. The result is a persistent curiosity about change. Scaling questions can be a useful tool for this form of inquiry because they quantify changes and provide ways to evaluate their impacts as well as forecast their futures.

Another compelling feature of the orientation to action is the assumption of personal agency, choice, and responsibility that it projects. Significant difficulties can prompt the experience of victimization, robbing a person of a sense of their ability to do anything in the face of challenges. The counselor's curiosity about actions taken by a client offers an antidote to a potentially smothering passivity by keeping the spotlight on personal agency.

It's typically easier to acknowledge that agency in the wake of favorable developments than in instances wherein the problem seems to have stayed the same or become worse. The careful, step-by-step unpacking of favorable developments typically shines a light on choices made by the client. Preferred developments are more easily overlooked when people are contending with significant obstacles, yet paradoxically, these situations also provide openings for acknowledging actions, however small, that have been taken in the face of challenges.

When preferred developments are elusive, a curiosity about coping tactics and skills— actions that have prevented things from getting worse—helps to keep hope alive and consolidates a foundation for constructive future dialogue.

Relationship challenges constitute a high percentage of the problems clients bring to therapy, and frequently long-entrenched patterns of relating make it especially difficult to act in novel ways, despite clear intentions to do so. In these cases, it's sometimes useful to try out new ways of responding in the safety of a therapeutic conversation as a precursor to making those changes beyond the consulting room door. Here, the coun- selor slips into the role of the other person and facilitates a careful debriefing of the role-play afterward. These are rehearsals for action, and a side benefit is the useful insights they generate that can be converted to new responses when brought back to the actual relationship.

Because in-session role-plays are somewhat remote approximations of what goes on in real life, there can sometimes be a significant gap between what unfolds in the session and what happens when a client attempts to respond differently to a key per- son in their life. In this situation, there is the opportunity to use the actual encounter outside the room as the focus of careful inquiry inside the room by counselor and client. As the client learns more about how these exchanges unfold and about their responses in the moment, they can use the information to respond differently in sub- sequent encounters.

These forays into the field are an example of what is sometimes called homework— between-session tasks that the client may engage in from week to week and that later become the subject of debriefs when the client reunites with their counselor. Some clients are highly motivated to engage in homework as a form of value-added activity associated with their therapy. Others prefer to reserve weekly sessions alone for doing the work. Still others may profess an interest in homework only to find that life takes over once they leave the consulting room. Like goal setting, the assignment of home- work is best done in careful collaboration with the client and in consideration of what is achievable given their current life circumstances.

CHAPTER ELEVEN DISCUSSION QUESTIONS

1. **Active ingredient.** The notion of the active ingredient prevalent in drug research falters when applied to counseling and therapy. What are some features distinguishing psychopharmacology from therapy that help to account for this?

2. **The buzzing confusion.** What did James (1890/1981) mean by the "buzzing confusion" that infants confront? What role might a theory play in instilling order into it?

3. **Theory and theoretical models.** What is the difference between theory generally speaking—as in the views that inform this book—and theoretical models of therapy?

4. **Causality.** The text clearly critiques causality as a framework for accounting for human action. How is the domain of action distinguished from other natural science contexts? Do you agree?

5. **The African violet queen.** The story of Erickson's work with his colleague's aunt is notably devoid of causal explanation for his client's behavior. Is this a shortcoming; does it neglect an important piece of the story? What might have been different if causal attribution played a more central role in Erickson's response to his client's dilemma?

6. **Cheerleading.** In what sense can offering explicit praise be seen as normative judgment? What advantages/disadvantages do you see in the alternative of posing questions that seek to thicken accounts of preferred developments?

7. **Expectancy of change.** The chapter argues that expectancy influences what we attend to and that what we attend to plays a large part in what is foregrounded or, in effect, rendered real. Provide an example of how this happens in your own interactions.

CHAPTER ELEVEN ACTIVITIES

1. **Disputing causality.** Form pairs. Speaker, identify some action in which you engaged; (a) account for it causally by pointing to events and circumstances that purportedly compelled it to happen, (b) replace the first set of causes by an equally plausible (but different) second set of causes, and (c) make a case for how the action seemed to have been an act of willful intention in defiance of purported causes. Debrief. Speaker and listener, what, if anything, shifted in your view of the action with the argument for and against its causal nature? Speaker, what did you like/dislike about seeing your action as caused by forces outside yourself? What did you like/dislike about seeing it as an expression of choice and intention?

2. **Adversity, coping, and agency.** Pair up. Speaker, discuss a situation in which you felt you were a helpless victim of circumstances. With the help of the listener, tally up the constraints stacked against you as a precursor to developing an inventory of what you did manage to do to get through (cope with) the situation despite the obstacles. Debrief. Both speaker and listener, what impact did acknowledging the constraints have on identifying coping behaviors? Speaker, did the identification of the steps you took to cope affect in any way your view of yourself as a victim in this situation?

3. **The constancy of change.** Form pairs. Speaker, share a description of a problem you currently face or have faced in the past. Speaker and listener together, examine the course of the problem across time—month to month, week to week, day to day, minute to minute. Debrief. Does the problem stay constant, or is it in flux? Speaker, what impact does it have on your sense of the problem to notice fluctuation/lack of fluctuation in the problem over time?

4. **Scaling change.** Pair up. Speaker, name a problem/challenge with which you are dealing. Listener, coach the speaker through a set of scaling questions to set benchmarks for (a) where the problem was at its worst and (b) where it is now. If it has improved, inquire as to which actions were taken to move it. If it has stayed the same or deteriorated, speculate about which actions might move the problem *one point* on the scale. Debrief. Speaker, what impact did the activity have on your experience of the problem? Listener, what were the challenges associated with posing the scaling questions?

5. **Thickening an account of a preferred development.** Pair up. Speaker, name some action you took that represented a favorable development (i.e., an exception) in relation to a problem with which you have been dealing. Listener, refrain from explicit praise, and instead engage in an inquiry to thicken the account of this development (sample questions are available in the Alternatives to Cheerleading section). Debrief. Speaker, what was it like to unpack the development and render a thicker account of it? How did it affect your view of your own agency? Listener, what challenges were associated with sticking to this line of inquiry?

6. **Projecting changes into the future.** Form pairs. Speaker, recount the same preferred development as in the previous activity. Listener, join with the speaker in projecting this development into the future (sample questions are available in the section titled Projecting Change Into the Future). Debrief. Speaker, what was it like to anticipate where these changes could take you? How did it affect your sense of hopefulness? Listener, what challenges were associated with sticking to this line of inquiry?

7. **Slowing down the image.** Pair up. Speaker, describe some action you engaged in that to some degree diminished a problem with which you have been contending. Listener, join the speaker in breaking down the action into fine detail, starting with what preceded it

and concluding with a look *back* on its impact on the problem and a look *ahead* and what it might say about the future of the problem. You may wish to consult questions listed in the section titled Slowing Down the Image. Debrief. Speaker, did anything become visible to you as a result of slowing down the frame? Listener, what challenges were associated with sticking to this line of inquiry?

8. **Enacting a relational exchange.** Form pairs. Speaker, describe a typical relationship scenario in which you are dissatisfied with how you respond to the other person. Speaker and listener, using the list outlined in the Rehearsal for Action: In-Session Enactments section, engage in an enactment. Debrief. Speaker, what difference, if any, did it make to have a chance to try an alternate response in this safe context? Listener, what were the challenges of facilitating this exchange?

Chapter 12

WORKING WITH THOUGHTS AND BELIEFS

INTRODUCTION

Cast your eyes about the various conflicts under way around the world at this time, and you will discover interminable disputes—some that have smoldered and raged for centuries—about *what is* and *what should be*. We all look at the universe through picture frames that determine what gets featured and what gets excluded. As Andersen (1992) put it, "there are as many versions of a situation as there are persons to understand it" (p. 61). Each of these various versions is associated with thoughts and beliefs about them. Some are energizing and hope inspiring, and others may promote discouragement and despair. Counseling conversations are a useful venue for laying these thoughts and beliefs on the table and joining clients in evaluating their effects and adopting more life-affirming ways of making sense of their situations and themselves.

Thoughts and beliefs, most often referred to as cognitions in the psychology literature, are the focus of this chapter. Like actions in the previous chapter and emotions in a chapter to follow, they are a subset of the stories that people tell and live. They don't represent the totality of lived experience. For many people, however, they play a very central role, so that the way they think exerts a powerful influence on how they feel and act.

> Monica has been waiting all afternoon for Jason to call. She shuts off the television, tosses the remote onto a nearby pillow, and slouches where she sits on the couch. Another glossy production featuring an ensemble cast with pearly white teeth and flawless skin. She feels restless and curiously discontented as she stands before the mirror, brushing her hair. Jason says his cell phone is acting up, but is that really what it's about? She looks at her reflection, grimacing at her complexion, baring

her uneven teeth. She squints to imagine what difference a new haircut would make, but to no avail. "No wonder he's not interested," she thinks. "He's probably off with someone else." Monica is tearful as a wave of sadness washes over her, and she notices a tight knot in her stomach. Her cat brushes Monica's elbow as she reaches to pour a cup of coffee. She grabs the cat roughly and deposits it on the floor with a thud, sending it running for safety in the next room. A few moments later, Jason arrives at the door, apologizing for his faulty cell phone. Monica launches into a verbal critique, and Jason leaves, abandoning his plan to spend the evening with her.

Monica's story shows how thoughts can be closely related to moods and in turn to actions associated with those moods. Her account also speaks to the relationship between cultural context and thinking—the way our thoughts are influenced by messages in the wider culture. Monica's scenario will provide an occasional reference point throughout this chapter, which is devoted to conversation practices for engaging clients around their thoughts and beliefs. The skills introduced in this chapter are useful for inviting a critical examination of unhelpful thinking patterns and joining with clients in replacing these. The chapter will also introduce an alternate approach to working with thoughts that involves changing the relationship with mental events—as opposed to changing the thoughts themselves.

As we saw in the introduction to Section 5 of this book (Promoting Change), people's experience is both diverse and interrelated. In other words, we respond to the world through thinking, feeling, and acting as well as physiologically and in other ways. This is the *diversity*. The *interrelationship* shows in the way that changes in any one of these areas affect what people experience in the others. In this chapter, the focus of that change is thinking. The chapter introduces skills for helping clients (a) identify thoughts and beliefs, (b) evaluate their impact, and (c) develop alternative thoughts and beliefs more closely aligned with their purposes. In contrast to Chapter 11, it's the thoughts associated with actions rather than the actions themselves that are the central focus. In other words, change the thoughts and beliefs, and the actions will change.

This chapter introduces a variety of skills for working with thoughts and beliefs:

1. identifying and linking event, thought, and consequence;
2. naming and discerning self-talk;
3. tracing negative moods to problematic thoughts;
4. evaluating the impact of thoughts;
5. linking thoughts to beliefs;

6. disputing negative thoughts and beliefs;

7. generating alternative beliefs;

8. developing thought records; and

9. relating with acceptance to unhelpful thoughts and beliefs.

THE MEDIATING ROLE OF THOUGHTS

There are always many stories to tell about any single event. Every situation we encounter is subject to multiple interpretations. And each of these interpretations, expressed in how we think about what's going on, has a different impact on how we feel and act. Box 12.1 describes a situation encountered by Dario, who self-identifies as shy. Notice how the various thoughts available to him have a direct impact on his experience of the event, which is characterized here in terms of his mood and actions.

BOX 12.1

The Fallout of Dario's Thoughts

Dario is invited to a party by a schoolmate named Charles whom Dario just recently met. At the party, Dario does not recognize anyone he knows. He is standing alone when he is spotted by Charles. They begin to talk. Charles abruptly cuts off their exchange midsentence to greet someone else arriving at the door.

Thought	Feeling	Action
I'm boring and can't hold someone's attention for more than a few sentences.	Sadness, self-critique	Withdraw from socializing, and adopt a passive demeanor.
Charles is rude and insensitive.	Anger, indignation	Leave the party.
Charles is feeling a little overextended, multitasking in his role as host, and can't afford to linger on one conversation.	Mild disappointment, compassion	Continue to circulate, introducing himself to other guests.

Of course Dario's feelings and actions are just two dimensions of Dario's experience at the party; there might have been many more listed here. As Greenberger and Padesky (1995) point out, thoughts may be accompanied by images (e.g., of being slapped in the face) and memories (e.g., of being spurned at a high school dance). And emotional responses often have a clear relationship to physiological states—for instance, anger might be accompanied by an elevated pulse rate and anxiety by sweaty palms. The point is that Dario's thoughts play a mediating role between the encounter with Charles and his overall experience of the party.

Ellis (2007) calls a situation that provokes problematic thoughts the "activating event" and the corresponding ripple effect the "consequences." The things we tell ourselves mediate between the two and usually arise spontaneously. For this reason, Aaron Beck (Beck & Weishar, 2005) uses the term "automatic thoughts" to describe thoughts that arise in the moment and contribute to negative moods and destructive actions. Box 12.2 illustrates how this sequence plays out for Monica, a sequence uncovered in the exchange between Monica and her therapist in the next section.

BOX 12.2

Monica: Event, Thought, Consequence

Activating Event	Automatic Thoughts	Consequences
Boyfriend fails to call	He won't call. My afternoon is ruined. He isn't interested in me. The relationship is over.	Feels gloomy and irritable Becomes tearful Experiences a heaviness in her chest Treats her cat roughly Argues with Jason

---

Of course carefully constructed breakdowns like those in Boxes 12.1 and 12.2 are not available to Dario or Monica in moments when they're awash in difficult feelings. Later, in relating these events to therapists, they may be similarly caught up in their emotional responses and may continue to have difficulty noticing the sequence of event, thought, and consequence playing out. A key feature of problematic self-talk is that it arises automatically outside of our awareness. In the longer term, a key task is to notice it in the moment to make an active choice around it, but for starters, it has to be recognized. To engage Dario or Monica in evaluating the outcome of their thought processes in preparation for adopting alternatives, they need help stepping back and examining the sequences that culminate in negative consequences. Once negative self-talk is identified, a person can commence being on the lookout for it, with the intention of replacing it with more useful thoughts. But getting there usually involves some patient teasing out of as-yet-unnoticed and -unnamed thoughts as a precursor to examining how they are operating.

LINKING ACTIVATING EVENT, THOUGHT, AND CONSEQUENCE

Helping Clients Identify Self-Talk

When Monica recaps the events of her weekend afternoon, the therapist learns they culminated in a fierce argument with Jason before he left prematurely. The linkage between thoughts and their consequences may appear obvious to therapists who stand on the outside looking in, but clients are living these challenging sequences. From their vantage points the landscape is less clearly defined. In the example below, the therapist invites Monica to step back and examine the sequence of occurrences that led to her feelings of sadness and anxiety, her rough treatment of her cat, and eventually the conflict with Jason. Thinking about her thoughts—also known as metacognition (Salvatore, Conti, Fiore, Carcione, Dimaggio, & Semerari, 2006; Thériault & Gazzola, 2008; Whelton, 2004)—is not something Monica is used to doing, so she could use some help. Notice there is an educational dimension to the exchange in that the therapist points out the way thoughts arise automatically in response to situations. You might also notice a certain patient persistence on the therapist's part, coaxing a more detailed account of what unfolded on Saturday afternoon. As she adopts a fine-grained view of the events, Monica gains insight into a frequently repeated sequence of events she hasn't previously identified.

> *Therapist:*   *Seems like all afternoon you were expecting to hear from Jason.*
>
> *Monica:*   *I was bored silly. He said he'd call.*
>
> *Therapist:*   *And he didn't. You mentioned shutting off the TV in frustration. What did you say to yourself at that moment?*

Monica: *Well, I was alone. I'm not sure I said anything.*

Therapist: *Of course. I didn't mean to suggest you were talking to yourself! What I meant is that you came to some conclusions when Jason didn't call. In a sense you said these to yourself, although not out loud.*

Monica: *Okay, I can see that.*

Therapist: *Sometimes that's called self-talk. We all do it in response to events. Something happens, we have an automatic thought that affects how we feel, what we say and do next.*

Monica: *Well, I guess I said, "He's not going to call."*

Therapist: *"He's not going to call." And did you come to any conclusions about what that meant?*

Monica: *I guess I figured it was proof he's not interested. That he doesn't want a relationship with me.*

Therapist: *Okay, the thought, "He doesn't want a relationship." Anything else?*

Monica: *I don't know. It just got me thinking I might as well get ready to be alone—again.*

Therapist: *So when Jason didn't call, some automatic thoughts came up. You told yourself he's not interested in you and the relationship has probably run its course. And how did that affect your mood, do you think?*

Discerning Implicit Self-Talk

Monica and her therapist were able to name some self-talk fairly readily—in this sense, it was explicit. This simplified the task of reviewing the sequence of events with her. Same for Nadia, who bitterly announces, I'm a loser through and through; I never have and I never will get anything right. Statements like these "totalize" (White & Epston, 1990) Nadia's identity—they paint her as one big problem. When self-talk is explicit, the process of seeking alternatives (to be explored below) can begin. But in some cases the thoughts and beliefs contributing to negative outcomes are less clear-cut, calling for additional skills in identifying implicit self-talk.

When self-talk is not immediately apparent, the therapist may need to read between the lines to discern possible assumptions lurking among the words spoken, offering these back to the client for the client's evaluation. Box 12.3 provides examples of implicit thoughts and beliefs.

BOX 12.3

Reading Between the Lines

Statement (What the Client Says)	Implicit Thought/Belief (The Meaning That Appears to Hover Between the Lines)
My brother James got into the program, but I don't see the point of applying. I mean, I'm no James. I can just imagine their faces looking over my portfolio.	I'm not as smart as my brother James, and I'm bound to be rejected. People reviewing my file will be shocked or amused that I bothered to apply.
They asked me to come along for their ski weekend, but I wouldn't dare. I've only skied about 10 or 15 times, and I still can't figure out how those racers manage to make it through those moguls.	I need to be able to ski like an expert to go on a social skiing outing. People are more concerned with my expertise than in inviting me for my company.

In the examples provided in Box 12.3, it appears that some unhelpful thoughts and beliefs are being spoken implicitly and lie behind the client's words. To avoid interpreting clients' experience on their behalf, it's helpful to verify hunches with them:

Example 1:

> *Seems like you end up comparing yourself to your brother James. When you do that, what do you tell yourself?*
>
> *What kinds of assumptions about your academic prospects do you come to when you compare yourself to your brother?*
>
> *Sounds like some brotherly competition. What does that lead you to tell yourself about your chances of getting into grad school?*

Example 2:

> *Can you hear a message in what you're saying about what level of expertise it takes to be welcomed into this social circle?*

> *I wonder if you're caught up by a voice that suggests the weekend is about athleticism rather than socializing.*
>
> *My impression is you're under the grip of an idea about what it takes to be an acceptable skier and maybe even an acceptable friend.*
>
> *What do you think you might be telling yourself about how the others would respond if you don't prove to be an expert downhiller?*

Problematic thoughts may also be more implicit than explicit when a person is sharing some negative mood without naming the thoughts associated with it. Here counselor and client might mutually identify self-talk by working backward, from mood to thought. Box 12.4 provides a list of many moods people often identity as negative; these can be keys to discovering counterproductive automatic thoughts.

BOX 12.4

Moods

People use a wide variety of words to describe their moods. Descriptions of negative moods are signposts to instances wherein problematic automatic thoughts may be at play.

Depressed	Afraid	Frightened
Sad	Embarrassed	Panicky
Insecure	Disgusted	Ashamed
Jealous	Scared	Frustrated
Nervous	Angry	Disappointed
Enraged	Mad	Humiliated
Anxious	Hurt	Confused
Envious	Guilty	Bored

The description of a negative mood that consistently recurs provides an opening to ask about the situations associated with the mood—a chain of inquiry that leads to the thoughts accompanying the situations. For instance, Luise is an experienced administrative clerk who experiences distressing bouts of anxiety that hamper her ability to cope with day-to-day responsibilities. On further inquiry, it becomes clear this anxious mood comes up at work but not at home or elsewhere. More specifically, Luise says she gets anxious when coworkers come into her work space, where her computer screen is on view for them to peruse.

As Luise and her counselor continue to explore these situations, it becomes evident she's concerned they'll spot errors in her work. Her counselor asks the following:

> *What do you tell yourself in those situations?*
>
> *What kinds of thoughts kick in at that moment?*
>
> *What do you say to yourself about what would happen if they spotted errors?*

Luise tells herself, *They'll see my work and find out I'm unqualified.* On further exploration, Luise identifies the thought, *I'll get fired and will have to find a job in the middle of an economic downturn.* This is despite the fact that she has years of experience and has frequently received commendations for her work. In this case, Luise's negative mood has prompted an exploration of the thoughts associated with it.

In seeing the connection between thought and mood, Luise is primed to adopt alternative thoughts. One common way this priming is done involves the therapist's branding the client's thoughts as irrational. However, this centers the therapist's point of view, leaving Luise out of an evaluation of her own experience. Just as important, it also overlooks that it is the distress that certain thoughts generate—not their purported logic or rationality—that is the issue at hand (see Box 12.5). A more collaborative way forward with clients whose thoughts appear to be contributing to negative moods is to join them in a critical reflection on the connection between (a) what they tell themselves and (b) how they feel. This helps them to gauge the impact of particular self-talk, which sets the stage for doing something about it.

BOX 12.5

An Alternative to the Rational-Irrational Dichotomy

It's questionable whether a mother who risks her very survival in snatching her child from the grip of a rabid grizzly is acting rationally, yet such things happen from time to time and are depicted as praiseworthy acts of heroism. Rationality has its place, but it is a dubious universal standard against which to judge all human action, thought, or belief. The familiar rational-irrational dichotomy celebrates one particular mode of engaging with the world while denigrating other ways of being. In a groundbreaking work, Carol Gilligan (1982) persuasively illustrated how Western psychological models have tended to depict rationality as the epitome of moral reasoning. Gilligan showed that whereas men often use rational, abstract, and rule-bound processes to come to moral decisions, women more often prioritize their concern for relationships over rationality in making key decisions. In other words, counseling practices that promote rationality to the exclusion of other ways of being may be inadvertently dismissive of people's preferred ways of engaging with the world. The point here is not to criticize rationality but simply to argue against the exclusive status it is sometimes accorded. People of all cultural backgrounds engage with the world in a multiplicity of ways, and as mentioned earlier, it is a thought's tendency to provoke *distress* rather than its purported rationality that should rightly be the focus of practice.

A second concern with the rational-irrational dichotomy is that it overlooks how people holding to unhelpful thoughts and beliefs are often responding to messages that can be traced to family members, educational institutions, world religions, and popular media, among other sources. For instance, judging ourselves against normative standards is something advertisers encourage us to do on an ongoing basis. In this case, it may indeed be arguable that we *do* fall short! Self-judgment may not be helpful, but it is not necessarily irrational.

A final concern with the rational-irrational dichotomy is that it raises the question, *Who gets to decide?* This is similar to the quandary presented by the phrase *distorted cognitions.* Assigning these terms positions the counselor as the arbiter of what is true and right, excluding the client's voice from the evaluation. A more useful practice is to join clients in a mutual investigation of the effects of certain thoughts and beliefs on their moods and actions.

So although much of the literature on cognition features the rational-irrational dichotomy, this text offers skills for helping clients to distinguish thoughts and beliefs that are helpful to them versus those that are unhelpful or hurtful. The focus is therefore on the *impact of the thought or belief in a person's life* rather than its purported veracity or adherence to some standard of rationality. This shift in language has only a minor impact on ideas and practices associated with cognition that you may have encountered previously. But given the key role that language plays in constructing experience, the distinction makes for some very significant differences in the experience of clients.

GAUGING THE IMPACT OF AUTOMATIC THOUGHTS

When noticing the apparently negative repercussions of automatic thoughts, it can be tempting to point these out directly to clients. In doing this, however, therapists center themselves as experts on their clients' experience. It's therefore more helpful to solicit clients' observations of the impact of particular thoughts.

Why not let the client decide? Handing this evaluation back to clients not only sidesteps the pitfalls of branding thoughts on their behalf but also prepares them for entertaining alternatives. People's taking the time to reflect on the fallout—on their self-image, energy, hopefulness, relationships, and so on—of automatic thoughts associated with problematic experience cannot help but deepen their commitment to making changes.

Another compelling reason to leave this evaluation to clients is that in some cases, our interpretations may be out of step with theirs. For instance, Aisha says she tells herself, *You'll never make it,* when struggling over her studies for a legal bar exam. It would be easy to assume the impact of this self-talk is negative and thus to press forward with a plan to replace it. But when asked, Aisha reports this thought ignites her energy to work harder. What at first blush appears to be an unhelpful thought turns out to be anything but. Box 12.6 provides examples of questions that can be used to help clients evaluate the repercussions of particular self-talk on their moods and actions.

The example below shows how this plays out with Monica. This exchange follows from the identification of the thoughts, *Jason is not going to call,* and, *Jason doesn't want a relationship.* The therapist follows up by inviting Monica to gauge the impact of these thoughts.

Therapist:	Okay, so you told yourself he wouldn't call. And not only that—that he wasn't interested in the relationship at all. What kind of mood did that put you in?
Monica:	You don't want to go there. Just ask Patches!
Therapist:	Patches?
Monica:	My cat, Patches. I practically threw her on the floor.
Therapist:	So what kind of mood is that?
Monica:	Not sure. I could feel a knot in my stomach. I was edgy.
Therapist:	Edgy. Edgy as in . . . ?
Monica:	I felt stressed. I was anxious.
Therapist.	Okay, anxious. Anything else?
Monica:	And sad, I guess. It was a very depressing moment. I went a long time without a boyfriend, and I don't want that again.
Therapist:	So the thoughts that he wouldn't call and that he wasn't interested led you to feel anxious and sad? Is that about right?
Monica:	Yeah, I'd say so.

Therapist: *Is that something you'd like to change?*

Monica: *Feeling anxious and sad? Sure, but how?*

Therapist: *I'm wondering if we could revisit those automatic thoughts and see if there might be other things you could tell yourself in situations like the one on Saturday afternoon.*

BOX 12.6

Inviting Clients to Evaluate the Impact of Thoughts

When clients are at the center of evaluating the impact of self-talk, they will appreciate more fully the consequences of certain thought patterns. This is motivating as well: It helps them to identify and experience their own distress rather than responding to the counselor's observations about it.

When you get thinking that, how do you end up feeling?

Where do those thoughts take you?

How does that thought pattern play out: what mood does it give rise to?

What happens when you tell yourself that?

What are the repercussions of that idea?

Would you say a belief like that leads you to feel more or less hopeful [energized, content, etc.]?

What have you noticed about the feelings that come up for you when that thought takes hold?

If you look at the overall sequence of things, from the thought that comes up, to the emotion associated with it, to the action that follows, what do you notice?

Ultimately, the goal of this form of conversation about problematic thoughts is to support clients in *replacing* unhelpful thoughts with helpful ones. In some cases, gauging the negative fallout of certain ways of thinking may be sufficient to proceed in joining clients as they adopt alternate thoughts—a practice outlined later in this chapter. But more often, thoughts that come up in one instance reflect broader patterns with extended histories. In effect, the thoughts are expressions of particular patterns of meaning making—sweeping beliefs that may have held sway for many years. Changing the self-talk in the moment may sometimes also involve altering patterns of meaning.

THE RELATIONSHIP BETWEEN AUTOMATIC THOUGHTS AND GLOBAL BELIEFS

The thoughts that come to mind in response to events are not mere random neurological firings; they reflect particular meanings that hold sway over a person and are typically representative of broader, global beliefs that deserve attention if the task at hand is to replace negative thoughts. Global beliefs, sometimes known as schemas (DeRubeis, Tang, & Beck, 2001), are present across multiple situations and contribute to the repeated onset of unhelpful automatic thoughts in particular contexts.

The word *global* is included here to distinguish these clusters of meaning from single, context-specific beliefs—say, the belief that a neighbor is on vacation or that the car needs gas. If thoughts are like sentences, global beliefs are the stories in which those sentences are imbedded. Or to put it differently, global beliefs are tunes or melodies, whereas thoughts are akin to the notes of which they are made. Looked at in isolation, problematic thoughts often look absurd and easy to refute. However, they often make sense, hurtful as they may be, when the camera view widens and they're understood in terms of the beliefs informing them.

When what appears to be the same set of circumstances gives rise to contrasting thoughts for different people, global beliefs will be clues to the difference, as the example of Helmut and Isabel illustrates. They've both been told by prospective employers that the hiring committee would like to interview them one more time before making a decision. Their thoughts around this event are strikingly different, however. The difference is more easily understood when considering the beliefs contributing to their self-talk.

	Event: Hiring Committee Wants One More Interview Before Decision	
	Global Belief	*Situation-Specific Thought*
Isabel	I'm competent at most things I take on and tend to have an edge on my peers.	I've successfully jumped through another hoop, and I'm getting closer to being hired.
Helmut	I'm never good enough; I always seem to fall short of the mark.	They're having their doubts about me and want to make sure they don't make a mistake.

Global beliefs are broader in scope than specific thoughts and are less likely to be named by clients. Problematic ones may be built on harsh critiques and normative judgments that we become adept at avoiding because of their unpleasantness, even while they influence our thoughts, feelings, and actions. They are also often stubbornly entrenched, making sweeping truth claims, as it were, and defying all challengers.

It's often important to engage clients at the level of global beliefs when joining them in challenging negative thoughts, or else you may find you've changed a note but that the melody remains essentially the same. The transcript below demonstrates how the exploration of Monica's automatic thoughts illuminates broader beliefs associated with distressing thought patterns that arise in similar situations.

Therapist:	*Monica, seems to me we're starting to get a picture of how the sequence unfolded for you: The call didn't come through, some thoughts arose, and you were plunged into a dark place. Is it all right if we take a closer look at those thoughts?*
Monica:	*Sounds okay to me. Where do we start?*
Therapist:	*Well, it seems you quickly concluded that Jason wouldn't call. Is that because he typically doesn't call when he says he will?*
Monica:	*No, not sure I'd say that.*
Therapist:	*Okay, so it's not as though you have a history of that?*
Monica:	*No, I wouldn't say so.*
Therapist:	*What else did you say you were thinking? What other conclusions did you come to?*
Monica:	*I guess I assumed it meant he wasn't interested. The relationship was toast.*
Therapist:	*You concluded the relationship was over. How does that sound to you now as we reflect on it?*
Monica:	*Over the top, definitely. We have our ups and downs, but I think we have a fairly solid thing going. It's just these moods I get into.*
Therapist:	*So this comes up at other times? I wonder if you're saying that his not calling triggered it, but it's a thought that arises in various other contexts too?*
Monica:	*Yeah, it's not like it was a new idea. I often get that feeling. When we go out, I notice he always seems to be checking out other women.*
Therapist:	*And what do you tell yourself then?*
Monica:	*That they're hotter than me!*

> *Therapist:*   *As in . . . ?*
>
> *Monica:*   *They're better looking. Sometimes when I'm out with him I see my reflection in a window and I hate my hair, I look fat.*
>
> *Therapist:*   *You feel unattractive? And what do you find yourself saying to yourself about you and Jason?*
>
> *Monica:*   *That he's losing interest because of my looks.*
>
> *Therapist:*   *Sounds like the idea that your relationship hinges on your physical attractiveness and that you don't make the grade.*
>
> *Monica:*   *Crazy, isn't it?*
>
> *Therapist:*   *I'm not sure I'd call it crazy, but I can see where it takes you. Do you think this is the case for women and men? Do you think Jason is up against the same stuff?*
>
> *Monica:*   *No, it's different for men. They can get by on their charm. Their looks just aren't so critical.*

An occupational hazard in working with thoughts is the tendency to be poised at all times to refute any thoughts that appear to be contributing to negative experience on the client's behalf. Like the practice of unilaterally branding thoughts as irrational, this leaves clients out of a reflexive evaluation of their experience. Notice here that the therapist checks to see if this scenario occurs repeatedly ("Is that because he typically doesn't call?"). Depending on Monica's account of things, this could turn into a conversation about her growing certainty that her relationship with Jason is on its last legs—an entirely different conversational direction. Instead, however, Monica indicates that her thoughts don't jive with her overall evaluation of things ("Over the top, definitely"). This leads to a further exploration of how things unfolded. Monica seems to indicate a familiar pattern ("It's just these moods I get into"), which the therapist confirms ("So this comes up at other times?"). From here the conversation turns to beliefs that transcend this one situation: (a) Monica isn't attractive, (b) Jason's commitment hinges on her physical beauty, and (c) the attractiveness of women hinges on their appearance, whereas for men, charm will suffice. These are broader beliefs that appear to be contributing to Monica's thoughts and to the dark moods associated with them.

At this point, Monica and her therapist have journeyed a long way from a tearful weekend afternoon. Where to from here? When people notice the negative repercussions of global beliefs and automatic thoughts on their moods and actions, it is sometimes all they need to do to embrace alternatives. Ultimately, the objective in working with unhelpful or hurtful thoughts and beliefs is to replace them with helpful ones. But sometimes they need to be disabled by challenging the claims that the beliefs make.

CHALLENGING THE TRUTH CLAIMS OF THOUGHTS AND GLOBAL BELIEFS

Strongly held thoughts and beliefs are like eyeglass clip-ons: They color everything we look at. When they are unhelpful or hurtful, that color is dark indeed. Unfortunately, supporting clients in discarding unhelpful thoughts and beliefs is rarely as easy as suggesting they simply remove the lenses. Thoughts and beliefs make powerful "truth claims" (White & Epston, 1990) about people and their situations. What for counselors is like colored lenses may be regarded by clients as the way things are.

This section presents two approaches to inviting clients to dispute what is taken for granted in preparation for identifying alternative ideas and beliefs more suited to their purposes and values.

1. **Identifying exceptions to unhelpful thoughts and beliefs.** As mentioned in Chapter 10, exceptions always deserve inquiry because a person may *already* possess the knowledge, skills, and resources they need to overcome problematic thoughts and beliefs.

2. **Disputing problematic thoughts and beliefs through Socratic dialogue.** Joining with clients in critical examinations of unhelpful self-talk and inviting them to generate alternative perspectives loosens the hold of pervasively problematic beliefs.

Identifying Exceptions to Unhelpful Thoughts and Beliefs

In working with thoughts and beliefs, the objective is to arrive at helpful replacements for problematic self-talk. So it makes sense to first check in with clients on the chance they are already equipped with helpful alternatives. This may involve identifying recent exceptions to the problematic self-talk or delving further into past situations in which thoughts and beliefs did not hamper the client. In the example below, Maria first helps Jorge to identify exceptions in the past. Notice how this discovery alerts them both to the occasional exceptions happening more recently.

> *Maria:* Jorge, it sounds like a visit home for the weekend is a potential minefield for you.
>
> *Jorge:* That pretty much captures it. Not so much with my mother, but put me in a room with my father for more than a few minutes and things go off the rails.
>
> *Maria:* You've described how the conversation runs dry at best and turns into an argument at worst. Do you remember some of the automatic thoughts you identified as coming up in those moments?

Jorge: He'll ask me something about my life, and I'll be convinced he doesn't really want to know.

Maria: Yup, that one rings a bell. I remember you describing how you tell your-self in those instances that his intentions aren't what they seem.

Jorge: I get fixed on this idea that he's out to shame me. That when he asks me about what I'm up to—not something he does a lot of, mind you—he's doing it to make fun of me or put me down.

Maria: And where does that lead?

Jorge: Nowhere pleasant! I get defensive; he gets confused; it all unravels.

Maria: Is it always this way? Have your conversations with your father ever been satisfying?

Jorge: It feels like never, but I suppose not. They've been disastrous in the past few months.

Maria: Were there times when he showed more interest, then? When you clicked better?

Jorge: That would be pushing it! No, clicking is not the right word. It's always been awkward. But somehow it didn't used to get to me the way it does now.

Maria: What did you used to tell yourself when your dad tried to engage you in conversation?

Jorge: That he was trying, anyway. He's not much of a conversationalist, espe-cially when it's not his chosen topic.

Maria: So you told yourself, "He's trying."

Jorge: His intentions are good. He's just clumsy about it, that's all.

Maria: "His intentions are good." And what difference did that make?

Jorge: I'd take him up on his questions, tell him a little about what was going on. It didn't always go very far, but I walked away feeling okay about it.

Maria: So instead of, "He has ulterior motives," something more like, "His inten-tions are good, he cares—but clumsily!"

Jorge: That's about right.

Maria: Have you been able to remind yourself of that lately?

Jorge: Funny you mention it, I'm just remembering, there was a stretch of talk on Sunday that felt different.

In the preceding exchange, Maria begins by reminding Jorge of the self-talk they have previously identified. She then confirms its negative consequences ("And where does that lead?") before checking for exceptions ("Have your conversations with your father ever been satisfying?"). Finding an exception, she checks to see what Jorge's previous self-talk was when things went better ("What did you used to tell yourself?"). Notice she methodically restates the problematic thoughts, as well as the alternative thoughts, to support Jorge in charting his way forward. Having identified exceptions to the unhelpful self-talk in the past, she gauges the impact ("And what difference did that make?") before checking to see if any exceptions have occurred more recently ("Have you been able to remind yourself of that lately?"). Chances are Jorge might have overlooked the example that comes to mind ("There was a stretch of talk on Sunday that felt different") if it were not for the exploration of earlier, more successful, conversations with his father.

In this example, Maria and Jorge have not had to work at generating *alternatives* to the problematic thoughts; instead they reclaimed some already within Jorge's repertoire. As they continue to work with this, they will develop strategies for Jorge to access this self-talk in the thick of the exchanges that, as he says, have been going off the rails.

In cases wherein clients *can't* identify alternative self-talk, it can be helpful to coax them to consider other options. This starts with what is sometimes known as "disputing" problematic thoughts (Dryden, 2009; Ellis, 2007) and has the effect of loosening the grip of unhelpful thoughts and beliefs.

Disputing Problematic Thoughts and Beliefs Through Socratic Dialogue

You may have noticed that when someone straight-out challenges something you have shared, it invites you to fortify your position, placing each of you on a different side of an argumentative divide. Clearly this would not be constructive in a therapeutic conversation. More useful is Socratic dialogue, a scaffolded inquiry designed to gently dismantle unhelpful thoughts and beliefs.

Socrates was the Greek philosopher featured in Plato's *Dialogues* who had mastered the art of using questions to help people evaluate their propositions. Socratic dialogue helps break the spell of unhelpful thoughts and beliefs by unmasking their improbable claims. When done effectively, it is the client doing the unmasking in the form of a critical examination gently guided by the counselor.

There are a number of things worth noticing in the example below, featuring Dario from Box 12.1 in this chapter. First, notice how the counselor invites

Dario to examine his thoughts for their impact on his mood and actions rather than challenging them outright as irrational. Second, the counselor does not take on the role of rating the validity of the thoughts Dario articulates but instead invites Dario to take a position (White, 2007) on them—that is, to evaluate whether he agrees with and is reconciled to the conclusions he comes to. Finally, there is a didactic quality to this exchange. Dario is unaccustomed to examining his own process this way, so the counselor breaks things down, repeats highlights, and introduces terms and concepts without interrupting the flow of the exchange.

Therapist:	*Would it be okay if we lingered for a moment on that exchange at the party you referred to earlier?*
Dario:	*Sure. What about it?*
Therapist:	*You mentioned the host seemed to tune out in midsentence and then moved on just as you were starting to talk about something of interest to you. Is that about right?*
Dario:	*[nods]*
Therapist:	*You said you concluded that Charles found you boring.*
Dario:	*[sighs]*
Therapist:	*I'm aware that at the present time, you're having difficulty entertaining any other possible interpretation of what his actions meant.*
Dario:	*It's kind of obvious, isn't it?*
Therapist:	*Less so to me than to you, I think. How about if we look a little more closely? At what stage of the party did that happen?*
Dario:	*Oh, I guess I'd been there about 20 minutes. People were still arriving.*
Therapist:	*Was it a big party? I remember you said they had a "monster home."*
Dario:	*Oh yeah. Lots of room, lots of folks.*
Therapist:	*I imagine there were quite a few people showing up at the door, then, right around the time you and Charles were snatching a bit of conversation?*
Dario:	*Steady stream. They came close to running out of space for the boots. Yeah, the guests were piling in around that time.*
Therapist:	*Would you say the host took his job seriously?*
Dario:	*As host? Yeah, I'd say so. He seemed pretty intent on making sure everyone got settled in.*

Therapist:	I guess I'm getting the image of someone pulled in various directions, especially toward the front door, where there was a parade of people arriving, minute by minute. Where do you think his head would have been in the moment you and he were talking?
Dario:	[pauses to reflect] Distracted I suppose. Drifting towards the guest arriving.
Therapist:	And what difference does it make to notice that as you reflect?

By the end of this exchange, Charles's response looks less like evidence of Dario's being boring and more like the typical behavior of a person playing host at a crowded party. The therapist does not proclaim this view, however, but rather hands it all back to Dario to evaluate.

The focus so far in the exchange with Dario is on his automatic thoughts at the party. Earlier we looked at the relationship between automatic thoughts and global beliefs—a distinction worth bearing in mind here because disputing Dario's thoughts at the party may not be enough if they're associated with a well-entrenched belief generalizable to other situations. We saw this with Monica, whose thoughts about Jason's not calling and what she took to be his disinterest in the relationship were related to beliefs about her physical appearance and even more broadly with beliefs about the requirements for female (versus male) attractiveness. In Dario's case, the unhelpful thoughts arising in his encounter with Charles also seem to be part of a larger pattern. As the conversation continues, the therapist makes linkages between the self-talk at the party and other negative thoughts Dario has reported. This turns the talk toward disputing a global belief that appears to link these various situations.

Therapist:	I'm wondering if you notice anything familiar about the way you reacted to Charles. I'm thinking about how you reported feeling after that exchange at the pub on the weekend and about where you ended up after visiting your mother last week.
Dario:	I'm not sure I know what you mean.
Therapist:	Well, do you remember what you identified as some recurring thoughts when your friends at the pub started checking their cell phones for messages? And the negative thoughts you described on your visit to your mother's?
Dario:	I see where you're going. I guess in every case, I felt someone didn't want to be with me. I'm not someone people are attracted to or want to be with. Sad fact, but true.
Therapist:	The truth, or some habitual belief that crowds out other interpretations of events and plunges you into a dark space?

> *Dario:* It seems pretty real to me.
>
> *Therapist:* I appreciate that for you, it just feels like the way things are. That must be difficult to live with day to day. Do you figure this is just something you have to reconcile to—there's no getting around the facts, and you just have to learn to live with them?
>
> *Dario:* I'm not sure about that. I'm tired of this feeling. I've just had it. That's why I'm here.

Here, Dario identifies a belief about being unlovable that seems to pervade the various events linked by related negative thoughts. Global beliefs like Dario's can be very painful and call for sensitive, compassionate responses. This does not rule out further Socratic dialogue, however; these harsh self-judgments can also be the subject of careful inquiry to pry their grip off of some purported indisputable truth. As the conversation continues, the therapist asks about Dario's various friends and family members, inviting Dario to contemplate the many gestures of care and friendship they have shown. The discussion erodes the stability of the problematic belief about being fundamentally unlovable. This prepares Dario to access alternate thoughts at moments such as his encounter with Charles.

GENERATING ALTERNATIVE THOUGHTS AND BELIEFS

Although separated here so they can be looked at sequentially, the generation of alternative beliefs often happens simultaneously, or at least tightly on the heels of, the various approaches to challenging truth claims. In the two examples above, the disputing of problematic thoughts and beliefs lays the foundation for identifying alternative beliefs that are more effective in the moment at hand.

Generating Beliefs Embedded in Exceptions

In the example of identifying exceptions above, Maria as counselor helps Jorge to identify instances wherein he and his father seem to have had meaningful exchanges. The alternative beliefs at play were named at that moment as "his intentions are good." In helping Jorge to consolidate the self-talk that made a helpful difference at the time, the two of them identify the alternative belief that his father at least tries, that his intentions are good. This is a belief that supports Jorge in his pursuit of intimacy with his father. Is it more rational, closer to the truth? The question falsely suggests there is a single right answer and, in any case, misses the critical point: The belief fortifies Jorge in reclaiming a yearned-for connection. After helping Jorge to identify his use of this belief in the past, Maria ensures Jorge names the belief explicitly here so he can carry it into further encounters with his father.

Generating Beliefs Arising From Disputation

The second mode of challenging beliefs explored above was disputing problematic thoughts and beliefs. Rather than identifying exceptions, this involves putting cracks in the beliefs to make way for different perspectives. This happened when Dario—with some carefully scaffolded inquiry from his counselor—identified reasons *other* than boredom why the host cut off a conversation midsentence. He concluded Charles was distracted by his hosting duties. This exchange prepares Dario and his counselor to consider what alternative self-talk might be more useful in situations such as the party:

Counselor:	*So what sort of self-talk would fit with that?*
Dario:	*With remembering he has hosting duties?*
Counselor:	*I was thinking this is different than telling yourself that Charles is not interested. What would you be telling yourself instead?*
Dario:	*That he's got other things to attend to, I guess. I'd be thinking there are other reasons for how he's responding. It's not just about me.*
Counselor:	*"It's not just about me." How would you carry that forward into the party?*
Dario:	*I guess I'd be less on the lookout for proof people found me uninteresting. I'd pay more attention to what's going on for the other person.*
Counselor:	*So what might you tell yourself if the next person you start talking to seems distracted?*
Dario:	*Oh, maybe that they've got some worries on their mind. Or they're as uncomfortable as me!*

The generation of alternative self-talk, above, also provided leverage to revisit the global belief that Dario and his counselor named—that no one is interested in him:

Therapist:	*Dario, do you remember how we identified a few situations wherein similar unhelpful thoughts about being boring come up?*
Dario:	*[nods] The pub, the visit with my mother. Yeah.*
Therapist:	*We figured these all had something in common—the belief that, as you put it, "no one wants to be with me." Could this alternative self-talk*

> you're describing now make a difference? Would reminding your-
> self, "It's not all about me," help to counter that belief taking over in
> those other situations?
>
> Dario: Could be.
>
> Therapist: How do you think it would help?
>
> Dario: It would turn my focus more to what is going on for the other per-
>   son. Get me out of myself a bit. Worth a try anyway.

You may be feeling by now that the various stages and components of working with thoughts and beliefs can be difficult to hold in your mind all at once; the same is true for clients not accustomed to making sense of their experience in this way. For that reason, it can be useful to invite clients to chart out their experience between sessions as a way to provide a concrete record of thoughts and beliefs as well as the contexts in which they arise.

CONSTRUCTING THOUGHT RECORDS

There is a reason for the modifier *automatic* to describe unwelcome thoughts that arise in specific contexts and sabotage us, to our dismay. Thought patterns are like well-worn neural pathways. Our thoughts will naturally flow along them like water to a trench until we can establish substitute neural routes (Beaudoin, 2009; Hanson, 2009; Siegel, 2012). This does not happen merely by discussing alternative thoughts and beliefs; they have to be put to service repeatedly until they supersede the unhelpful ones and become habitual. Thought records are useful tools for supporting this process because they document the instances in which these alternative neural pathways will be exercised. In effect, they are inventories of unhelpful thoughts and beliefs, as well as help-ful alternatives, and the contexts in which they arise (DeRubeis et al., 2001; Greenberger & Padesky, 1995).

A thought record can be filled out retrospectively, on the basis of memory, in a session, but it is more accurate if clients take them home and complete them during the week. In these cases, it's a good idea to introduce the record within a session so clients can pose any questions they might have about the meaning of the categories or the process of completing the record. It can then be taken away, to be completed daily, or even hour by hour, to track thoughts and beliefs and to monitor their consequences. Box 12.7 features an excerpt of a thought record constructed by Jorge to track his various encounters with his father.

BOX 12.7

Jorge's Thought Record

Situation	Automatic Thoughts	Mood and Mood Strength	Evidence for Unhelpful Self-Talk	Counterevidence	Alternative Thought/ Belief	Mood Revisited
Talking to Dad on phone	"He's probably watching TV, waiting to get off."	Anxious 64	He seems distracted.	He always sounds distracted on the phone, no matter whom he's talking to.	"He's making an effort."	18
Arriving home for the weekend	"We're sure to have a blowout."	Anxious, stressed 83	We argued last week, and I still feel angry.	Our phone call went well enough; he said he's looking forward to seeing me.	"This visit has good potential for mending fences."	25

In this case, Jorge's thought record is focused specifically on situations involving his father. For each situation, he tracks the automatic thoughts that come up and rates the mood associated with these, 1 to 100 with 100 being most negative. Jorge then notes both the evidence and the counterevidence for the unhelpful self-talk. Next, he notes alternative thoughts/beliefs he was able to access that are more helpful and in line with his purposes, which are to make a connection with his father. Finally the record lists the change in his mood that comes about with the substitution of the alternative belief.

Depending on a client's apparent level of engagement with this process, thought records can be introduced in their entirety or broken down into smaller steps to provide time for clients to absorb the concepts and begin to notice thoughts and beliefs at work. Jorge's record, illustrated here, is retrospective; a similar chart could be used in anticipation of various key situations to review possible alternatives to unhelpful self-talk before the situations are encountered.

MINDFULNESS PRACTICE AND COGNITION

To this point, the chapter has focused on challenging and replacing particular thoughts and beliefs that contribute to negative moods as well as actions. This proactive and to some extent adversarial (reflected in terms such as *challenge* and *dispute*) approach to unhelpful thought patterns is widely represented in the research literature and is popular among practitioners because of its orderly and somewhat linear structure (Beck, 2005; Dobson & Dozois, 2001; Hollon & Beck, 2004).

In recent years, a worldview associated with Eastern thought and particularly mindfulness practice has been seeding counseling, therapy, and psychology with alternate practices for orienting to thoughts and beliefs that cause distress (cf. Germer, Siegel, & Fulton, 2005; Harris, 2009; Hayes, 2004; Linehan, 1993, 1994; Segal, Williams, & Teasedale, 2002). These approaches involve what might be called an *accommodative* rather than an *adversarial* orientation to problem experience (cf. Kwee, 2010). This section of the chapter introduces some of these practices. Readers unfamiliar with mindfulness and its Eastern roots may want to consult Appendix 4 on mindfulness, meditation, and breath work. If you are already familiar with mindfulness practices and their origins, you may want to read on.

Incorporating Mindfulness When Working With Thoughts and Beliefs

The practice of mindfulness is closely associated with Buddhist psychology, a unique form of psychological research with a 2,500-year history, which Wallace (2001) describes as an insight-oriented "contemplative science" (p. 211).

Mindfulness, characterized by Germer et al. (2005) as (a) awareness (b) of present experience, (c) with acceptance, is central to this empirical investigation of the mind. In insight-oriented meditation (Kabat-Zinn, 2005; Kornfield, 2000), practitioners examine the field of awareness, observing how all mental phenomena—thoughts, feelings, physical sensations, memories, images, and so on—come to the foreground and then leave it. None of these are permanent or substantial but rather part of the ever-shifting landscape of consciousness. This insight has useful implications for persons caught up in what were earlier referred to as truth claims—intransigent thoughts that make hurtful proclamations about their identities and prospects in life. As Germer (2005b) puts it, when we observe the mind, what we see "is not some absolute truth; rather, we see through the delusion of our conceptualizations. We learn to hold our constructions more lightly" (p. 26).

Mindfulness practice applied to unhelpful thoughts and beliefs is therefore not about *debating* cognitions but rather holding them more lightly, adjusting one's relationship with them, acknowledging their presence without assigning them monolithic truth status. As useful as challenging and replacing unhelpful thoughts and beliefs can be, this offers a different way forward that may be particularly useful in certain situations:

1. **A person prefers an accommodative orientation to experience.** For some people, an adversarial approach to their mental events is experienced as fostering a combative relationship with self (Kabat-Zinn, 1990). Instead, they prefer an attitude of acceptance that relieves distress by diminishing internal conflict.

2. **Attempts to replace unhelpful cognitions have been ineffective.** In some cases, attempts to replace unhelpful cognitions simply don't work. A person continues to experience problematic self-talk and global beliefs that endure, and the continued effort to challenge these brings on distress.

3. **Have the wisdom to change the things I can and accept the things I can't.** Life does come with certain inevitabilities, and no amount of revised self-talk can take these away: pain, illness, aging, death. In some cases it may be more helpful to learn to live peaceably with a recurring thought or belief than to attempt to eradicate it.

Loosening the Grip of Unhelpful Cognitions

Earlier we looked at the totalizing claims to our identities or prospects that some thoughts and beliefs make—they convey a static and fixed portrait of circumstances and the self that, on scrutiny, doesn't hold up. The Zen teacher Joko Beck captures a very different view of the flow of experience by depicting each self as akin to whirlpools in the river of life: "Water entering one whirlpool quickly passes through and rejoins the river. . . . Though for short periods, it seems to be distinguished as a separate event, the water in the whirlpools is just the river itself" (cited in Kabat-Zinn, 2005, p. 174).

This observation is fairly easily grasped at the intellectual level; it becomes a fundamental insight with transformative power when directly experienced through the practice of meditation. This is a key point worth emphasizing here: Therapeutic approaches associated with mindfulness traditions are frequently linked to regular meditation practice for counselors and clients alike (cf. Germer et al., 2005; Hick, 2009; Segal et al., 2002). Inviting clients to reflect on the ephemeral quality of thoughts and beliefs is one thing; having them experience it profoundly is another and may require the repeated revisitation of mental events that happens with ongoing meditation.

In working from a mindfulness perspective, problematic thoughts and beliefs become the subject of dispassionate examination. This becomes an opportunity to notice the impermanent nature of all mental phenomena—both positive and negative—along with the transitory quality of self. The transcript below demonstrates an excerpt of a conversation between Thea and her counselor. Thea is 27 and works as a legal secretary at a medium-sized law firm. She describes herself as an anxious person with low self-esteem, both of which qualities are exacerbated in a workplace where she is surrounded by aggressively competitive lawyers. She describes a sense of despair as she tries to keep up, without much success, with the rapid-fire banter in the office.

Thea and her counselor have previously identified unhelpful global beliefs, such as the notion that she is slow-witted and intellectually inferior to most people she knows. In specific situations, this converts into various automatic thoughts such as, "He's laughing because he thinks I'm stupid," "They're deliberately trying to show me up by talking in legal jargon," and so on. As the excerpt below shows, Thea's attempts to replace this self-talk have not been satisfying. As her counselor explores Thea's efforts at disputing the unhelpful thoughts and beliefs, they identify an alternate relationship with the problem (and herself) that resonates more with Thea's values.

Counselor:	*How have you been doing with identifying the automatic thoughts as they come up?*
Thea:	*Not bad, not bad. I'm more aware of them, that's for sure.*
Counselor:	*That sounds like a good thing. Can you give me an example?*
Thea:	*I was having coffee with my friend Lynn on Tuesday. She started talking about something in the newspaper, and I got confused. Right away I noticed it: that sinking feeling I told you about. So I paid attention to my self-talk: the usual stuff about not being smart.*
Counselor:	*Okay, you identified the automatic thoughts. Were you able to replace them?*
Thea:	*I guess so. I told myself I have lots of qualities and that everyone is different—the things we've gone over.*
Counselor:	*And what effect did that have?*
Thea:	*I suppose it lifted the feeling slightly, but to tell you the truth, it reminded me of my Uncle Frank.*
Counselor:	*Uncle Frank?*
Thea:	*He's a stonemason. I've seen him working on old buildings. Sometimes he's busy trying to shore up the foundation with cement while up above him, bits of stone are raining down on him. The wall is crumbling!*
Counselor:	*Wow—that's a vivid image! Can you tell me more about that?*
Thea:	*It's like I get into a battle in my head: me against the self-talk. I'm all busy trying to reassure myself. So busy I can hardly hear what's going on around me. On a good day I go home feeling okay*

> *because I've convinced myself I'm okay, and then I show up at work next day and some smartass lawyer talks circles around me, and I feel bad all over again. I don't know if I'm up to all the fighting.*
>
> Counselor: *Tell me more about what you mean by "the fighting."*
>
> Thea: *The fighting to hold onto some kind of self-image I guess. I'm tired of it. Why can't I just be me?*

At this point, Thea talks about how her meditation practice helps her to let go of "the bickering in her head." She describes the never-ending parade of thoughts, feelings, images, and so forth that pass through her awareness and of her efforts to acknowledge these without judgment and return to her breath.

> Counselor: *You and your breath. I get an impression of peacefulness from your description. Does that fit?*
>
> Thea: *I guess so. It sure isn't enlightenment, though. [laughs]*
>
> Counselor: *What is it about how you relate to all of that mental activity when you're meditating that's different from what goes on with Lynn and your friends or at the office?*
>
> Thea: *It feels like a break. A break from all that trying to be this or that. I just watch the bubbles.*
>
> Counselor: *Tell me about the bubbles.*
>
> Thea: *All those thoughts—they're like bubbles floating by, and then they go "poof" and are gone. And I'm still sitting there. They're not me.*
>
> Counselor: *So you're more than this thought or that thought.*
>
> Thea: *There are always going to be thoughts going through my head, and I can watch them, but I don't have to agree with them or disagree with them. No fighting. I can just accept them for what they are. It doesn't solve anything. But maybe there's nothing to solve.*

This exchange points to a new direction in Thea's work with her counselor—a movement from disputing unhelpful thoughts and beliefs to living with them in a new way. As their conversations continue, they will explore the many facets of self that Thea experiences at different times and in different contexts. Thea will focus on the notion, "I am not my thoughts" (Teasdale et al., 2000, p. 616), not favoring one thought over the other. Instead, she will cultivate a nonjudgmental, compassionate relationship with all of them, aided by her meditation practice. Below are examples of various questions her counselor might pose to support Thea in continuing to examine the flow of her lived experience.

> *Is this the only set of thoughts you have about yourself, or do other ones come up in different contexts?*
>
> *What other views of yourself do you see arising in the course of a day?*
>
> *Have you noticed a connection between certain views of yourself and certain contexts?*
>
> *If you pay attention to the negative self-talk, how long does it tend to last before receding to the background?*
>
> *Where does the negative self-talk go when more favorable views come to the foreground?*
>
> *What have you noticed about how your personality shifts along with various contexts? When do you find you're more [confident, outgoing, optimistic, kind, etc.], and when are you less [confident, outgoing, optimistic, kind, etc.]?*
>
> *Which version of yourself was in the foreground at that moment—the [outgoing, optimistic, kind, etc.] version or the [withdrawn, pessimistic, selfish, etc.] version?*
>
> *Are there times when you grow tired of defending or stoking particular views of yourself? Do you tire of being full of yourself?*
>
> *Have you ever had the experience of letting go of yourself? If so, what's that like for you? Is that something you'd like to experience more?*
>
> *It sounds like you let go of your image of yourself yesterday—what would others have witnessed? If not an invisible person, what would they have seen? How do you feel about that version of yourself?*

Notice that unlike the attention to altering self-talk or global beliefs explored earlier, the focus here is almost exclusively on simply observing the changeability of mental events and of the version of self associated with them. As Teasdale and colleagues (Teasdale et al., 2000) put it, "the emphasis is on changing the awareness of and relationship to thoughts" (p. 616). The awareness is facilitated by encouraging a reflexive view that deliberately separates person and mental events in much the same way as does the practice of externalizing the problem that was first introduced in Chapter 7.

This reflexive awareness reveals the ephemeral or transitory aspect of Thea's thoughts and beliefs, which in turn leads to possibilities for her to relate to them differently. A fundamental finding of Buddhist psychology is that what we take to be the self rests on the sum of all subjective experience, including thoughts, feelings, sensations, memories, images, and so on. With increased awareness of how all of these are in constant flux (like the river described by Beck above) comes a different relationship to mental events, a loosening of the grip on a rigid or fixed sense of identity. For some clients, the result of this is a liberation—in some measure—from self-judgment and the relentless pressure to be somebody in particular.

A mindfulness orientation to dealing with problematic thoughts and beliefs provides an alternate route to what is perhaps the more familiar approach of disputing and replacing automatic thoughts and global beliefs. Here the relief from distress comes not from identifying more favorable thoughts and beliefs but rather from a shift in the *relationship* with all thoughts and beliefs and the recognition that they are all part of the endless flow of consciousness.

CHAPTER TWELVE RECAP

In this chapter we looked at the mediating role that thoughts and beliefs have between the events people encounter and their responses to those events, including their ensuing moods and the actions they take. In this sense, thoughts and beliefs play a powerful role in shaping experience. They often do this outside of people's awareness, with self-talk arising spontaneously in the moment. For this reason, an initial task is to help clients notice negative self-talk and its fallout.

When clients are invited to gauge the negative impact of particular thoughts, it prepares them to replace those thoughts with constructive alternatives. However, this possibility is sometimes constrained by global beliefs—clusters of meaning that are expressed in individual thoughts across a range of contexts. So it is often necessary to address not only the thoughts but the beliefs associated with them so that clients don't revert to a sort of default setting under the influence of entrenched and unchallenged ideas.

Once thoughts and beliefs have been clearly identified and their modi operandi have been compellingly uncovered, it's helpful to challenge them to loosen their grips, poke holes in their truth claims. The chapter reviews two approaches to doing that. For starters, it's always useful to check if a person has *already* had success in relation to the problematic thoughts and beliefs. Identifying exceptions can save a lot of effort searching for solutions when they are already at hand. When these are not evident, it's helpful to invite clients to dispute the thoughts or beliefs by gently guiding them through a critical analysis using Socratic dialogue.

The purpose of disputing unhelpful thoughts and beliefs is to weaken their grip in preparation for replacing them with alternatives. A close examination of exceptions—times when negative self-talk has not managed to prevail—will typically uncover counterclaims. When exceptions are hard to come by, alternative thoughts and beliefs can arise from the process of disputing the problematic ones. Either way, these processes generate helpful self-talk that deserves further cultivation.

Thought records are a useful tool for tracking all of this activity: monitoring the contexts in which self-talk arises, noting the associated moods, taking stock of evidence for and against thoughts and beliefs, documenting alternative beliefs, and so on. These can be completed retroactively in session, but it is more helpful if clients journal their experience between sessions to paint a fine-grained picture of self-talk and accompanying mood fluctuations.

Recently, mindful traditions have introduced alternatives to the disputational stance to cognitions featured at the outset of this chapter. For some people, an accommodative relationship to experience is a better fit—perhaps because their attempts to dispute unhelpful thoughts have been ineffective or because they prefer a less combative relationship with their experience. Mindfulness traditions derive from Buddhist psychology, whose long history of contemplative practice points to the ever-changing quality of the mind, including thoughts and beliefs, and the fluid nature of the self. Although these ideas are not difficult to grasp intellectually, the insight they afford is more experiential in nature and arises from sustained observation of mental phenomena. For both counselors and clients, mindfulness-oriented work is therefore more likely to be effective if accompanied by regular meditation practice.

CHAPTER TWELVE DISCUSSION QUESTIONS

1. **Reflection on your own ideas and beliefs.** Think back to a time in your life when you were not coping well with the challenges you faced, feeling and acting in ways out of step with your preferences. What were some of your global beliefs at that time about yourself, about your situation, about your prospects, and so on? Write these down one side of a page and compare them with a second column that outlines your thoughts and beliefs about the same things at a time when you were thriving. In sharing, you may choose to maintain confidentiality about the situations themselves and speak about only the thoughts and beliefs.

2. **Automatic thoughts.** For one of the global beliefs identified in Question 1, describe a scenario in which the belief might express itself as an automatic thought in response to the situation at hand. What impact would the thought likely have on your mood? What action might follow in this situation from such an automatic thought?

3. **Automatic thoughts and global beliefs.** Discuss the relationship between automatic thoughts and global beliefs. What distinguishes them? How do the latter influence the former? Give examples.

4. **Alternative beliefs.** What are examples of alternative beliefs to those listed in Discussion Question 2? What impact do you imagine them having?

5. **Shifting identity.** Discuss the various facets of your identity that express themselves at different times. Include consideration of variations in your mood and disposition.

Discuss how this ties into the observation of the ephemeral quality of self found in mindfulness traditions.

6. **Disputation and accommodation.** Disputation and accommodation represent different sorts of relationships with problems or concerns. Can you identify contexts in which you favor one and contexts wherein the other seems like the more appropriate response? What characterizes, for you, the difference between these contexts?

CHAPTER TWELVE ACTIVITIES

1. **Reading between the lines: Implicit thoughts and beliefs.** Form pairs. Speaker, identify some situation or experience that repeatedly causes you distress or unhappiness. Describe the situation or experience, sharing your opinions about it. Speaker and listener, team up to identify implicit thoughts and beliefs imbedded in the statements associated with this situation or experience. You can take a cue from the questions following Box 12.3. Debrief. Speaker, what was it like to notice the thoughts and beliefs that lurk behind your position? Listener, which challenges were associated with helping the speaker to identify these?

2. **Tracing negative moods to self-talk.** Pair up. Speaker, identify a recurring negative mood that troubles you from time to time. Listener, join the speaker in tracing these moods back to the self-talk that accompanies them. Debrief. Speaker, what was it like to identify—possibly for the first time—self-talk associated with negative moods? Even if you have previously identified this, what difference did it make to be reminded of the role of your thoughts in generating the mood? Listener, which challenges were associated with scaffolding this inquiry with the speaker?

3. **Identifying exceptions to automatic thoughts.** Pair up. Speaker, identify a situation in which your own self-talk gives rise to negative moods and unhelpful responses to the situation. Lay out a clear account of the self-talk. Speaker and listener, collaborate to identify exceptions to this self-talk: times when the speaker has adopted perspectives that have more helpful repercussions. Compare the alternate thoughts and beliefs with the problematic ones. Discuss. Speaker, was it difficult to identify exceptions? Did the exceptions seem convincing to you? What impact did it have on your mood to remind yourself of the exceptions? Listener, what were the challenges associated with identifying exceptions?

4. **Disputing automatic thoughts and generating alternatives.** Form pairs. Speaker, identify a situation in which your own self-talk gives rise to negative moods and unhelpful responses to the situation. Lay out a clear account of the self-talk. Listener, use Socratic dialogue to poke holes in the self-talk's claims, and support the

speaker in generating plausible alternative perspectives that have more helpful repercussions. Discuss. Speaker, was it difficult to let go of the negative self-talk? Did the alternative views seem convincing to you? What impact did it have on your mood to entertain the alternative views? Listener, what were the challenges associated with identifying alternative self-talk? To what degree did you find yourself in a rhetorical position, attempting to convince the speaker of counterclaims?

5. **Identifying global beliefs that contribute to unhelpful automatic thoughts.** Form pairs. Speaker, identify a situation in which your own self-talk gives rise to negative moods and unhelpful responses to the situation (perhaps the same situation as above). See if you can identify related but not identical situations in which you seem to think the same things with roughly the same negative consequences for your mood. Listener, support the speaker in examining potential global beliefs that link these various situations. Debrief. Speaker, were you able to identify any global beliefs linking the situations in which the automatic thoughts come up? If so, what was this like for you? Which possibilities might it suggest? Listener, what were the challenges associated with helping the speaker link automatic thoughts to global beliefs?

6. **Developing a thought record.** Use the following table to chart your own automatic thoughts in a situation that gives rise to problematic self-talk.

Situation	Mood	Automatic Thoughts	Evidence for Unhelpful Self-Talk	Counterevidence	Mood Revisited
Who, what, where, when?	*Name your mood(s) and rate from 0 to 100 to capture the strength of the feelings.*	*What were you telling yourself that led you to feel this way?*	*What evidence supports the problematic thoughts?*	*What evidence supports a counterclaim?*	*Rate your mood from 0 to 100 on entertaining counterevidence.*

7. **Observing mental events.** Find a quiet place to sit for 10 minutes uninterrupted. Adopt an upright posture, and fix your eyes on a spot a few feet in front of you, or let your eyelids grow heavy and close. Turn your attention to your senses. First pay attention to the sensation of your body in your seat, your feet on the floor. Then notice sounds in the room and beyond. Finally turn your attention to your breathing by noticing the gentle rising and falling of your diaphragm in response to intakes and exhalations of breath. When thoughts come up to distract you, notice them but do not judge them. Let them be, and return to the breath. Debrief in pairs. What was this like for you? Did you notice anything that is normally in the background of your awareness? Was it difficult to follow the directions? Did you find your mind wandering? What sorts of mental events came up? What learning do you walk away with?

Chapter 13

WORKING WITH EMOTIONS AND VALUES

INTRODUCTION

"How does that make you feel?" This familiar phrase is probably the most often cited example of a counseling question among the general public and among many practitioners as well. Counseling involves conversations with people about things that deeply matter to them, and when things deeply matter, emotion is close at hand. Johnson (2004) observes, "Emotions, like an internal compass, orient us to our world and provide us with crucial information about the personal significance of events" (p. 65). That significance may not always be clear and unambiguous, but the display of emotions alerts us that something is at stake and deserving of further curiosity.

There are other reasons, too, why emotion plays such an important role in counseling. The safety of the counseling relationship contributes to the accessing and expression of feelings that may have been locked away and dormant for a prolonged time. These can be powerful moments. This brings, for some, a profound sense of relief and, for others, a sudden flash of insight into experience obscured by a formerly indecipherable jumble of thoughts and feelings. The turning to and acceptance of a long-avoided emotion can feel like the naming of the elephant in the room; it can provide a sense of reassurance that a difficult feeling will not engulf us, and can promote a welcome moment of reconnection with self and others.

The expression of emotions, like all human expression, is inescapably cultural in the sense that what people get emotional about and how they display feeling vary across historical time frames and geographical regions, as well as from person to person (Gergen, 2001; Harré, 1986; Harré & Parrot, 1996; Stearns & Stearns, 1988). This by no means contradicts their biological dimensions (Griffith & Griffith, 1994;

Griffiths, 1997; Hanson, 2009; Siegel, 2012). The emotional brain centers have evolved over many millennia, and feelings play a key role in helping alert us to dangers and mobilize us for action, among other things. But understanding emotion as an adaptive, evolutionary phenomenon does not suggest a client's tears or hand-wringing speak for themselves. Emotional responses are cultural expressions of meaning (J. Bruner, 1986, 1990; Gergen, 2001), and as we have seen throughout this book, meaning is a malleable phenomenon, never a fixed given. The meanings we attach to events and the feelings that accompany them are subject to ongoing reinvention. To assume emotional expression uncovers some purported bedrock subverts the fluidly constructive process of therapeutic conversation.

Recent innovations in brain-scanning technologies are generating thousands of new pages on the neurological origins of human responses, including emotions. As enlightening as some of these findings are, they can distract therapists from the task at hand in conversations with people seeking to alter their relationships with aversive experience. J. Bruner (1990) captures the issue at hand:

> The engine in the car does not "cause" us to drive to the supermarket for the week's shopping, any more than our biological reproductive system "causes" us with very high odds to marry somebody from our own social class, ethnic group, and so on. (p. 21)

Biology, including brain biology, is part of the context in which human action is performed; biology is not destiny.

These caveats notwithstanding, emotion is a potent force, a vivid expression of what it means to be human, a key dimension of all our most celebrated works of art. As Goleman (1995) puts it, "our deepest feelings, our passions and longings, are essential guides. . . . Our species owes much of its existence to their power in human affairs" (p. 3). Counseling devoid of emotion is mere information exchange with little transformative power. Therapeutic conversations unfold against a back-drop of feelings and present many situations in which it can be helpful to invite those feelings to the foreground as an alternative to the focus on actions or thoughts seen in the two preceding chapters. This chapter explores a variety of approaches to working with emotions to achieve some of the following tasks:

- identifying exceptions to problematic emotions,
- creating safety for the exploration and expression of emotional material,
- inviting an exploration of emotions,
- using immediacy to bring emotion into the room and into the body,
- reflecting on feelings to dis-solve them, and
- turning toward emotion with nonjudgment and equanimity.

Reflection 13.1

Think back to a time when you responded to some event in a heart-over-head way—that is, with a spontaneous outburst of emotion. In which ways was the connection with and expression of that emotion helpful? In which ways was it hurtful? If you could revisit the situation, is there a way you might revise how you dealt with it?

CULTURE AND EMOTION

Dramatic advances in brain science are contributing to our understanding of how the brain plays such a key role in experiences that we may not experience as cerebral in any way. Emotion is certainly one of these, and so is music. For instance, Daniel Levitin's (2007) studies show the key role of neurological pathways in the processing and appreciation of music. In a sense, we're hardwired to experience certain melodies as catchy. At the same time, his work shows that what the brain recognizes as catchy varies from culture to culture. Brains don't develop separately from their environment, and the way they process music or (to get back to the topic at hand) emotion is always dependent on cultural context.

In her in-depth studies produced while living among the Inuit of Canada's north, anthropologist Jean Briggs (1971, 1999) vividly portrays a wide variety of emotions unfamiliar to non-Natives—emotions for which she had to invent English terms to name them for readers. Briggs's writings capture her puzzlement but also her exhilaration at the rich diversity of human experience. Lofland (1985) also demonstrates the diversity of emotional expression in showing how in regions where infant mortality rates are high, there is not the outpouring of grief at an infant's death that is more common in contexts wherein the death of an infant is a rare and unexpected event.

The work of anthropologists is useful to counselors because it provides the reminder that the cultural context—geographic, linguistic, socioeconomic, gendered, and so on—is never identical for two people. What looks or sounds like a readily identifiable nonverbal—tears, laughter, a lowered voice, and so forth—will always have a meaning exquisitely specific to the person at hand. So will different people's emotional responses to what appear to be identical situations: the death of a father, for instance:

- Tricia responds with an outpouring of anguish and tears. The event is cause for deep grief and disorientation. She requests leave from work and spends many weeks mourning and regrouping.

- Ivan meets the event with calmness—some might call it stoicism. He is seen to smile and laugh at the funeral. He reports feelings of relief and gratitude.

Further exploration reveals that Tricia's father assumed sole care for her from childhood, dying unexpectedly from an undetected heart condition. Ivan's 93-year-old father passed away after more than a decade of suffering and disorientation with Alzheimer's. In each case, how Tricia and Ivan respond makes sense to us as we hear more: a tribute to the shared dimensions of emotion that binds us as humans. Yet their experiences differ strikingly: a reminder that how people respond emotionally to events is a function of their unique cultural contexts. Feelings bring us together and promote intimate honesty; at the same time, they are a potent expression of a person's unique cultural positioning and deserve the same curious and thoughtful exploration as other aspects of experience.

Reflection 13.2

Have you ever met someone whose expression of emotion seemed to differ from yours—for instance, they laugh at things that don't seem funny to you or appears to speak with agitation about a topic that strikes you as somewhat inconsequential? Are there ways of making sense of these differences as cultural: in terms of not simply ethnicity or nationality but gender, socioeconomic class, sexual orientation, age, and so on?

BALANCING UNIVERSALIST AND RELATIVIST VIEWS OF EMOTION

The question of whether emotions are universal or relative has preoccupied theorists for a very long time (Burgoon, Buller, & Woodall, 1996). This is of course a key question for practitioners because if feelings are universal, then I as counselor can assume I know what you as client are experiencing once I identify the emotion associated with it. On the other hand, if emotions are relative, then I as counselor may never be quite sure of what is going on for you as client because what looks to me like a familiar emotion will be different for you than it is for me, due to your unique context.

It probably comes as no surprise that I advocate a both/and position and think both perspectives have merit. Certainly there are ways in which emotion can be understood as an adaptive response associated with particular regions of the brain. This primary evolutionary quality of emotion often links people across cultural contexts—think of the fear or grief that binds diverse survivors of a disaster, even when they can't communicate verbally due to language differences. If we weren't able to identify with the emotions clients share in session, we couldn't convey empathy and develop a trusting relationship. But it is also worth remembering that our inhabiting shared territory does not mean our experience is identical. Even researchers leaning toward a universalist view of emotions (cf. Keltner, Ekman, Gonzaga, & Beer, 2001) concede that although people of diverse backgrounds may use similar facial expressions, they differ in the meaning they ascribe to them. Scherer, Banse, and Wallbot (2001) found that when speaker and listener are of different cultural backgrounds, it gets harder for the listener to infer the emotions expressed by the speaker. The expression of an emotion in response to an event is tied to the meaning of that event in the local culture, which may or may not parallel the meaning ascribed by someone from outside the context. So as fundamentally human as emotions may seem, they can also be understood as "cultural performances" (Gergen, 2001) characterized by humanity's rich diversity.

For these various reasons, it makes more sense to both convey empathic acknowledgment of clients' feelings and be ever open to what makes their experiences unique. The universalist view reminds us of our shared humanity, but it is the relativist perspective that reminds us that ultimately, our cultural backgrounds are always somewhat distinct from one another's. Besides, that expectation of some difference encourages a stance of cultural curiosity that teases out experience-near description and intensifies therapeutic conversations. From this point forward, the chapter examines a variety of ways of working with emotion to suit the context of the person at hand—approaches as diverse as stepping into them or choosing alternatives.

CHOOSING ALTERNATE EMOTIONS

The notion of choosing emotions may provoke a double take for some readers, and it's interesting to reflect on why. There are long-standing ideas in both counseling and the wider culture that assign a sort of bedrock status to emotion, something *given* but never *chosen*. Various strands of psychological theory give rise to images of people operating out of deep unconscious forces that reveal themselves in moments of emotional expression (Gergen, 1994; Monk, Winslade, Crocket, & Epston, 1997)—moments that are then taken to speak an indisputable truth. This perspective oversimplifies the relationship between culture, meaning, and emotion and can persuade practitioners to go for the affect—to provoke the expression of feelings on the naïve assumption that this gets at what is real and is thus inherently healing, regardless of context. To depict emotion as speaking a truth that somehow trumps all others is to do a disservice to the voices and judgment of clients, treating them as mere emotional conduits rather than discerning subjects of their lives.

There may be no way to escape sickness and aging, loss and death, but there are many choices available for responding to these. Therapeutic conversations are a venue for exploring and acting on these choices, a place for collaborating with clients seeking to feel something different. As we shall see, this may involve turning toward the emotion as a means of transforming one's experience of it. But sometimes an emotion is a tired and troubling response that persists despite being reflected on, rendered symbolically, and cogently linked through in-depth analysis to events long past. Sometimes a client just wants to feel something different, and this chapter starts with practices for supporting clients in doing that.

Feel Something Different

The language we use to describe feelings says something about the power we attribute to emotion: "It had me in its grip," "It took hold of me," "It hit me like a ton of bricks," "I was overcome by it." In the presence of an intense emotion, it seems that a force bigger than us is in control and there are no other ways of responding available. Depending on the context, it may require patient and persistent work with clients to help them access alternate responses. But as we've seen elsewhere, alternate responses are often *already* part of a person's existing repertoire, and the task at hand may be no more complex than identifying these and building on them.

When seeking exceptions to problematic actions or thoughts, we search for instances when a person has chosen to behave or think differently. People don't typically have the experience of choosing feelings in quite the same way: The image of someone who wills their own happiness or contentment is typically associated with a sage or meditation master who's spent a lifetime learning how to moderate her mood. More typically, changes in feeling states are the by-product of choices we make in other domains: We talk to ourselves differently (as in daily affirmations, self-talk, attitude adjustments, etc.), or we act differently (as in slowing down, getting more active, reaching out to others, etc.), with the result that our moods change. Because of this, the identification of exceptions proceeds a little differently in the realm of feeling than it does with actions and thoughts.

Inquiring about times when problematic emotions have been absent will typically uncover factors under a person's control that they can address in the present circumstances. Understanding what has been different in those preferred contexts, for example, around relationships, lifestyle choices, living arrangements, self-talk, attitudes, and so forth, helps to isolate choices they can now make to re-create the contexts.

Box 13.1 illustrates three scenarios in which a client presents some emotional experience as problematic. In each case, client and counselor are able to identify exceptions to these feelings. Notice that in the context associated with the exceptions, there is always some element of choice on the part of the client—not a simple and direct choice to feel something different per se but a choice that influences the client's emotional life. One thing client and counselor need to discern is whether this alternate context is sufficiently similar to the current one to be of use. Assuming the choice that made or makes a difference in the other context is currently available to the client, the client is presented with an option for altering the problematic emotions.

BOX 13.1

Exceptions to Problematic Feelings

Problem	Exception	What Was Different	Choice Available in Current Circumstance
Anxiety. Lorraine is in the midst of a very busy term at college. She says she's "fretting" all the time; she's started biting her fingernails and is experiencing insomnia.	Prior to returning to college, Lorraine was employed in a hectic workplace, with multiple responsibilities. She says that generally she "coped well" and anxiety was not a significant issue for her.	In her previous job, Lorraine took out a gym membership and worked out every 2nd day. She says that as long as she kept fit, the harried work lifestyle "didn't get to her."	Lorraine commits to renewing a lapsed fitness routine, vowing to work out at least every 2nd day despite her busy schedule.
Jealousy. Javier's last girlfriend cheated on him. He says he's been caught up in feelings of jealousy related to his current	Some days, Javier says he notices the things Mia does to show her love and affection for him. These remind him that their	When Javier looks for proof of Mia's commitment, he sees it in a multitude of things she does for him that	Javier says he will trust his senses more, to notice how Mia relates to him instead of confusing her with a previous

(Continued)

(Continued)

Problem	Exception	What Was Different	Choice Available in Current Circumstance
girlfriend, Mia, who took a new job in an office full of men. He and Mia have been fighting frequently and Javier is concerned the relationship is at risk.	relationship is solid and that he can trust her displays of caring as evidence of her commitment.	demonstrate her caring. He turns this into self-talk in moments of jealousy, reminding himself that Mia displays her loyalty to him on a regular basis.	girlfriend. When feeling jealous, he will ask himself, What do your eyes see?
Grief. Sally, a nurse, lost a child to stillbirth. She saw a counselor about this and feels she's done all the processing she can do. In her job on the neonatal ward, she is constantly witnessing the joy of new parents and finds that despite herself this brings up deep feelings of loss.	Sally is often seconded for weeks at a time to a different ward of the hospital. She finds that in an environment where she is not constantly witness to the birth of children, her sadness and grief are not activated, and she generally feels more content.	In this situation, the exception is about working in a different physical context. The choice involved is in Sally's accepting the intermittent secondments and relocating to the other floors of the hospital, where she is not exposed to childbirth on a daily basis.	Sally feels she's done what she can to "work through" her grief over losing a child, and it may accompany her, to some extent, for the rest of her life. She decides to apply for a transfer to a different hospital ward.

The intention of Box 13.1 is not to suggest that dealing with problematic feelings is a tidy, linear process. Exceptions can provide doorways into other useful territories; getting to those territories and inhabiting them more fully typically takes time and effort. Nevertheless, it's a journey that can be helpfully facilitated by a therapist and one that does not necessarily involve delving into or solving emotions. Sometimes doing something different, as in the examples in Box 13.1, is sufficient to alter circumstances in line with client preferences.

However, in the complex realm of feelings, the identification of exceptions is not always sufficient for making a difference. For instance, in some situations, it's the attempts to tune *out* or turn *off* emotion that itself becomes a problem. Here a more helpful way forward may look very different from the search for exceptions depicted above. It involves turning *toward* the emotions, and this calls for sensitivity and responsivity on the part of the therapist.

Reflection 13.3

Have you ever experienced an issue that caused you emotional distress that did not seem to diminish no matter what degree of insight, understanding, explanation, or other forms of processing you brought to it? If this distress has since diminished, was this related to a change in context? If it has not diminished, what happens when you reflect on exceptions to this distress in your past? Can you identify contextual differences that might be transferable to the situation you are in now?

EMOTIONAL EXPRESSION IN SESSION: STRONG BREW

Perhaps due to that enduring image mentioned earlier of therapy as a venue for emotional catharsis, therapists in training sometimes gravitate toward interventions aimed at accessing emotion. But the expression of feelings is not *inherently* therapeutic, and the inclination to go for the affect risks exacerbating a client's sense of vulnerability and damaging a working relationship. Emotion is strong brew and should be handled with care for a variety of reasons.

Safety Considerations Around Emotional Sharing

It can be very difficult to sit with strong feelings such as fear, anger, anxiety, and grief, so we all effectively cope with these emotions by drawing on the more evolutionarily recent, executive functions associated with the neocortex region of the brain (Goleman, 1995; Siegel, 2012). We compartmentalize emotions, and we moderate them with self-talk, as seen in Chapter 12. This does not necessarily imply emotional cutoff or repression; indeed, it can be highly functional behavior in a social world where blatant emotional outbursts can threaten or alienate others. It is also an effective way to cope with painful experience that might otherwise overwhelm us, making it impossible to engage with daily tasks. Because of these caveats, it's worth reflecting on a number of considerations before instigating interactions that could be emotionally painful for clients:

- Do you have a shared understanding of the purpose of delving into emotional territory?

- Which sorts of emotions is the conversation likely to elicit? Are these potentially painful feelings?

- Has the client indicated a willingness to delve into painful territory?

- Have you mutually explored and consolidated strategies for coping with or being in the presence of strong or painful emotions?

- In a situation wherein a client is feeling particularly fragile around a topic, have you mutually agreed on a pass rule—that the client should feel free to tell you when they would prefer not to explore further?

In the safety of a therapeutic relationship, many powerfully helpful moments are associated with the sharing of strong feelings. The naming of one's struggle in the presence of a compassionate witness alone can provide a profound sense of relief as well as acknowledgment. As well, this sharing may enable clients to listen to an internal voice, as it were, that has long been ignored. Or they may discover that they can go on, and possibly even thrive, in the presence of feelings they feared and avoided at a cost to their relationships with themselves and others. When that safety is absent, however, therapeutic trust can be shattered, and counseling can inadvertently be a venue for the reperpetration of harmful experience.

Counselor Avoidance of Emotional Content

For the same reasons that clients may steer away from strong emotion, so may counselors. Therapeutic conversations call for the will and readiness to sit with difficult material. If a counselor is reluctant to hear about painful experience, chances are the conversation will never go there, even though such sharing might be useful in the moment at hand.

One possible outcome of a counselor's avoiding emotion is an exchange primarily centered on information gathering. Although the gathering of information has its place in the overall process, a conversation that steers clear of the difficult aspects of a client's subjective experience begins to feel like it's not going any-where. It lacks color and resonance, like a painting or musical composition devoid of human expression.

Another version of avoidance is to welcome emotion of whatever intensity—but only so long as it is *positive* emotion. This translates into conversations that invariably turn toward the celebration of good news. This could manifest as a persistent curiosity about some difficult emotion's *absence*—in other words, a relentless quest for exceptions—and avoidance of any exploration of the difficult feeling itself.

> Anthony: *I'm starting to notice I'm not as accepting as I'd thought about what she did. I seem to be short-tempered and irritable around her. I haven't confronted her about the affair, but I'm not sure it's such a small deal after all. I can feel this anger welling up in me; sometimes I feel I'm going to explode.*
>
> Counselor: *Are there times when the anger is not there? Do you ever manage to just put it aside and connect with her the way you did before all this happened?*

There may be a point when it would be useful for the client to put anger aside; however, it appears in this situation that a turning toward that anger could be use-ful for the following reasons:

- There is a risk of harm. What does "explode" mean, and is there a chance the client could be blindsided by this emotion if he doesn't deal with it in some way?

- It seems likely that the client and his partner will have difficulty working things through and mutually moving on from the affair if he is feeling but not expressing significant resentment and anger.

There are various reasons why it can be unhelpful to "feed" a destructive emo-tion (Dalai Lama & Cutler, 2000), but turning toward an emotion can be at the service of understanding it and learning to be in its presence. This opens up a variety of options for the client in responding to his partner, not to mention insur-ing against a potentially harmful outburst. Emotions are part of the totality of lived experience; without some degree of acknowledgment and processing, they some-times lurk on the fringes of awareness and may impede efforts to move forward in accordance with values and intentions.

A counselor's aversion to strong feelings—either out of difficulty coping with them personally or perhaps out of an impulse to protect the client—may also express itself in rescuing responses:

> *Clive:* *I just can't stop feeling down on myself. I look at my life, and all I see is failure. No friends, no job. What's the point? What's there to look forward to? Life is just one miserable day after another.*
>
> *Counselor:* *I hear that things are difficult, but remember, your parents and your brother are there for you. Besides, you lost that job through no fault of your own. You're a talented fellow with lots of prospects for the future.*

A response like this conveys the message, Buck up, Mister; it ain't so bad. It discourages the client from naming his experience, perhaps to the point that he will withhold the depth of his despair—a serious concern in the case of potentially suicidal clients (see Appendix 3). An alternative here is scaffolded inquiry that helps Clive discover hopeful possibilities in his circumstances without the counselor's haranguing.

Avoiding emotion in therapeutic dialogue can also lead to conversations that feel flat. In these cases, it can be helpful for counselor to step back and reflect on their participation in relation to the content of the exchanges:

- What seems to deeply matter to this person? Am I generous and open about exploring that?

- Am I inviting the client to share a rich account of their subjective experience of the issues raised? Do I project a willingness to hear more about their struggles?

- What is particularly difficult here for this client? Have I acknowledged that? Does the client perceive my empathy and compassion?

- Do I sense that there are feelings in the room that we aren't talking about?

- Do I notice my own discomfort arising at times in these conversations? If so, which territory in particular seems to promote this discomfort?

- Are there aspects of the client's situation that overlap with my own? Does the client's story push my buttons in any way?

Developing the ability to join clients in their sharing of powerful emotion is not a matter of mastering *technique;* it calls on counselors to cultivate familiarity and comfort with their own experience. To some degree this ability is developmental; it accrues as we age and are exposed to diverse life events—including loss, hurt, and conflict. Indeed, it's also an aptitude that typically develops over time in the role of counselor itself, but it is an ability that needs to be honed so that counselors are prepared to journey alongside their clients.

Reflection 13.4

Have you ever felt so emotionally raw that you felt the need to shut down rather than to process the feelings? Do you remember if anyone ever encouraged or urged you to speak about what was going on for you at this time when you did not feel ready? If so, what was that like?

USING IMMEDIACY: IDENTIFYING EMOTION IN THE HERE AND NOW

From Abstract Language to Experience in the Moment

When clients speak of their emotional experience, they enrich their descriptions of what's going on for them. Yet there is a difference between putting words to a feeling and being with the feeling in the moment, in the room, in the here and now. The practice of using immediacy involves bringing the emotion into the room and locating it in the body. Engaging in a task focused on an emotion is useful because it moves the conversation from the abstract to the concrete.

In the following example, Jorge has had a fateful weekend. With the assistance of some preparatory conversations with his counselor Maria, Jorge went into the weekend determined to come out to his parents. It didn't exactly unfold according to the script: Instead of being a prepared announcement over dinner, it emerged out of a mild argument with his father when he and his parents were driving to the supermarket. To Jorge's surprise, his father acknowledged he knew his son was gay and said that although he couldn't understand it, he accepted it. Jorge and his parents shed some tears together, and the weekend ended well. Yet Jorge says he isn't experiencing the sense of relief he'd expected, and he's made reference to a heaviness he's felt intermittently since the visit with his parents.

Maria: *Jorge, you mentioned earlier what you called a "heaviness" and how it's come up a lot since the weekend. Sounds like you've been dragging yourself around. I'm wondering whether, as you talk to me now, you'd like to turn your attention directly to that heaviness.*

Jorge: *In what way? I'm not sure I know what you mean.*

Maria: *We've been talking about the heaviness as something out there. Would you like to see if you can notice it here and now, in your body?*

Jorge: *We could give it a try, I guess. How, though?*

Maria: *You were describing to me your walk by the canal with Richard. He was bubbly and talking about celebrating with friends, and you said you couldn't get into it.*

Jorge: *Yeah, I sensed his relief and excitement but wasn't really feeling it myself.*

Maria: *What happens when you picture that moment? Do you have an image of where you were?*

Jorge: *We stopped and were leaning over the railing. He was chucking leftover bits of his bun onto the water for the ducks. [They review the situation for a moment, capturing the scene and reconstructing what was said.]*

Maria: *And you said that's when you first noticed the heaviness. Do you feel it now at all?*

Jorge: *A little, I guess.*

Maria: *What happens when you stay with that scene now and turn your attention inward? You could close your eyes if you'd like—up to you.*

Jorge: *[closes his eyes]*

Maria: *What do you notice when you pay attention to what's going on in your body?*

Jorge: *It's my arms and legs. They feel dense, heavy. Like they're weighing me down.*

Maria: *Okay. Anything else?*

Jorge: *My chest, too. It's like it's blocked up. Full, almost like when your stomach is full.*

In this example, the feeling (heaviness) being examined has already been named explicitly. Jorge initially put words to the feeling, although to this point he and Maria only understand it in abstract terms. The exchange provides an opportunity to be in more direct, sensory contact with the feeling. Notice that Maria revisits the incident associated with the heaviness briefly and invites Jorge to picture it to bring it into the here and now. This prepares the two of them to work with it further—an example is provided later in the chapter.

Using Immediacy in Response to Nonverbals

As mentioned, Jorge was explicit in his reference to a nebulous feeling—the heaviness. This is not always the case. In some situations, the emotions at hand have not yet been named and are conveyed nonverbally instead. You may have had the experience yourself of not noticing how you were feeling about a situation until you started telling a partner or friend about it. Your words quicken, your volume picks up, your pitch rises, and suddenly you perceive an agitation—anxiety, anger, frustration, disgust, and so on—that you hadn't been able to pin down. When this happens in a therapeutic conversation, it provides an opportunity to draw attention to an emotion that appears to be manifest in the immediate moment but has not been explicitly named. In this example, Maria is wearing her other hat and is client to counselor Daniel.

Daniel: And how has Azim been able to reduce that load?

Maria: I'm not sure what you mean.

Daniel: You were saying it's important that your relationship is democratic. Remember you told me that story about the time your mother had the knee operation and your father tried to take over the child rearing? How things fell apart and you all the paid the price?

Maria: Absolutely. My mother took it all on.

Daniel: So I was wondering what role Azim's taken up with your comprehensive exams coming next month.

Maria: [pauses] He does what he can. His job runs him into the ground. When he comes home he's just spent. And of course it's hockey season. [Maria begins to speak more quickly and forcefully, with what looks like some version of a sneer on her face.] You can't interrupt a hockey game for mere mortal affairs like diaper changing, can you? [rolls her eyes and looks aside] He does what he can.

Daniel: Maria, I hear you saying Azim does what he can, and I also sense you're saying other things by the way you're telling me about this now. I'd like to catch the full message you're sharing here. What do you notice when you pay attention to how you're feeling in this moment?

Maria: [pauses, turns her attention inward, sighs heavily]

Daniel: What does that sigh say?

Maria: [long pause] I guess I'm fed up.

Daniel: Fed up? What do you notice in your body right now?

Maria: I feel tight. Wound up. Exasperated.

Daniel: Okay, a few other things going on for you right now. Are there any words that particularly fit to capture what's going on for you?

Maria: I'm pissed off. Angry! I'm sick of the imbalance. I'm angry at Azim.

The use of immediacy draws attention to what the counselor may feel is present but unspoken. It gives counselors a chance to check in with clients to confirm impressions and ensure they are not misreading what they are witnessing. Here, Daniel is only truly inquiring about his hunch that there is more going on if he is open to hearing differently—otherwise his intervention is just a stylized version of telling Maria what's really going on.

If Maria were to maintain she is not upset with her partner Azim's behavior, one possible response would be to respectfully acknowledge her clarification. This does not mean Daniel must necessarily immediately let go of his impression, however. His one-step-removed view has the potential to be useful to Maria. If he finds he has a persistent sense Maria is agitated or angry, he can put the impression in his back pocket, to be visited at another time. Alternately, he could choose in the moment to be transparent about why he's asking and press further. This happens in the scenario below, after Maria says she's feeling neutral about the situation with Azim.

> Daniel: *Okay, thanks. I can hear you saying there's not much going on, yet I feel like I'm noticing more than you're saying.*
>
> Maria: *Like what?*
>
> Daniel: *I wouldn't want to say what it is: I think you'd know better, and that's why I ask.*
>
> Maria: *What are you noticing, then?*
>
> Daniel: *Well, I see you rolling your eyes and hear what seems like a sarcastic tone from you. I watch you sighing. It feels like there's emotion in the room that you're not pointing to. But maybe I'm reading too much into it. I wonder if you have any ideas about where I might be getting that impression?*

The skills Daniel is employing here are essentially paraphrasing what he feels Maria is conveying nonverbally and confirming his understandings with her. He's describing his read of Maria's experience and inviting her to correct his impression so that he can coordinate his reading with hers. He could put a name to his impression (anger, frustration, etc.), but then he wouldn't know what Maria might have called it—if anything at all—so he restrains himself here, despite the temptation.

In the counseling literature, there are a number of ideas associated with exchanges like this that although widely upheld, are out of step with a collaborative orientation to practice. They include the notion that clients may be in denial regarding certain purported truths about their experience and are resistant to exploring particular topics. This view is associated with the skill of "confrontation" (cf. Corey, 2005; Egan, 2002; Hackney & Cormier, 2008; Ivey & Bradford Ivey, 1999; Young, 2009). This is certainly one way of making sense of exchanges like the one between Daniel and Maria. But the notion that clients need confronting leads to a view of counselors as "reality adjusters" (Strong & Zeman, 2010, p. 333) and therefore positions counselors as the arbiters of reality.

Approaching what appears to be a discrepancy between what clients say and how they say it with a spirit of curiosity can be useful to both clients and counselors. When done skillfully, the inquiry centers clients' voices, paying tribute to their powers of discernment. By inviting Maria to evaluate what is transpiring, Daniel does not "point out incongruence" so much as initiate a dialogic interaction (Strong & Zeman, 2010) that brings forth ever thicker, experience-near accounts. From this point, there are various possibilities for going forward.

BOX 13.2

Inviting Emotional Exploration

Emotions speak powerfully, but not always clearly, as the great Irish singer/songwriter Van Morrison's song title "Inarticulate Speech of the Heart" aptly captures.

Sometimes when a client expresses strong feelings, the emotion may flow almost predictably and understandably from the content of the dialogue. Here, a reverential silence or perhaps some empathetic words of acknowledgment are ways to honor the gravity of the moment. But at other times, the moment may be pregnant with undeciphered meaning. This can take many forms: an unexpected tear or sob, for instance. Sometimes the counselor senses emotion but cannot pin it down or perceives what appears to be a discrepancy between what a client says and how they say it. All of these can be examples of what Katz and Shotter (1996) call an "arresting moment," a juncture for "reflection and further articulation, which allows clients to 'gesture' toward the uniqueness of their lives" (Lowe, 2005, p. 69). Here, the counselor's gentle curiosity may support the client in making sense of what is initially a baffling sensation or outburst as well as encourage a further exploration of some emotion.

To have conversations that make room for the breadth and depth of peoples' experience, counselors have to be prepared to sit in the presence of sometimes painful material and create an atmosphere of safety as they invite emotional exploration:

Would it be okay if we explored this further?

How about if we exercise a pass rule: You can let me know if there are things you don't want to talk about at this time?

(Continued)

(Continued)

Would you be interested in staying with this feeling right now so we can come to understand it better?

What do you notice when you just allow yourself to breathe into that feeling without judging it or trying to change it?

If your tears [laughter, closed fists, trembling knees, deep breaths, and so on] *could speak, what would the words be?* (Andersen, 1993)

You said you felt devastated. Could you take me inside that word?

I feel I'm noticing a real shift in your feelings right now; could you tell me more about what's going on for you?

What would you call the feeling that's washing over you [that came into the room] *just now?*

I'm aware I'm feeling confused between what you're telling me and what I think my eyes are seeing.

What's going on inside right now?

If that [anger, surprise, excitement, sadness] *had an important message for you at this moment, what would it be saying?*

You seem to be experiencing a lot of [feeling] *right now. I'm wondering if you can connect this feeling with other times and places in your life.*

What do you think this feeling says about what's important to you at this time in your life?

The naming of emotion and engagement with emotion in the here and now are helpful but are only steps along the path in working with emotion productively. At this point, there are various ways to proceed. In the example below, the heaviness that Jorge referred to is in the room following the use of immediacy by Maria, providing an opening for Jorge to explore the feeling and come to understand it more fully.

DIS-SOLVING EMOTIONAL KNOTS THROUGH EXAMINATION AND REFLECTION

Emotions aren't solved the way logical puzzles are. Feelings operate according to rules outside of the world of binaries and proofs. Left unexamined, they can act as impenetrable knots that contribute to destructive habits and hurtful interactions, even while banished from awareness. The notion of being stuck helps to capture this experience, a familiar dilemma that eludes language. The practice of immediacy helps to shed light on unspoken feeling, and it is through bringing emotion into language, reflecting on it, and orienting to it in new ways that useful shifts occur. Emotion is not solved, perhaps, but dis-solved (Anderson, 1997; Anderson & Goolishian, 1988) instead: When engaged, emotion transforms through a process that enlists both head and heart.

Maria:	*So the heaviness is in your limbs, and you feel it in your chest too. Are you okay staying with it?*
Jorge:	*Sure. It's not as though it's horrible or painful.*
Maria:	*Okay, nothing too extreme. How would you describe it? Is this a feeling you've experienced before or something new to you?*
Jorge:	*[pauses to reflect] It reminds me of when I moved out to go to college.*
Maria:	*Did you experience the heaviness then?*
Jorge:	*Yeah, or something like it. It's kind of a sad feeling, like the end of something.*
Maria:	*The end of something.*
Jorge:	*When I moved out I had this sense that I was leaving my childhood behind in some way. It was exciting, but it was sad too. Those were good years, and that period of my life was ending.*
Maria:	*Hmmm. The end of an era. A rite of passage. Something like that?*
Jorge:	*Yeah, it's a feeling I get in the spring sometimes. I'm happy to see the snow melting, but there's something about how when you move on, you leave things behind too.*
Maria:	*And now? Does any of this connect with now?*
Jorge:	*I guess I figured I'd done the moving out, but I wonder. There was something binding me to my parents with that secret between us. When I'd go home on weekends, it was like we were reliving the old days—for better and worse, mind you! I don't think it'll be like that again. Ever.*
Maria:	*More passages.*
Jorge:	*I think my dad's going to have to greet me on my terms now. I'm not quite the chip off the old block he was counting on.*
Maria:	*Sounds like that's maybe a bittersweet thing?*
Jorge:	*For sure. That weekend was key for me; I wouldn't want to go back. It means I can move on with my life in new ways.*
Maria:	*And at the same time, you're leaving some things behind.*

> *Jorge:*   *I guess that's why I haven't really felt any flood of relief the way I expected to.*
>
> *Maria:*   *There's some loss in it too. Some sadness.*

The counselor Maria's role in the example above is subtle and facilitative. She invites Jorge to stay with the emotion and to examine it. In asking if this is a new feeling or a familiar one, Maria helps Jorge to make connections with a past time when he felt something similar. Linking the two events allows Jorge and Maria to reflect on what makes them both similar and distinct, shedding new light on the heaviness that Jorge has been experiencing in recent days.

In Jorge's example, as he indicated ("It's not as though it's horrible or painful"), the feeling of heaviness is not so aversive that he is inclined to avoid it. Sometimes the exploration of distressing emotion is more challenging than this, however. If someone has spent years, and a great deal of mental energy, avoiding aversive feelings, it may be difficult to stay with them once they're invited forward. In these cases, of course, the first consideration should be about the costs and benefits of moving the conversation into emotional territory. The Considerations in Assessing Trauma section in Chapter 9 provides several ideas about doing this with an ethic of care.

It's important to note that any practices for helping clients engage with emotion should be about helping them find more useful ways of dealing with the emotion. The skills described here are not founded on the assumption that getting emotional is somehow inherently healing or that growth comes from opening wounds. That said, there are times when counselor and client may see merit in staying with an emotion despite the inclination to shut down or turn away. The following section offers ideas about supporting clients in doing this.

Reflection 13.5

Did you ever have the experience of just sitting with a distressing feeling, adopting a patient and tolerant attitude in the face of it rather than scolding yourself for feeling that way or trying to purge yourself of the emotion? If so, what was that like for you? If not, how does such a prospect sound when you reflect on it?

TURNING TOWARD DIFFICULT EMOTION

Chapters 11 and 12 presented various options for altering problematic experience by changing patterns of action or self-talk. Sometimes, a shift in actions—doing something different—resolves a problem with the fringe benefit of an elevated mood, with no need to address the mood explicitly (cf. Berg & Dolan, 2001; de Shazer, 1994; O'Hanlon, 2000). In other cases, a change in thinking precipitates a change in feeling—an observation that has spawned a wide range of related schools of therapeutic practice (cf. Beck & Weishar, 2005; Ellis, 2007; Meichenbaum, 1985).

In effect, then, the practices introduced in the preceding two chapters involve changing negative affect by adopting proactive strategies. The client takes control of action or thought, which alters mood. In many cases, this is a helpful option and may be sufficient. As Harris (2009) suggests, "if control is possible and assists valued living, then go for it" (p. 26). However, the inclination to turn away from or avoid difficult emotion sometimes takes the form of destructive behavior that exacerbates rather than diminishes problems (Harris, 2009; Morgan, 2005). In these situations, the attempt to control or suppress emotions may paradoxically prolong distress (Hayes, 2004), increasing the emotions' frequency and negative fallout (Cioffi & Holloway, 1993; Clark, Ball, & Pape, 1991).

The mindfulness-oriented practices introduced in Chapter 12 offer an alternative to turning away from or changing problematic experience. Instead, they encourage a change in one's relationship with the experience rather than a change in the experience itself (Germer, Siegel, & Fulton, 2005). In the preceding chapter, we saw this in the practice of being present nonjudgmentally to problematic cognitions rather than disputing them. This is in contrast to the habit of "experiential avoidance" (Germer, 2005a; Hayes, 2004), which frequently exacerbates problems even while the client is attempting to escape them. Morgan (2005) describes this alternative response as "turning towards life." In the case of emotion, it involves orienting to the emotion without judgment, being present to the immediate moment with acceptance and compassion (Kabat-Zinn, 1990, 2005).

In a therapeutic context, this begins with identifying the emotion. The client may be the first to do this, or perhaps the counselor employs the skill of using immediacy, demonstrated above, to turn attention to the emotion. The following exchange (condensed and segmented for purposes of illustration) demonstrates some of the practices that may then follow in inviting a client to turn toward an emotion. These include the following:

1. Invoke the client's evaluation of current attempts to control the emotion.

2. Speculate about the option of altering the relationship with the emotion by turning toward it.

3. Direct attention to the embodied emotion in the here and now.

4. Coach the use of breath.

5. Recruit the senses to study the emotion without judgment.

6. Direct attention to shifts in the relationship with the emotion.

7. Debrief.

In the following example, Alliyah has expressed frustration about her attempts to deal with the anxiety that keeps her up at night, tightens her back muscles, and contributes to a feeling of fatigue that she says is disproportionate to the actual amount of work she does in a regular day. She keeps to a regular fitness program and has done extensive work adopting self-talk to counter the dread-inducing voice of the anxiety. In other words, attempts to control or turn away from the emotion through action- and thought-oriented strategies have not been successful. Alliyah still contends with anxiety and has become discouraged and pessimistic.

1. **Invoke the client's evaluation of current attempts to control the emotion.**

> *Counselor:* *Sounds like you've been working hard at this, Alliyah. What would you say the outcome has been of your various attempts to control the anxiety?*

Turning toward or accepting emotions can seem like a radical step for someone who has worked hard to avoid or control them. To get clients onside with this alternate practice, it can be helpful to invite them to reflect on the outcome so far of their unsuccessful attempts to deal with the emotion.

2. **Speculate about the option of altering the relationship with the emotion by turning toward it.**

> *Counselor:* *Seems like your efforts to escape the anxiety or turn your back on it haven't been fruitful. How about if we try something different? I'm wondering if you'd be open to turning* toward *the anxiety and finding a way to relate to it differently?*
>
> *Alliyah:* *I'm not so sure I want to experience more of the anxiety. I find it distressing.*
>
> *Counselor:* *Exactly. Yet it keeps coming back. So I'm proposing finding a way to be in its presence differently, without* that *distress.*
>
> *Alliyah:* *Well, nothing else is working. But how?*
>
> *Counselor:* *Well, we could start with using your breath as a support. Remember, this is about reducing your discomfort, not increasing it. I could coach you through this, and you should feel free to stop anytime if you want—just say so.*

It makes a lot of sense to try to escape difficult emotions, so it is not surprising that for many clients, the notion of turning toward them might raise concerns. It is difficult to know what difference this can make until actually trying it (likely repeatedly), but it can be helpful to clarify up front that this is not a trial by fire exercise and that in orienting differently, the emotion will be less aversive than it has been. Notice the counselor does not say "reducing the anxiety" but rather "reducing your discomfort" because as mentioned, this approach is about relating differently without actively trying to change emotions. Reminding clients that they should feel free to discontinue the process at any time will typically assuage concerns.

3. **Direct attention to the embodied emotion in the here and now.**

Counselor: *As you talk about the anxiety, I wonder what you notice coming up in your body, here in the room, in the present moment?*

Alliyah: *I sense a knot. A knot in my stomach area. It's like a hard clenching, a tightness, a holding.*

This is a good point at which to invite the client to close their eyes if they are comfortable doing that (some people are not). As mentioned above, it will be easier to notice the presence of an emotion in the body when there is some sense of the emotion's presence in a client's nonverbals or the intensity of their language. For many clients it's an enlightening surprise to notice they can locate the emotion somewhere in the body—most often in the head, chest, or abdomen.

4. **Coach the use of breath.**

Counselor: *As you become aware of the knot, you also notice your breath as a backdrop to this awareness. Notice the rise and fall of your chest and abdomen with each passing breath. Turn toward that knot with your breath, breathing into and around it, feeling the fullness of your breath while staying present to the knot.*

The breath is a frequently ignored backdrop to every living moment. Clients not accustomed to attending to their breath may need some additional preparation for this activity. For more on working with the breath, see Appendix 4.

5. **Recruit the senses to study the emotion without judgment.**

Counselor: *Take the time to be present to the knot, to observe it without judging it—all the while breathing into it. Don't try to push it away or change it; just let it be. Examine it; get to know it. Does it have boundaries? Texture, color, shape? Does it stay the same, or is it changeable?*

It's often surprising how what might seem like an abstract feeling can be experienced more vividly through sensory recruitment—that is, by inviting someone to engage with it as an object that can be examined through the senses. The practice has the additional feature of externalizing the problem as seen in Chapter 7, putting distance between the client and the emotion, opening space to examine and reflect on it. The questions posed here could be for the client's personal reflection, or alternately the client could answer them aloud as the guided process unfolds.

6. **Direct attention to shifts in the relationship with the emotion.**

> Counselor: *Notice what's going on for you as you keep breathing, staying present to the knot without trying to change it or push it away. What comes up? What seems familiar? What feels different? How are you feeling about the knot right now? What are you thinking about the anxiety?*

Paradoxically, it is often the avoidance of emotion that gives it power over us (Germer, 2005a), like the fearful mystique that builds up around an offscreen villain. Once that villain comes on-screen, he fails to match the mystique because imagination trumps reality (think of how rarely the shark actually appears on-screen in the classic film *Jaws*). Typically clients will discover that being in the presence of the emotions is not as excruciating as they imagined. This is the beginning of a shift in their relationship with the emotions.

7. **Debrief.**

> Counselor: *What did you notice about your experience of the anxiety when you met it this way: being present to it, breathing into it, not turning away but not embracing it either? What are you learning about how the anxiety operates throughout your week? What's changing in your relationship with the anxiety over time?*

Notice that the debrief might focus on the practice just concluded, or it might include a broader discussion if the client has been engaging with the emotion through meditation or other practices over a more extended time. Modifying one's relationship with an emotion does not happen instantaneously, any more than our relationships with people are built on the basis of one brief encounter.

Although the intention of turning toward a problematic emotion is not to remove it or reduce it, clients will often have the experience of "symptom reduction" in the wake of these practices (Harris, 2009). It's important here to emphasize the paradoxical nature of acceptance: that it "is not acceptance if it is done in order to reduce aversive feelings" (Ciarrochi & Bailey, 2008, p. 100). It's worth noting that to accept an aversive experience is not to embrace it but simply to meet it with compassionate nonjudgment. It's the shift in the relationship that brings about a reduction in distress (Germer, 2005b).

Like the practices for changing thought patterns introduced in Chapter 12, revising relationships with emotions by turning toward them and accepting them takes time. It involves various engagements with emotion in session, followed by debriefs that afford clients the opportunity to reflect on their experience. And it involves turning toward the emotions between sessions as well, perhaps with the help of breathing exercises or practices such as meditation or body scans (Kabat-Zinn, 2005; Segal, Williams, & Teasedale, 2002). The outcome of these activities is experiential learning—the accumulation of insight built not on abstract theorizing but on direct attention to lived experience (Ciarrochi & Bailey, 2008; Germer et al., 2005). The insights that frequently arise include the following:

1. Difficult emotions are part of the experience of living.

2. We can't control precisely what, when, and where we will feel things. Feelings arise in response to internal and external events, often without conscious awareness.

3. Breathing into a feeling or sensation supports us in remaining in its presence.

4. Each feeling has a beginning, middle, and end; it comes and it goes. The feeling is absent before its onset, and it crests before waning and departing.

5. When we allow ourselves to be present to our emotions, breathing into them, meeting them with compassion rather than turning away from them, we discover they will not engulf us. They lose power over us as we come to see them as part of the ever-changing flow of mental events.

6. Progress is achieved not through pushing a difficult emotion away but by being with it without judgment. This is not about liking the emotion but merely about accepting it as part of the field of experience, one character in the endless parade of mental activity. The result is a shift in relationship that makes it possible to be more fully present to one's life.

Turning toward problematic or aversive emotion provides a strikingly different option than identifying situations in which the emotion has been absent. Yet—depending on the particularities of the context at hand—both approaches offer helpful ways forward for people contending with difficult feelings.

CHAPTER THIRTEEN RECAP

Like the two chapters that preceded it, this chapter has presented options for intervening in relation to a particular aspect of clients' experience—in this case, emotional experience. There are various reasons why the domain of feelings is so strongly associated with counseling and psychotherapy. Emotions are powerful expressions of people's subjectivity: They speak loudly and forcefully, even when they are less than fully formed and difficult to translate into words.

When considered in evolutionary terms, the emotional centers of the brain developed prior to areas devoted to language and other cognitive functioning. One's emotional response to an event, coupled with physiological changes, momentarily precedes the cognitive processing of the situation. There is an adaptive aspect to this response that contributes to ensuring personal safety, and in some cases the emotional response is associated with a perceived danger, for instance, that is no longer a threat to the person in question. In other words, as compellingly as emotion speaks, it is not the spokesperson for a fundamental truth and deserves reflection on the part of clients, just as thoughts do.

The visceral and embodied nature of emotion has the power to connect people across diverse cultural backgrounds, and indeed research does suggest that certain patterns of emotional expression are virtually universal. At the same time, there is a large body of literature documenting the diversity of human emotional experience across historical eras and geographical divides. Given the merits of both these universalist and relativist views of emotion, it makes sense to empathically acknowledge clients' expressions of feeling while also continuing to be curious about what is unique about their own emotional experiences.

The chapter looked at a variety of practices for working with emotion. These begin with the consideration of whether the client has already had success in relation to problematic feelings. For some people, reflecting on and processing emotion does not necessarily lead to relief of distress. In these cases, a more helpful response might be to simply identify contexts wherein the distress has been absent and to create those conditions (which might involve acting or thinking differently) in the current circumstance.

At other times it may be more helpful to join a person in engaging in some way with difficult feelings because they do not necessarily dissipate or transform when ignored. Yet there are good reasons why we all occasionally avoid being in the presence of painful emotion. For this reason, the practitioner should exercise sensitivity and care in inviting the client into emotional territory. On the therapist's side, avoidance may also occur from time to time, and it is worth examining because it is difficult to invite clients to move in close to their experience when the facilitator is hesitant to go where the journey will lead.

Sometimes emotion is spoken about as a distant and abstract phenomenon. At other times, it appears clients are conveying emotions without naming them through their nonverbal expression. In both instances, the practice of immediacy may be useful. Immediacy involves inviting a person to focus on the emotion and to notice it in the immediate present, in the here and now, in the body. This can bring the feelings into the room, rendering them available for more up-close examination.

There are many ways to proceed in working with emotion once it is rendered accessible. The experience of reflecting on feelings and connecting them to other times and places can shed light on stuck feelings. This reflection on emotion can contribute to its making sense in the wider context of one's life and effect a change that dis-solves it or at least diminishes its aversive dimensions.

Another option for working with emotion associated with mindfulness traditions is less about understanding and more about nonanalytic, nonjudgmental acceptance. This involves turning toward emotion, often with the support of the breath, to learn to be in its presence with equanimity. Orienting to emotion in this way is neither about changing nor about figuring out feelings. However, a paradoxical outcome of this practice is that a transformation occurs nevertheless with the discovery that one can live in peaceful tranquility with what may have formerly threatened to be all consuming. In addition, the practice reaps insight into one's experience, even though it involves letting feelings be rather than deliberately seeking to understand them.

CHAPTER THIRTEEN DISCUSSION QUESTIONS

1. **The importance of emotion in therapy.** Emotion can be expressed without being named and carried without being in the foreground of awareness. How do these observations relate to the importance of attending to emotion in therapy?

2. **What clients feel versus what they say.** A person's expression of emotion is sometimes regarded as truer than the words they share. Do you agree with this premise? What are the potential consequences for collaborative meaning making if the counselor privileges clients' shows of feeling over their spoken accounts?

3. **Ignoring emotion.** What are the potential downsides for a person of ignoring their emotional responses to events and situations?

4. **The idea of emotional expression as fundamentally healing.** The chapter reminds readers that it is not operating from the assumption that getting emotional is somehow inherently healing or that growth comes from opening wounds. Are these assumptions you hold or that you have witnessed in professional communities or popular culture? What are your thoughts about the role emotional expression plays in dealing with challenges?

5. **The role of the breath.** What is it about the breath that makes it a central focus of so many meditative traditions? What have you noticed about the connection between breathing and calming or relaxing?

CHAPTER THIRTEEN ACTIVITIES

1. **Emotion and incongruent verbals and nonverbals.** Pair up. Speaker, choose a topic that you feel strongly about—this could be anger, joy, resentment, attraction, and so forth. In relating your experience of this topic, deliberately project nonverbals that are contrary to the messages of the words you use. Listener, use paraphrasing and other basic skills to help the speaker relate their account. Debrief. Speaker, what was it like to have your verbals and nonverbals misaligned? Listener, what challenges were associated with coordinating meaning when the verbals and nonverbals were not congruent?

2. **Immediacy I: From abstract language to specific embodied experience.** Form pairs. Speaker, talk about something that has been or continues to be associated with strong emotion for you, but keep it at a distance by speaking about it in abstract terms. Listener, invite the speaker to connect with the feeling by reflecting on the situation that gave rise to the emotion. Invite the speaker to notice the presence of the emotion in their body. Debrief. Speaker, what difference, if any, did you notice when you switched from abstract talk to specific reflection on an incident and its affect on you? Listener, which challenges were associated with helping the speaker to get closer to the experience and the associated emotion?

3. **Immediacy II: Invoking embodied experience.** Form pairs. Speaker, talk about a topic you feel strongly about, as in Activity 1. Listener, support the speaker in relating their experience, paying special attention to nonverbals. Bring the nonverbals to the speaker's attention and invite them to attend to the emotion in their body. Debrief. Speaker, what shifted, if anything, when you were invited to notice your nonverbals and to attend to the emotion in the here and now? Listener, which challenges were associated with helping the speaker to get closer to the emotion in this way?

4. **Being present to an embodied emotion.** Pair up. Speaker, as in the previous activities, identify and speak about something about which you feel strongly. Listener, follow the steps in the section titled Turning Toward Difficult Emotion to coach the speaker through a process of being nonjudgmentally present to and breathing into the emotion. Debrief. Speaker, what was it like to be present to the emotion as a witness? Is there any aspect of it that appears new to you from this vantage point? Listener, which challenges were associated with helping the speaker to remain nonjudgmentally present to an embodied emotion?

5. **Attending to the breath.** Pair up. One person coaches the other through attending to the breath by inviting them to notice the breath (a) at the nostrils and on the upper lip, (b) in the rising and falling of the chest, and (c) in the diaphragm. You may draw from additional material on breath work in Appendix 4. Use descriptive language to assist your partner in examining the breath in this fine-grained way. Debrief. Coach, what did you do to help promote a quiet and reflective examination? What were the challenges in doing this? Partner, what, if anything, new did you notice about your breath in doing this?

Chapter 14

WORKING WITH STORIES

INTRODUCTION

Counseling is a storytelling craft. Clients consult therapists with stories about their lives and identities, and clients and therapists join together in weaving new, helpful stories for moving forward. The accounts clients share bear many of the characteristics of well-formed narratives: They feature a central character (the client), in relationship to others, encountering and responding to a series of challenges over time. The events they recount are linked by a plot as it were that has some degree of coherence in the way it weaves together what might otherwise be a series of disparate events (Frank, 1995; Lindemann-Nelson, 2001; White & Epston, 1990).

These accounts are not necessarily *fully* coherent, however, as Maria in the role of client displayed in her early meetings with Daniel, sifting through a jumbled mass of thoughts and feelings. One of the many gifts of therapy is that it provides people with a venue to bring order to their experience by reflecting on it with the help of a compassionate witness. Yet despite discontinuities and contradictions, there are also recognizable patterns amid the accounts clients share. When people are in distress, the patterns typically foreground struggles as they relate stories that often characterize themselves as faltering or failing in the face of seemingly intractable problems (White, 2004a). This was the case for Jorge on meeting his counselor Maria and recounting a problem-saturated story that featured his shortcomings as a student and a son. When therapeutic conversations are helpful, the stories clients tell and the stories they perform change. The patterns of meaning they identify among seemingly identical events have different shapes—more energizing, life affirming, optimistic—and the meanings they perform are more congruent with their values and purposes.

As we've seen in various ways throughout this book, it's not the facts of the matter but the meaning made of them—woven together in storied form—that constitutes experience. Viktor Frankl (1984) powerfully demonstrated this in his memoir of life in a German concentration camp. He showed that for those who held onto a story about their internment as a trial that would fortify them, or a challenging detour en route to reuniting with loved ones, the experience was bearable. For others, who made meaning of their harsh treatment only as needless suffering in preparation for inevitable death, the experience was crushing, and the repercussions for mental, physical, and spiritual health were devastating.

Stories, meaning, and experience are intimately related. White (2007) puts it this way: "It is the structure of narratives that provides the principal frame of intelligibility for acts of meaning-making in everyday life" (p. 80). To make sense of events, we story them, weaving threads of sensation, memory, thought, feeling, and action into coherent wholes. It is meanings, woven together in narratives, that constitute our experience—the lived realities we play out in the way we act, think, and feel.

Listening to clients' account as stories helps to situate them where they live—in their cultural worlds. We notice the sources people draw on to make sense of the events of their lives, including religious traditions, education systems, literature, psychology, and popular culture, to name a few. This vast repertoire of cultural discourse makes for a huge variety of storying options, but it constrains options, too—delimiting which representations, which ways of being, are legitimated and which are marginalized. Understanding experience as storied makes it possible to join people in expressing their unique meanings while simultaneously attending to how that expression always unfolds in influential cultural milieus. Engaging at the level of story therefore captures the cultural/relational quality of experience (J. Bruner, 1990; Gergen, 2006, 2009; Polkinghorne, 1988) and counteracts long-standing traditions of individualism.

Working with story offers another advantage: It captures the temporal flow of life as lived. Lives, like stories, have beginnings, middles, and endings. Each individual moment is colored by what has come before and shapes the view of what will come next. Therapeutic conversations display this temporal flow. Clients report events that unfold over time: reflecting on times past, recounting recent developments, and speculating about what lies ahead. The construct of story accommodates the kinetic and evolving aspect of lived experience.

Understanding therapeutic conversation as a storying activity creates options for integrating the skills presented to this point in the text. When therapeutic conversations are understood in storied terms, each of those skills is seen to be at the service of helping clients narrate their lives in useful ways. The delicate care given early on to reading and confirming meaning reflects the importance of evoking vivid description while keeping clients at the center of the storying process that is therapy. Following the chapters on reading and confirming meaning, attention turned to highlighting client preferences in assessing their situations. This practice ensures that clients not only narrate what they find troublesome but narrate what they yearn for and imagine because ultimately it is their hopes and aspirations that will inform which actions to commit to, which stories are worth pursuing.

Looked at through the lens of story, it's also easy to see how more recent book chapters on influencing are equally consistent with the task of supporting clients in performing preferred narratives. Chapter 10 is about how to facilitate story change while ensuring the client is the primary scriptwriter, as it were. The practices introduced in Chapters 11 to 13 are all about helping clients to adopt actions, thoughts, and feelings congruent with their purposes and intentions—in other words, to more fully perform preferred narratives through the ways they act, think, and feel. Having therefore provided a roadmap for breaking client experience down into manageable chunks, the book now introduces ideas and practices for putting those chunks together by intervening at the level of story.

The chapter has two main objectives. First, it examines the anatomy of narrative to shed light on how it links events together through time. Second, it shines a light back on previous chapters and demonstrates how the practices introduced to this point can be extended through the vehicle of story. In other words, movement in the domains of actions, thoughts, and feelings can be linked or storied to bring further coherence to therapeutic gains.

STORY AND CULTURE

The storying of experience is inherently a cultural activity because we turn to the cultures we inhabit to evaluate our identities and interpret the events of our lives. *How should I live? Am I a good father? What constitutes success? Does my situation warrant worry or stress?* We take a cue from the discourses around us to select the spin to put on our experiences. As mentioned above, there are many spins available; they're contained in a vast storehouse of stories, including the canons of world religions such as the Bible, Koran, Talmud, and Bhagavad-Gita or novels, films, television shows, blogs, songs, folktales, histories, legislation, educational curricula, advertisements, and so on.

We live amid a marketplace of stories, but that doesn't suggest the stories compete for our attention on a level playing field. Getting exposure for any particular spin by circulating it widely through society typically requires power and influence (a situation that's changing incrementally with the democratization afforded by the Internet). And the credibility afforded various stories varies, too, depending on the prestige associated with the institutions that disseminate them (cf. Foucault, 1979, 1980).

Whether they explicitly champion particular causes or offer gentle parables, these cultural stories are never neutral. To offer any particular expression and to cast it in a particular light is to make a statement about what is worthy of attention and what is not. This is what the author Salman Rushdie (1983) was referring to in suggesting that every story is a form of censorship. Any account privileges what it stands for and blinds us to alternative versions. We live our lives against a taken-for-granted (White, 2007) backdrop of cultural narratives that implicitly validates some accounts and marginalizes others. As discussed elsewhere, this calls for counselors to support clients in critical reflection to step back from entrenched beliefs because as Hoffman (1992) says,

> once people subscribe to a given discourse—a religious discourse, a psychological discourse, or a discourse around gender—they promote certain definitions about which persons or what topics are most important or have legitimacy. However, they themselves are not always aware of these imbedded definitions. (cited in Freedman & Combs, 1996, p. 122)

Staying mindful of the relationship between story and culture provides a range of possibilities for working with clients striving to make new meanings and perform new stories in the face of challenges they're up against. This might include keeping an eye out for dominant stories that may "recruit" them into acting in ways out of step with their intentions (Jenkins, 1990, 2009; White & Epston, 1990). It could also involve supporting clients as they challenge cultural narratives hampering their efforts to step toward their preferred outcomes. As we'll see below, the construct of story brings both of these themes to the foreground for Maria, creating the opportunity for her to both identify and challenge discourses influencing the way she interacts with her partner Azim. The addition of a narrative perspective makes visible the relational/cultural aspects of Maria's experience and introduces options for extending the work on thoughts and beliefs she and her counselor Daniel engaged in earlier (see Chapter 12).

DECONSTRUCTION: TRACING PROBLEMS TO CULTURAL STORIES

You may notice the words *thoughts* and *beliefs* most often appear in the place of another word, *cognitions,* throughout this text. The choice is deliberate and relates to the distinction between an individualist and a cultural view of people. Although roughly synonymous with *thought*, the word *cognition* is often paired with other words such as *brain* and *neurons*. It's a term used to highlight what goes on inside the head—to the relative exclusion of social processes (J. Bruner, 1990). This individualistic, intrapsychic emphasis was touched on earlier with Hoffman's (2002) image of people isolated from one another in their private bathyspheres. The word *cognition* is a workable tool when examining self-talk in isolation from context but is less useful for depicting people as social beings, drawing on a cultural array of perspectives available to them.

A cranium-bound view of the messages Maria is subject to about women as primary caregivers might characterize her thoughts as distorted cognitions. This overlooks the ways in which she draws consciously and unconsciously from a cultural repertoire of stories to make sense of her life. Widening the lens to incorporate a cultural view of Maria, her cognitions look less like distortions and more like accurate representations of dominant ideas. On closer inspection, we see that her thoughts (and our own) are not hatched in the head but reflect the enveloping cultural context. In this sense, cognition is a social process. This does not rule out practices for working with self-talk that are focused mostly at the individual level, a few of which were explored in Chapter 12. But understanding cognitions as fragments of cultural stories opens up a range of additional conversations that might not arise otherwise.

The practice of tracing thoughts and beliefs back to their origins is sometimes referred to as "deconstruction" (White, 1991) because it dismantles ideas constructed, as it were, over years (sometimes decades, often centuries) in culture's meaning-making factories: mass advertising, world religions, school systems, popular media, the professions of medicine and psychology, and so on. A deconstructive conversation looks at where beliefs come from, zooming the camera lens back to a wide-angle view. This has the curious effect of robbing ideas of their monolithic status by unveiling their constructed origins.

Because of the taken-for-granted quality of entrenched beliefs, deconstructive conversations require a persistent and focused curiosity on the counselor's part. Prior to examining deconstruction at work in a conversation between Daniel and Maria, here are a few road signs to direct you:

1. **Emphasize that thoughts and beliefs are ideas with origins (i.e., stories), not mere facts.** Facts and stories are different entities. One of the useful things about the construct of story is that stories are malleable and subject to change. Nevertheless, the stories that surround us are often invisible to us, and it is easy to slip back into thinking of a problematic thought as merely the way things are. This is where counselors can help through the language they use to characterize the idea in question.

2. **Name the idea explicitly.** As in other ways of disputing unhelpful thoughts, it helps to put words to the idea and to lay it out on the table where it can be examined critically.

3. **Trace the idea to the wider culture.** Locating the idea in culture separates it from the client's identity, externalizing it and creating space for critical reflection.

4. **Don't stop at individuals.** When examining the origins of our thoughts and beliefs, it can be a revelation to notice they can be traced to other people. But sometimes the inquiry stops prematurely—we attribute problems to others and get caught up in an unconstructive blame game. In helping clients in zooming out, one task is to invite them to go beyond individuals sources and to consider broader cultural origins.

5. **Locate ideas in institutional sources.** Certain institutions (mass advertising, world religions, school systems, etc.) in society act as factories for dominant stories. Identifying the origins of thoughts more specifically accentuates their culturally constructed natures. It also reinforces that particular versions of the world serve certain interests and overlook or contradict other interests.

6. **Invite the client to name and justify their position on the problematic cultural idea.** Because an idea is seen to originate in the culture does not imply the client will inevitably take issue with it. Our cultures are also the source of many cherished ideas and practices, after all. Are they problematic for the client? Inquiring into the justification for a critique helps the client to clarify where they stand, making it possible to break from a problematic pattern.

7. **Invite the client to name and justify their position on an alternate idea.** Inquiring into the justification for a preference helps people to articulate and consolidate their values.

You may remember that in her conversations with her counselor Daniel, Maria has been talking about the dilemmas of raising a child and being a partner to Azim while completing graduate school. Previously Daniel worked with Maria to amplify certain actions she'd taken. These were exceptions—instances where, despite her discomfort, Maria took more space for herself and handed additional responsibility to Azim. Although this was somewhat useful, Daniel noticed Maria's continuing to be pulled back to a sort of default helping mode she appeared to resent. At another time, Daniel picked up on Maria's nonverbals, which led to her identifying she felt angry about taking on more than her share of the load. Given that it is clear Maria is disgruntled with what she calls "imbalance" in the relationship, Daniel initiates a deconstructive conversation. He invites Maria to trace ideas about her role to the wider culture as a way to prepare her to critically reflect on them and to challenge them.

Daniel: I notice you sighing heavily when you speak about your responsibility as a mother, caregiver, partner.

Maria: Yeah, it's all a bit much.

Daniel: Do you think this is just the way things are, or would you be interested in challenging these ideas about a woman's role?

1. Emphasize that thoughts and beliefs are ideas with origins, not mere facts.

Maria: Challenging, sure. Easier said than done, though. It just seems to be in my bones.

Daniel: You seem to be under the sway of some pretty big ideas. If you had to list them, what would you say some of these assumptions are about a woman's role?

2. Name the idea explicitly.

Maria: Well, I guess for starters, the woman is the primary caregiver even when she has a partner. [pauses] But I don't really believe that.

Daniel: Okay, you don't really believe it, but I guess you're saying that this belief continues to come up and influences the way you feel and act, even though you "don't really believe" it?

Maria: Yup. Default setting.

Daniel: So, "the woman is the primary caregiver even when she has a partner." Are there other ideas related to this?

2. Name the idea explicitly.

Maria: I guess something about the man as the breadwinner. He needs his space; he's busy providing—all that stuff.

Daniel: Even if you're providing as much as he is.

Maria: For sure. I didn't say it made sense! [laughs]

Daniel: Did you invent these ideas?

3. Trace the idea to the wider culture.

Maria: *Invent them? You must be kidding.*

Daniel: *Okay, so where do you think you picked them up?*

Maria: *They're in the air! I don't know. My parents certainly modeled them. My father literally used to come home, grab a beer, and put his feet up—even when my mother worked 8:00 to 5:00 as a legal secretary.*

Daniel: *Okay, maybe* they *invented these ideas?*

4. Don't stop at individuals.

Maria: *You're giving them too much credit. Nope, it was pretty typical.*

Daniel: *So they didn't invent these ideas about the separation of gender roles, or about how a woman has to nurture while the man provides, and all that. Where did they pick the ideas up?*

5. Locate ideas and beliefs in institutional sources.

Maria: *Oh, TV for one thing.*

Daniel: *It was the way families were depicted on TV shows. Were the shows produced with women's concerns in mind?*

Maria: *They were designed to make money! To tell stories people would watch and to of course attract advertisers.*

Daniel: *Do you think the advertisers supported the messages?*

Maria: *Sure, long as it sold their products.*

5. Locate ideas and beliefs in institutional sources.

Daniel: *Okay, so this classic division of roles is sprayed all over the media, and it sells products. Anywhere else in society that the gender roles are so sharply divided?*

Maria: *Religion, I guess. Most religions make a big deal of distinguishing between the genders, and usually women get the short end of things.* [further discussion]

Daniel: So what's your take on this idea of women as the supreme caregivers? It seems it's an idea that gets around! That suit you okay?	6. Invite the client to name and justify their position on the problematic cultural idea.
Maria: It's objectionable!	
Daniel: Objectionable? What do you find objectionable about it?	
Maria: Why should women take on that role exclusively? It's unjust. I've got quite a bit on my hands, thank you, and I could use some damn help.	
Daniel: So it doesn't fit with your ideas about justice and fairness. How do you prefer to make sense of women's roles in families and relationships?	7. Invite the client to name and justify their position on an alternate idea.
Maria: I'm not sure I have a one-size-fits-all answer to that. Some women like to be caregivers, and that's their prerogative. But so do some men. I don't see that we need to have cookie-cutter roles.	

Of course this exchange represents a condensed version of a conversation that would normally take longer to unfold and clearly has more yet to come. The practice of deconstruction has the quality of unmasking ideas that may never have previously been questioned because they were taken to be the way things are. This can take time.

The ungluing of person and problem that deconstructive curiosity precipitates can take a variety of forms. Here are a number of additional questions that frame problems as threads of cultural stories:

Do you remember when and where this idea entered your life? What made you vulnerable to it at that time?

How does this assumption get circulated? Where do you most often run into it? In what contexts does this come up most often?

Who benefits most from this idea? What role do they play in keeping it alive? Whose interests are not served by this idea?

> *Has this always been a widely held belief, or did it arise at some particular time for some particular reasons?*
>
> *Why do you think this notion gets so much credence? How does it gain its credibility? Are there communities that don't buy into it?*

As noted above, this inquiry has a built-in externalizing quality to it. It separates Maria as a person from ideas recruiting her into interactions with her partner that are out of step with values that (with her counselor's help) she is beginning to articulate more clearly. At first blush, externalizing questions appear to remove the "locus of control" (Ajzen, 2002) from the client, but look closer and you will see they do the opposite. As Maria is able to stand back from ideas about how she should be in relationship, she is less likely to respond automatically, more able to make choices in the moment. Further questions can help her consolidate her ability to do this:

> *Who else do you know who shares this (emerging) perspective? Are there ways you can support each other when you feel you're losing sight of your values?*
>
> *What difference does reflecting on this now have when you're in the thick of it with Azim?*
>
> *Are there ways you can remind yourself of these alternative ideas about your roles when you find yourself slipping into old patterns?*
>
> *Is Azim aware of all this thought you're giving to these issues? What would it take to invite him into the conversation?*

Reflection 14.1

Have you ever had the experience of being on the inside of certain practices to the extent you didn't notice the ideas or beliefs on which they rested? This could be practices associated with workplaces, cultural subgroups, religious traditions, families of origin, and so on. Sometimes it's physical separation or the passage of time that affords the distance to notice what was formerly invisible. Sometimes that noticing happens in a flash, precipitated by a particular incident. If this has happened for you, would you say the distancing or externalizing from the ideas and beliefs allows you to exercise more or less personal choice in relation to them?

The Ripple Effect of Deconstruction

The last question above regarding Azim is a telling one because as Maria begins to step more fully into her preferred ways of being, there will be reverberations elsewhere in her life—a phenomenon that inevitably occurs when people make changes. For Maria, those reverberations may be most pronounced with her partner Azim because their existing patterns of relating have arguably worked in his favor. For one thing, Maria's new insights may mean he is asked to wash more dishes, cook more meals, change more diapers! One can imagine he might react with a degree of push back. On top of this, it's worth remembering that Azim also inhabits a cultural context that influences his ideas and attitudes. Having spent the first few years of his life in a country where male-female relations are more sharply delineated, he grew up accustomed to an asymmetry in gender roles even more pronounced than the ones Maria is currently challenging. In other words, he's under the influence of some powerful gender-focused discourses as well. Fortunately, the separation of person from cultural discourses that accompanies a storied view provides new avenues for constructive conversation. Rather than attributing their differences to (individual) spite or selfishness, Maria and Azim can explore the various cultural influences that contribute to their contrasting expectations.

Interrogating the Discourses Informing Counselor Practices

The inquiry into the cultural origin of ideas, employed above with clients, can also be helpful for counselors when they sense their practice is out of step with deeply held values or they sense a disjuncture in their relationship with a client. If you consider that the discipline of counseling and psychotherapy constitutes a culture in *itself*, then practitioners are always responding under the influence of professional discourses, including theories, institutional protocols, ethics codes, regulatory guidelines, and so on. Like Maria, therapists are also subject to acting in accordance with the taken for granted, sometimes without reflection. Similar deconstructive questions to those that supported Maria in choosing a place to stand amid many options can be used by therapists to help them adjust their practices when they sense impasses in their efforts to collaborate with clients:

> *Which stories about people and problems and how to intervene am I drawing on to inform my work with this client, and how resonant are they with my client's view of the world?*

> *Which ideas are driving my interventions? Can I trace what I'm saying and doing to the influence of particular theories or other sources?*

> *Are there ways my theory-informed practices are hampering me in interacting in a manner I believe will be most helpful?*
>
> *Are my practices guided primarily by adherence to a model or by the particular circumstances of my client?*
>
> *Whose view of problems and therapeutic change is being privileged in my interactions with my client and whose is being muted?*
>
> *What do the ideas behind my practice lead me to see and what (and who) do they render invisible?*

Well-constructed professional and theoretical discourses may have the appearance of being comprehensive, but they can't begin to match the complexity of people's lives or the nuance of interactions with clients. Although theories and models provide useful frameworks, collaborative practice also relies heavily on responsiveness (Paré & Lysack, 2004; Shotter, 1995; Strong, 2010) to the person in the chair opposite. And no two persons are identical. Sometimes the most useful way forward is to unhitch from a preset belief or protocol, and questions like those above can help make that happen.

In addition to facilitating attention to the cultural aspect of experience, the focus on story or narrative makes it possible to engage with the temporal dimension of experience in a way that other, more-narrow constructs do not. Life as lived is a flowing process—more like a movie and less like a snapshot. Stories share this quality: They feature characters moving through time. This presents options for making meaning across the arcs of people's lives.

THE TEMPORAL DIMENSION OF STORIES

Stories—like lives—have beginnings, middles, and endings. It's the plot of the story that links the various events within it and helps us make sense of events preceding whatever is happening in the moment as well as anticipate what will come next. All it takes is one unexpected event—a plot twist—and suddenly the meaning of past events and the picture of future events is instantaneously revised. No doubt you've witnessed this in films in which a character portrayed (until that point) as an innocent party is suddenly revealed to be the killer: Immediately the significance (i.e., the *meaning* and not the actual words spoken) of all of the dialogue preceding this moment changes in a flash. We shift in our seats, too, in anticipation of a different set of events to come.

This points to a peculiar feature of narratives: the two-way relationship between their individual parts and the overall story. As J. Bruner (1996) puts it, "the events recounted in a story take their meaning from the story as a whole. But the story as a whole is something that is constructed from its parts" (p. 122). A simpler way to put it: Change a part and you change the whole. This has significant implications for the practice of therapy.

BOX 14.1

Changing the Past, Altering the Future

The anthropologist Edward Bruner (1986) captured the temporal dimension of story and how the parts interact in his research on the accounts of the status of American Indians at different moments in the 20th century. Bruner tracked dominant ideas about this cultural subgroup in the 1930s and 1940s and compared them to perspectives more prevalent at the time he was writing. Note the two readings about the past, present, and future of American Indians:

Reading 1: **Early 20th Century**	**Reading 2:** **Late 20th Century**
Past: *Glory*	Past: *Exploitation*
Present: *Disorganization*	Present: ~~*Disorganization*~~
Future: *Assimilation*	*Resistance*
	Future: *Resurgence*

Notice that if you change the reading of the text in the present, it affects how both the past is read and the future is imagined. In Bruner's example, when people (in the 1930s/1940s) made sense of Native Americans as disorganized, they understood the group as being on track for assimilation and the loss of all attributes of a glorious past. But the reading Bruner identified as emerging a few years later was quite different. It presented a view of American Indians not as disorganized but as engaged in resistance to oppressive attempts to eradicate their traditions. With this take on their present circumstances, the whole story alters significantly. The view of the group's past changes dramatically and is seen as an oppressive violation of fundamental human rights. Equally altered is the view of what might come next for Native Americans—a perspective that fuels protest and the embrace of indigenous identity. Story is more than the mere sum of action, thought, or emotion; it encompasses all of these and has the power to precipitate momentous shifts in understanding, inciting whole nations to change.

(Continued)

(Continued)

The temporal aspect of stories has important practical implications for counselors and clients because therapeutic conversations are inevitably about the various stories available to make sense of where clients have come from, where they are now, and where they are headed next. A change in the here and now reverberates out both backward and forward. Bruner (1986) put it this way: "Story as a model has a remarkable dual aspect—it is both linear and instantaneous" (p. 153). Nora's story (Box 8.7 in Chapter 8) is a compelling example of this, showing how a revision of a person's past can have momentous consequences for their experience of the present.

The same sort of story revision across time frames described in Box 14.1 happens all the time in conversations with clients. Consider Maria again: She came home from work and handed her child Kyla over to her partner Azim so that she could have a shower (Chapter 11). When Maria is caught up in self-critique—one feature of which she and her counselor Daniel identified as mother guilt—she is inclined to view this event as evidence of *selfishness*. From the vantage point of this reading of the text, she turns to look at her *past* and sees her decision to go to graduate school as a *betrayal* of her daughter Kyla. When she looks ahead to the *future*, she sees *alienation* from a resentful daughter suffering from attachment issues due to her mother's intermittent absence from the home.

Put it all together, and the plot or dominant theme of this story might be called, Maria, the Bad Mother. When Maria talks to her counselor Daniel about handing Kyla over to Azim, she is vulnerable to using the incident as fodder for more unhelpful self-talk and more negative emotions related to her role as a parent. Maria is boxed in by a single story.

The novelist Chimamanda Adichie (TED) talks about what she calls the "danger of a single story," describing how when we limit ourselves to one view of people or things, we sacrifice countless options and render cookie-cutter views of people. This is a reminder of the importance of double listening touched on earlier, and here it is Daniel who keeps alternate views available by refusing the invitation (Jenkins, 1990) to portray Maria's actions as evidence of ill-intentioned or incompetent parenting. Instead, he becomes curious about how Maria managed this exchange with Azim while avoiding the flare-ups that had been plaguing their encounters recently (see Slowing Down the Image section, Chapter 11). His question draws a double take from Maria, the way plot twists do. She needs some additional help from Daniel to make sense of what he is asking because she is anticipating a conversation about bad mothering rather than avoiding flare-ups.

For Daniel, curiosity flows naturally from noticing an exception in Maria's account of a conflict-ridden relationship with her partner. As they talk it through, Maria and Daniel begin to make sense of this event as *sharing the parenting load*—a very different reading than the bad mother theme described above. This version of a recent event is an alternate vantage point from which to look backward and forward in time. Contemplating her earlier decision to return to school, Maria may begin to remember her determination to ensure her financial independence, to develop professional skills, to share parenting in an egalitarian marriage. As people engage in restorying conversations, they begin to unearth sensations and memories that don't fit with a dominant problem story. When Maria looks ahead to the future, she may be able to access the image of herself as a working professional, a role model of autonomous womanhood for Kyla, both providing and receiving support from a partner equally engaged in their daughter's upbringing.

Reading Number 1	**Reading Number 2**
Past: *Betrayal of Kyla*	**Past:** *Move toward self-determination*
Present: *Shirking of motherly duties*	**Present:** *Sharing the load*
Future: *Alienation from daughter*	**Future:** *Offering daughter an empowering role model*

A change in one part of the story reverberates in both directions. At least it has the potential to do that: The revised reading presented above for illustrative purposes did not occur in one single flash for Maria but was the product of patient and persistent exploration guided by Daniel, who employed a variety of questions to scaffold the process. The instantaneous enlightenment described by various spiritual traditions is a rare phenomenon, and even then it is typically the culmination of very substantial engagement with some question (Watts, 1957/1999). So too for therapeutic conversations: The meanings we make of our lives have deep roots extending out into the contexts we inhabit and stretching back in time. The sort of deconstructive inquiry seen in the preceding section is a bit like chopping at the roots of *problematic* narratives. Its source of nourishment cut off, the tree drops leaves and limbs, opening up alternate views for contemplation. A complementary practice more focused on surfacing *preferred* narratives starts with honing in on exceptions, the way Daniel did in his conversation with Maria. The next section explores that practice in more detail.

IDENTIFYING EXCEPTIONS: THREADS OF ALTERNATE STORIES

As we've seen elsewhere in this text, exceptions invariably provide useful openings for further exploration. There are many ways to describe an exception:

1. an instance when the problem is absent,

2. a preferred development,

3. an act of personal agency,

4. an expression or performance of meaning aligned with client values and intentions, or

5. an initiative.

Amplifying exceptions by encouraging clients to perform more of them—whether it's actions taken, things they are telling themselves (i.e., self-talk), or emotional states they are accessing—is a way of building upon positive developments but fails to fully capitalize on the extent of possibilities exceptions present. By joining people in making further meaning around exceptions, the developments become incorporated into their understandings of their lives and identities.

Reflection 14.2

Think about some problem you're dealing with, however small, as a reference point for this reflection. Can you identify an exception in relation to this problem—something you said, did, felt, and so forth that stood outside the problem and was more in line with your preferences? Note this does not have to suggest your victory over the problem, just an instance of something more in line with how you'd like things to be. Now consider the difference between being urged to do more of this and being led on a patient exploration of what you accomplished with questions like the following:

What difference did this exception make on your mood or energy level or hopefulness?

How did you manage to accomplish this in the face of the challenges involved?

Are there other events in the past that might have served as predictors that you'd do this?

If you did more of this in the future, how might the landscape of the problem change?

Drawing again on the temporal view that the construct of story provides, exceptions can be understood as threads of alternate stories. The image of an elongated thread is a reminder that meaningful expressions (as opposed to absurd non sequiturs, for example) don't come out of nowhere: They have histories behind them that shed further light on where people are coming from, and they set up expectations about what is next to come.

The Role of Double Listening in Restorying

There are always exceptions available as openings to alternate stories. Consider the following:

How did the client get here today, despite what they're up against?

What does this say about their desire for change?

However, this is not to say that a client mired in difficulties, discouraged by an apparent failure to deal with challenges, will readily *notice* an exception when it occurs. Nor is it likely they will plunge (without prompting) into a detailed account of the alternate understandings an exception speaks to—even if they are able to discern it. Hopeful and life-affirming stories are not simply unveiled in therapeutic conversations like this year's shiny new car model at an auto show. Restorying is a methodical process made possible through the counselor's double listening—"listening for traces in conversations that reflect people's hopes, values, preferences, knowledges and skills" (Young, 2011, p. 153). Double listening involves adopting an appreciative ally stance (Madsen, 2007), orienting to the client's story with the expectation of encountering threads of alternate stories.

We will look at how the counselor identifies exceptions through double listening in the example below of Maria as counselor working with Jorge. The two sections to follow will feature the proactive practices that follow from identifying exceptions: (a) developing thick description of exceptions and (b) linking exceptions through time.

A lot has happened for Jorge since he began his conversations with Maria. He has started looking into university programs and is coming close to a decision about switching into graphic design. This was one of a variety of goals he set with Maria, and he has acted on a number of others as well. He's eating better and avoiding caffeine, and he started going to the gym twice a week with Richard. His insomnia is mostly behind him. It would be a stretch to say he's thrown himself at his engineering studies, but he is getting adequate marks on the knowledge that his grades will have some influence on his future prospects. Jorge and Richard are getting along well. Perhaps most significant of all, Jorge has come out to his parents—a central issue that has occupied the better part of several conversations with Maria. Despite reporting a certain amount of satisfaction about these developments, Jorge tells Maria he continues to feel a lingering disappointment in himself. He says it's ironic: For years he felt bitter, convinced they would not love him for who he was, and now he feels guilty they are displaying an unexpected nonjudgment that he "doesn't deserve." He can't celebrate that things are more open with his parents because he feels he ditched them for years and made no effort to stay connected. To his dismay, he's avoiding the Sunday dinners that he committed to making a regular part of his week.

When Jorge engages with his life under the influence of this account, events are linked thematically into a plot that features him as an ungrateful son, undeserving of his parents' unconditional love. In this version of things, Jorge as central character does not explicitly display the values he assures Maria that he stands for. In fact, in his account he's more like the passive recipient of events, witnessing a situation happening to him without a sense of being able to make choices about how to act, think, or feel. The events as Jorge reports them constitute a series of developments over time—a thread in that sense, but of a problem-saturated story highlighting his perceived personal failures and passivity, promoting pessimism and a descending spiral of self-recrimination.

BOX 14.2

The Thread of a Problem-Saturated Account

Every story excludes some events and interpretations of situations and highlights others. In the graphic representation below of Jorge's discouraged account of his situation, problem-focused events and readings of events are represented by the capital letter *X* and tied together by a continuous line. Linked together, the *X*s trace one particular coherent way to make sense of Jorge's life, reflecting a theme or plot highlighting what Jorge currently perceives as his failings. This reading renders invisible *other* events and interpretations of events (represented by question marks) that the current story obscures.

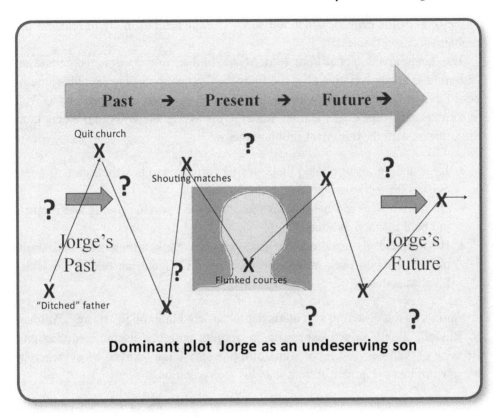

When Jorge casts his eyes back in time, they follow a dominant thread, and he recalls these details, among others, represented by the *X*s in Box 14.2:

- He stopped speaking to his father for almost a year: "I ditched him."
- He dropped out of church and hasn't been back: "I dumped the whole damn congregation and never even contacted the parish priest."
- He sent his parents a letter: "I was too damn selfish to just pick up the phone."
- He had several shouting matches with his father: "I was just one big shit disturber."
- He flunked half his courses in his second year: "And they were paying my tuition."

Like the example of Maria supplied earlier in this chapter, Jorge's account not only colors past events but is predictive of certain kinds of future events (the *X*s to the right of the center), which are so far unexplored but likely to reaffirm the problem-focused theme.

The landscape looks different to Maria in her role as Jorge's counselor. Listening as an appreciative ally, she finds the dominant plotline excludes a number of events she has borne witness to already in previous conversations as well as some events Jorge does mention, but only in passing and without noticing their discordance with the dominant problem theme:

- Jorge and his sister pooled their meager resources to buy their parents a television for their anniversary.
- He spent a weekend helping his father paint the porch, missing an art opening he'd planned to attend.
- He withheld his usual acerbic film criticism while sitting with his family through back-to-back movies on their new TV featuring one of his least-favorite actors.

Maria's double listening also alerts her to "absent but implicit" (Carey, Walther, & Russell, 2009) values expressed in Jorge's current, discouraged account. Because of that, her reading of some of the events Jorge takes to be evidence of his unworthiness is quite different than his interpretation.

- *Stopped speaking to his father.* Jorge earlier described how conversations with his father were getting more and more mutually dismissive and verging on aggression. Maria hears this as Jorge's preserving his dignity as well as avoiding interactions that might lead to irrevocable cutoff from his father.
- *Dropped out of church.* Maria hears this as Jorge's protesting the messages discounting his sexuality and lifestyle that were broadcast from the pulpit.
- *Sent a letter.* Maria hears this as Jorge's reaching out by a safe medium when speaking seemed likely to descend into conflict.
- *Had shouting matches.* Maria wonders what sort of self-respect it took on Jorge's part to not buckle down and defer to his patriarchal father's views.
- *Flunked courses.* Maria is curious how he managed to get the marks he did get, considering his discovery that engineering held little interest for him.

Note also that Maria does not automatically assume her versions of events will fit for Jorge. She holds them lightly, as subject to evaluation by Jorge, rather than unilateral conclusions about the truth of his circumstances. Double listening uncovers possibilities, but developing them will involve a dialogic process. Box 14.3 provides a view of these alternate events, and readings of events, that provide rich opportunities for restorying.

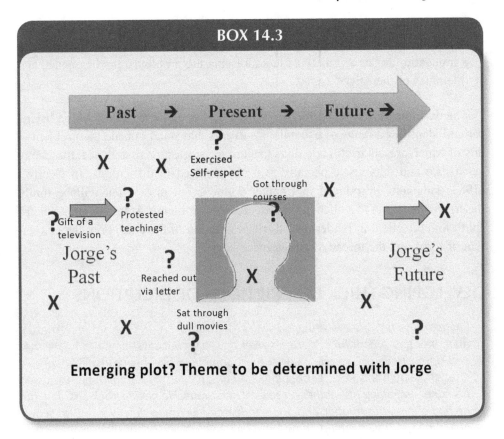

BOX 14.3

Past → Present → Future →

?

X   X   Exercised Self-respect

Got through courses X

? Gift of a television ? Protested teachings ?   X

Jorge's Past   ?   Jorge's Future

Reached out via letter X

X   X

Sat through dull movies ?

Emerging plot? Theme to be determined with Jorge

It is not uncommon for therapists to witness events unstoried by people that suggest alternate ways of making meaning of their current situations and indeed of their lives and identities more generally. Maria could provide Jorge with a neatly encapsulated summary of all the exceptions she notices and link them together with a resonant theme—in effect selling him on a more hopeful and constructive version of his situation. She decides otherwise, however, because she plans to join him in a careful examination of his experience—what Epston (2008) calls "co-research." Maria's facilitative role is crucial, but Jorge has to be at the center of the process to take ownership of the storying. So she will begin by getting curious about *just one exception* as a precursor to weaving an alternate story with Jorge. White (2007) describes exceptions as the starting points of "re-authoring conversations" in which the therapist introduces questions that

encourage people to recruit their lived experience to stretch their minds, to exercise their imagination, and to employ their meaning-making resources. People become curious about, and fascinated with, previously neglected aspects of their lives, and as these conversations proceed, these alternative storylines thicken, become more significantly rooted in history, and provide people with a foundation for new initiatives in addressing the problems, predicaments, and dilemmas of their lives. (p. 62)

The example of Maria and Jorge explored here demonstrates how Maria listens for and identifies a range of exceptions—events that stand outside the problem— any of which present useful openings to alternate stories. At first glance, these may seem pale and dubious, especially to a client mired in difficulties. In Geertz's (1983) language, introduced in Chapter 9, the event most often will be thinly described compared to a client's vivid account of problems. At this point, it's help-ful to join the client in rendering a thick description of the exception, the equiva-lent of fortifying the thread of an alternate story.

DEVELOPING THICK DESCRIPTIONS OF EXCEPTIONS

> *Shaofan says he's always struggled with relationships. A 28-year-old heterosexual man, he's had a handful of partners over the years but says they always seem to end up mistreating him. He says, "I must somehow like being treated badly, or else why would this keep happening?" When Shaofan was a child, he witnessed his father assaulting his mother on several occasions. He never struck Shaofan, but he had a ferocious temper, and Shaofan learned to tiptoe quietly in his presence. Shaofan says, "I've been tiptoeing ever since." He avoids confrontation at all costs, saying his passivity ends up "killing the chance of a relationship." He says he keeps his resentments bottled up and finds it's difficult to get close to people because of all the things that aren't said.*

Shaofan will provide the focus for this section, which introduces further skills in developing alternate stories with clients. In the example below, the therapist joins Shaofan in rendering a thick description of one particular event involving an exchange between Shaofan and his friend Emilio. As mentioned, the construct of story has a breadth to it that encompasses the various aspects of experience (actions, thoughts, feelings) isolated in Chapters 11 to 13. The questions posed by Shaofan's therapist are highly intentional, aiming for an experience-near account of the event that captures these various dimensions of Shaofan's experience and also situates him as the agent of the development he describes. As you can see, Shaofan doesn't initially perceive that agency, but that changes as the conversation unfolds. In a sense, the event starts out as an exception or preferred development only in the eyes of his counselor and becomes a development that Shaofan can embrace and take ownership of as the segment concludes.

Before reviewing the first part of that exchange, here's a list of milestones along the path. For clarity's sake, these are laid out in linear fashion; in practice they might not necessarily appear in such a tidy, linear sequence. Notice again that the event is described as an exception up front for simplicity's sake, but it only truly becomes an exception *for the client* once the client experiences it that way.

1. **Identify an exception.** This is any event that appears to stand outside the problem description, a preferred development. In the example below it is an action, but it could be a thought, feeling, image, memory, and so on.

2. **Develop a thick description of the development.** As seen in Chapter 9, thick description gets inside a person's experience, understanding actions as initiatives expressive of intentions, meanings, purposes, and values. Thick descriptions also incorporate various dimensions of experience, including those featured in this text's chapters on influencing practices: actions, thoughts, and feelings.

3. **Invite the client to name the development.** Problems are typically given all sorts of names by mental health practitioners and the people with whom they are associated: Why shouldn't preferred developments receive equal treatment? Naming an exception makes it more substantial and concrete. It also adds further significance to the event because the naming itself is an act of meaning making.

4. **Solicit the client's evaluation of the development and invite them to justify it.** Therapists can get understandably excited about developments to the extent that they get ahead of their clients. This provides a double check that the event is indeed a development preferred by the client and ensures the counselor is engaged in collaborative influence and not merely pitching their spin at the client. Asking the client to justify their stand further consolidates their values in relation to the event.

At this point in the exchange below, Shaofan is reporting on a recent encounter with his roommate Emilio, whom Shaofan describes as having a forceful personality. Notice he sees his interactions with Emilio as more of the same—that is, passive submission to mildly abusive behavior. The problem story obscures alternate readings. His therapist witnesses the account from a different vantage point and becomes curious about an apparent exception that Shaofan gradually comes to perceive as well.

Shaofan:	He was all worked up because he was going to have Debbie over later for supper and I was late getting back from work, and he was thinking I was gonna do the vacuuming. My turn I guess. I've kinda lost track.	Shaofan (S) shares the tail end of his account of yesterday's encounter with his roommate.
Therapist:	Debbie?	
Shaofan:	Someone he's been seeing lately. I haven't met her yet. Sounds all right from what I've heard so far. I told him the buses have been running way off schedule with that rotating strike, but in one ear and out the other.	
Therapist:	Sounds like he wasn't sympathetic.	Therapist (T) paraphrases.
Shaofan:	He gets into his usual rant: "You promised you'd be here at 4:30; all you think about is yourself." The usual four letter words, blah, blah, blah.	
Therapist:	Ouch. Not the perfect way to end a workday. How did you respond?	T conveys empathy and inquires regarding response versus effect.
Shaofan:	You know me and conflict. It stressed me out! I didn't raise my voice or get defensive. I just spread open the newspaper.	S sees this in problem terms as avoiding conflict.
Therapist:	No vacuuming?	
Shaofan:	Nope. Just started reading aloud.	
Therapist:	Reading aloud?	T (1) identifies apparent exception and (2) begins to elicit thick description of the development.
Shaofan:	About the strike! While he kept talking.	
Therapist:	[laughs] So you let the newspaper article talk for you.	
Shaofan:	I guess you could say that.	
Therapist:	How did that go over?	T asks about the effect of the development, further (2) thickening the account.

Shaofan:	*It quieted him down—eventually. Took a while. He got the message.*	
Therapist:	*How was that for you?*	
Shaofan:	*Sweet peace. It was a relief to hear the end of the rant. I felt pretty stressed though. It was the usual thing: I was tense, like all through my body.*	T understands this as an exception: an initiative in the face of a recurring challenge. Not so yet for S.
Therapist:	*How did you manage to keep reading despite that?*	
Shaofan:	*What do you mean?*	
Therapist:	*You mentioned how stressed you were. What did it take to stick with reading the article, even with Emilio's voice droning in the background?*	T (2) further thickens the description of the development by eliciting. The picture of an action in the face of a constraint.
Shaofan:	*I guess I was stubborn!*	At this point, for S, stubbornness is a failing and is not commendable.
Therapist:	*So you stubbornly held your ground. Is that a fair description of what you did?*	T tentatively names the initiative, borrowing some of S's words.
Shaofan:	*Battle of the Alamo. Yeah, I guess.*	S confirms characterization.
Therapist:	*What were you telling yourself that helped you stick to your script while Emilio tried to talk over you?*	T solicits an account of thoughts to render a thicker description of event.
Shaofan:	*I was in the right.*	
Therapist:	*So you reminded yourself you were in the right and stood your ground.*	T restates and recaps to reinforce the emerging description.
Shaofan:	*I don't control the buses! There was nothing I could do about it. Besides, who says I need to arrive at the crack of the hour? [sighs] I'm tired of it.*	S justifies versus critiques his response.
Therapist:	*Can you tell me more about being "tired of it"?*	
Shaofan:	*I'm fed up with all the speeches.*	

Therapist:	*What feeling goes along with that?*	T (2) seeks further thick description.
Shaofan:	*I'm mad, I guess.*	T solicits an account of feelings to expand account of holding his ground.
Therapist:	*Mad at . . . ?*	
Shaofan:	*My roommate! Emilio.*	
Therapist:	*I can hear it in your voice. Do you feel it as you share this story with me?*	T directs attention to the body to further thicken the account.
Shaofan:	*[pauses, turning attention inward] Yeah, I suppose I do.*	
Therapist:	*So you're saying that instead of turning away from this conflict, you got stubborn and responded by holding your ground. You said it helped you to remind yourself that you were in the right. And you're aware of feeling mad at Emilio. That's different, isn't it?*	T recaps and restates to consolidate this account of the development. T speculates the development is a change.
Shaofan:	*Well, it's different that I said it anyway.*	S (cautiously) confirms the newness.
Therapist:	*Okay, sharing it is different, but you've noticed feeling it before. This sounds like a new turn of events, or am I wrong?*	T names this as new on the belief that at this point in the conversation, S is able to see it that way as well.
Shaofan:	*No, that sounds fair to me.*	
Therapist:	*What would you call all of this? Reading the paper aloud when Emilio expects you to rush and grab the vacuum.*	T (3) invites S to name the development.
Shaofan:	*Call what?*	Not surprisingly, S needs coaching.
Therapist:	*Well, we've been having a lot of conversations about your challenges with conflict, your tendency to, as you've described it, "swallow it," and the negative fallout of that. Yesterday, it seems we're agreeing, you took a new step. I'm just wanting to mark the event by giving this new step a name.*	T carefully scaffolds the question to help S process the developments and to increase the chances of his coming up with an answer. T (3) again invites the client to name the development.

Shaofan:	*[pauses to think it through] How about "speaking my mind"?*	
Therapist:	*"Speaking my mind." Might make a good song title. Is this a good thing? What do you think?*	T (4) solicits S's evaluation of the event.
Shaofan:	*Yeah, I'd say so.*	
Therapist:	*Why? What makes it a good thing in your mind?*	T seeks justification of the evaluation.
Shaofan:	*Because I have a right to speak.*	S confirms he favors the account.
Therapist:	*A right?*	T seeks to thicken this response.
Shaofan:	*I haven't done anything to deserve all his rants.*	S adds a layer.

With the shifts in understanding that occur though therapeutic dialogue, it's fair to say that clients literally "move" as they story their experience in novel ways (Duvall & Béres, 2011; White, 2007; Winslade, 2009). That movement is evident here, although it is still early in the exchange. Shaofan opens by reporting further evidence of what he takes to be a deep-rooted personality problem, the outcome of childhood trauma. A few minutes later, he is celebrating—albeit mildly—a development that defies that pathology-focused description. Notice his therapist is patient and systematic, scaffolding the inquiry to support Shaofan in making that movement.

The product of the inquiry is thick description of Shaofan's interacting with his roommate: not an account of someone mechanically acting out pathology but rather an account of a man beginning to honor his own voice in the face of conflict. The description is thick because it features Shaofan's values and intentions and captures what he did, thought, sensed, and felt as part of this development. Returning to the metaphor of an exception as the thread of an alternative story, the thread has been thickened and fortified through questions that assume Shaofan's agency while inviting descriptions of thoughts, feelings, sensations, and so on:

Action: Reading the paper aloud over Emilio's berating of him.

Thoughts: I'm in the right; I'm tired of it; I don't deserve it.

Feelings: Anger, stress.

Sensations: Bodily tension.

Shaofan's counselor is intent on ensuring that what might otherwise be a blip on Shaofan's screen is rendered in vivid detail because this is a description, *well grounded in events*, of Shaofan that has far more potential to move him to helpful places than the problem-saturated account from which he is accustomed to drawing. This exchange has been broken down painstakingly for instructional purposes, so it's worth adding that there is no fixed formula for thickening exceptions. As in the learning of any new skills, it may provide comfort to have a linear sequence to follow. But to some degree, the thickening of meaning depicted above happens whenever we bring a persistent curiosity to people's accounts and orient to them as agents of their lives, acting from purpose and intention in the face of challenges.

Reflection 14.3

Can you think of anyone in your life who has an abiding faith in you as a person, who seems to anticipate your successes when they talk to you and turns your conversations with them into platforms for updating them on your latest achievements? Picture one of these talks with them. Are there ways in which these conversations make more visible that which lingered in the corners of your experience? What do you see when you look at your life through their eyes? Is this merely a superficial shot in the arm, or does the view of yourself brought forward by this person fortify you in more substantial ways for tackling the challenges that life throws at you?

The thread of an alternate story is more substantial after this brief exchange with Shaofan, but it hasn't yet been traced to places on the timeline of his life. It will be helpful to uncover further examples of the sorts of steps he took here, and the values and purposes they speak to, to bring a robustness to this emerging alternate account. After all, his problem account is particularly robust. He can readily point to any number of examples stretching back to childhood to make the case for his deficits and shortcomings. When exceptions have been identified and richly described and characterized, it's useful to connect them with other developments within a person's lived experience as part of the continuing project of foregrounding histories lost to memory and imagination. To see these practices in action, let's return to the conversation between Daniel and Maria.

LINKING EXCEPTIONS THROUGH TIME

Daniel evoked a rich description from Maria of a single event—her handing her infant to her partner to take a shower after a day at work—by inviting her to explore the actions, thoughts, and feelings surrounding the development and by inviting an account of Maria's purpose and value to the foreground. In the course of their conversation, the meaning Maria ascribed to the event morphed from shirking her motherly duties to sharing the parenting load. Daniel and Maria generated thick description of this key exception. This is a substantial shift, but one that's up against a persistent version of events with a long and enduring history in Maria's life: a story about what it takes to be a good partner and a good mother, for starters. And this entrenched version of things goes well beyond those two particular claims to some of the broader cultural discourses about gender roles that we saw earlier in the chapter. The point is that the shifts in meaning accomplished by Daniel and Maria in this single exchange are noteworthy but vulnerable to being washed away in the waves of more familiar problem-supporting meanings Maria is subject to on an ongoing basis. Identifying exceptions is a hopeful beginning, and thickening them is a helpful follow-up, but to more fully consolidate preferred developments it helps to take a history of them, as it were, and locate them in broader patterns of lived experience.

The exchange below represents a continuation of the conversation between Daniel and Maria. Here, an exception has been identified (handing over Kyla), named (sharing the parenting load), and thickly described. At this point, Daniel supports Maria in making links between this event and other related events in her life. This is the transformation mentioned earlier between one vivid (but static) snapshot to a moving image more representative of the flow of lived experience over time.

Daniel:	Hmmm. Okay, "sharing the load." I'm still trying to get a handle on how it was you did that, given the messages you describe about women as caregivers. Was this a breakthrough moment, or would you say you've shared the load before?
Maria:	With Azim, not so much, I realize now as we talk about it more.
Daniel:	Can you think of other times when you found ways to share a load that you were carrying all by yourself?
Maria:	Well, at home I suppose. When I was growing up.
Daniel:	Got an example?
Maria:	I've got three brothers, as you know, and they've come a long way, but man, could they be slackers in the kitchen.
Daniel:	You got stuck holding the dish towel?
Maria:	Exactly! Meals would end, they'd disappear, and there I'd be tidying up. No questions asked.

Daniel: *Your parents didn't say anything about it?*

Maria: *Not 'til I did.*

Daniel: *Tell me about that.*

Maria: *One night we had a bunch of family over—big spread (my mom's quite the cook), dishes everywhere—and the visitors all took off early to go to a show or something. Around that time my brothers and my father all piled into the yard to play horseshoes.*

Daniel: *Horseshoes?*

Maria: *Family tradition. [laughs] Don't ask!*

Daniel: *What did you do?*

Maria: *I looked at my mom and looked at the mess, and I just lost it. I went straight out to the horseshoe pit and started picking up the horseshoes, one by one. When I had all four, I took them inside and dumped them in the sink.*

From a single account of sharing the load, Maria has now described two events, separated in time and linked by a theme. The thread of the alternate story lengthens. It's a story featuring the following:

1. a protagonist	1. Maria
2. taking action	2. demanding a sharing of the load (challenging gender specifications)
3. in accordance with values	3. based on ideas about equity and fairness
4. in the face of challenges	4. in the context of dominant social practices and discourses about women as caregivers, and family and acquaintances who upload these
5. over time.	5. at various periods in her life.

The connecting of these two events is the beginning of a process of linking various events—some previously mentioned and some yet to be uncovered. Notice how each question solicits an additional event, which is then characterized further by making meaning of it—for instance, asking about values, abilities, intentions, and so on associated with the event. You will find examples of further questions for characterizing events and linking them below.

Following each characterization, the counselor can seek further events that speak to whatever is being characterized. The inquiry therefore alternates between (a) identifying concrete instances and rendering an account that includes actions, thoughts, feelings, and so forth and (b) making additional meaning of these instances by characterizing them further: asking questions that situate the person as an agent at the center of the event itself. Put more simply, this is essentially the practice of thick description but across time and place. Here's how it unfolds with Maria.

1. **Identify exception.** Handing over Kyla.

2. **Characterize it.** "What would you call this?" (sharing the load)

3. **Identify another instance of sharing the load.** "Can you think of another time you shared the load?" (horseshoe incident)

4. **Characterize new event.** T (3) again invites the client to name the development. "Wow, I'm left with the picture of all the males in your family standing around relaxing in the yard and you march up and take away their toys! What did it take to do that?" (Maria concludes she is someone who likes to call it like it is.)

5. **Identifying another instance of calling it like it is.** "Is that something you do? Have there been other times when you've called it like it is?" (challenged internship supervisor who was not making space for student input in case conferences)

6. **Characterize new event.** In this case, asking which *values* Maria was upholding. "What made it important enough to you that you took the risk to say that to your supervisor?" (thinks fairness and justice are important at work and elsewhere)

7. **Identify a hypothetical future instance of this appearing in her relationship with Azim.** "Is it fair to say you're upholding this sense of justice in your relationship with Azim?" (Maria agrees.) "If this were to continue, what might I see next year if I checked in on you and your family?" (will be attending a bimonthly book club she will start up with female friends, leaving Kyla with Azim on those nights)

Box 14.4 illustrates graphically how these questions unfold: Notice the questions and answers alternate between identifying events and characterizing events by soliciting further meaning around the events, as well as traveling backward and forward in time.

BOX 14.4

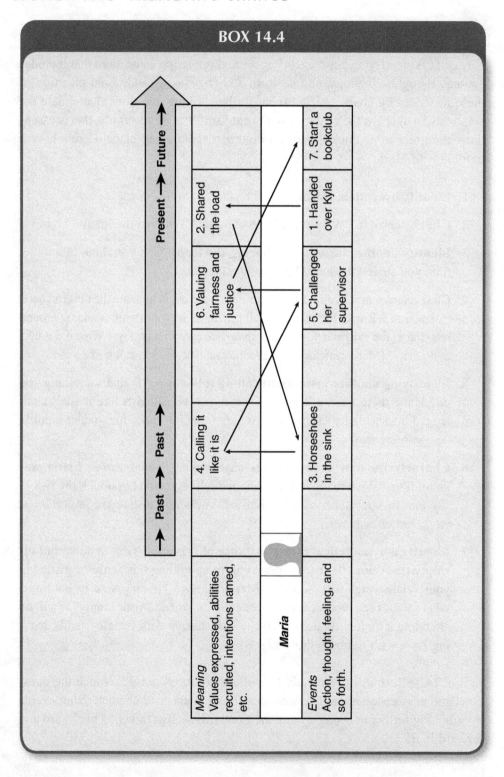

Making meaning around values starts with assuming that someone's actions are expressions of something they deem to be of worth:

> *What would you say you valued so much that you took those chances?*
>
> *What do you think your tears said about how important this was to you?*
>
> *Sounds like you've been upholding some principles through all of these examples. Which words would you put to your philosophy behind these steps?*

The thick description of preferred developments is always simultaneously a revisioning of a person's identity. This occurs through asking people about how initiatives speak to their skills, abilities, knowledges, and so on:

> *Sounds like some skills you maybe never knew you had! What would you call the ability you've been honing?*
>
> *What did it take to do these things when you consider what you were up against all those years?*
>
> *When you look at the steps you've taken at various times that you're describing here, what does it say about your ability to contend with big challenges in your life?*
>
> *What would you say you've learned, and how has it changed you?*

Getting at purposes and intentions is another way to characterize exceptions, highlighting themes that can be traced to other events in people's lives:

> *What do you think you were up to in doing that?*
>
> *What was behind that development for you—what were you trying to achieve?*
>
> *That helpful self-talk you described sounds like it served a very different purpose than all that self-criticism you described earlier.*
>
> *Can you tell me more about what inspired you to take that step?*

When a client relates more than one event without a chance for the two of you to characterize them individually, there is always the opportunity to invite them to name what the events share as a way of articulating an emerging theme:

> *So these two things—that incident on the baseball diamond and your talk with your teacher: What would you say they have in common?*

> *If these are two examples of a different way of doing things, what would you call it?*

> *This pair of initiatives of yours: What would you say they stand for?*

Restorying conversations are exhilarating tours of people's preferred universes. The questions above provide some guidelines but should not be seen to imply the journey is linear or even predictable. The unfolding of each new anecdote provides new themes that can be further linked across time, creating a rich tapestry of events and associated meanings. Notice this is far more than a process of reframing: It is something closer to the uncovering of alternate histories formerly obscured by problem accounts. These alternate histories differ from the dominant histories clients typically present in some key ways:

1. They feature people as agents of their lives rather than passive recipients of misfortune.

2. They uncover intentions, purposes, and values that make sense of people's actions.

3. They foreground competencies, abilities, and resources rather than categorizing and itemizing deficits.

4. They depict persons as cultural/relational beings by situating developments in context.

5. They provide a holistic view of a person, connecting the various dimensions of experience isolated in Chapters 11 to 13.

Naming the Emerging Story

In addition to characterizing events as they are uncovered, there is also the opportunity to do the same sort of meaning making across all of the events as a way of capturing the theme or plot of the whole emerging, alternate story. One way to do this is to invite clients to identify the "project" (Freedman & Combs, 1996) they are up to in the changes they are currently undertaking. The word *project* brings cohesion to a series of initiatives and suggests a person's intentionality at the same time. A playful alternative is to characterize a person as living out their biography, with recent preferred developments standing for a new chapter:

> *Here's a fun one for you: Suppose someone were writing your biography—everything in your life up to the developments you and I have been talking about in our past few conversations. And because books always work best in chapters, they're*

> *dividing the story up that way. And just like any other biography, they're looking for natural places to stop and start chapters and looking for chapter titles that speak to new phases of your life. What name would they put to the chapter that covers the developments you and I have been talking about lately?*

Like other restorying questions, answering this one requires reflection and creation on the part of clients. This is a characteristic of the practice of working with story: It goes beyond replacing problematic actions, thoughts, and feeling with helpful ones and actively engages clients in making new meaning of the developments they are undertaking.

CHAPTER FOURTEEN RECAP

In many respects, this chapter offers options for synthesizing the skills presented throughout this text—both conceptually and practically. At the conceptual level, understanding therapeutic conversation as a coauthoring process helps practitioners to recalibrate their interventions by asking one question: Is what I am saying/doing contributing to the shared construction of a more helpful story grounded in the client's lived experience?

The reminder that the meanings made in therapy need to be grounded in lived experience points to the distinction between (a) patiently crafted, co-constructed stories rich in detail and anecdotal content versus (b) Pollyanna-like spins full of unobtainable promises that are not founded on the details of people's lives. Working with story is working with lived history, reclaiming events previously excluded from reflection, and making sense of developments in a manner contrary to the thrust of dominant problem-focused accounts.

One of the advantages of thinking in terms of story is the reminder that experience does not happen in a vacuum: People are relational beings, and their lives unfold in cultural contexts. The story construct encourages an examination of the grand narratives that circulate societies, watchful of the way they may influence people to act, think, and feel in ways out of step with their preferences and values. Conversations that trace these influences help to deconstruct unhelpful narratives, creating space for other, more helpful accounts.

Another advantage of the narrative construct is the way it accommodates for the temporal flow of lived experience. Stories have a fascinating part-to-whole quality about them: A change in any part alters the whole and vice versa. This presents fertile opportunities for therapeutic conversations in which speculating about preferred futures can reshape the here and now, and reflecting newly on times past can change the view of both the present and the future.

Preferred developments—exceptions—in people's lives are portals into alternate universes of meaning. The process of restorying begins with identifying and thickly describing exceptions. Thick description captures various dimensions of experience such as actions, thoughts, and feelings, and it also situates people as agents of their lives, taking value-laden initiatives in the face of challenges. Any single exception provides a useful starting point for linking to other events, characterizing these in turn. The outcome of this systematic shared inquiry is the generation of rich meanings congruent with people's preferences and intentions, in contrast to the problem-focused stories they frequently bring to therapy.

CHAPTER FOURTEEN DISCUSSION QUESTIONS

1. **Power and dominant discourses.** What does it mean to suggest that the stories that compete for our attention don't do so on a level playing field?

2. **The cultural origins of thoughts and beliefs.** Identify some key sources of dominant ideas about, for example, self-worth, success, beauty, and intelligence in the wider culture. Make a list of some of the key messages associated with these institutions in the form of statements ("An intelligent person is . . . ").

3. **Cultural messages and global beliefs.** Following on the question above, what are examples of potentially unhelpful views of themselves a person might have under the influence of these dominant messages?

4. **The temporal dimension of stories.** Identify either (a) a favorable change in the way you view some aspect of yourself that alters your view of particular incidents in the past or (b) a change (for the better) in the way you make sense of some incident in the past that alters your story about yourself as a whole.

5. **The construct of story as integrative.** What does it mean to say the narrative metaphor is integrative and potentially encompasses both the conceptual overview and the skills introduced throughout the text?

6. **Restorying as historical revision.** What is the difference between a historical revision and the creation of an appealing fiction?

CHAPTER FOURTEEN ACTIVITIES

1. **Zooming out: tracing a self-critical view to cultural origins.** Form pairs. Speaker, identify some critique of yourself that you find problematic. Together, develop a rich description of the idea behind the critique, and trace it to the wider culture. Where does this idea arise? Is it associated with any particular institutions? What purpose does it serve in society? Debrief. Speaker and listener, what were the challenges associated with tracing the critique to some cultural source and linking it to some institutional source? What difference did it make to notice the critique's cultural origins?

2. **Thick description of an exception.** Form pairs. Speaker, identify some challenge or problem you are willing to discuss, and after providing an overview of it, team up with the listener to identify an exception. Listener, draw on the questions below and invent some of your own to help the speaker develop a thick description of the exception.

   Which action, thought, feeling is associated with this exception?

   What does it say about what the speaker values?

   Which skills or abilities were exploited by the speaker in accomplishing this exception?

   Which intentions of the speaker does this initiative speak to?

   Debrief. Speaker, what was it like to have this exception thickly described? Listener, what were the challenges associated with generating thick description?

3. **Characterizing an exception.** Pair up. This is a continuation of the preceding activity. Speaker and listener, join together in speculating about how this exception might be characterized. What does it speak to? What theme stands out when you consider this initiative in the context of the challenge(s) the speaker is or was facing? Debrief. Did you generate more than one theme? What difference did coming up with a theme make to the experience/perception of the exception?

4. **Linking exceptions through time.** Pair up. This is a continuation of the preceding activity. Listener, working with the exception described above, draw from the questions below and generate your own questions to help the speaker link the exception to another exception in their life.

   Have there been other instances of [name the theme or characterization you came up with from Activity 4] in your life? Tell me about one.

   Listener, help the speaker to generate a thick description of this other exception, drawing on the questions supplied in Activity 2 and inventing some of your own. Debrief. Speaker, what impact did it have to identify a second exception linked to the first? Listener, what were the challenges associated with linking these two exceptions around a shared theme?

5. **Naming the theme of an emerging story.** Form pairs. This is a continuation of the preceding activity. Listener and speaker, see if you can enumerate any other exceptions associated with the ones already identified. Speaker, try out a variation of the chapter title question at the end of this chapter to help the speaker identify an emerging theme associated with the linked exceptions you have both identified. Debrief. Speaker, what was it like naming a book chapter title and what impact, if any, did it have on your experience of the issues at hand? Listener, what were the challenges associated with helping the speaker name a global theme to characterize the changes represented by the various exceptions you identified?

Chapter 15

ENDINGS AND BEGINNINGS

INTRODUCTION

Coming to the end of a working collaboration with clients can be a bittersweet experience. The good news is that they've made some changes, taken some steps, transformed in some measure their ways of being in the world. But discontinuing therapy also means the end of what is often a rich and meaningful relationship for therapist and client alike, so it comes with a sense of loss as well. There is no fixed meaning for what is sometimes ominously (Young, 2009) referred to as "termination"; like any other moment in time, the end of a series of therapeutic conversations offers possibilities for constructive meaning making—looking back on the territory traveled and looking ahead to new horizons. It is an ending but, perhaps more important, a beginning.

This chapter brings the book to a close with an exploration of some of those possibilities. It begins with ideas for helping clients consolidate their gains by reviewing their journeys and sharing the changes they have made with an audience both real and imagined. It also introduces conversational practices for carrying useful change into the future and anticipating the almost inevitable backslides to come in preparation for responding constructively when problems make return visits.

WHEN IS IT OVER? DETERMINING WHEN TO END THERAPY

As we've seen, some therapeutic work is highly concrete and focused on specific steps and goals. On the other hand, some clients may be looking to be heard and witnessed without the expectation of clearly demonstrable outcomes. In the former case, determining when things are preparing to wrap is a matter of referring to the objectives. Indeed, need for closure may be mandated by an agency or other institution that funds a fixed number of sessions. In the latter case, that decision is less clear-cut. Either way, ending therapy is often a loaded issue for a variety of reasons and deserves careful exploration with clients, preferably with lead-up time so the topic gets the attention it deserves (Murdin, 2000; Young, 2009).

> *When we started these conversations, we put a lot of energy into developing a picture of where you wanted to go and the steps you'd be taking to get there. Seems to me you've accomplished a lot of that. How about if we review some of those goals and outcomes to take stock of anything that might be left?*
>
> *You and I have been reflecting on a number of significant changes you've made; I'm wondering if you might be thinking it's getting to the time to take a break from this process and put those changes to work.*
>
> *When I think of all the steps you've taken and the way you're engaging with some of those challenges head-on, I have a hunch you may be feeling ready to fly solo.*

For some clients, the prospect of ending a constructive partnership is understandably anxiety provoking; they may feel the gains they've made are fragile and not likely to stand up without the ongoing support of their therapists. These concerns deserve acknowledgment and can be assuaged through a review of their accomplishments (more on this below). They can also be addressed by "fading" (Young, 2009, p. 303) the work out incrementally, putting more time between sessions and giving clients a chance to see how they're coping with less regular consultation. An added benefit of this approach is that clients are less likely to experience a possible resumption of more regular sessions as failure. And if they cancel sessions scheduled at longer intervals because regular life takes over, they may justifiably interpret this as a sign of the progress they've made.

Besides lengthening the interval between final sessions, there is always the option to schedule a check-in session at some fixed date in the future after the last of the regular sessions. This provides the chance to review any learnings and to fine-tune in response to complications or new circumstances that have arisen in the client's life. In lieu of scheduling an appointment, it can help to remind the client, "You know where I am," as a way of reassuring them that further consultation is conceivable. A concern sometimes raised in relation to this invitation is the notion that it might promote dependency on the part of client; I think this perspective denigrates the client's judgment and initiative in seeking assistance in relation to challenges. In any case, I have found it more common for clients to get taken up in activity to the extent that a prescheduled check-in session gets canceled—a sign to me that they are coping with challenges and engaged with their lives.

It's not only clients who may have a reluctance to end the work; endings can be challenging for therapists as well. Therapeutic practice is an intense and intimate experience that contributes to the lives of practitioners as well as the people with whom they work. Saying good-bye understandably may be tinged with some degree of mutual loss (Goodyear, 1981). For therapists, this loss is sometimes heightened because it's associated consciously or unconsciously with other significant losses in their lives (Capuzzi & Gross, 2007; Ward, 1984). Alternately, practitioners may feel reservations about clients' completing because they see it "as an index of the counselor's success or failure" (Cormier & Hackney, 2007, p. 74). These responses deserve attention and are worthy topics for supervisory conversations. Finally, counselors' reservations may come from concern that clients are not yet ready and could benefit from further conversations. This is a legitimate concern and points to the importance of reflecting with clients on where they have been and where they are going. Therapy is a journey of sorts, and the metaphor of a rite of passage provides a useful framework for examining that journey with clients as a way both to evaluate whether it's time to stop meeting and to prepare for what's coming next.

THE ENDING OF THERAPY AS A RITE OF PASSAGE

If you think about our most widely performed cultural rituals—baptisms, bar mitzvahs, graduation ceremonies, weddings, and so on—they often mark a passage from one era or phase of life to the next. All cultures develop means of paying homage to important milestones, giving them substance and meaning through public expression. The closure of a sustained series of therapeutic conversations also constitutes a significant life transition equally worthy of being marked and celebrated.

Borrowing from the work of the French anthropologist Arnold van Gennep (1960), White and Epston (1990) and Duvall and Béres (2011) frame therapeutic practice as a contemporary cultural "rite of passage." The metaphor encompasses first what van Gennep called a separation phase, a distancing from a former state or way of being—think of clients as they first arrive to participate in a therapeutic conversation. At this point, clients' descriptions of their lives are thin, in the sense that discouragement often renders invisible their expression of values, purposes, and intentions in the face of challenges.

Following this separation phase, clients can be understood as entering into what van Gennep (1960) called the liminal or betwixt-and-between phase, characterized by "discomfort, confusion, disorganization, and perhaps heightened expectations for the future" (White & Epston, 1990, p. 7). This is a period of change involving a "migration of identity" (Duvall & Béres, 2011, p. 40) to the extent that clients move to new understandings of who they are and new ways of performing their identities as a consequence of their active participation in the therapeutic process.

In van Gennep's (1960) third and final phase of this rite of passage, people reenter society, but as transformed persons. Transplanting the metaphor to therapeutic practice, this is where clients are when the topic of ending enters the conversation. At this point, clients and therapists have rendered thick description of clients' lives that foregrounds their purposes and renders sensible thoughts, feelings, and actions formerly couched in the language of deficit. The intention here is not to suggest that every series of counseling exchanges contributes to monumental migrations of identity. But as Stephen Gilligan likes to say, people are "up to something big" when they decide to engage in therapeutic conversations. The rite-of-passage metaphor helps to honor that. Coming to the end of a series of therapeutic conversations is more like a phase of transition than a fixed event (Hackney & Cormier, 2008), and reflecting on the transition can be useful preparation for whatever is to come next.

Reflection 15.1

Which rites of passage have you experienced in your own life? Think of a crisis or challenge you encountered that brought about growth and change in your life. Do you remember where you were at as it began? Did you experience a stretch of disorganization and confusion in the midst of a period of transition while you dealt with it? In which ways did your identity shift as a consequence? Which aspects of yourself did you leave behind, and which new features of who you are today emerged from that period?

TAKING STOCK OF LEARNINGS

For Maria, the conversation that unfolded around a single event—handing Kyla over to Azim—led to identifying and characterizing (sharing the load, calling it like it is, valuing fairness and justice) a series of developments. By the time she and Daniel are preparing to wind down their work together, she is well equipped to reflect on what she's learned. Daniel facilitates this to support Maria in taking forward those learnings. Notice how the questions he generates borrow from the rite-of-passage metaphor in highlighting the change Maria has undergone.

With the changes you've been making, what would you say is one piece of yourself or way of being that you're leaving behind you as you go forward?

What is it about this piece that no longer fits for you?

Do you have any images to help characterize the difference between who you are now and who you were the first day you came to see me?

What have you learned? What are some key tips you'd share with others going through similar challenges?

How would you describe what's different about your relationship with yourself now?

Which priorities have risen to the surface?

Which skills and abilities have you uncovered that were dormant or at least not very visible to you before?

Questions like these continue the process of ensuring people are actively engaged in their own development, critically reflecting on the steps they've taken. The significance of these events can be further emphasized with practices for celebrating, documenting, and soliciting witnesses to their journeys.

CELEBRATING, DOCUMENTING, AND SOLICITING WITNESSES TO CHANGES

Like other key rites of passage we are inclined to celebrate through public ritual, the completion of therapy is an event that deserves formal acknowledgment. As the anthropologist Victor Turner (1986) wrote, "the hard-won meanings should be said, painted, dance, dramatized, put into circulation" (cited in Freedman & Combs, 1996, p. 237). Just what form this acknowledgment and circulation might take is dependent on client preferences. Asking a client to return to a last session with some small object representing the transformation they've undergone or presenting one to a client can be a way to mark the journey symbolically. When young persons or families are involved, the culminating session can be deliberately shaped around marking the passage, complete with speeches and even the sharing of a cake (Bertolino & O'Hanlon, 2002).

A printed certificate can be a playful acknowledgment of a young person's accomplishments (Freeman, Epston, & Lobovits, 1997; White & Epston, 1990). Complete with ornate, frilly borders and legalistic phrasing (e.g., "This is to attest that the aforementioned young person has hereby achieved . . ."), certificates add an official quality to the conquering of such daunting challenges as "tantrum taming" (Bertolino & O'Hanlon, 2002) and "fear-busting" (Freeman et al., 1997).

A good part of what gives stories their substance and credibility is the degree to which they are documented: Think wedding photo albums, framed degrees, home movies of first baby steps, and so on. Ludwig Wittgenstein (1953) famously said that there is no "private language"; the same might be said of the transformations that clients make in the course of therapeutic work. White and Epston (1990) pioneered practices of therapeutic letter writing that have since been widely taken up by practitioners in a variety of creative ways (cf. Bertolino, 2010; Epston, Maisel, & Borden, 2004; Freeman et al., 1997; Hurley, 2007; Nylund & Thomas, 1994; Paré & Majchrzak Rombach, 2003; Penn & Frankfurt, 1994). Letters to clients highlighting accomplishments and resources solidify therapeutic gains. They also offer a welcome alternative (White & Epston, 1990, call them "counter-documents") to long-standing traditions of filling file folders with paper chronicling what has been going wrong in peoples' lives.

Letters that pose wonderings about preferred developments invite clients to participate actively in their successes and simultaneously celebrate their achievements (cf. Paré & Majchrzak Rombach, 2003). In Daniel's letter to Maria at the close of her therapy, notice the use of experience-near vocabulary and a tentative stance that invites her to make further meaning of events, carrying the work forward beyond the last session:

Dear Maria,

As promised, I'm writing this short note to reflect on our work together. It's been a pleasure to witness the changes you've undertaken over these past few months, starting with your announcement (do you remember that early conversation?) that you were "Fed up. Baffled. Messed up. Crazy" and culminating in our inspiring talk on Monday night. Your resounding pledge in favor of fairness and sharing the load is something I will take back to my own relationships.

I won't attempt to summarize all the ground we covered or the various changes you made, but I wanted to leave you with some wonderings as you continue on your journey. I was imagining Kyla in particular as a young woman about 25 years from now, recounting her mother's story to a friend with admiration. I was thinking of a friend's struggling with the sorts of stresses of young family and career that you yourself have been contending with recently. What do you imagine Kyla would say about what you did—not only to cope but to thrive on those challenges? What might she say about what she personally witnessed as she watched you from day to day and about how the changes you made affected her as your daughter?

> *Just when you thought your work with me was over! I wish you all the best in your future endeavors and look forward to the possibility of one day encountering you as a colleague upon your completion of your program.*
>
> *Daniel*

In addition to documenting Daniel's witnessing of Maria's initiatives, this letter recruits an imaginary witness—Maria's daughter Kyla at some point in the future. It's not uncommon for people to have difficulty acknowledging their accomplishments directly—probably due to discourses about bragging and humility—and it is often easier to solicit descriptions of achievements by inviting clients to look at themselves through the eyes of admiring others. The following questions (starting with my favorite) do that by inviting an imagined audience and encouraging further conversations with potential witnesses:

> *Whom do you know who'd be most likely to predict the changes you've been making? What would that person tell me about what they know about you that would help me understand the accuracy of the predictions?*
>
> *Who would be most interested to hear about these developments? What would he or she find interesting about them? How could you catch up this person?*
>
> *Who will be most affected by the changes you've made? Is this person aware of the changes, or do you plan to talk to them about what's been going on?*

When Daniel asked Maria who would be least surprised by the steps she'd taken, a detailed exchange ensued about her now deceased grandmother, with whom Maria had had a special relationship since she was a child visiting her grandparents' farm every summer. Through her grandmother's eyes, Maria was able to point not only to overlooked personal attributes of hers but to a series of events scattered over a number of years that portray the commitment to justice and fairness more recently identified in her conversations with Daniel.

Reflection 15.2

Think of something you accomplished that you're proud of. It could be concrete, as in something you created, or more abstract, as in a shift in a way of being in the world. Perhaps it was a public achievement, or maybe it was something more private pertaining to your relationship with yourself or someone close to you. Whom do you know who would have been most likely to predict that you'd accomplish this? What would they say about you that would explain that prediction? What difference does it make to reflect on yourself through the eyes of an admiring other?

It can be useful to solicit living witnesses to preferred developments in clients' lives as a way of marking their passage—for example, writing a letter to parents, teachers, or school administrators documenting steps taken by a young person in relation to some challenge (Metcalf, 2008; Winslade & Monk, 1999; Winslade & Williams, 2012). Inviting friends or families to a session is a particularly direct way of doing this (Freedman & Combs, 1996). These sorts of encounters are rife with possibility but also pose some risks if not carefully facilitated—after all, they're intended to celebrate and circulate accomplishment, not to air grudges or to initiate couples or family work. As Freedman and Combs (1996) put it, "problems are maintained through language and social interaction" (p. 239); when others are brought into the consulting room it's not for just *any* conversation. When Jorge invited his partner Richard to a session toward the end of his work with Maria, the questions Maria posed to Richard framed the conversation in a way tailored to the objectives she and Jorge had previously laid out:

> *Richard, what changes have you noticed in Jorge since he and I first started meeting?*
>
> *Are there any qualities of his that have been highlighted for you as you've watched him dealing with a variety of challenges in his life?*
>
> *What have you learned or discovered about Jorge that you hadn't formerly known?*
>
> *How have you been affected personally by the changes Jorge has been making?*
>
> *Is there anything you admire in Jorge that perhaps you haven't had a chance to share with him directly to this point?*

Creating a forum for persons close to the client to witness the changes they've made has more than one purpose. Besides providing a venue for celebrating the clients' achievements, it's also an opportunity to catch friends and loved ones up on the migration of identity mentioned earlier to prepare them to respond differently in accordance with the changes made. Spreading the news (Freedman & Combs, 1995) about the changes made increases the chances that what comes back at clients will fortify their recent initiatives.

PREPARING FOR NEXT STEPS

Toward the end of therapeutic work, it's also a good idea to look ahead and prepare for what is coming next. This includes getting ready for the possibility of setbacks, a practice sometimes known as relapse prevention. Box 15.1 provides some ideas for useful lines of questioning.

BOX 15.1

Preparing for Setbacks

Life unfolds in cycles. When clients have largely moved out of problem-saturated stories and into ones more in line with their preferences and values, day-to-day living does not then become an extended free lunch. Life will continue to throw challenges at them—sometimes the same challenges that brought them in initially. It can be helpful to join with clients in speculating about this by looking ahead at the possibility and asking questions that invite them to draw on recent learnings to deal with what comes up.

How will you know that [X] is creeping back into the picture next time?

What are the situations [contexts, people, times of day, etc.] *in which [X] is most likely to reappear?*

How will you respond differently next time your boss pushes your buttons?

What answer will you have for jealousy next time it whispers in your ear?

Which sorts of things do you do that minimize the chances of [X] coming around?

How will you remember to reconnect with your breath next time that feeling comes on?

What have you learned about your ability to deal with [X] that will help you if [X] does reappear?

What do you think will be different when you run into [X] again?

What's in your refitted toolbox to help you deal with [X]?

Can you paint me a vivid picture of what I'd be watching if I saw you running into [X] next time, based on the things you've been learning?

If you were laying out research findings, which data could you trot out to share with [X] to remind [X] of your successes dealing with it?

Whom do you know who would be a supporter at a time when [X] reappears?

More often than not, problems have developed well-worn neural grooves, as it were (Hanson, 2009; Siegel, 2012). They are habitual sequences of thought, feeling, and action we readily fall back into, especially when surrounded by familiar social cues. These cues trigger automatic responses that find us acting in ways out of sync with renewed intentions for change. The most powerful of these cues is the people who surround us. After all, people act according to their readings of each other; depending on how others read us, there's the potential to initiate circular patterns that can either reinforce preferred stories or encourage repeat performances of problematic ways of being (Tomm, 1998).

As seen above, preparing to catch people up on changes is one way to minimize the chances of falling back into unhealthy or destructive habits. However, there are limits to the degree we can change others. In some cases, changing one's lifestyle may mean changing one's social circle as well. Therapeutic change often entails some degree of loss at the same time as it opens the horizon to new possibilities.

> *Are there certain circles of friends who are most likely to encourage the drinking's return?*
>
> *Which situations are most likely to tempt you to start using again?*
>
> *Who do you figure stands against trouble in your life, and who stands with it?*
>
> *Who do you most associate with your old lifestyle, and who fits with your new lifestyle?*
>
> *Can you name the people in your circle of support?*
>
> *Who's in the front row of the audience for these new performances? Who's more interested in a return engagement from the old you?*

Reflection 15.3

Can you think of a circle of people who act as the life support system of the preferred developments in your life? In which ways do they witness your accomplishments and mirror them back to you? What difference does this make to you? Are there others who are more like the life support system of problems? What is it about socializing with them that drags you back to a way of being out of step with your current values, purposes, and intentions?

In conversations leading up to the end of their work together, Daniel and Maria identified two distinct social circles of Maria's. One she associated with what she called "the 'burbs"—a lifestyle of clearly defined gender roles where moms stay home and rule the household. The other group, a newer circle of friends, included gay and straight couples in lifestyles underrepresented on magazine covers in supermarket checkout counters. In the process of reviewing her values with Daniel's help, Maria came to understand why she was increasingly drawn to this second group—a realization that came with a sense of both loss of an identity she was gradually shedding and excitement about what lay ahead. She also realized that some of Azim's family—including, in particular, his parents—would likely continue to have expectations that didn't fit for her about her role as partner to Azim and mother of Kyla. These being important people in Maria's life, Maria committed to continuing to respectfully explain to them her point of view about her role as a woman, she hoped with Azim's support.

For Jorge, the prospect of discontinuing his conversations with his counselor Maria was worrisome. He'd first gone to her at a very vulnerable time, and despite making what he called "huge headway," he was concerned that without his weekly meetings, he'd quickly lose his way. Maria suggested they experiment with spreading the sessions out—first to biweekly and then to monthly as Jorge found himself increasingly busy with plans for moving in with Richard and gathering the paperwork for his application package to a graphic design program. At one of their monthly meetings, they decided it might make more sense for Jorge to take a break from the regular sessions to get some of these things done, with a plan to have a check-in 4 months later. A few days before that follow-up meeting, Maria recognized Jorge's voice in her voicemail at her internship site. He was calling to cancel and left her the following message:

> *Maria, sorry to do this at short notice. I know we were on for Tuesday, but things are crazy right now. We're painting the apartment, and I'm putting the finishing touches on my portfolio for one of my graphics courses. I'm doing well, learning a lot, and get this—Richard is now part of the Sunday dinners at my parents'. Go figure! Hey, thanks for all those heartfelt conversations and good luck with your own studies. 'Til we meet again . . .*

CHAPTER FIFTEEN DISCUSSION QUESTIONS

1. **Determining when to end.** Some agencies tie termination to completion of goals set out at the very beginning of the work with clients. What are pros and cons to this policy?

2. **Fading sessions out.** An alternative to an abrupt finish is to reduce the frequency of sessions before final termination. What do you see as the advantages and disadvantages of this approach?

3. **The construct of termination.** Some of the literature puts a substantial emphasis on the delicacy of ending therapy, emphasizing the potential for creating insecurity in clients in its absence. Although this perspective pays homage to the therapeutic relationship, it

leaves other perspectives out for making sense of and proceeding with endings with clients. What are some of those overlooked other perspectives?

4. **Rites of passage.** What is the potential utility of thinking of endings as the third phase of a rite of passage?

5. **Your rites of passage.** Think of some substantial change that has occurred in your own life—perhaps a challenge you overcame, a transformation in lifestyle, the move from being single to being in a relationship or the ending of a long-term relationship, a shift of geographic location or career, and so forth. Guided by the description of rites of passage under the section heading The Ending of Therapy as a Rite of Passage, describe richly what was going on for you in the three stages you went through.

6. **Ritual and ceremony.** What difference do ritual and ceremony make to marking events and celebrating them? What is missing from key events that are not ritualized? What is added when there is an element of ritual or ceremony included?

7. **Ritual and ceremony around your own life passages.** Which rituals or ceremonies have been marked, or been noticeably absent, in relation to your own passages? What difference has the inclusion/exclusion of ritual made?

8. **Letters.** What is it about letters that distinguishes them from spoken words? What are the potential benefits and risks associated with these differences when used in conjunction with therapeutic practice?

9. **Witnesses.** What are the pros and cons of inviting witnesses to a session to get an additional view of developments? Which challenges might be associated with this practice, and how could therapists prepare for them?

CHAPTER FIFTEEN ACTIVITIES

1. **Exploring rites of passage.** Form pairs. Speaker, describe briefly a rite of passage you passed through at some time in your life. Listener, guided by the questions under the heading Taking Stock of Learnings, and inventing your own, scaffold an inquiry that helps the speaker to identify the things they learned during this transition in their lives. Debrief. Speaker, what was it like to make sense of this transition as a rite of passage and to discover skills and learnings associated with it? Listener, what were the challenges associated with helping the speaker identify skills and learnings?

2. **Therapeutic letters.** Listener, based on hearing the account of your partner's rite of passage in the preceding activity, write a short letter to acknowledge their passage and the learnings and accomplishments associated with it. Share the letter with the speaker.

Debrief. Speaker, what impact does it have to see some of your accomplishments acknowledged in print? Listener, what were the challenges associated with composing the letter?

3. **Accomplishments through the eyes of another.** Listener, based on the developments described by the speaker in the preceding two activities, pose the following questions: Who do you know who'd be most likely to predict the changes you've been making? What would they tell me about what they know about you that would help me understand the accuracy of their predictions? Guide the speaker through a detailed account of this other person's view of them. Debrief. Speaker, what was it like to see yourself through the eyes of an admiring other? Did you identify qualities you might have had trouble naming yourself? Listener, what were the challenges associated with using this question line to draw out an expanded description of the speaker?

4. **Relapse prevention.** Listener, continuing to build on the previous activities, interview the speaker about the possible return of the problem, guided by the questions in Box 15.1, Preparing for Setbacks. Debrief. Speaker, what difference do these questions make to your preparedness for dealing with setbacks? Do they uncover any steps you have already taken since the transition you've been describing? Listener, what were the challenges associated with helping the speaker to prepare for setbacks?

GLOSSARY

Absent but Implicit: The unspoken expression of value and purpose that can be read between the lines of client accounts or problems and difficulties.

Accountability: The ability to account in the sense of being able to provide a rationale for what counselors say and do. This involves being transparent with clients about what informs questions and statements and giving clients an opportunity for input into the therapeutic direction.

Agency: Sometimes referred to as personal agency, associated with what is called free will: volition, deliberate choice. Agency can be contrasted with passivity and the notion of determined action.

Alternate Story: An interpretation, account, description of events in contrast to the problem version and more in line with client preferences, hopes, values, and so forth. Exceptions can be understood as threads of alternative stories. An alternate story is sometimes referred to as a subordinate story line because it is (initially) in the shadow of a dominant problem-saturated account.

Automatic Thought: Self-talk arising in the moment in response to situations. The term is generally associated with problematic thoughts.

Co-construction of Meaning: In dialogue, meanings that are not merely shared between conversational partners but are also constructed in the moment. When there is more than one person participating, the meaning is, in effect, co-constructed.

Cognition: A thought/belief or the process of thinking. See Chapter 14 for reflections on how *cognition* has different associations than *thought/belief*.

Collaborative Influence: Supporting clients to move toward their preferred outcomes, rather than versions of health or wellness prescribed by the counselor, or a theory, or society at large. This form of influencing is decentered and involves leading from behind.

Confirming Understanding: Explicitly or implicitly inviting the client to correct the counselor's reading of what the client intends to convey. If there were no power differential involved, this step would be less necessary because it could be assumed clients would instantly object to what they took to be misreadings of their experience.

Culture: Indicating a complex concept, the word that is used to characterize both the social groupings we inhabit and the discourses and practices that are predominant within those social groupings.

Curiosity: An orientation to conversations that invokes a rich description of experience from the other. Curiosity leads us to approach conversations the way an anthropologist approaches an unfamiliar culture. It translates into questions that seek to evoke a fuller depiction of the meanings and traditions of the other.

Deconstruction: A conversational practice that involves exploring the origins of thoughts and ideas, tracing them back to their cultural origins. The practice externalizes in that it helps separate people from problematic identity claims not previously questioned or challenged.

Dialogue: Two-way conversation that evolves and transforms on the basis of contributions from both conversational partners. Dialogue is mutually responsive, co-constructive talk.

Discourse: Both a noun and a verb: as a noun, a belief, story, or body of knowledge that circulates within the wider culture or within a specific subculture or institutional context; as a verb, discourse is *performed* as well. People engage in discourse with each other, and therapeutic conversations are prime sites for constructive discourse.

Double Listening: All accounts of problems are also accounts of people's taking initiatives in the face of challenges and obstacles, exercising skills and abilities amid constraints, expressing implicitly what they hope for and value. Double listening involves listening as an ally, keeping an ear open for traces of all of these in a client's account.

Empathic Understanding: The ability to identify what is of most consequence for the client. This requires care-filled listening and often a reading of what is not overtly spoken but lies between the lines.

Exception: In simple terms, an instance when the problem is absent. Assuming the client has been part of naming what is problematic, this implies an exception is a preferred development. Making further meaning of exceptions, they can also be understood as personal initiatives or expressions of agency. They are examples of people's taking steps aligned with their values and intentions.

Experience: To be contrasted with the facts of the matter, one's lived reality. The facts may stay the same, but experience is changeable, a function of the meanings made of events.

Externalizing: Initially coined by White and Epston (1990), a linguistic practice that separates clients from problems and reduces blame and totalizing.

Global Belief: An unquestioned opinion, view, or perspective about one's identity, relations, life in general, and so forth that is influenced by cultural stories or discourses.

Harmonizing Talk: Jointly settling on language, including metaphors and turns of phrase, that is useful and resonant for discussing the issues at hand. This involves arriving at ways of speaking about things that are close to the experience of the client. These may include extensions or spins from the counselor so long as they are negotiated with the client.

Hearing: Distinguished by Harlene Anderson and Sue Levin (Anderson, 1997; Levin, 2006) from mere listening. Hearing involves dialogue—it is a mutual negotiation of meaning, a striving for a shared understanding.

Intentionality: Marks practice as conscious and ethical, guided by rationales for the actions taken, both verbal and nonverbal. When we practice with intentionality we do more than simply respond from the gut—we make decisions about the impact of our actions on the clients who consult us.

Leading From Behind: Keeping close to client meanings, evoking the client's values and preferences and relying on these as a compass for the direction of the work.

Mapping the Influence of the Problem: Asking questions that help to elaborate the effect of the problem on the client in various contexts.

Matching Client Language: Speaking in a manner that promotes mutual understanding by adjusting to the client's vocabulary and level of language use.

Meaning: A person's subjective experience in relation to a word, event, or series of events. Although words come to some extent with some predetermined meanings, the product of cultural consensus, each person puts their own spin on the meaning as well, as in, What does *love* mean to you? The meaning of an event or series of events is more than the facts of what happened; instead, it is the sense made of them, the story told about them, by the person in question.

Metacognition: Thinking about thoughts, adopting a reflexive posture in relation to one's cognitions.

Multistoried: Characterizing both lives and identities in the sense that many interpretations or meanings can coexist, with different versions' assuming dominance at different times.

My House: Strong's (2001) term for the meanings, knowledges, beliefs, values, discourses, theories, and so forth, the counselor brings to the conversation.

Narrative: Also known as story—akin to a web of meanings in that it brings continuity and coherence to what otherwise can be experienced as discontinuous and discrete events. It is in narrating experience that we ascribe meaning to it. Narratives are never neutral because they always foreground some elements and background others. They are expressions of subjectivity, and although they can be understood as conceptual frames or viewpoints, they can also be performed: In this sense they are meaning in action.

Not Knowing: A stance involving the deliberate suspension of preunderstandings (professional theories and models, personal biases, hypotheses, etc.) in the service of the client. Not knowing is an orientation to the other rather than a statement of the degree of one's personal knowledge (Anderson & Goolishian, 1993).

Not Understanding: Gurevitch's (1989) term, used in a manner similar to Anderson's (1997) not knowing. This implies not a literal ignorance but a stance of openness to surprise and further discovery.

Our House: Strong's (2001) term for the meanings co-constructed with the client, the product of dialogue between My House and Your House.

Pathologizing: Defining a client in terms of deficit, sickness, deviance, and so forth; developing formal labels of pathology and using these to categorize clients and make sense of their experience; ascribing purportedly causal links between a client's traumatic experience and their perceived deficits.

Plot: When making sense of people's experience in storied terms, the thematic continuity between the events as they recount them. Plot is a web of meaning that coheres otherwise disparate events.

Power: Not so much a quality that resides in an individual as a function of a relationship. In this sense, power exists between people. A position of power in relation to another may mean greater leverage or access to resources, a louder voice, more weight being assigned to one's utterances, and so forth. *Power with* suggests a sharing of the advantages of power to the other's advantage, whereas *power over* suggests imposition of meaning or abuse of power to the other's detriment.

Problem-Saturated Story: The dominant account of a client's life and identity shared by a client who is struggling with life challenges. Problem-saturated stories tend to render exceptions difficult to discern—one of various ways to explain the utility of a therapist's second pair of eyes.

Recapping: Periodically taking stock of the unfolding conversation, providing a summary of the most recent portion of the exchange. Effective recapping captures meaning: It includes the facts but is also rich with descriptions of the client's experience of those facts. Recaps contain a mixture of restating and paraphrasing.

Reflexivity: Holding a mirror up to one's practice, life as it were—being mindful and self-aware, observing what one is doing and reflecting on it critically.

Relational Responsiveness: The quality of being attentive to the other person in the relationship and responding in accordance with what the other brings forward (Paré & Lysack, 2004). The metaphor of coordinating with a dancing partner captures a sense of the skills associated with relational responsiveness.

Responsivity: The process or practice of choosing one's words and actions in consideration of the words and actions of the other person in a relationship.

Restating: Using the client's language in responding to their utterances. Typically in restating we seek to capture both content and process—an experience-near description of the client's experience.

Schema: See *Global Belief.*

Self-Disclosure: A counselor's sharing with the client details about the counselor's personal life, emotional experience, and so on.

Self-Talk: In effect, things we tell ourselves: the thoughts that arise, most often automatically, in response to events.

Socratic Dialogue: The use of questions to invite someone to reflect on their position, weighing out its consequences, playing out an argument to its conclusion, and so forth.

Story: See *Narrative.*

Summarizing: Providing an account of an entire conversation by way of achieving closure or introducing a new conversation. Like recaps, summaries include factual detail but are also rich with descriptions of the client's *experience* of the facts. Summaries contain a mixture of restating and paraphrasing.

Tentative Posture: Closely related to a not-knowing orientation: telegraphing to the client that the counselor's understandings are not closed or final and that the counselor's view of the client's experience is always open to the client's scrutiny and correction.

Thought: Also known as a cognition, something we tell ourselves. A thought is to a global belief somewhat like a sentence is to a story.

Totalizing: Defining something or someone in fixed and delimited terms, making out some perceived quality or feature to be the *all* of the client or thing. Pathologizing is typically a totalizing process.

Totalizing Description: Usually of identity, a bounded and fixed description that leaves no room for other versions, other possibilities—often problem or pathology focused.

Tracking the Story: Asking clarifying questions to ensure that you have the details right. These may be factual details, but more important, they are meanings. Meanings are what experience is made of and comprise thoughts, feelings, values, hopes, fears, and so forth.

Unpacking Resonant Language: In this sense, to explore words that appear to have special significance for the client in more detail, to open up the language further, to tease out a richer and fuller description.

Your House: Strong's (2001) term for the meanings, knowledges, beliefs, values, discourses, theories, and so forth that the client brings to the conversation.

APPENDIX 1

ASSESSMENT

In many instances, agencies have staff members specifically devoted to an intake assessment that precedes linking clients to therapists. This arrangement can be used to link clients with appropriately skilled practitioners, but it also leads to counselors' inheriting one particular take about their clients before they even meet them. Working with prior assessments calls for a skillful balancing act: It involves taking a cue from pregathered facts and thus saving a certain amount of time while simultaneously inviting clients to recount their stories face to face so that counselors hear clients' experience in the clients' own words.

Alternately, counselors may be called on to conduct formal assessments themselves at the front end of their work with clients. In some cases, the structure of these assessments may be rigidly predetermined; in other instances, practitioners have some leeway as to what they will include in assessment documentation. This appendix (adopted from Madsen, 2007) supplies ideas for possible sections to include or characteristics to look out for in conducting assessment. The following are a couple of points worth noting about assessment: (a) It is ongoing, and the picture inevitably expands and changes with repeated conversations with clients, and (b) assessment is not just about what information is committed to paper; it is about how counselors position themselves relative to the people with whom they work. The notes below deliberately manifest an orientation that centers client preferences and highlights their competencies and resources.

Source: Adapted from Madsen, W. (2007). *Collaborative therapy with multi-stressed families*, (2nd ed.). New York: Guilford Press.

IDENTIFYING INFORMATION

This section is for basic contact information and client demographics. It should include cultural characteristics, broadly speaking—for instance, age, ethnicity, sexual orientation, class, and so on. Sometimes these factors are only highlighted when clients are from a nondominant group, which further entrenches social hierarchies. As seen throughout this book, persons' lived experience is inextricably related to their cultural contexts. Gaining an understanding of clients' multiple cultural identities is a key aspect of assessment.

DESCRIPTION OF THE CLIENT IN CONTEXT

This provides a picture of the client in relational and contextual terms. It's often useful to include a genogram here (see Chapter 9), which is useful for tracking family and other close relationships as well as providing background to current circumstances (dates of births and deaths, divorces, graduations, and other key milestones). This section is valuable for noting any key community supports as well, including friends, neighbors, and social agencies. As seen in Chapter 8, knowing the contexts clients inhabit tells us what they are responding to. This could include various forms of abuse, conditions of poverty or violence, and so on. Foregrounding these helps to render people's actions more sensible because it clarifies the circumstances of their lives.

PRESENTING CONCERNS

Client concerns—sometimes referred to as presenting problems—are at the heart of the assessment process. Given that counseling is about addressing distress or some expressed need, the presenting concern is a description of which forms these take. How this is documented can vary immensely, from dry depictions of deviations from some arbitrary norm ("the client demonstrates significantly flat affect") to descriptions that foreground clients' concerns in their own words ("Josh says the 'spark' he felt when he first went back to school 'has been snuffed' and that he feels a 'heaviness' throughout his body on most days, particularly in the evenings").

A useful addition to this section is a separate account of the presenting concern as related by a referring source, which may come in the form of a diagnosis. It can be enlightening to determine how this description corresponds to or differs from how clients describe their concerns. As seen in Chapter 9, it is also useful to learn about the client's response to the referral source's description of the presenting problem(s).

CLIENT PREFERENCES AND COMPETENCIES

The flip side of presenting concerns, client preferences tell us, *What does this person hope for? What is their image of a better life?* The picture of client preferences is usually directly tied to presenting problems (i.e., the absence of the problem), but skillful questioning can also uncover rich descriptions of preferred territories of living (see Chapter 7).

Client competencies are gifts they can draw on to get to those preferred territories and are well worth noting. This can include skills applied in relation to specific concerns such as the use of humor to defuse family tensions. But people are "weirdly abled" (Freeman, Epston, & Lobovits, 1997) in all kinds of delightful ways, and learning about these abilities not only renders a richer picture of who they are but also uncovers resources that might prove useful in all kinds of unexpected ways.

CONTEXT OF PRESENTING CONCERNS

This section fleshes out a picture of how the concern operates in various domains of the client's life. It includes details about where and when the problem presents itself and how the client and those around him or her respond to it. In addition to actions, the context includes emotions, thoughts, and beliefs as well as the broader meaning making the client does in relation to the problem. Questions here uncover the "life support systems" of problems—situations, locations, people around whom the problem thrives, for instance. They also highlight the support systems that account for exceptions to the problem—the contexts in which clients' preferred ways of being are able to thrive.

CLIENT EXPERIENCE WITH HELPERS

Asking about their experience with helpers conveys to clients that their subjective experience of services is of key importance. Learning about how previous work has unfolded is useful for two other reasons. First, it provides insight into what has *not* gone well, reducing the chances of duplicating ineffective or distressing interactions that might get the therapy off to a poor start, not to mention hampering the development of a productive relationship. Second, information about the client's *successful* experience with other care providers helps to avoid reinventing the wheel because it provides a detailed account of interventions that may well prove useful in the current circumstances.

RELEVANT HISTORY

All of the preceding information in this appendix provides a rich backdrop to soliciting an account of clients' relevant history. *Relevant* is a key word here: There is always an infinite amount of information that could conceivably be gathered; it is more useful to foreground events directly related to the presenting concerns. This should include both accounts of the negative repercussions of problems and also accounts of success in relation to problems. As the word *history* suggests, this section is about capturing a time line of events from a time before the problem became a problem to the current day.

MEDICAL INFORMATION

It is not uncommon for relational, emotional, and cognitive experience to be affected by medical issues. Gathering medical information involves identifying illnesses or conditions that may have repercussions for the client's broader well-being as well as keeping track of medications currently and previously taken.

MENTAL STATUS

The content of this section is frequently required by licensing regulations and includes categories such as appearance and behavior, general orientation, thought content and organization, attention, concentration, intellectual functioning, memory, judgment and insight, and mood and affect. These categories are focused on the individual, and the information recorded here makes a lot more sense in the context of the other information gathered as part of the broader assessment.

RISK FACTORS AND SAFETY FACTORS

Counselors and therapists have a responsibility—ethical, legal, and regulatory—to ensure that clients are not at risk of perpetrating serious harm on themselves or others. Gauging the likelihood of this occurring is typically part of an overall assessment. Appendix 2 explores risk to others (violence and abuse), and Appendix 3 deals with risk to self (suicidality). A useful adjunct to determining which risks are at play is to also look for indications that clients have means of countering risk within their behavioral, emotional, and cognitive repertoires—what might otherwise be called "signs of safety" (Turnell & Edwards, 1999; Turnell & Hogg, 2007).

DIAGNOSIS

In many jurisdictions and work settings, assessment is linked to the practice of diagnosis. I almost wrote "inescapably linked," but as Madsen (2007) points out, some practitioners abstain from diagnosis on the basis of objections to its potentially stigmatizing influence and disillusionment with its clinical utility. Chapters 8 and 9 address the topic of diagnosis in a variety of ways. A shorthand summary of that discussion is that for some clients, diagnosis comes with a sense of relief that their suffering apparently has an explanation; at the same time, a diagnostic category renders a thin description of people, directing attention to what is not working, and obscuring that which is. It's important to ensure diagnoses do not define clients.

Linking a range of symptoms to a category in the *Diagnostic and Statistical Manual of Mental Disorders* (text revision) (American Psychiatric Association, 2000)—the most recent edition at the time of this writing—is a critical step in connecting clients with medications to relieve their distress. But although psycho-pharmaceuticals can contribute substantially to improving quality of life, they are also massively overprescribed in North America (Duncan, Miller, & Sparks, 2004; Gergen, 1990; Paris, 2010; Strong, 2009; Whitaker, 2010). In situations wherein diagnosis is required as part of assessment, it is useful to remember that assigned categories do not represent the totality of experience but are rather conceptual tools for action and part of a broader picture of a person's life. As discussed in Chapter 9, engaging clients in critical reflection on diagnostic labels signals the importance of their subjective experience and helps them to understand the diagnosis within their own frames of reference.

APPENDIX 2
SIGNS OF ABUSE

To provide help for young people who are being abused or are at risk of abuse, it's important to identify the abuse at the outset. There are various reasons why a young person may not name the abuse explicitly. They may fear reprisal, or they may be trying to avoid the inevitable disruption of their lives or the lives of their family that would accompany disclosure; they may be silent out of loyalty; they may have the impression that the abuse is normal or otherwise not worthy of reporting; they may be convinced that they won't be believed.

REPORTING ABUSE

It is not uncommon for practitioners, especially those new to practice, to be reluctant to report when they learn of or strongly suspect abuse, for some of the following reasons:

- lack of understanding of the dynamics of abuse,
- belief that it may be an isolated incident,
- lack of knowledge of reporting requirements and procedures,
- fear of reprisals from the family toward the child,
- concerns about disrupting a therapeutic relationship,
- belief that nothing will happen anyway,
- belief that the child can be helped without reporting, and
- respect for the family's right to privacy.

The reporting of abuse is a legal responsibility. It is entrenched in legislation and associated with the ethical duty to protect, which is reflected in a wide variety of ethics codes, though the codes may vary somewhat in the fine print. It's helpful to remember that legislation and protocols regarding abuse are designed to protect young persons and are not founded on punitive premises. The safety of whoever is at risk should be the primary consideration in guiding decisions concerning abuse or suspected abuse. As in any situation that involves risk, it is always a good idea to consult with colleagues both to generate multiple perspectives and for support.

Although definitions vary from jurisdiction to jurisdiction, abuse generally falls into four categories: physical abuse, sexual abuse, emotional abuse, and neglect. The signs of these are diverse, and any purported indicators are not *evidence* that abuse is occurring; however, certain patterns of presentation deserve further inquiry. This appendix differentiates these four categories and provides some preliminary notes on recognizing abuse.

EMOTIONAL ABUSE

The word *abuse* typically conjures up images of physical or sexual violence, but significant harm can be perpetrated on young people without physical contact. Some level of emotional abuse is involved in all types of maltreatment of a child, but it can also occur alone. Emotional abuse is the persistent emotional maltreatment of a child and can take various forms. It might involve conveying to children they are worthless or unloved, inadequate, or valued only insofar as they meet the needs of another person. It might also include deliberately silencing children or relentlessly belittling what they say or how they communicate. Although family members or caregivers are most often associated with emotional abuse, it can also arise in peer interactions (Kochenderfer-Ladd & Ladd, 2001). The term *bullying* has become commonplace to describe forms of abuse perpetrated by peers in face-to-face scenarios (Craig & Pepler, 2007) and increasingly through the Internet—a phenomenon known as "cyberbullying" (Keith & Martin, 2005).

Emotional abuse might include having dramatically unrealistic developmental expectations of a child: demanding the completion of tasks far beyond their current capability or severing them from social interaction or learning opportunities out of an inflated impulse to protect them from purported harm. It could also include witnessing severe emotional maltreatment or physical or sexual abuse.

When meeting with young persons and their caregivers, counselors sometimes witness abusive interactions right in the room; more often, however, it is things said or done that suggest patterns of emotional maltreatment may be occurring on a regular basis. It's important to remember there is no uniform way a young person might be expected to present if being subjected to emotional abuse or any other form of abuse for that matter. Indications that deserve further attention include suicide attempts, extreme aggressiveness or passivity, or an apparent delay in emotional or psychological development.

PHYSICAL ABUSE

Physical abuse involves physical mistreatment or physical injury of a child. It could include such actions as throwing, kicking, burning, or cutting a child; striking a child with a closed fist; shaking a child under age 3; interfering with a child's breathing; and threatening a child with a deadly weapon.

Further inquiry is warranted when children present with unexplained bruises, bites, burns, broken bones, or black eyes. Likewise if parents or caregivers offer conflicting or unconvincing accounts of the injuries or refuse to offer an explanation altogether. If parents or caregivers describe children as "evil" or advocate harsh physical discipline, it is worth learning more about what is going on at home. And of course here as with any form of abuse, a previous history of abuse is reason to be vigilant for signs of maltreatment or violence.

SEXUAL ABUSE

Sexual abuse involves the inappropriate sexual touching of a minor. It could include intentionally touching the child, directly or through the clothing, and it could also include permitting, compelling, or encouraging a child to engage in sexually touching someone else. This sort of activity should be distinguished from the touch of a parent or caregiver for the purposes of providing hygiene, child care, and medical treatment or diagnosis.

This form of abuse could also include involving children in looking at pornography or witnessing sexual activity as well as enlisting young people in the production of pornography or grooming them for sexual exploitation—for example, through the Internet. Although adult males are the most frequent perpetrators of sexual abuse, it can also be committed by women and other children.

Among the signs that warrant further inquiry, a child has difficulty walking or sitting, suddenly refuses to participate in gym or physical activities, demonstrates developmentally incongruent sexual knowledge or behavior, or becomes pregnant or contracts a venereal disease (particularly if underage).

NEGLECT

Though no less consequential, neglect differs from the other categories in that it focuses more on what is *not* done by caregivers. Neglect is the persistent failure to meet a child's basic physical and/or psychological needs, to the extent it is likely to result in the serious impairment of the child's health or development. Neglect can occur during pregnancy as a result of maternal substance abuse. With children, neglect could include a caregiver's failing to

- protect a child from harm or danger;
- provide adequate food, clothing, and shelter;
- ensure that the child receives adequate supervision; and
- provide access to appropriate medical care or treatment.

Neglect can also include a failure to provide or respond to a child's basic emotional needs and is frequently but not necessarily associated with caregiver substance abuse. Judgments of the scope of care need to take into account contextual factors such as family income: Poverty may lead to reduced resources without constituting neglect.

Abandonment is another aspect of neglect. This involves deserting a child and leaving them without necessities of life such as food, water, shelter, clothing, hygiene, and medically necessary health care. Criminal activity or incarceration of a parent or guardian does not necessarily suggest abandonment, but a pattern of criminal activity or repeated long-term incarceration may be associated with abandonment of a child.

Among signs to look out for in relation to neglect or abandonment are the following: a child is frequently absent from school, begs or steals food from classmates, or lacks clearly needed medical attention or clothing.

It is important to emphasize that this appendix is intended to provide some preliminary descriptions of forms of abuse to support novice counselors in beginning to think about it and look out for it. None of the indicators described here prove abuse is occurring, and as mentioned elsewhere, the decision to act on suspicions of abuse should always be done in consultation with colleagues and, when appropriate, with clients as well.

APPENDIX 3

ASSESSING FOR SUICIDALITY

The questions of how to anticipate and respond to suicidality are prevailing concerns of counselors in training, and appropriately so, given the responsibility to protect clients from self-harm. Nevertheless, it is important to remember that suicide is a very rare circumstance among clients, and counselors are typically surrounded by experienced colleagues and supervisors who can and should be consulted whenever questions of suicidality arise. In addition, specialized training in assessing risk of and responding to suicidality is widely offered and is a recommended adjunct to basic counselor training—both for the skills and knowledge it adds to a practitioner's repertoire and also for the reassurance that comes with being prepared for circumstances. This brief appendix provides a snapshot glimpse at the issue of suicidality and is not intended as a substitute for either collegial consultation or specialized training.

RISKS AND INDICATORS OF SUICIDALITY

The prevailing taboo about talking about suicide extends to sharing with others that one is considering taking one's life. Clients who are suicidal will only occasionally announce this outright. It is important for counselors to anticipate the risk of suicidality by evaluating the context of clients' situations and by reading into clients' comments. Among contextual considerations that suggest increased risk of suicide are the following:

- a history of suicide attempts or self-harm or a family history of same;
- psychiatric disorders, especially mood and psychotic disorders;
- substance abuse; and

- severe triggering events (job or financial losses, relationship ruptures, death of loved ones, etc.).

Of course these alone do not suggest a risk of suicide; some clients in these circumstances may be at no risk of self-harm. Assessing risk is a holistic process that involves attending to various cues. The preceding list becomes far more significant when coupled with the following:

- expressions of hopelessness or despair,
- selling or giving away possessions,
- dramatic mood swings,
- intense anger or rage,
- severe illness,
- significant social isolation, and
- physical or sexual abuse.

It's important to be fully open to exploring the topic of suicidality; if counselors are reticent, they convey the message to clients that they should keep their feelings under wraps. Instead, direct and explicit language acknowledges that self-destructive impulses are not abnormal, and it sends the signal that it's okay to share these and explore them further. A common misconception is that talking about suicide will impart the idea to a client or increase the chances that a client will follow through; there is no evidence to support this. There are many ways into this conversation that involve picking up on what the client has said or shown without needing to resort to a highly literal question such as,

Are you feeling actively suicidal?

Are you feeling hopeless about the future?

I've noticed you've said several times, "what's the point?" and I wondered if that meant you're thinking that life isn't worth living anymore.

That self-critical voice sounds very loud and harsh right now. Does it ever suggest to you that you should end your life?

Do you ever find yourself wishing it would just all be over?

Does it ever get so bad you think of taking your life?

Because suicide is subject to such widespread taboo, and because the emotion associated with it is hard to stay present to, it's best to gradually but systematically explore the topic with clients, picking up on their cues rather than raising suicide in an abrupt manner that might cause them to blurt out a denial. Nevertheless, the answer concerning whether someone is contemplating taking their own life is critical, and it's important to persist with questioning if the client responds in a manner that does not rule out the possibility.

SUICIDE INQUIRY

Most people have concluded at some time in their life that life is not worth living. This alone does not constitute active suicidality, however, and it is important to pursue a further inquiry when clients indicate they have been considering serious self-harm or suicide. The following are key considerations:

Suicidal ideation. Suicidal ideation includes thoughts and feelings about taking one's life. Gauging the extent of these is an important first step. How often do they think about killing themselves, for how long at a time, and how intense are these thoughts and feelings? Tools such as scaling questions (see Chapter 9) are useful here for assessing the scope of suicidal ideation.

Suicide plan. Does the client have a specific plan for killing themselves? This includes inquiring into when they anticipate doing this and at what location. Have they taken steps to prepare for this? Have they rehearsed the scenario or engaged in related nonlethal injurious behaviors?

Lethality of method. Does the client have a particular idea about how they might take their life? How lethal is this method (e.g., firearms vs. over-the-counter pain medication)?

Access to means. Another important question is whether the client has access to the means by which they intend to kill themselves. Does their plan involve firearms or prescription medications? If so, do they have access to a gun and ammunition? Have they stockpiled pills?

Intent. To what degree does the client seem seriously to be contemplating these steps? Are they ambivalent or determined to die? What circumstances (such as family or loved ones) may be contributing to hesitation?

PROTECTIVE FACTORS

Alongside apparent intentions to commit suicide, many clients also display a range of protective factors that diminish the risk substantially. Commitment to their families—especially children—or pets can fortify their determination to see out the bad patch they are in. Perhaps they indicate future plans that they continue to cherish despite their dark mood. They may have a strong social network available to support them. Protective factors may also include religious beliefs that discourage suicide or coping abilities that have seen clients through previous difficult circumstances.

RESPONDING TO SUICIDE RISK

There is no formal, fail-safe protocol for deciding that a suicide risk is imminent and in need of an active response. The most important thing is to consult with a supervisor or experienced colleagues to make a judgment call about how to respond. Clients too may be part of this consultation in cases in which the counselor determines that they are in a position to participate in decision making about their welfare. In these cases, clients should be engaged directly about the scope of the risk they are facing and steps they can take to reduce it. One option is to widen the circle by inviting clients to recruit friends and family into a circle of active support. It can also be useful to solicit an active commitment from clients to contact you or someone close to them before they act on any self-destructive impulses. This agreement might also include arrangements for limiting access to means of self-harm.

As clients will know, based on the discussion about the limits of confidentiality at the outset of therapeutic work, the risk of suicide is one of the rare circumstances that may occasionally call for the breaking of confidentiality. Nevertheless, this should be explained again in circumstances wherein the counselor chooses to inform someone directly about a client's suicidal state. In this case, the disclosure of information is motivated by the intention to protect clients from harm. Conveying this will often temper client concerns; nevertheless in some cases a client may feel their right to their own self-determination is being violated. This is an example where the counselor's ethical and professional obligations trump the client's expressed wishes.

Typical persons to contact in these circumstances include a spouse, roommate, or close family member. In situations in which suicide seems particularly imminent, it may be necessary for one of these key persons to accompany the client to a hospital emergency room or psychiatric intake.

APPENDIX 4

MINDFULNESS, MEDITATION, AND THE BREATH

WHAT IS MINDFULNESS?

Mindfulness as a construct, a practice, and a psychological process has its roots in Eastern psychology and more specifically the "contemplative science" (Wallace, 2001, p. 211) of Buddhism. A central observation of this tradition is that despite cultural variations that help to account for the infinite variety of human experience, we all encounter certain inevitabilities, such as pain, illness, ageing, and eventually death. As a result, we suffer.

The Buddhist response to the ubiquitous phenomenon of suffering is multifaceted; however, mindfulness plays a central role and has much to offer to counseling and therapy (Germer, Siegel, & Fulton, 2005). Mindfulness suggests a different approach to dealing with problematic experience than the proactive, adversarial one associated with challenging or disputing problematic cognitions detailed in much of Chapter 12. Mindfulness relieves suffering not by changing phenomena but by altering one's relationship with them (Germer et al., 2005). Germer (2005b) puts it this way:

> Mindfulness is a skill that allows us to be less reactive to what is happening in the moment. It is a way of relating to all experience—positive, negative, and neutral—such that our overall level of suffering reduces and our sense of well being increases. (p. 4)

One way to get at the meaning of the term *mindfulness* is to consider the absence of mindfulness that is a familiar feature of most people's days. Here are examples of this:

- eating a sandwich while working on a computer or communicating on a mobile device,
- being introduced to someone and taking no notice of their name,
- driving a car while ruminating about something that happened yesterday, and
- failing to notice a child's newly developed skill because of preoccupation with tomorrow's meeting.

What these examples share is what they are lacking. They portray an absence of awareness of, and attention to, the present moment. Being mindful is often equated with being awake (Kabat-Zinn, 2005) and can be contrasted with the automatic way we frequently engage in our daily activities. The word *mindfulness* has a variety of meanings as it is commonly used, including (a) a theoretical construct, (b) the practice of cultivating mindfulness such as meditation, and (c) a psychological process of being mindful (Germer et al., 2005).

Another key feature of mindfulness is nonjudgment. To orient to experience with mindfulness is to see it, hear it, feel it, smell it, taste it, imagine it, remember it, just as it presents itself, with no ambition to change it or make it better. It is what it is. Putting these together, Germer et al. (2005) characterize mindfulness as (a) awareness, (b) of present experience, (c) with acceptance.

As you can see, this orientation is less about change and more about presence without judgment to whatever presents itself. Judgment is a form of scorecard that constantly ascribes differential value to aspects of experience. Mindfulness dispenses with that scorecard to make room for experiencing what is before us in its fullness. In fact, if one were to distill a single key finding of Buddhist psychology, it is that dissatisfaction arises from attaching to experience. Attachment—sometimes called grasping—is something we all do a great deal of the time and is associated with both pleasurable and aversive phenomena. It happens when we grasp onto a pleasurable experience and wish it will go on forever, and it happens when we cling to the desire that an aversive experience will end. Either way, attachment leads to dissatisfaction or suffering. The central Buddhist premise and a key insight of mindfulness practice is that the relief of suffering is associated with letting go, or perhaps more accurately, *letting be*.

MEDITATION AND THE BREATH

Meditation is a practice common to all of the major spiritual traditions. It takes many forms but generally involves directing attention inward while sitting, standing, walking, or lying down. In the tradition of mindfulness, which has been taken up with vigor in the West in recent years (cf. Hanson, 2009; Kabat-Zinn, 2005; Kornfield, 2000; Levine, 2011), attention is turned to the rising and falling of the breath, typically at either the nostrils or the diaphragm.

The key role of the breath in inducing relaxation, focus, and equanimity has been thoroughly documented for thousands of years and is most fully developed in the multifaceted discipline of yoga. Herbert Benson, a medical researcher at Harvard University, played a seminal role in drawing North American attention to the benefits of breath work and meditation when he demonstrated their role in influencing the autonomous nervous system and lowering blood pressure (Benson, 1975). Another medical practitioner, Jon Kabat-Zinn (cf. 1990, 2005), has more recently contributed to the meteoric rise of interest in mindfulness in the West and has been influential in the development of approaches to psychotherapy that borrow from mindfulness traditions (cf. Germer et al., 2005; Hayes, 2004; Linehan, 1993; Segal, Williams, & Teasedale, 2002).

There are many approaches to meditation deriving from a wide variety of traditions. Some involve attention to mental images or the recitation (aloud or silent) of words or phrases. As mentioned, the breath is a key resource in most traditions and, like the heartbeat, represents an uninterrupted backdrop to all living moments. In the traditions associated with mindfulness, the breath is an anchor rather than the one-pointed target of focused concentration found in some meditation approaches. It acts as a stabilizing home base to come back to when the mind boards a "train of thought" (Paré, Richardson, & Tarragona, 2009) and loses the quality of reflexive self-awareness. Returning to the breath supports the purpose of attending to the full scope of experience, moment by moment. Breath work is therefore the means to a greater end: the cultivation of a nonjudgmental, compassionate relationship with all that passes across the field of awareness:

> Mindfulness meditation encourages a gentle focus on immediate present experience, observing bodily sensations, mental impressions, feeling states and so on as they appear moment-to-moment. Attention is directed with kindness and equanimity towards whatever objects of mind or body appear. As each impression arises it is not clung to nor pushed away but simply experienced and let be, making space for the next impression to arise and fall away. There is a quieting of the interpretative and conceptual mind, a deliberate quest for a non-discursive lived experience. Narrative creation, which relies on imagination and memory, is muted as meditators seek to reduce the proliferative thinking and rumination that often fills the mind. (Percy, 2008, p. 358)

The mental states achieved by meditation contribute to a temporary alteration of autonomic nervous system indicators such as heart rate and oxygen consumption among various others and have been shown to have a favorable impact on sleep patterns, concentration, blood pressure, and a range of other factors (Benson, 1975; Kabat-Zinn, 2005). Recent research indicates the changes are more than transitory: Improvements in brain scanning and other technologies have demonstrated that the brain is malleable and subject to transformation well into adult life (Hanson, 2009; Siegel, 2012). The phenomenon of neuroplasticity suggests that mindfulness practice encourages the proliferation of particular neural connections along with the atrophy of others.

Mindfulness therefore offers a range of helpful possibilities for therapeutic work, both through encouraging a gentle attention in the moment during therapeutic conversations and through supporting clients in the development of their own meditation practices. Mindfulness practice also contributes to therapists' skills in listening and attending (Baer, 2003; Hick, 2009) and can play a central role in professional self-care.

REFERENCES

Ajzen, I. (2002). Perceived behavioral control, self-efficacy, locus of control, and the theory of planned behavior. *Journal of Applied Social Psychology, 32*(4), 665–683.

American Psychiatric Association. (1952). *Diagnostic and statistical manual of mental disorders.* Washington, DC: American Psychiatric Association.

American Psychiatric Association. (2000). *Diagnostic and statistical manual of mental disorders* (4th ed., text revision). Washington, DC: Author.

Andersen, T. (1987). The reflecting team: Dialogue and meta-dialogue in clinical work. *Family Process, 26,* 415–425.

Andersen, T. (1992). Reflections on reflecting with families. In S. McNamee & K. Gergen (Eds.), *Therapy as social construction* (pp. 54–68). Newbury Park, CA: Sage.

Andersen, T. (1993). See and hear, and be seen and heard. In S. Friedman (Ed.), *The new language of change* (pp. 303–322). New York, NY: Guilford.

Andersen, T. (1995). Reflecting process; acts of informing and forming; you can borrow my eyes, but you must not take them away from me. In S. Friedman (Ed.), *The Reflecting Team in Action* (pp. 11–37). New York, NY: Guilford.

Anderson, H. (1997). *Conversation, language and possibilities: A postmodern approach to therapy.* New York, NY: Basic Books.

Anderson, H. (2007). The heart and spirit of collaborative therapy: The philosophical stance—"A way of being" in relationship and conversation. In H. Anderson & D. Gehart (Eds.), *Collaborative therapy: Relationships and conversations that make a difference* (pp. 41–59). New York, NY: Routledge.

Anderson, H. (2009). Collaborative practice: Relationships and conversations that make a difference. In J. Bray & M. Stanton (Eds.), *The Wiley handbook of family psychology* (pp. 300–313). Oxford, UK: Wiley.

Anderson, H., & Gehart, D. (Eds.). (2007). *Collaborative therapy: Relationships and conversations that make a difference.* New York, NY: Routledge.

Anderson, H., & Goolishian, H. (1988). Human systems as linguistic systems: Preliminary and evolving ideas about the implications for clinical theory. *Family Process, 27*(4), 371–393.

Anderson, H., & Goolishian, H. (1993). The client is the expert: A not-knowing approach to therapy. In K. Gergen & S. McNamee (Eds.), *Therapy as social construction* (pp. 25–39). London, UK: Sage.

Arthur, N., & Collins, S. (2010). *Culture-infused counseling* (2nd ed.). Calgary, Canada: Counselling Concepts.

Audet, C. T., & Everall, R. D. (2010). Therapist self-disclosure and the therapeutic relationship: A phenomenological study from the client perspective. *British Journal of Guidance & Counselling, 38*(3), 327–342. doi:10.1080/03069885.2010.482450

Austin, J. L. (1965). *How to do things with words* (2nd ed.). Cambridge, MA: Harvard University Press.

Bachar, E. (1998). Psychotherapy—An active agent: Assessing the effectiveness of psychotherapy and its curative factors. *Israel Journal of Psychiatry and Related Sciences, 35*(2), 128–135.

Baer, R. A. (2003). Mindfulness training as a clinical intervention: A conceptual and empirical review. *Clinical Psychology: Science and Practice, 10*(2), 125–143.

Baird, B. N. (2005). Clinical writing, treatment records, and case notes. In B. Baird (Ed.), *The internship, practicum, and field placement handbook* (pp. 101–121). Upper Saddle River, NJ: Prentice.

Bakhtin, M. M. (1981). *The dialogic imagination: Four essays* (M. Holquist, Ed.). Austin: University of Texas Press.

Bakhtin, M. M. (1986). *Speech genres and other late essays* (V. W. McGee, Trans.). Austin: University of Texas Press.

Baruth, L. G., & Manning, M. L. (2007). *Multicultural counseling and psychotherapy: A lifespan perspective* (4th ed.). Upper Saddle River, NJ: Pearson Merrill Prentice Hall.

Bavelas, J. B. (2012). From the lab to the therapy room. Microanalysis, co-construction, and solution-focused therapy. In C. Franklin, T. Trepper, W. J. Gingerich, & E. E. McCollum (Eds.), *Solution-focused brief therapy: From practice to evidence-informed practice* (pp. 144–162). Oxford, UK: Oxford University Press.

Bavelas, J. B., Coates, L., & Johnson, T. (2000). Listeners as co-narrators. *Journal of Personality and Social Psychology, 79*(6), 941–952.

Bavelas, J. B., McGee, D., Phillips, B., & Routledge, R. (2000). Microanalysis of communication in psychotherapy. *Human Systems, 11,* 47–66.

Beaudoin, M. N. (2009). The SKILL-ionaire in every child: Boosting children's socio-emotional skills through the latest in brain research. Bradenton, FL: Booklcker.com.

Beck, A. T. (2005). The current state of cognitive therapy: A 40-year retrospective. *Archives of General Psychiatry, 62,* 953–959.

Beck, A. T., & Weishar, M. (2005). Cognitive therapy. In R. Corsini & D. Weddings (Eds.), *Current psychotherapies* (7th ed.). Belmont, CA: Brooks/Cole.

Beels, C. (2001). *A different voice: The rise of narrative in psychotherapy.* Phoenix, AZ: Zeig, Tucker, and Theisen.

Benson, H. (1975). *The relaxation response.* New York, NY: Avon.

Béres, L. (2009). Mindfulness and reflexivity: The no-self as reflective practitioner. In S. Hick (Ed.), *Mindfulness and social work: Reflective practice and interventions* (pp. 57–75). Chicago, IL: Lyceum Books.

Berg, I. K. (1994). *Family based services: A solution-focused approach.* New York, NY: Norton.

Berg, I. K., & de Shazer, S. (1993). Making numbers talk: Language in therapy. In S. Friedman (Ed.), *The new language of change: Constructive collaboration in therapy* (pp. 5–24). New York, NY: Guilford.

Berg, I. K., & Dolan, Y. (2001). *Tales of solutions: A collection of hope-inspiring stories.* New York, NY: Norton.

Berger, P., & Luckmann, T. (1967). *The social construction of reality: A treatise in the sociology of knowledge.* New York, NY: Doubleday.

Bertolino, B. (2010). *Strengths-based engagement and practice.* Boston, MA: Allyn & Bacon.

Bertolino, B., & O'Hanlon, B. (2002). *Collaborative, competency-based counseling and therapy.* Boston, MA: Allyn & Bacon.

Beutler, L. E., Moleiro, C., & Talebi, H. (2002). Resistance in psychotherapy: What conclusions are supported by research. *Journal of Clinical Psychology, 58*(2), 207–217. doi: 10.1002/jclp.1144

Bickman, L. (1999). Practice makes perfect and other myths about mental health services. *American Psychologist, 54*(11), 965–978.

Bischoff, M. M., & Tracey, T. J. G. (1995). Client resistance as predicted by therapist behavior: A study of sequential dependence. *Journal of Counseling Psychology, 42*(4), 487–495. doi: 10.1037/0022-0167.42.4.487

Biswas-Diener, R. (2010). *The practice of positive psychology coaching, in practicing positive psychology coaching: Assessment, activities, and strategies for success.* Hoboken, NJ: John Wiley. doi: 10.1002/9781118269633.ch8

Bobele, M., Servin-Guerrero Lopez, S., Scamardo, M., & Solorzano, B. (2008). Single-session/walk-in therapy with Mexican-American clients. *Journal of Systemic Therapies, 27*(4), 75–89.

Bohart, A., & Tallman, K. (1999). *How clients make therapy work: The process of active self-healing.* Washington, DC: American Psychological Association.

Bohart, A. C. (2006). The active client. In J. C. Norcross, L. E. Beutler, & R. F. Levant (Eds.), *Evidence-based practices in mental health: Debate and dialogue on the fundamental questions* (pp. 218–226). Washington, DC: American Psychological Association.

Briggs, J. (1971). *Never in anger: A portrait of an Inuit family.* Cambridge, MA: Harvard University Press.

Briggs, J. (1999). *Inuit morality play: The emotional education of a three-year old.* New Haven, CT: Yale University Press.

Bronfenbrenner, U. (1977). Toward an experimental ecology of human development. *American Psychologist, 32,* 513–531.

Bronfenbrenner, U. (1979). *The ecology of human development: Experiments by nature and design.* Cambridge, MA: Harvard University Press.

Brown, C., & Augusta-Scott, T. (Eds.). (2007). *Narrative therapy: Making meaning, making lives.* Thousand Oaks, CA: Sage.

Brown, L. (2006). Still subversive after all these years: The relevance of feminist therapy in the age of evidence-based practice. *Psychology of Women Quarterly, 30,* 15–24. doi: 0361-6843/06

Bruner, E. (1986). Ethnography as narrative. In V. Turner & E. Bruner (Eds.), *The anthropology of experience* (pp. 139–158). Chicago: University of Illinois Press.

Bruner, J. (1986). *Actual minds, possible worlds.* Cambridge, MA: Harvard University Press.

Bruner, J. (1990). *Acts of meaning.* Cambridge, MA: Harvard University Press.

Bruner, J. (1996). *The culture of education.* Cambridge, MA: Harvard University Press.

Burgoon, J. K., Buller, D. B., & Woodall, W. G. (1996). *Nonverbal communication: The unspoken dialogue.* New York, NY: McGraw-Hill.

Calder, C. (Ed.). (2008). *Contemporary risk assessment in safeguarding children.* Lyme Regis, UK: Russell House.

Campbell, A., & Hemsley, S. (2009). Outcome Rating Scale and Session Rating Scale in psychological practice: Clinical utility of ultra-brief measures. *Clinical Psychologist, 13*(1), 1–9.

Campbell, J., Rose, L., Kub, J., & Nedd, D. (1998). Voices of strength and resistance: A contextual and longitudinal analysis of women's responses to battering. *Journal of Interpersonal Violence, 13*(6), 743–762.

Cantwell, P., & Holmes, S. (1994). Social construction: A paradigm shift for systemic therapy and training. *Australian and New Zealand Journal of Family Therapy, 15*(1), 17–26.

Caplan, P. J. (1996). *They say you're crazy: How the world's most powerful psychiatrists decide who's normal.* New York, NY: Da Capo Press.

Capps, D. (1998). *Living stories: Pastoral counseling in congregational context.* Minneapolis, MN: Augsburg Fortess.

Capuzzi, D., & Gross, D. R. (2007). *Counseling and psychotherapy: Theories and intervention* (4th ed.). Upper Saddle River, NJ: Pearson.

Carey, M., Walther, S., & Russell, S. (2009). The absent but implicit: A map to support therapeutic enquiry. *Family Process, 48*(3), 319–331.

Chun, K. M., Organista, P. B., & Marin, G. (Eds.). (2003). *Acculturation: Advances in theory, measurement, and applied research.* Washington, DC: American Psychological Association.

Churchill, W. (1993). *Struggle for the land: Indigenous resistance to genocide, ecocide and expropriation in North America.* Monroe, ME: Common Courage Press.

Ciarrochi, J. V., & Bailey, A. (2008). *A CBT practitioner's guide to ACT.* Oakland, CA: New Harbinger.

Cioffi, D., & Holloway, J. (1993). Delayed costs of suppressed pain. *Journal of Personality and Social Psychology, 64,* 274–282.

Clark, D. M., Ball, S., & Pape, D. (1991). An experimental investigation of thought suppression. *Behaviour Research and Therapy, 29,* 253–257.

Coates, L. (1997). Causal attributions in sexual assault trial judgements. *Journal of Language and Social Psychology, 16,* 278–296.

Coates, L., Bavelas, J. B., & Gibson, J. (1994). Anomalous language in sexual assault trial judgements. *Discourse and Society, 5*(2), 191–205.

Coates, L., & Wade, A. (2007). Language and violence: An analysis of four discursive operations. *Journal of Family Violence, 22*(7), 511–522.

Cochran, J., & Cochran, N. H. (2006). *The heart of counseling: A guide to developing therapeutic relationships.* New York, NY: Thomson Brooks/Cole.

Corey, G. (2005). *Theory & practice of counselling and psychotherapy* (7th ed.). Belmont, CA: Thomson Brooks/Cole.

Cormier, S., & Hackney, H. (2007). *Counseling strategies and interventions* (6th ed.). Boston, MA: Allyn & Bacon.

Craig, W. M., & Pepler, D. J. (2007). Understanding bullying: From research to practice. *Canadian Psychology, 48*(2), 86–93.

Crocket, K. (1999). Supervision: A site of authority production. *New Zealand Journal of Counseling, 20,* 75–83. [Unapproved editorial changes corrected as Errata (2000), *New Zealand Journal of Counseling, 21,* 85–87.]

Crocket, K. (2004). Storying counselors: Producing professional selves in supervision. In D. Paré & G. Larner (Eds.), *Collaborative practice in psychology and therapy.* Binghamton, NY: Haworth.

Crocket, K. (2010). Rescuing speech: Teaching a writing aesthetic for counseling practice. *Journal of Poetry Therapy: The Interdisciplinary Journal of Practice, Theory, Research and Education, 23,* 73–86.

Dalai Lama, XIV, & Cutler, H. C. (2000). *The art of happiness.* New York, NY: Riverhead Books.

Dalmiya, V. (2002). Why should a knower care? *Hypatia, 17*(1), 34–52.

Daly, K. D., & Mallinckrodt, B. (2009). Experienced therapists' approach to psychotherapy for adults with attachment avoidance or attachment anxiety. *Journal of Counseling Psychology, 56*(4), 549–563.

Davies, B. (1991). The concept of agency. *Postmodern Critical Theorizing, 30,* 42–53.

de Jong, P., Bavelas, J. B., & Korman, H. (n.d.). Unpublished manuscript using microanalysis to observe co-construction in psychotherapy.

de Jong, P., & Berg, I. K. (2007). *Interviewing for solutions.* Belmont, CA: Thomson.

de Shazer, S. (1985). *Keys to solution in brief therapy.* New York, NY: Norton.

de Shazer, S. (1988). *Clues: Investigating solutions in brief therapy.* New York, NY: Norton.

de Shazer, S. (1991). *Putting difference to work.* New York, NY: Norton.

de Shazer, S. (1993). Creative misunderstanding: There is no escape from language. In S. Gilligan & R. Price (Eds.), *Therapeutic conversations* (pp. 81–94). New York, NY: Norton.

de Shazer, S. (1994). *Words were originally magic.* New York, NY: Norton.

de Shazer, S., & Dolan, Y. (2007). *More than miracles.* Binghampton, NY: Haworth.

Derrida, J. (1976). *Writing and difference* (A. Bass, Trans.). Chicago, IL: University of Chicago Press.

DeRubeis, R. J., Tang, T. Z., & Beck, A. T. (2001). Cognitive therapies. In K. S. Dobson (Ed.), *Handbook of cognitive behavioral therapies* (2nd ed., pp. 349–392). New York, NY: Guilford.

Detwiler, J. B., & Whisman, M. A. (1999). The role of homework assignments in cognitive therapy for depression: Potential methods for enhancing adherence. *Clinical Psychology: Science and Practice, 6*(3), 267–282. doi: 10.1093/clipsy.6.3.267

Dobson, K. S., & Dozois, D. J. A. (2001). Historical and philosophical bases of the cognitive-behavioural therapies. In K. S. Dobson (Ed.), *Handbook of cognitive-behavioural therapies* (2nd ed., pp. 3–39). New York, NY: Guilford.

Donnellan, M. B., & Robins, R. W. (2010). Resilient, overcontrolled, and undercontrolled personality types: Issues and controversies. *Social and Personality Compass, 4*(11), 1070–1083.

Drew, P., & Heritage, J. (1993). *Talk at work.* Cambridge, UK: Cambridge University Press.

Dryden, W. (2009). *Skills in rational emotive behavior counselling and psychotherapy.* London, UK: Sage.

Duba, J. D., Graham, M. A., Britzman, M., & Minatrea, N. (2009). Introducing the "basic needs genogram" in reality therapy–based marriage and family counseling. *International Journal of Reality Therapy, 29*(2), 15–19.

Duncan, B., & Miller, S. (2000). *The heroic client: Doing client-directed, outcome-informed therapy.* San Francisco, CA: Jossey-Bass.

Duncan, B. L., Miller, S. D., & Sparks, J. A. (2004). *The heroic client: A revolutionary way to improve effectiveness through client-directed, outcome-informed therapy* (Rev. ed.). San Francisco, CA: Jossey-Bass.

Duncan, B. L., Miller, S. D., Wampold, B. E., & Hubble, M. A. (Eds.). (2010). *The heart and soul of change: Delivering what works in therapy* (2nd ed.). Washington, DC: American Psychological Association.

Duvall, J. (2010, May 27). *Introduction to the Youth Services Bureau of Ottawa walk-in clinic.* Ottawa: Youth Services Bureau of Ottawa.

Duvall, J., & Béres, L. (2011). *Innovations in narrative therapy: Connecting practice, training, and research.* New York, NY: Norton.

Efran, J. S., Lukens, R. J., & Lukens, M. D. (1988). Constructivism: What's in it for you? *Family Therapy Networker, 12*(5), 27–35.

Egan, G. (1995). *The skilled helper: A problem management approach to helping* (6th ed.). Pacific Groves, CA: Brooks/Cole.

Egan, G. (2002). *The skilled helper: A problem-management and opportunity-development approach to helping* (7th ed.). Pacific Groves, CA: Brooks/Cole.

Ellis, A. (2007). *Overcoming resistance: A rational emotive behavior therapy integrative therapy approach.* New York, NY: Spring.

Epston, D. (1989). *Collected papers.* Adelaide, Australia: Dulwich Centre.

Epston, D. (1993). Internalized other questioning with couples: The New Zealand version. In S. Gilligan & R. Price (Eds.), *Therapeutic conversations* (pp. 183–189). New York, NY: Norton.

Epston, D. (1999). Co-research: The making of an alternative knowledge. In *Narrative therapy and community work: A conference collection.* Adelaide, Australia: Dulwich Centre.

Epston, D. (2001). Anthropology, archives, co-research and narrative therapy. In D. Denborough (Ed.), *Family therapy: Exploring the fields' past, present and possible futures* (pp. 177–182). Adelaide, Australia: Dulwich Centre.

Epston, D. (2008). *Down under and up over: Travels in narrative therapy.* Chippenham, UK: Antony Rowe.

Epston, D., Maisel, R., & Borden, A. (2004). *Biting the hand that starves you.* New York, NY: Norton.

Epston, D., & Marsten, D. (in press). "What doesn't the problem know about your son or daughter?" Providing the conditions for the restoration of a family's dignity. *International Journal of Narrative Therapy and Community Work.*

Fook, J., & Gardner, F. (2007). *Practising critical reflection: A resource handbook.* Maidenhead, UK: Open University Press.

Foucault, M. (1965). *Madness and civilization.* New York, NY: Vintage.

Foucault, M. (1979). *Discipline and punish: The birth of the prison.* New York, NY: Vintage.

Foucault, M. (1980). *Power/knowledge: Selected interviews and other writings 1972–1977* (C. Gordon, Ed. & Trans.; L. Marshall, J. Mepham, & K. Soper, Trans.). New York, NY: Harvester Wheatsheaf.

Fox, N. J. (2003). Practice-based evidence: Towards collaborative and transgressive research. *Sociology, 37*(1), 81–104.

Frame, M. W. (2000). Constructing religious/spiritual genograms. In R. E. Watts (Ed.), *Techniques in marriage and family counseling* (pp. 69–74). Alexandria, VA: American Counseling Association.

Frances, A. (2012, May 11). *Diagnosing the D.S.M.* Retrieved from http://www.nytimes.com/2012/05/12/opinion/break-up-the-psychiatric-monopoly.html?ref=us

Frank, A. W. (1995). *The wounded storyteller: Body, illness, and ethics.* Chicago, IL: University of Chicago Press.

Frank, A. W. (2004). *The renewal of generosity: Illness, medicine, and how to live.* Chicago, IL: University of Chicago Press.

Frankl, V. (1984). *Man's search for meaning.* New York, NY: Pocket Books.

Freedman, J., & Combs, G. (1996). *Narrative therapy: The social construction of preferred realities.* New York, NY: Norton.

Freeman, J., Epston, D., & Lobovits, D. (1997). *Playful approaches to serious problems: Narrative therapy with children and their families.* New York, NY: Norton.

Freeman, J. C., & Lobovits, D. (1993). The turtle with wings. In S. Friedman (Ed.), *The new language of change: Constructive collaboration in psychotherapy* (pp. 188–225). New York, NY: Guilford.

Freire, P. (1972). *Pedagogy of the oppressed* (Myra Bergman Ramos, Trans.). New York, NY: Herder and Herder.

Friedman, S. (1993). Escape from the furies: A journey from self-pity to self-love. In S. Friedman (Ed.), *The new language of change: Constructive collaboration in therapy* (pp. 251–277). New York, NY: Guilford.

Fulton, P. (2005). Mindfulness as clinical training. In C. K. Germer, R. D. Siegel, & P. R. Fulton (Eds.), *Mindfulness and psychotherapy* (pp. 55–72). New York, NY: Guilford.

Gabbard, G. O., & Crisp-Han, H. (2010). Teaching professional boundaries to psychiatric residents. *Academic Psychiatry, 34*(5), 369–372.

Gadamer, H.-G. (1988). *Truth and method* (Rev. ed., J. Weinsheimer, Trans.). New York, NY: Continuum.

Gazzola, N., & Stalikas, A. (2003). Can Carl Rogers teach us anything about interpretation? *Client-Centered and Experiential Psychotherapies, 2*(4), 242–257.

Geertz, C. (1976). "From the native's point of view": On the nature of anthropological understanding. In K. Basso & H. Selby (Eds.), *Meaning in anthropology* (pp. 221–237). Albuquerque: University of New Mexico Press.

Geertz, C. (1983). *Local knowledge.* New York, NY: Basic Books.

Gehart, D., & Paré, D. A. (2008). Suffering and the relationship with the problem in postmodern therapies: A Buddhist re-visioning. *Journal of Family Psychotherapy, 19*(4), 299–319.

Gergen, K. J. (1985). The social constructionist movement in modern psychology. *American Psychologist, 40,* 266–275.

Gergen, K. J. (1990). Therapeutic professions and the diffusion of deficit. *Journal of Mind and Behavior, 11*(3/4), 353–367.

Gergen, K. J. (1994). *Realities and relationships: Soundings in social construction.* Cambridge, MA: Harvard University Press.

Gergen, K. J. (2001). *The saturated self* (2nd ed.). New York, NY: Perseus.

Gergen, K. J. (2006). The relational self in historical context. *International Journal for Dialogical Science, 1*(1), 119–124.

Gergen, K. J. (2009). *An invitation to social constructionism* (2nd ed.). London, UK: Sage.

Germer, C. K. (2005a). Anxiety disorders: Befriending fear. In C. K. Germer, R. D. Siegel, & P. R. Fulton (Eds.), *Mindfulness and psychotherapy* (pp. 152–172). New York, NY: Guilford.

Germer, C. K. (2005b). Mindfulness: What is it? What does it matter? In C. K. Germer, R. D. Siegel, & P. R. Fulton (Eds.), *Mindfulness and psychotherapy* (pp. 3–27). New York, NY: Guilford.

Germer, C. K., Siegel, R. D., & Fulton, P. R. (Eds.). (2005). *Mindfulness and psychotherapy.* New York, NY: Guilford.

Gilligan, C. (1982). *In a different voice: Psychological theory and women's development.* Cambridge, MA: Harvard University Press.

Goffman, E. (1961). *Asylums: Essays on the social situation of mental patients and other inmates.* New York, NY: Doubleday.

Goldstein, J. (2002). *One dharma.* New York, NY: HarperCollins.

Goleman, D. (1995). *Emotional intelligence: Why it can matter more than IQ.* New York, NY: Bantam.

Goodman, N. (1978). *Ways of worldmaking.* Hassocks, UK: Harvester Press.

Goodman, T. A. (2005). Working with children: Beginner's mind. In C. K. Germer, R. D. Siegel, & P. R. Fulton (Eds.), *Mindfulness and psychotherapy* (pp. 197–219). New York, NY: Guilford.

Goodyear, R. K. (1981). Termination as a loss experience for the counselor. *Personnel and Guidance Journal, 59*(6), 347–350. doi:10.1002/j.2164-4918.1981.tb00565.x

Greenberg, G. (2010). *Manufacturing depression: The secret history of a modern disease.* New York, NY: Simon & Schuster.

Greenberger, D., & Padesky, C. A. (1995). *Mind over mood: A cognitive therapy treatment manual for clients.* New York, NY: Guilford.

Griffith, J. L., & Griffith, M. E. (1994). *The body speaks: Therapeutic dialogues for mind-body problems.* New York, NY: Basic Books.

Griffiths, P. E. (1997). *What emotions really are: The problem of psychological categories.* Chicago, IL: University of Chicago Press.

Guanaes, C., & Rasera, E. (2006). Therapy as social construction: An interview with Sheila McNamee. *Interamerican Journal of Psychology, 40*(1), 123–132.

Gurevitch, Z. D. (1989). The power of not understanding: The meeting of conflicting identities. *Journal of Applied Behavioral Science, 25*(2), 161–173.

Guterman, J. Y. (2006). *Mastering the art of solution-focused counselling.* Alexandria, VA: American Counseling Association.

Hackney, H., & Cormier, S. (2008). *The professional counselor* (6th ed.). Boston: Allyn & Bacon.

Hall, E., Hall, C., Stradling, P., & Young, D. (2006). *Guided imagery: Creative interventions in counselling and psychotherapy.* Thousand Oaks, CA: Sage.

Hamid, S. (2000). Culture-specific syndromes: It's all relative. *Visions: BC's Mental Health Journal, 9,* 5–8.

Hancock, F., & Epston, D. (2010). Becoming a narrative practitioner: A participatory view of narrative therapy teaching. Unpublished manuscript.

Hanson, R. (2009). *Buddha's brain: The practical neuroscience of happiness, love, and wisdom.* Oakland, CA: New Harbinger.

Hardy, K. V., & Laszloffy, T. A. (1995). The cultural genogram: Key to training culturally competent family therapists. *Journal of Marital and Family Therapy, 21*(3), 227–237.

Hare-Mustin, R. (1994). Discourses in the mirrored room: A postmodern analysis of therapy. *Family Process, 33,* 19–35.

Harkaway, J. E., & Madsen, W. C. (1989). A systemic approach to medical non-compliance: The case of chronic obesity. *Family Systems Medicine, 7,* 42–53.

Harper-Jaques, S., McElheran, N., Slive, A., & Leahey, M. (2008). A comparison of two approaches to the delivery of walk-in single session mental health therapy. *Journal of Systemic Therapies, 27*(4), 40–53.

Harré, R. (Ed.). (1986). *The social construction of emotions.* Oxford, UK: Blackwell.

Harré, R., & Parrot, W. G. (Eds.). (1996). *The emotions: Social, cultural, and biological dimensions.* London, UK: Sage.

Harris, R. (2009). *ACT made simple.* Oakland, CA: New Harbinger.

Hayes, S. (2004). Acceptance and commitment therapy, behavioral frame theory, and the third wave of behavioral and cognitive therapies. *Behavior Therapy, 35,* 639–665.

Hertlein, K. M. (2002). Lose your marbles. *Journal of Clinical Activities, Assignments & Handouts in Psychotherapy Practice, 2*(2), 119–121.

Hick, S. (Ed.). (2009). *Mindfulness and social work: Reflective practice and interventions.* Chicago, IL: Lyceum Books.

Hoagland, S. L. (1991). Some thoughts about "caring." In C. Card (Ed.), *Feminist ethics* (pp. 260–261). Lawrence: University of Kansas Press.

Hoffman, L. (1993). *Exchanging voices.* London, UK: Karnac.

Hoffman, L. (2002). *Family therapy: An intimate history.* New York, NY: Norton.

Hoffman-Hennessy, L., & Davis, J. (1993). Tekka with feathers: Talking about talking (about suicide). In S. Friedman (Ed.), *The new language of change: Constructive collaboration in therapy* (pp. 345–373). New York, NY: Guilford.

Hofmann, S. G., Sawyer, A. T., Witt, A. A., & Oh, D. (2010). The effect of mindfulness-based therapy on anxiety and depression: A meta-analytic review. *Journal of Consulting and Clinical Psychology, 78*(2), 169–183. doi: 10.1037/a0018555

Hofstede, G. (2001). *Culture's consequences* (2nd ed.). Thousand Oaks, CA: Sage.

Hollon, S. D., & Beck, A. T. (2004). Cognitive and cognitive behavioral therapies. In M. J. Lambert (Ed.), *Bergin and Garfield's handbook of psychotherapy and behavior change* (pp. 447–492). New York, NY: John Wiley.

Holzman, L. (Ed.). (1999). *Performing psychology: A postmodern culture of the mind.* New York, NY: Routledge.

Horowitz, A. V., & Wakefield, J. C. (2012). *All we have to fear: Psychiatry's transformation of natural anxieties into mental disorders.* New York, NY: Oxford University Press.

Horvath, A. O., & Greenberg, L. S. (Eds.). (1994). *The working alliance: Theory, research and practice.* New York, NY: John Wiley.

Horvath, A. O., & Symonds, B. D. (1991). Relation between working alliance and outcome in psychotherapy: A meta-analysis. *Journal of Counseling Psychology, 38*(2), 139–149.

Howard, G. S. (1991). Culture tales: A narrative approach to thinking, cross-cultural psychology and psychotherapy. *American Psychologist, 46*(3), 187–197.

Hoyt, M. (Ed.). (1994). *Constructive therapies.* New York, NY: Guilford.

Hubble, M., Duncan, B., & Miller, S. (1999). *The heart and soul of change: What works in therapy.* Washington, DC: American Psychological Association.

Hudson O'Hanlon, W., & Weiner-Davis, M. (1989). *In search of solutions: A new direction in psychotherapy.* New York, NY: Norton.

Hurley, E. (2007). Establishing non-criminal records. *International Journal of Narrative Therapy and Community Work, 3,* 3–10.

Hyun-nie, A., & Wampold, B. E. (2001). Where oh where are the specific ingredients? A meta-analysis of component studies in counseling and psychotherapy. *Journal of Counseling Psychology, 48*(30), 251–257.

Isaacson, W. (2007). *Einstein: His life and universe.* New York, NY: Simon & Shuster.

Iversen, R. R., Gergen, K. J., & Fairbanks, R. P., II. (2005). Assessment and social construction: Conflict or co-creation? *British Journal of Social Work, 35,* 689–708.

Ivey, A. E., & Bradford Ivey, M. (1999). *Intentional interviewing and counseling* (4th ed.). Pacific Grove, CA: Brooks/Cole.

Ivey, A. E., Ivey, B. D., & Zalaquett, C. P. (2009). *Intentional interviewing and counseling: Facilitating client development in a multicultural society.* Belmont, CA: Brooks/Cole.

James, W. (1981). *The principles of psychology.* Cambridge, MA: Harvard University Press. (Original work published 1890)

Jenkins, A. (1990). *Invitations to responsibility: The therapeutic engagement of men who are violent and abusive.* Adelaide, Australia: Dulwich Centre.

Jenkins, A. (2009). *Becoming ethical: A parallel, political journey with men who have abused.* Dorset, UK: Russel House.

Johnson, S. M. (2004). *The practice of emotionally-focused couple therapy* (2nd ed.). New York, NY: Brunner-Routledge.

Kabat-Zinn, J. (1990). *Full catastrophe living: Using the wisdom of your body and mind to face stress, pain, and illness.* New York, NY: Dell.

Kabat-Zinn, J. (2005). *Coming to our senses: Healing the world and ourselves through mindfulness.* New York, NY: Hyperion Books.

Karasu, T. B. (1986). The specificity against nonspecificity dilemma: Toward identifying therapeutic change agents. *American Journal of Psychiatry, 143,* 687–695.

Katz, A., & Shotter, J. (1996). Hearing the patient's "voice": Toward a social poetics in diagnostic interviews. *Social Science and Medicine, 43*(6), 919–931.

Keith, S., & Martin, M. (2005). Cyberbullying: Creating a culture of respect in a cyber world. *Reclaiming Children and Youth, 13*(4), 224–228.

Keltner, D., Ekman, P., Gonzaga, G. G., & Beer, J. (2001). Facial expression of emotion. In R. J. Davidson, K. R. Scherer, & H. H. Goldsmith (Eds.), *Handbook of affective sciences* (pp. 415–432). Oxford, NY: Oxford University Press.

Kessler, M. (1994). What gets clients better: The need for verification. *International Journal of Communicative Psychoanalysis & Psychotherapy, 9*(1), 11–17.

Knight, C. (2012). Therapeutic use of self: Theoretical and evidence-based considerations for clinical practice and supervision. *Clinical Supervisor, 31*(1), 1–24. doi: 10.1080/07325223.2012.676370

Kochenderfer-Ladd, B., & Ladd, G. W. (2001). Variations in peer victimization: Relations to children's maladjustment. In R. Juvonen & S. Graham (Eds.), *Peer harassment in school: The plight of the vulnerable and victimized* (pp. 25–48). New York, NY: Guilford.

Kornfield, J. (2000). *After the ecstasy, the laundry.* New York, NY: Bantam.

Kosutic, I., & McDowell, T. (2008). Diversity and social justice issues in family therapy literature: A decade review. *Journal of Feminist Family Therapy, 20*(2), 142–165. doi: 10.1080/08952830802023292

Kuehl, B. P. (1995). The solution-oriented genogram: A collaborative approach. *Journal of Marital and Family Therapy, 21*(3), 239–250.

Kvale, S. (1983). The qualitative research interview: A phenomenological and a hermeneutical mode of understanding. *Journal of Phenomenological Psychology, 14*(2), 171–197.

Kwee, M. G. T. (Ed.). (2010). *New horizons in Buddhist psychology: Relational Buddhism for collaborative practitioners.* Chagrin Falls, OH: TAOS Institute.

Lambert, M. J. (Ed.). (2004). *Bergin and Garfield's handbook of psychotherapy and behavior change* (5th ed.). New York, NY: John Wiley.

Lambert, M. J., & Bergin, A. E. (1994). The effectiveness of psychotherapy. In A. E. Bergin & S. L. Garfield (Eds.), *Handbook of psychotherapy and behavior change* (4th ed., pp. 143–189). New York, NY: John Wiley.

Larner, G. (1996). Narrative child family therapy. *Family Process, 35,* 423–440.

Law, I., & Madigan, S. (1994). Introduction to power and politics in practice. *Dulwich Centre Newsletter, 1,* 3–6.

Lee, C. C. (Ed.). (2006). *Multicultural issues in counseling: New approaches to diversity* (3rd ed.). Alexandria, VA: American Counseling Association.

Lee, C. C., Burnhill, D. A., Butler, A. L., Hipolito-Delgado, C. P., Humphrey, M., Muñoz, O., & Shin, H. (2009). *Elements of culture in counseling.* Upper Saddle River, NJ: Pearson.

Lee, C. C., & Ramsey, C. J. (2006). Multicultural counseling: A new paradigm for a new century. In C. C. Lee (Ed.), *Multicultural issues in counseling: New approaches to diversity* (3rd ed., pp. 3–11). Alexandria, VA: American Counseling Association.

le Guin, U. K. (1984). *A wizard of Earthsea.* New York, NY: Bantam.

Lempert, B. (1996). Women's strategies for survival: Developing agency in abusive relationships. *Journal of Family Violence, 11,* 269–290.

Levinas, E. (1985). *Ethics and infinity: Conversations with Philip Nemo* (R. A. Cohen, Trans.). Pittsburgh, PA: Duquesne University Press.

Levine, N. (2011). *The heart of the revolution: The Buddha's radical teaching on compassion, forgiveness, and kindness.* New York, NY: HarperCollins.

Levine, S. (1987). *Healing into life and death.* New York, NY: Random House.

Levitin, D. J. (2007). *This is your brain on music.* New York, NY: Penguin.

Liebenberg, L., & Ungar, M. (2008). *Resilience in action: Working with youth across cultures and contexts.* Toronto, Canada: University of Toronto Press.

Lindemann-Nelson, H. (2001). *Damaged identities, narrative repair.* Ithaca, NY: Cornell University Press.

Linehan, M. M. (1993). *Cognitive-behavioural treatment of borderline personality disorder.* New York, NY: Guilford.

Linehan, M. M. (1994). Acceptance and change: The central dialectic in psychotherapy. In S. C. Hayes, N. S. Jacobson, V. M. Follette, & M. J. Dougher (Eds.), *Acceptance and change: Content and context in psychotherapy* (pp. 73–90). Reno, NV: Context Press.

Lipchik, E. (1994). The rush to be brief. *Family Therapy Networker, 18*(2), 34–39.

Lipchik, E. (1999). Theoretical and practical thoughts about expanding the solution-focused approach to include emotions. In W. A. Ray & S. de Shazer (Eds.), *Evolving brief therapies: Essays in honor of John Weakland* (pp. 157–172). Galena, IL: Geist and Russell.

Lipchik, E. (2002). *Beyond technique in solution-focused therapy: Working with emotions and the therapeutic relationship.* New York, NY: Guilford.

Lock, A., & Strong, T. (2010). *Social constructionism: Sources and stirrings.* London, UK: Cambridge University Press.

Lofland, L. H. (1985). The social shaping of emotion: The case of grief. *Symbolic Interaction, 8*(2), 171–190.

Lonner, W., Dinnel, D., Forgays, D., & Hayes, S. (Eds.). (1999). *Merging past, present, and future in cross-cultural psychology: Selected papers from the Fourteenth International Congress of the International Association for Cross-cultural Psychology.* Lisse, the Netherlands: Swets & Zeitlinger.

Lopez, S. L. (2008). *Positive psychology: Exploring the best in people* (Vols. 1–4). Westport, CT: Praeger.

Lowe, R. (2005). Structured methods and striking moments: Using question sequences in "living" ways. *Family Process, 44,* 65–75.

Luborsky, L., Mintz, J., Auerbach, A., Christoph, P., Bachrach, H., Todd, T., Johnson, M., Cohen, M., & O'Brien, C. P. (1980). Predicting the outcome of psychotherapy: Findings from the Penn Psychotherapy Project. *Archives of General Psychiatry, 37,* 471–481.

MacCluskie, K. (2010). *Acquiring counseling skills: Integrating theory, multiculturalism, and self-awareness.* Upper Saddle River, NJ: Pearson.

Madigan, S. (2011). *Narrative therapy.* Washington, DC: American Psychological Association.

Madsen, W. (1999). *Collaborative therapy with multi-stressed families.* New York, NY: Guilford.

Madsen, W. (2007). *Collaborative therapy with multi-stressed families* (2nd ed.). New York, NY: Guilford.

Mahalik, J. R. (1994). Development of the client resistance scale. *Journal of Counseling Psychology, 41*(1), 58–68. doi: 10.1037/0022-0167.41.1.58

Malinen, T., Cooper, S., & Thomas, F. (Eds.). (2012). *Masters of narrative and collaborative therapies.* New York, NY: Routledge.

Martin, D. J., Garske, J. P., & Davis, M. K. (2000). Relation of the therapeutic alliance with outcome and other variables: A meta-analytic review. *Journal of Consulting and Clinical Psychology, 68*(3), 438–450.

Matthews, G., Deary, I., & Whiteman, M. C. (2009). *Personality traits.* New York, NY: Cambridge University Press.

McAuliffe, G. (2007). *Culturally alert counseling.* Thousand Oaks, CA: Sage.

McKee, R. (1997). *Story: Substance, structure, style, and the principles of screenwriting.* New York, NY: ReganBooks.

McNamee, S. (2004). Social constructionism as practical theory: Lessons for practice and reflection in psychotherapy. In D. A. Paré & G. Larner (Eds.), *Collaborative Practice in Psychology and Therapy* (pp. 9–21). New York, NY: Haworth.

McNamee, S., & Gergen, K. J. (Eds.). (1992). *Therapy as social construction.* London, UK: Sage.

Mearns, D. (1997). *Client-centred counseling training.* London, UK: Sage.

Meichenbaum, D. (1985). *Stress inoculation training.* New York, NY: Pergamon Press.

Metcalf, L. (2008). *Counseling towards solutions.* Somerset, NJ: John Wiley.

Miraglia, E., Law, R., & Collins, P. (2006). *Learning commons—What is culture?— Baseline definition.* Retrieved from http://www.wsu.edu.gened/learn-modules/top_culture/cullture-defintion.html

Monk, G., Winslade, J., Crocket, K., & Epston, D. (1997). *Narrative therapy in practice: The archaelogy of hope.* San Francisco, CA: Jossey-Bass.

Monk, G., Winslade, J., & Sinclair, S. (2008). *New horizons in multicultural counseling.* Thousand Oaks, CA: Sage.

Morgan, S. (2005). Depression: Turning towards life. In C. E. Germer, R. D. Siegel, & P. R. Fulton (Eds.), *Mindfulness and psychotherapy* (pp. 130–151). New York, NY: Guilford.

Mroczek, D. K., & Little, T. D. (Eds.). (2006). *Handbook of personality development.* Mahwah, NJ: Lawrence Erlbaum.

Murdin, L. (2000). *How much is enough: Endings in psychotherapy and counselling.* London, UK: Routledge.

Myerhoff, B. (1986). Life not death in Venice. In E. Bruner & V. Turner (Eds.), *The anthropology of experience.* Chicago: University of Illinois Press.

Nelson, T. S. (Ed). (2010). *Doing something different: Solution-focused brief therapy practices.* New York, NY: Routledge.

Newman, C. F. (Ed.). (2004). *Suicidality.* New York, NY: Guilford.

Niolan, P. H., Whitaker, D. J., Feder, L., Campbell, J., Wallinder, J., Self-Brown, S., & Chivers, S. (2009). A multicomponent intervention to prevent partner violence within an existing service intervention. *Professional Psychology: Research and Practice, 40*(3), 264–271. doi: 10.1037/a0013422

Noddings, N. (2002). *Educating moral people: A caring alternative to character education.* New York, NY: Teachers College Press.

Norcross, J. C. (2001). Purposes, processes, and products of the task force on empirically supported therapy relationships. *Psychotherapy: Theory, Research, Practice, Training, 38,* 345–356.

Nylund, D., & Thomas, J. (1994). The economics of narrative. *Family Therapy Networker, 18*(6), 38–39.

O'Connell, B. (1998). *Solution-focused therapy.* London, UK: Sage.

Ofer, Z., Williams, M. H., Lehavot, K., & Knapp, S. (2009). Psychotherapist self-disclosure and transparency in the Internet age. *Professional Psychology: Research and Practice, 40*(1), 22–30. doi: 10.1037/a0014745

O'Hanlon, B. (2000). *Do one thing different.* New York, NY: HarperCollins.

O'Hanlon, W. H. (1993). Take two clients and call them in the morning: Brief solution-oriented therapy with depression. In S. Friedman (Ed.), *The new language of change: Constructive collaboration in therapy* (pp. 50–84). New York, NY: Guilford.

Papadopolous, L., Bor, R., & Stanion, P. (1997a). Genograms in counseling practice: A review (Part 1). *Counseling Psychology Quarterly, 10*(1), 16–26.

Papadopolous, L., Bor, R., & Stanion, P. (1997b). Genograms in counseling practice: A review (Part 2). *Counseling Psychology Quarterly, 10*(2), 135–148.

Paré, D. A. (1995). Of families and other cultures: The shifting paradigm of family therapy. *Family Process, 34*(1), 1–19.

Paré, D. A. (1996). Culture and meaning: Expanding the metaphorical repertoire of family therapy. *Family Process, 35*(1), 21–42.

Paré, D. A. (2001). Finding a place to stand: Reflections on discourse and intertextuality in counseling practice. In *Theoretical issues in psychology: Proceedings of the International Society for Theoretical Psychology 1999 Conference.* Norwell, MA: Kluwer Academic.

Paré, D. A. (2002). Discursive wisdom: Reflections on ethics and therapeutic knowledge. *International Journal of Critical Psychology, 7,* 30–52.

Paré, D. A. (2008). Invited response to chapter five: Discourse, positioning, and deconstruction. In G. Monk, J. Winslade, & S. Sinclair (Eds.), *New horizons in multicultural counseling* (pp. 137–139). Thousand Oaks, CA: Sage.

Paré, D. A., & Larner, G. (Eds.). (2004). *Collaborative practice in psychology and therapy.* Binghampton, NY: Haworth.

Paré, D. A., & Lysack, M. (2004). The oak and the willow: From monologue to dialogue in the scaffolding of therapeutic conversations. *Journal of Systemic Therapies, 23*(1), 6–20.

Paré, D. A., & Lysack, M. (2006). Exploring inner dialogue in counsellor education. *Canadian Journal of Counselling, 40*(3), 131–144.

Paré, D. A., & Majchrzak Rombach, M. A. (2003). Therapeutic letters to young persons. In C. F. Sori & L. Hecker (Eds.), *The therapist's notebook for children and adolescents* (pp. 199–203). Binghampton, NY: Haworth.

Paré, D. A., Richardson, B., & Tarragona, M. (2009). Watching the train: Mindfulness and inner dialogue in therapist skills training. In S. Hick (Ed.), *Mindfulness and social work* (pp. 76–91). Chicago, IL: Lyceum Books.

Paris, J. (2010). *The use and misuse of psychiatric drugs: An evidence-based critique.* West Sussex, UK: Wiley.

Parker, I. (Ed.). (1999). *Deconstructing psychotherapy.* New York, NY: Routledge.

Parker, I., Georgaca, E., Harper, D., McLaughlin, T., & Stowell-Smith, M. (1996). *Deconstructing psychopathology.* London, UK: Sage.

Parry, A. (1991). A universe of stories. *Family Process, 30,* 37–54.

Pedersen, P. (1995). The culture-bound counsellor as an unintentional racist. *Canadian Journal of Counselling, 29*(3), 197–205.

Pedersen, P. B. (1991). Multiculturalism as a generic approach to counseling. *Journal on Counseling and Development, 70,* 6–12.

Pedersen, P. B., Draguns, J. G., Lonner, W. J., & Trimble, J. E. (2008). *Counseling across cultures* (6th ed.). Thousand Oaks, CA: Sage.

Penn, P., & Frankfurt, M. (1994). Creating a participant text: Writing, multiple voices, narrative multiplicity. *Family Process, 33,* 217–231.

Pennebaker, J. (1997). *Opening up: The healing power of expressing emotions.* New York, NY: Guilford.

Percy, I. (2008). Awareness and authoring: The idea of self in mindfulness and narrative therapy. *European Journal of Psychotherapy and Counselling, 10*(4), 355–367.

Peterson, C. (2006). *A primer in positive psychology.* New York, NY: Oxford University Press.

Piaget, J., & Inhelder, B. (1962). *The psychology of the child.* New York, NY: Basic Books.

Pichot, T., & Dolan, Y. N. (2003). *Solution-focused brief therapy: Its effective use in agency settings.* Binghamton, NY: Haworth.

Piercy, F. P. (2002). Birthday letters: A ritual to connect parent and child. *Journal of Clinical Activities, Assignments & Handouts in Psychotherapy Practice, 2*(4), 41–45.

Polkinghorne, D. (1993). Postmodern epistemology of practice. In S. Kvale (Ed.), *Psychology and postmodernism* (pp. 147–165). Newbury Park, CA: Sage.

Polkinghorne, D. E. (1988). *Narrative knowing and the human sciences.* Albany: State University of New York Press.

Ponterotto, J. G., Casas, J. M., Suzuki, L. A., & Alexander, C. M. (Eds.). (2010). *Handbook of multicultural counseling* (3rd ed.). Thousand Oaks, CA: Sage.

Pope-Davis, D., & Coleman, H. (Eds.). (2001). *The intersection of race, class, and gender in multicultural counseling.* Thousand Oaks, CA: Sage.

Prochaska, J. O., Norcross, J. C., & DiClemente, C. C. (1994). *Changing for good.* New York, NY: Morrow.

Reich, J. W., Zautra, A. J., & Hall, J. S. (Eds.). (2010). *The handbook of adult resilience.* New York, NY: Guilford.

Reynolds, V. (2009). An ethic of resistance: Frontline worker as activist. *Women Making Waves, 19*(1), 1–5.

Reynolds, V. (2010). A supervision of solidarity. *Canadian Journal of Counseling and Psychotherapy, 44*(3), 246–257.

Rober, P. (2002). Constructive hypothesizing, dialogic understanding and the therapist's inner conversation: Some ideas about knowing and not knowing in the family therapy session. *Journal of Marital and Family Therapy, 28*(4), 467–478.

Robinson, T. L. (2005). *The convergence of race, ethnicity, and gender: Multiple identities in counseling.* Upper Saddle River, NJ: Pearson.

Robinson-Wood, T. L. (2009). Extending cultural understanding beyond race and ethnicity. In C. C. Lee, D. A. Burnhill, A. L. Butler, C. P. Hipolito-Delgado, M. Humphrey, O. Munoz, & H. Shin (Eds.), *Elements of culture in counseling* (pp. 31–41). Columbus, OH: Pearson.

Rogers, C. (1992). The necessary and sufficient conditions of therapeutic personality change. *Journal of Consulting and Clinical Psychology, 60*(6), 827–832. (Original work published 1957)

Rønnestad, M. H., & Orlinsky, D. E. (2005). Therapeutic work and professional development: Main findings and practical implications of a long-term international study. *Psychotherapy Bulletin, 40,* 27–32.

Rønnestad, M. H., & Skovholt, T. M. (2003). The journey of the counselor and therapist: Research findings and perspectives on professional development. *Journal of Career Development, 30,* 5–44.

Rose, N. (1990). *Governing the soul: The shaping of the private self.* New York, NY: Routledge.

Rose, N. (1998). *Inventing our selves: Psychology, power and clienthood.* New York, NY: Cambridge University Press.

Rosen, A., & Callaly, T. (2005). Interdisciplinary teamwork and leadership: Issues for psychiatrists. *Australian Psychiatry, 13*(3), 224–241.

Rosenhan, D. L. (1973). On being sane in insane places. *Science, New Series, 179*(4070), 250–258.

Rothman, A. D., & Nowicki, S. (2004). A measure of the ability to identify emotion in children's tone of voice. *Journal of Nonverbal Behaviour, 28,* 67–92.

Rumi, J. (1995). *The essential Rumi* (C. Barks with A. Moyne, J. Arberry, & R. Nicholson, Trans.). San Francisco, CA: HarperSanFrancisco.

Rushdie, S. (1983). *Shame: A novel.* Toronto, Canada: Random House.

Salaman, E., Grevelius, K., & Andersson, M. (1993). Beware the siren's song: The AGS commission model. In S. Gilligan & R. Price (Eds.), *Therapeutic conversations* (pp. 330–343). New York, NY: Norton.

Saleebey, D. (2008). Commentary on the strengths perspective and potential applications in school counseling. *Professional School Counseling, 12*(2), 68–75.

Salvatore, G., Conti, L., Fiore, D., Carcione, A., Dimaggio, G., & Semerari, A. (2006). Disorganized narratives: Problems in treatment and therapist intervention hierarchy. *Journal of Constructivist Psychology, 19,* 191–207.

Scherer, K. R., Banse, R., & Wallbot, H. G. (2001). Emotion inferences from vocal expression correlate across languages and culture. *Journal of Cross-Cultural Psychology, 32,* 76–92.

Schön, D. (1983). *The reflective practitioner: How professionals think in action.* New York, NY: Basic Books.

Scott, J. C. (1990). *Domination and the arts of resistance: Hidden transcripts.* New Haven, CT: Yale University Press.

Scott, J. C. (2009). *The art of not being governed: An anarchist history of upland Southeast Asia.* New Haven, CT: Yale University Press.

Segal, Z. V., Williams, J. M. G., & Teasedale, J. D. (2002). *Mindfulness-based cognitive therapy for depression: A new approach to preventing relapse.* New York, NY: Guilford.

Sevenhuijsen, S. (1998). *Citizenship and the ethics of care: Feminist consideration on justice, morality and politics.* London, UK: Routledge.

Sfard, A. (1998). On two metaphors for learning and the dangers of choosing just one. *Educational Researcher, 27*(2), 4–13.

Shaffir, R. (2000). *The Zen of listening: Mindful communication in the age of distraction.* Wheaton, IL: Quest.

Sharry, J., Darmody, M., & Madden, B. (2008). A solution-focused approach. In S. Palmer (Ed.), *Suicide: Strategies and interventions for reduction and prevention* (pp. 184–202). New York, NY: Routledge/Taylor & Francis.

Shotter, J. (1993). *Conversational realities: Constructing life through language.* London, UK: Sage.

Shotter, J. (1995). In conversation: Joint action, shared intentionality, and ethics. *Theory & Psychology, 5*(1), 49–73.

Siegel, D. (2012). *The developing mind, how relationships and the brain interact to shape who we are* (2nd ed.). New York, NY: Guilford.

Slive, A., & Bobele, M. (2011). *When one hour is all you have: Effective therapy for walk-in clients.* Phoenix, AZ: Tucker and Theisen.

Sloan, T. (2009). Personality theories. In I. Prilleltensky & S. Austen (Eds.), *Critical psychology: An introduction* (2nd ed., pp. 57–74). Thousand Oaks, CA: Sage.

Smith, C. (2004). Relational attunement: Internal and external reflections on harmonizing with clients. In D. A. Paré & G. Larner (Eds.), *Collaborative practice in psychology and therapy*. Binghampton, NY: Haworth.

Smith, D. (1991). Hermeneutic inquiry: The hermeneutic imagination and the pedagogic text. In E. G. Short (Ed.), *Forms of curriculum inquiry* (pp. 187–210). Albany: State University of New York Press.

Smith, G. (1995). *The protectors' handbook: Reducing the risk of child sexual abuse and helping children to recover.* London, UK: Women's Press.

Snyder, C. R., & Lopez, S. J. (Eds.). (2009). *Oxford handbook of positive psychology* (2nd ed.). New York, NY: Oxford University Press.

Snyder, C. R., Lopez, S. L., & Pedrotti, J. T. (2010). *Positive psychology: The scientific and practical explorations of human strengths.* Thousand Oaks, CA: Sage.

Soanes, C. (Ed.). (2003). *The Oxford compact English dictionary* (2nd ed.). Oxford, UK: Oxford University Press.

Sommers-Flanagan, J., & Sommers-Flanagan, R. (1995). Intake interviewing with suicidal patients: A systematic approach. *Professional Psychology: Research and Practice, 26*(1), 41–47.

Sori, C. F., & Hecker, L. L. (Eds.). (2008). *The therapist's notebook: Vol. 3. Homework, handouts, and activities for use in psychotherapy.* New York, NY: Routledge.

Southwick, S., Litz, B., Charney, D., & Friedman, M. J. (Eds.). (2012). *Resilience and mental health: Challenges across the lifespan.* New York, NY: Cambridge University Press.

Speedy, J., Jones, M., Jones, F., Jones, J., Jones, P., & Jones, J. (2005). Failing to come to terms with things: A multi-storied conversation about poststructuralist ideas and narrative practices in response to some of life's failures. *Counselling and Psychotherapy Research, 5*(1), 65–73.

Speight, S. L., Myers, L. J., Cox, C. I., & Highlen, P. S. (1991). A redefinition of multicultural counseling. *Journal on Counseling and Development, 70,* 29–36.

Spence, D. S. (1982). *Narrative truth and historical truth: Meaning and interpretation in psychoanalysis.* New York, NY: Norton.

Spitzer, R. L. (1981). The diagnostic status of homosexuality in *DSM III:* A reformulation of the issues. *American Journal of Psychiatry, 38*(2), 210–215.

Stearns, C. Z., & Stearns, P. W. (1988). *Emotions and social change.* New York, NY: Homes and Meier.

Stein, D. M., & Lambert, M. J. (1984). On the relationship between therapist experience and psychotherapy outcome. *Clinical Psychology Review, 4,* 127–142.

Strong, S. R. (1969). Counseling: An interpersonal influencing process. *Journal of Counseling Psychology, 15,* 215–224.

Strong, T. (2000). Collaborative influence. *Australian and New Zealand Journal of Family Therapy, 21*(3), 144–148.

Strong, T. (2001). "My house", "your house", and "our house": Discursive thoughts on optimizing dialogue in therapy. *Journal of Clinical Activities & Handouts in Psychotherapy Practice, 1*(4), 41–55.

Strong, T. (2002). Collaborative "expertise" after the discursive turn. *Journal of Psychotherapy Integration, 12,* 218–232.

Strong, T. (2009, April). Book review: Pharametucial reasoning, by Andrew Lakoff. *Context,* 39–41.

Strong, T. (2010). Staying in dialogue with CBT. *European Journal of Psychotherapy and Counselling, 12*(3), 243–256.

Strong, T. (n.d.). [Brief therapy and the *DSM:* 13 possible conversational tensions]. (Unpublished manuscript).

Strong, T., & Paré, D. A. (Eds.). (2004). *Furthering talk: Advances in the discursive therapies.* New York, NY: Kluwer Academic/Plenum.

Strong, T., & Zeman, D. (2005). "Othering" and "selving" in therapeutic dialogue. *European Journal of Psychotherapy, Counseling and Health, 7,* 245–261.

Strong, T., & Zeman, D. (2010). Dialogic considerations of confrontation as a counselling activity: An examination of Allen Ivey's use of confronting as a microskill. *Journal of Counseling and Development, 88,* 332–339.

Strupp, H. H., & Hadley, S. W. (1979). Specific versus nonspecific factors in psychotherapy. *Archives of General Psychiatry, 36,* 1125–1136.

Stuart, R. B. (2004). Twelve practical suggestions for achieving multicultural competence. *Professional Psychology: Research and Practice, 35*(1), 3–9. doi: 10.1037/0735-7028.35.1.3

Sue, D. W., Ivey, A., & Pedersen, P. (2009). *A theory of multicultural counseling and therapy.* Pacific Grove, CA: Brooks/Cole.

Sue, D. W., & Sue, D. (2003). *Counseling the culturally different: Theory & practice* (4th ed.). New York, NY: John Wiley.

Sue, D. W., & Sue, D. (2008). *Counseling the culturally diverse: Theory and practice* (5th ed.). Hoboken, NJ: John Wiley.

Surrey, J. L. (2005). Relational psychotherapy, relational mindfulness. In C. Germer, R. Siegel, & P. Fulton (Eds.), *Mindfulness and psychotherapy* (pp. 91–110). New York, NY: Guilford.

Sutherland, O., & Strong, T. (2012). Response to commentary: Is collaboration a viable target for family therapists? *Journal of Family Therapy, 34,* 1–8. doi: 10.1111/j.1467-6427.2012.00585.x

Sykes Wylie, M. (1994). Panning for gold. *Family Therapy Networker, 18*(6), 40–49.

Teasdale, J. D., Segal, Z. V., Williams, J. M. G., Ridgeway, V. A., Soulsby, J. M., & Lau, M. A. (2000). Prevention of relapse/recurrence in major depression by mindfulness-based cognitive therapy. *Journal of Consulting and Clinical Psychology, 68,* 614–623.

Thériault, A., & Gazzola, N. (2008). Feelings of incompetence among experienced therapists: A substantive theory. *European Journal of Qualitative Research in Psychotherapy, 3,* 19–29.

Thomas, A. J. (1998). Understanding culture and worldview in family systems: Use of the multicultural genogram. *The Family Journal, 6*(1), 24–32. doi: 10.1177/106648079806061005

Thomas, F. N. (2007). Simpler may not be better: A personal journey with and beyond systemic and solution-focused practices. *Journal of the Texas Association for Marriage and Family Therapy, 12*(1), 4–29.

Thomson, L. (1998). *Personality type.* Boston, MA: Shambhala.

Tilsen, J., & Nylund, D. (2008). Psychotherapy research, the recovery movement and practice-based evidence in psychiatric rehabilitation. *Journal of Social Work in Disability & Rehabilitation, 7*(3/4), 340–354.

Todd, N., & Wade, A. (1994, Fall). Domination, deficiency, and psychotherapy, Part I. *Calgary Participator,* 37–46.

Todd, N., & Wade, A. (2004). Coming to terms with violence and resistance: From a language of effects to language to responses. In T. Strong & D. Paré (Eds.), *Furthering talk: Advances in the discursive therapies* (pp. 145–161). New York, NY: Kluwer.

Tomm, K. (1987b). Interventive questioning: Part I. Reflexive questioning as a means to enable self-healing. *Family Process, 26,* 3–13.

Tomm, K. (1998, Fall). When you and your teen don't get along. *Family Health,* 39–42.

Tomm, K., & Lannamann, J. (1988). Questions as interventions. *Family Therapy Networker, 12*(5), 38–41.

Tronto, J. (1993). *Moral boundaries: A political argument for an ethic of care.* New York, NY: Routledge.

Turnell, A., & Edwards, S. (1999). *Signs of safety: A solution and safety oriented approach to child protection casework.* New York, NY: Norton.

Turnell, A., & Hogg, S. E. V. (2007). Compassionate, safe and rigorous child protection practice with biological parents of adopted children. *Child Abuse Review, 16,* 108–119. doi: 10.1002/car.941

Ungar, M. (2005). *Handbook for working with children and youth: Pathways to resilience across cultures and contexts.* Thousand Oaks, CA: Sage.

Ungar, M. (2006). *Strengths-based counseling with at-risk youth.* Thousand Oaks, CA: Corwin Press.

van Gennep, A. (1960). *The rites of passage.* Chicago, IL: University of Chicago Press. (Original work published 1909)

Vygotsky, L. (1986). *Thought and language.* Cambridge, MA: MIT Press.

Wade, A. (1997). Small acts of living: Everyday resistance to violence and other forms of oppression. *Contemporary Family Therapy, 19,* 23–39.

Wade, A. (2007). Despair, resistance, hope: Response based therapy with victims of violence. In C. Flaskas, I. McCarthy, & J. Sheehan (Eds.), *Hope and despair in narrative and family therapy* (pp. 62–64). New York, NY: Routledge.

Walitzer, K. S., Dermen, K. H., & Connors, G. J. (1999). Strategies for preparing clients for treatment: A review. *Behavior Modification, 23*(1), 129–151. doi: 10.1177/0145445599231006

Wallace, B. A. (2001). Intersubjectivity in Indo-Tibetan Buddhism. *Journal of Consciousness Studies, 8*(5/7), 209–230.

Walsh, R. A. (2008). Mindfulness and empathy: A hermeneutic circle. In S. F. Hick & T. Bien (Eds.), *Mindfulness and the therapeutic relationship* (pp. 72–88). New York, NY: Guilford.

Walter, J., & Peller, J. (2000). *Recreating brief therapy: Preferences and possibilities.* New York, NY: Norton.

Wampold, B. (2010). *The basics of psychotherapy: An introduction to theory and practice.* Washington, DC: American Psychological Association.

Wampold, B. E. (2000). Outcomes of individual counseling and psychotherapy: Empirical evidence addressing two fundamental questions. In S. D. Brown & R. W. Lent (Eds.), *Handbook of counseling psychology* (4th ed., pp. 711–739). New York, NY: John Wiley.

Wampold, B. E. (2001). *The great psychotherapy debate: Models, methods, and findings.* Mahwah, NJ: Lawrence Erlbaum.

Wampold, B. E., Mondin, G. W., Moody, M., Stich, F., Benson, K., & Ahn, H. (1997). A meta-analysis of outcome studies comparing bona fide psychotherapies: Empirically, "all must have prizes." *Psychological Bulletin, 122,* 203–215.

Ward, C. C., & Reuter, T. (2011). *Strength centred counselling.* Thousand Oaks, CA: Sage.

Watters, E. (2010). *Crazy like us: Globalizing the American psyche.* New York, NY: Free Press.

Watts, A. (1957/1999). *The way of zen.* New York, NY: Random House.

Weiner-Davis, M. (1993). Pro-constructed realities. In S. Gilligan & R. Price (Eds.), *Therapeutic conversations* (pp. 149–157). New York, NY: Norton.

Weiner-Davis, M., de Shazer, S., & Gingerich, W. (1987). Building on pre-treatment change to construct the therapeutic solution: An exploratory study. *Journal of Marital and Family Therapy, 13*(4), 359–363.

Weingarten, K. (1998). The small and the ordinary: The daily practice of a postmodern narrative therapy. *Family Process, 37,* 3–16.

Whelton, W. J. (2004). Emotional processes in psychotherapy: Evidence across therapeutic modalities. *Clinical Psychology and Psychotherapy, 11,* 58–71.

Whitaker, R. (2010). *Anatomy of an epidemic: Magic bullets, psychiatric drugs, and the astonishing rise of mental illness in America.* New York, NY: Random House.

White, M. (1984). Pseudo-encopresis: From avalanche to victory, from vicious to virtuous cycles. *Family Systems Medicine, 2,* 150–160.

White, M. (1991). Deconstruction and therapy. *Dulwich Centre Newsletter, 3,* 21–67.

White, M. (1995). *Re-authoring lives: Interviews and essays.* Adelaide, Australia: Dulwich Centre.

White, M. (1997). *Narratives of therapists' lives.* Adelaide, Australia: Dulwich Centre.

White, M. (2000). Re-engaging with history: The absent but implicit. In M. White (Ed.), *Reflections on narrative practice* (pp. 35–58). Adelaide, Australia: Dulwich Centre.

White, M. (2003). Narrative practice and community assignments. *International Journal of Narrative Therapy and Community Work, 2,* 17–56.

White, M. (2004a). Addressing personal failure. In M. White (Ed.), *Narrative practice and exotic lives: Resurrecting diversity in everyday life* (pp. 149–232). Adelaide, Australia: Dulwich Centre.

White, M. (2004b). Folk psychology and narrative practice, Part I. In M. White (Ed.), *Narrative practice and exotic lives: Resurrecting diversity in everyday life* (pp. 59–84). Adelaide, Australia: Dulwich Centre.

White, M. (2004c). Working with clients who are suffering the consequences of multiple trauma: A narrative perspective. *International Journal of Narrative Therapy and Community Work, 1,* 44–75.

White, M. (2007). *Maps of narrative practice.* New York, NY: Norton.

White, M., & Epston, D. (1990). *Narrative means to therapeutic ends.* New York, NY: Norton.

White, V. (2001). Applying postmodern theory to assessment and collaborative counseling plan development. In K. Eriksen & G. McAuliffe (Eds.), *Teaching counselors and therapists: Constructivist and developmental course design* (pp. 203–218). Westport, CT: Bergin & Garvey.

Wiener, J., & Rosen, D. H. (2009). *The therapeutic relationship: Transference, counter transference, and the making of meaning.* College Station: Texas A&M University Press.

Wilkins, P. (2000). Unconditional positive regard reconsidered. *British Journal of Guidance & Counseling, 28*(1), 23–36.

Winslade, J. (2009). Tracing lines of flight: The implications of the work of Gilles Deleuze for narrative practice. *Family Process, 48,* 332–346.

Winslade, J., & Monk, G. (1999). *Narrative counselling in schools: Powerful and brief.* Thousand Oaks, CA: Sage.

Winslade, J., & Williams, M. (2012). *Safe and peaceful schools: Addressing conflict and eliminating violence.* Thousand Oaks, CA: Sage.

Wittgenstein, L. (1953). *Philosophical investigations* (G. E. Anscombe, Trans.). Oxford, UK: Blackwell.

World Health Organization. (n.d.). *Mental health, human rights and legislation: WHO's framework.* Retrieved from http://www.who.int/mental_health/policy/fact_sheet_mnh_hr_leg_2105.pdf

Wylie, M. S. (1994). Morality and therapy. *Family Therapy Networker, 18*(3), 10–12.

Yapko, M. D. (2003). *Trancework: An introduction to the practice of clinical hypnosis* (3rd ed.). New York, NY: Brunner-Routledge.

Yonan, J., Bardick, A. D., & Willment, J. H. (2011). Ethical decision making, therapeutic boundaries, and communicating using online technology and cellular phones. *Canadian Journal of Counselling and Psychotherapy, 45*(4), 307–326.

Young, K. (2008). Narrative practice at a walk-in therapy clinic: Developing children's worry wisdom. *Journal of Systemic Therapies, 27*(4), 54–74.

Young, K. (2011). When all the time you have is now: Re-visiting practices and narrative therapy in a walk-in clinic. In J. Duvall & L. Béres (Eds.), *Innovations in narrative therapy* (pp. 147–166). New York, NY: Norton.

Young, M. (2009). *Learning the art of helping: Building blocks and techniques.* Upper Saddle River, NJ: Pearson.

Yuen, A. (2007). Discovering children's responses to trauma: A response-based narrative practice. *International of Narrative Therapy and Community Work, 24,* 3–18.

Yuen, A. (2009). Less pain, more gain: Explorations of responses vs. effects when working with the consequences of trauma. *Explorations: An E-Journal of Narrative Practice, 1,* 6–16.

Zalaquett, C. P., Fuerth, K. M., Stein, C., Ivey, A. E., & Ivey, M. B. (2008). Reframing the "DSM-IV-TR" from a multicultural/social justice perspective. *Journal of Counseling and Development, 86*(3), 364–371.

Zimmerman, K. J. (2011). Commentary: Is collaboration a viable target for family therapists? *Journal of Family Therapy, 33,* 215–223. doi: 10.1111/j.1467-6427.2011.00535.x

INDEX

ABOUT THE AUTHOR

David Paré, PhD, is a full professor in the Faculty of Education at the University of Ottawa, where he teaches counseling and psychotherapy. A licensed counseling psychologist, David is also the director of the Glebe Institute, A Centre for Constructive and Collaborative Practice, in Ottawa.

David is the coeditor of two books about collaborative practices in counseling and therapy: *Collaborative Practice in Psychology and Therapy* (with Glenn Larner) and *Furthering Talk: Advances in the Discursive Therapies* (with Tom Strong).

⊗SAGE research**methods**

The essential online tool for researchers from the world's leading methods publisher

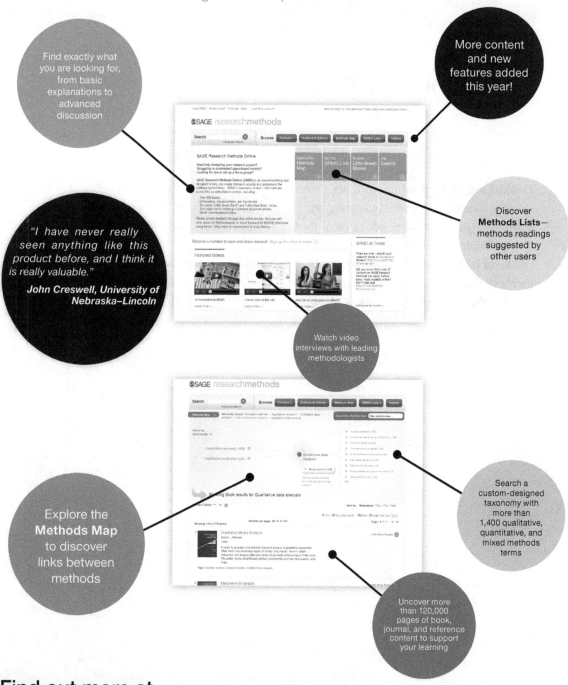

Find exactly what you are looking for, from basic explanations to advanced discussion

More content and new features added this year!

Discover **Methods Lists**—methods readings suggested by other users

"I have never really seen anything like this product before, and I think it is really valuable."

John Creswell, University of Nebraska–Lincoln

Watch video interviews with leading methodologists

Explore the **Methods Map** to discover links between methods

Search a custom-designed taxonomy with more than 1,400 qualitative, quantitative, and mixed methods terms

Uncover more than 120,000 pages of book, journal, and reference content to support your learning

Find out more at
www.sageresearchmethods.com

CPSIA information can be obtained
at www.ICGtesting.com
Printed in the USA
FSHW01n1755300718
50909FS